"This book offers a stimulating and original way to explore the Roman world of Luke-Acts by way of recent archaeological finds in Roman Britain. Here the military community of Vindolanda, the traders and financiers of Roman London, and the rural community which produced the curse tablets of Uley—all brought to life by a disciplined archaeological imagination—provide windows into the lives and loves of Luke's characters and original readers."

—LOVEDAY ALEXANDER
Emeritus Professor of Biblical Studies, University of Sheffield

"In this remarkable book, Richard Cleaves shows—more clearly than anyone has before—the broad interconnections and parallels between the literacies of Roman Britain and those of the contemporaneous eastern Mediterranean. More than this, he maps the shared concerns, interests, anxieties, and habits that allow us to imagine the common ground across which religious communication and mutual understanding must have taken place in the first centuries AD."

—GREG WOOLF
Leon Levy Director of the Institute for the Study of the Ancient World, New York University

"Cleaves brings realism to an understanding of Luke-Acts by presenting first-hand, near-contemporary evidence of types of people, practices, and ideas seen in the biblical texts. The astonishingly preserved real people of Roman Britain bring new and illuminating depth to a reading of Luke-Acts."

—PETER OAKES
Rylands Professor of Biblical Criticism and Exegesis, University of Manchester

"It only rarely happens that an interpreter conceives of a totally new and highly significant approach to a biblical text. Yet this is what Richard Cleaves has done with *Imagining Luke-Acts in Roman Britain*. In an academic setting where research into the beginnings of Christianity in the first century CE has been focused solely on the Mediterranean world, Cleaves has had the daring insight to ask, and to go a long way towards answering, how Britain might have featured in the process. . . . The result is not just a scholarly triumph, but a major contribution to bringing the British people into startling and unexpected conjunction with the dawn of Christianity."

—PHILIP F. ESLER
Portland Chair in New Testament Studies, The University of Gloucestershire

Imagining Luke-Acts in Roman Britain

MATRIX
The Bible in Mediterranean Context

PREVIOUSLY PUBLISHED VOLUMES

Richard L. Rohrbaugh
The New Testament and Social-Science Criticism

Markus Cromhout
Jesus and Identity

Pieter F. Craffert
The Life of a Galilean Shaman

Douglas E. Oakman
Jesus and the Peasants

Stuart L. Love
Jesus and the Marginal Women

Eric C. Stewart
Gathered around Jesus

Dennis C. Duling
A Marginal Scribe

Jason Lamoreaux
Ritual, Women, and Philippi

Ernest Van Eck
The Parables of Jesus the Galilean

Bruce J. Malina and John J. Pilch
Handbook of Biblical Social Values (3rd ed.)

K. C. Richardson
Early Christian Care for the Poor

Douglas E. Oakman
The Radical Jesus, the Bible, and the Great Transformation

Jerome H. Neyrey, SJ
By What Authority?

Imagining Luke-Acts in Roman Britain

Through the Eyes of the People of the Bloomberg Tablets, the Vindolanda Tablets, and the Uley Tablets

RICHARD CLEAVES

CASCADE *Books* • Eugene, Oregon

IMAGINING LUKE-ACTS IN ROMAN BRITAIN
Through the Eyes of the People of the Bloomberg Tablets, the Vindolanda Tablets, and the Uley Tablets

Matrix: The Bible in Mediterranean Context 15

Cascade Books
An Imprint of Wipf and Stock Publishers
199 W. 8th Ave., Suite 3
Eugene, OR 97401

www.wipfandstock.com

PAPERBACK ISBN: 979-8-3852-6288-5
HARDCOVER ISBN: 979-8-3852-6289-2
EBOOK ISBN: 979-8-3852-6290-8

Cataloging-in-Publication data:

Names: Cleaves, Richard, author.

Title: Imagining Luke-Acts : through the eyes of the people of the Bloomberg tablets, the Vindolanda tablets, and the Uley tablets / Richard Cleaves.

Description: Eugene, OR: Cascade Books, 2026. | Matrix: The Bible in Mediterranean Context 15. | Includes bibliographical references and index.

Identifiers: ISBN: 979-8-3852-6288-5 (paperback). | ISBN: 979-8-3852-6289-2 (hardcover). | ISBN: 979-8-3852-6290-8 (ebook).

Subjects: LCSH: Bible.—Luke—Criticism, interpretation, etc. | Bible.—Acts—Criticism, interpretation, etc. | Bloomberg tablets. | Vindolanda tablets. | Uley tablets. | Romans—Great Britain.

Classification: BS2589 C55 2026 (print). | BS2589 (epub).

For Lake, Margot, Griff, Sylvie, Edith, and Dilys
in the hope that one day Luke–Acts and Roman Britain
will catch their imagination

"Archives are enchanting because they function as gateways to history. For the uninitiated, archives might seem more akin to sepulchres or mausoleums than repositories for remnants of life, memories and lived experiences. But occasionally—and more often than expected—one can experience an almost overwhelming sense of closeness. Here, the archive is merely a means to an end, supplying documents that hold previously unknown information, allowing the researcher of the past to 'walk' through a lost world."

—Rebecka Lennartsson, "Notes on 'Not Being There'"

"Reading texts always involves some effort to go beyond the level of the words on the page, beyond even the wider 'factual' circumstances to which they relate . . . and to penetrate into the field of the personal. Only thus can understanding occur as part of a genuine meeting of persons, and our own personhood be modified by it."

—Trevor Hart, "Imagination and Responsible Reading"

Archival "ethnography is the eye of the needle through which the threads of the imagination must pass."

—Paul Willis, *The Ethnographic Imagination*

Contents

Permissions

Bloomberg Tablets. Figure 2, Londinium c. 80 CE, is from Susan Wright, *Archaeology at Bloomberg*, 23, © MOLA/Judith Dobie. Figure 3, Presentation Stylus, is from MOLA Blog, © Andy Chopping. Figure 5 is from Roger S. O. Tomlin, *Roman London's First Voices*, 24, © MOLA. Figures 4, 6 7, 8 are from Roger S. O. Tomlin, *Roman London's First Voices*, © MOLA, photographs Andy Chopping/drawings Roger S. O. Tomlin. The texts are quoted from *RIB* and are published under a Creative Commons 4.0 International License, https://creativecommons.org/licenses/by/4.0/; they were drawn, transcribed, translated and interpreted by Roger S. O. Tomlin and are used with his permission.

Vindolanda Tablets. Figures 9, 10, 11, images from Vindolanda, © The Vindolanda Trust and used with permission. Figures 12, 13, 14, 15, images of *Tab. Vindol. II* 291; *III* 574; *II* 343; *II* 344, © The Trustees of the British Museum. The texts are quoted from *RIB* and are published under a Creative Commons 4.0 International License, https://creativecommons.org/licenses/by/4.0/. They were transcribed, translated and interpreted by Alan Bowman and David Thomas with contributions by J. N. Adams (*Tab. Vind.* II and III), John Pearce (*Tab. Vind.* III), and Roger S. O. Tomlin (*Tab. Vind.* IV).

Uley Tablets. Figures 16 and 17, images of the Temple of Mercury by Steve Smith, are used with kind permission of Museum in the Park, Stroud. Figure 18, the head of the cult statue of Mercury, © The Trustees of the British Museum. Figure 19, Tab. Uley 72: photograph, © The Trustees of the British Museum; drawing by Mark Hassall from *Britannia* 10 (1979), p. 343, © Cambridge University Press. Figure 22, *Tab. Uley* 2: photograph © The Trustees of the British Museum; drawing by Roger S. O. Tomlin from *Britannia* 23 (1992), p. 311, © Cambridge University Press. The texts are from Roger S. O. Tomlin, *The Uley Tablets*, © Roger S. O. Tomlin who transcribed, translated and interpreted them; they are used with his permission.

Nestle-Aland, Novum Testamentum Graece, 28th Revised Edition, edited by Barbara and Kurt Aland, Johannes Karavidopoulos, Carlo M. Martini, and Bruce M. Metzger in cooperation with the Institute for New Testament Textual Research, Münster/Westphalia, © 2012 Deutsche Bibelgesellschaft, Stuttgart. Used by permission.

Biblia Sacra Iuxta Vulgatam Versionem, Third Revised Edition, edited by Robert Weber, © 1969 and 1983 Deutsche Bibelgesellschaft, Stuttgart. Used by permission.

Figures

Tables

Preface

THOSE WHO VISIT BRITAIN and those who live in Britain are never far from Roman remains be they evident in place names, roads, town plans, archaeological sites, or museum displays. In the mind's eye it is possible not only to recreate a lost world but to reanimate the people who left their mark long ago. In recent decades a treasure trove of business transactions, personal letters, and even pleas to the local god, have been discovered, transcribed, translated and published. In fragments of writing, little larger than a post card, it is possible to get to know people by name and glimpse something of their social, cultural, political and ritual life. With our inward ear it is as if we can hear their voices as they communicate to each other.

In exploring Roman Britain, very few people have made the connection between the world of Roman Britain and the world of the New Testament. If only one has the eye to see, there are so many connections to be made, as a glance at Table 2 will show. As the events described in the New Testament were unfolding, the Romans invaded Britain (43 CE). By the time that invasion was complete (c. 83 CE), the earliest books of the New Testament had been written and were in circulation.

The recent publication of three sets of writings from early Roman Britain has the potential to throw light on the way Luke's Gospel and the Acts of the Apostles were received by their first audiences. The traders, merchants and financiers of the Bloomberg tablets (published 2016), the women as well as men of the military community of the Vindolanda tablets (published 1983–2019 and ongoing), and the members of a rural community who in times of crisis turned to the nearby temple dedicated to Mercury (published in part 1993–2022, and in full 2024) were not only the kind of people we meet in Luke-Acts, but also the contemporaries of its first readers. Drawing on the insights of archival ethnography, it is possible to develop an understanding of these people through their very own hand-written documents. Just as an ethnographer undertakes a "scientific description of peoples and cultures with reference to their particular customs and characteristics," (COD) so an archival ethnographer uses the commonplace, every day detail in that written record to develop an understanding of people from long ago. With such an understanding of people from an urban, a military and a rural community in Roman Britain we can imagine how they themselves, or people such as these, might have read texts from Luke-Acts had they become followers of the Way of Jesus.

Chapter one is a necessary justification of this approach to Luke-Acts. It begins by making connections between the eastern Mediterranean world of Luke-Acts and Roman Britain, demonstrating the way the two extremities of the Roman empire have a shared history and to some extent a shared cultural encyclopedia. It goes on to explore the shift in the study of Roman Britain from the reconstruction of a narrative history to a focus on material culture, people and society. It then describes the way a similar shift has prompted the development of archival ethnography in accessing the world of the New Testament in the eastern Mediterranean and goes on to propose the use of that approach in accessing the world of the New Testament in Roman Britain. This does not entail a historical study of the arrival of Christianity in Roman Britain. Instead, it involves imagining a reading of Luke-Acts through the eyes of the people of a city-based trading community, a fort-based military community, and a temple-oriented rural community. The next part of this opening chapter will, therefore, consider the nature of the multi-faceted imagination such an approach requires. With an exploration of the assumptions made regarding Luke–Acts in the light of recent scholarship, the Introduction draws to a close, outlining the shape of our imagined reading of Luke-Acts in Roman Britain.

In Chapters two, three and four we examine each set of writings in turn, get to know the people responsible for them, and imagine how they and people like them might have responded to Luke and to Acts, as followers of the Way of Jesus. In the study of Luke-Acts generalizations are often made about the world of the Roman Empire. The reading of texts from Luke-Acts offered here is unique in that it adopts the methodology of archival ethnography, using *realia* from early Roman Britain to access that world. Chapter five brings together insights gleaned from our imagined reading of Luke-Acts, concluding with suggestions for the way in which these three archives can be used in further study of New Testament texts. Further resources are available at www.lukeactsinromanbritain.co.uk.

Acknowledgments

THIS BOOK IS ENTIRELY dependent on the painstaking work over many years of archaeologists, conservationists, photographers, curators, epigraphers and many more. My first thanks, therefore, must go to all those responsible for their discovery and publication. *The Bloomberg Tablets* were excavated by the Museum of London Archaeology, with the support of Bloomberg LP. The tablets were photographed by Andy Chopping and drawn, transcribed, translated and interpreted by Roger S. O. Tomlin. They are on display in the London Mithraeum at the Bloomberg building and in the London Museum.

The Vindolanda Tablets continue to be excavated by the Vindolanda Trust, led initially by Robin and Patricia Birley, subsequently by Anthony and Heide Birley, and currently by Andrew and Barbara Birley; they were photographed in infra-red originally by Alison Rutherford and since by many others. They have been transcribed, translated and interpreted by Alan Bowman and David Thomas with contributions by J. N. Adams (*Tab. Vindol.* II and III), John Pearce (*Tab. Vindol.* III), and Roger S. O. Tomlin (*Tab. Vindol.* IV). They are displayed imaginatively in Vindolanda and in the British Museum.

The Uley Tablets were excavated by The Committee for Rescue Archaeology in Avon, Gloucestershire and Somerset, later renamed the Western Archaeological Trust, and subsequently by the Birmingham University Field Archaeology Unit. The tablets were conserved and unrolled by Simon Dove of the Department of Prehistoric and Romano British Antiquities of the British Museum. They have been drawn, transcribed, translated and interpreted by Roger Tomlin, who published them initially in *The Uley Shrines: Excavation of a Ritual Complex*, one-by-one in *Britannia*, the journal of The Roman Society, and completely in *The Uley Tablets*. They are on display in the British Museum, and described in displays at the Museum in the Park, Stroud.

Since 2019, the Bloomberg Tablets and the Vindolanda Tablets have been available to all on the web site, "Roman Inscriptions of Britain," created by Scott Vanderbilt and part of the LatinNow project. I have delighted in the photographs of the original tablets and the links to the British Museum Online Collection's greater range of photographs; and I have drawn extensively on the full commentary and notes that accompany each tablet. I look forward to the publication of the Uley Tablets on *RIB*. Displays of the tablets themselves have caught my imagination. My thanks go to Roger Tomlin for his encouragement and permission to use his work so extensively.

Second, my thanks must go to those who made this research possible, especially to the Kirby Laing Foundation who funded the PhD on which this book is based, and to my supervisor, Professor Philip F. Esler, Portland Chair in New Testament Studies at the University of Gloucestershire. His encouragement, guidance and support has been invaluable throughout. Thank you to Professor Greg Woolf, Leon Levy Director of New York University's Institute for the Study of the Ancient World and Professor of Ancient Mediterranean Studies and to Professor Peter Oakes, Rylands Professor of Biblical Criticism and Exegesis at the University of Manchester, and other readers for their helpful guidance and support in revising my PhD thesis in readiness for publication. Thank you to all at Wipf and Stock for their guidance and support. Thank you to Chris Jones-Jenkins for preparing the Map and to Phil Cleaves for adapting it for this book.

Luke-Acts caught my imagination a long time ago and so my thanks go back a long way: to my parents, Reg and Dilys, who helped me do a school project on Paul's missionary journeys when I was eight years old, and made sure I did not miss an episode of the BBC's ten-part series, *Paul of Tarsus*, researched and written by Joy Harrington, filmed on location in Crete and starring Patrick Troughton, who went on to become the second Dr Who; to Alan White, who inspired my Junior Church group to write our own paraphrase and commentary on Luke's Gospel after *the New English Bible* was published; to Arthur Ireson and Malcolm Lomax for their O and A Level courses on the Synoptic Gospels and for prompting me to write a short dissertation on *The Theology of Luke's Gospel* for Leicester's Jonathan North awards; to Classics teachers messrs Mosley and Kinder for introducing me to Latin and Greek; and to history teachers, Ed Rayner and

Peter Greaves, and Leicester University's Centre for English Local History, who introduced me to W. G. Hoskins, archaeology, local history and the deserted medieval villages of Leicestershire; to Denys Whiteley and George Caird who at Oxford University introduced me to the study of Paul and the New Testament in the context of the world of the time; to Paul Clark who accompanied me on a tour of many of the sites visited by Paul; to Tudur Jones and Alwyn Charles who in the University College of North Wales and at Coleg Bala-Bangor introduced me to the importance of the reception history of biblical texts; to the Congregational Churches of Harden, Minsterley, Pontesbury and Highbury, Cheltenham with whom I have made connections between the world of the New Testament and today's world; to Ann Jeffers, Janet Wootton, Jason Boyd and other colleagues and students of the Congregational Institute for Practical Theology, who have joined me in exploring the world of the New Testament on our doorstep in Roman Britain; to the Tantur Institute and Henry Carse who introduced me to the archaeology and history of the Holy Land in a way that enabled me to make connections with the work of W. G. Hoskins; to Roger Box, coin collector and guide at Chedworth Roman Villa, who introduced me to the world of Roman coinage; to Fernando Coronato of Centro Nacional Patagónico CONICET, who introduced me to Christopher Tilley's *A Phenomenology of Landscape*; to Alice Brown who introduced me to Wordsworth and his *Poems of the Imagination*; and to the University of Gloucestershire's International Centre for the Study of the Bible, the annual lecturers, colleagues in the Graduate Seminar and particularly those in the Latin reading group as we had the disturbing experience of reading Tacitus' *Agricola* as the full horror of the Russian invasion of Ukraine became apparent.

Throughout, imagination has played a key part: whether in Athens when I wrote in my journal of imagining the situation as Paul addressed the Athenians, or in anticipating my first visit to the Holy Land, when I wrote of "letting my historical imagination loose." I finish my thanks with words that speak as much to today's world as they did when they were originally written. In his foreword to Joy Harrington's *Paul of Tarsus*, the book of the TV series, Roy McKay, BBC Head of Religious Broadcasting, commended "the time and thought she gave not only to the biblical record in The Acts and the Epistles but also to the social, political, and religious background of the age"; he went on to observe that "an imaginative understanding of the early years of the Christian Church can be a help to realistic appreciation of the religious situation in our own day."

A particular thank you to my wife Felicity who accompanied me on many site visits and made sure I started . . . and finished my book; and to my sons and their families for their encouragement and help, Dave and Rebecca, Phil and Lynsey. The final word must go to my grandchildren. When showing them the book I was writing, one of them asked "Who is it for?" As I tried to explain as simply as I could that it was for those interested in the New Testament, and for those interested in Roman Britain, their eyes glazed over. "Yes, but who is it *for*?" came the weary response. "Each book I read says inside the cover it is *for* someone." And so I have followed Luke's good example and included a personal dedication, which in my case is especially for my grandchildren.

Abbreviations

4QpapLXXLevb	Cave 4 Qumran Papyrus Septuagint translation of Leviticus
CIL	*Corpus Inscriptionum Latinarum* (1863 and ongoing)
COD	*Concise Oxford English Dictionary* (12th ed., 2011)
Dessau ILS	H. Dessau, *Inscriptiones Latinae Selectae* (1892–1916)
GNB	Good News Bible
LXX	The Septuagint Greek translation of the Hebrew Scriptures
MOLA	Museum of London Archaeology
NA28	Nestle-Aland *Novum Testamentum Graece*, 28th edition (2012)
NRC	New Roman Cursive
NRSV	New Revised Standard Version (1989)
NRSVue	New Revised Standard Version updated edition (2021)
OLD	*Oxford Latin Dictionary*. Edited by A. Souter et al. 1968
ORC	Old Roman Cursive
P.Amh. II 77	*Amherst Papyri* (1900–1): Petition to the Epistrategus
P.Oxy	*Oxyrhynchus Papyri* (1898–)
PAS	Portable Antiquities Scheme
RIB	Roman Inscriptions of Britain Online
RIC	Roman Imperial Coinage
SBLGNT	Society of Biblical Literature Greek New Testament (2010)
THGNT	Tyndale House Greek New Testament (2017)
SD	Sylloge of *Defixiones* from the Roman West (2022)
Tab. Lond. Bloomberg	*Tabulae Londinienses Bloomberg*, the Bloomberg tablets
Tab. Vindol.	*Tabulae Vindolandenses*, the Vindolanda tablets
Tab. Uley	*Tabellae Uley*, the Uley tablets

Tab. Sulis	*Tabellae Sulis*, the Bath tablets
UBS 4,5,6	United Bible Societies Greek New Testament fourth edition (1994), fifth edition (2015), sixth edition (2025)

The Texts

Transcripts and translations of the tablets are quoted throughout the book. The Appendix contains a select catalogue of key texts that are referred to in Chapters 2, 3, and 4. They are reproduced here for ease of reference. However, they tell only part of the story. The transcripts and translations were published alongside photographs, drawings, introductions, notes and commentary for each tablet. When studying any tablet it is essential to refer to the full publication. The Bloomberg tablets and the Vindolanda tablets (together with the Bath curse tablets) are available online at "Roman Inscriptions of Britain" (*RIB*): https://romaninscriptionsofbritain.org/. The Uley tablets have been published in Roger S. O. Tomlin, *The Uley Tablets* and in due course will appear, together with all other curse tablets from Britain, in *RIB*. Images of the Bloomberg tablets and the Uley tablets are available at British Museum Online Collections (https://www.britishmuseum.org/collection/). I am indebted to the work of Alan Bowman and David Thomas on the Vindolanda tablets, and of Roger Tomlin on the more recent Vindolanda tablets, the Bloomberg tablets, and the Uley tablets. In expressing my gratitude I must stress that the comments on the tablets in the course of this book are my own interpretation of their work and I take responsibility for any shortcomings there may be. I have made every effort to reproduce the texts here and in the body of this book as they appear in *RIB* as revised in 2024 and 2025, and in Roger S. O. Tomlin, *The Uley Tablets* (2024); once again any failings are my responsibility and I stress that reference must be made to the full publication of the original tablets.

Key Conventions Used in the Transcripts

For those new to Latin Epigraphy the LatinNow website, including Alan Bowman, Alex Mullen and Anna Willi's two-volume *Manual of Roman Everyday Writing*, an interactive ebook, is a good place to start.[1] For a more in-depth introduction, see Alison Cooley's *Cambridge Manual of Latin Epigraphy*. In her helpful introduction to editorial conventions in the study of ancient Latin texts, Cooley emphasises that "it is crucial not to mislead the reader into thinking that letters in a text are more legible than they really are."[2] The following table brings together conventions used by Alan Bowman, David Thomas and Roger Tomlin in their publication of the Vindolanda tablets, and of Roger Tomlin in his publication of the Bloomberg tablets and the Uley tablets.[3] In the original publications underdots are used to indicate doubtful or partially preserved letters. I have followed Roger Tomlin's practice in *Britannia Romana* and omitted them "for the sake of simplicity."[4]

(i), (ii)	Bloomberg and Vindolanda: separate columns of text (type 2 wax tablets; ink tablets). Uley: unrelated fragments or texts of the same lead tablet.
(a), (b)	Uley: inner face (where the text begins), outer face (where the text ends).
(abc)	letter(s) omitted by abbreviation, or a symbol explained.
[abc]	lost or damaged letter(s) restored.
[[abc]]	letter(s) erased, crossed out or over-written in the original.
<abc>	letter(s) erroneously omitted in the original.
{abc}	superfluous letters in the original.
\abc/	Uley: interlinear addition, letters added between the lines.
ABC	Uley: letter(s) read but not understood.
[.], [..]	Bloomberg: trace of one, or two letters. Uley: lacuna of one, or two letters.
[.. ? ..]	Bloomberg: trace of at least three letters.
[...]	Bloomberg: lacuna in the text of uncertain length.

1. "LatinNow"; Mullen and Bowman, *Scripts and Texts*; Willi, *Writing Equipment*.

2. Cooley, *Manual of Latin Epigraphy*, 350–360.

3. Bowman, *Life and Letters*, 100; Tomlin, *Roman London's First Voices*, 7; Tomlin, *The Uley Tablets*, 80–82.

4. Tomlin, *Britannia Romana*, xv–xvi.

<table>
<tr><td>[ ]</td><td>Vindolanda and Uley: lacuna of uncertain number of letters.</td></tr>
<tr><td>[c.4]</td><td>Vindolanda: estimate of the number of letters missing in a lacuna.</td></tr>
<tr><td>.</td><td>Uley: illegible letter.</td></tr>
<tr><td>..</td><td>Uley: two illegible letters.</td></tr>
<tr><td>...</td><td>Uley: three (or more illegible letters).</td></tr>
<tr><td>]</td><td>text missing to the left.</td></tr>
<tr><td>[</td><td>text missing to the right.</td></tr>
<tr><td>. . .</td><td>the text is broken or incomplete at the top or bottom.</td></tr>
<tr><td>uacat</td><td>space left in the original.</td></tr>
<tr><td>traces</td><td>incomplete and illegible letters.</td></tr>
<tr><td>?</td><td>uncertain transcript or translation: see commentary.</td></tr>
<tr><td>(!)</td><td>divergent spelling: see commentary.</td></tr>
<tr><td>m1, m2</td><td>Vindolanda: distinguish different hands in original.</td></tr>
<tr><td>►</td><td>Vindolanda: interpunct, a medial point between words in original.</td></tr>
<tr><td>á</td><td>Vindolanda: acute accent over a vowel represents an 'apex' in original, marking a long vowel</td></tr>
<tr><td>ab|cd</td><td>line break in the middle of a word</td></tr>
<tr><td>ab |cd</td><td>line break following a complete word</td></tr>
</table>

CHAPTER 1

Introduction

Imagining Luke–Acts in Roman Britain

"We see into the life of things."

—Wordsworth, *Poems of the Imagination*

From the East to the Outermost Island of the West: Imagining Luke–Acts in Roman Britain

IN MANY WAYS THE peoples, cultures, and societies of the Mediterranean world and of the island of Britain were as different in the time of the New Testament as they are today. At the most basic level of communication, the common language of the eastern Mediterranean was Greek and that of the west, Latin. And yet, for all the differences between east and west, there are many points of contact in a shared history. Establishing the connection between the eastern and western provinces of the Roman Empire demonstrates the way a study of Roman Britain opens a window on to the world of the New Testament.

A Shared History Between the Mediterranean World of Luke–Acts and Roman Britain

A year after establishing the province of Syria, Pompey captured Jerusalem in 63 BCE, put an end to the Hasmonean dynasty, and established Roman control of *Iudaea* through the "friendly" kingdom of the Herodian dynasty.[1] As Rome's power extended eastwards with Pompey's campaigns, so it extended westwards in Julius Caesar's Gallic war campaigns. Although Julius Caesar withdrew his army from Britain following the campaigns of 55 and 54 BCE, it seems as if he established close ties with "friendly" kingdoms in the southeast of Britain. As trade developed over the next century, so too did "mobility of people between Britain and the Roman world": it is possible that sons of those friendly kings were educated in Rome.[2] John Creighton suggests they may well have met with the sons of the Herodian dynasty in what he describes as "the Augustan kindergarten."[3] Similarities between the iconography of Philip's coins in Caesarea Philippi[4] and the coins of southeast Britain, notably of Tincomarus of the Atrebates[5] whose presence in Rome is mentioned by Augustus in *Res Gestae* 32,[6] add weight to the view that "the southeast was now, economically at least, part of the Roman world."[7]

As Paul's travels began, Claudius invaded Britain in 43 CE, initiating a conquest that would be completed by the Flavians forty years later.[8] The triumph of Claudius, the only one between the triumph of Germanicus, son of Tiberius, in 17 CE and the triumph of Titus over *Iudaea* in 71 CE,[9] was commemorated in places visited by Paul. In Pisidian Antioch, a statue had been dedicated to Claudius c. 45–46 CE, "for his safety and victory in Britannia" (*pro incolumitate / eius et victoria / Britannica*).[10] Another statue was erected in honor of Publius Anicius Maximus from Pisidian Antioch, c. 45–50 CE; as camp prefect (*praefectus castrorum*) of *legio II Augusta* under the command of Vespasian he had been "honored with a mural crown

1. Jagersma, *History of Israel*, 105–37.

2. Cunliffe, *Britain Begins*, 363–64.

3. Creighton, *Coins and Power*, 117–25.

4. Hendin, *Guide to Biblical Coins*, 228–32.

5. van Arsdell, *Celtic Coinage*, plate 17, Atrebates, Regni & Belgae.

6. Cooley, *Res Gestae Divi Augustae*, 96–97, 253–54.

7. Cunliffe, *Britain Begins*, 367; S. James, *Exploring World of Celts*, 47–48; Leins and Farley, "*A Changing World*," 122–24.

8. D. J. Mattingly, *An Imperial Possession*, 87–127; Salway, *History of Roman Britain*, 55–126; S. Hill and Ireland, *Roman Britain*, 13–26; Ireland, *Roman Britain Sourcebook*, chaps. 3–7; Todd, *Roman Britain*, 43–115. "Roman Britain."

9. Beard, *Roman Triumph*, 69–70.

10. Standing, "Claudian Invasion and Victoria Britannica," 281–82; Tomlin, *Britannia Romana*, 14–15.

and untipped spear for his service in Britannia" (*honorato / corona murali et / hasta pura ob bellum / Britannic(um)*.[11] In Corinth there is evidence of "the direct worship of the personified goddess *Victoria Britannica*" in a statue of Tiberius Claudius Dinippus who is described as "augur, priest of Victoria Britannica" (*auguri, sac[erd(oti)\ Victor(iae) Britannic(ae)*, 49 CE.[12] Fragments survive of the triumphal arch erected in Rome c. 51 CE to honor the triumph of Claudius by the Roman Senate and People "because he had received the surrender of eleven British kings, defeated without the loss of any men, and brought barbarian peoples beyond the Ocean for the first time under the rule of Rome" (*SENATVS. PO[pulusque.] RO[manus q]VOD | REGES. BRIT[annorum XI devictos sine] | VLLA.IACTVR[a in deditionem acceperit | GENTESQVE.B[arbaras trans oceanum] | PRIMVS. IN DICI[onem populi romani redegerit]).* Built as an integral part of his restoration on a monumental scale of the aqueduct, Aqua Virgo, it seems to have been a celebration of Claudius's mastery of water in his conquest of the peoples on the other side of the ocean.[13] Images of the arch appeared on coins throughout the empire.[14]

The conquest of Britain is for Josephus all the more notable because it involved overcoming the perils of the Ocean. According to Josephus, shortly after the failure of the Boudica revolt in 61 CE, Agrippa II warned the would-be rebels in Jerusalem not to take up the sword: "consider the defenses of the Britons, you who feel so sure of the defenses of Jerusalem. They are surrounded by the Ocean and inhabit an island as big as the land

11. P. Anicius Maximus: https://www.roman-britain.co.uk/people/p-anicius-maximus/; A. R. Birley, "Officers of Second Augustan Legion," 105 including picture; Pollard and Berry, *Complete Roman Legions*, 86; Tomlin describes Pisidian Antioch as "a little Rome built on seven hills, a Latin-speaking enclave in the Greek east," *Britannia Romana*, 10–11.

12. Standing, "Claudian Invasion and Victoria Britannica," 284–87: photo, 285; Tomlin describes this as one of "at least ten inscriptions honouring Dinippus in similar terms (*Britannia Romana*, 13–14). Heilig suggests that this is "archaeological evidence for Claudius and his victory over Britannia being celebrated in a very public—and cultic!—way in Corinth during the exact time that Paul was active there." He uses that, with a photo, as "evidence for a contemporary historical background of Paul's use of the triumph metaphor in 2 Cor. 2:14" (*Apostle and the Empire*, 63–70).

13. The inscription is as redrawn by G. Gatti in 1942 and is reproduced by A. A. Barrett who also describes the arch's incorporation into Agua Virgo ("Claudius' British Victory Arch," 12, 16–19); Hingley, *Conquering the Ocean*, 92–93; Salway, *Roman Britain*, 86; Tomlin, *Britannia Romana*, 16–17. Cf. Suetonius, *Claudius* 21.181.

14. South Warwickshire Hoard 1114, 1115: Ireland, *South-Warwickshire Hoard*, 32. Cf. "*OCRE*": RIC I (second edition) Claudius 34. Map (Figure 1) 12.

which we inhabit; yet the Romans crossed the sea and enslaved them, and four legions keep that huge island quiet."[15] The Judean revolt of 66 CE was suppressed by Vespasian, who had played a significant part in Claudius's conquest of the south of Britain; to quell the revolt of Shim'on ben Kosiba Hadrian turned to Severus, governor of Britain (130–133/34 CE), "in an operation that," according to Richard Abdy, "spanned the entire length of the Roman world."[16]

Crucifixion is one mark of the brutality of the Roman Empire. In Latin literature it is often described as a common punishment and yet the skeletons of only two victims of crucifixion have ever been discovered, one in Jerusalem and the other in a late first to early second-century Roman roadside settlement on the *Via Devana* in Fenstanton, near Cambridge. The twenty-five to thirty-five year old male victim had suffered disease, traumatic injury and may have been shackled. Tied to a cross bar, his feet had been nailed on either side of an upright to secure them during his prolonged and agonizing death. He would consequently have been unable to ease the pain by moving his feet. Nonetheless, his body had been respectfully buried on its back, with hands clasped at the pelvis, presumably by family or friends. In the report of their discovery in 2018, David Ingham and Corinne Duhig describe the way the positioning of the nail "penetrating the right heel bone (*calcaneum*) horizontally, exiting below the protrusion called the *sustentaculum tali*" was identical to the positioning of the nail in the burial of Yehochanan found at Giv'at ha-Mivtar in north Jerusalem in 1968. The Cambridgeshire crucifixion is the best-preserved example of this form of execution, throws light on its practice and demonstrates its prevalence across the empire.[17]

That shared history between the Mediterranean world of Luke–Acts and Roman Britain is evident in the following chronological table comparing significant events in Rome, in the Eastern Mediterranean world of Luke–Acts and in Roman Britain:

15. Josephus, *Bellum Iudaicum* II.378, 160.

16. Abdy, *Legion*, 38–39; Jagersma, *History of Israel*, 159.

17. *Ingham and Duhig, Crucifixion in the Fens*, 25–29; Lewsey, "Evidence of a Roman Crucifixion"; Abdy, *Legion*, 274. Radiocarbon dating gives a 68 per cent probability of a date between 210 and 340 CE, and a 95 per cent probability of a date between 130 and 360 CE. For a survey of the literature on crucifixion, including reference to the Jerusalem skeleton, see Hanson and Oakman, *Palestine in the Time of Jesus*, 85–89; Reed, *Visual Guide to the New Testament*, 92–93; Walker, *In Steps of Jesus*, 177.

Date	Rome[18]	E. Mediterranean[19]	Britain/Britannia[20]
Sixties BCE	60 BCE, Pompey, Crassus and Caesar form triumvirate.	63 BCE, Pompey takes *Iudaea.*	
Fifties BCE		55 BCE, Antipater, father of Herod, procurator of *Iudaea.*	55 BCE, Caesar's first campaign. 54 BCE, Caesar's second campaign. Hostages taken to Rome.
Forties BCE	49–48 BCE, civil war between Pompey and Caesar. 44 BCE, Caesar killed. 43 BCE, Mark Antony, Lepidus, Octavian, triumvirate. 42 BCE, Mark Antony and Octavian defeat Brutus and Cassius at Philippi.	Antipater's sons, Phasael and Herod rule in Jerusalem and Galilee respectively. Philippi becomes a *colonia*	Commios, friendly king of Rome; start of southern dynasty, Atrebates. Growing trade between Rome and southeast of Britain.
Thirties BCE	31 BCE, Octavian defeats Antony and Cleopatra at Actium.	40–37 BCE, Herod campaigns in *Iudaea.* 37 BCE, Herod appointed king of the *Iudaei* in Rome. 37–4 BCE reign of Herod, king of the *Iudaei.*	34 BCE, Octavian considers campaign in Britain, but nothing comes of it.

18. Woolf, *Rome*; Beard, *SPQR*.

19. Jagersma, *History of Israel*; Grabbe, *Judaism*; Josephus, *Jewish War*; Bruce, *Acts*; Walton and Wenham, *Exploring the New Testament*, vol. 1. For an alternative chronology based on the letters of Paul, see Campbell, "Chronology."

20. Salway, *History of Roman Britain*; D. J. Mattingly, *An Imperial Possession*; B. Jones and Mattingly, *Atlas of Roman Britain*. See Map (Figure 1).

Date	Rome	E. Mediterranean	Britain/Britannia
27 BCE - 14 CE	Augustus	Sons of friendly king, Herod, educated in Rome: Alexander; Aristobulus; Philip; Herod Antipas; and grandson Agrippa. c. 4 BCE, birth of Jesus (Luke 1–2). 4 BCE, death of Herod. 4 BCE–33/34 CE, Philip, tetrarch of Ituraea and Trachonitis (Luke 3:1). 4 BCE–39 CE, Herod Antipas, tetrarch of Galilee (Luke 3:1). 4 BCE– 6 CE, Archelaus, ethnarch of *Iudaea*. 6 CE: failed rebellion of Judas the Galilean (Acts 5:37); direct Roman rule of *Iudaea*: appointment of governor. c. 8 CE: 12-year-old Jesus visits Jerusalem (Luke 2:41–51).	27 BCE, Octavian (Augustus) considers campaign in Britain, but nothing comes of it. 26 BCE, Augustus considers campaign in Britain, but nothing comes of it. Sons of friendly kings from southeast Britain, including sons of Commius, Tincomarus, Epillus and Verica, educated in Rome as trading links grow. Tribes minting coins: Atrebates, Trinovantes, Iceni, Durotriges, Cantiaci, Catuvellauni, Dobunni, Corieltavi. See Map.

Date	Rome	E. Mediterranean	Britain/Britannia
14–37 CE	Tiberius	26–37 CE, Pontius Pilate, governor of *Iudaea*. c. 28 CE, Jesus' ministry begins in fifteenth year of Tiberius (Luke 3:1—22:46). 27/28 CE, Agrippa has a son, Agrippa, educated in Rome. 31/32 CE, after trial by Pilate and Herod Antipas, death and resurrection of Jesus (Luke 23–24). Pentecost; first communities of followers of the Way established (Acts 1–11). 34 CE, death of Philip the tetrarch.	Descendants of Commios and Tincomarus, friendly kings in southeast Britain (Atrebates); Cunobelinus, king of eastern dynasty (Trinovantes), followed by Adminius (Cantici). Trading links continue to grow as sons of friendly kings educated in Rome. See Map.
37–41 CE	Gaius Caligula	37/38 CE, Agrippa, son of Herod, given Ituraea and Trachonitis. 40 CE, Herod Antipas exiled to Gaul. Agrippa and Petronius, governor of Syria, prevent Gaius placing statue of himself in Jerusalem temple.	Adminius exiled from Britain by Cunobelinus. Gaius initiates but abandons campaign against Britain.

Date	Rome	E. Mediterranean	Britain/Britannia
41–54 CE	Claudius	Agrippa aids Claudius and is made King over the whole area once ruled by his father, Herod. 44 CE, Agrippa dies (Acts 12:20–25). Kingdom becomes a Roman province, ruled by governors. 49 CE Agrippa II appointed king of Chalcis and given oversight of Jerusalem temple. 49 CE: Claudius expels *Iudaei* from Rome (Acts 18:2). c.47–57 CE: Paul and others establish communities of followers of the Way in eastern Mediterranean. (Acts 13:1—21:26). 51–52 CE: Gallio proconsul of Achaia (Acts 18:12).	40–43 CE, Cunobelinus dies, flight of Verica to Rome. 43 CE, conquest of Britain begins. 43–46 CE, Vespasian victorious across the south. 47 CE, conquest of south and east of Britain complete (Map 1 and 16–26). Province of Britannia established (Cantiaci, Atrebates, Dumnoni, Durotriges, Trinovantes, Catuvellauni, Iceni, Dobunni, Corieltavi). Campaigning meets resistance from Silures, Demetae, Cornovii, Decangli, Ordovices, Brigantes. See Map. Londinium established as a trading port (Map 1). c. 43–53 CE, one Bloomberg tablet. 49 CE, Camulodunum becomes a *colonia* (Map 16). c. 50 CE, friendly Rulers: Togidubnus (Atrebates); Prasutagus (Iceni); Cartimandua (Brigantes). See Map.

Date	Rome	E. Mediterranean	Britain/Britannia
54–68 CE	Nero	54/55 CE: Agrippa II given jurisdiction in Galilee. c. 57 CE: Paul arrested and tried in Caesarea by governors, Felix and Festus, and by Agrippa II; appeals to emperor (Acts 23:23—26:32). c. 60 CE: Paul under arrest in Rome (Acts 28:11–31). Pre 66 CE, in Jerusalem Agrippa II warns *Iudaei* not to rebel, referring to Britannia and implicitly the failure of the Boudica revolt. 66 CE war of the *Iudaei*. Sixties CE, earliest suggested date for Luke–Acts	53–65/70 CE, fifteen Bloomberg tablets. 60/61 CE, campaign against Ordovices as far as Ynys Mon̂ (Map 32) cut short by death of Prasutagus, precipitating Boudica revolt. Camulodunum, Verulamium, Londinium (Map 16, 17, 1) destroyed by fire. Boudica defeated at Manduessedum (Map 30). c. 61 CE, the three urban centers quickly rebuilt, leading to consolidation of southeast Britannia.
68 CE	Year of the four emperors Nero, Galba, Otho, Vitellius.	Vespasian and son, Titus, campaign against *Iudaei.*	

Date	Rome	E. Mediterranean	Britain/Britannia
69–79CE	Vespasian, Start of Flavian dynasty.	70 CE, fall of Jerusalem and destruction of temple. 73 CE capture of Massada, last outpost of *Iudaei*. Seventies – eighties CE, middle date suggested for Luke-Acts.	65/70–80 CE, Twenty-eight Bloomberg tablets. 71–73 CE, vigorous campaigning resumes under the Flavians. 71–73 CE, Brigantes defeated. 73–77 CE, Silures defeated. Network of small forts and roads secures western frontier of Britannia (Map 47, 48, 49, 50, 10, 9, 8, 7, 26, 27, 28, 29). 76 CE, Agricola appointed governor of Britannia. 77/78 CE, Agricola completes conquest of Decangli and Ordovices. 78/79 CE, Agricola secures hold over Brigantes and Parisi and moves north. See Map.
79–81 CE	Titus, Flavian dynasty	Seventies – eighties CE, middle date suggested for Luke-Acts.	79/80 CE, Agricola campaigns further north. See Map.

Date	Rome	E. Mediterranean	Britain/Britannia
81–96 CE	Domitian, Flavian dynasty	Seventies – eighties CE, middle date suggested for Luke–Acts.	80–90/5 CE, thirty-one Bloomberg tablets. 82/83 CE, battle of *Mons Graupius* completes conquest of Britain. See Map note. c. 85 CE, monumental arch constructed in Rutupiae (Map 18). 85–130 CE, Vindolanda Tablets from a sequence of wooden forts at Vindolanda (Map 2).
96–98 CE	Nerva		Glevum a *colonia* (Map 26).
98–117 CE	Trajan	Early second century CE, late date suggested for Luke–Acts.	75–125 CE, earliest Uley curse tablet (Map 3).
117–138 CE	Hadrian	134–135 CE, Sextus Julius Severus transferred to *Iudaea* to suppress the Second rebellion of *Iudaei* led by Shim'on bar Kosiba. c. 135 CE, Babatha hides family documents in cave by the Dead Sea.	122 CE, Hadrian's Wall. (See Map 36, 37, 38, 2, 39, 41, 40). 130/1–132/3 CE, Sextus Julius Severus, governor of Britannia.
100s –200s CE.			Second – third centuries CE, Uley tablets written in Old Roman Cursive.

Date	Rome	E. Mediterranean	Britain/Britannia
200s –300s CE.	306–337 CE, Constantine	313 CE, edict of Toleration, Milan. 314 CE, three from Britannia attend Council of Arles.	End of third century CE, martyrdom of Aaron and Julius as followers of the Way in Isca Silurum (Map 28), and of Alban in Verulamium (Map 17). After 296 CE, Britannia becomes a civil diocese of four provinces Fourth century CE, Uley tablets written in New Roman Cursive.
400s CE	410 CE, sack of Rome.		409 CE, end of Roman rule in Britain.

Table 1. Key dates connecting Rome, *Iudaea* and the Eastern Mediterranean, and Britain/Britannia

Accessing a Cultural Encyclopedia of the Roman World of Luke–Acts in Roman Britain

In Britain one is never far from interesting Roman remains and imaginatively curated museum displays.[21] Rarely, if ever, is any connection made with the world of the New Testament, and yet connections that bring to life the cultural encyclopedia of the Roman dimension of that world are hidden in plain sight as can be seen in the following table (asterisks indicate museums):

21. Although out of print, the best guide to Britain's Roman remains is Wilson, *A Guide to Roman Remains in Britain*. Less detailed, but also good is Allen and Bryan, *Roman Britain*. "Roman Britain" includes an A–Z of Places of Roman Britain.

Location	Map	Features	Luke–Acts
Roads	See Map (Figure 1): approx.	Evident in the six major trunk roads in England and Wales:	Throughout Luke–Acts.[22]
	1–41	to north (A1), Ermine St	
	1–21	to south coast (A3),	
	1–24 and 9	to west (A4 and A 40),	
	1–31	to Wroxeter (A5) Watling St cont'd,	
	1–6	to northwest (A6) not shown.	
		And in other named roads:	
	37–41	the Stanegate	
	20–25/26	Ermin Way	
	24–46	Fosse Way	
	16–47	Via Devana	
	9–48	Sarn Helen	
	26–9	Via Julia Maritima	
Londinium Bloomberg Tablets	1	The Bloomberg tablets are on display where they were discovered at The London Mithraeum beneath Bloomberg's European headquarters; and at the Museum of London where the full story of Roman London is told.[23]	

22. Kloppenborg, "Luke's Geography." Note: details are more accurate in Luke towards the coast and in Acts.

23. S. M. Wright, Archaeology at Bloomberg; "London Mithraeum"; "London Museum."

Location	Map	Features	Luke-Acts
Vindolanda and the Tablets	2	The Vindolanda tablets are on display in Vindolanda, and at the British Museum.[24]	
Uley and the Tablets	3	The location of the Temple of Mercury on the Hill of *Aruerius* and the adjacent hill fort and burial chamber can be explored. Finds are displayed at the nearby Museum in the Park, Stroud and the tablets themselves, the head of Mercury, figurines and other artefacts in the British Museum.	
Bath* (Aquae Sulis)	55	Classical temple dedicated to Sulis Minerva: virtual reality presentations visualize ritual and sacrifices.[25]	Classical temples found in cities mentioned in Acts: Lystra (Acts 14:8–18); Athens (Acts 17:16–34); Ephesus (Acts 19:21–41).
Caerleon* (Isca)	28	Fortress of *legio II Augusta*: amphitheater, baths, barracks, centurions' quarters, *contubernia* and bread ovens.[26]	Centurions: Luke 7:1–10; 23:47; Acts 10:1—11:18; 22:25–26; 23:23; 24:23; 27:1–44. Feeding of 5000 Luke 9:14 (cf. John 6:15).

24. "Roman Vindolanda Fort and Museum"; R. Birley, *Vindolanda: Daily Life*; "The British Museum"; Hobbs and Jackson, *Roman Britain*.

25. Cunliffe, *Roman Bath*; Wilson, A Guide to Roman Brita*in*, 158–70; Cousins, *Sanctuary at Bath*; Allen and Bryan, *Roman Britain*, 74–76; Davenport, *Roman Bath*; "Roman Baths of Bath."

26. Knight, *Caerleon*; Wilson, *A Guide to Roman Britain*, 302–14; Allen and Bryan, *Roman Britain*, 144–46; Manning, *Roman Wales*, 31–43; Howell, *Silures*, 73–76

Location	Map	Features	Luke–Acts
Gloucester* (Glevum or Colonia Nervia Glevensis)	26	Life-size, mounted statue of Nerva marked 1900th anniversary of status as a *colonia*. Roman grid street plan and course of walls evident in city center, and in museum.[27]	Philippi a *colonia*: Acts 16:12, 11–40; cf. Phil 3:20.

27. Copeland, *Roman Gloucestershire*, 62–64; Wilson, *A Guide to Roman Britain*, 170–77; Allen and Bryan, *Roman Britain*, 82–84. Crummy and Hurst, *Coloniae of Roman Britain* was published to commemorate the 1900th anniversary of Gloucester becoming a *colonia*. R. Rowe imagines followers of the Way meeting outside the walls of second century Glevum in the context of a Libertus detective mystery (*Ghosts of Glevum*). "Museum of Gloucester."

Location	Map	Features	Luke–Acts
Caerwent (Venta Siulurm)	29	Walled town with layout of streets in *insulae*, shops fronting the main street. Foundations of forum and basilica (including tribunal, where magistrates heard civil cases); temple; courtyard houses; craftworker houses, workshops and shops. Artefacts exhibited in Newport Museum and Art Gallery (Map 4).[28] Similar interiors re-created in Cirencester, St Albans and Museum of London.[29] Honorific inscription to Tiberius Claudius Paulinus.[30]	The kind of courtyard houses and craftworker houses where early followers of the Way in Acts would have met.[31] Street called Straight in Damascus and city walls (Acts 9:11, 23–25). Tribunal in Philippi (Acts 16:20),[32] Corinth (Acts 18:12–17) and Caesarea (Acts 25:6, 17). Visiting Antioch in Pisidia (Acts 13:13–52; 14:21–23; and possibly 16:6; 19:1) Paul probably saw the honorific inscription

28. Brewer, *Caerwent*, 48–53; Wilson, *A Guide to Roman Britain*, 359–70; Allen and Bryan, *Roman Britain*, 148–49; Manning, *Roman Wales*, 57–71; Guest, "Forum-Basilica Caerwent"; Howell, *Silures*, 76–86; "Newport Museum Archaeology."

29. "Verulamium Museum"; "Roman London Gallery"; "Corinium Museum."

30. *RIB* 311; Brewer, *Caerwent*, 11; Tomlin, *Britannia Romana*, 243–44.

31. Pritchard, *Atlas of the Bible*, 174–75; Oakes, *Reading Romans in Pompeii*, 1–97; Oakes, *Empire, Economics, and the New Testament*, 3-62.

32. Keener, *Acts*, 403.

Location	Map	Features	Luke-Acts
		Evidence of early followers of the Way in Britannia: a *Chi Rho* symbol etched on a pewter bowl deposited in an urn in a Caerwent house,[33] a place associated with two of Britannia's three third century Christian martyrs, Julius and Aaron.[34] Another Caerwent house has features resembling what might be expected in a house church.[35]	to Publius Anicius Maximus, commended for his part in Claudian invasion of Britain,[36] which is very similar to honorific inscription and statue to Tiberius Claudius Paulinus in Caerwent.
Chedworth*	5	Evidence of early followers of the Way in *Chi Rho* symbol etched into slabs around the spring at Chedworth. Reconstructed villa rooms illustrate stratification of society.[37]	The meal brings together different strata of society (Luke 14:15–24; 22:27).

33. House IX.7N: Brewer, *Caerwent*, 23; "Chi Rho Dish Caerwent"; "Newport Museum Archaeology."

34. A. Breeze, "British Martyrs Aaron and Julius"; Wilson, *A Guide to Roman Britain*, 359–70; Allen and Bryan, *Roman Britain*, 148–49; B. Jones and Mattingly, *Atlas of Roman Britain*, 295; J. R. Davies, "OT Personal Names," 3, 14–15.

35. House V.22N: Brewer, *Caerwent*, 23.

36. CIL III 6809; A. R. Birley, "Officers of Second Augustan Legion," 105, including picture; Pollard and Berry, *Complete Roman Legions*, 86.

37. Cleary, *Chedworth Roman Villa*, 97–98; R. Goodburn, *Roman Villa, Chedworth*, 28.

Location	Map	Features	Luke-Acts
Cirencester* (Corinium)	25	SATOR square etched on the wall of a house in Cirencester, perhaps suggesting early followers of the Way met in this house.[38] Reconstructions of interior of houses.	Followers of the Way meet in houses (Acts 12:12; 16:40).
Chichester* (Noviomagus Regnorum) Fishbourne Palace*	21 and 22	Inscription to Togidubnus,[39] a friendly king of Rome whose palace was possibly at nearby Fishbourne,[40] which has features reminiscent of Herodian palaces.[41] Children of friendly kings from Britain educated in Rome.[42]	Herodian dynasty educated and at home in Rome: Herod the Great (Luke 1:5); Herod Philip (Luke 3:1); Herod Antipas (Luke 3:1,19; 9:7–9; 13:31–35; 23:6–15; Acts 4:27); Herod Agrippa I (Acts 12:1–23); Herod Agrippa II (Acts 25:13—26:32).

38. Wilkes, "SATOR Square"; Atkinson, "'SATOR' Word-Square"; Atkinson, "Cirencester Word-Square"; Stevenson, *A New Eusebius*, 7–8; Tomlin suggests "the truth may be that it is simply a word-square" (*Britannia Romana*, 378–79).

39. *RIB* 91: *[N]eptuno et Minervae | templum | [pr]o salute do[mus] divinae | [ex] auctoritat[e Ti(beri)] Claud(i) | [To]gidubni r[eg(is) m]agni Brit(anniae) | [colle]gium fabror(um) et qui in eo | [sun]t d(e) s(uo) d(ederunt) donante aream | [. . . Pud]ente Pudentini fil(io).* To Neptune and Minerva, for the welfare of the Divine House by the authority of Tiberius Claudius Togidubnus, great king of Britain, the guild of smiths and those therein gave this temple from their own resources, Pudens, son of Pudentinus, presenting the site. Tomlin, *Britannia Romana*, 33–34.

40. Cunliffe, Fishbourne Roman Palace; Wilson, *A Guide to Roman Britain*, 68–77; Allen and Bryan, *Roman Britain*, 24–25.

41. Cunliffe, *Fishbourne Roman Palace*; Wilson, *A Guide to Roman Britain*, 77.

42. Creighton, *Coins and Power*, 117–25, cf. Celtic coinage from southeast Britain.

Location	Map	Features	Luke–Acts
Colchester* (Camulodunum, or Colonia Claudia Victricensis)	16	The magnificent Norman Castle Keep, home to Colchester's Roman Museum, was built on the foundations of the *colonia's* temple dedicated to the divinized Claudius and set within a colonnaded plaza. A ceremonial gateway celebrated Claudius's many achievements. A theater and chariot racing stadium.[43]	Visiting Antioch in Pisidia, a *colonia*, Paul would have seen its temple dedicated to divinized Augustus, set within a colonnaded plaza, and its ceremonial gateway celebrating Augustus's achievements with *Res Gestae:*[44] Acts 13:13–52; 14:21; and possibly 16:6; 19:1.
Fenstanton, Cambridgeshire	14	The Cambridgeshire Crucifixion.[45]	Crucifixion (Luke 23:26–49).
Leicester* (Ratae Corieltavorum)	63	Leicester's Jewry Wall Museum tells the story of Roman Leicester, and of the household responsible for the Leicester curse tablet. Milestone illustrates road network.[46]	Followers of the Way meet in houses (Acts 12:12; 16:40). The meal brings together different strata of society (Luke 14:15–24; 22:27). Road network throughout.

43. Crummy, *City of Victory: Colchester*, 59–61, and passim; Wilson, *A Guide to Roman Britain*, 210–28; Allen and Bryan, *Roman Britain*, 103–7; "Colchester Castle."

44. Crossan and Reed, *In Search of Paul*, 178–83; Walker, *In Steps of Paul*, 78–81, 87–90; Cooley, Res *Gestae Divi Augustae*, 13–16.

45. Ingham and Duhig, *Crucifixion in the Fens*, 25–29; Lewsey, "Evidence of a Roman Crucifixion"; Abdy, *Legion*, 274; cf. Hanson and Oakman, *Palestine in the Time of Jesus*, 85–89; Reed, *Visual Guide to the New Testament*, 92–93; Walker, *In Steps of Jesus*, 177.

46. "Jewry Wall"; Savani et al., *Roman Leicester.*

Location	Map	Features	Luke–Acts
Manchester* (Mamucium)	6	Early evidence of followers of the Way in Britannia: *SATOR* square cut into the shoulder of an amphora fragment in Manchester.[47]	
Richborough* (Rutupiae)	18	Gateway to Britannia, with monumental arch (c. 85 CE) marking completion of the conquest of Britannia.[48]	The triumph in Britannia was celebrated in Corinth (Acts 18:1–17) and Pisidian Antioch (Acts 13:13–52; 14:21; and possibly 16:6; 19:1).
St Albans* (Verulamium)	17	Although in a very different geographical location, this is the best-preserved Roman theater in Britain. There are also reconstructions of the interior of homes and workshops. Evidence of followers of the Way in the martyrdom of Alban.[49]	The theatre in Ephesus (Acts 19:21–41). Craft workers' homes; workshops of those involved in building.

47. B. Jones and Mattingly, Atlas *of Roman Britain*, 295, 297.

48. Wilmott and Smither, "Fort at Richborough," 147–48; Watson, "Roman Britain in 2020 Southern," 147–48; Sherwood, "Roman Gateway"; Allen and Bryan, *Roman Britain*, 40–41; Wilson, *A Guide to Roman Britain*, 39–45.

49. "Verulamium Museum"; Niblett, *Verulamium*; Allen and Bryan, *Roman Britain*, 112–15; Wilson, *A Guide to Roman Britain*, 228–41.

Location	Map	Features	Luke–Acts
Caerhun Segontium Tomen y Mu̓r	48 49 50	A network of roads, linking forts, secured occupation, and the western frontier. Dramatic earthworks of auxiliary forts can be explored in Caerhun and Tomen y Mu̓r (Map 48, 50) where a Roman Will was discovered; and the barracks, *via principalis, praetorium* and *principia* of a stone fort in Segontium. Map 49.[50]	Road network throughout Luke–Acts.

Table 2. A select gazetteer of places in Britain that open a window on to the world of the New Testament

The Roman galleries of the British Museum, London, are a rich source of material not only for Roman Britain[51] but also for the world of the Bible.[52] The iconography of coins serves as an illustrated cultural encyclopedia of pre-Roman Britain and imperial Rome. The story of southeast Britain in the late Iron Age and of Rome from 194 BCE to 164 CE is told in three coin hoards: the Hallaton Hoard (Harborough Museum, Market Harborough),[53] the South Warwickshire Hoard (Market Hall Museum, Warwick)[54] and the Llanvaches Hoard (National Roman Legion Museum,

50. Wilson, *A Guide to Roman Britain*, 339–52; Allen and Bryan, *Roman Britain*, 144, 146–47, 160–61; Guest, *Roman Frontiers in Wales*, 63–79, see map on p. 67; Tomlin, "A Roman Will"; Tomlin, *Britannia Romana*, 227–28. Hopewell, *Roman Roads*, 38–63. Allen and Brian describe Sarn Helen, the Roman road linking north and south Wales was part of that network from Caerhun through Tomen y Mu̓r, Dolaucothau, and Caerfyrddin to Castell Nedd (Map (Figure 1) 48, 50, 10, 9, 8) (*Roman Britain*, 161–62).

51. Hobbs and Jackson, *Roman Britain*.

52. T. C. Mitchell, *Bible in British Museum*; B. H. Edwards and Anderson, *Through the British Museum*.

53. Score, *Conquest Period Ritual Site*; Score, *Story of Hallaton Treasure*; "Hallaton Treasure." Map (Figure 1) 13.

54. Ireland, *South-Warwickshire Hoard*; Dingle, "*Market Hall Museum*." Map (Figure 1) 12.

Caerleon).[55] The story is told in the Portable Antiquities Scheme website,[56] in many local museum displays and in major displays in the Ashmolean museum, Oxford,[57] and the British Museum, London.[58]

Since 2005, moves to recognize the entire frontier of the Roman Empire as a world heritage site are a reminder of the rich diversity and shared cultural heritage that span the whole empire.[59] By 161 CE Aelius Aristides of Smyrna spoke of the way "an encamped army, like a rampart, encloses the civilized world in a ring . . . from the settled areas of Aethopia to the Phasis, and from the Euphrates in the interior to the great outermost island towards the west," i.e. to Britain.[60]

Beyond Narrative History: Giving Voice to the Voiceless in Roman Britain

The shift from a focus on narrative history to material culture, people and society in the study of Roman Britain connects with recent studies of the New Testament that have a similar focus and give rise to the development of archival ethnography. In the mid twentieth century historians sought to produce a narrative history of Roman Britain by drawing on a historical imagination in the sense understood by R. G. Collingwood.[61] Collingwood speaks of "certain fixed points," and Hoskins of "facts," which are then supplemented by the imagination so ensuring that what is produced is not "imaginary" but in a proper sense "historical." That is precisely what Collingwood had done in his contribution to the first volume of *the Oxford History of England*, weaving together ancient texts and recent archaeological discoveries to create a narrative history of Roman Britain, supplemented

55. "Llanvaches Roman Coin Hoard." Map (Figure 1) 11.

56. "PAS"; Moorhead, *Roman Coinage in Britain*.

57. "Ashmolean Museum Coins."

58. "British Museum, Department of Coins."

59. D. J. Breeze, ed. "Collection: Frontiers of the Roman Empire"; D. J. Breeze et al., *African Frontiers*; D. J. Breeze et al., *Eastern Frontiers*; D. J. Breeze and Guest, *Roman Frontiers in Wales*; D. J. Breeze, *Frontiers Hadrian's Wall*; D. J. Breeze, *Frontiers Hinterland of Hadrian's Wall*; D. J. Breeze et al., *History of Frontier Studies*; D. J. Breeze, *Frontiers of Imperial Rome*; Abdy, *Legion*, 23.

60. Aristides mid-2nd century 26, 80–84; D. J. Breeze, *Frontiers of Imperial Rome*, 20.

61. Collingwood, *The Idea of History*, 242.

by thematic chapters.[62] It became a pattern for subsequent histories of Roman Britain.[63] By the time Collingwood's Oxford History was replaced in 1981 by Peter Salway, scholars had begun "to question many of the apparently fixed points in the accepted picture of Roman Britain";[64] nonetheless, Salway produced a narrative history in the same way, supplemented by thematic chapters.[65] The narrative of Collingwood, Frere, Salway and many others was influenced by Francis Haverfield's 1905 lecture, *The Romanization of Roman Britain.* Drawing on archaeological, linguistic and historical evidence he had argued that "the Empire . . . Romanized the province, introducing Roman speech and town-life and culture."[66] Frere spoke of "Romano-British culture" not as "a replacement of cultures" but as a "synthesis" arising from "the impact of the civilization of Rome upon the Celtic people of Britain."[67] For Salway "Romanization" was not "a conscious spreading of Roman amenities at Roman expense"; rather, it entailed "appropriation" as influential individuals and families identified "themselves with Roman political and social culture."[68] A different approach has emerged in the twenty-first century. David Mattingly structured his history of Roman Britain around military, urban and rural communities; rejecting the notion of Romanization he focused on the discrepant identities to be found within those different communities, seeking to give voice to people experiencing the power of empire and its implications for their identity in a Britannia that he describes as *An Imperial Possession.* While he too draws

62. Collingwood and Myres, *Roman Britain*: the machinery of government; the people; the towns; the countryside; industry and commerce; art; religion.

63. Frere includes narrative chapters 1–8, 15–16; thematic chapters 9–14 on administration, towns, countryside, trade and industry and the Romanization of Britain (*Britannia*, first published, 1967; 3rd edition extensively revised 1987). Todd offers a narrative history bringing together ancient texts and the most recent archaeological discoveries and insights (*Roman Britain*: first published in 1981; revised in 1997 and 1999).

64. Salway, *Roman Britain*, vii.

65. Salway offers a narrative history (3–501), followed by thematic chapters on the assimilation of Britain (505–38); the historical geography of Roman Britain (539–72); town and country (573–614); the economy (615–64); religion and society (665–739) (*Roman Britain*). Revised and abridged as Salway, *Oxford Illustrated Roman Britain*; and published without illustrations in abridged form as Salway, *Roman Britain.* The narrative section was further condensed as Salway, *Roman Britain Short Introduction.* Cf. S. Hill and Ireland, *Roman Britain.*

66. Haverfield, *Romanization of Roman Britain*, 79.

67. Frere, *Britannia*, 295.

68. Salway, *History of Roman Britain*, 83.

on a historical imagination to weave together the ancient texts and archaeological discoveries, he also makes use of that kind of geographical and archaeological imagination described by Tilley and Shanks.[69] In *Britannia Romana*, Roger Tomlin draws on inscriptions to illustrate the history and character of Roman Britain.[70]

In the study of Roman Britain, the application of a historical imagination as understood by Collingwood is problematic: the "fixed points" and "facts" are few and far between. There are only a few references to Britain in the works of four Roman historians: Caesar,[71] Tacitus,[72] Suetonius,[73] and Cassius Dio,[74] while Augustus mentions the presence of two friendly kings in Rome.[75] Translations of the main texts have been brought together in Stanley Ireland's *Roman Britain: A Sourcebook*.[76] The geography and people of Britain are briefly described by Caesar,[77] Tacitus,[78] Pliny the Elder,[79] and Strabo.[80] The British section of the Antonine Itineraries maps the Roman roads that were established by the mid second century CE.[81] The following

69. D. J. Mattingly structures his history around The Military Community, The Civil Communities, and The Rural Communities of Britain in the Roman Empire, *An Imperial Possession*; he offers an alternative paradigm to "Romanization" (*Imperialism*, 269–76); Shanks and Tilley, *Reconstructing Archaeology*.

70. Tomlin uses inscriptions in stone and in wood to give a chronological account from 43 CE to 212 CE in chapters 1–8; and in the Third and Fourth Centuries in chapters 13–14; and to reflect on Soldier and Civilian, Government and Administration, Economy and Society, Gods and Men, in chapters 9–12, *Britannia Romana*.

71. Caesar, *Bellum Gallicum*, H. J. Edwards ed. and trans., *The Gallic War*; in translation: Warner, *War Commentaries of Caesar*.

72. Tacitus, *Agricola; Historiae* 1–3, 4–5; *Annales* 1–3, 4–6, 11–12, 13–16. In translation: *Agricola*; *The Annals*; *The Histories*.

73. Suetonius, Gaius Caligula, Claudius, Nero, Vespasian: *Lives of the Caesars*, vols. I and II, translated by J. C. Rolfe. In translation: C. Edwards, *Lives of the Caesars*.

74. Cassius Dio, *Roman History*, Books 39, 40, 49, 53, 59, 60, 62, 66, Cary and Foster, *Roman History*.

75. *Res Gestae* 32: Cooley, *Res Gestae Divi Augustae*, 96–97, 253–54.

76. Ireland, *Roman Britain Sourcebook*.

77. Caesar, *Bellum Gallicum* IV.7, 12, 13; V.12, 13, 14.

78. Tacitus, *Agricola* 15, 102.

79. Pliny the Elder, *Natural Histories:* IV.102, 104.

80. Strabo, *Geography*: I.4.1,3; II.5.8; IV.5.5.

81. B. Jones and Mattingly, *Atlas of Roman Britain*, 23–29: see further Chapter 2 on Britain and the Roman Geographers.

table correlates the main primary sources, dates and the early periods of Roman influence and rule in Britannia:

Period	Dates	Author	Works, dated
Invasions of Caesar	55, 54 BCE	Julius Caesar (102–44 BCE)	*Bellum Gallicum* IV.20–38; V.1–23 (c.51 BCE).
		Cassius Dio (c. 150–235 CE)	*Roman History* XXXIX.51–53; XL.1–4 (200–222 CE).
Caesar to Claudius	54 BCE – 43 CE	Julius Caesar	*Bellum Gallicum* VII.75, 76, 79.
		Aulus Hirtius (one of Caesar's officers)	Caesar's *Bellum Gallicum* VIII 6, 7, 10, 21, 23, 47, 48 (c. 43 BCE).
		Strabo (c. 64 BCE – 25 CE)	Γεωγραφικά, II.5.3 and 8 (c. 7 BCE or 17–18 CE).
		Cassius Dio	XLIX.38.2; LIII.22.5; LIII.25.2; LIX.25.1–3.
		Augustus (63 BCE – 14 CE)	*Res Gestae*, 32 (c. 14 CE).
		Tacitus (c. 56/57 – c. 120 CE)	*Annales* II.24 (115–120 CE).
		Suetonius (c. 70 – c. 122 CE)	*Caligula* 44, 46 (c. 117–127 CE). Inferences can be made from study of late Iron Age or Celtic coins from southeast Britain.[82]

82. Creighton, *Coins and Power*, 174–215; van Arsdell, Celtic Coinage; "Celtic Coin Index"; "Iron Age Coins." See Map note (Figure 1).

Period	Dates	Author	Works, dated
Invasion of Claudius	43 CE	Suetonius	*Claudius* 17, 24.
		Cassius Dio	LX.19–23.
Claudius to Boudica Revolt	43–60/61 CE	Suetonius	*Vespasian* 4, *Nero* 18
		Tacitus	*Annales* XII.31–40, XIV.29–39; *Agricola* 15, 16 (98 CE)
		Cassius Dio	LXII.1–12.
From Boudica revolt to completion of the occupation	60/61–c.83 CE	Tacitus	*Agricola*, 5, 8, 9–38; *Historiae* I.9, II.11, 57, 59–60, 65, 66, 86, 97, III.22, 44, 45, IV.68 (from 105 CE).
		Cassius Dio	LXVI.20.1–3.

Table 3. The chief primary sources for the history of Roman Britain

From the departure of Agricola (c. 83 CE) to the building of Hadrian's wall (122 CE) "there is an almost total dearth of literary evidence."[83] Although there are rich archaeological resources, not least in coins, inscriptions, and material culture, there are few written texts apart from our three archives.[84] The confidence once shown in writing "a history of Roman Britain" has now been called in question. The focus is not so much on narrative history as on material culture. The editors of *The Oxford Handbook of Roman Britain* (2016) offer a bare chronological outline limited to ancient historical texts:[85] after brief surveys of the way the history of Roman Britain has been written and of recent developments in archaeology, the handbook goes on to explore the variety of sources of knowledge, focusing on material culture, and the study of society and people. The aim is not to achieve a narrative history but to encounter those who have left their mark on the

83. Ireland, *Roman Britain Sourcebook*, 92–94.

84. The intention is "to make every published inscription from Roman Britain accessible to all" in the online "*RIB*"; "PAS"; Ireland, *Roman Britain Sourcebook*.

85. Millett et al., *Oxford Handbook Roman Britain*, xxvii–xxxvi.

landscape and on its archaeology and so give voice to people who have hitherto been voiceless.[86] As can be seen in the next section, that very approach has proved fruitful in the study of New Testament texts.

Accessing the World of the New Testament in the Eastern Mediterranean

Writing tablets, papyri and material culture from the early Roman Empire have the potential to help us address a problem that, in the words of George Caird, "constantly besets readers of the Bible. We do not live in the world of the . . . New Testament, we are unacquainted with what to . . . contemporaries . . . were familiar, everyday objects or experiences, and it is therefore easy for us to miss the affinities which imposed themselves on the inward eye of the biblical writers" and, one might add, the New Testament's first readers.[87] According to John Dominic Crossan and John Reed, it is possible to understand a New Testament person's world not so much by going where they actually were as by going where, in the vagaries of time and place, their world "is still preserved most fully and can still be seen most clearly."[88] Much has been written to address that problem on the basis of that principle in the last fifty years. Whether those studies focused on the *Iudaei* before and after the fall of Jerusalem[89] or on the Roman Empire,[90] they have all engaged with the world of the eastern Mediterranean.[91]

86. Millett et al. group contributors under four headings: the nature of the evidence (1–13); society and the individual (14–23); forms of knowledge (24–33); and landscape and economy (34–41) (*Oxford Handbook Roman Britain*). This contrasts markedly with the chronological approach of Malcolm Todd, *Companion to Roman Britain*. Hingley combines a focus on material culture, archaeology and ancient texts in his account of the Roman invasion of Britain, *Conquering the Ocean*.

87. Caird, *Language and Imagery*, 145.

88. Crossan and Reed, *In Search of Paul*, 317; cf. Crossan and Reed, *Excavating Jesus*. Jonathan Reed does this for the whole of the New Testament (*Visual Guide to the New Testament*).

89. Grabbe, *Judaism; Neusner* et al., *Judaisms and Their Messiahs*; Neusner and Chilton, *Judaism in the New Testament*; Vermes, *Jesus in Jewish World*.

90. Carter, *Roman Empire and the New Testament*; Horsley, *Paul and Empire*; Crossan and Reed, *In Search of Paul*; Crossan and Reed, *Excavating Jesus*.

91. Barclay, *Jews in the Mediterranean*; Bailey, *Paul through Mediterranean Eyes*; Elliott, *Social Scientific Criticism*; Esler, *First Christians in Their Social Worlds*; Esler, *Early Christian World*; Hanson and Oakman, *Palestine in the Time of Jesus*; Malina, *Windows on Jesus' World*; Neyrey, *Imagining Jesus*; Neyrey and Stewart, eds., *Social World of the*

In her study of *Papyri and the Social World of the New Testament*,[92] Sabine Huebner seeks "a better understanding of the structural, social, and cultural conditions that the protagonists of the New Testament, as well as its early readers, experienced in their everyday lives" by adopting what she describes as "micro-approaches" focused on the Egyptian papyri. "Dated official and private letters, tax receipts, census returns, petitions, wills, marriage contracts, and land leases alongside a wealth of other documents . . . permit the ordinary people of the ancient world to speak to us just as they spoke to one another."[93] Entering into the social world of Roman Egypt she encounters contemporaries of the people of the New Testament and its first readers. Immersing herself in the world of the papyri and heeding the voice of "those who never appear in ancient literature – artisans, peasants, shepherds, and fishermen, their wives and children," Huebner draws on the census system to explore Luke 2:1–3, the place of women in Luke 24:9–11, the family and household of a craftsman in Matthew 13:55, travel by the lower classes in Luke 1:39 and an occupation on the margins of society in the world of the shepherds of Luke 2:8–10.[94] While focused on specific papyri, Huebner's choice of papyri is necessarily random.

Bruce Longenecker's approach is more focused. Accessing "the first-century world through the material remains" of Pompeii and Herculaneum *In Stone and Story* brings New Testament texts into conversation with the people responsible for those frescoes, inscriptions, graffiti and other artefacts.[95] By "placing early Christian discourse in its historical setting" he hopes its force "will be more apparent."[96] His focus on the material culture of Pompeii and Herculaneum is in accord with recent approaches to the history of Rome and of Roman Britain.[97] He connects a wide variety of New Testament texts with what he describes as "protocols" of popular devotion, social prominence and household effectiveness.[98]

In *Reading Romans In Pompeii*, Peter Oakes drills down into one specific location in Pompeii and the people whose lives can be glimpsed

---

New Testament; Oakes, *Rome in Bible*; Stegemann and Stegemann, *Jesus Movement*.

92. Huebner, *Papyri*.

93. Huebner, *Papyri*, 2–3.

94. Huebner, *Papyri*, 3 and chapters 3–7.

95. Longenecker, *In Stone and Story*, 24.

96. Longenecker, *In Stone and Story*, 7.

97. Woolf, *Rome*, xi; Millett et al., eds., *The Oxford Handbook of Roman Britain*.

98. Longenecker, *In Stone and Story*, ix–x, 286–90.

there: the block of houses known as the Insula of the Menander, and especially the house of the stoneworkers, the house of the cabinet-maker, a bar, and the house of the Menander itself.[99] While little more is known of the individuals mentioned in Romans 16 than their names and, occasionally, occupations, much is known about the people associated with the Insula of the Menander. Oakes re-creates a craftworker-led house-church in Pompeii[100] and imagines how they might have read Romans 12;[101] he goes on to consider what a slave bath-stoker, a poor stoneworker, a sexually exploited slave, and a craftworking house-church host might have made of the great themes of Romans: the God of justice, the gospel of survival, the redemption of the body, the Jewish salvation of a holy people.[102] He uses this model craftworker-led house church as "a device" to seek an understanding of the inter-relations of people "within first-century Christian groups" and thereby sense how they might have read specific New Testament texts, not least those to do with economics and empire.[103]

This approach involves something akin to ethnography. An ethnographer bases their study of a particular people on fieldwork among them and interaction with anthropological literature and ideas. In *Notes on Not Being There*, Rebecka Lennartsson asks whether ethnography can "ever be used to describe and understand a lost world." She suggests that an ethnographer of the past can work in archives "which function as gateways to history"; indeed, it is in the archive that one can "experience an almost overwhelming sense of closeness" and "walk through a lost world."[104] Ethnographic methods enable Lennartsson to study the sex trade in eighteenth century Stockholm by focusing on the documentary record of a notorious ball at the royal palace on 10 April 1768.[105] At a "narrative level" attention to detail gives "a feel for the period and people one wishes to approach," but more is needed. At a "communicational level" she seeks to establish the "situational

99. Oakes, *Reading Romans in Pompeii*, 1–45: the Insula of the Menander is in Region I, Block 10; the House of Menander is Region I, Block 10, House 4; the House of the Stoneworker is I.10.6; the House of the Cabinetmaker is I.10.7; the bar is I.10.2–3.

100. Oakes, *Reading Romans in Pompeii*, 69–97.

101. Oakes, *Reading Romans in Pompeii*, 98–126.

102. Oakes, *Reading Romans in Pompeii*, 132–74.

103. Oakes extends this approach to Philippians and 1 Thessalonians (*Empire, Economics, and the New Testament*, 4–5). Oakes and Kent, "Entering Early Christianity" is an online resource using the same methodology and engaging with 1 Corinthians.

104. Lennartsson, "Notes on Not Being There," 109.

105. Lennartsson, "Archival Ethnography."

context" of the time long ago with an awareness of "the cultural filter of the modern-day researcher." Throughout, there needs to be an awareness of what is not said, "the less pronounced cultural information that is not immediately disclosed." This "connotational level" involves "two general but interlinked procedures: contextualization, and the search for clues."[106] In a related study, Lennartsson maintains that "analysis and interpretation are the tasks of scholarship, rather than relating as thoroughly and objectively as possible a historical course of events."[107]

Philip Esler has developed archival ethnography in a study of Babatha and her family.[108] In 1961, Yigael Yadin discovered in a cave by the Dead Sea a "leather pouch containing thirty-five legal documents dated from 94 CE to 132 CE written in Aramaic and Greek, relating to Babatha and her family."[109] In *Babatha's Orchard*, Esler offers an imaginative reconstruction of their lives as they drew up four documents around the sale of a date palm orchard on the shores of the Dead Sea in Maoza in Nabatea, across the water from Engedi in Judea. While not based on "direct observations of living people," it is *ethnography* in that it is based on giving "an account of the everyday life of a particular group" which amounts to an "exploration of a particular world of experience."[110] It is not simply to do with exploring the legal and social systems reflected in a set of legal documents. It "involves imagining that one was present where and when the document was signed and, like a modern day ethnographer, was able to observe what those present were saying and doing and to ask them to clarify any points of uncertainty."[111] It is *archival* in the sense that it seeks to enter into the lives of those people through the detailed and careful study of an archive of legal documents concealed by a Judean woman fleeing Roman soldiers at the end of the Shim'on ben Kosiba revolt in 135 CE. Subsequently, Esler draws on another document from the same archive to lead us into the world of that Judean family and their relationship with a centurion who loaned money to Babatha's second husband.[112] He then invites us to reflect on the way people living by the Dead Sea who were familiar with that kind of relationship

106. Lennartsson, "Notes on Not Being There," 110–11.

107. Lennartsson, "Archival Ethnography," 91.

108. Esler, *Babatha's Orchard*.

109. Esler, *Babatha's Orchard*, xv; Yadin, *Bar-Kokhba*, 222–53.

110. Esler, *Babatha's Orchard*, 4.

111. Esler, *Babatha's Orchard*, 22. Cf. Esler, "Righteousness of Joseph," 2.

112. Esler, *Babatha's Orchard*.

might have read Matt 8:5–13.[113] The context in which four Judean wedding contracts were drawn up enables him to explore how "a first century Christ-follower would have made sense of the narrative in Matt 1:18–25."[114] Esler thereby "reveals the potential of archival ethnography conducted on legal documents to push the understanding of New Testament texts in fresh directions."[115] Recent discoveries make it possible to adopt that methodology in Roman Britain.

Archival Ethnography and the World of the New Testament in Roman Britain

Since 2024 three archives of written material from Roman Britain enable us to "walk through a lost world"[116] and glimpse the everyday lives of particular people in the province of Britannia.[117] They enable us to engage with contemporaries of the first readers of the New Testament, allowing them "to speak to us just as they spoke to one another."[118] We can bring Luke–Acts "into conversation with" people responsible for those documents and read the text through their eyes.[119] We can draw on the insights of archival ethnography, engage with particular groups of people and explore their world of experience, alert to those small details that function as clues to an understanding not only of their interactions with each other but of the way they might respond to Luke–Acts.[120]

Discovered in excavations at the site of the Bloomberg European Headquarters in the City of London from 2010–2014, the Bloomberg tablets are the most ancient writings to have been discovered in Britain and the most recent to have been published. Dating mainly from the forties to the eighties CE, they are the first documents to be discovered in Britain that are contemporary with the events narrated in the New Testament and its earliest books. Wax tablets, they include financial and legal documents, and the

113. Esler, "Reading Matthew by the Dead Sea."

114. Esler, "Righteousness of Joseph," 2.

115. Esler, "Righteousness of Joseph," 39.

116. Lennartsson, "Notes on Not Being There," 109.

117. Esler, "Reading Matthew by the Dead Sea"; Esler, "Righteousness of Joseph."

118. Huebner, *Papyri*, 3. Cf. R. Cleaves, "Reading the New Testament in Roman Britain."

119. Longenecker, *In Stone and Story*, 24.

120. Esler, *Babatha's Orchard*, 22–25.

correspondence of traders, merchants, craft-workers, financiers, freedmen, and slaves of mid-first century London.[121]

Discovered first in 1973 and in excavations ever since, and published in 1983, 1993, 2003, 2010 and 2019, the Vindolanda tablets are ink-on-wood writing tablets from a military community in a frontier fort at the end of the first century and the beginning of the second century. They include the administrative documents of auxiliary cohorts, together with the military and personal correspondence of men and women in the fort.[122]

During excavations in 1977, 1978 and 1979 many lead curse tablets were discovered in a temple dedicated to Mercury on the Cotswold escarpment at Uley, overlooking the River Severn. Written by people with Roman and Celtic names they emanate from a non-elite, non-military rural community in Roman Britain; they were published periodically from 1993 and in full in 2024;[123] similar tablets were discovered during excavations of 1978–1983 in the sacred spring of the temple dedicated to Sulis Minerva in Bath and others in non-military settings in the southern half of Britain.[124]

When Robin Birley unearthed the first of the Vindolanda tablets in 1973, he and the newly formed Vindolanda Trust turned to Alan Bowman and David Thomas, papyrologists with experience of the Greek and Latin papyri of the John Rylands Library, Manchester, who have worked on them ever since. More recently, they have been joined by Roger Tomlin who published the Bath curse tablets in 1988, the first Uley tablets in 1993 (and since in *Britannia*), and the Bloomberg tablets in 2016.

Not only is the cursive script of the Bloomberg tablets, the Vindolanda tablets and the Uley tablets identical to that of the papyri, the form of each set of documents is replicated across the empire. In the *Manual of Everyday Roman Writing*, volume 1, Alex Mullen and Alan Bowman indicate where collections of such scripts can be found and go on to introduce

121. Tomlin, *Roman London's First Voices*. Map (Figure 1) 1.

122. Available online at www.romaninscriptionsofbritain.org/tabvindol; Bowman, *Life and Letters*; A. R. Birley, *Garrison Life*. Map (Figure 1) 2.

123. Originally published in Woodward and Leach, *Uley Shrines Excavation*, 113–30; subsequently published in *Britannia*; brought together in Sánchez Natalías, "Curse Tablets against Thieves," 344–66; and fully published in 2024; Tomlin, *The Uley Tablets*. Map (Figure 1) 3.

124. *SD* 205–*SD* 460, Sánchez Natalías, *Sylloge Defixiones*, 265–383; tablets from Bath: *SD* 206–*SD* 335 (267–329); the Bath tablets were originally published in Tomlin, *Tabellae Sulis* and are available online at www.romaninscriptionsofbritain.org/tabsulis. Map (Figure 1) 55.

the characteristics of Old Roman Cursive (ORC) and New Roman Cursive (NRC), explaining how to read these everyday texts.[125] In volume 2, Anna Willi explores the things Romans wrote with, styluses, ink and other accessories; and the things they wrote on, wax tablets, wooden tablets, papyrus, parchment, lead and other metal tablets, and other surfaces.[126] She reflects on the way interest has shifted from quantifying the extent of literacy in the Roman world, to a focus on the cultural context of different types of literacy.[127] The wax tablets of the archive of Iucundus the banker in Pompeii[128] are similar to the Bloomberg tablets and their form as financial and legal documents akin to the Babatha papyri with their sealed inner text and open outer text.[129] Ink-on-wood tablets from a military context similar to Vindolanda have been found in Egypt and in Vindonissa, Switzerland;[130] one written and signed by Shim'on ben Kosiba was found in the Cave of Letters by the Dead Sea in the early 1960s.[131] Lead curse tablets in Greek and in Latin have been found the length and breadth of the empire from the fifth century BCE to the fifth century CE, including more than 60 from the well of the palace at Caesarea Maritima,[132] fourteen from Syrian Antioch including one against Babylas the grocer,[133] and one aimed at five people bearing names associated with the followers of Jesus in Jerusalem.[134] A comprehensive catalogue of Latin curse tablets, A *Sylloge of* Defixiones *from the Roman West*, was published by Celia Sánchez Natalías in 2022.[135]

Sabine Huebner is quite explicit, "Papyri and ostraca found outside Egypt, as well as wooden writing tablets such as the Vindolanda tablets from northern Britain, . . . or the Bloomberg tablets from London, show many similarities in terminology with the Egyptian papyri, testifying to a common mindset and shared understanding across the Roman

125. Mullen and Bowman, *Scripts and Texts*, 1:23–40, 41–62, 63–71.

126. Willi, *Writing Equipment*, 32–65.

127. Willi, *Writing Equipment*, 14. Cf. Woolf, "Ancient Illiteracy?," 41.

128. Cooley and Cooley, *Pompei and Herculaneum*, 277–86.

129. Esler, *Babatha's Orchard*, 103–4.

130. An inventory of wooden writing tablets Bowman and Thomas, *Vindolanda: Latin Tablets*, 33–35; available online at Bowman and Thomas, *Tab. Vindol. I.*

131. Yadin, "Expedition to Judean Desert," 41–43.

132. Burrell, "Curse Tablets Caesarea"; Burrell, "Herod's Caesarea." Cf. a curse against a dancer from the theater Mastrocinque, "Defixio from Caesarea."

133. Hollman, "Curse Tablet from Antioch."

134. Daniel and Sulimani, "New Curse Tablet from Jerusalem."

135. Sánchez Natalías, *Sylloge Defixiones*.

provinces."[136] In *More Light from the Ancient East,* Arzt-Grabner, Kloppenborg and Kreinecker include a number of the Bloomberg and Vindolanda tablets, arguing that they are of value in developing an "understanding of early Christ groups."[137]

None of the three sets of writing from Roman Britain constitutes an "archive" in the sense used by Esler of the Babatha archive. Speaking of the Vindolanda tablets, Bowman, Thomas, and Tomlin "refrain from using the term 'archive' which in its strictest sense should refer to a group of documents written, received or compiled by the same individual(s)."[138] Esler, however, suggests an archive "can refer either to a place containing records, documents, or other materials of historical interest or to a collection of such documents."[139] It is in this last sense that we can think of each of these sets of writings as an archive. Each is a manageable size and is associated with a particular location and with specific people, many of whom are named. They emanate from an urban, a military and a rural context.

Drawing on the micro-approaches of Sabine Huebner into the everyday lives of the Roman provincial middle and lower classes using the Egyptian papyri, and the archaeological approaches of Bruce Longenecker in the context of Pompeii and Herculaneum, and of Peter Oakes in re-creating a craftworker-led house church in Pompeii's Insula of Menander, I shall adapt the archival ethnography of Rebekka Lennartsson and Philip Esler and imagine how people from each of those communities might have read Luke–Acts. That will involve giving "an account of the everyday life of" three disparate groups which "amounts to an exploration of their particular worlds of experience."[140] It will involve more than simply exploring the financial and business world of those traders, merchants and financiers, the world of that military community in Vindolanda, and the world of those engaged in that specific ritual practice in Uley. It will involve imaginatively entering into the lives of the people who were engaged with each other in writing those texts. It requires the cultivation of an imagination that is multi-faceted yet grounded in history. It is important to reflect on the kind

136. Huebner, *Papyri*, 7, Arzt-Grabner et al., *More Light from Ancient East.*

137. Arzt-Grabner et al., *More Light from Ancient East*, 9, 33, 190–95, 202, 218–19.

138. Bowman et al., "Vindolanda Tablets, IV (Online)," 230.

139. Esler, *Babatha's Orchard*, 13; Abdy describes the Vindolanda tablets as "an ancient archive" (*Legion*, 229); Tomlin describes the Bath tablets and the Uley tablets as archives (*Britannia Romana*, 335); "archive" is defined as "a collection of historical documents or records" (COD, 68).

140. Esler, *Babatha's Orchard*, 4.

of imagination we need as we adapt the methodology of archival ethnography in studying New Testament texts.

Archival Ethnography, the New Testament, and the Place of the Imagination

At its most basic, Mary Warnock suggests, imagination is "that which creates mental images."[141] Perhaps more helpful is Leslie Stevenson's observation that "the most basic notion of imagination" involves "having an image or concept of something not presently perceived."[142] It gives one "the ability to think of something that one has never perceived, but which others have perceived and told one about." Through the study of documents, we can access the people responsible for them as imagination gives us "the ability to think about a particular mental state of another person, whose existence one infers from perceived evidence."[143]

It is important, however, not to limit our understanding of imagination. "The imagination," argues Graham Ward, "admits no boundaries. It infiltrates all human understanding."[144] It cannot therefore be pinned down. Trevor Hart maintains it is better thought of "as *a way of thinking, responding and acting* across the whole spread of our experience, not some arcane "thing" with a carefully specified and limited remit."[145] As such, imagination is "the faculty which makes sense of things, locating particular bits and pieces within larger patterns, and in doing so goes beyond what is given, filling gaps, painting bigger pictures."[146] As an innate aspect of what it means to be human, it enables us to venture beyond the data with which we are presented and make sense of it. It is through our imagination that we find the words and metaphors we need to make sense of, and talk about, not only ideas and concepts but also emotions and feelings. Imagination is, therefore, "our means of interpreting the world" not only of the present but also the past.[147]

141. Warnock, *Imagination*, 10.

142. L. Stevenson quotes the first sense given in the *Oxford English Dictionary* ("Imagination," 238).

143. L. Stevenson, "Imagination," 239–41: Conceptions 1, 1b, 1d.

144. Ward, *Unimaginable*, 184.

145. Hart, *Between Image and Word*, 5.

146. Hart, "Imagination," 319.

147. Warnock, *Imagination*, 194.

Drawing on a Historical Imagination

Our imagined reading of Luke–Acts must take history seriously. History has to do with the lives of people who lived, and events that happened, in the past. The historian's imagination enables them to "create mental images" of that past and to make sense of it. According to R. G. Collingwood, "the historian's picture of his subject, whether that subject be a sequence of events or a past state of things, thus appears as a web of imaginative construction stretched between certain fixed points provided by the statements of his authorities." There is, however, a danger the historian must guard against lest the picture that emerges becomes a flight of fancy, far removed from the data. Their imagination must not be arbitrary; it must be informed by the data, by its wider interpretation and by the wider context. "If these points are frequent enough and the threads spun from each to the next are constructed with due care, always by the *a priori* imagination and never by merely arbitrary fancy, the whole picture is constantly verified by appeal to these data and runs little risk of losing touch with the reality which it represents."[148]

In *The Making of the English Landscape* W. G. Hoskins put those principles into practice: to write the history of a landscape "requires a combination of documentary research and of fieldwork . . . slowly one pieces together from the records, from the archaeological finds in the local museum, and from the evidence of one's own eyes, what has happened."[149] That whole process, to use Mary Warnock's definition, depends on "that which creates mental images" i.e. imagination. Hoskins appeals to Wordsworth to justify his method. In his *Guide through the District of the Lakes* one of the first sections has to do with the "Aspect of the Country, as affected by its Inhabitants" in which Wordsworth "begins by asking the reader to envisage what the landscape, finished by the great impersonal forces of Nature and awaiting its first human inhabitants, looked like in its primeval freshness."[150] Wordsworth uses a number of key phrases in establishing what it is the reader must do: "form to himself an image," "he may see or hear in fancy," he "may think" of things that happened "with no human eye to notice, or human heart to regret or welcome the change." For Hoskins, such a work of imagination, however, must be supplemented with the careful gathering of

148. Collingwood, *The Idea of History*, 242.

149. Hoskins, *Making of English Landscape*, 15, 297.

150. Hoskins, *Making of English Landscape*, 17.

data: "one needs to be a botanist, a physical geographer, and a naturalist, as well as an historian, to be able to feel certain that one has all the facts right before allowing the imagination to play over the small details of a scene."[151]

Collingwood speaks of "certain fixed points," and Hoskins of "facts," which are then supplemented by the imagination so ensuring that what is produced is not "imaginary" but in a proper sense "historical." By drawing on this "historical imagination" the historian can create a narrative history. However, our imagined reading of Luke–Acts requires us to enter into the everyday lives of the people of Londinium, Vindolanda and the rural area around Uley's temple of Mercury and then to bring them into conversation with Luke–Acts. Something more is needed. To that "historical imagination" we must add a sociological, an ethnographic and a cultural imagination.

Drawing on a Sociological, an Ethnographic, and a Cultural Imagination

A sociological imagination involves a shift of focus from narrative to people. C. Wright Mills argued that "the sociological imagination enables us to grasp history and biography and the relations between the two within society."[152] It is what helps us to engage with the people responsible for the documents we are studying. A sociological imagination "enables its possessor to understand the larger historical scene in terms of its meaning for the inner life and the external career of a variety of individuals."[153] In his *Ethnographic Imagination*, Paul Willis argues that as ethnography provides "the empirical and conceptual discipline" it becomes "the eye of the needle through which the threads of imagination must pass."[154] Adopting an ethnographic imagination in the sense advocated by Willis, Lennartsson suggests that "to identify or empathize with informants may be seen as an aid to understanding, rather than an obstacle to objectivity and stringency."[155]

That in turn calls for the exercise of a cultural imagination as we endeavor to address the gap between the cultures of today and the cultures of the world of the New Testament. Culture is embodied in symbols

151. Hoskins, *Making of English Landscape*, 19.

152. Mills, *Sociological Imagination*, 6.

153. Mills, *Sociological Imagination*, 5.

154. Willis, *Ethnographic Imagination*, viii.

155. Lennartsson, "Archival Ethnography," 92.

understood instinctively by those who are part of that culture. It is not that the people of a particular culture necessarily have an intellectual understanding of the symbols which give expression to their culture: rather, they emerge from a shared imagination. They live those symbols in their own imaginations as they share with each other. Graham Ward argues that "exploring the imagination enables us to assess what is going on in a given cultural situation: what is going on beneath and yet through the symbolic." It is in that sense that imagination "infiltrates all human understanding." Such a cultural imagination is intertwined inextricably with cultural values and with a sociological imagination that has to do not only with people as individuals but with "the way we institutionalize and organize" society.[156]

Drawing on a Geographical and an Archaeological Imagination

It is only possible to imagine Luke–Acts through the eyes of those responsible for the Bloomberg tablets, the Vindolanda tablets and the Uley tablets because archaeologists and others have excavated each of those locations. Significant developments in archaeology since the 1960s have not only provided a great deal more data based on rigorous scientific analysis but also drawn on the imagination in innovative ways.

Emerging from the work of antiquarians of the eighteenth and nineteenth centuries archaeology had, by the mid twentieth century, become more methodical in the hands of expert practitioners such as Mortimer and Tessa Wheeler and Kathleen Kenyon. The advent of radiocarbon dating in the 1950s led to a more scientific approach in the 1960s.[157] Drawing on developments in the social sciences and particularly in anthropology, this *new archaeology* combined the rigor of scientific research with an objectivity based on data and statistics. One of its advocates, Lewis Binford, spoke of the way "the tremendous quantities of data which the archaeologist controls"[158] can be harnessed, as it were in laboratory conditions, to offer anthropological insights into the processes of cultural change and evolution.[159] Talk of the "processes of cultural change" gave rise to the alternative label, *processual archaeology*. The move away from an inductive approach to

156. Ward, *Unimaginable*, 184–85.

157. Hingley, "Early Studies in Roman Britain"; Millett, "Roman Britain since Haverfield"; Perring, *London in Roman World*, 17–21.

158. Binford, "Archaeology as Anthropology," 224.

159. Gamble, *Archaeology: The Basics*, 24–30.

data based on common sense to "a consciously deductive philosophy, with the attendant emphasis on the verification of propositions through hypothesis testing" had "far-reaching consequences for archaeology."[160] Significantly, the excavations leading to the discovery of the Vindolanda tablets (since 1973 and continuing),[161] the curse tablets of the temple of Mercury in Uley (1976–1979),[162] and of the sacred spring in Bath (1978–83)[163] and the Bloomberg tablets (2010–2014),[164] have all been undertaken with this scientific rigor. The combination of dendrochronology with radiocarbon dating by the 1990s makes precise dating of the Bloomberg tablets and the Vindolanda tablets possible.[165]

There was, however, a reaction to *the new archaeology*. Introducing an article by Jacquetta Hawkes on *the Proper Study of Mankind*, the editor of *Antiquity* sounded a note of caution: "as more and more scientific aids to archaeology are provided and used, the archaeologist may seem to be concerned with, and seem to be happy to be concerned with, an increasingly detailed study of trees without pausing to look at the wood of which they are a part."[166] Jacquetta Hawkes called for the use of the imagination on the interface between the objectivity of the scientific archaeologist and the public: "the link between the archaeological artefact and popular accessible writings is the imaginative *personality* trained in the humanities."[167] For the things of the past to connect with the present, an imaginative but informed popularizer is needed to bridge the gap between the scientific archaeologist focused on the minutiae of the past and the person who seeks to connect with that past.

160. Binford and Binford, "Archaeological Perspectives," 18.

161. Bowman, *Life and Letters*; "*RIB*" 2019.

162. Woodward and Leach, *Uley Shrines Excavation*; "Centre for Study of Ancient Documents"; Sánchez Natalías, *Sylloge Defixiones SD* 354–440 (344–366); Tomlin, *The Uley Tablets*.

163. Cunliffe, *Roman Bath*; Cousins, *Sanctuary at Bath*; Davenport, *Roman Bath*; Tomlin, *Tabellae Sulis*.

164. Tomlin, *Roman London's First Voices*; "*RIB*."

165. Gamble, *Archaeology: The Basics*, 63–66. N.B. — it is the archaeological context that can be precisely dated, giving the latest date for each tablet: Tomlin, *Roman London's First Voices*, 5, 31–51; https://romaninscriptionsofbritain.org/tabvindol/vol-II/introduction.

166. Hawkes, "Proper Study of Mankind," Introduction.

167. Hawkes, "Proper Study of Mankind," 261.

In 1987 Michael Shanks and Christopher Tilley published *Reconstructing Archaeology: Theory and Practice*,[168] questioning whether the natural sciences could provide an adequate model for the social sciences and whether "the most certain knowledge is mathematical and deterministic in conception."[169] The archaeologist needs to be aware of the way their own experience shapes their understanding. As "the particular perspective from which an object or event is viewed is an integral part of the object of study" it follows that "values cannot be eradicated from archaeology." They need to be made explicit and then subjected to "critical scrutiny."[170] "Accepting archaeology as practice, truth as constituted in practice, is to accept truth as precarious, written into political relations."[171] This emphasis on the importance of a critically reflective archaeology led to what has been described as *interpretive archaeology*, or *post-processual archaeology*.[172]

This approach puts people and their experience center stage, as Tilley argued in *A Phenomenology of Landscape*: "the key issue in any phenomenological approach is the manner in which people experience and understand the world."[173] Timothy Darvill speaks of the way Tilley "melded anthropology with social theory to create a new application of cultural relativism for the interpretation of spaces and places."[174] As Hoskins had transformed the study of the English landscape a generation before, so Tilley had a similar impact on a new generation. "To understand a landscape truly it must be felt. . . . To convey some of this feeling to others it has to be talked about, recounted, or written and depicted."[175] That requires the use of what Tilley describes as *the geographical imagination*: "people are immersed in a world of places which the geographical imagination aims to understand and recover – places as contexts for human experience, constructed in movement, memory, encounter and association."[176]

168. Shanks and Tilley, *Reconstructing Archaeology.*
169. Shanks and Tilley, *Reconstructing Archaeology*, 34.
170. Shanks and Tilley, *Reconstructing Archaeology*, 66–67.
171. Shanks and Tilley, *Reconstructing Archaeology*, 67.
172. Gamble, *Archaeology: The Basics*, 34–39.
173. Tilley, *Phenomenology of Landscape*, 11.
174. Tilley, Review of *Phenomenology of Landscape.*
175. Tilley, Review of *Phenomenology of Landscape*, 31.
176. Tilley, *Phenomenology of Landscape*, 15.

It is an *archaeological imagination* that brings together these different elements, enabling the historian to engage with people of the past and the way in which they related to each other.

> To recreate the world behind the ruin in the land, to reanimate the people behind the sherd of antique pottery, a fragment of the past: this is the work of the archaeological imagination, a creative impulse and faculty at the heart of archaeology, but also embedded in many cultural dispositions, discourses and institutions commonly associated with modernity. The archaeological imagination is rooted in a sensibility, a pervasive set of attitudes towards traces and remains, towards memory, time and temporality, the fabric of history.[177]

Clive Gamble is adamant: "Archaeology is about excitement. It is about intellectual curiosity and finding ways to turn that curiosity into knowledge about people in the past." It is an archaeological imagination that "allows us to go where we can never travel, to the past, and to think about time and objects in very different ways to our everyday experience."[178] For Tilley and Shanks, a greater interaction with artefacts will draw people into an imaginative engagement with the past that enables them to relate to their own present and future.[179] The archaeological imagination has to do with our own experience, identity, and future: "There is thus an accompanying exhortation to look beyond the academic discipline of archaeology through memory practices, tradition and innovation to a (modern) human condition and to find ways that the archaeological imagination may enhance and enrich human experience now and for the future."[180] It is precisely because "students can reflectively think, and work to re-enact in their minds the world of the artefact" that they "gain historical knowledge from artefacts," suggests Clare Jarmy.[181] When enabled to take an "imaginative leap" and connect with history in a way that engages them with their own lives and their own future, education becomes transformative. "Seeing artefacts plays its part in this transformation, allowing for the re-enactment of history in the mind of the student, a rare chance for doing so away from the more prescribed curriculum of the classroom. In taking this imaginative leap, she

177. Shanks, *Archaeological Imagination*, 25. Cf. Cousins, *Sanctuary at Bath*, chap. 3.

178. Gamble, *Archaeology: The Basics*, 1.

179. Shanks and Tilley, *Reconstructing Archaeology*, chap. 4.

180. Shanks, *Archaeological Imagination*, 149.

181. Jarmy, "*Neath Moth-Eaten Rag*," 425.

creates historical knowledge. In doing so, she does not simply learn some history: she becomes an historian."[182]

Texts as Artefacts That Come to Life in the Imagination

The artefacts we are going to engage with are texts. To look at a Bloomberg wax writing tablet on display at the foot of the Bloomberg tower on the way into the London Mithraeum, or in the London Museum[183] or at an ink-on-wood Vindolanda tablet on display in Vindolanda[184] or in the British Museum,[185] or at a Uley curse tablet in the British Museum[186] is to be in the position of the one who first wrote that text and, in the case of the first two, of the one who first read it. We truly engage with those tablets not only when we seek an understanding of what is written on them but also when we draw on our multi-faceted imagination and encounter the people responsible for them. Linda Maloney has described such an approach as "fact-based imaginative empathy."[187]

What Richard Gordon said of Tomlin's work on the curse tablets could also be said of his work on the Bloomberg tablets and, with Bowman and Thomas, on the Vindolanda tablets: "In attempting to contextualize 'indigenous' curse-texts in Latin it is important not merely to provide the best text one can manage and take material aspects and provenience into account, as is nowadays standard procedure, but also, in an act of historical imagination, to take seriously the situation of the writers as they represented it to themselves. . . ."[188] This is the raw material from which we can develop an archival ethnography that, to adapt Trevor Hart, "enables the genuine particularity of the other to 'come to life' in our own imagination." It is as if one becomes in his words "a surrogate member of the relevant human group." Something happens when one engages imaginatively with such texts: "reading texts always involves some effort to go beyond the level

182. Jarmy, "*Neath Moth-Eaten Rag*," 438.

183. S. Wright, *Archaeology at Bloomberg*; "London Mithraeum"; "London Museum."

184. "Vindolanda & Roman Army Museum."

185. "British Museum Roman Britain Gallery"; Hobbs and Jackson, *Roman Britain*, 58–61, 76–78.

186. "British Museum Roman Britain Gallery"; Hobbs and Jackson, *Roman Britain*, 78–80.

187. Maloney and Reimer, *Acts*, lxi.

188. Gordon, "Imaginative Force," 129.

of the words on the page, beyond even the wider "factual" circumstances to which they relate (insofar as these can be discovered by the methods of careful objective study), and to penetrate into the field of the personal. Only thus can understanding occur as part of a genuine meeting of persons, and our own personhood be modified by it."[189]

Before engaging in our imagined reading, it is necessary to consider assumptions we will make concerning Luke–Acts: unity and authorship; date and genre; first readership or audience; relationship with the empire and its many complexities.

Luke–Acts Then and Now: Assumptions Behind an Imagined Reading

Drawing on archival ethnography and an imagined engagement with the people of the Bloomberg tablets, the Vindolanda tablets and the Uley tablets, we are going to focus on Luke's Gospel and the Acts of the Apostles. Together they form the longest continuous piece of writing by a single author in the New Testament. Luke's Gospel tells of the life and teaching, the death and resurrection of Jesus, taking the readers to Jerusalem; Acts gives an account of the first followers of the Way of Jesus[190] as they witness to Jesus from Jerusalem to Rome and to "the ends of the earth" (Acts 1:8). Among the first followers of Jesus, we encounter traders and merchants such as we meet in the Bloomberg tablets, the military personnel and their wives and families whom we meet in the Vindolanda tablets, and people from rural settings who made use of practices akin to those involving the curse tablets of Uley.

It has been argued by Larry Hurtado that the first followers of Jesus were "distinctively text oriented,"[191] and that "the earliest Christian artefacts" were papyrus documents of the biblical books read and listened to as the first followers of Jesus gathered to worship.[192] We are therefore justified in imagining a follower of the Way of Jesus, one of those traders or

189. Hart, "Imagination," 326.

190. I shall use this description of the first followers of Jesus as it is frequently used by Luke to describe them and their communities: Acts 9:2; 18:25, 26; 19:9, 23; 22:4, 14; 24:22. Cf. Matthews, *Acts*, xiv.

191. Hurtado, "A Bookish Religion," 141.

192. Hurtado, *Earliest Christian Artifacts*.

merchants "circulating around the urban networks of the empire,"[193] arriving with a codex including Luke and Acts in his baggage to share with groups of followers of the Way. Conversant in Greek and Latin our trader would have been able to give a running translation of the text to the group of Latin speakers, among whom may have been some with knowledge of Greek.[194]

We have some indication of what that might have looked like. The Old Latin texts that pre-date Jerome's Vulgate stem "from a period when Latin and Greek speakers within the Church were in close communication."[195] One example is to be found in *Codex Bezae* (c. 400 CE) which contains on opposite pages the Greek and Old Latin text of the Gospels (in the order Matthew, John, Luke (ευαγγελ(ιον) κατ(α) λουκαν: *euang(elium sec (undum) lucan*), Mark, 3 John, and Acts (πραξις αποστολων: *actus apostolorum*).[196] It reflects two earlier bilingual manuscripts, one of the gospels (in the order Matthew, Mark, John, Luke), and another of Acts.[197] That is of particular interest as the Latin is on the left and the Greek on the right of the same page, arranged in such a way as to be exactly parallel. It is suggested that it was written for a Latin speaker who was learning Greek.[198] The use of the Vulgate alongside the Greek text and NRSV in biblical quotations (a practice adopted throughout) gives an approximate indication of how these texts would have been understood in a Latin speaking context.[199]

193. Woolf, "Female Mobility," 352.

194. Greek-derived names appear in *Tab. Lond. Bloomberg* 23, 67; *Tab. Vindol. II* 311, 361, *III* 581, 610; *Tab. Uley* 52 contains Latin formulas transliterated into Greek letters.

195. Houghton, *Latin New Testament*, 155–56: see chapter 6 for an account of the text of the early Latin New Testament. Jerome's fifth century *Vulgate* was a revision of earlier Latin texts. The earliest old Latin manuscript from North Africa, *Vetus Latina 1*, predates the third-century Cyprian. Houghton indicates that the Old Latin was translated "around the end of the second century, and the Vulgate, a revision made two hundred years later," *Textual Commentary UBS 6*, 10*.

196. *Codex Bezae* (Cambridge, University Library, MS Nn.2.41).

197. Houghton, *Latin New Testament*, 28. See *The Laudian Acts.*

198. Holford, "Travels of Laudian Acts."

199. Biblical quotations make use of *Nestle-Aland, Novum Testamentum Graece*, 28th Revised Edition edited by Barbara and Kurt Aland et al. 2012; *Biblia Sacra Iuxta Vulgatam Versionem*, Third Revised Edition, edited by Robert Weber. 1983. *New Revised Standard Version Bible* 1989.

The Unity and Authorship of Luke-Acts

While it is possible to read Luke and Acts separately, similarity of language, length, and structure, together with the shared dedication to Theophilus justify the assumption that they constitute a two-volume work,[200] and that the common name, Luke–Acts, is appropriate.[201] The earliest manuscript to include parts of Acts and the four gospels is Chester Beatty P. 45 from the third century CE.[202] Luke is named as a companion of Paul in Phlm 24 and 2 Tim 4:11; in Col 4:14 he is identified as "the beloved physician"; whether the "we passages" of Acts imply that the writer, at least of those passages, was a companion of Paul (16:10–17; 20:5—21:18; 27:1—28:16) is a moot point.[203] Within the text itself the author is anonymous.[204] For ease of reference we will refer to the author of Luke–Acts as Luke.[205]

The Date of Luke-Acts

While some have dated Luke–Acts in the 60s CE,[206] the consensus until recently has dated it in the 70s–80s,[207] arguing that Luke–Acts "shows a

200. Keener, *Acts*, 76–77; Witherington, *Acts*, 4–8; Wolter, *Luke I*, 30–35; Talbert, *Reading Acts*, 3; C. K. Barrett, *Acts Volume* 2, cxi–cxiv; Green, "Luke–Acts?," 101–19; Green, *Gospel of Luke*, 6–10; Matthews, *Acts*, 1–4; Cadbury *Making of Luke-Acts*, 1–11. Pervo sees Acts "as a sequel to Luke," suggesting Luke did not plan the two in advance (*Acts*, 20). Maloney and Reimer are ambivalent about the unity of Luke and Acts and so refer to the author of Acts as Lukas (*Acts*, lv).

201. Cadbury, *Making of Luke-Acts*, 10–11.

202. Hurtado, *Earliest Christian Artifacts*, 37–38, 220, 234. "Manuscript P45 Center for the Study of New Testament Manuscripts" 2022.

203. Keener argues that "the narrator indicates his presence with the group by using the first-person plural" (*Acts*, 383–85); Pervo argues that "'we' is most often a sign of late composition and is rather better attested in fiction than in works of unquestioned accuracy. . . . The first plural brings the readers into the story" (*Acts*, 7, 392–96); Mount sees it as a fictional construct ("Acts"); after summarizing three positions (the author's presence, the use of an eye-witness source, a literary creation) Talbert concludes "the question is moot at the moment" and for the purposes of his commentary, inconsequential (*Reading Acts*, 148).

204. Recent commentaries survey the arguments: Wolter, *Luke I*, 4–11; Brawley, *Luke*, 5–6; Keener, *Acts*, 48–51; Pervo, *Acts*, 5–7; Matthews, *Acts*, 1–4; Matthews and Reid, *Luke 1–9*, xlviii.

205. Wolter, *Luke I*, 10; Keener, *Acts*, 50.

206. Robinson, *Redating the New Testament*, 86–117; Seccombe, "Dating Luke–Acts."

207. Keener prefers the seventies (*Acts*, 46–48); Witherington the late seventies to

remarkable knowledge of the general conditions of life in the eastern Mediterranean at the time of Paul,"[208] and reflects the world of the Flavian dynasty, not least in its description of legal proceedings.[209] While Luke–Acts is in circulation by the second half of the second century there is little evidence of links between Luke–Acts and earlier Christian writers.[210] There is a fluidity in the manuscript tradition of Luke, even more pronounced in Acts, that suggests an "open book that was subject to re-working."[211] It can be argued that Luke–Acts does not make use of Paul's letters[212] or of Josephus.[213] More recently, the beginning of the second century has been proposed on the grounds that Luke–Acts does draw on the *Antiquities* of Josephus, the corpus of Pauline letters, the separate group of Pastoral Epistles and the works of Clement, Ignatius, and Polycarp,[214] and may constitute a response to the teachings of Marcion.[215] Others argue that the description of the Roman military in Luke–Acts reflects an early second century context.[216] If the message of Trajan reflected in literature, building projects, and visual media

early eighties (*Acts*, 60–63); Wolter early eighties (*Luke I*, 11–12); Bruce late seventies to early eighties (*Acts*, 9–18); Alexander the eighties ("Acts Oxford Commentary," 1061); Esler mid to late eighties or early nineties (*Community and Gospel in Luke–Acts*, 27–30); Schaberg and Ringe 85–90 CE ("Luke," 497); Reimer end of the first century CE (*Women in Acts*, xii).

208. Alexander, "Acts Oxford Commentary," 1028.

209. Witherington, *Acts*, 62; Esler, *Community and Gospel in Luke–Acts*, 28–29.

210. Bruce, *Acts*, 10–12; C. K. Barrett, *Acts Volume 2*, lxiii–lxxii.

211. Matthews and Reid, *Luke 1–9*, lvi. The Alexandrian text is found in *Codex Sinaiticus* and the "Western" Text in *Codex Bezae*. See Wolter, *Luke I*, 1–4; Bruce, 1990, 69–80; Metzger has a detailed introduction to the textual tradition of Acts (*Textual Commentary*, 222–36), and detailed comments on Luke and Acts (*Textual Commentary*, 108–66, 236–445; Houghton has a brief overview of the textual tradition and then detailed comments on both Luke and Acts (*Textual Commentary UBS 6*, 119–94, 279–329); Pervo has an introduction to the text of Acts (*Acts*, 1–4) and comprehensive notes on textual variants throughout the commentary.

212. Wolter, *Luke I*, 9–10; Esler, *Community and Gospel in Luke–Acts*, 28.

213. Bruce, *Acts*, 43–44.

214. Pervo, *Dating Acts*; Pervo, *Mystery of Acts*, 9–12; Pervo, *Acts*, 3–12; D'Angelo, "ANHP Question," 47–48, 66–68; Matthews and Reid, *Luke 1–9*, lv–lvii; Matthews, *Acts*, 22–23; Maloney and Reimer, *Acts*, lv–lvii; Mount, "Acts."

215. Tyson, *Marcion and Luke–Acts*; Knox, *Marcion and the New Testament*; cf. Matthews and Reid, *Luke 1–9*, lv.

216. Zeichmann, "Military Forces in Judaea," especially 107–12; Zeichmann, *Roman Army and the New Testament*, 49–107.

was that "victory belongs to Rome, and the world is better off for it,"[217] that offers, it is suggested, the context in which to read Luke–Acts.[218] As John Knox acknowledged in the work that influenced one of the proponents of a second century date,[219] while such a date "has a certain *a priori* probability" "unfortunately, the evidence is too meagre either to disprove or prove."[220] In the absence of compelling evidence, Talbert concludes that Acts "can have been written anytime between the early sixties and the early second century."[221] Either of the earlier dates (sixties CE or seventies to eighties CE) enables us to imagine Luke–Acts through the eyes of the people of the Bloomberg tablets (forties to eighties CE) and the Vindolanda tablets (eighties to the twenties of the second century CE); any of the possible dates are appropriate for the Uley tablets (between the second and fourth centuries CE). For our purposes it is acceptable to leave this question unresolved.

The Genre of Luke–Acts

Different views have been put forward regarding the genre of Luke–Acts. Is it historical writing akin to Greco-Roman historical writing?[222] Does it narrate "an epoch of the history of Israel"?[223] Is it "popular history," albeit with more fiction than history,[224] or in today's terms a historical novel "based on real events"?[225] Does it take the form of a Greco-Roman novel?[226] Is it "a foundational epic for the early Christian church," doing for the story of the church what Virgil's *Aeneid* had done for the story of Rome?[227] Is the preface as one would expect in a literary work[228] or in the kind of technical or sci-

217. Dupertuis and Penner, *Engaging Early Christian History*, 11.

218. Dupertuis and Penner, *Engaging Early Christian History*; Penner and Stichele, *Contextualizing Acts*; Billings, *Acts and Roman Imperialism*.

219. Tyson, *Marcion and Luke–Acts*, 11.

220. Knox, *Marcion and the New Testament*, 166.

221. Talbert, *Reading Acts*, 2.

222. Keener, *Acts*; Witherington, *Acts*, 39.

223. Wolter, *Luke I*, 30–31.

224. Pervo, *Acts*, 18.

225. Maloney and Reimer, *Acts*, lvii.

226. Schwartz, "Trial Scene"; Pervo, *Profit with Delight*; Pervo, *Dating Acts*; Witherington offers a critique of Pervo (*Acts*, 376–81).

227. Bonz, *Past as Legacy*, 25–29, 189–93.

228. Bonz, *Past as Legacy*, 129–32; cf. 40–42.

entific handbooks familiar to the craftworkers and "middle-brow" readers among the followers of the Way of Jesus?[229] Is it more concerned "with what a character should say, or how a situation should unfold, than by any principle of 'accuracy'"?[230] Does it follow "two over-riding principles guiding ancient authors of historical narrative . . . imitation of previous models, and idealization in the service of crafting suitable prose"?[231] Is it creative writing depicting an idealized Paul as "an emblem of those manly virtues that constituted the common moral currency of the early Roman Empire"?[232] Or is Luke in accord with Paul's letter in depicting Paul "in emasculating ways" as "violable and beatable"?[233] Is it "a succession narrative": in Luke giving an account of the founder of the community" and in Acts "a narrative about Jesus' successors"?[234] Is it a biography akin to Greco-Roman biographies?[235] Is Luke the biography of an individual, Jesus, and Acts the biography of a people?[236] Richard Burridge argues that it bears comparison with, among other biographies, Tacitus's life of his father-in-law, Agricola, governor of Britannia c. 77–83 CE. *Agricola* is much the same length as Luke; shows little interest in Agricola's early life, instead focusing on the six years that are most significant; devotes a disproportionate amount of space to the final battle Agricola was involved in; and throughout has a polemical purpose.[237] Given this connection with Britannia our imagined reading will regard Luke and Acts (in that it focuses on Peter, Stephen, Philip and Paul) as historical writing akin to ancient biography. It will take seriously the dedication to Theophilus (Luke 1:1–4).

229. Alexander, "Luke's Preface."

230. Matthews, *Acts*, 12–17.

231. Matthews, *Acts*, 17.

232. Schellenberg, *Abject Joy*, 8; Schellenberg, "Beatings and Imprisonments"; cf. Lentz, *Luke's Portrait of Paul*, 105.

233. Lawrence, "Appearance and Health," 148–50; citing Wilson, *Unmanly Men in Luke-Acts*, 153, 156.

234. Talbert, *Reading Acts*, 9.

235. Talbert, *Reading Acts*, 14, 255–58; Burridge, "Genre of Acts"; Burridge, *What Are the Gospels?*.

236. Talbert, *Reading Acts*, 14.

237. Burridge, *What Are the Gospels?*, 151–52, 156–212.

The First Readership or Audience of Luke–Acts

For whom was Luke–Acts written? Few would now argue, with Caird, that Luke–Acts was written entirely for those outside the Christian community as "the first great *apologia* for the Christian faith."[238] Witherington suggests it was written in "an apologetic manner" "to a person of some social status to help them in "the uphill struggle" to become or remain a Christian."[239] Was it written for a predominantly Gentile community of followers of the Way[240] or for a community made up of "a mixture of Judean and Gentile, in which each group is significant"?[241] Was it written "to explain and defend" a well-established community of followers of the Way, rather than "nurture a young and fragile" community?[242] Was it written for an audience of "higher education than many others, with a wide knowledge of the north Aegean Greek culture and familiarity with the Septuagint"?[243] Was it written "with the perspective of a high status patron in mind, whether real or imaginary"?[244] Was its purpose to provide such a reader with "a lasting image of a man noble and virtuous when tested by the perils of travel"?[245] Was the "most excellent Theophilus" (κράτιστε Θεόφιλε: *optime Theophile*, Luke 1:3) an individual of high standing,[246] perhaps the patron of the work, or any "friend of God"?[247] Was Luke–Acts written for women such as Lydia as much as for men such as Theophilus?[248] Was Luke–Acts written not so much for a specific community but generally with all Christians in mind?[249]

238. Caird, *Luke*, 14.

239. Witherington, *Acts*, 379.

240. Fitzmyer, *Acts*, 59.

241. Esler, *Community and Gospel in Luke–Acts*, 31. Cf. Maloney and Reimer, *Acts*, lvi.

242. Pervo, *Acts*, 22.

243. Keener, *Acts*, 51.

244. Matthews, *Acts*, 5; cf. Matthews and Reid 2021, 3; Schaberg and Ringe, "Luke," 494.

245. Schellenberg, "Danger, Paul and Travel," 143; Schellenberg, "Beatings and Imprisonments"; cf. Lentz, *Luke's Portrait of Paul*, 168–72. Contrast Lawrence, "Appearance and Health," 148–50.

246. Witherington, *Acts*, 63.

247. Keener, *Acts*, 51.

248. Kahl, "Reading Luke Against Luke."

249. Bauckham, "For Whom Were Gospels Written?."

Was it written "as much for the non-believer as the believer"?[250] Is it possible to be specific? Is there within the text an indication of the diverse variety of people among those who were the first followers of the Way and so among those who were the first to read Luke–Acts?[251] We will assume that it was written for people who had already become followers of the Way of Jesus and accept Wolter's argument that it is "very probable that the Gospel of Luke was written not only *in the knowledge* that there were Christian communities everywhere in the Roman provinces, but also that in the view of its author its content was also relevant to every single . . . one of these communities."[252]

Luke–Acts, Rome, and Empire

What relationship does Luke–Acts have with the Roman Empire? Is it "pro" or "anti"? Or is such a distinction too simplistic?[253] In his survey of Luke–Acts scholarship, Steve Walton suggested in 2002 there had been five ways of looking at Luke–Acts and its view of the Roman Empire and he went on to suggest a sixth.[254] Luke–Acts

1. serves as political apologetic, defending the church to would-be Gentile converts from the wider Roman world.[255]
2. offers a political apologetic that works the other way round, defending the Roman world to those who follow the Way of Jesus, emphasizing "the positive aspects of Roman involvement in the history of the church."[256]
3. serves to "legitimate" the involvement in a church community of Romans "serving the empire in a military or administrative capacity" and so to "demonstrate that faith in Jesus Christ and allegiance to Rome were not mutually inconsistent."[257] There is a persuasiveness

250. Lentz, *Luke's Portrait of Paul*, 171.

251. Kahl, "Reading Luke Against Luke"; Brawley, *Luke*, 7; Matthews, *Acts*, 82–91.

252. Wolter, *Luke I*, 29. Cf. Bauckham, "For Whom Were Gospels Written?"; Bauckham, *The Gospels for All Christians*.

253. Billings, *Acts and Roman Imperialism*.

254. Walton, "Luke's View of Roman Empire."

255. Caird, *Luke*, 14; Bruce, *Acts*, 23–25; Conzelmann, *Acts*.

256. Walaskay, *Political Perspective of Luke*, 64.

257. Esler, *Community and Gospel in Luke-Acts*, 210.

about the rhetoric of Acts, and by implication Luke, that highlights "the compatibility between its concerns and values and those of the Roman Empire."[258] Luke presents Paul "as a man of high social status and moral virtue" who personifies what would have been recognized, by the first reader/hearer of Acts, as the classical cardinal virtues."[259] What is important for Luke is "Roman power exercised in proper fashion."[260]

4. helps followers of the Way of Jesus in the "conduct" of their lives, by giving an account of the writer's own "allegiance" to that Way. It enables them to live within the realities of the world of the Roman Empire and equips them should it be necessary to "witness" to the Way of Jesus in Roman legal proceedings.[261] There is, thus, a "compatible, symbiotic relationship between Christianity and Rome" in which "synagogues, houses and public places" serve as "workplaces God has selected for Christians to work programmatically from Jerusalem to Rome."[262]

5. has no interest in the politics of the Roman Empire and has instead a different focus on Jesus and God.[263]

6. offers its readers "a strategy of critical distance from the empire." There is a complexity in Luke–Acts, suggesting "co-operation and mutual respect" where that is possible; where there is opposition from Rome, calling "the state back to its former ways" and calling the church "to bear faithful witness to Jesus'.[264]

Post-colonial biblical criticism has had its impact in recent years: developments since 2002 have been summarized by Matthew Skinner.[265] Beneath the surface of what appears to be a pro-Roman work, argues

258. Matthews, *Acts*, 45; cf. 45–56; cf. Schaberg and Ringe, "Luke," 496; Schellenberg, "Danger, Paul and Travel," 145; Schellenberg, *Abject Joy*, 7–8; Talbert, *Reading Acts*, 123–24.

259. Lentz, *Luke's Portrait of Paul*, 3; cf. Schellenberg, "Beatings and Imprisonments."

260. D. R. Edwards, "Surviving Roman Power," 187.

261. Cassidy, *Christians and Roman Rule*; Cassidy, *Jesus, Politics, and Society*; Cassidy, *Society and Politics in Acts*.

262. Robbins, "Luke–Acts," 221. Cf. Robbins, "Social Location."

263. Jervell, *Theology of Acts*.

264. Walton, "Luke's View of Roman Empire," 106.

265. Skinner, "Acts in Relation to Empire"; cf. Kochenash, "Taking Bad with Good."

Brigitte Kahl, is a subtext that subverts the empire by focusing on Christ's claims to lordship over against Caesar's.[266] John Dominic Crossan describes "the logic of Jesus' Kingdom program" as "a mutuality of healing (the basic spiritual power) and eating (the basic physical power) shared freely and openly." Such a program "built a *share*-community from the bottom up as a positive alternative to Antipas's Roman *greed*-community established from the top down."[267] Christoph Heilig contrasts Tom Wright's espousal of a coded "anti-imperial subtext-hypothesis" in Acts and Paul's letters[268] with John Barclay's view that "the Roman Empire was insignificant to Paul."[269] He then proposes a third way that sees Paul as "a highly engaged observer of current political events" and so takes seriously the historical context of empire in understanding Paul's use of metaphorical language, for example to do with triumph.[270]

Luke–Acts, suggests Gary Gilbert, can be thought of as a counter to the kind of Roman propaganda found in the *Res Gestae* of Augustus.[271] For Marianne Palmer Bonz Luke–Acts offers "a rival vision of empire" to the one so powerfully described in Virgil's *Aeneid*.[272] In a post-colonial feminist reading, Margaret Aymer suggests Luke–Acts is a "reimagination of a divine imperial inbreaking," "written in the rhetoric of an occupied and colonized people imagining an empire stronger and more powerful than that which oppresses them."[273] Luke–Acts has the potential to destabilize Roman interests and is effectively saying that Rome does not have the last word.[274] Barbara Reid understands Luke to be countering "Roman imperial values by offering Jesus' service in humility as a contrast to imperial power and arrogance," whereas Shelly Matthews holds that Luke is "reinscribing imperial power rather than overturning it."[275] They do not, however, ac-

266. Kahl, "Acts."

267. Crossan, *God and Empire*, 118.

268. N. T. Wright, "Paul's Gospel Caesar's Empire."

269. Barclay, "Roman Empire Insignificant to Paul."

270. Heilig, *Apostle and the Empire*, 5–13, 139.

271. Gilbert, "Roman Propaganda." The heading of the Latin text of Augustus" *Res Gestae* reads *rerum gestarum divi Augusti*: the Greek text reads πράξεις τε καὶ δωρεαὶ Σεβαστοῦ θεοῦ Cooley, *Res Gestae Divi Augustae*, 58–59. "The best attested title for [Acts] is Πράξεις Ἀποστόλων see Pervo, *Acts*, 29–30.

272. Bonz, *Past as Legacy*, 129–93.

273. Aymer, "Acts Women's Bible Commentary," 544.

274. Skinner, "Acts in Relation to Empire," 116.

275. Matthews and Reid, *Luke 1–9*, 45.

cept that "Luke is making an explicit and subversive contrast between the "good news" of Jesus and the "good news of Rome": instead, Luke's aim is "to reassure his readers rather than to incite them to engage in politically subversive action." At the same time narratives to do with wealth and poverty show a real "concern for the suffering caused by imperial practices of economic extraction."[276]

It is Luke's very emphasis on reassuring people of standing who have become followers of the Way that suggests to Shelley Matthews that there were those among the first followers of the Way who stood out against Roman values more explicitly. She advocates "reading against the grain" in order to discern within the text of Luke–Acts indications of more subversive elements among the first followers of the Way.[277] Confronted with the "powerfully unsettling phenomenon" of the coming of the Spirit at Pentecost (Acts 2) and at other times, Luke endeavors "to write an orderly account" (Luke 1:4) that points his readers "in the direction of order, clarity and security."[278] By "taming" the Way and making it acceptable to those within the power-structures of the Roman Empire, Luke has nonetheless preserved echoes of prophetic voices that can still be heard by close attention to the text.

Robert Brawley speaks of the hidden dimensions of hierarchies of dominance which are subverted in Luke's gospel as "major concerns for law and order that belong to the ruling classes . . . are likewise subverted."[279] Drawing on an intertextuality that puts texts from the world of the Roman Empire alongside the New Testament, Warren Carter suggests "the interactions" between "God's empire and Rome's empire" are "complex and multivalent" ranging across "coexistence and accommodation, opposition and conflict, imitation and mimicry." He sets the Gospels over against the Roman Empire as they present us with "God who will "out-Caesar" Caesar to become the supreme ruler of the world."[280]

Others suggest that for Luke it is the other way round. Kazuhiko Ymazaki-Ransom argues that Luke has a negative view of Rome not in reaction to Rome's oppression of the people of God, but rather in affirmation

276. Matthews and Reid, *Luke 1–9*, 73–74.

277. Matthews, *Acts*, 82–91. Cf. Reid, "Do You See This Woman?."

278. Matthews, *Acts*, 83.

279. Brawley, *Luke*, 3.

280. Carter, *Jesus and the Empire*, chaps. 1 and 5: Kindle edition locations 121 and 1587.

of the sovereignty of God and the Lordship of Christ which is denied by the "demonic powers" of Rome.[281] For Kavin Rowe it is not that Jesus challenges the lordship and sovereignty of the emperor but that the emperor challenges the lordship and sovereignty of the God of Israel and Jesus.[282] To follow the Way of Jesus, he argues, involves "a different way of life" in which "basic patterns of Greco-Roman culture are dissolved" and the world is turned upside down without overthrowing Roman imperial power: "new culture, yes — coup, no."[283]

Aymer again speaks of "Luke's more conciliatory stance toward the Roman occupation and imperialization on behalf of the "kingdom" or empire of God. Both of these have implications for the growth of the Jesus movement."[284] Such "a pattern of fundamental tension" can be seen throughout the New Testament, according to Peter Oakes, and is "inherent in early Christian attitudes to Rome,"[285] not least in Acts where "Luke's Rome is a mixture of efficiency, openness, justice, cruelty, and corruption."[286] In Luke–Acts the church balances different identities and refuses to be identified with "empire": at its heart, for Eric Barreto is "a radical inclusivity, a profound hospitality for all" and a gospel that "does not simply seek to shape our behavior" but "to challenge our very assumptions about *identity*."[287] Loveday Alexander suggests a nuanced approach: while Luke seeks to demonstrate the legality of Christian practice to a Roman readership, "Paul's message embodies an alternative political vision that is profoundly subversive." Becoming a Christian involves an identity that embodies an alternative political vision.[288]

The Complexities of Luke–Acts

Matthew Skinner suggests there is a "messiness" about current Luke–Acts scholarship. He concludes by suggesting this is no bad thing and that "the

281. Yamazaki-Ransom, *Roman Empire in Luke*, 201–2.
282. C. K. Rowe, *World Upside Down*, 103–16.
283. C. K. Rowe, *World Upside Down*, 91.
284. Aymer, "Acts Women's Bible Commentary," 536.
285. Oakes, *Empire, Economics, and the New Testament*, 165.
286. Oakes, *Empire, Economics, and the New Testament*, 177.
287. Barreto, "Gospel on the Move," 186.
288. Alexander, "Luke's Political Vision."

complexities deserve greater attention."[289] In pointing the way forward he suggests moving away from the attempt to identify Luke's original readers towards a focus on, among other things, "the general cultural setting of the broader Roman world." In Luke–Acts there is a rich diversity of ways in which people who follow the Way of Jesus negotiate their relationship with the Roman Empire. It is this very "multidimensionality" and even "inconsistency" that, in his view, lends verisimilitude to the narrative of Luke–Acts.[290]

Far from being a weakness, it is that very uncertainty about authorship, date and original readership that becomes a strength for Joel Green in his commentary on the Gospel of Luke. He "proceeds under the assumption that our ability or inability to identify the author of the third Gospel is unimportant to its interpretation."[291] Instead, he focuses on the narrative itself and argues that modern interpreters need "to engage as fully as possible in an exploration of the cultural presuppositions Luke shared with his contemporaries."[292]

That approach is broadly followed by Robert Brawley in his Social Identity commentary on Luke. In his opinion "little can be said about the place or time of composition," other than that it reflects the world of the late first century CE: "what counts is what turns out to be true in the narrative world."[293] For him the narrative read, as it were, by a first-time reader becomes all important. At the same time, he argues, "Luke's narrative employs a cultural encyclopedia that is unavailable to interpreters without substantial familiarity with the history of antiquity."[294] Understanding that cultural encyclopedia "requires immersion in historical studies," though "even at their best modern interpreters can never understand the New Testament world as it "really was."[295] For Brawley that involves drawing on social-scientific approaches and focusing on the social identity not so much of the implied reader/hearer of Luke–Acts as of the people "who appear in Luke's narrative."[296]

289. Skinner, "Acts in Relation to Empire."

290. Skinner, "Acts in Relation to Empire," 125.

291. Green, *Gospel of Luke*, 20.

292. Green, *Gospel of Luke*, 12.

293. Brawley, *Luke*, 6–7.

294. Brawley, *Luke*, 7.

295. Brawley, *Luke*, 8–9.

296. Brawley, *Luke*, 10.

It is as we re-enact in our mind's eye the history of the traders and merchants of Londinium, the military community of Vindolanda and the rural community around the temple dedicated to Mercury at Uley, that we shall be in a position to imagine Luke–Acts through the eyes of such people and understand better the way Luke–Acts interacts with questions of empire.

An Imagined Reading of Luke–Acts

Our imagined reading will bring the people who appear in Luke's narrative into conversation with the people responsible for the Bloomberg tablets, the Vindolanda tablets and the Uley tablets. It will assume that the gospel of Luke and the book of Acts are a single work which we will refer to as Luke–Acts, written by a single author we will refer to, for ease of reference, as Luke. The precise dating and the identity of the intended readership or audience we will regard as open questions. We will assume that Luke–Acts was written in a way that has similarities with ancient biographies; and that it was written not simply for its original readership but for followers of the Way of Jesus wherever they may be found. Focusing on individuals whose lives we momentarily glimpse in their writings and on the way they might have read Luke–Acts will enable us to contribute to current debates about the New Testament and empire.

Seeing into the Life of Things: Imagining Luke–Acts in Roman Britain

Studying texts and inscriptions from the Greco-Roman and Judean worlds of the eastern Mediterranean while employing anthropological insights and ideas from the social sciences,[297] enables us to identify the kind of things to expect in what Robert Brawley describes as a "cultural encyclopedia":[298] first century personality, kinship and social location; gender; honor and shame; reciprocity and patron-client relations; the poor and the rich; economics and debt; table-fellowship; ceremonies; sickness and healing; city

297. Esler, *Community and Gospel in Luke–Acts*; Esler, *First Christians in Their Social Worlds.*; Malina, *Windows on Jesus' World*; Malina, *New Testament World*; Neyrey, ed., *Social World of Luke–Acts*; Neyrey, *Imagining Jesus*; Neyrey and Stewart, eds., *Social World of the New Testament.*

298. Brawley, *Luke*, 7–9.

and countryside.[299] These are among the themes that emerge from a reading of our archives from Roman Britain.

In the remainder of this book, each of the three archives will function as a "gateway to history" as we explore "a particular world of experience," re-enact a moment of history, take an imaginative leap and get to know named people. Chapters 2, 3 and 4 will each begin with a brief introduction to the people concerned, after which we will introduce the tablets, piecing together what is known of that corpus of texts, the location in which they were created and the people who wrote them. We will then draw on the archival ethnography developed by Lennartsson and Esler, taking into account the insights of Huebner, Longenecker and Oakes and in our mind's eye imagine, first, the people whose very handwritten words have survived in the texts we are studying; and, second, how people such as these, drawn to follow the Way of Jesus, might have read texts from Luke–Acts, finding some familiar and others challenging. We will then finish each chapter by drawing conclusions regarding the way they might have negotiated the world of the Roman Empire.

In Chapter 2, imagining Luke–Acts through the eyes of the people of the Bloomberg tablets will take us to passages to do with money and possessions; honor and shame; reciprocity and debt; patrons and clients; slaves and masters; the rich and the destitute; Roman law and literacy. We will see how much of the world of Luke–Acts would be familiar to them, and we will explore how the Way of Jesus would challenge many of their assumptions.

Chapter 3 will introduce us to three groups of people whose writings have been preserved at Vindolanda: women present in the fort; centurions and other officers; and their commanding officers. As we imagine each group in turn, we will be taken to passages in Luke–Acts to do with women of agency; the military and local people; Roman law; travel and identity; festivals and feasting; sickness and death; honor and shame; patrons and clients; masters and slaves and the reversal of roles.

Chapter 4 will begin with an introduction to the temple of Mercury and will ask whether the lead tablets deposited there should be regarded as curse tablets or prayers for justice. Imagining the people responsible for the tablets will take us to passages to do with temples; ritual practice; cursing; and praying.

299. Esler, *Community and Gospel in Luke-Acts*; Neyrey, ed., *Social World of Luke-Acts*; Neyrey and Stewart, eds., *Social World of the New Testament*.

Chapter 5 will reflect on the way the people we have encountered might have negotiated the Way of Jesus in the context of the Roman Empire. It will highlight the potential there is in Roman Britain for the use of archival ethnography in studying Luke–Acts and other New Testament texts.

As we draw on the insights of archival ethnography, we must nurture a multi-faceted imagination. It will be an imagination that "creates mental images"[300] and "allows us both to express and to understand ideas."[301] It will be *a historical imagination* that appeals to data, "runs little risk of losing touch with the reality which it represents,"[302] and entails a "fact-based imaginative empathy."[303] It will be *an ethnographic imagination* that allows us "to empathize" with the people we encounter[304] and *a sociological imagination* that "enables us to grasp history and biography and the relations between the two within society."[305] It will be an imagination that gives us "the ability to think about" particular people whose existence is inferred from the evidence we have to hand.[306] It will be *a geographical imagination* that immerses us "in a world of places" and "aims to understand and recover" them in such a way that they become a context for human experience.[307] It will be *an archaeological imagination* that seeks "to recreate the world behind the ruin in the land, to reanimate the people behind the" artefact in a way that "enables us to make sense of our relationship with the past . . . and [its] relationship to our sense of self and identity."[308] It will be an imagination which "makes sense of things, locating particular bits and pieces within larger patterns, and in doing so goes beyond what is given, filling gaps, painting bigger pictures."[309] It will be an imagination informed by the data available and so it will be an imagination that guards against becoming a flight of fancy.[310] It will be an imagination that hears with the inward ear

300. Warnock, *Imagination*, 10.

301. Warnock, *Imagination*, 72.

302. Collingwood, *The Idea of History*, 242.

303. Maloney and Reimer, *Acts*, lxi.

304. Lennartsson, "Archival Ethnography," 92.

305. Mills, *Sociological Imagination*, 6.

306. L. Stevenson, "Imagination," 239–41: Conceptions 1, 1b, 1d.

307. Tilley, *Phenomenology of Landscape*, 15.

308. Shanks, *Archaeological Imagination*, 25.

309. Hart, "Imagination," 319.

310. Collingwood, *The Idea of History*, 242; Willis, *Ethnographic Imagination*, viii.

and sees with the inward and inner eye.[311] Our imagined reading must meet three criteria. It must be justifiable in the locations and with the writings chosen, informed by careful study of the data available, and warranted by close attention to the biblical text.

The imagined reading of Luke–Acts I will share will necessarily be my imagined reading. As he came to the end of his celebration of imagination Graham Ward extended an invitation to his readers. It is one I would extend to you: "the exercise of my imagination as a writer is an invitation to exercise your mind as a reader."[312] Let your imagination take you via these writings from the ancient world to an encounter with the people responsible for them and through their eyes to a fresh encounter with Luke–Acts. The artefacts under consideration may be described as "things." They include not only the stylus wax writing tablets of Londinium, the ink-on-wood writing tablets of Vindolanda and the lead tablets of the rural community around the temple of Mercury on the Hill of *Aruerius* at Uley; among those artefacts we must also count a notional codex of Luke–Acts. As we look beyond those "things" into the lives of those responsible for them, may we have that kind of imagination Wordsworth spoke of in his *Poems of the Imagination* and "see into the life of things."[313]

311. Poems of the Imagination XXVI, Preface to the edition of 1815, *Poems of the Imagination* XXIX, XII, XIX, Wordsworth, *Poetical Works*, 164, 753, 166, 149, 157.

312. Ward, *Unimaginable*, 237.

313. Wordsworth, *Poetical Works*, 164: *Poems of the Imagination* XXVI, "Lines Composed a few miles above Tintern Abbey," line 49.

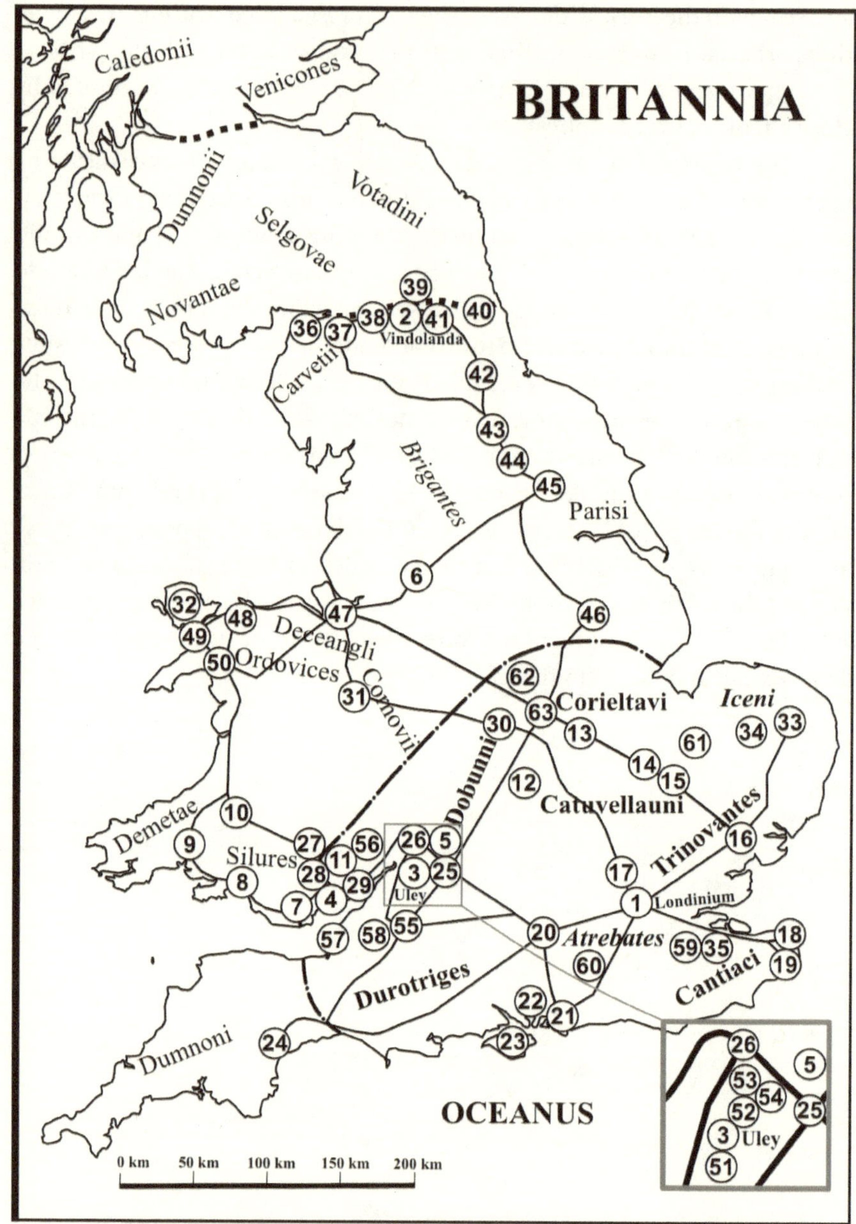

Figure 1. Map of Britannia drawn by Chris Jones-Jenkins and revised by Phil Cleaves showing locations mentioned in the text; Celtic peoples, coin production, and friendly kings; extent of curse tablets; key roads.

Map of Britannia

Chapter 1: Introduction

1	Londinium	Llundain	London*
2	Vindolanda		Chesterholm*
3	Temple of Mercury on the Hill of *Aruerius*		Uley
4		Casnewydd	Newport*
5	Chedworth Villa		Chedworth*
6	Mamucium	Manceinion	Manchester*
7		Caerdydd	Cardiff
8	Nidum	Castell Nedd	Neath
9	Moridunum	Caerfyrddin	Carmarthen
10	Luventium	Dolaucothau	Gold Mines*
11	Llanvaches Hoard		Caerleon*
12	South Warwickshire Hoard		Warwick*
13	Hallaton Hoard		Market Harborough*
14			Fenstanton
15	Duroliponte	Caergrawnt	Cambridge

Chapter 2: The Bloomberg Tablets

1	Londinium	Llundain	London*
16	Camulodunum		Colchester*
17	Verulamium		St Albans*
18	Rutupiae		Richborough*
19	Dubris	Dofr	Dover
20	Calleva Attrebatum		Silchester
21	Noviomagus Regnorum		Chichester*
22			Fishbourne Palace*
23	Vectis Insula	Ynys Wyth	Isle of Wight
24	Isca Dumnomniorum	Caerwysg	Exeter*
25	Corinium Dobunnorum		Cirencester*
26	Glevum	Caergloyw	Gloucester*

27	Burrium	Brynbuga	Usk
28	Isca	Caerllion ar Wysg	Caerleon*
29	Venta Silurum	Caerwent	Caerwent
30	Manduessedum		Mancetter
31	Viroconium Cornoviorum		Wroxeter*
32	Mona Insula	Ynys Môn	Anglesey
33	Venta Icenorum		Caistor St. Edmund
34	?Epocuria		Unknown location of fort among Iceni
35	Verlucionium		Unknown location of Five-acre wood in Kent

Chapter 3: The Vindolanda Tablets

2	Vindolanda		Chesterholm*
36	Maia		Bowness
37	Luguvalium	Caerliwelydd	Carlisle*
38	Briga		Unknown location of fort near Vindolanda.
39	Vercovicium		Housesteads*
40	Segedunum		Wallsend*
41	Coria		Corbridge
42	Vinovia		Binchester
43	Cataractonium	Catraeth	Catterick
44	Isurium Brigantum		Aldborough
45	Eboracum	Caerefrog	York*
46	Lindum		Lincoln*
47	Deva	Caer	Chester*
48	Canovium	Caerhun	Conwy Valley
49	Segontium	Caernarfon	Caernarfon
50		Tomen y Mûr	

Chapter 4: The Uley Tablets and Other Curse Tablets

3	Temple of Mercury on the Hill of *Aruerius*		Uley
51	Uley Bury Hill Fort		Uley
52	Uley Long Barrow	Hetty Pegler's Tump	Uley
53	Nympsfield Long Barrow		Nympsfield
54	Woodchester Villa		Woodchester
55	Aquae Sulis Temple of Sulis Minerva	Caerfaddon	Bath*
56	Temple of Nodens		Lydney Park*
57	Temple, unknown		Brean Down
58	Temple, unknown		Pagans Hill
59	Temple, unknown		East Farleigh, Kent
60	Temple, unknown		Farley Heath, Surrey
61	Temple, unknown		Hockwold, Norfolk
62	Temple, unknown		Ratcliffe-on-Soar
63	Ratae Corieltavorum	Caerlŷr	Leicester*

Numbered entries are locations mentioned in the text. Welsh place names are listed as they predate English names, often date to shortly after the period of the Roman occupation, and occasionally derive from Celtic place names adopted by the Romans. Those marked with (*) have a good museum or visitor center.[314]

The names in large lettering indicate tribal society in Britain in the first century CE.[315] Tribes minting coins are shown in bold: Atrebates, Trinovantes, Iceni, Durotriges, Cantiaci, Catuvellauni, Dobunni, Corieltavi.[316] Those with friendly rulers, c. 50 CE, are italicized: Atrebates (Togidubnus), Iceni (Prasutagus), Brigantes (Cartimandua).[317]

314. Cleary, *Map of Roman Britain*; B. Jones and Mattingly, *Atlas of Roman Britain*. Hingley lists the meaning of the ancient name, the role of the site, and the visible remains (*Conquering the Ocean*, 266–67).

315. B. Jones and Mattingly, *Atlas of Roman Britain*, 45; Todd, *Roman Britain*, 31; Salway, *History of Roman Britain*, 36; D. Mattingly, *An Imperial Possession*, 49. Hingley lists the names of peoples, their location and their possible meaning (*Conquering the Ocean*, 268).

316. Van Arsdell, *Celtic Coinage*; B. Jones and Mattingly, *Atlas of Roman Britain*, 55.

317. B. Jones and Mattingly, *Atlas of Roman Britain*, 141; Hingley, *Conquering the Ocean*, 68.

The major roads marked are mentioned in the text and mostly based on the Antonine Itineraries.[318]

Curse tablets have been found to the south and east of the broken line. Those found in temples are identified.[319]

Mons Graupius is 325 kilometers to the north of Vindolanda, near Aberdeen in the Grampian mountains.[320] Hadrian's Wall from Bowness to Wallsend (122 CE) post-dates the Vindolanda tablets.[321] The Antonine Wall, from the Firth of Clyde to the Firth of Forth, marked the northern frontier of the Roman Empire for a short period in the middle of the second century CE.[322]

318. B. Jones and Mattingly, *Atlas of Roman Britain*, 23–28, 94, 98, 100; Cleary, *Map of Roman Britain*; Guest, *Roman Frontiers in Wales*, 36; Hopewell, *Roman Roads*; Mattingly, *An Imperial Possession*, 264; Salway, *History of Roman Britain*, 124.

319. Sánchez Natalías, *Sylloge Defixiones*, 77; McKie, *Living and Cursing*, 14–15; Tomlin, *The Uley Tablets*, 5.

320. Cleary, *Map of Roman Britain*; B. Jones and Mattingly, *Atlas of Roman Britain*, 75, 76.

321. Cleary, *Map of Roman Britain*; B. Jones and Mattingly, *Atlas of Roman Britain*, 114–15; Breeze, *Frontiers Hadrian's Wall*, 48.

322. Cleary, *Map of Roman Britain*; B. Jones and Mattingly, *Atlas of Roman Britain*, 122–23.

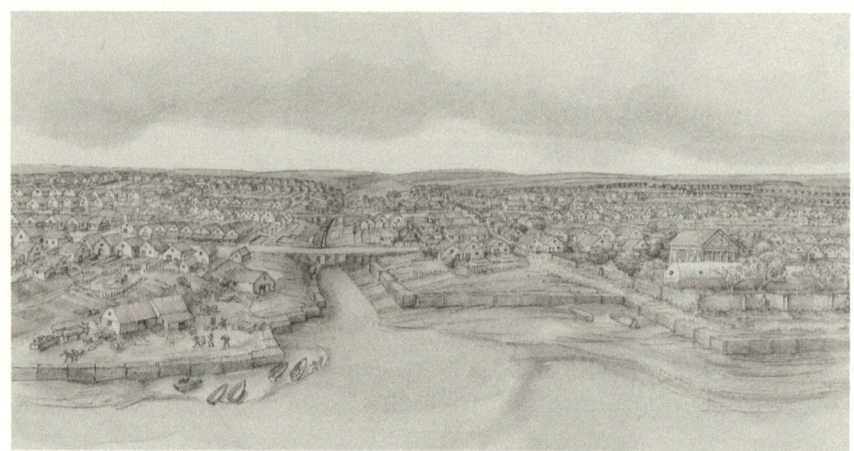

Figure 2. Londinium c. 80 CE. View from south of the Thames, at the mouth of the Walbrook. This conjectural reconstruction shows the timber waterfronts along the Thames and boats beached on the foreshore, timber bridges over the Walbrook and the densely built-up town on both sides of the valley; east of the Walbrook is the temple and baths complex (far right foreground), with the forum and basilica in the distance (top right). The first crossing of the Thames would be to the right of this picture, at the location of the modern London Bridge. © MOLA/Judith Dobie.[1]

1. S. Wright, *Archaeology at Bloomberg*, 23.

CHAPTER 2

Imagining Luke–Acts in an Urban Community

Through the Eyes of the People of the Bloomberg Tablets

> "the sociological imagination enables us to grasp history and biography and the relations between the two within society."
>
> —C. Wright Mills, *The Sociological Imagination*

Introducing the People of the Bloomberg Tablets

WITHIN THIRTY YEARS OF the Claudian invasion of Britain in 43 CE much had happened.[2] The one-time legate of *legio II Augusta*, Vespasian, had put down the Judean revolt and subsequently taken power in Rome as emperor. Londinium had grown up around the bridge that spanned the Thames at its first crossing point. Whether it was established as a supply-base for the military occupation of Britain, as Dominic Perring argues[3] or, as Richard Hingley suggests, it was "founded by a community of traders who wished to exploit the location of the port" it was of considerable economic significance. Evidence unearthed recently suggests it developed as a result of "an ambitious urban programme."[4] It has been described by Dominic Perring as "a place dominated by the political establishment" and

2. See Table 1. See Map (Figure 1) 1, 16–28.
3. Perring, *London in Roman World*, 68–70.
4. Hingley, *Londinium: A Biography*, 25–32.

"a creature of Roman political purpose."[5] A significant port, Londinium attracted traders, merchants and bankers who recorded their transactions on wax tablets. Titus had proved unreliable in his moneylending and was in danger of appearing shameful.[6] Gratus, the freedman of Spurius, was in possession of a loan note for 105 denarii; he could realize its cash value by claiming that sum from Tibullus, the freedman of Venustus, or by selling the loan note on to a third party.[7]

One dated tablet makes it clear that traders forced to flee the burning city during the Boudica revolt (60–61 CE) returned and resumed business as soon as the revolt had been quelled. Gaius Valerius Proculus of Londinium contracted on 12 October 62 CE to make twenty deliveries of provisions by 13 November to Marcus Rennius Venustus in Verulamium (St Albans), thirty-five kilometers away, at a charge of one quarter denarius for each load. The full sum would be paid on condition that all twenty loads were delivered.[8] From these tablets it is clear, as David Johnston observes, that "credit played a vital part in the Roman economy, and payments were often made without coinage."[9] The merchants and traders we meet in the Bloomberg tablets brought an economic system recognizable across the empire, built on patronage, honor and shame, reciprocity and debt.

Let's imagine that, sometime in the last quarter of the first century CE, a merchant who has been drawn to follow the Way of Jesus arrives with a codex or codices including Luke and Acts in his baggage to share with a group of followers of the Way of Jesus. A mixed group of rich and poor, slave and free, women and men, locals and new arrivals, it includes people such as those we encounter in the Bloomberg tablets. To imagine Luke–Acts through their eyes is to encounter it as its first audience would have done.

To ensure such an imagined reading is justifiable in mid-first-century Londinium we will first introduce the Bloomberg tablets, exploring what exactly they are. That will then enable us to draw on our adaptation of

5. Perring, *London in Roman World*, 30. Cooley notes the major role of immigrants and the absence of local elite ("Role of the Non-Elite," 104).

6. *Tab. Lond. Bloomberg* 30, 43–53 CE; Tomlin, *Roman London's First Voices*, 120–23. Appendix Chapter 2.

7. *Tab. Lond. Bloomberg* 44, 8 Jan. 57 CE; Tomlin, *Roman London's First Voices*, 152–55. Appendix Chapter 2.

8. *Tab. Lond. Bloomberg* 45, 21 Oct. 62 CE; Tomlin, *Roman London's First Voices*, 156–59. Appendix Chapter 2. Map (Figure 1) 17.

9. Johnston, *Roman Law*, 102.

archival ethnography and imagine life among the merchants and traders responsible for the Bloomberg tablets. We will then be able to imagine how people such as these might have responded to Luke–Acts as they would have encountered much that was familiar and much that would challenge them. It is finally in those challenges that we shall consider how they might have negotiated the Way of Jesus through their world of finance and trade.

Introducing the Bloomberg Tablets and Other Stylus Writing Tablets of Londinium

2016 saw the publication of 405 stylus writing tablets from the middle of the first century CE, of which more than eighty are legible.[10] Discovered during excavations (2010–2014) on the site of Bloomberg's European Headquarters in the City of London, they are the earliest pieces of writing to be discovered in Britain: some are contemporary with events in the New Testament.[11]

The fragments of wax tablets were preserved in anaerobic conditions beside the Walbrook, a tributary of the Thames that has long-since disappeared. An early priority of the Romans had been to bridge the Thames, easing communication between the south-east coast and Camulodunum (Colchester), the first Roman capital, and Verulamium (St Albans) to the north and Calleva Atrebatum (Silchester), to the west.[12] A town quickly grew up on each side of what is now London Bridge.[13] A grid of north-south and east-west roads developed on both sides of the Walbrook between two hills, Cornhill and Ludgate hill.[14] To alleviate flooding the banks of the Walbrook were shored up with double walls, infilled with rubbish from further east; the land was levelled using similar detritus. Most of the Bloomberg tablets had been destroyed and were used in that infill.[15]

10. Tomlin, *Roman London's First Voices.*

11. See Table 4.

12. Camulodunum, Verulamium, Calleva Atrebatum, Map (Figure 1) 16, 17, 20.

13. Perring et al., *Archaeology Roman London*; Perring, *Roman London*; Rowsome, *Heart of the City*; Clark and Sheldon, *Londinium and Beyond*; J. Hill and Rowsome, *Roman London and Walbrook*; S. Wright, *Archaeology at Bloomberg*; Hingley, *Londinium: A Biography*, 25–50; Perring, *London in Roman World*, 63–86. For a map of Londinium see Rowsome, *Londinium Map*. Figure 2.

14. Perring, *London in Roman World*, 72–74.

15. Tomlin, *Roman London's First Voices*, 32.

Wooden shops and workshops fronted the main roads with living accommodation behind: strip houses, they had wattle and daub walls and thatched roofs.[16] By 60 CE the housing was as closely packed as in Herculaneum.[17] Excavations at the adjacent 1 Poultry site in the 1990s produced evidence of craftworkers, such as leather workers and tentmakers enabling the Museum of London to recreate wooden dwellings, a pottery shop and a tavern.[18] Advances in dendrochronology since 1983 make it possible to date wooden remains from first century Londinium to within ten years.[19]

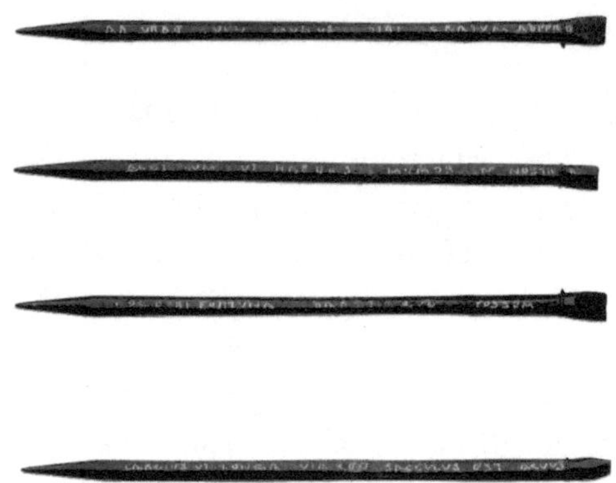

Figure 3. Presentation stylus from the Bloomberg excavations. Note the flattened end, serving as an eraser, a common feature of wax tablet styluses. Photograph: Andy Chopping. Inscription highlighted: Roger S. O. Tomlin. From MOLA blog, © MOLA/Andy Chopping.

ab urbe v[e]n[i] munus tibi gratum adf(e)ro |acul[eat]um ut habe[a]s memor[ia]m nostra(m) |rogo si fortuna dar[e]t quo possem |largius ut longa via ceu sacculus est (v)acuus

I have come from the City [? Rome]. I bring you a welcome gift |with a sharp point that you may remember me. |I ask, if fortune allowed, that I might be able (to give) |as generously as the way is long (and) as my purse is empty.[20]

16. Perring, *London in Roman World*, 72–74, 204–5.

17. Rowsome, *Heart of the City*, 26.

18. J. Hill and Rowsome, *Roman London and Walbrook*; Rowsome 2001; cf. Perring, *London in Roman World*, 214.

19. Tyers, "Tree-Ring Dates"; Tomlin, *Roman London's First Voices*, 5. The dating scheme developed in 1 Poultry was used in the Bloomberg excavations. The decision to use the corporate name "Bloomberg" in the formal designation of the Bloomberg tablets artificially separates them from the tablets discovered beside the Walbrook, especially at 1 Poultry.

20. "I Went to Rome"; Willi, *Writing Equipment*, 33–38.

Among the 200 styluses discovered on the Bloomberg site one, inscribed on four faces, seems to have been brought by a trader from Rome (Figure 3), suggesting "the importance of travel from the Continent in spreading Latin in Londinium."[21] Of the 300 stylus tablets previously found in London, nineteen have been published:[22] seven were discovered by the Walbrook and four at 1 Poultry.[23] They confirm Tacitus's description of Londinium as a place *copia negotiatorum et commeatuum maxime celebre* (most renowned for its abundance of merchants and of traded goods).[24] Business resumed immediately following the Boudica revolt.[25]

Made locally of imported coniferous timber, mostly silver fir that had previously been used in casks and barrels, the stylus writing tablets were on average *c.* 140 mm wide by *c.* 110 mm high.[26]

Type 1 tablets were plain on one side and recessed and filled with blackened beeswax on the other. The text was written in lower cursive letterforms as the stylus disclosed the white of the wood through the blackened wax. It is the resulting scratch marks on the wood that can be deciphered today with the help of photography (Figure 4).

Type 2 tablets were recessed on both sides, one with a single panel, the other with two panels separated by a space used for the seals of witnesses.

21. Cooley, "Role of the Non-Elite," 108, 112–14; Wilson, "Latin, Literacy and Roman Economy," 81–87.

22. Frere and Tomlin, *RIB II Fasc. 4*, 11–21 and since 1986 published in Britannia. Tomlin lists and describes the tablets published prior to 2016 (*Roman London's First Voices*, 287).

23. Tomlin, "1 Poultry Stylus Writing Tablets."

24. Tacitus, *Annales* xiv.33.

25. *Tab. Lond. Bloomberg* 45 is evidence of that swift rebuilding: Tomlin, *Roman London's First Voices*, 156–59. Appendix Chapter 2.

26. D. Goodburn and Humphreys, "Waxed Stylus Writing Tablets." This is slightly larger than A6 (148.5 mm x 105 mm).

Figure 4. *Tab. Lond. Bloomberg* 29 as it may have originally appeared: a letter from Taurus to Macrinus about Catarrius taking beasts of burden. Traces of earlier (and/or corrected) text have been removed and lost text conjecturally reconstructed. Appendix Chapter 2. © MOLA (photograph Andy Chopping/drawing Roger S. O. Tomlin.

taurus macrino domino | carissimo salute | scias me domine recte esse | quod tu sis inuicem cupio | cum uenerat catarrius et | iumenta aduxerat conpedia | quae messibus tribus reficere | non possum adfueram ehre | ad diadumenum set ille | superuenit unum diem

Taurus to Macrinus his dearest lord, | greetings. | Know that I am in good health, | which I desire that you are too. | When Catarrius had come and had taken the beasts of burden away, | investments which I cannot | replace in three months, | I was at (the house of) Diadumenus yesterday, | but he (Catarrius) arrived unexpectedly for a single day . . .[27]

27. Tomlin, *Roman London's First Voices*, 16.

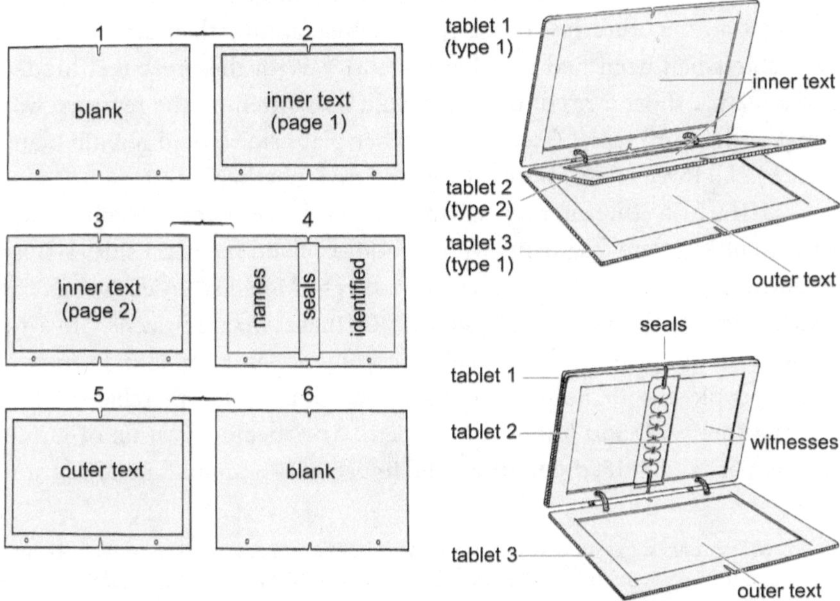

Figure 5. Schematic reconstruction of a triptych—two type 1 tablets enclosing a type 2, hinged together—used for a legal document. Left - diagram showing the three tablets: the text was duplicated (inner and outer) and witnesses wrote their names to the left of their seals on the type 2 tablet (on face 4) which enclosed the inner text (faces 2 and 3), their names being identified to the right by patronymic, military subunit, etc. (after *Tab. Vindol.* 1, 45, fig. 9). Right - schematic reconstruction (after Speidel, *Vindonissa*, 22, fig. 7, adapted for the Bloomberg tablets). © MOLA.[28]

In correspondence, two type 1 tablets were hinged using two small holes on one long side to form a diptych; they would be tied together using the two notches in the middle of the long sides with the wax-filled recesses facing each other. On one plain side the addressee's name and sometimes address would be etched in capitals using a pointed stylus.[29] In legal and financial documents a type 2 tablet was inserted between two type 1 tablets to form a triptych (Figure 5).

The name was in the same way etched on the plain side of tablet one (face 1) and the start of the document written through the wax on the other side (face 2). The rest of the document was written on the single recessed panel of the second (type 2) tablet (face 3). The witnesses, often seven in

28. Tomlin, *Roman London's First Voices*, 24, citing Speidel, *Vindonissa*.

29. Webley, "Styli"; Willi, *Writing Equipment*, 49–55.

number, would write their names to the left and further identification to the right on the other side of the type 2 tablet, adding their seals once the two tablets had been tied together (face 4).[30] With the inner text hidden and sealed, a short form of the text would be written on the recessed wax panel of the third tablet (face 5). The other plain side would remain blank (face 6). All three tablets were hinged and tied together.[31]

Of the forty-three items of correspondence among the Bloomberg tablets, twenty-five are fragments with an addressee on the plain side. Six use an epistolary formula: e.g. "you will give this to Metellus" (*Metello dabis*);[32] sixteen identify the addressee by name.[33] Of these two are citizens,[34] five are of Celtic origin possibly from Gaul,[35] and one possibly has Iberian roots.[36] Three people are identified by occupation: Optatus the merchant,[37] Tertius the ?brewer,[38] and Junius the cooper.[39] The specific location of Junius the cooper is identified, opposite (the house of) Catullus.[40] Londinium is

30. Marshman suggests that the use of a signet ring was a marker of identity and status and indicative of literacy ("Making Your Mark in Britannia," 172, 191).

31. Tomlin, *Roman London's First Voices*, 15–30.

32. *Tab. Lond. Bloomberg* 1; Tomlin, *Roman London's First Voices*, 60–61. Cf. 2 (62–63), 4 (66–67), 14 (86–87), 16 (90–91), 24 (106–7).

33. *Tab. Lond. Bloomberg* 1; Tomlin, *Roman London's First Voices*, 60–61 Metellus. Cf. 2 (62–63) Gratus the son of Junius; 3 (64–65) Tiberius Claudius Danucus, Cornelius S[.]tta ...; 4 (66–67) Luguseluus the son of Junius; 5 (68–69) Martialus son of Ambiccus; 6 (70–71) Mogontius; 7 (72–73) Optatus; 8 (74–75) Jucundus son of Flavius; 9 (76–77) Julius; 10 (78–79) Florus; 11 (80–81) Sabinus son of Pirinus; 12 (82–83) Tertius; 13 (84–85) Namatobogius the son of [...[linagius]; 14 (86–87) Junius; 15 (88–89) Atticus; 16 (90–91) Bassus.

34. *Tab. Lond. Bloomberg* 3; Tomlin, *Roman London's First Voices*, 64–65 Tiberius Claudius Danucus, Cornelius S[.]tta....

35. *Tab. Lond. Bloomberg* 4; Tomlin, *Roman London's First Voices*, 66–67 Luguseluus, Junius (a Latin name concealing a Celtic element). Cf. 5 (68–69) Ambiccus, 6 (70–71) Mogontius, 13 (84–85) Namatobogius.

36. *Tab. Lond. Bloomberg* 11; Tomlin, *Roman London's First Voices*, 80–81, Pirinius.

37. *Tab. Lond. Bloomberg* 7; Tomlin, *Roman London's First Voices*, 72–73: Optato *neg(otiatori)*.

38. *Tab. Lond. Bloomberg* 12; Tomlin, *Roman London's First Voices*, 82–83: *Tertio bracea|vacat rio*. For an explanation of conventions used in transcribing and translating the tablets see The Texts, xxiii-xxv.

39. *Tab. Lond. Bloomberg* 14; Tomlin, *Roman London's First Voices*, 86–87: *Iunio cupario*.

40. *Tab. Lond. Bloomberg* 14 Tomlin, 2016, 86–87: *dabes Iunio cupario | contra Catullu<m>*.

identified as the destination of three letters,[41] of which one is addressed to Mogontius[42] and another to [. . .]inus of tribunician rank.[43] Of the remaining eighteen items of correspondence three have little more than the names of the sender, the addressee or a third person[44] and two defy classification.[45] In one letter Bellus seems to write "angrily,"[46] and in another it appears that "Frontinus is able"[47] but nothing else is decipherable. Two have military associations: one refers to Classicus, prefect of the sixth cohort of Nervii. He is probably the Treveran, Julius Classicus who went on to command a cavalry *ara* in the Batavian revolt of 70 CE. A relative of the newly appointed governor of Britain, Julius Classicianus, he was brought in with his auxiliary cohort as reinforcements after the Boudica revolt.[48] Another names a fort garrisoned in the aftermath of the Boudica revolt, "the fort of ?Epocuria" in "(the canton of) the Iceni," mentioning that Julius Suavis has accepted something for himself.[49] The creation of small forts such as this, linked by a network of roads, was the mechanism used to subdue the local peoples.[50]

41. *Tab. Lond. Bloomberg* 6, 18, 24; Tomlin, *Roman London's First Voices*, 70–71, 94–95, 106–7.

42. *Tab. Lond. Bloomberg* 6; Tomlin, *Roman London's First Voices*, 70–71 *Londinio Mogontio.*

43. *Tab. Lond. Bloomberg* 18; Tomlin, *Roman London's First Voices*, 94–95.

44. *Tab. Lond. Bloomberg* 26; Tomlin, *Roman London's First Voices*, 110–11, Calventius Ingenuus; 36 (136–37), the Latin Carus, or a Celtic name incorporating caro-]; 40 (144–45] Nigellio.

45. *Tab. Lond. Bloomberg* 42; Tomlin, *Roman London's First Voices*, 148–49; 43 (150–51).

46. *Tab. Lond. Bloomberg* 28; Tomlin, *Roman London's First Voices*, 114–15.

47. *Tab. Lond. Bloomberg* 34; Tomlin, *Roman London's First Voices*, 132–33.

48. *Tab. Lond. Bloomberg* 33; Tomlin, *Roman London's First Voices*, 130–31; for a reconstruction of the tomb of the imperial procurator, C. Julius Classicianus see Perring, *London in Roman World*, 107.

49. *Tab. Lond. Bloomberg* 39; Tomlin, *Roman London's First Voices*, 142–43. Appendix Chapter 2. Map (Figure 1) 34.

50. Cf. Guest, *Roman Frontiers in Wales*, 69.

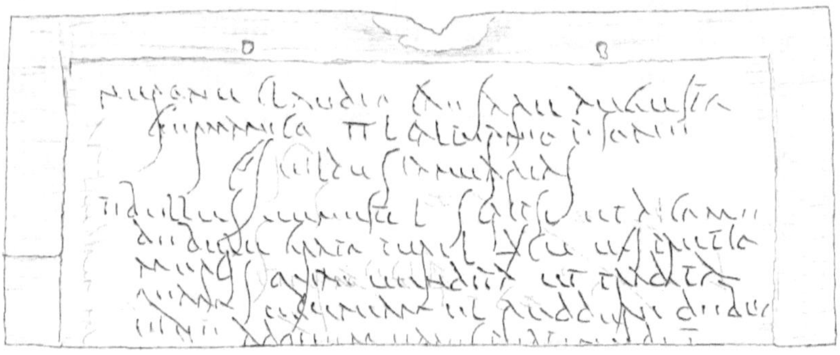

Figure 6. *Tab. Lond. Bloomberg* 44. A loan note of Tibullus the freedman of Venustus, 8 January, 57 CE. W 137.3 × H (56.2) × Th R: 7.6 × Th F: 4.6 mm. Appendix Chapter 2. © MOLA (phograph Andy Chopping/drawing Roger S. O. Tomlin.)[51]

The remaining five letters have to do with honor and shame in the world of trade and finance: we meet Vialicus, the freedman of Secundio, and hear of the slave of ?Marcus Salvius M[. . .] . . . as they negotiate a loan;[52] Taurus who complains to Macrinus that Catarrius "had taken the beasts of burden away";[53] Titus who is in danger of appearing shameful (*turpis*) to his peers;[54] Atticus who is concerned that someone is slow in

51. Tab. Lond. Bloomberg 44; Tomlin, *Roman London's First Voices*, 152–55. Appendix Chapter 2.

52. *Tab. Lond. Bloomberg* 27; Tomlin, *Roman London's First Voices*, 112–13. Appendix Chapter 2.

53. *Tab. Lond. Bloomberg* 29; Tomlin, *Roman London's First Voices*, 116–19. Appendix Chapter 2. Cf. 32 (128–29) for another transaction involving a beast of burden.

54. *Tab. Lond. Bloomberg* 30; Tomlin, *Roman London's First Voices*, 120–23. Appendix Chapter 2.

paying his debt;[55] and an unknown person who has concerns about the repayment of a loan.[56]

Of the fourteen financial and legal documents, five are loan notes or notes of hand like the *chirographum* of the slave of ?Marcus Salvius:[57] one drawn up by Tibullus, the freedman of Venustus, with Gratus the freedman of Spurius, on 8 January 57 CE;[58] another by Atticus addressed to Narcissus (the slave) of Rogatus the Lingonian;[59] a third promises, in the presence of the bodyguard Rusticus, to act "in good faith" (*fide*)[60] and refers to "the principal" and "the interest" (*sortis siue us{s}urae*);[61] and a fourth by Communis on 15 March 82 CE;[62] a fifth retains only the words that indicate the loan note can be sold on to a third party, (*a[d] quem ea res | [pertinebit]*).[63] A contract is drawn up between citizens Marcus Rennius Venustus and Gaius Valerius Proculus on 21 October 62 CE for the delivery of twenty loads of provisions by 13 November from Londinium to Verulamium.[64] A receipt to do with a farm was drawn up by Florentinus, a slave,

55. *Tab. Lond. Bloomberg* 31; Tomlin, *Roman London's First Voices*, 124–27. Appendix Chapter 2.

56. *Tab. Lond. Bloomberg* 35; Tomlin, *Roman London's First Voices*, 134–35. Appendix Chapter 2.

57. *Tab. Lond. Bloomberg* 27, where the note of hand is implied in a letter; Tomlin, *Roman London's First Voices*, 112–13. Cf. 57. In all it seems that 25 tablets have to do with loans.

58. *Tab. Lond. Bloomberg* 44; Tomlin, *Roman London's First Voices*, 152–55. Appendix Chapter 2.

59. *Tab. Lond. Bloomberg* 55; Tomlin, *Roman London's First Voices*, 178–81. Appendix Chapter 2.

60. Meyer describes the way "good-faith contracts . . . could be undertaken by men who were not Roman citizens, or by mixed citizen/non-citizen groups . . . – purchase/sale (*emptio-venditio*), leasing/hiring (*locatio-conductio*), agency (*mandatum*), and partnership (*societas*)" ("Law and Latinization," 192, 194); Johnston argues "it was open to a judge to find that the failure of a party to act in accordance with ordinary commercial standards was not consonant with good faith. The standard of good faith therefore gave the contract extraordinary vitality and flexibility" (*Roman Law*, 96). Cf. the appeal of the innocent man from overseas, *Tab. Vindol. II* 344. Appendix Chapter 3.

61. *Tab. Lond. Bloomberg* 56; Tomlin, *Roman London's First Voices*, 182–83. On the reverse of this type 2 document is the name of a witness, Rusticus, the bodyguard.

62. *Tab. Lond. Bloomberg* 53; Tomlin, *Roman London's First Voices*, 174–75.

63. *Tab. Lond. Bloomberg* 54; Tomlin, *Roman London's First Voices*, 176–77. Cf. 44 (152–55) and 55 (178–81).

64. *Tab. Lond. Bloomberg* 45; Tomlin, *Roman London's First Voices*, 156–59. Appendix Chapter 2.

on the orders of his master, Sextus Cassius.[65] Four are fragments with only the date remaining.[66]

Unlike the correspondence, the financial and legal documents would have been triptychs but only one of the above documents is a type 2 document, naming Rusticus as a witness on the reverse.[67] There are eleven more type 2 tablets which include on the one side lists of witnesses and on the other fragments of the inner text of a legal or financial document. Three appear to have been loan notes,[68] five have been cancelled, one with a line drawn through the lists of witnesses[69] and four with lines drawn through the inner text.[70] One identifies Attius the son of Optatus at Durobrivae (Rochester, Kent) as a thief and might have been a joke, a parody or "even a wooden curse tablet" against Attius.[71] Two of the eleven identify witnesses by military rank as cavalrymen: *decuriones* Primus, Billiccus (son) of Vannius,[72] Longinus, troop of the decurion Mar[. . .], Agrippa, troop of the decurion Silvanus, Verecundus, troop of the decurion Silvanus.[73] On the grooved side of one tablet it appears as if an unnamed slave of a named

65. *Tab. Lond. Bloomberg* 50; Tomlin, *Roman London's First Voices*, 168–69. Appendix Chapter 2. Cf. Johnston, *Roman Law*, 78–80.

66. *Tab. Lond. Bloomberg* 46; Tomlin, *Roman London's First Voices*, 160–61; 47 (162–63), 48 (164–65) by someone of the first cohort of Vangiones, 49 (166–67), 52 (172–73).

67. *Tab. Lond. Bloomberg* 56; Tomlin, *Roman London's First Voices*, 182–83.

68. *Tab. Lond. Bloomberg* 61; Tomlin, *Roman London's First Voices*, 194–97; 62 (198–201), use of the word *accepit* ("he has received") suggests a loan note; 64 (204–5); 68 (214–15).

69. *Tab. Lond. Bloomberg* 58; Tomlin, *Roman London's First Voices*, 186–89: Vegetus, (son) of Tutor is named on the ungrooved face; Mercator and Reductus are the only names recognized as witnesses.

70. Figure 7, *Tab. Lond. Bloomberg* 55; Tomlin, *Roman London's First Voices*, 178–81. Appendix Chapter 2. Cf. *Tab. Lond. Bloomberg* 61; Tomlin, *Roman London's First Voices*, 194–97 "money on loan" is mentioned on the grooved side followed by reference to Primus and Billiccus (son) of Vannius, and to decuriones; 64 (204–5) including (seal) of Audax or Audacius; 65 (206–7), (seal) of Marius, (seal) of Paullus, (seal) of Saccus, (seal) of Verecundus; 68 (214–15), two witnesses are named, Tiberius and ?(son) of Aprilius. Figure 7, *Tab. Lond. Bloomberg* 55. Appendix Chapter 2.

71. *Tab. Lond. Bloomberg* 59; Tomlin, *Roman London's First Voices*, 190–91.

72. *Tab. Lond. Bloomberg* 61; Tomlin, *Roman London's First Voices*, 194–97.

73. *Tab. Lond. Bloomberg* 62; Tomlin, *Roman London's First Voices*, 198–201: the only tablet to follow the usual layout, name to the left of the seal and identification to the right. The word *tur(ma)* is written differently each time suggesting each witness who was literate wrote their name and identification themselves.

master has been deliberately erased.[74] Extensive re-use makes it impossible to say what some tablets were for.[75]

Eight tablets are accounts: on one occasion we see slaves acting as their masters' agents, checking off items as they were paid for, one costing 65 denarii, another 6 denarii;[76] one is described as "the account of Crispus" (*ra[t]io Crispi*) and has to do with various items of beer (*cerues[a]*), one of which amounts to 7 denarii for 105 units;[77] one speaks either "of the Romans" or "of Roman *somethings*";[78] one notes that Ammonicus owed 30 denarii (*(denarios) XXX debet Ammonicus*), mentions "Pactumeius the son of ?Adenhus," and identifies 106 denarii as the "?total";[79] on one tablet all that is left is the numeral 40, *XXXX*;[80] on another, the barred[81] numeral 200 (CC);[82] on another unidentifiable barred numbers;[83] on another it is simply the "total: 20 denarii" *(acced(unt) (denarii) XX)* that remains.[84] Such accounts involved correlating the painted labels *(tituli picti)* on containers such as amphorae and barrels used extensively in trade with a written record;[85] the ubiquity of such trade at this time is indicative of a widespread competence in what might be described as commercial literacy.[86] The Bloomberg tablets enable Alison Cooley to hypothesize "that

74. *Tab. Lond. Bloomberg* 60; Tomlin, *Roman London's First Voices*, 192–93: *ser(u)us*; alternatively Serus might be a rarely found name.

75. *Tab. Lond. Bloomberg* 63; Tomlin, *Roman London's First Voices*, 202–3: Abot[...], Iuni[us], Nama[tobogius], Num[...], Surunus are witnesses while the ungrooved face has been extensively re-used; 66 (208–9), Macrinus, Deuillus.

76. *Tab. Lond. Bloomberg* 70; Tomlin, *Roman London's First Voices*, 218–19; other items are unchecked; entries follow a standard format: slave's name, master's name, numeral, costing in denarii: ?Catullus the slave of Romanius Faustinus, [name] the slave of Senecio.

77. *Tab. Lond. Bloomberg* 72; Tomlin, *Roman London's First Voices*, 222–25.

78. *Tab. Lond. Bloomberg* 75; Tomlin, *Roman London's First Voices*, 230–31.

79. *Tab. Lond. Bloomberg* 76; Tomlin, *Roman London's First Voices*, 232–33.

80. *Tab. Lond. Bloomberg* 69; Tomlin, *Roman London's First Voices*, 216–17.

81. CC with a line above each C. Cf. Cooley, *Manual of Latin Epigraphy*, 358.

82. *Tab. Lond. Bloomberg* 73; Tomlin, *Roman London's First Voices*, 226–27.

83. *Tab. Lond. Bloomberg* 74; Tomlin, *Roman London's First Voices*, 228–29.

84. *Tab. Lond. Bloomberg* 71; Tomlin, *Roman London's First Voices*, 220–21.

85. Cf. barrel head of wine barrel with markings indicating producer, trader, quantity, and value, Bloomberg, London: with markings: Tomlin, "Roman Britain in 2018," 505–6.

86. Woolf, "Ancient Illiteracy?," 38–41. Cf. Ferrándiz, "What Is Law?"; Blair et al., suggests that the barrel marked Tiirtiius is a possible example ("Wells and Bucket-Chains," 13).

incoming traders initially introduced sophisticated Latin literate practices" to Londinium during the fifties CE.[87] Elizabeth Meyer argues that the legal framework around trade and commerce "did not drive people to learn Latin, but Latin helped provincials to use the law and to get ahead."[88]

Three tablets appear to be writing exercises in literacy and numeracy suggesting the importance of schooling, as they perhaps represent "the exercises of an apprentice or pupil."[89] A type 1 tablet clearly has the letters of the alphabet pricked into the plain side and scratched into the wax surface.[90] Two type 1 tablets were found together, each containing grids and numerals on both the plain recessed sides: it appears they were the two leaves of a diptych.[91]

Among these tablets are the first writings discovered in Britain that are contemporary with the events narrated in Acts. The following table categorizes the tablets in date order and correlates them with passages in Acts.[92]

1 Poultry/ Bloomberg Period/Date	Type	Tab. Lond. Bloomberg Number	Luke-Acts
2 phase 1 43–53 CE	Letters	30.	44 CE, Herod Agrippa I dies (Acts 12:23). Paul's travels begin (Acts 13:1—18:28). 51–52 CE, Gallio proconsul of Achaia (Acts 18:12).
2 phase 2 53–60/61 CE	Letters	44 (57 CE).	Paul's travels continue

87. Cooley, "Role of the Non-Elite," 109; cf. Wilson, "Latin, Literacy and Roman Economy," 81–87.

88. Meyer, "Law and Latinization," 195.

89. Wolff, "Education in Latinization," 174; cf. Meyer, "Law and Latinization," 195; Wilson, "Latin, Literacy and Roman Economy," 95–96.

90. *Tab. Lond. Bloomberg* 79; Tomlin, *Roman London's First Voices*, 240–43.

91. *Tab. Lond. Bloomberg* 77, 78; Tomlin, *Roman London's First Voices*, 234–35, 236–39.

92. Tomlin, *Roman London's First Voices*, 5, 288–93; Bryan et al, "The Archaeological Context"; Bruce, *Acts*, 92–95.

1 Poultry/ Bloomberg Period/Date	Type	Tab. Lond. Bloomberg Number	Luke-Acts
	Financial/ Legal	1, 2, 17.	(Acts 19:1—21:26); Paul taken in Jerusalem (21:27—23:22) and held in Caesarea (Acts 23:23—26:32); 52–59 CE, Felix governor of *Iudaea* 59–61 CE, Festus governor of *Iudaea*. Paul taken to Rome (Acts 27:1—28:15).
2 phase 3 (early) 60/61–62 CE	Financial/ Legal	45 (62 CE).	Paul in Rome
	Alphabet	79.	(Acts 28:16–31).
2 phase 3 (late) 62–65/70 CE	Letters	3, 4, 18, 31.	Sixties CE, earliest suggested date for Luke-Acts.
	Witnesses list	58, 59.	
	Accounts	69.	
	Numerals	77, 78.	
3 phase 1 (early) 65/70–80 CE	Letters	5, 6, 7, 8, 9, 10, 11, 19, 20, 21, 22, 26, 32, 33, 34, 35, 36, 37.	
	Financial/ Legal	46, 47, 54, 55, 56.	Seventies to eighties CE, middle date suggested for Luke-Acts.
	Witnesses list	60, 61.	
	Accounts	70, 71, 72.	
3 phase 1 (late) 80–90/95 CE	Letters	12, 13, 14, 15, 16, 23, 27, 28, 29, 38, 39, 40, 41, 42, 43.	

1 Poultry/ Bloomberg Period/Date	Type	Tab. Lond. Bloomberg Number	Luke-Acts
	Financial/ Legal	48 (67 CE), 49 (85 CE), 50 (64 CE), 51 (76 CE), 52 (85–95 CE).	Seventies to eighties CE, middle date suggested for Luke-Acts.
	Witnesses list	62, 63, 64, 65, 66.	
3 phase 1 (undifferentiated) 65/70 -90/95 CE	Letters	24	
4 phase 1 90/95–125 CE	Financial/ Legal	53 (82 CE)	Early 2nd century CE, late date suggested for Luke-Acts.
	Witnesses list	67	
Unstratified	Letters	25	
	Witnesses list	68	

Table 4. The Bloomberg tablets compared with Luke-Acts. Note the periods and dates in the first column refer to the archaeological context in which the tablets were discovered, offering an approximation of the latest probable date of the tablets themselves.[93]

The Bloomberg tablets are in a similar format to the financial documents of Lucius Caecilius Iucundus in Pompeii, of which 153 are legible;[94] and of the Sulpicii, the Murecine archive, found outside Pompeii and recording activities in the port of Puteoli.[95] The financial system we encounter in the Londinium of the Bloomberg tablets would have been familiar to travelers across the empire.[96]

93. Tomlin, *Roman London's First Voices*, 5.

94. Cooley and Cooley, *Pompeii and Herculaneum*, 277–86.

95. Andreau, *Banking and Business*, 71–77.

96. Andreau, *Banking and Business*, 50–63.

It is impossible to draw a clear distinction between financial and legal documents as many of the former make use of legal terminology. The establishment of Britannia as a province under a consular governor shortly after Claudius's invasion[97] saw, in some measure, "the arrival of the codified legal system of Roman law,"[98] albeit with local variations.[99] As Alison Cooley argues, "the Bloomberg tablets demonstrate . . . the complex implementation of the Roman legal system that allowed financial agreements to be strengthened via a written document, and the immediate adoption of sophisticated forms of writing."[100] Jurisdiction was the responsibility of the emperor and exercised through the governor who from Vespasian's time acted through a *legatus iuridicus*, of whom five are known and two were legal experts.[101] While there is no evidence of any code specific to Britannia, the Bloomberg tablets and other stylus tablets from Londinium enable us to glimpse the way Roman provincial law was lived and worked out in practice.[102] David Johnston is clear that they "are significant in showing the diffusion of Roman legal institutions in Britain as early as the fifties CE."[103]

According to Paul du Plessis twelve "have implications for our understanding of the provincial application of Roman law."[104] The contract between Venustus and Proculus[105] is an instance of *lex locationis*, whereby Venustus "places" a job that Proculus undertakes to perform.[106] The pre-

97. Salway, *Roman Britain*, 87–89.

98. de la Bédoyère, *Real Lives of Roman Britain*, 66–67.

99. Johnston is clear, "The evidence therefore supports a remarkable penetration of Roman legal culture wide throughout the empire" but "within the empire there were local variations" (*Roman Law*, 10–14).

100. Cooley, *Role of the Non-Elite*, 106.

101. C. Salvius Liberalis Nonius Bassus, part of the circle of the younger Pliny, was appointed c. 79 CE; his successor was L. Iavolenus Priscus: Frere, *Britannia*, 183; for an account of Roman law in Britannia see du Plessis, "Provincial Law in Britannia."

102. Du Plessis, "Provincial Law in Britannia," 459: there is more evidence in the Vindolanda Tablets and indirectly in the Curse Tablets. Cf. Johnston, *Roman Law*, 17–18.

103. Johnston describes the tablets including "acknowledgements of debt and payment, a contract for delivery, and references to interest on debt and to guaranteeing debt, as well as to some features of Roman civil procedure" (*Roman Law*, 18).

104. *Tab. Lond. Bloomberg* 27, 29, 30, 35, 44, 45, 50, 51, 55, 57, 62, 70: du Plessis, "Bloomberg Tablets and Roman Law."

105. *Tab. Lond. Bloomberg* 45; Tomlin, *Roman London's First Voices*, 156–59. Appendix Chapter 2.

106. Frier, *Roman Law of Contracts*, ch. V, part A; du Plessis notes that "the consensus underlying the contract of letting and hiring seemingly only admitted the existence of

liminary judgement dated 22 October 76 CE (*praeiudico*) anticipates a full hearing on 9 November to settle a case between Litugenus and Magunus.[107] One document involves entering into a legal "undertaking" (*sponsion|em facere*) and contending in "judgment" (*iudicio certare*),[108] while another includes part of a legal formula, *actum* (executed) but nothing more.[109]

Stylus writing tablets were important in the execution of Roman law from the period of the republic through to the empire.[110] Whereas the Greeks had used papyrus, Rome, Italy and then the provinces used stylus writing tablets in the conduct of legal affairs. The triptych, with its inner and outer texts and formulaic language, signed and sealed by around seven witnesses, was characteristic of financial and legal transactions throughout the empire.[111] "The charge," for example, "was generally written down on tablets or mini-tablets (*libelli*); when a case was dismissed, one phrase used was "tablets shall be destroyed" (*solventur . . . tabulae*)."[112] Whether in legal or financial documents the written word not only recorded but also effected something real: the loan note, *chirographum*, with its formulaic, *scripsi* (I have written) had actual value and sufficed for payment.

Whether, as Meyer suggests, the use of a similar style of "inner" and "outer text" signed by witnesses in so many of the papyri of the Babatha documents from the Cave of Letters by the Dead Sea was a deliberate statement by Babatha and her family, "adopting the forms she thinks most likely to win Roman approval,"[113] or as Hannah Cotton argues her practice in a

---

a single (sometimes written) record of the agreement, but the jurists felt it necessary to emphasize the bilateral nature of letting and hiring by using two distinct terms," that is to say, *lex locationis*, from the perspective of the one placing the job, and *lex conductionis*, from the perspective of the one carrying out the job ("Roman Concept of Lex Contractus," 80–81). Cf. Johnston, *Roman Law*, 115–17; Johnson defines *locatio conductio* as "the contract of hire or letting, whether of a thing, of services, or of a task to be done" (*Roman Law*, 194).

107. *Tab. Lond. Bloomberg* 51; Tomlin, *Roman London's First Voices*, 170–71. Appendix Chapter 2.

108. *Tab. Lond. Bloomberg* 57; Tomlin, *Roman London's First Voices*, 184–85. Appendix Chapter 2.

109. *Tab. Lond. Bloomberg* 67; Tomlin, *Roman London's First Voices*, 210–11: a type 2 tablet with identifiers in the second column that could indicate citizenship, or possibly be the patronymics of non-Romans, . . . of Mansuetus, . . . of Sextus, . . . of Neo, . . . of Aristus.

110. Meyer, *Legitimacy and Law*.

111. Meyer, *Legitimacy and Law*, 9.

112. *Justinian Digest* II.13.1.1, "Justinian Digest" 2023.

113. Meyer, *Legitimacy and Law*, 192–93.

document from 94–99 CE, pre-dating Roman jurisdiction in 106 CE, was simply Nabataean,[114] the documents have a similar format.[115]

In the Bloomberg tablets of first century Londinium we meet ninety-two persons by name[116] and encounter the legal and financial world that spans the Roman Empire. There are Roman and Celtic names, though probably from Gaul rather than Britain; citizens and non-citizens; masters, freedmen, slaves, and slaves of slaves. There are householders, craftworkers, merchants and traders involved in a financial and banking system built on the use of loan notes and dependent on cultural values shared across the empire. There are people involved in transporting goods and at least one person involved in farming; there are officers and troopers from the Roman army and administrators too. All are men. While not an "archive" in the strictest sense, these letters, financial and legal documents, accounts and writing exercises give a voice to those who lived and did business in Londinium in the second half of the first century CE. They enable us to glimpse their individual lives and the way in which they interacted with each other. People such as these were among the first readers of Luke–Acts.

Imagining Merchants, Traders, and Financiers from First-Century Londinium

The part slaves and freedmen play in the financial dealings of first century Londinium is glimpsed in what remains of Secundio's letter to his freedman, Vialicus.[117] Secundio asks Vialicus to receive a note of hand,

114. Cotton, "Guardianship of Jesus Son of Babatha"; Yadin, *Documents from the Bar Kokhba Period*, pts. 1–4; Esler, *Babatha's Orchard*, 94–220. Compare inner and outer texts in Figure 5 and Yadin, *Bar-Kokhba*, 229–31.

115. Esler, *Babatha's Orchard*, 234–53. Reimer describes the use among Jewish people in Palestine and the Diaspora of such "duplicate documents" in a wide range of business and legal contexts in the first two centuries CE. However, her conclusion that "the duplicate documents constitute a central sign of Jewish resistance to Roman rule" is called in question by the evidence from Londinium, Pompeii and elsewhere (*Women in Acts*, 2–6).

116. Tomlin, *Roman London's First Voices*, 51–57. Another 14 names cannot be recognized, the names of 4 emperors and 8 consuls appear in the dates, and 11 names appear as patronymics.

117. *Tab. Lond. Bloomberg* 27; Tomlin, *Roman London's First Voices*, 112–13. Appendix Chapter 2. Cf. on slavery and the Roman economy: Woolf, *Rome*, 97–101; Andreau, *Banking and Business*, 64–70; on slavery and Roman society: Bradley, *Slavery and Society*; on slavery and Roman law: Johnston, *Roman Law*, 51–54; on Roman slavery and the

(c<h>irographum) of an unnamed slave of a Roman citizen, *M(arci?) S[a] luii M[... ...]tandi*. A *chirographum* is, according to the second century Gaius, the hand-written note that serves as a written contract (*litterarum obligatio*) when there is no verbal contract (*stipulatio*) in that person's name.[118] A form of contract appropriate for non-citizens or foreigners (*peregrini*), it serves as a loan or payment for goods or services. In the world of manufacturing, commerce and business slaves could work directly for their master, as their master's agent in a shop or workshop, or for themselves managing a *peculium*, an amount of money or property for which they were responsible.[119] David Johnston notes that the *peculium* ("a fund of property entrusted to a slave or to a child in the power of a paterfamilias, but which nonetheless remained the property of the paterfamilias") "was designed as a means of balancing the interests of those involved in trade by imposing on a paterfamilias some liability for his dependants, but not too much."[120] Working directly for his master, a slave might have administered the household and

New Testament: Harrill, *Slaves in the New Testament;* and Powery, "Roman Slavery and the New Testament"; on slavery in Luke: Matthews and Reid, *Luke 10–24*, 478–81. Woolf suggests Cato the elder, in his treatise *On Farming* (c. 160 BCE), "offers a thoroughly Roman model of slavery" in which "slaves offered a core workforce that could be worked exceptionally hard, the sick and old could be easily disposed of, no idle mouths need be tolerated, and the workforce could be increased or decreased in size easily enough" (*Rome*, 98–99). Bradley surveys the range of occupations undertaken by slaves, and concludes that, apart from military service, it was "virtually limitless" (*Slavery and Society*, 57–80). He is critical "of those that take a largely economic approach to Roman slavery" as that approach "diverts attention from the broad cultural significance slavery held in Roman society at large" (*Slavery and Society*, 15–16); in that context, "Roman slaves . . . were bought and sold like animals, were punished indiscriminately, and violated sexually; they were compelled to labor as their masters dictated, they were allowed no legal existence, and they were goaded into compliance through cajolery and intimidation. They were the ultimate victims of exploitation" (*Slavery and Society*, 178–79).

118. Gaius, *Institutiones* 3.134: "Institutiones": *Praeterea litterarum obligatio fieri uidetur chirografis et syngrafis, id est, si quis debere se aut daturum se scribat, ita scilicet, si eo nomine stipulatio non fiat. quod genus obligationis proprium peregrinorum est* (Furthermore, a liability arisen from a written document is seen to take effect with a document in a person's own handwriting and signed by both parties; that is, if anyone writes that he owes a debt it is thus obvious, even if no verbal contract in his name has taken effect; this type of liability is particularly for foreigners). On the oral contract of *stipulatio* see Johnston, *Roman Law*, 92–94. He defines stipulation as "a contract entered into orally by formal exchange of corresponding question and answer" (*Roman Law* 194).

119. Andreau, *Banking and Business*, chap. 5; Woolf, *Rome*, 97; Johnston, *Roman Law*, 119–25.

120. Johnston, *Roman Law*, 122, 194.

its expenses as a steward (*dispensator*), or served as agent, (*servus actor*), perhaps in moneylending.[121]

In this instance the unnamed slave is responsible for drawing up the *chirographum* and is acting for Marcus Salvius. The payment of the loan is to be made "to the freedman Vialicus" (*liberto Vialico*). As a freedman he could act as an agent (*institor*) in his own right. People could lend him money and use him as an intermediary to lend money. The form of address suggests a close relationship with Secundio as former master and now patron.[122] Either Vialicus is in partnership with his patron Secundio who asks him to accept the *chirographum* as a loan, perhaps as payment for goods or services; or Vialicus acts as an intermediary for the Roman citizen, Marcus Salvius, who may have been a financier. Andreau suggests that between the aristocracy and those professional men who are "town dwellers with a specialized trade, such as artisans, traders and bankers," characteristic of pre-industrial societies, there is a third group of entrepreneurs or merchant-financiers involved in money-lending and maritime loans, possibly at high interest. Noting the complexities of Roman financial life and the way money so often passed "from the wealthy to the slightly less so," Andreau suggests there were deals between professional bankers and between bankers and other kinds of financiers: there were "various ways lenders and borrowers were brought together sometimes involving professional bankers."[123] Amidst all the complexities of this hierarchical world of finance and banking "usurers and moneylenders must have existed throughout the Empire."[124]

We can imagine Vialicus needing a loan for goods or services he is providing. He turns to Secundio, formerly his master, now his patron, to act as an intermediary with those to whom Vialicus is supplying goods or from whom he is seeking a loan. Secundio has secured a loan from Marcus Salvius who has arranged for his slave to write a *chirographum*, a loan note. Secundio now writes to Vialicus to ascertain whether he is prepared to receive the *chirographum*.

121. Andreau, *Banking and Business*, 64–67.

122. Andreau, *Banking and Business*, 64. On patronage see Woolf, *Rome*, 95–97. Johnston defines an *institor* as "a person appointed by the owner of a business as its manager" (*Roman Law*, 194).

123. Andreau, *Banking and Business*, 50–60. Cf. Johnston, *Roman Law*, 102–5.

124. Andreau, *Banking and Business*, 62–63.

Two other freedmen, Tibullus and Gratus, maintained social and financial links with their former masters now patrons, Venustus and Spurius, perhaps as agents in the world of commerce.[125] Tibullus had purchased merchandise from Gratus which had now been delivered (*mercis quae uendita et tradita*).[126] Having already made a partial payment he completed the transaction and paid the outstanding sum on 8 January 57 CE not in coin but in a note of hand, *chirographum*. In the presence of witnesses he made the legally binding statement, "I have written and say that I owe" (*scripsi et dico me debere*) the sum of 105 denarii (*(denarios) CV*)," a sizeable amount.[127] The signed, witnessed, and sealed document was handed to Gratus in payment. Tibullus was now in debt to Gratus but he allowed for the possibility that the *chirographum* might be sold on or sub-contracted to a third party, using the legal formula, "this money I am due to repay him or the person to whom the matter will concern" (*quam pecuniam ei reddere debeo |eiue*[128] *ad quem ea res pertinebit*). Either Gratus or that third party, perhaps one of the ubiquitous moneylenders, would be able to call in the debt at some time in the future.[129] It is to be hoped for Tibullus's sake that they would act fairly and not seek an excessive profit![130]

125. Andreau, *Banking and Business*, 64. Cf. Johnston, *Roman Law*, 52–54.

126. *Tab. Lond. Bloomberg* 44; Tomlin, *Roman London's First Voices*, 152–55. Appendix Chapter 2.

127. Approximately £10,676 based on an eight-hour day at a rate of £12.71 per hour, the full UK living wage, April 2026. Reece refers to Matt 20:1–16 where a laborer is paid one denarius for a day's wage, on this basis £101.68 (*Coinage of Roman Britain*, 110). Cf. Abdy, *Legion*, 67. Abdy suggests this is a little less than half a year's pay for a legionary soldier (225 denarii) and a little more than half a year's pay of an auxiliary soldier (187½ denarii) (*Legion*, 63); cf. Perring, *London in Roman World*, 74.

128. Tomlin's translation identifies this word as *siue*, "or."

129. The same formula appears in *Tab. Lond. Bloomberg* 54 and 55: Tomlin, *Roman London's First Voices*, 176–77 and 178–81. It also appears in two other tablets from the Walbrook: *RIB 2(4)* no. 2443.15, *RIB II Fasc. 4*; and Tomlin, "Girl in Question."

130. *Tab. Lond. Bloomberg* 44; Tomlin, *Roman London's First Voices*, 152–55. Appendix Chapter 2.

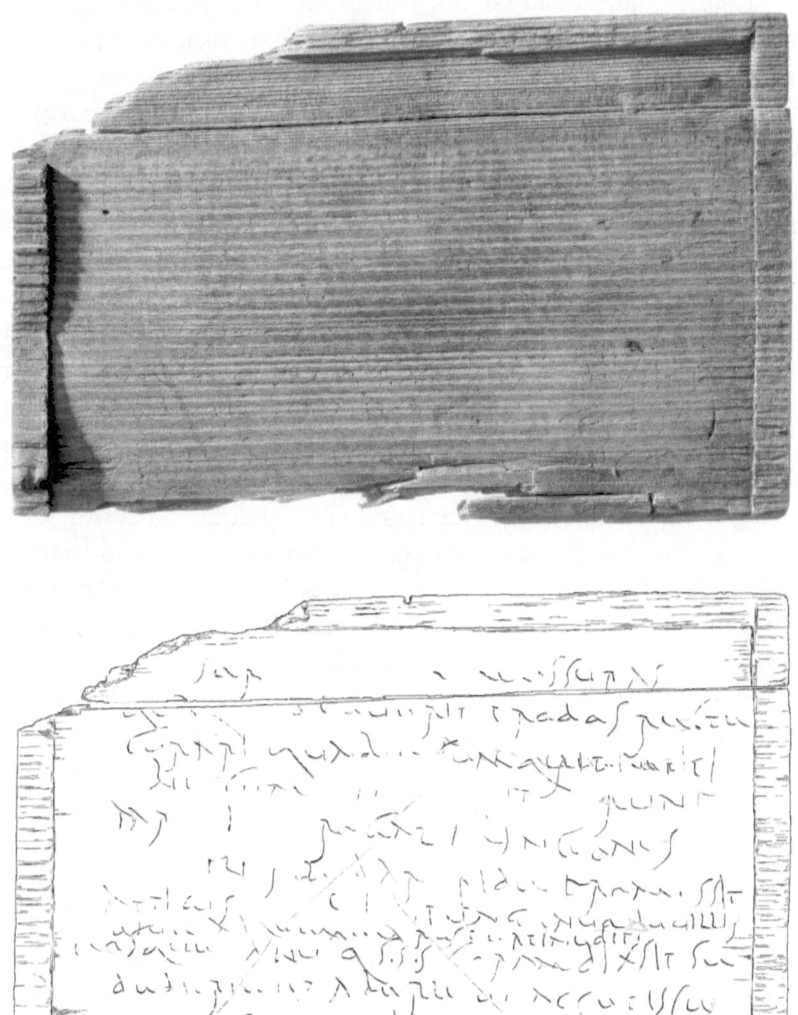

Figure 7. *Tab. Lond. Bloomberg* 55. A loan note of Atticus that has been cancelled with two diagonal lines. W 146.0 × H (77.8) × Th R: 8.2 × Th F: 5.8 mm. Appendix Chapter 2. © MOLA (phograph Andy Chopping/drawing Roger S. O. Tomlin.)[131]

131. *Tab. Lond. Bloomberg* 55; Tomlin, *Roman London's First Voices*, 178–81. Appendix Chapter 2.

Unlike Tibullus and Gratus, Atticus and Narcissus are both slaves, working directly in the service of their masters or as their master's agents in a shop or workshop. We can imagine the moment Atticus, unable to write himself, has a scribe write out a *chirographum* assuring Narcissus (in his own right or acting for Rogatus), that he will pay the principal of the loan plus any interest (*[et] sor[tem et eorum u]s{s}uras*) "properly managed" in "good (coin)" (*probos recte |curari*).[132] He further emphasizes his reliability by stating that he has made this promise "properly, truly and faithfully" (*[rec]te [p]robe dari fide promis{s}it*). The wording implies that the loan may be passed on to someone else (*eiue ad quem ea res pertinebit*). As many as seven witnesses scrutinize the document, check that the inner text corresponds to the outer text and add their names and seals. The loan note is now ready to be taken to Narcissus as he acts for Rogatus, a Lingonian, perhaps a cavalryman in a recently formed auxiliary cohort of Lingonians, serving alongside cohorts of Nervii and of Vangiones.[133] That Atticus is a man of honor is emphasized throughout: explicit reference to good coin and to proper, true, and faithful dealing not only sets the financial arrangement firmly within the context of the Roman legal practice of "good-faith contracts," but serves also as a reminder that shameful conduct is always a possibility.[134] Subsequently, the loan was settled and the *chirographum* cancelled as two lines were scored along the diagonals of the tablet. It is not clear whether such lines effected the cancellation of the loan or were "merely a visual representation of the fact that it is no longer in force" ensuring it will no longer be used.[135]

Witnesses of a legal or financial transaction, such as the cavalrymen, Longinus, Agrippa and Verecundus,[136] Rusticus, the bodyguard (*singu[?laris]*),[137] Verecundus, Marus, Paullus, and Saccus, had clearly written in their own hand suggesting that each was expected to write their own name and add their own seal.

132. *Tab. Lond. Bloomberg* 55; Tomlin, *Roman London's First Voices*, 178–81. Cf. *Tab. Lond. Bloomberg* 56; Tomlin, *Roman London's First Voices*, 182–83.

133. *Tab. Lond. Bloomberg* 55; Tomlin, *Roman London's First Voices*, 178–81. Cf. Tab Lond. Bloomberg 33 (Nervii) and 48 (Vangiones).

134. Meyer, "Law and Latinization," 192, 194; Johnston, *Roman Law*, 96. See above, Chapter 2, n. 60.

135. Cotton, "Cancelled Marriage Contract," 66. On coin production in Claudian Britain, see Box, *Plated Roman Denarii*.

136. *Tab. Lond. Bloomberg* 62; Tomlin, *Roman London's First Voices*, 198–201.

137. *Tab. Lond. Bloomberg* 56; Tomlin, *Roman London's First Voices*, 182–83.

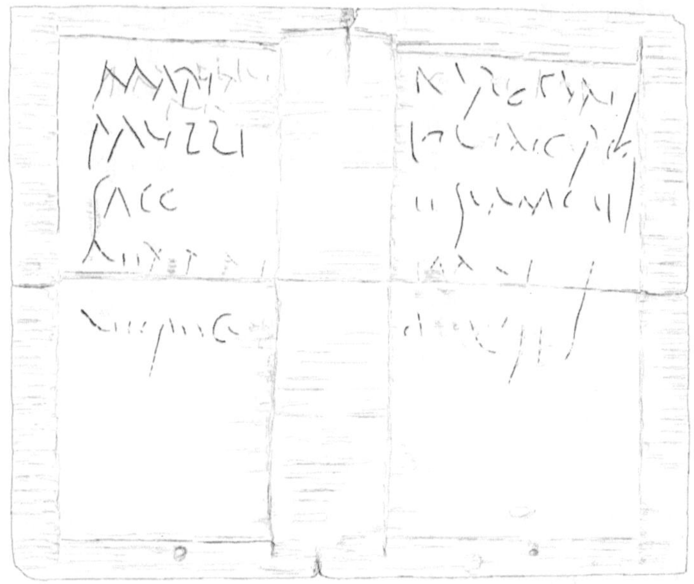

Figure 8. *Tab. Lond. Bloomberg* 65. A grooved face for signatures and seals of witnesses: Marius, Paullus, Saccus, Verecundus. W 137.5 × H 114.6 × Th R: 9.0 × Th F: 5.7 × W seal-groove: 22.2 mm. Appendix Chapter 2. © MOLA (phograph Andy Chopping/drawing Roger S. O. Tomlin).[138]

138. *Tab. Lond. Bloomberg* 65; Tomlin, *Roman London's First Voices*, 206–7. Keener

In financial documents such as these we can see that the empire-wide system of finance, commerce, and banking, with its comparatively high level of literacy, had arrived as Londinium was being established.[139] Yet within a couple of years of Tibullus handing his *chirographum* to Gratus it seemed in danger. What had become the capital of Claudius and Nero's Britannia, Camulodunum, together with Verulamium and Londinium, had fallen to Boudica.[140] The revolt, however, was short lived: the Bloomberg evidence suggests the reconstruction of Londinium began, and commerce and trade resumed, immediately.[141]

In Marcus Rennius Venustus and Gaius Valerius Proculus we meet two Roman citizens who follow the law of letting and hiring (*lex locationis*)[142] and enter into a contract for the delivery of goods following an earlier part payment.[143] On 12 October 62 CE Venustus contracts with Proculus that "he bring from Verulamium by the ides of November (13 November) twenty loads of provisions at a transport-charge of one quarter denarius for each" (*ut intra |Idus Nouembres perferret a* ⟦*Londi*⟧ | *5 Verulamio penoris onera uiginti |in singula (denarii) quadrans uecturae*). A condition is attached, though difficult to decipher: an initial part payment will be followed by the full payment once the final load is delivered. While another tablet refers to the use of beasts of burden, *iumenta*,[144] these loads were probably conveyed in a wagon. This is a vivid cameo of the way business was conducted and transport arrangements made, not least in the picture it gives of a traveler

speaks of "the Romanness of Paul's name" (*Acts*, 334); a traveler around the Mediterranean world, a visitor to "the Latin-speaking enclave" of Pisidian Antioch, to Corinth which "in the first century used Latin as its official language" (Tomlin, *Britannia Romana*, 11, 13), and a prisoner in Rome, Paul may well have had some command of Latin. Were he to have written his name in Latin, it would perhaps have looked something like this. Appendix Chapter 2.

139. Johnston, *Roman Law*, 18.

140. For Iceni, see Map (Figure 1); Camulodunum, Verulamium, Londinium, Map (Figure 1) 16, 17, 1.

141. Tomlin, *Roman London's First Voices*, 55–56.

142. Du Plessis, "Roman Concept of Lex Contractus," 80–81; Johnston, *Roman Law*, 115–17, 194. See above, Chapter 2 n. 106.

143. *Tab. Lond. Bloomberg* 45; Tomlin, *Roman London's First Voices*, 156–59. Appendix Chapter 2.

144. *Tab. Lond. Bloomberg* 29; Tomlin, *Roman London's First Voices*, 116–19. For reconstruction, Figure 4. Appendix Chapter 2.

regularly making the thirty-five-kilometer journey between Verulamium and Londinium.[145]

If Tertius the ?brewer (*bracearius*)[146] was the Domitius Tertius who is the addressee of a Carlisle stylus tablet we glimpse long-distance trade with the military on the northern frontier.[147] The appearance of the name Tertius on the base of a barrel dated c. 63 CE[148] suggests that he was in business with Iunius the cooper (*cupario*), who lived opposite (the house of) Catullus.[149] Keeping accounts was important in such a business. The account (*ratio*) of Crispus, perhaps a tavern owner, records dealings in beer (*ceruesa*) (*rat[i]o Crispi cerues[a]*[150] involving a named agent, Butus.[151] Exploring the Celtic roots of *bracearius* and *ceruesa*, Adams suggests this was "an activity drawn from the local population."[152] That Londinium's traders were involved with local people is evident from another tablet that relates to trade with a local farm: in September or November, 64 CE Florentinus, slave to the citizen, Sextus Cassius [. . .]tus, wrote as his agent, at the order of his master (*scrips[i] iussu domini*), acknowledging receipt of two payments of rent from a farm (*accepisse pension|es duas ex fundo*).[153] With Dominic Perring, it is reasonable to suppose, however, that the lifestyles

145. See Antonine Itinerary, Route II where the mileage is recorded as 21 Roman miles, and the real distance, 22 miles (35 kilometers): B. Jones and Mattingly, *Atlas of Roman Britain*, 25. Verulamium, Londinium, Map (Figure 1) 17, 1.

146. *Tab. Lond. Bloomberg* 12; Tomlin, *Roman London's First Voices*, 82–85; Adams suggests *bracearius* may derive from a Celtic word that has come down into modern Welsh, *bragdy*, (*New Vindolanda Tablets*, 562–63).

147. *RIB* 2443.4, found in a late Flavian context addressed to Domitius Tertius, brewer, at Carlisle: *RIB II Fasc. 4*, 14. Cf. Perring, *London in Roman World*, 215; Tomlin, *Britannia Romana*, 309–10. Map (Figure 1) 37.

148. The barrel was re-used at the base of Well 1 discovered at 30 Gresham Street: Blair et al., "Wells and Bucket-Chains," 13.

149. *Tab. Lond. Bloomberg* 14; Tomlin, *Roman London's First Voices*, 86–87. Cf. Perring, *London in Roman World*, 215.

150. Another Celtic word evident in modern Welsh as *cwrw*. Cf. J. N. Adams, "New Vindolanda Tablets," 563; J. N. Adams, "Language of Vindolanda Tablets."

151. *Tab. Lond. Bloomberg* 72; Tomlin, *Roman London's First Voices*, 222–25.

152. J. N. Adams, "New Vindolanda Tablets," 563.

153. *Tab. Lond. Bloomberg* 50; Tomlin, *Roman London's First Voices*, 168–69. Appendix Chapter 2. Cf. Woolf on slaves in the context of the agrarian economy (*Rome*, 98–100).

of these traders "were radically different to those of subject populations within the urban hinterland."[154]

The people of the Bloomberg tablets are all men. Enslaved women are mentioned in two other Walbrook tablets. A deed of sale on a stylus tablet discovered in nearby 1 Poultry records the purchase of an enslaved Gallic girl, Fortunata, for 600 denarii by Vegetus, assistant slave of Montanus, the slave of the August Emperor (Domitian or Trajan), and sometime assistant slave of Iucundus *(Vegetus Montani imperatoris Aug(usti) ser(vi) Iucundiani vic(arius))*.[155] This implies the presence in Londinium of slaves and freedmen involved in the administration of the province. He had bought and received Fortunata by means of mancipation (*emit mancipioque accepit*), "an archaic Roman survival older than coinage, in which the purchaser asserted his ownership in the presence of the vendor, five witnesses, and a man holding the scales which notionally weighed out the purchase price."[156] The "girl in question" was "transferred in good health" (*sanam traditam*) and was "warranted not to be liable to wander or run away" (*esse erronem fugitivam non esse praestari*).[157] In another Walbrook tablet discovered in 1927 "the writer gives instructions to "turn that girl into cash" (*diligenter cura(m) agas ut Mam puellam ad nummum redigas*).[158] This tablet confirms the impression of a stylus writing tablet discovered near the Walbrook at Lothbury in 1927 that there was a trade in slaves, including enslaved girls, in Britannia.[159]

Such a world functions best where honor is upheld, and shame is scorned. In the Bloomberg correspondence there is evidence of frustration and anger at the failings of others. Bell[. . .]us is provoked to respond "angrily . . ." (*rogo irate . . .*).[160] Taurus complains to Macrinus whom he greets as "his dearest lord" (*Taurus ⟦Taurinus⟧ Macrino domino* | vacat *[ca]riss[imo] salute<m>*) that Catarrius "had taken the beasts of burden away" (*iumenta a<b>duxerat*). That meant for Taurus the loss of investments that

154. Perring, *London in Roman World*, 30.

155. £50,016 in April 2023, see above, Chapter 2, n. 117. Tomlin, "Girl in Question"; Tomlin, *Britannia Romana*, 272–74.

156. Tomlin, "Girl in Question," 47; Cf. du Plessis, "Provincial Law in Britannia," 450; Johnston, *Roman Law*, 98, 194.

157. Tomlin, "Girl in Question." Cf. Perring, *London in Roman World*, 222–23; Johnston, *Roman Law*, 51.

158. *RIB* 2443.7: Tomlin, "Girl in Question," 49–50.

159. *RIB* 2443.7; *RIB II Fasc. 4*, 15.

160. *Tab. Lond. Bloomberg* 28; Tomlin, *Roman London's First Voices*, 114–15.

could not be replaced within three months (*conpe<n>dia | quae messibus tribus reficere | non possum [?adf]ueram*). To make matters worse Catarrius had arrived unexpectedly for a single day while Taurus was staying "at (the house) of Diadumenus" (*a[d D]iadumenum set ille |superuenit unum diem*).[161] Someone whose name is lost had given 200 denarii as a deposit (*arram*) when making a purchase and had been prompted to write a letter requesting that the recipient hand over what he owes perhaps because of a late payment.[162] There is an urgency on the part of Atticus in requesting that his correspondent should hand over "the 26 denarii in *victoriati*," a coin of the eastern empire worth half a denarius and no longer minted (*quam primum mit|tas (denarios) uiginti sex in uictoriat(is)*. The correspondence was perhaps between two partners who had stored coins for their value and may indicate trade with Greek cities of the east.[163] The importance of bread and of salt is suggested in the way he introduces his request, "I ask you by bread and salt" (*rogo [te] per panem et sal|em*).[164]

In the earliest of the Bloomberg tablets (43–53 CE) we meet Titus, a financier who is in danger of losing his honor.[165] The inner face of the tablet contains part of a letter that is addressed to Titus on the outer (plain) face; it calls him to task as a money lender. The first part speaks of him gaining a reputation in the forum for his money lending (. . . | *1 quia per forum totum |gloriantur se te faene|ras<s>e*). The writer goes on to warn Titus in no uncertain terms: "Therefore I ask you in your own interest not to appear *turpis* . . . you will not thus favor your own affairs . . ." (*itaque te rogo tua |causa ne tu turpis appar<e>|5 as in ...cus non sic |res tuas ?ama[bis] |et.put[a]s* traces). *Turpis* is the antithesis of honor, referring to shameful, disgraceful

161. *Tab. Lond. Bloomberg* 29; Tomlin, *Roman London's First Voices*, 116–19. For reconstruction, Figure 4. Appendix Chapter 2.

162. *Tab. Lond. Bloomberg* 35; Tomlin, *Roman London's First Voices*, 134–35. Appendix Chapter 2.

163. One *victoriatus* has been reported to PAS in the St Albans Area: "PAS," Record ID: BH-1DD9E4 – Victoriatus. An alternative interpretation is suggested by Johnson: "the tablet is referring to a payment of a value expressed in terms of Roman currency to be effected in non-Roman coins," perhaps "silver units of Epaticcus or Cunobelin." As such, it is evidence "that as late as the sixties CE Celtic coinage was an accepted supplement to state currency, even in areas such as London" ("Use of Celtic Coinage," 19).

164. *Tab. Lond. Bloomberg* 31; Tomlin, *Roman London's First Voices*, 124–27. Appendix Chapter 2. Cf. *Tab. Lond. Bloomberg* 15, 55; Tomlin, *Roman London's First Voices*, 88–89, 178–81, where the name Atticus also appears.

165. *Tab. Lond. Bloomberg* 30; Tomlin, *Roman London's First Voices*, 120–23. Appendix Chapter 2.

or dishonorable conduct and to people guilty of disgraceful behavior.[166] It is a word used in the Vulgate in Titus 1:11 and 1 Pet 5:2 (αἰσχροκερδῶς: *turpis*) and translated graphically by William Tyndale as "filthy" and in the NRSV as "sordid." With the world of finance and commerce the Romans have brought to Britain not only the world of literacy and patronage in business affairs but also the world of honor and shame. It is a world we are familiar with from the eastern Mediterranean.[167]

It is a world underpinned by a framework of law. In the record of legal action by someone who has "judicial authority" (*iudicio certare*)[168] reference to an "undertaking" (*sponsionem*) and the "management" (*procurationem*) of the case suggest some kind of economic and financial activity[169] that has to do with "aspects of legal representation."[170] According to Justinian's *Digest* "commercial agents" (*institores*) were "often though not always slaves" and "personal agents" (*procuratores*) were "mostly free people of higher standing."[171] As personal agents they "received instructions (*procuratio*) of a more general nature, and . . . were given a general remit to manage someone's affairs"; liability in the event of a dispute depended on the identity of the agent as *institor* or *procurator* and the nature of the contract.[172] That the fragmentary *Tab. Lond. Bloomberg* 57 has to do with a *procuratio* suggests that it was a key document in such a case establishing the relationship between two parties to a contract. This is an example of a first-century real-life situation codified by Ulpian (third century) and included in Justinian's *Digest* (sixth century CE).[173]

Another legal document includes the formal introduction to a "preliminary judgment" (*praeiudico*) by a judge appointed by the provincial governor, Sextus Iulius Frontinus, or by the *legatus iuridicus*, in the name of

166. *Tab. Lond. Bloomberg* 30; Tomlin, *Roman London's First Voices*, 122, Tomlin's translation, 'shabby," does not do justice to the force of the word *turpis*: *OLD*, 1994: 3, 4. Appendix Chapter 2.

167. Malina, *New Testament World*, chap. 1.

168. *Tab. Lond. Bloomberg* 57; Tomlin, *Roman London's First Voices*, 184–85. Appendix Chapter 2.

169. Tomlin, *Roman London's First Voices*, 56.

170. Du Plessis, "Bloomberg Tablets and Roman Law."

171. Du Plessis, *Letting and Hiring*, 55ff.

172. Du Plessis, *Letting and Hiring*, 58–59.

173. On the organization of businesses along these lines: Johnston, *Roman Law*, 118–30; on Ulpian and Justinian's *Digest*: Johnston, *Roman Law*, 18–28.

the emperor Vespasian.[174] Dated 22 October 76 CE, it anticipates litigation between Litugenus and Magunus coming to court on 9 November. It would appear from the reference to delegating "responsibility for (hearing a case)" (*operam dare*) that Londinium did not have the right to appoint magistrates at this time and so "jurisdictional competence"[175] lay with the emperor and would have been exercised by his representative, the provincial governor,[176] through his deputy (*legatus iuridicus*) who had responsibility for legal matters.[177] That Litugenus and Magenus were non-Romans with Celtic names, probably from Gaul, suggests that non-Romans had access to the Roman legal system.[178]

A stylus tablet discovered beside the Walbrook c. 500 meters to the north, dated 14 March 118 CE[179] records the resolution of a dispute over ownership of the five-acre wood Verlucionium in Kent (Map (Figure 1) 35) following a formal visit of the judge and the parties to the dispute (*cum ventum esset in rem praesentem*). It implies the formal registration of land in an earlier period, possibly after its confiscation during the Roman occupation of Britannia.[180] The wood had been acquired by Valerius Silvinus

174. *Tab. Lond. Bloomberg* 51; Tomlin, *Roman London's First Voices*, 170–71; Tomlin, *Britannia Romana*, 257–58; Frere, *Britannia*, 183; du Plessis, "Provincial Law in Britannia," 441–42; Perring, *London in Roman World*, 94. Johnston notes that "it seems likely, especially in cases that involved any great complexity, that some pre-trial discussion or negotiation, possibly involving advice from jurists, will have taken place before parties eventually appeared before the praetor" (*Roman Law*, 135). With regard to provincial practice, however, Johnston states "it was the provincial governor who exercised jurisdiction" normally without the use of a two-stage process (*Roman Law*, 144). Appendix Chapter 2

175. Du Plessis, "Bloomberg Tablets and Roman Law."

176. Tomlin, *Roman London's First Voices*, 170; Hingley, *Londinium: A Biography*, 68–71; Perring, *London in Roman World*, 91–95; de la Bédoyère, *Roman Britain*, 83–91; he lists the governors (*Roman Britain*, 87).

177. Du Plessis, "Provincial Law in Britannia," 441–42; Frere, *Britannia*, 183.

178. Du Plessis, "Provincial Law in Britannia," 442; Meyer, "Law and Latinization," 196–97.

179. RIB 2443.1914 March 118 CE. Found in 1986 in a second century Roman embankment east of the Walbrook at Throckmorton Street, c. 500 m to the north of the Bloomberg site. On land ownership and on the definition of boundaries, see Johnston 2020, 74–84. Meyer notes "that the wood was bought through *emptio*, the consensual contract of sale allowed to both citizens and non-citizens, but also the only contract allowed for provincial land by those who only possessed it rather than exercised *dominium* over it" ("Law and Latinization," 193).

180. Tomlin, "Five Acre Wood"; Tomlin, *Britannia Romana*, 258–59; Perring, *London in Roman World*, 179. Map (Figure 1) 35.

(or an earlier owner) and purchased in good faith by Julius Bellicus whose entitlement to the land was now being challenged in an action that "might have been brought by the Procurator asserting the Emperor's rights," by another private person or by the "*vicus* or *civitas* asserting a claim to land within its boundaries."[181] In an alternative interpretation, du Plessis suggests it "may have been the field notes of a land surveyor who was assessing the extent of the land for the purposes of land tax in the context of its recent sale."[182] In either case, the identification of the land with reference to two neighboring portions of land and an adjacent road, together with the format of the document with its sealed inner and unsealed outer pages, makes this document similar to the property deed of a date orchard belonging to Babatha on the shores of the Dead Sea.[183]

The formality of the legal and financial documents demonstrates the importance of the written word in the world of finance and of law:[184] a written document made real a payment in lieu of coinage, a contract for the purchase of merchandise or services and the decision of a court. Such written documents were authenticated by witnesses who wrote their own names and then sealed them.[185] This was a society built on debt that depended on honor and was established on patronage and slavery with relationships characterized by reciprocity.

Given that life was lived in the public eye, honor has been defined as "the value of a person in his or her own eyes *plus* that person's value in the eyes of his or her social group": it can be regarded as "a commodity accumulated by people in public life to increase their worth" and as such is "a limited good" that can be "ascribed at birth" and/or "achieved (and lost) throughout one's lifetime,"[186] as Titus knew only too well.[187]

181. Tomlin, "Five Acre Wood," 213–14.

182. Du Plessis, "Provincial Law in Britannia," 14.

183. P. Yadin 2: Esler, *Babatha's Orchard*, chaps. 5–7; Lewis, *Documents of Bar Kokhba*, 65–70. See above, Chapter 2, n. 115.

184. *Tab. Lond. Bloomberg* 44–57; Tomlin, *Roman London's First Voices*, 152–85; Meyer, "Writing in Legal Contexts"; Meyer, *Legitimacy and Law*. Another legal document dated to the late second or third century has to do with property ownership: *RIB* 2443.13, *RIB II Fasc. 4*, 18–19.

185. *Tab. Lond. Bloomberg* 58–68; Tomlin, *Roman London's First Voices*, 186–215.

186. Crook, *Reconceptualizing Conversion*, 67; citing MacMullen, *Roman Social Relations*, 62.

187. *Tab. Lond. Bloomberg* 30; Tomlin, *Roman London's First Voices*, 120–23. Appendix Chapter 2.

If honor was the pivotal social value, kinship was the central social institution.[188] Relationships can be described in terms of "reciprocity."[189] The Bloomberg tablets do not include personal correspondence and so there is no direct evidence of that "familial reciprocity" which is characteristic of family and other relationships in which the interests of the "other" are paramount. That would have been evident in the households and military communities we glimpse in the Bloomberg tablets and see in the extensive use of *frater* and *soror* in the Vindolanda correspondence.[190]

The financial and legal documents among the Bloomberg tablets reflect that "balanced reciprocity" that underpins trade and commerce and looks to an equivalent benefit for both parties to a contract or agreement.[191] The legal proceedings have to do with instances of its breakdown. In one tablet we see two contrasting forms of reciprocity side by side.[192] As they engage in a commercial transaction Tibullus and Gratus appear to be social equals in a relationship of "balanced reciprocity"; so too are their former masters, Venustus and Spurius. It would appear, however, that Venustus is in a relationship of "general reciprocity" with his former slave Tibullus, as is Spurius with his former slave Gratus. The implication is that they have exchanged goods that do not share equal value: theirs is a relationship of

188. Crook, *Reconceptualizing Conversion*, 68. Cf. Malina and Neyrey, "Honor and Shame."

189. Neyrey speaks of three types of reciprocity: "generalized reciprocity, disinterested concern for the other party; balanced reciprocity, mutuality in a balanced and symmetrical way; negative reciprocity, pure self-interest to the disadvantage of the other party" ("Ceremonies in Luke–Acts," 371–73). Crook considers that to be an over-simplification, and prefers Stegemann and Stegemann, *Jesus Movement* (*Reconceptualizing Conversion*, 54–59). I follow Stegemann and Stegemann, who speak of four types of reciprocity: familial reciprocity, to do with the household and kinship and amounting to a brotherly and sisterly love; balanced reciprocity, involving people of the same status and symmetrical relationships, not least in the exchange of goods and services; general reciprocity, involving people of unequal status and asymmetrical relationships, as between patron and client, teacher and student, rich and poor; negative reciprocity, involving relationships between strangers and enemies whereby one does to another what one does not want done to oneself (*Jesus Movement*, 34–36).

190. See below, Chapter 3, nn. 212, 213.

191. Cf Meyer who observes the *mutuum*, a form of contract obligating "the recipient to return the same amount and quality as what had been received," often expressed with "promises to repay in good faith," is found in a number of the Bloomberg tablets ("Law and Latinization," 193–94).

192. *Tab. Lond. Bloomberg* 44; Tomlin, *Roman London's First Voices*, 152–55. Appendix Chapter 2.

unequal status whereby one party remains subservient to the other. It is in this sense that Venustus and Spurius may be said to be patrons of Tibullus and Gratus respectively in that they have exchanged goods and services for honor, gratitude, and loyalty.[193]

By contrast, "negative reciprocity" forms part of the background to first century Londinium and in many ways is the elephant in the room. It is essentially self-centered, be it on the part of an individual or a group and involves a relationship in which one party seeks to benefit at the expense of the other, cheating them "out of a balanced exchange."[194] According to Cassius Dio it was "the confiscation of the large sums of money that Claudius had given to the foremost Britons" that contributed to the Boudica revolt. Decianius Catus, the procurator of the island, maintained they were loans which "were to be paid back." To make matters worse, Seneca "lent to the islanders 40,000,000 sesterces that they did not want," hoping to receive "a good rate of interest"; when, however, he demanded repayment of the loan all at once he "resorted to severe measures in exacting it."[195] Local peoples had been involved in trade with Rome since the time of Julius Caesar's expeditions to Britain (55 and 54 BCE); many, such as those responsible for the farm we read of in the Bloomberg tablets,[196] were part of the trading arrangements that were built on balanced reciprocity.[197] However, the loans described by Cassius Dio are evidence of a "negative reciprocity" that implies "the economic exploitation of Britain and the Britons."[198] Boudica's rebellion came to nought, the social and economic structures characterized by honor and shame, patronage and slavery and relationships of reciprocity were quickly re-established. The tensions arising from such "negative reciprocity," however, continued to simmer.

193. Crook, *Reconceptualizing Conversion*, 56–58; citing 34–37.

194. Crook, *Reconceptualizing Conversion*, 55–56; citing Sahlins, *Stone Age Economics*, 195; cf. 34–37.

195. Cassius Dio LXII.2, Cary and Foster 1914ff., Vol. VIII, 83. The equivalent of £830,000,000 today, see above, Chapter 2, n. 127.

196. *Tab. Lond. Bloomberg* 50; Tomlin, *Roman London's First Voices*, 168–69. Appendix Chapter 2.

197. Tab. Lond. Bloomberg 35 may indicate the prolonged use of Celtic coinage into the latter part of the first century CE: Johnson, "Use of Celtic Coinage." See above, Chapter 2, n. 163. Appendix Chapter 2.

198. D. J. Mattingly, *An Imperial Possession*, 293; cf. Perring, *London in Roman World*, 187, 191–202.

Imagining Luke–Acts in the Familiar World of Londinium

It was in the context of this kind of society, that Luke–Acts would have first circulated. Whether it was written for a particular individual or for a general audience, for a community that had roots among the *Iudaei* or the Romans, for a specific community or for all such communities, Luke–Acts was received by followers of the Way of Jesus from all strata of society.[199] They would have counted among their number local people as well as craftworkers like Tertius, householders like Catullus, tavern owners like Crispus, transport organizers like Marcus Rennius Venustus, Roman officers like Longinus, slaves like Florentinus and Fortunata, freedmen like Tibullus, patrons like Venustus and others involved in their world of commerce, finance, business and law. Our imagined readers of Luke–Acts would discover that many passages relate directly to the world they were familiar with beside the Walbrook in first century Londinium.

Orientation, Location and the Role of Eyewitnesses

The opening of Luke–Acts serves to orient readers from the outset. Whether or not the people we encounter in the Bloomberg tablets would have recognized a formal preface characteristic of biographical writing[200] or of scientific or technical handbooks,[201] they would have valued Luke's introductory words dedicated to "to the most excellent Theophilus" (κράτιστε Θεόφιλε: *optime Theophile* Luke 1:3; cf. Acts 1:1).[202] This is the language of honor and patronage that Taurus knew well as he wrote to "Macrinus his dearest lord" (*Macrino domino* | vacat *[ca]riss[imo]*):[203] it would suggest Luke–Acts was written for people such as themselves who were "not without means"

199. See above, Chapter 1, *The First Readership or Audience of Luke–Acts.*

200. Burridge observes that "Luke's use of a preface can be paralleled in Lucian and Philo, who have a paragraph each, and in Isocrates, Tacitus and Philostratus, who all have a more extended prologue" (*What Are the Gospels?*, 157–58, 189).

201. Alexander 1986; Wolter, *Luke I*, 43.

202. The use of the Vulgate alongside the Greek text and NRSV in biblical quotations (a practice adopted throughout) gives an approximate indication of how these texts would have been understood in a Latin speaking context. See above, Chapter 1, nn. 195–99.

203. *Tab. Lond. Bloomberg* 29. Appendix Chapter 2. Cf. the ink tablet 185: Tomlin, *Roman London's First Voices*, 116–19, 282–83.

and who "enjoyed a certain social prestige."[204] Among those who followed the Way of Jesus it would be reassuring to find centurions in Capernaum, Jerusalem and Caesarea (Luke 7:1–10; 23:47; Acts 10:1—11:18; 22:25–26; 23:23; 24:23; 27:1–44), householders and traders in Joppa, Philippi and Corinth (Acts 9:43; 16:14,40; 18:2,7), and people from their world of finance and trade in the stories of Jesus (Luke 7:41–43; 10:29–37; 12:41–46; 16:1–13; 19:1–10, 11–27).

The disputes between Cattarius and Taurus;[205] Litugenus and Magunus;[206] and Lucius Julius Bellicus and Titus Valerius Silvinus[207] would have required the kind of careful investigation Luke alludes to when he describes deciding "after investigating everything carefully from the very first, to write an orderly account" (ἔδοξεν κἀμοὶ παρηκολουθηκότι ἄνωθεν πᾶσιν ἀκριβῶς καθεξῆς σοι γράψαι: *visum est et mihi adsecuto a principio omnibus diligenter ex ordine tibi scribere*, Luke 1:3). In the resolution of each of those cases the testimony of witnesses would have been sought: financial and legal documents had legal force as they were witnessed by people such as Marius, Paullus, Saccus and Verecundus.[208] Our imagined readers would have realized the importance of a written account informed by those who had seen for themselves from the beginning, οἱ ἀπ᾽ ἀρχῆς αὐτόπται: *qui ab initio ipsi viderunt* (Luke 1:1–4).[209] They would have recognized the authority of those Jesus spoke of as "my witnesses" (μου μάρτυρες: *mihi testes*) in Jerusalem, Judea and to the ends of the earth (Acts 1:8; cf. Luke 24:48); the part played by "witnesses" as the story of the first followers of the Way was

204. Wolter, *Luke I*, 52.

205. *Tab. Lond. Bloomberg* 29; Tomlin, *Roman London's First Voices*, 116–19. Appendix Chapter 2.

206. *Tab. Lond. Bloomberg* 51; Tomlin, *Roman London's First Voices*, 170–71. Appendix Chapter 2.

207. *RIB* 2443.19; Tomlin, "Five Acre Wood."

208. *Tab. Lond. Bloomberg* 65; Tomlin, *Roman London's First Voices*, 206–7. Figure 8. Appendix Chapter 2.

209. Bauckham, *Jesus and the Eyewitnesses*, 116–24.

told;[210] and the key part played by those who had been "witnesses" from the very start (Luke 24:48; Acts 1:8, 22).[211]

The implication of what Luke writes is that Theophilus had already been instructed in the Way of Jesus but the purpose of Luke's writing is to establish the "truth" (ἀσφάλεια: *veritas*) of the matter (Luke 1:4) in a way that is convincing, giving a sense of "certainty" to something that has already been grasped.[212] More than historical veracity is at stake.[213] It is as if Theophilus is presented with something that will give him the "assurance"[214] that it is possible for him to be part of this movement while at the same time challenging him to live according to Luke's presentation of its Way. Encountering Luke–Acts as followers of the Way of Jesus, our imagined readers would not only be reassured that people of their standing were part of that movement but also challenged to follow the Way of Jesus as presented by Luke.

We can imagine them noticing things from the world they were familiar with. They were accustomed to using wooden writing tablets in keeping accounts and in correspondence: they would know exactly the kind of thing Zechariah requested when he asked for a writing tablet (πινακίδιον: *pugilaris* Luke 1:63). Luke lays down two markers at the very outset that establish the place and time of his narrative (Luke 1:5 and 3:1). His extended narrative around the birth of Jesus happens "in the days of King Herod of Judea" (ἐν ταῖς ἡμέραις Ἡρῴδου βασιλέως τῆς Ἰουδαίας: *in diebus Herodis regis Iudaeae* Luke 1:5) and his account of all that Jesus did and

210. Bauckham, *Jesus and the Eyewitnesses*, 271–79. In Matthews and Reid, Barbara Reid argues that "placing the women's names at the close of the account in Luke 24:10 . . . can be read . . . as following a protocol whereby the names of witnesses are given at the conclusion of their testimony" (*Luke 10–24*, 635); Shelley Matthews disagrees (*Luke 10–24*, 628–36).

211. Cf. Acts 2:32; 3:15; 4:33; 5:32; 10:39, 43; 13:31; 23:11.

212. Green, *Gospel of Luke*, 45.

213. Wolter, *Luke I*, 53.

214. Fitzmyer, *Luke I–IX*, 300; Esler, *Community and Gospel in Luke–Acts*, 222; cf. Matthews and Reid notice connotations that are missed in the NRSV, "The word ἀσφάλεια (v. 4) connotes assurance that the story told will be acceptable, rather than disturbing, to the reader's core values. The NRSV translation "truth" [following the Vulgate, *veritas*] misses this nuance" (*Luke 1–9*, 3). They quote Brigitte Kahl who "points out ἀσφάλεια/*securitas* was a core concept in Roman state ideology" ("Reading Luke Against Luke," 74–75).

taught (cf. Acts 1:1) is dated in a way familiar to Tibullus and Marcus Rennius Venustus:[215]

> In the fifteenth year of the reign of Emperor Tiberius, when Pontius Pilate was governor of Judea, and Herod was ruler, tetrarch, of Galilee, and his brother Philip ruler, tetrarch, of the region of Ituraea and Trachonitis, and Lysanias ruler, tetrarch, of Abilene
>
> Ἐν ἔτει δὲ πεντεκαιδεκάτῳ τῆς ἡγεμονίας Τιβερίου Καίσαρος, ἡγεμονεύοντος Ποντίου Πιλάτου τῆς Ἰουδαίας, καὶ τετρααρχοῦντος τῆς Γαλιλαίας Ἡρῴδου, Φιλίππου δὲ τοῦ ἀδελφοῦ αὐτοῦ τετρααρχοῦντος τῆς Ἰτουραίας καὶ Τραχωνίτιδος χώρας, καὶ Λυσανίου τῆς Ἀβιληνῆς τετρααρχοῦντος
>
> *anno autem quintodecimo imperii Tiberii Caesaris procurante Pontio Pilato Iudaeam tetrarcha autem Galilaeae Herode Philippo autem fratre eius tetrarcha Itureae et Trachonitidis regionis et Lysania Abilinae tetrarcha* (Luke 3:1)

The sixty-seven *IVDAEA CAPTA* coins reported to the Portable Antiquities Scheme[216] since 1995[217] suggest our imagined readers would quite possibly have an awareness of *Iudaea* following the defeat of the rebellion in 70 CE. The likes of Rogatus who is described as a Lingonian (*Lingonus*)[218] and Classicus, a prefect of the cohort of the Nervians (*Neruii*)[219] would associate those described In Luke–Acts as Ἰουδαίοι: *Iudaei* with people rooted in and adopting the customs of *Iudaea*. The use of *Iudaei* (Ἰουδαίοι) and *Iudaea* (Ἰουδαία) throughout is a reminder of the analogous use of terms such as *Lingonus* and *Nervii*.[220] Even if they had no further knowledge of

215. See especially: *Tab. Lond. Bloomberg* 44 (8 January 57 CE); 45 (21 October 62 CE); 50 (64 CE); 48 (67 CE); 51 (22 October 76 CE); 53 (15 March 82 CE); 49 (2–6 October 85 CE); 52 (85 CE or later), *RIB* 2443.19 (14 March 118 CE).

216. PAS is run by the British Museum and Amgueddfa Cymru – National Museum Wales to encourage the recording of archaeological objects found by members of the public in England and Wales: "PAS."

217. Vespasian (48), Titus (3), Domitian (1), Galba (1): "IVDAEA CAPTA Coins"; including two in the "Llanvaches Hoard": 2008.19H/19; 2008.19H/20. Esler includes sketches of all the IVDAEA CAPTA coin types in the British Museum (*Modelling Early Christianity*, 246–54).

218. *Tab. Lond. Bloomberg* 55 (c. 65/70–80 CE); Tomlin, *Roman London's First Voices*, 178–81. Appendix Chapter 2.

219. *Tab. Lond. Bloomberg* 33 (c. 65/70–80 CE); Tomlin, *Roman London's First Voices*, 130–31.

220. Brawley, *Luke*, 8; Mason, "Jews, Judaeans," 489–509, 511; contrast Matthews, *Acts* xiv; Novenson, "Ioudaios, Pharisee, Zealot," 168. Cf. the use of terms such as *cohors*

the *Iudaei* and their practices, the narrative of Luke–Acts contains within itself sufficient to give some rudimentary understanding of their practices, ritual and sacred texts. Our imagined readers are introduced to the temple, the God (θεός: *deus*) and Lord (κύριος: *dominus*), and rituals of the *Iudaei* at the very outset in Luke 1:6 and in 1–2, and to key moments in their history in Acts 7:2–53.

Honor Restored in the Cancellation of Debts

When a Pharisee was shocked at the way "a woman . . . who was a sinner" poured oil from an "alabaster jar of ointment" over the feet of Jesus during a meal, Jesus spoke of a moneylender (δανιστής: *fenerator*) and two debtors (χρεοφειλέται: *debitores*), one of whom owed 500 denarii and the other 50 denarii (Luke 7:41–42). This was the world of our imagined readers in which loans for similar sums of money were fully documented.[221] They were all too aware of the need for someone engaged in lending (*faenerare*) money to act with honor and to avoid the shameful behavior of Titus.[222] They would think of the formal cancellation of a loan note as lines were struck through the text[223] or through the names of the witnesses.[224]

There is a familiarity for our imagined readers in this parable: they knew that failure to repay a loan not only brought shame on the one responsible but could also provoke an angry response. The actions of the moneylender might have prompted them either to think of someone who

VIIII Batauorum and *cohors I Tungrorum* in the Vindolanda tablets.

221. *Tab. Lond. Bloomberg* 31: 26 and 10 denarii; 35: 200 denarii; 37: 300 denarii; 44: 105 denarii; 70: 16 ¼ denarii, 65 denarii and 6 denarii; 71: 20 denarii; 72: 5 denarii, 7 denarii, half denarius, one quarter denarius, one and a half denarii; 76: 30 denarii, total 106 denarii; two tablets mention figures that might refer to denarii: *Tab. Lond. Bloomberg* 22: cccc (400); 69: xxxx (40). In a study of the 102 Dead Sea legal papyri, Esler observes that nine (nearly 10 percent) are acknowledgements of debts for 20, 600, 1,170, 60, 300, 50, and 4 denarii and so indicate the widespread experience of debt in Judea at the end of the first and start of the second centuries CE ("Dead Sea Legal Papyri"). The similar proportion of financial documents acknowledging debt among the Bloomberg tablets, is a reminder that the experience of indebtedness spanned the Roman Empire from east to west. Cf. Johnston, *Roman Law*, 102.

222. *Tab. Lond. Bloomberg* 30; Tomlin, *Roman London's First Voices*, 120–23. Appendix Chapter 2.

223. *Tab. Lond. Bloomberg* 55. Appendix Chapter 2. Cf. 61, 64, 65, 68; Tomlin, *Roman London's First Voices*, 178–81, 204–7, 214–15.

224. *Tab. Lond. Bloomberg* 58; Tomlin, *Roman London's First Voices*, 186–89.

would have acted in that way or to think such action impossible.[225] They would surely have been struck not only by his remarkable generosity but also by the equally remarkable restoration of the one who had been shamed. The size of the cancelled debt accentuates the scale of the restoration as the shamed woman is to go in peace.[226] Her faith has saved her in that her honor is restored.[227] While this narrative may be about the equilibrium of society[228] with its hierarchies and subordination,[229] our imagined readers would be challenged by the question posed by Jesus at the end of the parable as he speaks of the love of the debtor for the moneylender who cancels the debt. It is as if relationships built on love offer an alternative basis for building community among those who follow the Way of Jesus.[230]

A Word of Honor

It is the central importance of love that prompts the parable of the Samaritan traveler. How one understands the parable depends on the way the "one who hears the parable identifies with the characters" in the narrative.[231] Our imagined readers might recognize in the Samaritan the kind of person contracted by Gaius Valerius Proculus to transport twenty loads of provisions on as many days from Verulamium to Londinium in the aftermath of the Boudica revolt.[232] The innkeeper assumes the Samaritan will come back when he returns with his beast of burden (κτῆνος: *iumentum*),[233] suggest-

225. Wolter, *Luke I*, 323 considers it "an action not completely unthinkable."

226. Wolter, *Luke I*, 323.

227. Reid rejects the view of a shamed woman as a male perspective and urges a different view of the woman that recognizes the generosity of her love ("Do You See This Woman?," 108–17). For an alternative perspective from a woman's point of view see below, Chapter 3, *Festivals and Feasting.*

228. Green, *Gospel of Luke*, 312.

229. Brawley, *Luke*, 94–97. Cf. Matthews and Reid, *Luke 1–9*, 238–44.

230. Schaberg and Ringe, however, consider this a distortion on the part of Luke that "displays real arrogance" ("Luke," 506).

231. Brawley, *Luke*, 118.

232. *Tab. Lond. Bloomberg* 45; Tomlin, *Roman London's First Voices*, 156–59. Appendix Chapter 2. Fitzmyer, *Luke X–XXIV*, 886: the distance from Jerusalem to Jericho was 29 kilometers; and from Verulamium to Londinium 35 kilometers, see above: Chapter 2, n. 145; Map (Figure 1) 17 to 1.

233. *Tab. Lond. Bloomberg* 29; Tomlin, *Roman London's First Voices*, 116–19. Appendix Chapter 2.

ing he was a regular traveler. The Samaritan uses the language of another loan note[234] when he promises to repay the innkeeper whatever he is owed above the initial payment of two *denarii*: ὅ τι ἂν προσδαπανήσῃς ἐγὼ ἐν τῷ ἐπανέρχεσθαί με ἀποδώσω σοι: *quodcumque supererogaveris ego cum rediero reddam tibi* (Luke 10:35). There is more to this dimension to the story than is sometimes allowed.[235] Our imagined readers moved in a world in which transactions were based on a respected person's word of honor articulated in the form of a loan note. They would see in the actions of the Samaritan an expression of that compassion (σπλάγχνα: *misericordia*) that had moved him on seeing the wounded man. That act of mercy is even more telling in the context of the aftermath of the Boudica revolt and ongoing tensions with the local population. Love is given value here in terms that would be understood by our imagined readers from that world of finance and commerce.

The Slave as Faithful and Prudent Manager

Imagining Luke–Acts through the eyes of the people of the Bloomberg tablets, we are conscious of the complex role of the slave and the freedman in the world of the Roman Empire.[236] Florentinus, the slave of Sextus Cassius, had a significant responsibility and was in charge of receiving two payments of rent from one or more farms.[237] Narcissus, the slave of Rogatus, seems to have been in charge of his master's affairs.[238] Catullus, the slave of Romanius Faustinus, and the slave of Senecio were acting as agents for their masters in managing their accounts.[239] Tibullus, the freedman of Venustus and Gratus the freedman of Spurius were working for their former masters now their patrons.[240] They clearly had positions of re-

234. *Tab. Lond. Bloomberg* 44: *quam pecuniam ei reddere debeo*; Tomlin, *Roman London's First Voices*, 152–55. Appendix Chapter 2.

235. Wolter, *Luke II*, 80.

236. Harrill, "Paul and Slavery," 302–3. Cf. Bradley, *Slavery and Society*, 75; Woolf, *Rome*, 97–101; Johnston, *Roman Law*, 51–54; Matthews and Reid, *Luke 10–24*, 400. See above, Chapter 2, n. 117.

237. *Tab. Lond. Bloomberg* 50; Tomlin, *Roman London's First Voices*, 168–69. Appendix Chapter 2.

238. *Tab. Lond. Bloomberg* 55; Tomlin, *Roman London's First Voices*, 178–81. Appendix Chapter 2.

239. *Tab. Lond. Bloomberg* 70; Tomlin, *Roman London's First Voices*, 218–19.

240. *Tab. Lond. Bloomberg* 44; Tomlin, *Roman London's First Voices*, 152–55.

sponsibility and were respected not only by their masters but also by those they traded with. Readers of Luke 12:41–48 from within this world would recognize that the slave who is respected and honored as "blessed" becomes the agent of his master when he is "put in charge of all his possessions" (ἐπὶ πᾶσιν τοῖς ὑπάρχουσιν αὐτοῦ καταστήσει αὐτόν: *supra omnia quae possidet constituet illum*)." In overall charge is a "faithful and prudent manager" (ὁ πιστὸς οἰκονόμος ὁ φρόνιμος: *fidelis dispensator et prudens*) who might well be understood as himself a slave with responsibility for his master's affairs. In the sale of the enslaved girl Fortunata,[241] Montanus is identified as the slave of Vegetus, himself a slave. As an imperial slave, like Vegetus, Montanus was possibly a *dispensator*, a steward with responsibility for handling imperial funds in the province. Given the setting of this parable "within the metaphorical field of the Roman household (*domus*) or family (*familia*),"[242] our imagined readers would recognize the honor accorded to a slave given such a position of responsibility. Equally, they would recognize in the slave who took advantage of his master's absence and beat other slaves, irresponsible actions that brought shame upon him. For our imagined readers "this parable emphasizes fidelity in [their] everyday world."[243] The "cultural realities" of these parables span the empire and can be glimpsed in the world of the Bloomberg tablets. While they would identify with the circumstances envisaged here, not least the elevated role of the slave-manager, the effect of the question Peter asks (Luke 12:41) is to prompt our readers to realize this message is for everyone.[244] They would agree that "from everyone to whom much has been given, much will be required; and from one to whom much has been entrusted, even more will be demanded" (Luke 12:48).

Appendix Chapter 2.

241. Tomlin, "Girl in Question," 41–51; Perring, *London in Roman World*, 223, 225.

242. Green, *Gospel of Luke*, 498.

243. Brawley, *Luke*, 133–34. Cf. Matthews and Reid, *Luke 10–24*, 399–403. From their "feminist perspective, equipped with recent scholarship on the violence of slave systems," Matthews and Reid are "suspicious of the many ways interpreters have downplayed Luke's violent slave logic" (*Luke 10–24*, 399–400); they advocate "the importance of centering a history of women in early Christianity on slave women rather than elite women" (*Luke 10–24*, 403).

244. Green, *Gospel of Luke*, 497 and 499.

Keeping Accounts

Eight of the Bloomberg tablets are accounts,[245] reflecting the kind of detailed record keeping that may have been required of the seven who were chosen to serve in Jerusalem (Acts 6:1–7). At the prompting of the Apostles, the seven are set apart by "the whole community of the disciples" to "wait at tables"[246] (διακονεῖν τραπέζαις: ministrare mensis), "keep accounts" (NRSV footnote) or "handle finances" (GNB).[247] Crispus[248] would have known what accounts were like and how important it was to keep them accurately in his tavern. So too would Catullus, the slave of Romanius Faustinus,[249] and Ammonicus and Pactumeius the son of Adenhus.[250] The people of the Bloomberg tablets may have understood this task to be one of keeping the kind of accounts they too were used to keeping. That would then imply a level of literacy on the part of the seven subsequently borne out in the narrative of Philip and the Ethiopian eunuch (Acts 8:26–40).

Occupation and Location

The narrative in Acts frequently refers to people by their trade and by their house, something Tertius, the brewer and Junius the cooper who lived opposite (the house of) Catullus would have immediately recognized. We encounter the room in Jerusalem where the disciples were staying (Acts 1:13) and later the house of Judas on the Street called Straight in Damascus (Acts 9:11), the house of Simon the tanner by the seaside in Joppa (Acts 10:6), Cornelius's house in Caesarea (Acts 10:22), and the house of Mary, the mother of John Mark (Acts 12:12); Paul visits Lydia, the dealer in purple cloth, in her house in Philippi (Acts 16:40), and stays with Aquila

245. *Tab. Lond. Bloomberg* 69–76; Tomlin, *Roman London's First Voices*, 216–33.

246. A translation followed in English from Tyndale to the New Revised Standard Version, New International Version, and English Standard Version.

247. F. F. Bruce follows this interpretation (*Acts*, 182). Cf., Silva, *Dictionary of the New Testament Theology*, 1:703; Aymer, "Acts Women's Bible Commentary," 540; Keener speaks of an "economic ministry" and "the ministry of resource sharing" and "economic ministry to the needy" (*Acts*, 217, 218, 222); Maloney and Reimer speak of "managing the community's finances" (*Acts*, 79). C. K. Barrett considers it an unlikely possibility *Acts Volume 1*, 311); Fitzmyer rejects it (*Acts*, 348–49).

248. *Tab. Lond. Bloomberg* 72; Tomlin, *Roman London's First Voices*, 222–25.

249. *Tab. Lond. Bloomberg* 70; Tomlin, *Roman London's First Voices*, 218–19.

250. *Tab. Lond. Bloomberg* 76; Tomlin, *Roman London's First Voices*, 232–33.

and Priscilla, fellow tentmakers in Corinth (Acts 18:2–3). When Paul visits the house of Titius Justus in Corinth, next door to the synagogue, its location is identified in the way the house of Junius the cooper is identified (Acts 18:7).[251] His visit to the house of Philip the Evangelist in Caesarea and subsequent stay at the house of Mnason of Cyprus uses a similar form of address (Acts 21:8, 16). Demetrius in Ephesus is known by his trade as a silversmith (Acts 19:24).

There is evidence in first century Londinium of leatherworkers, silversmiths and other craftworkers.[252] The traders, merchants and craft workers of mid-first-century Londinium were accustomed to traveling in pursuit of business.[253] They may have recognized in the traders and craft workers of Acts, not least Paul, artisans whose travels were "at least partially a function of economic opportunity."[254] Early on in Acts there is a shift from Jerusalem to "political and commercial hubs of the Roman Empire."[255] The encounter with householders and those engaged in the everyday life of those hubs would be familiar to our imagined readers: Londinium had become such a hub by 60 CE, with an approximate population of 10,000.[256]

Trade in Grain

There is evidence from the excavations in 1 Poultry that there was some import of grain.[257] Those who had come from Gaul or further afield had had to make a sea crossing to reach Londinium. They would have been familiar with the arrangements made for Paul's final voyages. The last voyage

251. *Tab. Lond. Bloomberg* 14; Tomlin, *Roman London's First Voices*, 86–87.

252. Gardner, "Metalworking Crucibles," 79–82; Cf. the discovery of uncut panels of tent among the quays of post Boudican Londinium: Perring, *London in Roman World*, 99–100, 213–16; J. Hill and Rowsome, *Roman London and Walbrook*. Cf. below, Chapter 3, *Festivals and Feasting*; *Tab. Vindol. III* 656.

253. Perring, *London in Roman World*, 195, 226–27.

254. Schellenberg, "Danger, Paul and Travel," 157.

255. Spencer, *Journeying through Acts*, 108.

256. Perring, "Recent Advances Roman London"; Rowsome argues that "the spatial and chronological development of Londinium would have been influenced not only by its topography, but by its role as an officially sanctioned entrepôt or privately initiated trading community, complex civil and military inter-relationships and administrative arrangements that may have flowed from its status" ("Mapping Roman London"). Cf. Rowsome, *Heart of the City*, 18–22; Rowsome, *Londinium Map*.

257. Hingley, *Londinium: A Biography*, 41; Perring, *London in Roman World*, 124–27.

to Phoenicia and Caesarea is on a ship with cargo (τὸν γόμον: *onus*) which was to be unloaded at Tyre (Acts 21:3). The first ship on Paul's last voyage to Rome was a ship of Adramyttius (Acts 27:2) that would be trading at ports along the coast of Asia.[258] The second ship found in Myra in Lycia was bound for Italy and probably part of the grain fleet from Alexandria (Acts 27:6).[259] The centurion rejects Paul's caution in sailing when the Mediterranean was about to be closed to shipping, preferring the advice of the pilot and the owner.[260] The kind of financial system reflected in the use of wax tablets as in the Bloomberg site, was also one that was used in shipping.[261] Some of the tablets discovered in the Murecine archive of the Sulpicii, bankers from Puteoli, were to do with credit extended in the shipping of goods.[262] The final amount would not be paid until delivery, but interim amounts needed to be paid through a banker. While there is no evidence of such banking arrangements around shipping in Londinium, the advance payment on the twenty loads being delivered from Verulamium over a period of a little over twenty days by Gaius Valerius Proculus is similar.[263] The ship wrecked on Malta is an Alexandrian ship with a cargo of wheat (Acts 27:38). The traders and merchants of first century Londinium were familiar with the kind of travel undertaken by Paul on land and sea.

258. Kloppenborg argues that Luke's knowledge of travel around this coast is accurate ("Luke's Geography"; 102).

259. Keener, *Acts*, 596–97; cf. Thompson, "Holy Internet."

260. Whether the authentic details in the narrative of Paul's last voyage and shipwreck are to be viewed as a historical record as Keener, *Acts*, 592–614, or as "a Lukan composition throughout," Maloney and Reimer, *Acts*, 331–39, is much debated. Pervo suggests Acts 27 "is best understood as a chapter from a religious novel" and maintains that "solutions that judge this material entirely factual or completely fictitious are questionable" (*Acts*, 645); see his full analysis, (*Acts*, 644–54). Praeder regards this narrative as both literary and theological: "In the sea voyage, storm, and shipwreck in Acts 27:1—28:16 Luke has chosen what could be called a characteristically Gentile story to conclude his Christian story of the sending of the salvation of God to the Gentiles. The result is an account of literary and theological character, with a literary relation to sea voyages in ancient literature and with a theological relation to the rest of Luke–Acts" ("Sea Voyages in Luke–Acts," 704).

261. Perring, *London in Roman World*, 203–4, 212–13.

262. Jones, *Bankers of Puteoli*, 103–17; Andreau, *Banking and Business*, ch. 6.

263. *Tab. Lond. Bloomberg* 45; Tomlin, *Roman London's First Voices*, 156–59. Cf. du Plessis, who suggests that a discussion about credit in *Tab. Vindol.* 343 "points to the existence of moneylenders or bankers who are able to credit accounts held in different places" ("Provincial Law in Britannia," 17). Figure 14 and appendix to Chapter 2.

The Importance of the Written Word

Trade in first century Londinium depended on a significant level of literacy which in turn depended on education.[264] The written word and the ability to read runs through Luke–Acts from the childhood of John (Luke 1:80) and Jesus (Luke 2:40, 52, 4:16) to the upbringing of Paul (Acts 22:3) and the letter-writing of the first followers of the Way (Acts 15:22–35). At the start and finish of Luke's Gospel writing tablets have a part to play, as Zechariah announces the name of his son John (Luke 1:63) and as an inscription is placed over the crucified Jesus (Luke 23:38). It is as the proceedings against Paul unfold in Caesarea, however, that the written word becomes all important in a legal context (Acts 25:26–27).

When Paul was brought into the audience chamber of Herod's palace in Caesarea to stand before King Agrippa and his sister Bernice it was not only with great pomp. There was a formality to the hearing in the presence of the leading men of the city and the tribunes of the five cohorts stationed there. Festus has brought Paul before them all in the presence of King Agrippa "so that, after we have examined him, I may have something to write – for it seems to me unreasonable to send a prisoner without indicating the charges against him" (Acts 25:26–27). Where commentaries on Luke–Acts maintain that it was, indeed, a formality expected in such cases, they cite the third century jurist, Marcianus and his second book on Appeals quoted in the sixth century *Digest* of Justinian:[265] *post appellationem interpositam litterae dandae sunt . . . ad eum, qui de appellatione cogniturus est, sive principem sive quem alium* (after an appeal has been lodged documents of referral are to be given . . . to the one who will hear the appeal, whether the emperor or his representative).[266] The need for a written record in legal proceedings would have been self-evident to people such as Litugenus and Magunus. In Londinium, as in Caesarea, responsibility

264. Cf. writing exercises *Tab. Lond. Bloomberg* 77–79; Tomlin, *Roman London's First Voices*, 234–43. Cooley, *Role of the Non-Elite*, 109; Hassall suggests Agricola may have been correct in suggesting the sons of leading local people received an education ("London: Britain's First University?," 117–20). Tacitus *Agricola* 21, *iam vero principum filios liberalibus artibus erudire*, 106; "he trained the sons of the leading men in the liberal arts," (tr. Harold Mattingley and J. B. Rives, *Agricola and Germania*, 15); Hingley, *Londinium: A Biography*, 37; Perring, *London in Roman World*, 203, 219–20. See above, Chapter 2, nn. 89, 90, 91.

265. Gaventa, *Acts*; Parsons, *Acts*; Witherington, *Acts*; Bruce, *Acts*; Conzelmann, *Acts*; Fitzmyer, *Acts*.

266. *Justinian Digest* XLI.6.1: "Justinian Digest."

for conducting a case and in delivering a judgment had been "given by the emperor" (*data ab |Ca[e]sare*).[267] The formality of legal proceedings[268] involved committing a "preliminary judgment" (*praeiudicium*) to writing.[269] Our imagined readers would recognize in this text the significance of the written record.

Negotiating the Way Through the World of First-Century Londinium

As we imagine people such as those responsible for the Bloomberg tablets encountering Luke–Acts it is clear they would have found much they would have been familiar with. They would have the assurance that among those who followed the Way of Jesus were people of similar status to themselves who continued to be involved in the world of trade and commerce. Like them they face a challenge as they seek to negotiate a way through the complexities of that world that is true to the teaching of Jesus in Luke's Gospel and modelled on the life of the first followers of the Way in Acts. There is throughout Luke a concern for the destitute and a disdain for the rich which finds expression in a commitment to share in Acts. The stratification of the Roman Empire that is always in the background in Luke–Acts is evident as much in first century Londinium as in the eastern Mediterranean. That the powerful are brought down by God, and the lowly lifted up, challenges our imagined readers who are part of a financial system built on a balanced reciprocity to adopt a familial reciprocity within the community they now belong to.[270] That gives rise to a radical generosity that involves sharing and the love of enemies. Being true to that Way while at the same time continuing their involvement in the world of trade and commerce is the challenge faced by the likes of Tibullus, Gratus, Narcissus and Titus.

267. *Tab. Lond. Bloomberg* 51; Tomlin, *Roman London's First Voices*, 170–71. Appendix Chapter 2.

268. Meyer, *Legitimacy and Law*.

269. *Tab. Lond. Bloomberg* 51; Tomlin, *Roman London's First Voices*, 170–71. Appendix Chapter 2.

270. As used by Crook, *Reconceptualizing Conversion*, 54, following Stegemann and Stegemann, *Jesus Movement*, 34–36. See above, Chapter 2, n. 189.

The Powerful Brought Down: the Lowly Lifted Up

If, as we have argued above,[271] people such as Venustus and Proculus, Litugenus and Magunus would find in Luke–Acts the reassurance they needed that there was room for them among those who followed the Way of Jesus, it is also clear that they would find much to challenge their everyday practices. In the coming of Jesus, anticipated by Mary before his birth, "the Lord" and the "God" of the *Iudaei*

> has shown strength with his arm; he has scattered the proud in the thoughts of their hearts. He has brought down the powerful from their thrones, and lifted up the lowly
>
> Ἐποίησεν κράτος ἐν βραχίονι αὐτοῦ, διεσκόρπισεν ὑπερηφάνους διανοίᾳ καρδίας αὐτῶν· καθεῖλεν δυνάστας ἀπὸ θρόνων καὶ ὕψωσεν ταπεινούς,
>
> *fecit potentiam in brachio suo dispersit superbos mente cordis sui deposuit potentes de sede et exaltavit humiles* (Luke 1:51–53)

Addressing the people of *Iudaea*, Zechariah speaks of being "saved from our enemies and from the hand of all who hate us" and being guided "into the way of peace" (εἰς ὁδὸν εἰρήνης: *in viam pacis* Luke 1:71, 79).

Schaberg and Ringe describe Mary's words as "the great New Testament song of liberation—personal and social, moral and economic—a revolutionary document of intense conflict and victory."[272] Matthews and Reid maintain that this song proclaims "divinely wrought vanquishing of the ruling powers, victory for God's own people in the past, and a vision for God's power and protection in bringing forth a different future." However, they differ in their understanding of the significance of the words to Luke: Reid understands it as "countering Roman imperial values," whereas Matthews "sees Luke reinscribing imperial power rather than overturning it."[273] Green suggests followers of the Way would be presented with "a break with existing standards," and a God who is on the side of the weak,[274] is opposed to forces of oppression wherever they may be found,[275] and "against socio-religious, politico-economic forces working in opposition

271. See above, Chapter 2, *Imagining Luke–Acts in the Familiar World of Londinium.*

272. Schaberg and Ringe, "Luke," 503.

273. Matthews and Reid, *Luke 1–9*, 45.

274. Green, *Gospel of Luke*, 100.

275. Green, *Gospel of Luke*, 114–15.

to" his purposes.[276] Brawley goes further to suggest that following the Way of Jesus amounts to "the end of hierarchical systems of domination" and offers "well-being for all" that cuts through "large complexes of such things as social, religious, economic, gender, and political dominance."[277] Kuecker maintains that "social dislocation" accompanies followers of the Way of Jesus as they put "obedience to the Word of Israel's God above Roman . . . social norms."[278] Would our imagined readers have to break with their world of trade and commerce?

If we imagine Luke–Acts being read by people such as the traders and merchants of Londinium, other elements of the narrative come to the fore. John, the forerunner of Jesus, counsels modified behavior on the part of the tax-collectors and soldiers of Rome (Luke 3:10–14), and the "worthy" (ἄξιός: *dignus*) centurion of Capernaum is commended by Jesus (Luke 7:4, 9, 10). For our imagined readers, as for "the most excellent Theophilus," there is a challenge in these words to a changed way of life within the world they knew. It is not rebellion that is called for but a radical critique.

Wolter sees in these words of Mary a "reversal of the powerful and the powerless"[279] that is "an old motif that is widely attested in the environment of the NT."[280] Though unaware of the Septuagintisms of Luke 1–2,[281] our imagined readers would perhaps have a heightened awareness of the implications of the words of Zechariah. Addressing the people of *Iudaea*, Zechariah speaks of being "saved from our enemies and from the hand of all who hate us" and being guided "into the way of peace" (εἰς ὁδὸν εἰρήνης: *in viam pacis* Luke 1:71, 79). For our imagined readers as much as for the *Iudaei* that way of peace would involve "acceptance of the proclamation of Jesus."[282]

What would our imagined readers in the last quarter of the first century CE make of such words in the wake of the failure of the Boudica rebellion in Britannia (60–61 CE) and of the rebellion of the *Iudaei* in Jerusalem (66–70

276. Green, *Gospel of Luke*, 104.

277. Brawley, *Luke*, 48.

278. Kuecker, "*Luke*," 110.

279. Wolter, *Luke I*, 96.

280. Wolter cites OT passages, Homer, Hesiod, Pindar, Euripides, Xenophon, Gnomologium Vaticanum, Herodianus Historicus, 1 Clement, and a third century CE papyrus, P. Oxy XXXI 2554, Fragment I.2 (*Luke I*, 96–97).

281. Fitzmyer, *Luke I–IX*, 312, 359, 377.

282. Wolter, *Luke I*, 114.

CE)? The implied reprimand to Titus (43–53 CE),[283] the *chirographum* written by Tibullus (8 January 57 CE),[284] and other loan notes,[285] show that financial and commercial practices established throughout the empire had been established from the outset in the newly founded Londinium. Whatever the causes of the Boudica revolt,[286] that system came under threat with the destruction of Camulodunum, Verulamium and Londinium.[287] The *chirographum* of Marcus Rennius Venustus (21 October 62)[288] indicates that Londinium recovered quickly after the suppression of the revolt. In the wake of these upheavals traders, merchants and bankers depended on continuity and stability. The ability of the powers that be to suppress revolt and keep order amidst the ensuing tensions was all important. The peace had to be enforced, however, as is suggested by the reference, in correspondence involving Julius Suavis, to a fort established in the canton of the Iceni in the aftermath of the revolt.[289] By the time that a preliminary judgment was given in the case between Litugenus and Magunus,[290] Vespasian was emperor and campaigning had resumed in the lands of the Silures to the west and the Brigantes to the north. Under the governorship of Petilis Cerialis (71–74 CE) and of Iulius Frontinus (74–78 CE), Tacitus maintains that it was the caliber of the commanders and of the armies that instilled fear into the local people as they lost hope and witnessed the subjugation of their lands.[291] He goes on to tell of the campaigns of his father-in-law, Agricola,

283. *Tab. Lond. Bloomberg* 30; Tomlin, *Roman London's First Voices*, 120–23. Appendix Chapter 2.

284. *Tab. Lond. Bloomberg* 44; Tomlin, *Roman London's First Voices*, 152–55. Appendix Chapter 2.

285. See above, Chapter 2, nn. 57-70.

286. See above, Chapter 2, n. 195.

287. Camulodunum, Verulamium, Londinium, Map (Figure 1) 16, 17, 1.

288. *Tab. Lond. Bloomberg* 45; Tomlin, *Roman London's First Voices*, 156–59. Appendix Chapter 2.

289. *Tab. Lond. Bloomberg* 39; Tomlin, *Roman London's First Voices*, 142–43. Appendix Chapter 2.

290. *Tab. Lond. Bloomberg* 51; Tomlin, *Roman London's First Voices*, 170–71. Appendix Chapter 2.

291. Tacitus, *Agricola* 17, . . . *magni duces, egregii exercitus, minuta hostium spes. et terrorem statim intulit Petilius Cerialis, Brigantum civitatem. . . . subiit sustinuitque molem Iulius Frontinus, vir magnus quantum licebat, validamque et pugnacem Silurum gentem armis subegit*, 104. (. . . the generals were great, the armies outstanding and the hopes of our enemies diminished. Petilius Cerialis at once struck terror into their hearts by attacking the state of the Brigantes. . . . Julius Frontinus took up and shouldered the heavy

governor of Britannia (77–83 CE) that brought an end to the conquest of Britannia with the battle of Mons Graupius. He puts into the mouth of Calgacus, a leader of the Britons, a critique of the ensuing peace that reflects contemporary criticism of Rome.[292]

> If the enemy is rich, they are greedy; if he is poor, they strive for glory. . . . To pillage, butchery and rape they give spurious names and call it empire (*imperium*); and where they bring about desolation they call it peace (*pax*).
>
> *si locuples hostis est, avari, si pauper, ambitiosi. . . . auferre trucidare rapere falsis nominibus imperium atque ubi solitudinem faciunt, pacem appellant.*[293]

Any who came to follow the Way of Jesus, however, and encounter Luke–Acts would be prompted by these words of Zechariah to seek a different kind of peace from the one described here by Tacitus.

There are elements in the parable of the ten pounds that would be familiar to our imagined readers (Luke 19:11–27). When a nobleman goes to a far country, summons ten of his slaves and gives them ten pounds (δέκα μνᾶς: *decem mnas*) to "do business" (πραγματεύσασθε: *negotiamini*), Narcissus, the slave, would recognize the role played by slaves in carrying out their master's business;[294] Optatus the *negotiator* would recognize the world of merchants.[295] Narcissus and Rogatus, slave and master, would also have recognized the part played by bankers and the importance of interest (Luke 19:23):[296] they would also have been aware of the custom of storing money in the ground.[297] There is, however, another element to the story that we can imagine them responding to: as the nobleman goes to a far country to seek royal power, he speaks of enemies who did not want him

---

burden, as great a man as the times allowed. He subdued by force of arms the strong and warlike nation of the Silures. . . . (trans. H.Mattingley and J. B. Rives, *Agricola and Germania*, 13).

292. Ogilvie and Richmond, trans., *Agricola*, 258: e.g. Pliny, *Natural History* 6.182, published in 79 CE. See Map (Figure 1) note.

293. Tacitus, *Agricola* 30.5, 112.

294. *Tab. Lond. Bloomberg* 55; Tomlin, *Roman London's First Voices*, 178–81. Appendix Chapter 2.

295. *Tab. Lond. Bloomberg* 7; Tomlin, *Roman London's First Voices*, 72–73. Cf. *OLD*, 1168: "One who engages in commerce, a wholesale trader or dealer."

296. *Tab. Lond. Bloomberg* 55. Appendix Chapter 2. Cf. *Tab. Lond. Bloomberg* 56; Tomlin, *Roman London's First Voices*, 178–83.

297. Abdy, *Romano-British Coin Hoards.*

to be king and of the brutal consequences that follow (Luke 19:12 and 27). Was this the kind of brute force they had been aware of in the defeat of the Boudica revolt? Would they have seen in this would-be king "an antitype of a follower of Jesus", whose command to slaughter his enemies is "the utter antithesis of enemy love and mercy" that characterizes the follower of the Way of Jesus?[298]

Concern for the Destitute, Disdain for the Rich

The people of the Bloomberg tablets engaged in everyday commerce and lived in a world of business that at times dealt in large sums of money and led to the accumulation of wealth. The 105 denarii owed by Tibullus to Gratus[299] is only a portion of the price of the merchandise which had been sold and delivered; Atigniomarus was in receipt of 300 denarii when he arrived in the city.[300] In a community of followers of the Way of Jesus our imagined readers, merchants and traders of first century Londinium, would be among the wealthiest.[301] Without any knowledge of the sacred texts of the *Iudaei*, they would recognize in the words read by Jesus in Nazareth at the start of his ministry a concern for the poor.[302] Jesus is

> to bring good news to the poor, . . . to proclaim release to the captives and recovery of sight to the blind, to let the oppressed go free, to proclaim the year of the Lord's favor.
>
> εὐαγγελίσασθαι πτωχοῖς. . . κηρύξαι αἰχμαλώτοις ἄφεσιν καὶ τυφλοῖς ἀνάβλεψιν, ἀποστεῖλαι τεθραυσμένους ἐν ἀφέσει, κηρύξαι ἐνιαυτὸν κυρίου δεκτόν.
>
> *evangelizare pauperibus . . . praedicare captivis remissionem et caecis visum dimittere confractos in remissionem praedicare annum Domini acceptum et diem retributionis.* (Luke 4:18–19)

298. Brawley, *Luke*, 155.

299. *Tab. Lond. Bloomberg* 44; Tomlin, *Roman London's First Voices*, 152–55. Appendix Chapter 2.

300. *Tab. Lond. Bloomberg* 37; Tomlin, *Roman London's First Voices*, 138–39.

301. Perring, *London in Roman World*, 222–26; cf. Esler, *Community and Gospel in Luke-Acts*, 173.

302. Wolter, *Luke I*, 200; Matthews and Reid, *Luke 1–9*, 131–33.

Implicit in the use of the word "poor" (πτωχός: *pauper*) is reference to "those reduced to total destitution," those who were "beggars, weak, powerless, landless, diseased, naked, hungry and destitute."[303]

By the time our imagined readers had absorbed the teaching of Jesus to his disciples they could have been in no doubt about his concern for the destitute and disdain for the rich. Those who are in extreme poverty and hungry are blessed unlike those who are rich and full now (Luke 6:20, 21, 24, 25). The measure of the ministry of Jesus is evident in the difference he makes to those who have nothing, the blind, the leprosy sufferers, the dead; and in the good news he brings to the poverty-stricken beggar (Luke 7:22). As Jesus sets out for Jerusalem and tells stories on the way, this message is pressed home. From the outset Londinium was a significant urban center of trade which recovered quickly from the devastation of the Boudica revolt. By the second half of the first century it had become a cosmopolitan city with a military presence, home to the provincial administration, with wealthy traders and artisans.[304] There were "dramatic differences between the inhabitants of Londinium in terms of wealth."[305] It was a place of poverty and feasting,[306] of slaves and free, with a trade in slaves involving slaves of some standing.[307] There is evidence of people from the indigenous population living in round houses, perhaps craftworkers moving in to take advantage of the new order of things, or enslaved people brought in to support the extensive building works.[308] As a provincial city the stratification of society evident across the empire would have been to the fore in Londinium: the urban poor of Londinium as of anywhere else "suffered extreme forms of economic, social and political deprivation. For them life was a very grim business."[309]

303. Paulraj, *Food Justice*, 85. See further 84–93 where Paulraj has established this meaning. The Vulgate's choice of *pauper* rather than *mendicus* suggests "the domestication of Luke's meaning began early and is now rampant." Esler, personal comment.

304. Hingley, *Londinium: A Biography*, 57–115; Perring, *London in Roman World*, 86–113.

305. Hingley, *Londinium: A Biography*, 68.

306. Hingley, *Londinium: A Biography*, 106–8.

307. Hingley, *Londinium: A Biography*, 69; Tomlin, "Girl in Question"; Frere et al., *Inscriptions of Roman Britain*, 15: 2443.7.

308. Hingley, *Londinium: A Biography*, chaps. 2–5; Perring, "Recent Advances Roman London," 23–30.

309. Esler, *Community and Gospel in Luke–Acts*, 179. Cf. Woolf, *Ancient Cities*, 398–400; Rowsome, *Heart of the City*, 32.

Alongside evidence of grain stored in building 13 on the 1 Poultry site,[310] we have a tantalizing glimpse of a trade in grain with the local population as one unnamed correspondent appeals to an equal as "lord brother" regarding a purchase of grain,[311] and as Florentinus, the slave of Sextus Cassius, confirms the receipt of two payments from a local farm.[312] Dependence on the surrounding countryside for a continuous supply of grain[313] made Londinium typical of urban centers across the empire: as elsewhere, "the hand of élite social control" was evident in first century Londinium which remained "resolutely alien" with its residents "enjoying lifestyles that were radically different to those of subject populations within the urban hinterland."[314] In such an extractive economy the rich man's accumulation of large surpluses for his own enjoyment "inevitably meant 'an accumulation of misery' for others."[315] Our imagined readers would recognize the folly of the rich man who pulled down his barns and built larger ones when his land produced abundantly. Jesus' warning "to be on your guard against all kinds of greed" (Luke 12:13–21) speaks into a world in which Titus was tempted to work for his own gain at the expense of others.[316] With their considerable wealth the people of the Bloomberg tablets would be challenged by the words of Jesus,

> So therefore, none of you can become my disciple if you do not give up all your possessions.
>
> *οὕτως οὖν πᾶς ἐξ ὑμῶν ὃς οὐκ ἀποτάσσεται πᾶσιν τοῖς ἑαυτοῦ ὑπάρχουσιν οὐ δύναται εἶναί μου μαθητής.*

310. Hingley, *Londinium: A Biography*, 41; Perring, *London in Roman World*, 124–27.

311. *Tab. Lond. Bloomberg* 38. In a note on *fussum* and another on *a Tincori*, Tomlin suggests there is a reference to grain and a hitherto unidentified location possibly associated with Tincomarus, king of the Atrebates (*Roman London's First Voices*, 140). J. N. Adams argues that *fussum*, past participle of *fundo*, "could be used of pouring grain" ("New Vindolanda Tablets," 556–57). Appendix Chapter 2.

312. *Tab. Lond. Bloomberg* 50; Tomlin, *Roman London's First Voices*, 168–69. Appendix Chapter 2.

313. Perring and Brigham, "Londinium and Its Hinterland," 151ff.

314. Perring, "Recent Advances Roman London," 21.

315. Brawley, *Luke*, 131; cf. Matthews and Reid observe that "the man's large landholdings and abundant harvest would set him apart from more than 90 percent of the population that lived in destitute, or near destitute, conditions" (*Luke 10–24*, 395).

316. *Tab. Lond. Bloomberg* 30; Tomlin, *Roman London's First Voices*, 120–23. Appendix Chapter 2.

> *sic ergo omnis ex vobis qui non renuntiat omnibus quae possidet non potest meus esse discipulus.* (Luke 14:33)

The invitation of destitute beggars, the maimed, the blind and the lame to the great feast (Luke 14:15–24) and the contrast between the rich man and Lazarus, the destitute, ulcerated, and hungry beggar[317] at the gate (Luke 16:19–31) leave our imagined readers in no doubt as to the identity of "the poor" and to the challenge facing them in table fellowship and the sharing of goods. In Luke–Acts God's power is set over against "the proud, the powerful and the rich,"[318] while his activity is "on behalf of the lowly and hungry."[319] Richard Pervo suggests that "the ethical focus of Acts is on the use of money."[320] However, as Shelly Matthews argues, "the gospel [and by implication Acts] gives no uniform way to respond personally and does not propose a comprehensive economic system."[321] Instead, Luke–Acts, and especially Acts, offers examples to follow, models to emulate. Whereas "much of Luke teaches by telling . . . Acts generally communicates by showing."[322] It is, therefore, quite possible to imagine our readers following in the footsteps of people from their world of finance, trade and commerce such as Zacchaeus (Luke 19:1–10), Lydia (Acts 16:14, 40), Aquila, Priscilla and Paul (Acts 18:1–3). In the generosity of sharing and of eating with people "of varied social strata" they would not so much be abandoning as redefining the "socio-religious and economic relations" of the world to which they were accustomed.[323] They would take seriously "the community-oriented character of the Way" and "that abhorrence of materialism in the form of greed" condemned by Paul as he quotes Jesus in his speech to the Ephesian elders (Acts 20:32–35).[324] They would be challenged to go into the "roads and lanes" beyond the comfort of the town with its ribbon development

317. Paulraj, *Food Justice*, 87.

318. Green, *Gospel of Luke*, 104.

319. Green, *Gospel of Luke*, 105.

320. Pervo, *Acts*, 19.

321. Matthews and Reid, *Luke 1–9*, 132–33.

322. Pervo, *Acts*, 19.

323. Paulraj, *Food Justice*, 196; Schaberg and Ringe suggest that "Luke shows special interest in the right use of possessions or resources by the wealthy (12:15–21; 16:19–31; 19:1–10)" ("Luke," 507).

324. Maloney and Reimer, *Acts*, 287; for them Acts 22:28 makes plain that Paul's "true status is not based on material wealth or its uses" (*Acts,* 304). Matthews and Reid, *Luke 10–24*, 460–61.

of streets,[325] to engage with those reduced to destitution (Luke 14:23)[326] following the example of Paul's spirit of radical generosity (Acts 20:35).[327]

Reciprocity, Debt and Love for Enemies

No sooner had Jesus spoken of the way the poor and hungry are blessed in contrast to those who are rich and full now, than he went on to speak of love for enemies. It is telling that he immediately sets that command in the context of a social world of which they are very much a part. The command to love your enemies addresses the world of the people of the Bloomberg tablets at two levels. First, theirs is a volatile world where memories of the initial military campaigns of Claudius's conquest are fresh, a world which is all too conscious of the rebellion led by Boudica and the Iceni peoples, the continued suppression of that revolt and the ensuing campaigns to the west and the north.[328] Talk of love for enemies is challenging on the active and contested frontier of the empire. Second, it addresses their world of credit and loan notes. The financial world of first century Londinium is built on lending and credit based on trust. A breakdown of trust and shameful behavior is condemned. Taurus feels justified in complaining to Macrinus his dearest lord, about the way Caturrius had come and taken away beasts of burden:[329] such behavior is not acceptable. When Titus seeks to profit unjustifiably from his loans, he is condemned as shameful.[330] Atticus is anxious that a payment be made promptly implying some delay.[331] Something provoked Bell[. . .]us to respond angrily.[332]

Steeped in the pivotal values of honor and shame, conducting business based on balanced or general reciprocity, and sometimes negative

325. Perring, "Recent Advances Roman London," 25. Cf. de la Bédoyère, *Real Lives of Roman Britain*, 40–41; Perring, *London in Roman World*, 171–79.

326. Paulraj, *Food Justice*, 87.

327. Pervo, *Acts*, 528–29.

328. See Table 1.

329. *Tab. Lond. Bloomberg* 29; Tomlin, *Roman London's First Voices*, 116–19. Appendix Chapter 2.

330. *Tab. Lond. Bloomberg* 30; Tomlin, *Roman London's First Voices*, 120–23. Appendix Chapter 2.

331. *Tab. Lond. Bloomberg* 31; Tomlin, *Roman London's First Voices*, 124–27. Appendix Chapter 2.

332. *Tab. Lond. Bloomberg* 28; Tomlin, *Roman London's First Voices*, 114–15.

reciprocity, our imagined readers of Luke–Acts would encounter a different kind of community among the followers of the Way of Jesus. Bringing together people of different ethnicities and of different strata in society, sharing possessions and eating at the same table, such a community is rooted in the teaching Jesus shares with his disciples in Luke 6:20–49. That it turns on its head many of the assumptions of first century urban life, not least in Londinium, is apparent in the opening blessings and woes (Luke 6:20–26). An alternative kind of community based on the love of enemies[333] finds expression in the words, "Do to others as you would have them do to you" (καθὼς θέλετε ἵνα ποιῶσιν ὑμῖν οἱ ἄνθρωποι ποιεῖτε αὐτοῖς ὁμοίως: *prout vultis ut faciant vobis homines et vos facite illis similiter* Luke 6:31). To imagine this passage being read by people who live in the world of Taurus following the loss of his beasts of burden or Atticus concerned at the non-payment of a loan is to realize that "the notion of giving with expectation to receive, as in 6:31," is as "thoroughly at home" in first century Londinium as in "ancient Mediterranean culture."[334] Jesus goes further: he caricatures the "balanced reciprocity" they were used to (Luke 6:32–34) and replaces it with a "familial reciprocity" that entails a generosity of love that reaches out to enemies too.[335] Such love of enemies amounts to doing good and lending, expecting nothing in return (Luke 6:35). For people of the Bloomberg tablets to belong to a community of followers of the Way of Jesus would be "a counter-cultural existence indeed," for their lives would be "based on an inverted understanding of their social world."[336]

The enemy love envisaged here by Jesus finds expression in the generosity of a forgiveness and a generous giving that makes for a very different kind of community. Such a community binds its members together as "children of the Most High" and mirrors the merciful Father Jesus discloses (Luke 6:35–49). This is what "comprises the ethical identity of Christian communities."[337] If it turns on its head the balanced reciprocity evident in the Bloomberg tablets, it even more clearly rejects the negative reciprocity

333. Brawley, *Luke*, 84–86; Matthews and Reid, *Luke 1–9*, 206–13.

334. Brawley, *Luke*, 85.

335. See above, Chapter 2, n. 189. Cf. Crook, *Reconceptualizing Conversion*, 54–59; Stegemann and Stegemann, *Jesus Movement*, 34–36.

336. Green, *Gospel of Luke*, 273. Matthews and Reid suggest that these are precisely the people addressed by Luke: "Luke's intended audience is the more well-to-do, like Theophilus (1:4), and Luke continually stresses that discipleship involves divestment and sharing" (*Luke 1–9*, 203).

337. Wolter, *Luke I*, 282.

that according to Cassius Dio contributed to the exploitation of the local population and the Boudica revolt.[338] The inability to pay back unreasonably large loans had led to the enslavement of local peoples, their resentment, and their subsequent revolt. Here we glimpse that kind of slavery consequent upon the inability to repay debts characteristic of urban life in the Mediterranean world.[339]

Such generosity and love of enemies is to the fore in the teaching Jesus shares with his disciples (Luke 6:20–49) and shapes their understanding of community (Acts 2:44–45; 4:32–37); it is also central to the prayer he invites them to make their own: "forgive us our sins, for we ourselves forgive everyone indebted to us" (*καὶ γὰρ αὐτοὶ ἀφίομεν παντὶ ὀφείλοντι ἡμῖν· καὶ μὴ εἰσενέγκῃς ἡμᾶς εἰς πειρασμόν: dimitte nobis peccata nostra siquidem et ipsi dimittimus omni debenti*[340] *nobis* Luke 11:4). The forgiveness of those who are in debt and "release from the earthly shackles of indebtedness"[341] would be a challenge for our imagined readers as they faced the kind of problems experienced by Taurus, Atticus and Bell[. . .]us.

Patrons and Clients, Slaves and Masters

Patronage involving that kind of "general reciprocity" that amounted to a "system of social control" whereby some were subservient to others,[342] was as evident in the dealings of merchants and traders in first century Londinium as in the eastern Mediterranean. It had to do with "the reciprocal exchange of goods and services" and involved "a relationship that was personal and of some duration," a relationship that was unequal "between parties of differing status" and so could develop into exploitation.[343] The *chirographum* in which Tibullus promises a part payment of 105 denarii to Gratus may have been simply between the two of them. Tibullus, however, identifies himself as the freedman of Venustus (*Venusti l(ibertus)*) and

338. Cassius Dio, *Roman History*, LXII.2, Vol VIII, 83.

339. Esler, *Community and Gospel in Luke-Acts*, 174. Cf. Bradley, *Slavery and Society*; Woolf, *Rome*, 97–101.

340. *Debeo* occurs in *Tab. Lond. Bloomberg* 35, 44, 53, 55, 76.

341. Oakman, "Jesus and Agrarian Palestine," 80; cf. Matthews and Reid, *Luke 10–24*, 365.

342. Crook, *Reconceptualizing Conversion*, 59–66; Stegemann and Stegemann, *Jesus Movement*, 34–36.

343. Batten, "God in James," 50; Crook, *Reconceptualizing Conversion*, 60–66.

Gratus as the freedman of Spurius (*Grato <S>puri l(iberto)*) suggesting they were both acting "as agents or partners" for their erstwhile masters who were now their patrons.[344] While able to engage in activities open to men born free, "a freedman had a particular legal status": maintaining social and financial links between a freedman and his patron was common practice.[345] We see here the unequal relationship between the patron and his freedman and at the same time the equal relationship between the two patrons and between the two freedmen.

Slaves had a different status and, as across the empire, were involved in the commerce and business of Londinium in various ways: as *arcarii* simply looking after cash as an assayer or money changer; *actores* acting as agent for their master in managing finances; or *dispensatores* running a business in parallel with their master, possibly advancing interest bearing loans.[346] It appears that the slave of ?M(arci) S[a]luii M[. . .] was acting as agent for his master in writing a *chirographum*; a letter enquires whether Vialicus the freedman of Secundio (*Secundionis liberto Vialico*) will accept the loan note.[347] As a slave, Florentinus was able to write and conduct business on behalf of his master, Sextus Cassius [. . .]tus.[348] Narcissus works as a slave on behalf of his master, Rogatus.[349] Montanus, "slave of the august emperor," in turn had "an assistant slave, Vegetus, (*Vegetus Montani imperatoris Aug(usti) ser(vi) Iucun|diani vic(arius)* who was able to purchase Fortunata, the enslaved girl who was in "good health and warranted not to be liable to wander or run away" (*sanam tradi|tam esse erronem fugitivam non esse |praestari*) for the large sum of 600 denarii.[350]

344. *Tab. Lond. Bloomberg* 44; Tomlin, *Roman London's First Voices*, 154. Appendix Chapter 2.

345. Andreau, *Banking and Business*, 64. Cf. Bradley, *Slavery and Society*, 77; Johnston, *Roman Law*, 52–54.

346. Andreau, *Banking and Business*, 64–65. Cf. Harrill, "Paul and Slavery," 302–3; Bradley, *Slavery and Society*, 75. See above, Chapter 2, n. 117.

347. *Tab. Lond. Bloomberg* 27; Tomlin, *Roman London's First Voices*, 112–13. Appendix Chapter 2

348. *Tab. Lond. Bloomberg* 50; Tomlin, *Roman London's First Voices*, 168–69. Appendix Chapter 2.

349. *Tab. Lond. Bloomberg* 55; Tomlin, *Roman London's First Voices*, 178–81. Appendix Chapter 2.

350. Tomlin, "Girl in Question," discovered in excavations at the adjacent 1 Poultry in 1994.

The alertness of the slaves who are awaiting their master's return from a wedding banquet leads to "the inversion of normal master-slave hierarchies of dominance"[351] as the master serves the slaves at the table (Luke 12:35–40). It is, however, a momentary act that does not lead to the abandonment of those hierarchies but instead to a greater alertness. The ensuing parable contrasts the "faithful and prudent manager" (ὁ πιστὸς οἰκονόμος ὁ φρόνιμος: *fidelis dispensator et prudens*) who is put in charge of his master's slaves with the slave who in such circumstances abuses the slaves, men and women, set under him (Luke 12:41–48). The challenge to our imagined readers is not so much to invert the hierarchies of their world as to live with fidelity and honor in the everyday world they knew well.[352]

There is an assumption in the dealings of those who are involved in such business arrangements that they will act with honor: that assumption gives weight to the parable of the dishonest manager in Luke 16:1–13. A rich man has a manager who has to give an "accounting" of his "management" (τὸν λόγον τῆς οἰκονομίας: *rationem vilicationis*). In anticipation of being dismissed as a result of charges that he was "squandering" (διασκορπίζων: *dissipasset)* the rich man's property, he writes off a portion of what is owed by a number of his master's debtors, inviting each to take their "bill" (τὰ γράμματα: *cautionem*). Fitzmyer's suggestion[353] that the manager was not acting dishonestly but rather arranging to repay that part of the excessive interest he had added to the loan, is rejected by Kloppenborg who observes that in contemporary loan documents from Egypt "the contract is always framed as an agreement between the lender and the borrower, even when, as is frequently the case, the lender's agent actually negotiated the contract."[354] The Bloomberg tablets demonstrate that those practices had reached the far frontiers of the western empire by the middle of the first century CE, adding weight to Kloppenborg's argument. Our imagined readers would be at home in the world of this parable.[355]

351. Brawley, *Luke*, 133.

352. Brawley, *Luke*, 134. Contrast Matthews and Reid: "insofar as this passage utilizes the corrupted and violent relationships endemic to slavery as rhetorical devices it is difficult to elicit uplifting theological insights from them" (*Luke 10–24*, 403).

353. Fitzmyer, *Luke X–XXIV*, 1097–98.

354. Kloppenborg, "Dishonored Master," 481.

355. Matthews and Reid, *Luke 10–24*, 456. Contrast Harrill who argues that the scene depicted here is "*literary*, not social description" and is based on Roman comedic writing about "the *servus* Callidus (clever or wily slave)" (*Slaves in the New Testament*, 66–83).

First, the relationship of patron and agent between the rich man (πλούσιος: *dives*) and his manager (οἰκονόμος: *vilicus*), is one that would be familiar to Tibulus, the freedman of Venustus as he promised to pay Gratus, the freedman of Spurius, acknowledging that the loan could be sold on to someone else.[356] This is precisely the kind of person envisaged in the story with access to "his master's wealth" who "acted as his agent in business affairs."[357]

Second, the manager is tasked with giving the rich man "an accounting (λόγος: *ratio*) of his "management" (τῆς οἰκονομίας: *vilicationis*). That detailed written records were kept of business dealings was something that Crispus took for granted as he kept an account (*ratio*) of the sale of beer.[358] He was not alone: eight of the Bloomberg tablets are "accounts."[359] Traders such as these would know precisely what was entailed in keeping an account of their business dealings.

Third the manager then calls for the bill (τὰ γράμματα: *cautionem*) to be produced. A legal term used in Justinian's *Digest*, a *cautio* was read at a hearing before Aemilius Papinian, praetorian prefect and jurist, using phrases (emboldened) Atticus uses in promising to pay Narcissus, the slave of Rogatus:[360]

> **I, Lucius Titius, have written that I have received** (*Lucius Titius scripsi me accepisse*) from Publius Maevius fifteen aureii paid to me from his home as a loan for consumption. These fifteen are **to be given in best coin** (*proba recte dari*) on the first of next month; for this, Publius Maevius has stipulated, and **I, Lucius Titius, have promised** (*spopondi ego Lucius Titius*). If on the day above written the sum has not been paid and given to Publius Maevius **or to him to whom the matter shall then belong** (*eive ad quem ea res pertinebit*) or no satisfaction has been made on its account, then, for as long as I thereafter take to pay, for every thirty days one denarius for every hundred shall be paid by way of penalty;

356. *Tab. Lond. Bloomberg* 44; Tomlin, *Roman London's First Voices*, 152–55. Appendix Chapter 2.

357. Green, *Gospel of Luke*, 590.

358. *Tab. Lond. Bloomberg* 72; Tomlin, *Roman London's First Voices*, 222–25.

359. *Tab. Lond. Bloomberg* 69–76; Tomlin, *Roman London's First Voices*, 216–33.

360. *Tab. Lond. Bloomberg* 55; Tomlin, *Roman London's First Voices*, 178–81. Appendix Chapter 2.

> for this, Publius Maevius has stipulated, and I, Lucius Titius, have promised.[361]

As we imagine people of the Bloomberg tablets reading this parable, we see immediately that "it has been drawn simply and directly from everyday life, from taken-for-granted suppositions about 'the way the world works.'"[362] All is not well with their world, however: Taurus had been cheated by Catarrius and was fearful of the loss of a significant investment in beasts of burden;[363] late settlement of an account, possibly by an intermediary, is worrying Atticus;[364] and he is not alone in being concerned about possible non-payment of outstanding debts.[365] Most significant is the warning a friend gives Titus not to "appear shameful" lest he damage his own affairs. It seems as if accusations about Titus had been circulating "through the whole market."[366] Whether they were justified or not, Titus is given the chance to set things right. In the Bloomberg tablets we witness the messiness of a business world where all does not always work to plan, where a manager of injustice (οἰκονόμος τῆς ἀδικίας: *vilicus iniquitatis*) could be singled out and where questions could be raised about the use of wealth arising from injustice (μαμωνᾶ τῆς ἀδικίας: *mamona iniquitatis*). It is in the context of that complexity that our imagined reading can throw light on what is a problematic parable. It neither presents the manager as a straightforward example to be followed,[367] nor simply as a representative of an extractive economic system to be rejected.[368] It is not so much a call for economic redistribution[369] as a guide for those navigating the Way of

361. *Justinian Digest* XII.1.40, "*Justinian Digest*" 2023; Watson 1998, 363. Wording similar to *Tab. Lond. Bloomberg* 55 is emboldened, and the Latin added. Appendix Chapter 2.

362. Green, *Gospel of Luke*, 589. Cf. Kloppenborg, "Dishonored Master," 486.

363. *Tab. Lond. Bloomberg* 29: Tomlin, *Roman London's First Voices*, 116–19. Appendix Chapter 2.

364. *Tab. Lond. Bloomberg* 31: Tomlin, *Roman London's First Voices*, 124–27. Appendix Chapter 2.

365. *Tab. Lond. Bloomberg* 35: Tomlin, *Roman London's First Voices*, 134–35. Appendix Chapter 2.

366. *Tab. Lond. Bloomberg* 30: Tomlin, *Roman London's First Voices*, 120–23. Appendix Chapter 2.

367. Wolter, *Luke II*, 260–71.

368. Brawley, *Luke*, 155–57.

369. Green, *Gospel of Luke*, 588–97.

Jesus while involved in that world of business. Perhaps there is an element of humor in the telling of the story.[370]

The sympathies of patrons, such as Venustus and Spurius, might lie with the wealthy man, while the sympathies of agents such as the freedmen, Tibullus and Gratus, might lie with the manager.[371] The manager's squandering of the rich man's property was the kind of shameful behavior Titus had been criticized for.[372] Titus, however, had been warned to change his ways; within the parable the agent is given no such warning. Perhaps the rich man, like other rich men in Luke's narrative,[373] was the one who was acting shamefully.

Our imagined readers would recognize the way the manager was seeking to enter into a reciprocal arrangement with the debtors he was helping in the hope of being received into their "homes" (δέξωνταί με εἰς τοὺς οἴκους αὐτῶν: *recipiant me in domos suas*). His generosity is predicated on the balanced reciprocity that expects something in return. The likes of Ammonicus, in debt for the sizeable sum of 30 denarii,[374] might feel sympathy for the way the debtors are treated by the agent. We can imagine our readers attributing to the rich man the observation that the manager had acted "shrewdly" (φρονίμως: *prudenter*) in securing a future for himself based on an anticipated welcome into the homes of those he had helped.[375]

Jesus' teaching, beginning at verse 8b, and not, as some suggest at verse 8a,[376] would speak directly to our imagined readers. It serves as a commendation of the likes of the traders and merchants of Londinium: as children of this age they are indeed more prudent (φρονιμώτεροι: *prudentiores*) in their dealings with their contemporaries than the children of light. Making reciprocal relationships even by means of wealth that comes from injustice will stand them in good stead for the future (ποιήσατε φίλους ἐκ τοῦ μαμωνᾶ τῆς ἀδικίας, ἵνα ὅταν ἐκλίπῃ δέξωνται ὑμᾶς εἰς τὰς αἰωνίους σκηνάς: *facite vobis amicos de mamona iniquitatis ut cum defeceritis recipiant*

370. Tannehill, *Luke*, 247.

371. *Tab. Lond. Bloomberg* 44; Tomlin, *Roman London's First Voices*, 152–55. Appendix Chapter 2.

372. *Tab. Lond. Bloomberg* 30; Tomlin, *Roman London's First Voices*, 120–23. Appendix Chapter 2.

373. Luke 12:13–21; 14:12; 16:19–31; 18:18–25; 19:1–10; 20:45–47; 21:1–4.

374. *Tab. Lond. Bloomberg* 76; Tomlin, *Roman London's First Voices*, 232–33.

375. Green, *Gospel of Luke*, 588–94; Fitzmyer, *Luke X–XXIV*, 1094–99; Brawley, *Luke*, 151–54.

376. Wolter, *Luke II*, 260–71.

vos in aeterna tabernacula Luke 16:9). Is it at this point that the humor comes to the fore? Our imagined readers would see themselves in these characters and initially take heart, sensing the reassurance they need. One could imagine them enjoying the fun of the story. The rich man, the manager and the three debtors are characteristic of an economic system that spans the empire; they too would struggle to negotiate their way through the complex world of first century Londinium. It is at that moment of reassurance that the challenge comes; as followers of the Way they are also "children of light." The teaching of Jesus that follows speaks directly into the world they knew so well: "whoever is faithful (πιστὸς: *fidelis*) in a very little is faithful also in much; and whoever is dishonest (ἄδικος: *iniquus*) in a very little is dishonest also in much" (Luke 16:10–13). The traders and merchants of Londinium would know full well the significance of those words in their world. The challenge is for them to negotiate the often messy world of patronage, honor, and shame of first century Londinium with fidelity and honor.[377] More than that they are to recognize that a slave cannot serve two masters. It is not possible to be a slave to God and to such wealth (οὐ δύνασθε θεῷ δουλεύειν καὶ μαμωνᾷ: *non potestis Deo servire et mamonae*, Luke 16:13b).

The force of this challenge is pressed home as our imagined readers go on to read of people who were "lovers of money" (φιλάργυροι: *avari* Luke 16:14) and of "the rich man (πλούσιος: *dives*) who was dressed in purple and fine linen, and who feasted sumptuously every day" in stark contrast to the destitute beggar (πτωχὸς: *mendicus*)[378] named Lazarus, "covered with sores," who lay at his gate (Luke 16:19–31). The reversal of roles at death is a reversal of status measured in terms of wealth and the lack of it: during his lifetime the rich man had received his "good things" (τὰ ἀγαθά: *bona*) "and Lazarus, in like manner, evil things (τὰ κακά: *mala*)." Such wealth could only be accumulated at the expense of the extreme poverty encountered in Lazarus. While Brawley suggests this was nothing less than a reversal of the all too prevalent "social hierarchies of dominance,"[379] our imagined readers could equally see it as Luke's challenge not to ignore the beggars

377. Brawley, *Luke*, 151–54; Kuecker, "*Luke*," 148–50; Green, *Gospel of Luke*, 588–97.

378. *mendicus*, meaning "a destitute person, beggar": *OLD*, 1098 used in the Vulgate here and at Luke 16:22 for πτωχὸς. Each other instance of πτωχὸς in Luke (4:18; 6:20; 7:22; 14:13, 21; 18:22; 19:8) is translated by the weaker *pauper*, meaning "poor," *OLD*, 1314.

379. Brawley, *Luke*, 156. Cf. 111.

they encountered in Londinium but to give them a place at the table in the community of the Way.[380]

In Zacchaeus (Luke 19:1–10) they meet with someone who responds to the challenge of Jesus and yet remains within their world of finance. While there is no mention of taxation in the Bloomberg tablets, the traders and merchants of Londinium would be able to recognize fair and honorable dealing in the world of business. When Zacchaeus promises to give half of his possessions to the destitute, he goes on to say, "and if I have defrauded (ἐσυκοφάντησα: *defraudavi*) anyone of anything, I will pay back four times as much" (Luke 19:8). Our imagined readers might see in Zacchaeus's practice that kind of disgraceful behavior that was in danger of bringing shame to Titus; they might see in Zacchaeus's changed behavior the kind of transformation, leading to restored honor, encouraged by the writer of the letter to Titus.[381] The consequence of that change in Zacchaeus's practice is the salvation (σωτηρία: *salus*) that comes to his house.[382] Our imagined readers might envisage such a salvation in the context of their everyday lives. In Zacchaeus they would see someone who became a follower of the Way of Jesus and sought to navigate the world of finance in the light of that commitment: "the point here is that it is possible for a rich person to experience salvation."[383]

As followers of the Way involved in the world of reciprocity and patronage, and of slaves and masters, they too might well find themselves arguing "as to which one of them was the greatest" (Luke 9:46–48). This after all was the mindset that shaped the social stratification of their world. Within the community of those following the Way of Jesus, however, things were to be different. Setting a little child (παιδίον: *puerum*) by his side, Jesus says that "whoever welcomes this child in my name welcomes me, and whoever welcomes me welcomes the one who sent me." In one of the more

380. Matthews and Reid argue that "One step toward the kind of conversion called for in the parable is to relate to poor persons as individuals with names, not an anonymous group 'the poor'" (*Luke 10–24*, 469). See below, *Festivals and Feasting*.

381. *Tab. Lond. Bloomberg* 30; Tomlin, *Roman London's First Voices*, 120–23. Appendix Chapter 2.

382. Wolter, *Luke II*, 349.

383. Matthews and Reid suggest that "Zacchaeus's story provides an answer to the question posed to Jesus in the episode with the rich ruler after Jesus remarks on the difficulty of a rich person entering the *basileia* of God." For Luke "riches are an obstacle to the *basileia* of God" as in 1:53; 6:24; 12:16–21; 14:33; 16:13, 19–23; 18:25. They do not, however, exclude the wealthy, but confront them with difficult choices (*Luke 10–24*, 507). Cf. Matthews and Reid, *Luke 1–9*, 131–33, 202–3.

fragmentary Bloomberg tablets *puer* is probably used as an informal term for "slave."[384] Among the followers of the Way of Jesus "the one who possesses the smallest prestige stands at the top" of the social ladder.[385] In Jesus' ensuing comment a "counterworld is constructed, which leads in this case to the ascriptions of social status being turned into their opposite":[386] "for the least among all of you is the greatest" (ὁ γὰρ μικρότερος ἐν πᾶσιν ὑμῖν ὑπάρχων οὗτός ἐστιν μέγας: *minor est inter omnes vos hic maior est*).

So imbued are the disciples with the cultural norms that are also evident in first century Londinium, however, that they continue to argue. A dispute arose among them as to who was the greatest at the close of the Passover meal Jesus shared with them (Luke 22:24–30). On this occasion Jesus draws on those cultural norms our imagined readers in Londinium would recognize, explicitly the way "patronage offered many models and metaphors for imperial rule."[387] He speaks of the way "the kings of the Gentiles lord it over them; and those in authority over them are called benefactors" (εὐεργέται: *benefici*). In their "patron-client relationships" benefactors like kings expected something in return, not least a recognition of high status and honor.[388] At this point, Jesus directly addresses the community of disciples around the table as he says, "but not so with you; rather the greatest among you (ἐν ὑμῖν: *in vobis*) must become like the youngest, and the leader like one who serves." After contrasting the one who serves at table and the one who is served, Jesus goes on to say that he is among them as "one who serves" (ὁ διακονῶν: *ministrator*). Jesus identifies with the one of low status, the one who serves, and expects that of his followers too.[389]

Luke writes in such a way that our imagined readers would recognize that Jesus "uses normal social protocols" from their world "in order

384. *Tab, Lond. Bloomberg* 43: Tomlin, *Roman London's First Voices*, 150; *OLD*, 1515. In a Leicester curse tablet, listing the names of twenty slaves in a courtyard house, the Greek παιδίον comes into Latin in the word *paedogogium* referring to the slave quarters: Tomlin, "Paedagogium and Septizonium"; Savani et al., *Roman Leicester*, 49.

385. Wolter, *Luke I*, 405.

386. Wolter, *Luke I*, 405–6.

387. Woolf, *Rome*, 96.

388. Brawley, *Luke*, 188; contrast Batten who suggests that the distinction between patronage and benefaction disappeared only in the late Roman Empire ("God in James," 51–54). Matthews and Reid suggest that Luke here adopts the perspective of an ancient elite discourse, wherein "benefactors are called not to become literal slaves but rather to understand themselves as metaphorical 'servants to all' while retaining their positions of 'authority over'" (*Luke 10–24*, 574–75).

389. Brawley, *Luke*, 189.

to insist that standard categories will not do"[390] within the community of those who follow the Way. It is within that community that in the context of the arguments over greatness and of the parable of the rich man and Lazarus "Jesus turns the social pyramid upside down."[391] At the same time, within the world of trade and commerce our imagined readers would be challenged to conduct their lives with that fidelity and honor their world expected.[392]

Generosity and Sharing

Concern for the destitute and disdain for the rich, the rejection of balanced reciprocity as a response to debt and the inversion of the social pyramids of patronage and of slavery find expression in the lives of the first followers of the Way of Jesus in Acts as they come together and "have all things in common" (εἶχον ἅπαντα κοινὰ: *habebant omnia communia* Acts 2:44). That meant "they would sell their possessions and goods and distribute the proceeds to all, as any had need." (καὶ τὰ κτήματα καὶ τὰς ὑπάρξεις ἐπίπρασκον καὶ διεμέριζον αὐτὰ πᾶσιν καθότι ἄν τις χρείαν εἶχεν: *possessiones et substantias vendebant et dividebant illa omnibus prout cuique opus erat* Acts 2:45). The sharing of possessions to meet the needs of all was something that would challenge our imagined readers of Acts within the community of those followers of the Way. Among these first followers of the Way "no one claimed private ownership of any possessions, but everything they owned was held in common." (οὐδὲ εἷς τι τῶν ὑπαρχόντων αὐτῷ ἔλεγεν ἴδιον εἶναι ἀλλ' ἦν αὐτοῖς ἅπαντα κοινά: *nec quisquam eorum quae possidebant aliquid suum esse dicebat sed erant illis omnia communia* Acts 4:32). Whether this was an ideal to work towards or an account of the beginnings from which there was inevitable decline, "such counter-cultural values continued to pervade ancient Christianity."[393]

This exemplifies the "radical generosity" which, together with "enemy love," the followers of the Way of Jesus are challenged to adopt. In

390. Green, *Gospel of Luke*, 767.

391. Green, *Gospel of Luke*, 391–92.

392. Matthews and Reid suggest this is Luke's purpose here (*Luke 10–24*, 575).

393. Keener, *Acts*, 173–77; Aymer maintains this amounted to "a political religious act that issued a strong challenge to the status quo" ("Acts Women's Bible Commentary," 537). Maloney and Reimer suggest the author "is certainly proposing a model for second-century Christian life in the urban centers of the empire as he knew them" (*Acts*, 40).

his social identity commentary on Luke and Acts,[394] Aaron Kuecker suggests that "Jesus' followers are invited to participate in Jesus' identity, as children of the Most High, particularly as they exercise enemy love and radical generosity."[395] Whereas he suggests that will result in their "social dislocation,"[396] our imagined readers might see that Acts follows on from Luke in giving them, along with "the most excellent Theophilus," the assurance that this is a practical course of action that they can be justified in following. Nonetheless, we can imagine the scale of the challenge for traders and merchants from Londinium drawn to follow the Way of Jesus. The social implications of "the countercultural values" within the community of the first followers of the Way of Jesus would be immense for the likes of Tibullus, Gratus, Vialicus and the unnamed slave of Marcus Salvius.

There are, however, people within the narrative of Luke–Acts they can look to who had risen to the challenge. Key to a "radical generosity" which meant that "there was not a needy person among them" (ἐνδεής τις ἦν ἐν αὐτοῖς: *quisquam egens erat inter illos*) was the distribution "to each as any had need" (διεδίδετο δνvvvv ἑκάστῳ καθότι ἄν τις χρείαν εἶχεν: *dividebantur autem singulis prout cuique opus erat* Acts 4:35). The attempt of Lucius Julius Bellicus to resolve the ownership of the five-acre wood Verlucionium suggests that the ownership of property had been clearly defined in mid-first-century Londinium, as it was across the empire,[397] and that it could subsequently be the subject of legal proceedings. It is quite possible that it had been acquired forcibly from the local people.[398] The generosity of Joseph of Cyprus might well be an inspiration to them. It was not that he had given all that he possessed: rather, he had "sold a field that belonged to him (ὑπάρχοντος αὐτῷ ἀγροῦ πωλήσας: *cum haberet agrum vendidit*) and then brought the money and laid it at the apostles' feet" (Acts 4.37). The generosity of Ananias and Sapphira might also have been an inspiration had it not been for their deceit. Ananias too had, with Sapphira his wife "sold a piece of property" (σὺν Σαπφίρῃ τῇ γυναικὶ αὐτοῦ ἐπώλησεν κτῆμα: *cum Saffira uxore sua vendidit agrum* Acts 5:1); however, with her knowledge he

394. Kuecker, "*Luke*"; Kuecker, "*Acts*."

395. Kuecker, "*Acts*," 211.

396. Kuecker, "*Acts*," 213–14.

397. Esler, *Babatha's Orchard*, 109–75, 241–53; cf. Perring, *London in Roman World*, 179.

398. *RIB* 2443.19 Tomlin, "Five Acre Wood." Cf. du Plessis who argues it was part of a detailed land survey for tax purposes ("Provincial Law in Britannia," 14).

"kept back some of the proceeds and brought only a part and laid it at the feet of the apostles." Ivoni Richter Reimer cites Judean papyri bearing the signatures of women in property ownership and the use of legal documents with an inner and outer text to suggest that the phrase "with Sapphira his wife" implies that Sapphira had a stake in the property and would have signed the document.[399] Consequently, Sapphira is complicit with Ananias in a shared decision to deprive the community of followers of the Way part of what they had committed to share.[400] What is at stake in the narrative is the deceit of both of them as Ananias "with his wife's knowledge kept back some of the proceeds" (καὶ ἐνοσφίσατο ἀπὸ τῆς τιμῆς, συνειδυίης καὶ τῆς γυναικός: *et fraudavit de pretio agri conscia uxore sua et adferens partem* Acts 5:2).[401] When exposed, that prompts a shame our imagined readers would recognize.[402] Were it not for that deceit Joseph of Cyprus and Ananias and Sapphira might have modelled the kind of generosity that would have been possible for them to emulate, even if it would be a challenge.[403]

The world we glimpse in the Bloomberg tablets is a world of trade and commerce in which property is owned and in which careful records of the sale of property are kept.[404] Among the followers of the Way in Jerusalem, there was "a daily distribution of food" to ensure the needs of all were met (ἐν τῇ διακονίᾳ τῇ καθημερινῇ: *in ministerio cotidiano*): that called for the kind of effective management of funds (διακονεῖν τραπέζαις: *ministrare mensis*) our imagined readers were used to and could emulate (Acts 6:2–7).[405] As in Luke so in Acts, community is established through ministry to the destitute (Luke 4:18; 7:22; 14:13, 21; 16:22–23; 18:22; 19:8), and the needy (Acts 4:35; 6:1–6; 11:29–30; 14:17). That it was possible to remain within the world with which they were familiar and yet at the same time adopt an identity that was countercultural is suggested as the narrative of Acts unfolds, not least in its reference to householders and artisans.[406]

399. Reimer, *Women in Acts*, 5–6. On such Judean papyri see Esler, *Babatha's Orchard*; *Dead Sea Legal Papyri*; *Reading Matthew by the Dead Sea*; *Righteousness of Joseph*.

400. On Sapphira see Reimer, *Women in Acts*, 2–29.

401. C. K. Barrett, *Acts Volume 1*, 262; Spencer, *Journeying through Acts*, 66; Witherington, *Acts*, 216.

402. *Tab. Lond. Bloomberg* 28, 29, 30, 35, 44, 55; see above, Chapter 2, nn. 179, 180.

403. Alexander, "Acts Oxford Commentary," 1034; Alexander, *Acts People's Commentary*, 47.

404. *RIB* 2443.19Tomlin, "Five Acre Wood."

405. See above, Chapter 2, *Keeping Accounts*.

406. See above, Chapter 2, *Occupation and Location*.

These are people of similar social strata to the traders and merchants of first century Londinium and the people they dealt with: as followers of the Way of Jesus they take seriously its countercultural values. Their stories offer assurance to our imagined readers that it was possible for them to follow the Way of Jesus.[407]

This "radical generosity" found expression in the collection for those followers of the Way adversely affected by famine in *Iudaea*.[408] It was "according to their ability" (*καθὼς εὐπορεῖτό τις*: *prout quis habebat*) that each "would send relief" (*διακονίαν πέμψαι*: *ministerium mittere*) supporting the collection organized by Barnabas and Saul (Acts 11:27–30). The delivery of another such collection personally led to Paul's arrest in Jerusalem (Acts 24:17). To give expecting nothing in return was a departure from the balanced reciprocity that characterized the dealings of the people of the Bloomberg tablets and defied "conventional sociocultural boundaries":[409] but it was eminently do-able by followers of the Way of Jesus who included in their number people who could be recognized among the traders and merchants of first century Londinium. It was this "radical generosity" that had been to the fore in Paul's words to the Ephesian elders as he quoted Jesus (Acts 20:33–35),[410] and was now in evidence as Publius, the land-owning "leading man of the island" (*τῷ πρώτῳ τῆς νήσου principis insulae*) of Malta saw to it that as Paul and his companions set sail people "put on board all the provisions" that were needed (*ἀναγομένοις ἐπέθεντο τὰ πρὸς τὰς χρείας*: *et navigantibus inposuerunt quae necessaria errant*, Acts 28:7–10). Whether this is a historical narrative,[411] or a "remarkably idyllic" text[412] it is "redolent with the language of benefaction, friendship, and reciprocity, the lubricants of Greco-Roman urban society"[413] and so connects with our imagined readers. Following the Way of Jesus may have been countercultural, but it was something that could draw people of the standing of Tibullus, Gratus and others of first century Londinium.

407. Schaberg and Ringe, "Luke," 496, speak of "an unrelieved tension" existing in Luke, and by implication Acts, "between the ideal and the accommodation, the radical attitude toward wealth and the moderate attitude."

408. Kuecker, "Acts," 231.

409. Spencer, *Journeying through Acts*, 132.

410. See above, Chapter 2, *Reciprocity, Debt and Love for Enemies*; cf. Maloney and Reimer, *Acts*, 287, 304; Pervo, *Acts*, 528–29.

411. Keener, *Acts*, 611–16.

412. Pervo, *Acts*, 671.

413. Pervo, *Acts*, 672.

Conclusion: Negotiating the Way with a Radical Generosity

With that "inward ear" of the imagination and the adaptation of archival ethnography we explored in Chapter 1, we have discovered clues that have enabled us to hear the voices of the people of the Bloomberg tablets. We are now in a position to draw conclusions that are justifiable in the context of mid-first-century Londinium and the discovery beside the Walbrook of so many wax tablets produced by merchants and traders, informed by a careful study of the tablets themselves, and warranted by close attention to the text of Luke–Acts.

The world of Luke–Acts is recognizable to the people of the Bloomberg tablets. It was a world of honor and shame, of property and debt, of fairness and corruption in trade and commerce, of patronage and slavery, set within a framework of law and of justice. And yet as we imagine Luke–Acts through the eyes of the people of the Bloomberg tablets we cannot help but see the many points at which the teachings of Jesus are countercultural, inverting their understanding of rich and poor, reciprocity and patronage. It is a world in which God brings down the powerful and lifts up the lowly, a world in which concern for the destitute and disdain for the rich find expression among the first followers of the Way of Jesus in sharing, having all things in common and meeting the needs of all. Our imagined readers from Londinium and its world of finance and commerce would find reassurance in Luke–Acts that people of like standing had from the first been counted among the followers of the Way of Jesus. At the same time, they would have been challenged to negotiate their everyday world with a radical generosity that was indeed countercultural.

Figure 9. Vindolanda as it is today.[1] The rectangular later stone fort in the shape of a playing card has four gates (N, S, E, W). The west gate (W) links the fort with the Vicus, the civilian settlement to the west (e). In the center is the *principia* (b), the large headquarters building, at the heart of which is the *aedes*, the shrine where the cohort's standards were guarded. Beyond is the *praetorium* (a), the home of the commanding officer, his wife, children and slaves. Towards the north are the barrack blocks (d), each for a century of eighty soldiers. The large area at the northern end of each is for the centurion and his staff. Each of the ten smaller pairs of rooms is the *contubernium* where each unit of eight soldiers has their sleeping quarters and storage space. Next to the West Gate are the grain stores (c). Excavations from the 1970s to the south of the west wall revealed a sequence of earlier wooden forts, the first (I, marked with dots) the same size as the visible stone fort and in roughly the same location. The second, (II/III, marked with dashes), almost doubled in size, and turned by ninety degrees. That fort was enlarged again and extended to the west (IV/V, marked with lines). The excavation trenches, to the south of the west wall, were at the location of the wooden *praetorium* of the enlarged Period II and III forts, yielding many of the ink-on-wood tablets; and of the barrack blocks, workshops, and South Gate of the even larger Periods IV and V forts. © The Vindolanda Trust.

1. "Vindolanda Trust"; "Vindolanda Fact-File Roman Forts"; R. Birley, *Vindolanda: Roman Frontier Fort*, colored plate 6, 52, 64, 93, 102, 108.

CHAPTER 3

Imagining Luke–Acts in a Military Community

Through the Eyes of the People of the Vindolanda Tablets

> "To recreate the world behind the ruin in the land, to reanimate the people behind the . . . fragment of the past: this is the work of the archaeological imagination."
>
> —Michael Shanks, *The Archaeological Imagination*

Introducing the People of the Vindolanda Tablets

On 18 May sometime in the late 80s or early 90s CE *cohors I Tungrorum*, based at Vindolanda, was under the command of Iulius Verecundus. Of the 752 men (including six centurions), 456 (including five centurions) were absent: forty-six were serving as guards of the governor; 337 (including two centurions) were at the office of Ferox at Coria; six were outside the province (including one centurion), nine were going ahead into Gaul (including one centurion), eleven were in York to collect pay, and forty-five at unspecified locations; one centurion was in Londinium and an individual soldier elsewhere. Only 296 (including one centurion) were resident in Vindolanda; of those, thirty-one were not fit for service: fifteen were sick, six were wounded and ten were suffering from inflammation of the eyes.[2]

2. *Tab. Vindol. II* 154. Appendix Chapter 3. Difficulties in the interpretation of this tablet underline the importance of reading the transcript and translation alongside the Introduction and the Commentary and Notes. Some figures are difficult to read, the references to locations outside the province, in Gaul and in York, are particularly difficult to

They played a key role in what had become the northern frontier zone of the province of Britannia. The decade following the Boudica revolt had seen the consolidation of the Roman presence in the southeast. As Vespasian came to power, three governors effectively completed the conquest of Britannia: Cerialis (71–73/4 CE) subdued the Brigantes, Julius Frontinus (73/74–77/78 CE) the Silures of south Wales, and Agricola (77/78–78/79 CE) the Ordovices of North Wales. More than 60 campaigning forts, linked by a network of roads and controlled from the legionary fortresses of Isca (Caerleon) and Deva (Chester) ensured the subjugation of the peoples of Wales[3] in spite of their valor and the difficult terrain (*super virtutem hostium locorum quoque difficultates*).[4] As Vespasian was succeeded by Titus and Domitian, five further seasons of campaigning by Agricola to the north culminated in the battle of Mons Graupius in the north of Scotland,[5] and the completion of the conquest of Britannia (78/79–83/84 CE).[6] Some of the most vicious hand to hand fighting had been undertaken by four cohorts of Batavians[7] and two cohorts of Tungrians[8] (*donec Agricola quattuor Batavorum cohortes ac Tungrorum duas cohortatus est, ut rem ad mucrones ac manus adducerent).*[9] Battles that had been a spectacle on an enormous

---

interpret. This summary also takes into account revised readings in the Appendix to *Tab. Vindol. III* as a result of the advent of digital scanning. Cf. Woolf observes that Ferox and Verecundus are the only two people named; those submitting and receiving the report would have known "how to identify the individuals in each category if needed" ("Ancient Illiteracy?," 35). Vindolanda, Coria, Map (Figure 1) 2, 41.

3. Guest, *Roman Frontiers in Wales*, 60–61. E.g. Tomen y Mûr, Isca, Deva, Map (Figure 1) 50, 28, 47.

4. Tacitus, *Agricola* 17.2, 104.

5. According to Ogilvie and Richmond, a misspelling of Graupius as Grampius by Francisco dal Pozzo (Puteolanus) in the first printed edition of *Agricola* (Milan, 1475–80? CE), prompted the Scottish historian, Hector Boecce (1465–1536) to name the mountains in that locality the Grampian mountains (*Agricola Text and Commentary*, 84, 251–52). Cf. Charlotte Higgins, *Under Another Sky*, 139. According to B. Jones and Mattingly, proposed sites for the battle include locations near Perth, Dundee, Aberdeen, and Inverness (*Atlas of Roman Britain*, 76). See Map (Figure 1) note.

6. D. J. Mattingly, *An Imperial Possession*, 87–109; Salway 2001, 91–126; Ogilvie and Richmond 1967; Todd, *Roman Britain*, 82–115. The occasion was marked by the construction of a monumental arch c. 85 CE at Rutupiae (Map (Figure 1) 18): Hingley, *Conquering the Ocean*, 163–64; Wilmott and Smither, "Fort at Richborough," 148; Allen and Bryan, *Roman Britain*, 41; Wilson, *A Guide to Roman Britain*, 40–41.

7. A. R. Birley, *Garrison Life*, 42–45.

8. A. R. Birley, *Garrison Life*, 45.

9. Tacitus, *Agricola* 36.1, 115–16.

and savage scale (*grande et atrox spectaculum*), were everywhere followed by a desolate silence (*vastum ubique silentium*).[10] Victory enabled Agricola to hand over to his successor a province that was peaceful and safe (*tradiderat interim Agricola successori suo provinciam quietam tutamque*).[11] He had overseen a building program, and cultivated a liberal education among the elite which in their naivety they called "civilization," when, according to Tacitus, it was part and parcel of their enslavement (*Idque apud imperitos humanitas vocabatur, cum pars servitutis esset*).[12] The aftermath of the conquest was not without tension, as is suggested by words Tacitus attributed to the British leader Calgacus: "To pillage, butchery and rape they give spurious names and call it empire (*imperium*); and where they bring about desolation they call it peace (*pax*)" (*auferre trucidare rapere falsis nominibus imperium atque ubi solitudinem faciunt pacem appellant*).[13]

As the Roman fleet circumnavigated the northern coast of Britannia, the army consolidated its position and *cohors I Tungrorum* built a wooden fort at Vindolanda (*c.* 85–92) on the Stanegate, a frontier road linking Coria (Corbridge) on the River Tyne and Luguvalium (Carlisle) on the River Eden.[14] The fort was rebuilt and enlarged by the part mounted *cohors VIIII Batauorum* (c. 92/95–105);[15] when they were sent to join Trajan's Dacian campaign *cohors I Tungrorum* returned (c. 105–122).[16]

The Vindolanda tablets date from that uneasy peace established subsequently under Domitian, Nerva and Trajan. By Hadrian's time hostilities flared again,[17] prompting his visit c. 122 CE and the erection of the frontier wall.[18] Whether it was built to regulate the movement of people and

10. Tacitus, *Agricola* 38.2, 117.

11. Tacitus, *Agricola* 40.3, 119.

12. Tacitus, *Agricola* 21.2, 106–7.

13. Tacitus, *Agricola* 30.5, 112, 257–58.

14. B. Jones and Mattingly, *Atlas of Roman Britain*, 100. Vindolanda, Coria, Luguvalium, Map (Figure 1) 2, 41, 38. The Stanegate road is marked on the Map (Figure 1); cf. B. Jones and Mattingly, *Atlas of Roman Britain*, 113; Salway, *History of Roman Britain*, 124.

15. "*Equitate*," *Tab. Vindol. III* 628; Bowman et al., *Vindolanda Writing-Tablets III*. Figure 9.

16. A. R. Birley, *Garrison Life*, 57–76.

17. A tombstone commemorating the centurion, Titus Annius of *I cohors Tungrorum* alludes to his death in the "war" at around the time of Hadrian's accession: Tomlin, "Vindolanda's Other Inscriptions," 209.

18. D. J. Mattingly, *An Imperial Possession*, 119–21; S. R. Jackson, *Roman Occupation of Britain*, 143–55; Salway, *Roman Britain*, 173–84.

facilitate economic relations in an extensive border zone, or to prevent the movement of people across a militarized frontier,[19] Hadrian's wall is a reminder of the tensions that prevailed in the world of Vindolanda.[20]

Each auxiliary cohort based at Vindolanda kept detailed records of their work, provisions, and equipment. Officers and their families corresponded on matters of professional concern and personal interest.[21] In the military documents, accounts, lists and letters of Vindolanda we meet the kind of people we encounter in Luke–Acts: women of standing; commanders of auxiliary cohorts; provincial governors; centurions; soldiers and slaves. We glimpse the world in which Luke–Acts began to circulate. Following the approach outlined in the Introduction, we will begin with a detailed introduction to the Vindolanda tablets. Given that the corpus of Vindolanda tablets is far greater than that of the Bloomberg tablets or the Uley tablets, we will then focus on three groups of people and the tablets associated with each: the women and documents to do with the management of the *praetorium;* centurions and documents to do with their administrative duties; the prefects and documents to do with their professional and personal lives. Drawing on our adaptation of archival ethnography, we will take an imaginative leap to see with our inward eye the women, centurions and prefects of Vindolanda and its neighboring forts. That will enable us to imagine Luke–Acts through the eyes of people such as these drawn to follow the Way of Jesus. The world we discover in Vindolanda is very much the world of Luke–Acts and yet at the same time it is a world challenged by Jesus in Luke and by the followers of the Way in Acts. We will finally ask how such people from a military community might have negotiated their relationship with the empire as readers of Luke–Acts. Does Luke imply that "Jesus and his followers did not contravene Roman law and were therefore

19. Bruhn and Hodgson, "Impact of Hadrian's Wall," 134.

20. D. J. Breeze suggests possible practical explanations for the wall: defense against invasion; protection against raiding; controlling civilian movement; keeping the peace. He also suggests alternative abstract reasons: for stability; for imperial containment; as a base of operations; as a reflection of the failure to conquer the rest of the world; as a monument to Hadrian ("Studying Roman Frontiers"). Cf. D. J. Breeze, "Impact of Rome"; D. J. Breeze, "Purpose of Hadrian's Wall"; D. J. Breeze, "Hadrian's Wall"; D. J. Breeze et al., *African Frontiers.* Bruhn and Hodgson are adamant, "rather than being an insignificant bureaucratic border transecting a homogeneous zone, the Wall destroyed pre-existing homogeneity and created a stark division between north and south, with the southern developments shielded by a generally impermeable barrier across which contacts took place at a limited number of supervised places" ("Impact of Hadrian's Wall," 153).

21. Bowman, *Life and Letters.*

not a threat to the empire"?[22] Did he seek to subvert the "major concerns for law and order that belong to the ruling classes"?[23] Or is the reality we glimpse as we engage in archival ethnography more nuanced?

Introducing the Vindolanda Tablets

The Vindolanda tablets are thin leaves of wood about postcard size and between 1mm and 3mm thick.[24] The cursive script is written in ink often with a split nib.[25] Cheap and easy to make, they sufficed where no papyrus was available. In many cases they were folded with the text preserved on the inner surfaces, sometimes with an address on the outer face.[26] As one auxiliary cohort left Vindolanda and another arrived, documents were broken up, sometimes burned, and discarded on the floors of administrative buildings and barracks only to be covered by layers of clay and turf as buildings were repaired and the wooden forts rebuilt and enlarged.[27]

Figure 10. Reconstructed ink pen with original nib and ink pot lid from Vindolanda. © The Vindolanda Trust.

By the mid second century the last of the wooden forts was replaced with a stone fort that remained in use until the departure of the Romans c. 410 CE. The stone fort and its accompanying civilian settlement (*vicus*) remained the focus of excavation through the 19th century and from 1929 under the direction of Eric and Margaret Birley and their sons Anthony

22. Esler, *Community and Gospel in Luke-Acts*, 205.

23. Brawley, *Luke*, 3.

24. Willi, *Writing Equipment*, 45–49. For original photographs see Figures 13 and 15.

25. Willi, *Writing Equipment*, 38–41. Figure 10.

26. Bowman, *Life and Letters*, 8-9; Bowman and Thomas, "Format of Vindolanda Tablets." For conventions used in transcripts see The Texts, xxiii-xxv.

27. R. Birley, *Vindolanda: Roman Frontier Fort*, 44.

and Robin, until a sequence of earlier wooden forts was discovered by Robin Birley in 1972.[28] Thirteen feet below ground level he unearthed the first wooden writing tablet in March 1973.[29] In the excavations of 1973 and 1974 many more wooden writing tablets were discovered, perfectly preserved in the anaerobic conditions that had resulted from the manner of their disposal. With the help of Alison Rutherford's infrared photography and papyrologists, Alan Bowman and David Thomas, 117 were transcribed, translated and published in 1983. Excavations by the Vindolanda Trust under the direction of Robin and Patricia Birley, with Anthony and Heide Birley, and in the next generation, Andrew and Barbara Birley, have led to the publication of 776 tablets.

Excavations	Publication	Date	Numbering
1973–1974	*Tabulae Vindolandenses I*	1983[30]	I 1–117
1985–1993	*Tabulae Vindolandenses II*	1994[31]	II 118–572
1991–1994	*Tabulae Vindolandenses III*	2003[32]	III 573–853
2001–2003	*Tabulae Vindolandenses IV part 1*	2010[33]	IV 854–869
	Tabulae Vindolandenses IV part 2	2011[34]	IV 870–889
2017	*Tabulae Vindolandenses IV part 3*	2019[35]	IV 890–893

28. Figure 9.

29. A. R. Birley, *Garrison Life*, 22; *Tab. Vindol. II* 346; Bowman and Thomas, *Vindolanda: Latin Tablets*, 132–35.

30. Bowman and Thomas, *Vindolanda: Latin Tablets*: 1–117. N.B.— this volume and its numbering is no longer referred to.

31. Bowman et al., *Vindolanda Writing-Tablets* II: 118–572. The first 117 tablets were revised and renumbered, starting with 118.

32. Bowman et al., *Vindolanda Writing-Tablets* III: 573–853. Some earlier texts were revised in an Appendix in the light of the advent of digital photography.

33. Bowman et al., "Vindolanda Writing-Tablets IV:1 Britannia," 854–69.

34. Bowman et al., "Vindolanda Writing-Tablets, IV:2 Britannia," 870–89 (including 882–89, *descripta*).

35. Bowman et al., *Vindolanda Tablets, IV:3* Britannia, 890–893.

Excavations	Publication	Date	Numbering
	Tabulae Vindolandenses IV	2019[36]	IV 854–893
1973–2019	Roman Inscriptions of Britain/ Inscriptions/Vindolanda Tablets.	2019[37]	118–893

Table 5. Excavation and publication dates of the Vindolanda Tablets[38]

The nature of the deep excavations of the early wooden forts with their anaerobic conditions, together with advances in dendrochronology make it possible to date the finds with a high degree of precision:[39] most tablets come from periods II and III.[40]

Period	Fort	Date	Cohort/Location of Finds
I	Primary fort c. 3.5 acres	c. 85–95 CE	*cohors I Tungrorum* Outside west wall
II	Enlarged fort c. 5 acres	c. 95–105 CE	*cohors VIIII Batauorum* *Praetorium*
III	Renovated fort	c. 100–105 CE	*cohors VIIII Batauorum* *Praetorium*

36. Bowman et al., *Tab. Vindol.* IV: 854–889.

37. *https://romaninscriptionsofbritain.org/tabvindol*: *Tab.* Vindol. II–IV. 118–893. All four volumes published online, including introductory matter, digital images, transcripts, translations, notes and commentary.

38. *https://romaninscriptionsofbritain.org/tabvindol.* Excavations are on-going, and finds are published in *Britannia.*

39. Hillam, "Tree-Ring Analysis."

40. Bowman et al. "remain committed to the view that confidence can be placed in the chronological framework of the periods of occupation and the different phases of fort construction, but that a number of anomalies in the attribution of individual tablets to particular periods or structures means that we should be cautious about basing interpretations of any particular text solely on archaeological data." "Vindolanda Tablets and their Context"; "Vindolanda Writing-Tablets IV:1 Britannia," 189–90.

Period	Fort	Date	Cohort/Location of Finds
IV	Rebuilt fort	c. 105–120 CE	*cohors I Tungrorum* and others, with additional and probably legionary establishment to the west. Barracks
V	Rebuilt fort	c. 120–130 CE	*cohors I Tungrorum* Workshop

Table 6. Periods of occupation of the Vindolanda wooden forts, indicating the cohort in residence and where the tablets were found[41]

While best preserved in Vindolanda, such ink-on-wood tablets are not limited to Britannia and the north west of the empire.[42] The discovery in 1961 of an Aramaic letter in the same format from Shim'on bar Kosiba leader of the second Judean revolt (134–135 CE), prompted Yigael Yadin to observe that "the practice of writing on wood was widespread throughout the Orient, and is often mentioned even in rabbinical literature."[43] Serena Amiratti argues that the presence of wooden wax tablets together with papyri in Pompeii and Egypt suggests that the choice between papyrus and wood may have been to do with the nature of the document.[44] Similar wooden writing tablets were used in Hittite texts for legal documents, accounts and letters.[45] That more wooden tablets have not been discovered in

41. A. Birley and Blake, *Vindolanda Research* 2005–2006, 3. For a description of the archaeological context of the tablets discovered in each period see https://romaninscriptionsofbritain.org/tabvindol/vol-II/introduction#arch-context https://romaninscriptionsofbritain.org/tabvindol/vol-IV/tablets-context. For diagrams of the *praetorium* at Period 2 and at Period 3, the barrack block, palatial building/schola at Period 4, and the workshop at Period 5 see R. Birley, *Vindolanda: Roman Frontier Fort*, 52, 64, 93, 102, 108, color plate 6. For a description taking into account the excavations published in *Tab. Vindol. IV* see https://romaninscriptionsofbritain.org/tabvindol/vol-IV/tablets-context.

42. Bowman, *Life and Letters*, 9; A. R. Birley, *Garrison Life*, 33.

43. Yadin, "Expedition to Judean Desert," 41–42; Haran, *Codex*, 1996, 219–22, including photo, Fig. 5.

44. Ammirati, "Use of Wooden Tablets."

45. Waal, "They Wrote on Wood."

the eastern Mediterranean and more papyri in the north western provinces of the empire is due in large measure to climate.[46]

Similar documents are to be found among Egyptian ostraca from auxiliary forts in Wâdi Fawâkhir[47] and Bu Njem:[48] daily reports and correspondence indicate that soldiers from the garrison were at work in various locations, arranging the provision of grain. There is a real connection here from one frontier to another:[49] "at the time pen-and-ink cursive Latin was being written in the same way all over the empire" albeit with "a huge range of individuality."[50]

Through their correspondence and detailed record keeping we glimpse the workings of the Vindolanda cohorts and of the households that occupied the *praetorium* and see a little of their lifestyle.[51] We get a feel for traders and the relationships they had with the military community as they sought to draw on its legal processes. We can recognize the dependence of the community on the production of great quantities of wheat and barley and of hides for their clothing.[52] We see not only the basic foodstuffs and clothing used by the military community,[53] but also the finer clothing, foodstuffs and furnishings treasured by the family who lived in the *praetorium*.[54] The domestic arrangements for the *praetorium* were highly developed, well documented and in Alan Bowman's words fit "very well into the context of the well-to-do Roman *familia*."[55] The way of life of the Mediterranean world was to be experienced in Britannia. A wide range of activities was dependent on a high level of literacy: "the management of men and resources, . . . the acquisition and redistribution of supplies, . . . the processing and exchange of information, . . . establishing and sustaining

46. Pearce, "Imagining Roman London"; Pearce, "Writing Tablets and Literacy," 46.

47. Guéraud, "Ostraca Grecs et Latins."

48. J. N. Adams, "Latin and Punic," 88.

49. Bowman, *Life and Letters*, 32.

50. Bowman, *Life and Letters*, 86.

51. Pearce, "Food in the Roman Army."

52. For an introduction to food supplies in a Roman fort, quantifying the amount of land required to grow grain and the amount of grain needed to feed men and animals see Dannell and Wild, *Longthorpe II*.

53. Cf. D. J. Breeze, "Life in the Fort" for a comparison of the diet of officers and men in a later Antonine fort.

54. Harlizius-Kluck, "Textile Technology"; Wild, "Vindolanda Textiles."

55. Bowman, *Life and Letters*, 62. Cf. Hingley, *Conquering the Ocean*, 185.

social relationships by officers, soldiers and their dependents."[56] Fundamental to trade,[57] literacy extended, at a basic level, to the lower ranks[58] and, as in Rome, to women among the elite.[59] It was, suggests Alan Bowman, "the intensive use of the written word that enabled the army to function with coherence in a large geographical area in a way which simply would not have been possible without it."[60] Ian Haynes argues that "the pen was more crucial to the success of the Empire's armies even than the sword."[61]

The dispersed nature of the army's presence on the northern frontier of the empire, evident in the Vindolanda tablets, has contributed to a re-evaluation of the Roman army.[62] The frontier was not defended by a series of heavily fortified, fully populated, forts. "The military presence," suggests Alan Bowman, "can be made to seem stronger and more pervasive than it actually is, numerically, to the scattered and less organized tribal units which might not perceive that forts were not always fully manned."[63] The fort was part of an extended community of people interacting with each other through the written word. Documents such as the Vindolanda tablets and the eastern Mediterranean papyri and ostraca have prompted recent scholarship on the Roman army to move "beyond organization, to illuminate soldiers' relationships with one another and with the local community."[64] The army is more than a military machine: it is a community of soldiers with disparate identities yet sharing a common identity as *milites* within the Roman Empire.[65]

56. Pearce, "Writing Tablets and Literacy," 45; Tomlin suggests "some common soldiers could read and write" albeit at a basic level ("Literacy in Roman Britain," 214); Speidel, "Learning Latin in Roman Army," 139. See Speidel, "Learning Latin in Roman Army."

57. Woolf, "Ancient Illiteracy?," 38–41. Cf. Ferrándiz, "What Is Law?."

58. Tomlin, "Literacy in Roman Britain," 214; Ingemark, "Literacy in Roman Britain," 25; D. J. Mattingly, *An Imperial Possession*, 199–204.

59. McDonnell, "Writing Manuscripts."

60. Bowman, *Life and Letters*, 42; Haynes, *Blood of the Provinces*, 313–36.

61. Haynes, *Blood of the Provinces*, 313.

62. Haynes, *Blood of the Provinces*, 10–20; D. J. Breeze, *Frontiers of Imperial Rome*. Cf. D. J. Breeze, "Impact of Rome" with reference to changed thinking regarding the later period of Hadrian's Wall.

63. Bowman, *Life and Letters*, 18.

64. Goldsworthy et al., *Roman Army as a Community*, 8. Cf. Zeichmann, *Roman Army and the New Testament*, chap. 2; Zeichmann, "Military Forces in Judaea"; Haynes, "Roman Army as Community," 8; Alston, *Soldier and Society*, 3–5.

65. James, "Community of Soldiers," 77–78. Cf. D. J. Mattingly, *An Imperial Possession*,

Imagining Sulpicia Lepidina, Claudia Severa and Other Women

Life in the *praetorium* of a frontier fort must have been uncomfortable, dangerous and lonely for the wives and families of the prefects.[66] "Accompanying their husbands in long distance relocations,"[67] they were, however, more than "faceless camp followers": they were "valued within the social structure of the group."[68] Shoes, clothing and jewelry discovered within the fort suggest the presence of other women in spite of the non-recognition of marriage for auxiliaries and legionaries. Only officers from the equestrian and senatorial orders were permitted to marry.[69] The range of shoes from the time of Lepidina and Cerialis suggests their household had five children aged between two and ten.[70]

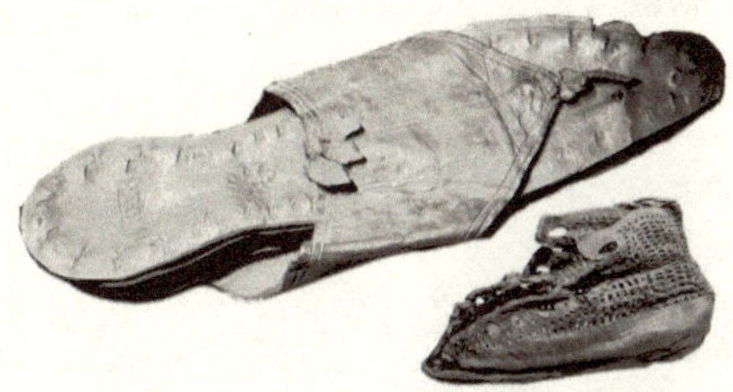

Figure 11. An expensive slipper found in the *praetorium* of Cerialis and Lepidina, probably belonging to Lepidina. It is stamped with vine leaves and two *cornucopiae* interlocked across an ear of corn, and also with his maker's mark by Lucius Aebutius Thales of Gaul.[71] A baby boot found in the same place and possibly belonging to one of the children of Cerialis and Lepidina. © The Vindolanda Trust.[72]

166–98 and 199.

66. Allason-Jones, *Women in Roman Britain*, 46.

67. Woolf, "Female Mobility," 359. Cf. Abdy, *Legion*, 38–39 on long-distance travel from one end of the empire to the other.

68. Greene, "Sulpicia Lepidina," 105.

69. Scheidel suggests that, because soldiers could co-habit with women and raise children, albeit without their having any legal rights, "non-recognition" of marriage might be a more precise term than the traditional "ban" ("Marriage," 417–18). R. Birley, *Vindolanda: Daily Life*," 21, 26; Bowman, *Life and Letters*, 75. Sherwin-White, *Roman Citizenship*, 248 on the legitimization of the offspring of such relationships. Cf. *Tab. Vindol. III* 670.

70. van Driel–Murray, "Leatherwork," 54–56.

71. B. Birley, "Curator's Favourite Shoes."

72. B. Birley, "Curator's Favourite Shoes."

For Sulpicia Lepidina, wife of Flavius Cerialis, prefect of *cohors VIIII Batauorum*, family celebrations, special days and feasting offered some relief. On 11 September (between 97 and 103) Claudia Severa, wife of Aelius Brocchus the prefect of a neighboring fort,[73] sent "her Lepidina" greetings, anticipating the day of the celebration of her birthday (*ad diem ´ |sollemnem natalem meum*).[74] She fears the day will be dull if her friend cannot come and so she is insistent that she attends, extending a warm invitation (*ibenter faciás ut uenias |ad nos iucundiorem mihi [diem] interuentú tuo facturá*). As she comes to the close of the letter she sends greetings not only from her husband, "my Aelius" but also from her "little son" (*filiolus*).[75] The affection she has for Lepidina is apparent in the final greeting in her own hand: "I shall expect you, sister. Farewell, sister, my dearest soul, as I hope to prosper, and hail" (vacat *sperabo te soror |uale soror anima |mea ita ualeam |karissima et haue*).

Figure 12. *Tab. Vindol.* II 291. Claudia Severa invites Sulpicia Lepdina to her birthday celebration. W 223 x H 96. Appendix Chapter 3. © The Trustees of the British Museum.

On another occasion Severa looks forward to a celebratory breakfast.[76] That birthday celebrations were an important part of the calendar at the *praetorium* is implied by the centurion, Clodius Super, addressing "his" Cerialis as a "brother" apologizing for missing Lepidina's birthday celebration.[77]

73. Possibly Coria, Map (Figure 1) 41: *Tab. Vindol. II* 292, cf. III Appendix: Bowman et al., "Vindolanda Writing-Tablets, IV:2 Britannia." Appendix Chapter 3.

74. *Tab. Vindol. II* 291, cf. III Appendix. Appendix Chapter 3.

75. Brocchus refers to his *filiolus* in an affectionate letter to Cerialis (*Tab. Vindol. III* 623). *Filiolus* appears in Mark 10:24; John 13:33; Gal 4:19; 1 John 2:1, 12, 18, 28; 3:7, 18; 4:4; 5:21.

76. *Tab. Vindol. III* 639.

77. *Tab. Vindol. III* 629. Appendix Chapter 3. Cf. *Tab. Vindol. II* 255.

Severa and Lepidina were in regular correspondence with each other and accustomed to meeting to deal with important matters. Writing from Briga where she is staying for the time being, Lepidina wants to discuss an important matter that cannot be broached in a letter.[78] Her husband, Brocchus, appears to have refused her permission to travel to Vindolanda, suggesting they meet at Coria, their home base. Severa is, however, determined to make the journey.[79] Once again she finishes the letter herself, taking up the pen and bidding farewell to her friend as "my sister, my dearest and most longed-for soul" (*ual]e mi soror |karissima et anima |ma desideratissima*).[80]

Brocchus writes with affection to Cerialis, passing on greetings from his wife, Claudia Severa,[81] asking that Cerialis greet Lepidina.[82] That Lepidina has an important part to play in the wider military community of the fort is suggested in letters that refer to her by name[83] and by the discovery of a letter addressed to her from another woman, Paterna.[84] This is evidence, suggests Elizabeth Greene, of "a distinct female milieu in this military community," lying "parallel to the otherwise dominant masculine structure inherent to the Roman army."[85]

The household of the *praetorium* lived in a way that would be recognized in elite households across the empire.[86] What can be said of such houses where the "householder had a significant public profile" can be said of the *praetorium*: "despite variety in their layout, residences were not devised simply to be private spaces for family members to retreat to after a

78. *Tab. Vindol. II* 292. Appendix Chapter 3. Briga is 70 km away according to A. R. Birley, *Garrison Life*, 136; in the vicinity of Vindolanda according to Bowman and Thomas, *Tab. Vindol. II* 2019b: *Tab. Vindol. II* 292. See Map (Figure 1) 38 for a conjectural location. Appendix Chapter 3.

79. *Tab. Vindol. II* 292, cf. III Appendix, Bowman and Thomas, *Tab. Vindol. II*. Coria, Map (Figure 1) 41. Appendix Chapter 3.

80. A third letter from Severa to Lepidina has only the final greeting, *Tab. Vindol. II* 293.

81. *Tab. Vindol. III* 626. Cf. II 244, III 622.

82. *Tab. Vindol. II* 247.

83. *Tab. Vindol. II* 227, 247, 257, 263 (*m2? dominam*), 274, 288, and *Tab. Vindol. III* 622, 627, 629.

84. *Tab. Vindol. II* 294. Appendix Chapter 3.

85. Greene, "Female Networks," 372. Abdy, *Legion*, 231. This contradicts the view of Schaberg and Ringe that "wealthy Roman women of the upper classes" were "without real decision-making authority and leadership" ("Luke," 498).

86. Bowman, *Life and Letters*, 62.

long day in the public arena."[87] Living in the *praetorium* a prefect's wife and even children would be an important part of "the social structure of the community."[88]

An inventory listing items of foodstuff, clothing, jewelry and furnishings hints at the luxury Cerialis and Lepidina enjoyed as they entertained in the *praetorium*: at 99⅝ denarii a pair of purple curtains (*uela purp(urea)* cost eight times as much as a leather saddle (*scordiscum*).[89] Inventories of tunic(s) (*tunicae*), two cloaks (*abollae*), Italian capes (*paenulae*), an outfit (*synthesis*) probably of clothing, perhaps of silver or some other fine ware, loose robes, half-belted tunics, underclothes, and vests suggests they dressed well.[90] The same writer lists valuables including a vase, rings and stones,[91] shoes and Gallic shoes.[92] Similar lists of textiles and clothing are found among the Egyptian papyri.[93] Artefacts discovered at Vindolanda suggest the clothing might have included purple and other bright colors and have been in a predominantly diamond twill pattern.[94] Their extravagance is evident in a diet that included spices,[95] roe deer, young pig, ham and venison;[96] and in their tableware comprising two shallow dishes, five side-plates, three vinegar-bowls, a platter, a single shallow dish, four bread-baskets, two cups, two bowls in a box, three egg cups, a strong-box (?) and a bronze lamp.[97] Similar luxury egg-cups (*ouaria*), from the dinner service of the wealthy Cornelius Gallus are listed in a Greek inventory in Egypt.[98] Two examples have been found in Pompeii and another in Boscoreale: "each has a small cup suitable for holding a boiled egg in the shell, and a

87. Longenecker, *In Stone and Story*, 212.

88. Greene, "Sulpicia Lepidina," 107. Cf. Abdy, *Legion*, 170–73.

89. *Tab. Vindol. III* 596, line 21. Cf. de la Bédoyère, *Gladius*, 133–34.

90. *Tab. Vindol. II* 195, 196.

91. *Tab. Vindol. II* 196.

92. *Tab. Vindol. II* 197.

93. Bowman and Thomas, *Tab. Vindol. II* 197, note line 3 with a reference to *P.Oxy 31.2599*, 31, http://papyri.info/ddbdp/p.oxy;31;2599.

94. A. R. Birley, *Garrison Life*, 139; Harlizius-Kluck, "Textile Technology."

95. A black jar labelled "1,884 coriander seeds" was found nearby: Tomlin, "Vindolanda's Other Inscriptions," 208.

96. *Tab. Vindol. II* 191. Cf. Pearce, "Food in the Roman Army."

97. Bowman and Thomas, *Tab. Vindol. II* 194, Introduction: *Tab. Vindol. II* 191, 194, 195 are by the same hand; 196, 197 may also be by the same person.

98. Oliver and Shelton, "Silver on Papyrus," 28.

geometric base which, when turned upside down, served as a dish rest."[99] That some items of homeware, clothing, shoes and textiles were acquired by Cerialis from neighboring auxiliary prefects, Tranquillus and Brocchus, suggests we glimpse here the lifestyle of those of equestrian rank.[100] This was what helped to reinforce their sense of identity.[101] Lepidina and Severa were women of high status with family connections similar to those of their husbands:[102] the *gentilica*, Sulpicia and Claudia, suggest that citizenship in Lepidina's family goes back to "the reign of the emperor Servius Sulpicius Galba (68–69 CE),"[103] while Severa's family acquired citizenship in the time of Claudius (41–54 CE), as had the tribune in Jerusalem, Claudius Lysias (Acts 22:28, 23:26).[104]

Observance of festivals through the year gave a structure to life in the *praetorium* at Vindolanda and contributed to that sense of shared identity among Roman auxiliaries.[105] Such ritual helped make sense of the power they represented.[106] A notebook from the time of Cerialis and Lepidina, records chickens (*pulli*) and geese (*anseres*) disbursed on specific dates from 11 (?) April 102 to 16 July 104 CE,[107] and probably consumed after their use in sacrifices.[108] Other disbursements (*expensa*) have to do with special events in the household of Cerialis and Lepidina and the observation of festivals, including possibly the *Matronalia* on 1 March and the birthday of Minerva on 21 March (*ad [sacrum n(atalem) Miner-/uae)*.[109] Onesimus, a Greek name common among slaves and freedmen, possibly a

99. Oliver and Shelton, "Silver on Papyrus," 28.

100. Bowman and Thomas, *Tab. Vindol. II* 196, Introduction; Abdy, *Legion*, 129–31.

101. Woolf, *Rome*, 253–54.

102. Bowman, *Life and Letters*, 50–52.

103. Bowman, *Life and Letters*, 51.

104. Greene suggests that "marriages were not always the product of dalliances with locals," more often, women came from the same tribes as their husbands ("Female Networks," 371). Abdy, *Legion*, 233–34.

105. Haynes, *Blood of the Provinces*, 198–206; Women in Roman Britain, 142; D. J. Mattingly, *An Imperial Possession*, 166.

106. Woolf, *Rome*, 137.

107. Bowman and Thomas suggest that *Tab. Vindol. III* 581 may be in the same hand as *Tab. Vindol. II* 191, 194, 196, 197 (*Tab. Vindol.* III.581, Introduction).

108. *Tab. Vindol. III* 581. Cf. Boman and Thomas, *Tab. Vindol. III* 582, note line a.i.2 and the reference to Chrisso the poultryman.

109. Bowman and Thomas, *Tab. Vindol. III* 581, Introduction and note line 71–72 and 76; another interpretation is offered by A. R. Birley, *Garrison Life*, 128–35; cf. line 45.

standard-bearer, is linked tentatively with the decoration of the standards (*rosalia signorum*).[110] Symbolic of "the unit's allegiance to the emperor and the soldier's allegiance to his unit," they stood in the *aedes principiorum*, the shrine at the heart of the fort that was immediately next to the *praetorium*.[111] Preparations were in hand on 1 May or June for a special lunch (*prandium*) to mark the "visit of the governor" (*aduentu consu[laris]*) and arrangements made for his bodyguards (*singulares*).[112] Dinner with Brocchus on 25 December and 1 January may have coincided with *Saturnalia*: on another occasion Brocchus invited Cerialis and Lepidina to stay once the *Saturnalia* were over, bidding his "dearest brother" farewell in his own hand (m2 *ua[le] mi frater |k[ari]ssime*.[113] Noting their enthusiasm for hunting, Birley suggests it was an occasion for the hunt.[114]

Beginning on 17 December, the household festival of *Saturnalia* went on for three to five days involving the role reversal of master and slaves.[115] In Vindolanda's *praetorium* slaves would be served by Cerialis and eat in style before the drinking, gaming and revels began.[116] Lepidina and their children would probably be present as the whole household exchanged presents, withdrawing later. Such role reversal gave slaves the opportunity to let off steam and the master of the household (Cerialis) the opportunity to neutralize potential threats.[117] It reinforced the status quo, serving to re-establish the hierarchies of the household and socialize newcomers into it.[118] A letter written by Severus to Candidus, the slave of a previous prefect, Genialis, arranging for delicacies to be available suggests it was a regular

110. Bowman and Thomas, *Tab. Vindol. III*: *Tab. Vindol.* 581, c.Back 88. Cf. *Tab. Vindol. III* 610 and Philem. 10–21; A. R. Birley, *Garrison Life*, 132; Goldsworthy, *Complete Roman Army*, 92.

111. Haynes, *Blood of the Provinces*, 218. On another occasion Masculis, a decurion, wrote to Cerialis and spoke of setting up a standard (*uexsillum*) at a shrine beside a crossroads: *Tab. Vindol.* 628. Figure 9.

112. Bowman and Thomas, *Tab. Vindol. III* 581, note line c.Back 95, 96; cf. *Tab. Vindol. II* 248. *RIB* 1713. The later tomb of a bodyguard of the governor was erected in Vindolanda by his widow (*RIB* 1713): Tomlin, "Vindolanda's Other Inscriptions," 209.

113. *Tab. Vindol. III* 622.

114. A. R. Birley, *Garrison Life*, 130, 147–51. Cf. *Tab. Vindol. II* 233, III 615, IV 861.27.

115. Beard et al., *Religions of Rome Volume 2*, 124–26.

116. Dolansky, "Celebrating the Saturnalia," 491.

117. Versnel, *Transition and Reversal*, 115–17.

118. Dolansky, "Celebrating the Saturnalia," 500; cf. Matthews and Reid, *Luke 10–24*, 401–2.

feature on the calendar at Vindolanda.[119] Remarkably for one of such high standing, Severus, a *cornicularius*,[120] addressed Candidus, a slave, in an informal and egalitarian way as "brother"(*frater*).[121]

The *Matronalia* was also significant for Cerialis, Lepidina and their household.[122] Commemorating "the founding of the temple of Juno Lucina, goddess of childbirth" on the Kalends of March, it was a feast day particularly for wives or mothers.[123] Anthony Birley suggests it had connections with the mother goddesses of the lower Rhineland and Batavia.[124] Celtic mother goddesses played a significant part in rites taken over by the Romans in Britannia too, not least in Vindolanda where five ritual dedications are to mother goddesses.[125] One can imagine the prominent role played by Lepidina among the wives and mothers of the military community in its three main components matching the *Saturnalia*: Cerialis would pray for the well-being of Lepidina and for their marriage; Lepidina, herself, would serve the household slaves with a special feast; Cerialis and Lepidina would then exchange gifts.[126] Above all the *Matronalia* "was a domestic observance that focused on the members of the *domus* [in this instance the *praetorium*] and their well-being": it underlined the part played by the *domina* as slave mistress in the household.[127] As in the *Saturnalia* the feasting with its role reversal served to reinforce the relationships within the household: the slaves had an afternoon of indulgence, the *domina* had a year of compliance. The involvement of Lepidina and Claudia in their respective festivals of *Saturnalia* and *Matronalia* helped secure their role as

119. *Tab. Vindol. II 301.*

120. A senior staff officer hoping for promotion to the rank of centurion: Goldsworthy, *Complete Roman Army*, 68. Cf. *Tab. Vindol. II* 301, Bowman and Thomas, *Tab. Vindol.* II.

121. *Tab. Vindol. II* 301, cf. III Appendix, Bowman and Thomas, *Tab. Vindol.* III; Haynes, *Blood of the Provinces*, 16.

122. *Tab. Vindol. II* 581, line 72, Bowman and Thomas, *Tab. Vindol.* II. Cf. Suetonius, *Vespasian* 19.270, 350.

123. A. R. Birley, *Garrison Life*, 130.

124. Anthony Birley offers an alternative chronology (*Garrison Life*, 130) which was subsequently rejected by Bowman and Thomas after further scrutiny of the tablets.

125. R. Birley, *Vindolanda: Daily Life*, 32.

126. Greene, "Women and Families," 250–52.

127. Dolansky, "Reconsidering the Matronalia," 193.

wives within the *praetorium* and the responsibility they had for the household and its management.[128]

In another informal household account book from the *praetorium* of Cerialis and Lepidina, a slave of the household lists food supplies over a few days in June (c. 100–105 CE) and makes provision on three occasions for a festival (*ad sacrum*).[129] On 25 June he refers to charitable donations (*stipes*) at a festival dedicated to a goddess (*ad sacrum |d<i>uae*), perhaps Fortuna, a deity popular in the army associated with that day.[130] The provisions include not only Celtic beer (*ceruesae*), a simple wine (*uini*) and a sour wine (*aceti*) associated with lower ranks,[131] but also Massic wine (*uini ..ssec(?)*), some of which may have been used in the offering to the goddess. Grain and pulses, sourced locally and further afield, were the staple diet of the Vindolanda cohorts; the purchase of pepper, a luxury, by or for Tagarminis, a low-ranking soldier, suggests there was a spirit of *convivium* and access to luxury items not only within the *praetorium*, but also among *milites*.[132]

Lepidina and Cerialis lived with the reality of ill health as soldiers were wounded and sick, many with eye problems.[133] Once Cerialis excused himself from some commitment referring to his son's state of health (*ualetudinem*).[134] When Lepidina suffered from a fever she sought help from another woman, Paterna, who wrote offering to bring two remedies (*ego duas an.[| 5 feram tibi*):[135] either she had access to her own or she brought something recommended by the *seplasarius*[136] or the *medicus*.

A hospital is implied in the strength report of *cohors I Tungrorum*[137] and mention is made of work on a hospital (*ualetudinarium*) in a day

128. Dolansky, "Reconsidering the Matronalia," 202. Cf. Abdy, *Legion*, 231.

129. *Tab. Vindol. II* 190.

130. A. R. Birley, *Garrison Life*, 135. Cf. Tomlin, *Britannia Romana*, 350.

131. Cf. Luke 23:36: at the crucifixion the soldiers offer Jesus 'sour wine" (ὄξος: *acetum*).

132. *Tab. Vindol. II* 184, Pearce, "Food in the Roman Army," 940–41. Cf. Tomlin, *Britannia Romana*, 297–309.

133. Cf. *Tab. Vindol. II* 154; Appendix Chapter 3. A. R. Birley, "Eye Disease"; Abdy, *Legion*, 170–73, 196; Tomlin, *Britannia Romana*, 295–96.

134. Bowman and Thomas, *Tab. Vindol. II* 227: this word is an interlinear addition (line b.2); an alternative interpretation of this fragment of a letter suggests Lepidina is writing to Cerialis out of concern for his health (Introduction).

135. *Tab. Vindol. II* 294. Appendix Chapter 3.

136. See below, Chapter 3 n. 220.

137. *Tab. Vindol. II* 154. Appendix Chapter 3.

report.[138] Another day report refers to a group of men building a residence (*hospitium*) for Marcus, the doctor (*medicus*):[139] as a *medicus ordinarius* he would probably have had the rank of a centurion.[140] One young *medicus*, 25 year-old Anicius Ingenuus, was honored by *cohors I Tungrorum* on a tombstone in the nearby Vercovicium (Housesteads) fort.[141] Vivian Nutton argues that medical services were provided by men with specific training, many of whom may have been Greek recruits with experience of medicine and access to Greek text books.[142]

When Lepidina arrived with Cerialis and *cohors VIIII Batauorum* they may have had their own *medicus* as Marcus would have moved on with his own cohort.[143] In an account and a letter from the time of Cerialis and Lepidina, Vitalis is identified as a "pharmacist" (*seplasarius*) whose responsibility was either to put together remedies for the soldiers or to put together treatments for doctors to administer.[144] A writing tablet in Luguvalium (Carlisle) mentions another *seplasarius*, Albanus, perhaps serving in a military hospital.[145] A rare Latin word originating in Seplasia, north of Naples, a place renowned for its medical ointments, it is sometimes translated "dealer in ointments."[146] Tomlin draws attention to the way *seplasariii* and *medici* are linked in an early Christian homily from late fifth or early sixth century CE, giving rise to the possibility they were associated with each other in medical treatment.[147]

138. *Tab. Vindol. II* 155.

139. *Tab. Vindol. II* 156. Bowman and Thomas as "medical orderly"; Baker translates *medicus* as "doctor" ("Medicine").

140. R. W. Davies, "Medici"; R. W. Davies, "Some More Medici."

141. *RIB* 1618; Nutton, "Medicine and Roman Army," 263. Tomlin, *Britannia Romana*, 294–295; Vercovicium, Map (Figure 1) 39. Cf. Abdy, *Legion*, 196–99.

142. Nutton, "Medicine and Roman Army," 264–65; Goldsworthy, *Complete Roman Army*, 100–101; A. R. Birley, *Garrison Life*, 47, 90; Cruse, A. Review of *Roman Medicine*, 503. Cruse cites evidence for military doctors in Roman Britain and medical practice common across the empire (*Roman Medicine*). Cf. Greek inscriptions: *RIB* 461, 3151; Latin inscriptions: *RIB* 1618, 1028.

143. In Colossians 4:14 Luke is referred to as ὁ ἰατρὸς ὁ ἀγαπητὸς: *medicus carissimus*.

144. *Tab. Vindol. III* 586 and IV 877; Tomlin, *Britannia Romana*, 295. Cf. Baker, "Medicine," 563; see Allason-Jones, "Health Care" for a fuller study of health care in the Roman North.

145. Tomlin, "Roman Britain in 1990," 300. Luguvalium, Map (Figure 1) 37.

146. *OLD*, 1738.

147. With reference to Mark 5:26 where *seplesarius* (spelled *simplassarios*) is used of the physicians who failed to help the woman with the issue of blood. Cf. Luke 8:43:

Tab. Vindol. III 591 may be "an inventory of medical supplies or a list of substances used for medical purposes" perhaps as an eye salve or in the treatment of wounds. There is also evidence that linen possibly soaked in honey was used in the treatment of eye conditions: *Tab. Vindol. III* 592 lists items with medicinal properties, including honey, beet and ointment (*mel |beta[...] |ung[...]*).[148]

Not long before their arrival in Vindolanda, *cohors VIIII Batauorum* had been campaigning north into Scotland. There is a tantalizing glimpse, albeit indirectly, of the cost of such campaigning and the grief it gave rise to. Among a small number of writing exercises[149] from the time of Lepidina and Cerialis is a quotation in capitals from Virgil, *Aeneid* 9.473: . . . |*interea pavidam volitans pinna|ta .ubem* m2 *seg.* vacat |. . .:[150] perhaps the children in the *praetorium* were taught by Lepidina.[151] It is suggested that the word *seg(niter)*, "slack," in a different hand is the teacher's critical comment on the writing exercise.[152]

The quotation is apt: written in a literary hand it speaks of a mother who had insisted on accompanying her son, Euryalus, as Aeneas and his followers arrive in Italy. The complete passage in the *Aeneid* (9.473–480) tells of the mother's devastation at the news of her son's tragic death.

> *Interea pavidam volitans pennata per urbem*
> *nuntia Fama ruit matrisque adlabitur auris*
> *Euryali. at subitus miserae calor ossa reliquit,*
> *excussi manibus radii revolutaque pensa.*
> *evolat infelix et femineo ululatu*
> *scissa comam muros amens atque agmina cursu*
> *prima petit, non illa virum, non illa pericli*

Tomlin, "Roman Britain in 1990," 300, n. 35. See below, Chapter 3, nn. 220, 221.

148. *Tab. Vindol. III* 592; Bowman and Thomas, *Tab. Vindol. III.*

149. *Tab. Vindol. II* 118–121; Bowman and Thomas, *Tab. Vindol. II*; *Tab. Vindol. IV* 854–856; Bowman et al., "Tab. Vindol. IV." Cf. *Tab. Vindol. II* 452. Appendix Chapter 3.

150. *Tab. Vindol. II* 118. Appendix Chapter 3. Bowman and Thomas list quotations from Virgil in military contexts, not least in Egyptian and Judean papyri, one from Herod's fortress at Masada (*Tab. Vindol. II* 118). Bowman wonders whether texts of Virgil were available at Vindolanda (*Life and Letters*, 88–89). Cf. R. Birley, *Vindolanda: Roman Frontier Fort*, 67. Cf. *Tab. Vindol. II* 452 contains the first line of *Aeneid* and was found in the barrack block suggesting it may have been a writing exercise for a soldier, see R. Birley, *Vindolanda: Roman Frontier Fort*, 97. Appendix Chapter 3.

151. A. R. Birley, *Garrison Life*, 144. Cf. Woolf, *Rome*, 254.

152. A. R. Birley, "Review of the Tablets," 38.

> *telorumque memor, caelum dehinc questibus implet.*[153]
>
> Meanwhile winged Rumor flew in haste through the settlement with her message and flitted right to the ear of Euryalus's mother. Poor lady, all warmth at once left her. The shuttle leapt from her hands and her skein of wool untwined. She dashed forth in distraction and terrible distress; and, wailing as women do and tearing her hair, she ran with mind deranged to the wall where stood the foremost ranks; she took no thought for the danger from the spears, no thought for the presence of men. And then she filled all the sky with her lament.[154]

With memories of battles still raw among those based in Vindolanda, perhaps Lepidina found solace in the poetry of Virgil, whose *Aeneid* "had penetrated deeply into popular culture."[155] She may well have known what it was to feel the color drain from her cheeks and for the skies to be filled with cries of grief as news flew through the streets of such a tragic loss.

A number of letters suggest that when *cohors VIIII Batauorum* moved on and *cohors I Tungrorum* returned, Priscinus was their prefect.[156] His wife had extended to an unknown correspondent "comfort just as a mother would do" (*consolaris |sicut mater faceret*), something that was appreciated by the letter writer, "indeed, my own heart [welcomed?] this sympathy (of yours)" (*hunc enim ▸ adfec|tum ▸ animus meus*).[157] At a later date, Julia Domna, Septimius Severus's Empress, was honored as *mater castrorum*, mother of the army camps, in recognition of the part she played alongside

153. Virgil, *Aeneid* 9.473–480, 146–149.

154. Virgil, *The Aeneid*, 240.

155. Bonz argues that "during his lifetime, Virgil was regarded as Rome's greatest living poet, not only by other writers but also by the general public. Very early he became a model author for grammarians and rhetors, and throughout antiquity his poems comprised one of the most widely used school texts. . . . Furthermore, evidence that the *Aeneid* had penetrated deeply into popular culture is to be found on the walls of excavated Pompeii, where some of its verses can still be seen, etched on the surfaces." (*Past as Legacy*, 61). Abdy maintains that the discovery of cavalry sports helmets used on parade and in displays not far from Vindolanda depicting scenes from Troy (late first to second or third century CE) is evidence of the popularity of such foundation myths in the army (*Legion*, 138–39).

156. Bowman and Thomas, *Tab. Vindol. II* 295–298; *Tab. Vindol. III* 636–638; A. R. Birley, *Garrison Life*, 152–55.

157. Bowman and Thomas, *Tab. Vindol. III* 663. Appendix Chapter 3. Cf. Bowman and Thomas *Tab. Vindol. III* 639: it is possible that Priscinus's wife's *gentilicium* and *cognomen* are on the reverse; A. R. Birley, *Garrison Life*, 153, suggests the name Varia, but this is rejected by Bowman and Thomas.

her husband in his military campaigns.[158] A similar role had been played by Agrippina (the Elder, d. 33 CE), granddaughter of Augustus when she had provided much needed practical support for her husband, the general Germanicus Caesar. According to Richard Abdy "Agrippina had shown that there was an opportunity for tough and charismatic Roman women to guide and support soldiers operating under difficult conditions."[159]

These were women with a mind of their own: they were women of agency whose contribution to the wider military community was valued beyond the immediate circle of their husbands and children.[160] In a letter to Cerialis Vitalis, a *decurion* of the Augustan *Ala* later stationed in Deva (Chester), asks to be remembered to his mistress, Lepidina (*dominam tuam a me salu/ta*), recognizing her contribution to the community as a whole.[161] In a letter that perhaps confirms that Cerialis and Lepidina had children Valatta, another woman, looks to Lepidina for support as she presents "her Cerialis" with a legal petition or some kind of request to do with a favor or patronage.[162] That would suggest that other women in the fort looked to her to act in their interests as an intermediary.[163]

The correspondence of Lepidina and Severa and other women indicates the significant part they played in the *praetorium* and beyond.[164] They contributed to the education of their children and had a hand in the management and oversight of the *praetorium* with its round of feasts and festivals. Not only did they have the affection and support of their husbands and women of similar standing, but they also had the respect of other officers and were a source of comfort and practical support for other women in the military community.

158. Abdy, *Legion*, 170.

159. Abdy, *Legion*, 171.

160. Greene, "Sulpicia Lepidina," 105. Cf. references to Ingenua, the recipient's daughter in *Tab. Vindol. III* 643. Ingenua is also named in *Tab. Vindol. III* 642.

161. *Tab. Vindol. II* 263; Bowman and Thomas, *Tab. Vindol. II*. Appendix Chapter 3. Deva, Map (Figure 1) 47.

162. Bowman and Thomas *Tab. Vindol. II* 257, Appendix III; Tomlin, "Vindolanda Tablets," 462. Michael Peachin points out that one in six of the petitions discovered among the Egyptian papyri were from women, to do with issues around violence, inheritance and dowry ("Vindolanda Tablets and Law"; 226). Appendix Chapter 3.

163. Greene, "Female Networks," 379–80; Abdy, *Legion*, 231.

164. Cf. *Tab. Vindol. II* 324.

Imagining Luke–Acts Through the Eyes of the Women Associated with Vindolanda

Women of High Standing and Women's Travels

Were women of the standing of Sulpicia Lepidina and Claudia Severa to become followers of the Way of Jesus, they would discover in Luke–Acts confirmation that it was for them and their peers.[165] Among those who followed Jesus as he "went on through cities and villages proclaiming and bringing the good news of the kingdom of God" (Luke 8:1–3) were Joanna, "the wife of Herod's steward Chuza" and others who were able to "provide for them out of their resources" (αἵτινες διηκόνουν αὐτοῖς ἐκ τῶν ὑπαρχόντων αὐταῖς: *aliae multae quae ministrabant eis de facultatibus suis).* They would recognize these women of means from "the higher levels of society"[166] and assume they were literate and able to manage resources.[167] We do not hear them, but their near contemporaries at Vindolanda give voice to the things they held dear.

While "the devout women of high standing" (τὰς εὐσχήμονας: *honestas)* along with "the leading men" of Antioch in Pisidia (τοὺς πρώτους τῆς πόλεως: *primos civitatis*) were incited by *Iudaei* to turn against Paul and the Way (Acts 13:50), not a few of "the leading women" (γυναικῶν τε τῶν πρώτων: *mulieres nobiles*) of Thessalonica were among those who heeded Paul and became followers of the Way (Acts 17:4). Though nothing else is said of her, Damaris is named alongside Dionysius the Areopagite as a follower of the Way (Acts 17:34). Elite women had "an informal, 'private' authority" that was based on their "birth, rank, family, reputation and social connections."[168] They would have been "members of a class in which women have access to the public sphere as well as control of dwellings

165. Kahl advocates reading Luke–Acts not only through the eyes of Theophilus and his peers but also through the eyes of Lydia and women of agency ("Reading Luke Against Luke").

166. Wolter, *Luke I*, 330–31; Green, *Gospel of Luke*, 320–21; Witherington, "On the Road, 138–39"; Caird, *Luke*, 116; Schaberg and Ringe, "Luke," 506; Matthews and Reid, *Luke 1–9*, 248–55; contrast de Boer, "Lukan Mary Magdalene," 144.

167. Confirming Matthews and Reid's conclusion: "Based on women's legitimate involvement in financial matters in the Roman world, we conclude that Luke regards women taking initiative to finance a religious movement as an acceptable practice." (*Luke 1–9*, 249). Cf. Abdy, *Legion*, 231.

168. Hemelrijk, "City Patronesses," 234.

suitable for housing communities of Jesus-followers."[169] The presence of such women among followers of the Way is indicative of their place "in the early assemblies as leaders and as funders."[170] Valued as they were "within the social structure" of the fort, and in the life and management of the *praetorium*,[171] we can imagine Sulpicia Lepidina and Claudia Severa seeing something of themselves in such women as the "the leading women" of Thessalonica and the "woman named Damaris" of Athens, who "were persuaded" and "became believers." As women Lepidina and Severa were accustomed to meeting with each other and with other women; they would perhaps have been drawn to the women who, in Lydia's company, gathered together outside the gate of Philippi, by the river, at a place of prayer,[172] and to the community of followers of the Way, presided over by Lydia in her house.[173] They would find grounds themselves for becoming followers of the Way.[174] They would presume the "relatives and friends" who made up Cornelius's household (οἶκος: *domus*) and came to follow the Way (Acts 10:2, 24, 48), included women of some standing.[175] When Publius, the leading man of Malta, entertained Paul and his companions for three days, they would imagine the involvement of his wife (Acts 28:7–10).

The first householder to welcome Jesus and the first followers of the Way was Martha who is presented as "a patron: prosperous, independent, ready to host this traveler" (Luke 10:38–42).[176] The first householder to welcome Peter after his escape from prison was "Mary, the mother of John, whose other name was Mark" (Acts 12:12), "a rich patron of the assembly

169. Maloney and Reimer, *Acts*, 245.

170. Aymer, "Acts Women's Bible Commentary," 543; cf. Maloney and Reimer, *Acts*, lix.

171. Greene, "Sulpicia Lepidina," 105; cf. A. R. Birley, *Garrison Life*, 103; R. Birley, *Vindolanda: Daily Life*, 21; Abdy, *Legion*, 171, 231. Cf. *Tab. Vindol. III* 629, II 257, 263.

172. Reimer, *Women in Acts*, 72–92.

173. Reimer, *Women in Acts*, 109–27. On Lydia see Ascough, *Lydia*; Reimer, *Women in Acts*, 71–149.

174. At the conclusion of her imagined reading of Acts 17:16–34 through the eyes of Damaris, Hannah Lents argues that naming Damaris alongside Dionysius the Areopagite "forces readers to ask where Damaris and her sisters fit into the narrative of Paul's speech" ("Paul's Areopagus Speech," 253). This is the kind of response our imagined readers might make.

175. This suggests a possible answer to the question posed by Maloney and Reimer, "How is it that a Roman centurion has relatives in this place, on what were from the Roman point of view the fringes of civilization?" (*Acts*, 151). Cf. Pervo, *Acts*, 267.

176. Green, *Gospel of Luke*, 435.

in whose home they meet."[177] The first householder to welcome Paul and companions was Lydia "from the city of Thyatira and a dealer in purple cloth" (πορφυρόπωλις: *purpuraria* Acts 16:14): welcoming them to her Philippi home she became a follower of the Way. In all three householders our imagined readers would have recognized women of agency.[178] While not householders themselves, the households of Lepidina and Severa were managed on a lavish scale: they knew those who traded in luxury cloth and the cost of purple curtains.[179] They would have seen in Martha a host who entertains;[180] in Mary a householder with an enslaved woman (παιδίσκη: *puella*), Rhoda;[181] and in Lydia a householder involved in trading luxury goods.[182]

177. Aymer, "Acts Women's Bible Commentary," 542; cf. Maloney and Reimer, *Acts*, 167; Pervo, *Acts*, 305.

178. Wolter notices that the first householders to welcome Jesus and Paul were women (*Luke II*, 83). Aymer suggests that "Mary underscores what the story of Tabitha also reveals, the insistent presence and leadership of women in the early church" ("Acts Women's Bible Commentary," 542). Maloney and Reimer suggest that Eunice, the mother of Timothy (Acts 16:1–3), was "in all likelihood . . . the head of the household of the Way in Lystra" (*Acts*, 211). Calpino suggests that Tabitha and Lydia are not untypical of women craft-workers and householders in the Roman Empire ("Crafting Gender in Acts," 222–26). On women householders in the Greco-Roman world and in early Christianity, see further Osiek et al., *A Woman's Place*; Lafosse, "Women and Children."

179. *Tab. Vindol. III* 596.

180. Matthews and Reid, *Luke 10–24*, 358

181. Aymer maintains that "Rhoda reminds us that, even in the Christian assembly, class oppression continues" ("Acts Women's Bible Commentary," 542). Reimer takes a different view, arguing that Rhoda is not identified as Mary's slave and therefore might be a member of the community of the followers of the Way who meet in Mary's house (*Women in Acts*, 240–43). Harrill argues that Luke deliberately uses a literary device from Roman comedy, depicting a running slave, *serva currens*, simply to add humor and heighten the tension of the narrative thus reinforcing "the institution and ideology" of slavery (*Slaves in the New Testament*, 59–66); Pervo supports this view (*Acts*, 306).

182. This reinforces the view that Luke's audience would associate purple with wealth: Keener, *Acts*, 391; Aymer, "Acts Women's Bible Commentary," 543. For a historical account of Lydia as an independent woman of means trading in a luxury good see Ascough, *Lydia*, 81. Cf. Hylen, *Women in the New Testament World*, 130. For a differing view of Lydia as a freedwoman engaged in a dirty trade associated with the urban poor see Reimer, *Women in Acts*, 105, 116, 126. Cf. Maloney and Reimer, (*Acts*, 219–20); regarding Acts as a novel, they go on to characterize Lydia as a wealthy householder (*Acts*, 221–28). Pervo suggests Lydia be perceived "as single, divorced or widowed . . . the head of her household, and a person of some means . . . not rich, but among early Christians . . . fairly well situated . . . with a limited place in the social world of her colony" (*Acts*, 403–4).

As the wives of prefects of auxiliary cohorts, Lepidina and Severa were used to traveling; their close friendship involved visiting each other with and without their husbands. Women such as these coming to follow the Way would recognize the journeys of Mary and Elizabeth as they shared their friendship with each other (Luke 1:26–56); the journeys Mary made with Joseph (Luke 2:1–7), with her son Jesus (Luke 8:19), and to Jerusalem (Acts 1:14);[183] and the journeys taken with Jesus to his death and beyond by the women who resourced Jesus' ministry (Luke 8:1–3; 23:49; 24:1–12).[184] Not only would they see in Priscilla and Aquila householders who shared the craft of tent-making with Paul and hosted a gathering of the followers of the Way in their home, but also a woman who with her husband and with Paul traveled to Ephesus where, as a woman of agency, Priscilla's words played a significant part in building up the Way (Acts 18:1–3, 24–28).[185] Indeed, Priscilla is named first in Acts 18:18, 26, possibly suggesting she was "more prominent."[186]

Personal experience and hearsay[187] would have made Lepidina, Severa and their peers aware of the perils of travel by sea. If, as we have imagined, they were familiar with Virgil's *Aeneid*, perhaps they would have recognized in the climax to Luke–Acts (Acts 27:1—28:16) "the travelogues, forecasts of storm and shipwreck, storm scenes, and concerns for safety in sea voyages in ancient literature."[188] As they might have followed the story of the Way

183. Cf. Jo-Ann Badley in Maloney and Reimer, *Acts*, 15–16.

184. Matthews and Reid suggest that such "a mixed-gender group" accompanying Jesus might have been unexceptional for Luke and his first readers (*Luke 1–9*, 250). Contrast Schaberg and Ringe, "Luke," 506.

185. Maloney and Reimer, *Acts*, 261–64. Pervo suggests Aquila and Priscilla "were evidently missionaries who specialized in the formation and nurture of house churches" (*Acts*, 451). Reimer suggests that as artisans Aquila and Priscilla were accustomed to traveling and so can be described as missionaries and teachers. The perception of them as fellow workers of Paul in Rom 16:3 bears out the view of Luke in Acts 18 that Priscilla as much as Aquila "can be recognized as a highly esteemed missionary who is understood as Paul's "co-worker" and who stands as an equal not only alongside Aquila, but also in the company of Paul and other missionaries" (*Women in Acts*, 208–19) .

186. Pervo, *Acts*, 451. Priscilla (or Prisca) is named first in Acts 18:18, 26; Rom 16:3 and 2 Tim 4:19; Aquila is named first in Acts 18:2 and 1 Cor 16:9; cf. Reimer, *Women in Acts*, 195–96. See Reimer, *Women in Acts*, 195–226.

187. Not long before their arrival in Vindolanda, the Roman fleet had sailed around the north of Britain, experiencing stormy seas. Tacitus, *Agricola* 10.6, 99, cf. 173– 174. See Map (Figure 1) note. For harbors on the east coast they might well have been familiar with, see B. Jones and Mattingly, *Atlas of Roman Britain*, 199.

188. Praeder, "Sea Voyages in Luke–Acts," 684; cf. 693: while the parallels are not

in Luke–Acts, they would have been reassured by the kindness of Julius, "a centurion of the Augustan Cohort" (Acts 27:1, 3, 31, 43) and the hospitality of Publius, "the leading man of the island" of Malta (Acts 28:7–10) that it was appropriate for them also to be followers of the Way.

Festivals and Feasting

With its festivals and feasting, life in the *praetorium* was organized in a way that would have been recognizable in elite homes across the empire. Lepidina and Severa knew their place and the place of their equals: at those feasts they knew who was invited and who was not. Jesus steps into the world of hospitality Lepidina and Severa were used to when he accepts Levi's invitation to "a great banquet in his house" (Luke 5:29) and eats with various Pharisees (Luke 7:36; 11:37; 14:1). Noting he was at home in the world of feasting and banqueting (Luke 5:33–39), they would have recognized the extravagance of the woman who honored Jesus by anointing his feet with ointment from an alabaster jar, seeing her positively (Luke 7:36–50).[189] Whether they were drawn to Mary or to Martha, they would have understood the welcome given to Jesus and his followers in their house (Luke 10:38–42). They would have welcomed Cornelius and his household (Acts 10:1–48); theirs was the kind of household Sergius Paulus the proconsul of Cyprus would have kept (Acts 13:7, 12); theirs was the kind of hospitality given by Publius, the leading man of Malta, to Paul and his companions (Acts 28:7).[190] In Caesarea as in Vindolanda, albeit on a smaller scale, governors come and go, and honored guests are welcomed (Acts 24–26): among them were the freedman Governor Felix in the company of his wife, Drusilla (Acts 24:24–27),[191] the equestrian Festus who welcomes Herod Agrippa II in the company of his sister, Bernice (Acts 25:13, 23).[192] The households

exact, by the first century CE "storm scenes were part of literary tradition and part of rhetorical training. Introduced into Greek literature by Homer . . . and instituted in Latin literature by Virgil, *Aeneid* 1.34–156."

189. Reid, "Do You See This Woman?," 116–17. For an alternative male perspective see above, Chapter 2, *Honor Restored in the Cancellation of Debts.*

190. See above, Chapter 2, *Generosity and Sharing.*

191. Maloney and Reimer suggest that Drusilla, wife of Felix, a Judean, and daughter of Herod Agrippa I, was in all likelihood not interested in the Way: (*Acts*, 315–16).

192. Maloney and Reimer suggest that "it is highly unlikely" that Paul ever met Agrippa II or Bernice (*Acts*, 323). They argue that their presence in the narrative is a literary device. Bernice is sister to Drusilla and Agrippa II and "serves as the last example

of Cerialis and Lepidina and of Brocchus and Severa enjoyed each other's hospitality. Hospitality such as they were accustomed to was something Jesus enjoyed at every turn (Luke 11:37). When they entertained, they would invite their friends, brothers, sisters, relatives, or rich neighbors in the expectation of an invitation in return. Theirs was a world of balanced reciprocity.[193]

Jesus' reflections on the tendency of guests to choose "the places of honor" and the dangers of being asked to move should someone "more distinguished" arrive amounted to the kind of wisdom they as hosts would take for granted (Luke 14:7–10). In Luke–Acts it is supremely at the meal table that it becomes apparent that the Way of Jesus is radically different.[194] Echoing the words of Mary as she had sung of the one who "has brought down the powerful from their thrones and lifted up the lowly" (Luke 1:52), Jesus speaks of the way "all who exalt themselves will be humbled, and those who humble themselves will be exalted" (Luke 14:11).

Even this was not entirely alien to Lepidina, Severa and their contemporaries. While they probably knew nothing of the yearly cycle of Judean festivals (Luke 2:41; 22:1–38; Acts 2:1; 12:3–4; 20:6,16; 27:9), their year was also shaped by the rhythm of ritual and festival. Twice each year, from 17 December to 22 December and on 1 March they shared in household festivals that momentarily inverted their social norms. The feasts of the *Saturnalia* and the *Matronalia*, and the way in which a *cornicularis* could address his slave as "brother,"[195] raised the possibility that slaves might be served by their master just as the master has his slaves "sit down and eat" as he serves them (Luke 12:37).[196] Accustomed to observing the *Matronalia*, they might see in Luke 1–2 a celebration of the motherhood of Elizabeth and Mary. It would come as no surprise that it is in that context that Mary, the mother of Jesus, articulates a principle that is to become a keynote of the teaching of Jesus (Luke 1:51–53; cf. 4:18–19; 22:24–27) and find expression among those who follow the Way in a community of sharing in the home and at the table (Acts 2:43–47). The God they encounter in her words

---

in Acts of an aristocratic woman sympathetic to Paul" (*Acts*, 327–30).

193. Crook, *Reconceptualizing Conversion*, 64–59; Stegemann and Stegemann, *Jesus Movement*, 34–36. See above, Chapter 2, n. 189.

194. Paulraj, *Food Justice*, 111; Klinghardt, "Meals in Luke," 111; Matthews and Reid, *Luke 10–24*, 423–27.

195. *Tab. Vindol. II* 301.

196. Described as an "outlandish" redefinition of household relations by Green, *Gospel of Luke*, 499. Cf. Matthews and Reid, *Luke 10–24*, 401–2.

"has scattered the proud in the thoughts of their hearts, has brought down the powerful from their thrones, and lifted up the lowly; he has filled the hungry with good things, and sent the rich away empty" (Luke 1:51–53). This is not, suggest Schaberg and Ringe, "the song of a victim but one that proclaims liberation with tough authority."[197]

There is, however, a major difference in the teaching of Jesus and the description in Acts of the first followers of the Way. The feasts of the *Saturnalia* and the *Matronalia* reinforced the hierarchies of the elite household, serving to provide a safety valve for any tensions and securing an ensuing year of compliance.[198] By contrast, the teaching of Jesus introduces a Way to follow throughout the year, a Way that finds expression in the new spirit of community established among those who follow the Way of Jesus.[199] The Way of Jesus extends beyond the household and invites those who follow it to become part of a new and differently ordered household. "When you give a banquet," Jesus goes on to say, "invite the destitute, the crippled, the lame and the blind" (*κάλει πτωχούς, ἀναπείρους, χωλούς, τυφλούς*: *voca pauperes debiles claudos caecos* Luke 14:13).

In *Food Justice and Hospitality in Luke–Acts: A Historical and Contemporary Interpretation*, Gideon Paulraj has demonstrated that "the *πτωχοί* in the Lucan world were beggars, weak, powerless, landless, diseased, naked, hungry and destitute."[200] The challenge intensifies as Jesus tells the parable of the great dinner for which those invited have excuses and so cannot attend. Angered, the master of the house sends his slave "into the streets and lanes of the town" to "bring in the destitute, the crippled, the blind, and the lame"; once they have been brought in there is still room, prompting the master to command the slave to go beyond the town into the surrounding countryside,[201] "Go out into the roads and lanes and compel people to come in, so that my house may be filled" (Luke 14:15–24).

Were the likes of Lepidina and Severa to join a community of those who followed the Way, they would be challenged by the teaching of Jesus in Luke and the example of the first communities in Acts to ensure that at its

197. Schaberg and Ringe, "Luke," 504.

198. Dolansky, "Celebrating the Saturnalia," 500; Dolansky, "Reconsidering the Matronalia," 202; cf. Matthews and Reid, *Luke 10–24*, 401–02.

199. Green, *Gospel of Luke*, 104–5; Brawley, *Luke*, 47; Paulraj, *Food Justice*, 201–8.

200. Paulraj, *Food Justice*, 85. Matthews and Reid speak of "the desperate condition of the poor" and of the hungry as those who are "chronically starving" (*Luke 1–9*, 202–3); cf. Matthews and Reid, *Luke 10–24*, 426–30.

201. Wolter, *Luke II*, 223.

heart the balanced reciprocity they were accustomed to would be replaced by a familial reciprocity that extends hospitality without expecting anything in return.[202] The move beyond the town to the surrounding countryside would have resonated with our imagined readers. While within the military community all were provided with food, they would have encountered extremes of destitution in their travels through the *vicus*, the settlement that grew up around the fort and beyond into the roads and lanes they were accustomed to traveling.[203] The community of those who followed the Way is open to all regardless of their social status and their capacity to reciprocate.[204] Lest there be any doubt about the extent of this challenge, the narrative goes on to speak of feasting and celebrating (Luke 15:6,9,23), and of the rich man "dressed in purple and fine linen" who "feasted sumptuously every day" and the destitute beggar "named Lazarus, covered with sores" who longed for the scraps that fell from the rich man's table (Luke 16:19–31). The likes of Lepidina and Severa would no doubt recognize the signs of opulence in the rich man's clothing[205] and in his feasting as they too were challenged to recall the destitute outside the walls of the fort.[206] This teaching makes real the commitment Jesus had made to the destitute, the captives, the blind and the oppressed in Nazareth (Luke 4:18–21) and all he reported to the messengers of John (Luke 7:18–23).

It is in Acts that the followers of the Way live out this kind of familial reciprocity in their sharing of all things (Acts 2:44–46; 4:32–37) and in their breaking down of ethnic and social barriers (Acts 10:1—11:18). Paulraj wonders whether Luke's omission in Acts of any refence to the destitute (πτωχόι: *pauperes*) is deliberate, implying that the followers of the Way lived out the paradigm outlined by Jesus in his Nazareth declaration (Luke 4:18), though he has to concede the problems remain with the plight of the Greek widows (Acts 6:1–6).[207] Reading of the first followers of the Way, our imag-

202. Crook, *Reconceptualizing Conversion*, 54–59; Stegemann and Stegemann, *Jesus Movement*, 34–36; cf. Neyrey, *Ceremonies in Luke-Acts*, 371–73. See Chapter 2, n.189.

203. *Tab. Vindol. II* 292. Appendix Chapter 3. Cf. 291. The women of the *praetorium* also accompanied the cohort when it was on the move.

204. Esler, *Community and Gospel in Luke-Acts*, 194; Green, *Gospel of Luke*, 550.

205. Green draws attention to the purple clothing and daily feasting as signs of opulence (*Gospel of Luke*, 605–10).

206. Matthews and Reid suggest that "one step toward the kind of conversion called for in the parable is to relate to poor persons as individuals with names, not an anonymous group 'the poor'" (*Luke 10–24*, 469).

207. Paulraj, *Food Justice*, 107–10.

ined readers would quickly become aware that fundamental to it is a table fellowship that is open to all, where all is shared and the needs of each are met. (Acts 2:43–47; 4:32–37).[208]

How would our imagined readers respond? They would find in Jesus one who shares their love of feasting but calls into question the values on which the world of their feasting is built. Would this be too great a challenge for them? Such a radically different way of life would seem to preclude their involvement in the Way. And yet, as we have seen, among the followers of the Way were some they would be at home with. Might they give expression to the teaching of Jesus in showing a concern for those they knew to be injured and unwell in the community of the fort? Might they extend their concern to those of a status beneath them within the military community and to those beyond the fort community in the *vicus* and surrounding countryside? The challenge was not simply to give "the scraps" that "fall from the table" but to devote their lives to "good works and acts of charity" as Tabitha had done (Acts 9:36).[209] There can be no escaping that the proclamation of the "good news to the destitute" is a key to Luke's meal narrations.[210] Faced with such a challenge they might have found in the narrative of the woman with "the alabaster jar of ointment" (ἀλάβαστρον μύρου: *alabastrum unguenti*) a model of remarkably generous love that would help them as they struggled with those challenges and sought to follow the Way of Jesus (Luke 7:36–50).[211]

Kinship in Turbulent Times

The message is reinforced as Jesus goes on to address the large crowds who had been following him, telling them that being a disciple of Jesus involves

208. Keener, *Acts*, 173–76; 202–3; Spencer, *Journeying through Acts*, 49–50; 65; Paulraj, *Food Justice*, 200–208.

209. Reimer suggests that Tabitha's example is an "incitement to action" (*Women in Acts*, 36–41). See further Reimer in Maloney and Reimer, *Acts of the Apostles*, 136–42, where she argues that "acts of charity" "encompass actions such as those that are mentioned in Matthew 25:35–36 and refer to the practice of justice" (*Acts*, 136–142, especially, 137). Aymer observes that "a woman of wealth and status," Tabitha is "the only woman specifically named "disciple" (μαθήτρια: *discipula*) in the . . . New Testament" ("Acts Women's Bible Commentary," 541). On Tabitha see Reimer, *Women in Acts*, 31–69.

210. Paulraj, *Food Justice*, 195.

211. Reid, "Do You See This Woman?," 112–19. Schaberg and Ringe consider this a failure on the part of Luke ("Luke," 505).

hating "father, mother, wife and children, brothers and sisters, even life itself"; it involves carrying the cross, counting the cost and giving up all possessions (Luke 14:25–33). The women of Vindolanda belonged to a community in which people addressed each other as *frater*[212] and *soror*:[213] far from home they understood their friendships and the loyalty they had to each other in familial terms. That sense of a broadening of family commitments Jesus espoused may have struck home to them in their context too (Luke 8:19–21).[214] Followers of the Way in their position might find it possible to live the kind of commitment Jesus envisages in their context and at the same time bridge the divides they were all too aware of.

In the calendar of festivals observed at Vindolanda, 25 June also played a significant part in the lives of Lepidina, her household and her friends. It was the day of the festival of the goddess Fortuna and involved the provision of charitable donations. Were the likes of Lepidina or members of her household drawn to become followers of the Way this practice may have prepared them a little not only for that spirit of sharing (Acts 2:43–47) but also for the commitment to share with those most in need (Acts 4:35; 11:29).[215] They would be drawn to the centurion of Capernaum who was commended for his love for and commitment to the local people (Luke 7:4–5), to Cornelius who "gave alms generously to the people" (Acts 10:2) and in particular to Tabitha who "was devoted to good works and acts of charity" (Acts 9:36).

Fortuna's emblem was a *cornucopia* signifying the provision of plenty, and a ship's rudder on a globe, often associated with *redux* to "give the Emperor a safe homecoming from his travels," and suggesting mastery of the sea.[216] They themselves would have experienced the perilous sea-crossing

212. *Frater*: *Tab. Vindol. II*, 210, 233, 236, 243, 247, 248, 250, 252, 255, 256 (App), 259, 260, 265, 289, 295, 297, 300, 301, 306, 309, 310, 311, 331, 343, 345, 347, 349, 352, 363, 364 (App), 370 (App), 417, 420, 451, 456? 508; *Tab. Vindol. III*, 611, 612, 614, 622, 623, 629, 630, 632, 642, 643, 646, 648, 664, 667, 669, 670, 693, 713, 730, 750, 756, 790, 844, 848; *Tab. Vindol. IV*, 868, 869, 875, 877, 888.

213. *Soror*: *Tab. Vindol. II*, 291, 292. 293, 310, 335, 389; *Tab. Vindol. III*, 635, 639, 661.

214. For "comparable redefinitions" of familial relationships in the ancient world see Wolter, *Luke I*, 345. Cf. Matthews and Reid who comment that "for those born into disadvantaged social positions, an invitation into a fictive family group with those in positions of power would be good news indeed. But the summons is very costly for anyone of higher status. It is they to whom the parables are addressed" (*Luke 10–24*, 434).

215. Cf. Gregson who suggests the practice of Jewish almsgiving is part of the context for the practice of sharing (*Everything in Common?*, 77).

216. H. Mattingly, *Roman Coins*, 161. "Llanvaches Roman Coin Hoard": Denarii of

to Britannia and may have heard reports from the fleet dispatched by Agricola around the northern coast of Scotland after the Battle of Mons Graupius. Bearing the name of Claudius, Severa may have been proud that the conquest of the peoples beyond the ocean begun by Claudius was now commemorated not only in the triumphal arch on the Aqua Virgo in Rome but in a new arch erected c. 85 CE at the point of entry to Britannia at Rutupiae (Richborough). "Nowhere," Tacitus comments noting the swirling ebb and flow of the tidal currents, "does the sea dominate more widely" (*nusquam latius dominari mare, multum fluminum huc atque illuc ferre*).[217] Encountering Luke–Acts they would be invited to see Jesus as the one who "commands even the winds and the water, and they obey him" (καὶ τοῖς ἀνέμοις ἐπιτάσσει καὶ τῷ ὕδατι, καὶ ὑπακούουσιν αὐτῷ: *et ventis imperat et mari et oboediunt ei* Luke 8:25). The words of Paul to all on board the ship as it became victim to the storm off the coast of Crete suggest that such was the authority those who follow the Way could call on: "I urge you now to keep up your courage, for there will be no loss of life among you, but only of the ship" (παραινῶ ὑμᾶς εὐθυμεῖν· ἀποβολὴ γὰρ ψυχῆς οὐδεμία ἔσται ἐξ ὑμῶν πλὴν τοῦ πλοίου: *suadeo vobis bono animo esse amissio enim nullius animae erit ex vobis praeterquam navis* Acts 27:22). Mastery of the sea was the prerogative not only of the emperor and the forces of Rome but even more so of Jesus and the followers of the Way.[218]

Sickness and Death

Lepidina and Severa belonged to communities where sickness was common. They had a concern for their sick children as the centurion had for

---

Nerva, 2008.19H/171; 2008.19H/181; 2008.19H/182; 2008.19H/190. Moorhead, *Roman Coinage in Britain*, 17 fig. 3 a coin of Domitian. "PAS": Denarius of Trajan, NLM–E8B04D.

217. Tacitus, *Agricola* 10.6, 99; cf. 173–74. Hingley sees this as the moment when "the conquest of ocean" is complete (*Conquering the Ocean*, 162–163). "Gateway to Britannia." See Map (Figure 1) note.

218. With Parsons, "Empowering, Empire-ing or Engaging?," 145; Parsons is critical of Carter who sees Acts 27 as symbolic of sovereignty over the Roman Empire (*Navigating Roman World in Acts 27*); cf. Carter, "Aquatic Display"; Praeder suggests that "Paul's promises of safety in Acts 27:21–26, 33–38 link the storm and shipwreck to the story of salvation in Luke–Acts." Paul's "supposed ability to deliver a speech during a raging storm . . . is something . . . he shares with Odysseus, Julius Caesar, the Greeks and the Trojans, Hannibal, the Argonauts, and Aeneas" ("Sea Voyages in Luke–Acts," 695–696). Cf. Pervo, *Acts*, 660–61. Hingley's association of the conquest of Britain with the mastery of the sea informs our imagined reading (*Conquering the Ocean*, 92–93, 162–63).

his slave (Luke 7:1–10), the widow for her son (7:11–17) and the parents for their sick daughter (Luke 8:40–56). When afflicted with a fever Lepidina had access at least to a *seplasarius* and possibly a *medicus* and on one occasion was pleased to receive two remedies to help her. The fever of Simon's mother-in-law and the desire for relief from it were familiar (Luke 4:38–39). Eyesight problems were prevalent among the men of the cohort and played a significant part in Luke's account of Jesus and his followers as he gave sight to the blind (Luke 4:18; 7:21–23; 14:13, 21; 18:35–43), and as Saul's temporary blindness was healed (Acts 9:8–19; 22:11–13). That they lived with people who were sick or injured would mean that they recognized the significance of the healing Jesus brought. They would have had an empathy with the woman "suffering from hemorrhaging for twelve years" who had "spent all she had on physicians" (ἰατροῖς: *medicos* Luke 8:43–48).[219] When a very early tradition identified Luke as "the beloved physician" (ὁ ἰατρὸς ὁ ἀγαπητὸς: *medicus carissimus*), our imagined readers in Vindolanda would recognize the kind of person the writer had in mind (Col 4:14).

The early Christian homily from late fifth century or early sixth century Africa cited by Tomlin as evidence for the linking of *medici* and *seplasauri* relates to the equivalent narrative in Mark 5:25–34. It speaks of a woman's frustration as "she said to herself, 'Why should I go to the doctors now at such cost and without any benefit? Why should I go to the pharmacist and seek useless prescriptions for juices from plants?'" (. . . *ait intra se "Vt quid mihi iam medicis egere, cum sumptu, sine fructu? ut quid mihi dictata inaniter quaerere pigmenta, ire per simplassarios?"*).[220] Indeed, in Luke–Acts

219. Note that the reference to physicians is absent from an early third century papyrus of the passage in Luke and other manuscripts too: Metzger, *Textual Commentary*, 121; Houghton, however, points out that in Luke 8:43 "the skill of the writing has led to the suggestion that this is the work of the evangelist". While the committees of UBS 4, 5 and 6 are "doubtful about this text," SBLGNT and THGNT support it (*Textual Commentary UBS 6*, 141–42).

220. "Sermo De Flvxv Sangvinis." The homily goes on to speak of the art of the *medici* but also the iron instruments that arouse fear: . . . *ait intra se "Vt quid mihi iam medicis egere, cum sumptu, sine fructu? ut quid mihi dictata inaniter quaerere pigmenta, ire per simplassarios? sequar tantos sanatos et laetantes angelos, accedo ad simplassarium corporis mei, pulso caelestis medici ianuam, tango fimbriam et accipio medicinam. si purpuram regiam tangit reus et efficitur de crimine mortis securus, ego si tetigero regem caelorum non fortasse insultabo artibus medicorum? si tetigero, inquit, salua ero. fide Christi tango, et finem profluenti sanguini pono: accedo ad limitem fimbriorum prosumpsit et ferramenta non metuam medicorum. hoc fecit quod praesumpsit, hoc inuenit quod credidit, hoc accepit quod petit, hoc aperuit quod pulsavit* . . . "she said to herself, "Why should I go to the doctors now at such cost and without any benefit? Why should I go to the pharmacist and

Lepidina and Severa would encounter familiar features of their everyday world. When they read of the woman with the "alabaster jar of ointment" (*ἀλάβαστρον μύρου*: *alabastrum unguenti* Luke 7:37) and the women preparing "spices and ointments" following the burial of Jesus (*ἀρώματα καὶ μύρα*: aromata et *unguenta* Luke 23:56),[221] they may have thought of the ointments available to them through the services of a *seplasarius*.

Lepidina and Severa lived in a world that knew the meaning of grief expressed so powerfully in Virgil's lament of a woman for her son lost in battle.[222] They would have an empathy with the parents who wept at the death of their daughter (Luke 8:52), with Jesus as he wept over Jerusalem and the scale of its imminent destruction (Luke 19:41–44),[223] and with the women of Jerusalem who wept as Jesus went to his execution (Luke 23:27). If, as seems possible, texts of Virgil's *Aeneid* were available to Lepidina and Cerialis and others in Vindolanda,[224] it may well be that the *Aeneid* was for them one of "the repositories of genuine wisdom concerning the meaning of the past and its implications for the present."[225] In the century and more since it had been written it had become established as "a coherent interpretation of the whole course of Roman history": its over-arching message was

---

seek useless prescriptions for juices from plants? I will follow after such angels who heal and bring delight. If a criminal touches the purple robe of a king and his release from a mortal crime is secure, will it not follow that I, if I touch the king of the heavens, will perhaps not have abused the arts of the doctors?" "When I touch, I will be healed," she said. "I touch with faith in Christ and I put an end to the flow of blood: I reached out to the edge of his clothes and it has benefitted me and I do not fear the iron instruments of the doctors." She did this because she anticipated it. She found this because she believed. She received this because she prayed. She opened this [door] because she knocked." The "iron instruments of the doctors" may be seen in the British Museum, the Ashmolean museum and in many other Roman museums in Britain. See Chapter 1, *Accessing a Cultural Encyclopedia of the Roman World of Luke–Acts in Roman Britain*.

221. Wolter, *Luke II*, 537–38; cf. Matthews and Reid, *Luke 10–24*, 621.

222. See above, Chapter 3, nn. 149-154. Zeichmann suggests the healing of Aeneas (Acts 9:34) is symbolic of the healing of the empire (*Roman Army and the New Testament*, 83). On the other hand, Matthews and Reid argue that they represent "the defeated, which is to say the feminized, people of Judaea" (*Luke 10–24*, 601–2). Pervo observes that the name "Aeneas" "is attested for Palestinian Jews from the second century BCE to the fourth century CE" (*Acts*, 253).

223. Seim notes "the turbulence and horror" of the destruction envisaged here ("Virgin Mother," 92). Cf. Matthews and Reid, *Luke 10–24*, 517–21. Our imagined reading accords with the reading strategy they advocate (*Luke 10–24*, 521).

224. Bowman, *Life and Letters*, 88–89. See above, Chapter 3 n. 150.

225. Bonz, *Past as Legacy*, 16.

"that Rome's eternal rule has been granted in accordance with divine will only if one accepts the divine legitimacy of Virgil's Jupiter."[226] Just as the opening words of the *Aeneid* capture the thrust of its message, so too the opening words of Luke and of Acts, establish the reliability of this alternative vision.[227] Marianne Palmer Bonz argues that the basic structure of Luke–Acts is a reflection of, and perhaps deliberately modelled on, the bi-partite structure of the *Aeneid.* Books 1–6 tell of Aeneas's journey to the shores of Italy and Books 7–12 tell of the battles and other trials to be overcome after their arrival in Italy. Within that overall framework is, she suggests, a tri-partite structure whereby the "keystone" section featuring Rome and Augustus is at the center in books 5–8, flanked by sections that "emphasize the obstacles that must be met and overcome in order for the mission to reach its ultimately successful conclusion," Aeneas's struggles with Dido (books 1–4) and his struggles with Turnus (books 9–12).[228] Luke–Acts likewise has a bi-partite structure, in Luke telling of the life, death, resurrection and ascension of Jesus, and in Acts beginning at the point at which Luke ends, telling of the outpouring of the Spirit, the continuation of the mission by the disciples and the spread of the Pauline mission to Rome itself.[229] Within that framework there is also a tri-partite structure, at the center of which is the trial, death, resurrection and ascension of Jesus and the outpouring of the Holy Spirit and the beginnings of the Way in Jerusalem (Luke 19:28—Acts 8:1), flanked by an account of the tribulations that beset Jesus from the outset and as he journeys to Jerusalem (Luke 1—19:28) and of the tribulations that beset his first followers as the Way moves to Rome (Acts 8:2—28:31).[230]

226. Bonz, *Past as Legacy*, 182.

227. Bonz, *Past as Legacy*, 40–41, 129–32; cf. *Tab. Vindol. II* 452 (Appendix Chapter 3), containing the first line of the introductory words of the *Aeneid.* Compare Luke 1:1–4 and Acts 1:1–8 with *Aeneid* 1 lines 1–8: "*Arma virumque cano, Troiae qui primus ab oris |Italiam fato profugus Lavinaque venit |litora—multum ille et terris iactatus et alto |vi superum, saevae memorem Iunonis ob iram, |multa quoque et bello passus, dum conderet urbem |inferretque deos Latio; genus unde Latinum |Albanique patres atque altae moenia Romae.*" "Arms and the man I sing, who first from the coasts of Troy, exiled by fate, came to Italy and Lavine shores; much buffeted on sea and land by violence from above, through cruel Juno's unforgiving wrath, and much enduring in war also, till he should build a city and bring his gods to Latium; whence came the Latin race, the lords of Alba, and the lofty walls of Rome." Tr. Fairclough.

228. Bonz, *Past as Legacy*, 58–59. Cf. Talbert, *Reading Acts*, 20.

229. Bonz, *Past as Legacy*, 182–83.

230. Bonz, *Past as Legacy*, 129–93.

Familiar with Virgil's *Aeneid*, might our imagined readers have recognized that for Luke "the divine plan ultimately calls for the eternal reign of the risen Jesus over a universally chosen community of believers"? Bonz suggests that "Luke–Acts presents a rival vision of empire with a rival deity issuing an alternative plan for universal human salvation, involving a very different sort of hero as the primary instrument for the implementation of that plan, a different concept of the chosen people, and a very different means by which conquest leads to inevitable victory."[231] It would seem that Luke goes out of his way throughout Luke and Acts to ensure that our imagined readers would encounter people very much like them, and so realize that "Luke's vision of peaceful internal conquest" is inclusive of those who are very much part of the Roman Empire. Yet, at the same time, they were presented with a view of the world radically different from the one they were accustomed to.

Women of Agency

The women whose writings are preserved in Vindolanda were women of agency. Traveling with auxiliary cohorts experienced in fierce fighting they were not simply fellow travelers. Living in the *praetorium* they played an important part in the social fabric of the military community.[232] The likes of Lepidina and Severa offered help to other women,[233] and other women could look to them for help in difficult circumstances.[234] We can imagine such women noticing in Luke–Acts the way women undertake significant tasks that also make a difference.[235] It is Mary who is the first to encapsulate the challenge Jesus brings to the status quo wherever that may be (Luke 1:46–55) and a woman, Anna the prophet, who is the first to "speak about" Jesus "to all who were looking for the redemption of Jerusalem" (Luke

231. Bonz, *Past as Legacy*, 182.

232. Greene, "Sulpicia Lepidina," 107.

233. *Tab. Vindol. II* 257; Appendix Chapter 3. Greene, "Female Networks," 379–80.

234. *Tab. Vindol. II* 294; Appendix Chapter 3. Greene, "Women and Families," 249–50.

235. Cf. Kahl who advocates reading Luke–Acts through the eyes not only of Theophilus and his like, but also through the eyes of Lydia and the women who made up the diverse communities of followers of the Way ("Reading Luke Against Luke," 83–88). D'Angelo imagines "real women" in the second century and concludes that in Luke–Acts men are assigned "the ministry of the word, and women "the ministry of benefactions and hospitality" ("ANHP Question," 66–69); cf. D'Angelo, "Women in Luke–Acts," 455.

2:38). It is a group of women, some of whom are of high standing, who resource Jesus' itinerant mission as "models of sharing" (Luke 8:1–3).[236] They and other women who had traveled with Jesus and accompanied him through the troubles of his final week are the first to share the message of his resurrection (Luke 24:8–10) and may be regarded as disciples.[237] Tabitha's life is spent doing good (Acts 9:36). Lydia, a dealer in purple cloth, is host to a community of followers of the Way (Acts 16:14–15, 40). Priscilla is a tentmaker, who with her husband hosts such a community, travels and teaches (Acts 18:1–3, 24–28).[238] It is not only Philip, one of the seven and "an evangelist" (Acts 6:1–6; 8:26–40) but also his four unmarried daughters who "had the gift of prophecy" (Acts 21:8–9).[239] Theirs was a partially literate world in which they saw to it that their children were taught to write: they might have assumed some literacy, not least on the part of the leading women they meet in Luke–Acts (Luke 8:1–3; Acts 13:50; 17:4) and might well assume that just as Zechariah could write (Luke 1:63), so too Mary's responsibility in nurturing her son was to ensure that he too would be able to read and, as Chris Keith argues, write (Luke 2:40, 52; 4:16).[240]

Imagining Cassius Felicio, Saecularis and Other Centurions and Officers

In Luke–Acts, we encounter centurions who figure, Esler suggests, "as a prototype of the government officials who will later show such interest in the Christian message."[241] The Vindolanda tablets throw light on the deal-

236. Schaberg and Ringe, "Luke," 497.

237. Karris, "Women and Discipleship in Luke," 28–33, 36–39.

238. Pervo notes that "these three are associated with fabric" and "in all three cases the activity is income-producing" (*Acts*, 255).

239. Maloney and Reimer, *Acts*, 290–91.

240. Keith argues that John 8:6,8 reflects a plausible historical tradition that Jesus could write ("Pericope Adulterae"); elsewhere he suggests that Jesus' literacy was not to the level of a scribal-teacher (*Jesus' Literacy*). In Codex Bezae the Latin equivalent of καταγράφω in John 8:6,8 is *scribo*: "*Codex Bezae* (MS Nn.2.41)," 238–39 (134v, 135r). To Keith's use of the Oxyrhynchus Papyri to illustrate the use of καταγράφω (in *Codex Bezae* the equivalent of *scribo*), might be added the use of *scribo* in the Bloomberg tablets and the Vindolanda tablets to refer to everyday writing: *Tab. Lond. Bloomberg* 23, 44, 50, 53, 55; *Tab. Vindol. II* 177, 212, 225, 260, 289, 300, 311, 312, 324, 334, 343, 364, 377; *Tab. Vindol. III* 611, 645, 647, 664, 665, 667, 670, 701, 706, 751, 832, 842, *Tab. Vindol. IV* 875, 893.

241. Esler, *Community and Gospel in Luke-Acts*, 37.

ings of centurions within the military community and with local people and traders. Centurions in auxiliary cohorts had often come up through the ranks and shared the same ethnic background as their men, though many came from wealthier families and local aristocracy.[242] Finds from Vindolanda suggest that centurions and their cavalry equivalent, decurions, may have had their wives living with them.[243]

Travel for centurions and other men was commonplace. On the day of the strength report of *cohors I Tungrorum*, five of the six centurions had traveled away from the fort, one in Londinium another outside the province, another in Gaul. 456 of the 752 men were also some distance away.[244] The letter Chrauttius wrote to "his brother and old messmate" (*suó fratri | contubernali antique*) was to be delivered "at London" to Veldedeius, "the groom of the governor" (*Londini |Veldedeio |equisioni co(n)s(ularis)*.[245] After chastising him for failing to write for such a long time, Chrauttius passes greetings on to other mutual acquaintances, chases up the shears he had bought from Virilis the veterinary doctor and asks to be remembered to "our sister Thuttena." An expenses account[246] from the *praetorium* of *cohors I Tungrorum* details a route described in the later Antonine itinerary from Eboracum (York) to Coria (Corbridge), passing through Isurium (Aldborough), Cataractonium (Catterick) and Vinovia (Binchester).[247] This suggests that "itineraries were used for official perambulations in which several centers might be visited in a given order."[248] The outward journey includes dates and on five occasions ¼ of a denarius is spent on wine. The substantial account for 94 ¾ denarii includes the cost of accommodation, wheat, salt, fodder, and vests together with wagon axles for a carriage.[249] The network of roads across the province and the empire facilitated the

242. Goldsworthy, *Complete Roman Army*, 73.

243. A. R. Birley, *Garrison Life*, 103; R. Birley, *Vindolanda: Daily Life*, 21.

244. *Tab. Vindol. II* 154, a strength report dated 18 May between 92 and 97 CE. Appendix Chapter 3. Cf. *Tab. Vindol. IV* 857, a similar strength report. For similar reports from other periods and other parts of the empire see Alston, *Soldier and Society*, 22–23.

245. *Tab. Vindol. II* 310: the name Veldedius appears on a leather offcut found nearby in association with a horse's chamfron (armor to protect a horse's head). Tomlin, "Vindolanda's Other Inscriptions," 209. Appendix Chapter 3.

246. *Tab. Vindol. II* 185.

247. Route I: B. Jones and Mattingly, *Atlas of Roman Britain*, 25; Map (Figure 1) 45; 44; 43; 42; 41.

248. B. Jones and Mattingly, *Atlas of Roman Britain*, 23. Cf. Abdy, *Legion*, 37–43.

249. *Tab. Vindol.* 185, Bowman and Thomas, *Tab. Vindol. II*.

exchange of correspondence, cemented relationships, and established an identity for those centurions, officers and men beyond the cohort they belonged to. It helped build a web whose strands secured power in the empire.[250] It also gave them knowledge of the wider world. Some knowledge of Rome with Domitian's recently erected arch commemorating the quelling of the Judean revolt by Titus can be assumed, not least because of the circulation of *Iudaea capta* coins.[251] With roots in Batavia and Tungria and retaining their ethnic identity and customs,[252] our imagined readers from *cohors I Tungrorum* and *cohors VIIII Batauorum* would recognize in the use of the word Ἰουδαῖοι: *Iudaei* people with an ethnic identity rooted in their homeland of *Iudaea* and shared customs and practices.[253] The narrative of Luke–Acts is written enabling those with no direct knowledge of the *Iudaei* to understand something of their background in the law and the prophets.

Extensive administrative responsibilities demanded advanced levels of numeracy and literacy from centurions.[254] Michael Speidel argues that "the complete absence of Germanic influences from the Latin of the Vindolanda tablets . . . betrays the surprisingly high level of linguistic competence of their authors."[255] A brief report of the day's duties (*renuntium*)[256] would be submitted by the *optio* in charge of a small group of men.[257] Many have been discovered:[258] the fullest relates to the century of Crescens (*Tab. Vindol.* III 574).

250. Woolf, "Rulers Ruled," sec. 25; Kolb, "Mobility," 120–23.

251. Vespasian (48), Titus (3), Domitian (1), Galba (1): IVDAEA CAPTA Coins, reported to PAS; and two in the "Llanvaches Hoard": 2008.19H/19; 2008.19H/20. Esler includes sketches of all the IVDAEA CAPTA coin types in the British Museum (*Modelling Early Christianity*, 246–54).

252. A. R. Birley, *Garrison Life*, 42–45.

253. Brawley, *Luke*, 8; Mason, "Jews, Judaeans," 489–509, 511; contrast Matthews, *Acts* xiv; Novenson, "Ioudaios, Pharisee, Zealot," 168. Cf. the use of Lingonian (Lingonus) and Nervians (Neruii) in the Bloomberg tablets: Tab. Lond. Bloomberg 55 and 33, see above, Chapter 2, nn. 218, 219, 220.

254. Goldsworthy, *Complete Roman Army*, 72; Bowman, *Life and Letters*, 79–94; Speidel, "Learning Latin in Roman Army," 142.

255. Speidel, "Learning Latin in Roman Army," 149.

256. A. R. Birley, *Garrison Life*, 80–85.

257. *Tab. Vindol. II* 127: century of Exomnius; 128, century of Crescens; 138, century of Felicio (cf. II 166, 168, 182, 193, III 578, 610); 148, optio Candidus of the century of Crescens; *Tab. Vindol. III* 575: century of Exomnius; 576, IV 849: century of Rufus. Cf. *Tab. Vindol. II* 129, 137, IV 870.

258. *renuntio Tab. Vindol. II* 127, cf. III Appendix; 128; 129, cf. III Appendix; 130;

Figure 13. *Tab. Vindol. III* 574. *Renuntium* report by Arcuittius, *optio* of the century of Crescens of Cohors VIIII Batavorum. W 83mm x H 82 mm. Appendix Chapter 3. © The Trustees of the British Museum.

More detailed reports were made of the work accomplished each day.[259] On one occasion, possibly when units from *cohors VIIII Batauorum* had joined *cohors I Tungrorum,* 343 men were in the workshops (*in officis*), twelve making shoes, eighteen building a bath house, others building a hospital; they sawed, plastered, moved rubble, worked with lead and clay, and made tents.[260] Centurions were also involved in commissioning work from skilled craftsmen (*fabri*) in the workshops (*fabricae*): Musurunus, a centurion, ordered a strap or webbing for the underpart of a vehicle from

135; 137; 138; 139; 146; 148; 152; 153; 458?; III 574, 576, 578; *renuntium Tab. Vindol. II* 545, cf. III Appendix; III 574; 575; 577; 579; *renuntius Tab. Vindol. II* 127; 130; 131; 133; 134; 135; 136; *renutium Tab. Vindol. II* 140; 141; 143; 147; 149; 151; 545?. Source: *RIB* Index of Latin words.

259. Abdy, *Legion*, 239–41.

260. *Tab. Vindol. II* 155, cf. III Appendix; Abdy, *Legion*, 182–83.

the workshop of the century of Firmus, *ocridem ► factam ad uetu|5 ram ► iussu Musuruni (centurionis)*.[261]

Centurions were able to make requests on behalf of their men: on one occasion, a decurion, Masclus, wrote to Iulius Verecundus requesting leave for some of his men and the return of a cleaving knife on loan to Talampus of the century of Nobilis.[262] Formal requests for leave (*commeatus*) were addressed to the prefect and emphasized the "worthiness" (*dignum*) of the one making the request.[263] In one of the most complete, Buccus addresses the prefect as "my lord" (*domine*) and commends "a worthy person to whom to grant leave" without specifying the purpose of the leave (*Buccus t.[|rogo domine dignum |me habeas cui des c[o]m|[m]eatum p.r.so ut possi[m] | 5 [c.6 ...]e.ere fa.[)*.[264] Andangius and Vel [. . .] work closely with the prefect Verecundus asking that Crispus the *mensor* be given lighter military service (*[amicum] nostrum nomi|[ne] Crispum mensorem |facias ut possit bene|10 ficio tuo leuius militare |e[t] genio tuo gratias age|[re d]ebemus* vacat).[265] Flavius Cerialis wrote in his own hand to his dearest, fortunate brother (*m2? uale mi feliciter(?) [frater].. [|karissime* vacat), an unnamed centurion based away from the fort, ordering his return to do a head-count of his soldiers or to arrange some kind of payment to other centurions.[266] The centurion, Clodius Super, wrote in a similarly intimate way to Flavius Cerialis as "my dearest lord and brother" (*domine frater |carissime*), expressing concern for his boys' well-being ahead of their transfer and asking for the provision of appropriate clothing.[267]

One of the key strengths of the Roman army was its division into small groups dependent on each other. A century, under a centurion, would be

261. *Tab. Vindol. IV* 862. Cf. *Tab. Vindol. II* 160, 182.

262. *Tab. Vindol. IV* 892. Cf. *Tab. Vindol. III* 586, an account, III 628 a letter from Masclus to Cerialis and an address, II 505.

263. Six addressed to Cerialis, prefect of *cohors VIIII Batauorum* (*Tab. Vindol. II* 166–171); one to Flavianus, prefect in command at an earlier date, (172); one to Priscinus, prefect of *cohors I Tungrorum* (173); and four which do not include the name of the addressee. Among those asking for leave are someone whose name ends in . . . danus of the century of Felicio (166), an unknown person from the century of Felicio (168), Gannalius (169); Expeditus (171); Aventinus (172); Messicus (175); and Buccus (176) each of whom belongs to an unidentified century.

264. *Tab. Vindol. II* 176.

265. *Tab. Vindol. IV* 891. Appendix Chapter 3.

266. *Tab. Vindol. II* 242, cf. III Appendix.

267. *Tab. Vindol. II* 255; "boys" in the sense of "slaves": *OLD*, 1515. Cf. *Tab. Vindol. II* 184 where overcoats and other commodities are being traded in the centuries of Ucenius (?) and Tullio.

made up of approximately ten *contubernia* of eight men sharing a tent or barrack room.[268] Connectedness is the key and is reflected in the way correspondents address each other. In one tantalizingly fragmented letter spanning three tablets,[269] it looks as if centurions and others shared together in the kind of military association or guild that prior to the discovery of the Vindolanda tablets had been evident only from the time of Septimus Severus (193–211 CE).[270] The writer addresses someone as "most loved" (*ka]r[is]|sime*), and seems to be making good some problem that has arisen by sending additional denarii in "individual wrappings" (*in cartas inse[- |ges*). Acknowledging his mistake (*mea erratio*) he appeals for support to preserve his honor, "so please believe me . . . that I retire thus so that my reputation is intact, which is the chief point" (*ita rogo credas mihi |m.....eme sic re|5 cedere ut integer |sim quod est primu(m)*). He goes on to clarify his reasoning: "And yet I want it to be clear to you that I am withdrawing neither from the mess nor from the club [/ association/guild] unless . . ." (*ac tamen uolo liqueat |tibi me nec a contiber|nio recedere nec a sco|5 la nisi c..ius rationem*). Sadly, the reason he gives has been lost. The writer defends himself to the "lord," *domi|no* referring to an occasion when he was seen at the "goldsmiths" or "the silversmiths" who may well have been based in Londinium (*apud auri|fices aut apud argen|5 tarios*). In what may be the conclusion to the letter mention is made again of the mess (*contibernium*) and the recipient is asked to pass greetings on to, among two others, Felicio, a centurion who is mentioned in a number of tablets.[271] We

268. *OLD*, 436. Cf. J. K. Knight, *Caerleon*, 42–43 (Map (Figure 1) 28); Alston, *Soldier and Society*, 21. See Figure 9.

269. *Tab. Vindol. III* 655, 656, 657. Appendix Chapter 3.

270. On *scholae* see *Tab. Vindol. III* 656, Bowman and Thomas, *Tab. Vindol. III*.

271. *Tab. Vindol. III* 655, 656, 657. Appendix Chapter 3. Bowman and Thomas comment that this is a very early reference to *scholae* usually associated with Severan times and later (*Tab. Vindol. III* 656 n. i.4–5). Richmond describes Guilds (*collegia*) as "worshipful associations of private soldiers and lower ranks for welfare and good fellowship" associated with Severan and later buildings ("Roman Legionaries," 133–34). According to Smith, in Severan times "they were also social clubs, enjoying occasional "feasts," and having a clubhouse, *schola*, within the camp perimeter for relaxation and entertainment" ("Army Reforms," 497). According to Goldsworthy, buildings in Lambaesis, North Africa have been "tentatively identified as the *scholae* or guild houses associated with particular ranks such as centurions" (*Complete Roman Army*, 88). Bowman and Thomas suggest that "goldsmiths and silversmiths were perhaps operating in London" (*Tab. Vindol. III* 656, n. ii.4–5). The temple of Neptune and Minerva was built by the authority of Tiberius Claudius Togidubnus, "great king of Britain," by the guild of smiths (*[colle]gium fabror(um)*: see Chapter 1, n. 39. For Felicio, *centurio* see *Tab Vindol.* II 138,166, 168, 182, 193, 242, III 578; for Felicio see 657, 698.

glimpse here that sense of mutual interdependence within a *contubernium* and a *schola* extending to the associations of silversmiths and goldsmiths in far off London; there is a warmth in the final greeting that suggests a sense of connectedness among colleagues set in a framework of honor and shame as the writer seeks to right a wrong. The same sense of connectedness is evident in the other letter by the same writer, in which he counts among his "messmates" (*[c]ontibernales*) someone with the Greek name, Elpis.[272]

Centurions had responsibility for the purchase of foodstuffs, trading with civilians: in Cerialis's time Surenus is mentioned in the context of the acquisition of chickens, while decurions are linked with beer.[273] The Vindolanda tablets show that coinage was in regular use and the main denomination referenced was the denarius.[274] Once, when *cohors I Tungrorum* returned to a much enlarged fort in Vindolanda c. 105–120 CE, sufficient grain was ordered to meet the dietary requirements of 2,000 soldiers for one day; Firmus ordered grain for legionary soldiers who were at the time in the fort;[275] Felicio the centurion ordered 45 pounds of bacon, and centurion Exominius is listed handling denarii in records kept by a civilian trader.[276]

Letters addressed to Cassius Saecularis (a centurion, decurion or *optio*) suggest he had responsibility for the supply of barley[277] and of timber[278] and may have been involved with local people as an "*interpres*," an agent or "interpreter in some transaction with non-Latin speakers."[279] Saecularius seems to have won the respect of those he dealt with: Curtius Super greets him as "his Cassius" (*Curtius Super Cassio suo |salutem*);[280] Vittius Adiutior, *aquilifer*

272. *Tab. Vindol. II* 346: this was the very first tablet to be discovered in 1973 and speaks of socks sent by one Sattua and of four pairs of sandals and two underpants. It finishes with similar superlative greetings: *[o]pto felicissimus uiuas*: I pray that you live in the greatest good fortune.

273. *Tab. Vindol. III* 581; cf. Abdy, *Legion*, 184.

274. Of the 233 references to coinage in the Vindolanda tablets, 194 mention denarii, one mentions a dupondius and thirty-eight mention the as: Bland, "Coin Hoards," 72.

275. *Tab. Vindol. II* 180, Bowman and Thomas, *Tab. Vindol. II*: Introduction.

276. *Tab. Vindol.* 182. Cf. *Tab. Vindol. IV* 861. For an assessment of the Roman military diet in general see R. W. Davies, "Roman Military Diet." For an assessment in the light of the Vindolanda evidence see Pearce, "Food in the Roman Army"; Whittaker, "Supplying the Army"; Abdy, *Legion*, 221–22.

277. *Tab. Vindol. II* 213.

278. *Tab. Vindol. II* 215.

279. Bowman and Thomas, *Tab. Vindol. II* 213, Commentary and Notes ii 1; Wilson, "Latin, Literacy and Roman Economy," 90.

280. *Tab. Vindol. II* 213.

of *II legio Augusta* based in Caerleon, extends "very many [greetings]" to him as his "little brother" (*fra|terclo suo plurimam*);[281] and another writes with cheerful familiarity, "I pray that you are enjoying the best of fortune and are in good health" *opto felicissimus bene ualeas*.[282] It was not only the staple diet the centurions were involved with: Felicio, a centurion with *cohors VIIII Batauorum* arranged a loan for the purchase of spices (*condimentorum*), gruel (*halicae*) and eggs (*oua*).[283] Such exotic spices suggest involvement with traders from the eastern Mediterranean.[284] They also had a part to play in arranging festivals. A letter written in the same hand as *Tab. Vindol.* II 213 and 214 and so associated with Saecularis speaks of arrangements for a priest to be sent to Verecundus, the prefect, about a festival (. . . |*sacerdotem quem |rogo ut ad Verecun|dum praef(ectum) de fes- |. . . | . . .)*.[285]

A letter from Octavius, probably a civilian trader, throws light on the trade undertaken by centurions and other officers.[286] It was found with two accounts and the appeal of an overseas trader in the barrack block c. 105–120 CE.[287] Described as "the most impressive and extensive letter found at Vindolanda so far,"[288] it is a business letter written in haste using technical financial terms and spellings influenced by the sound of words.[289] It throws light on the world of honor and shame present on the northern frontier as much as in the eastern Mediterranean.[290] Indeed, Anthony Birley suggests Fatalis (line 22) was a legionary centurion born in Rome who served in Britannia with *legio II Augusta* and *legio XX Victrix* and finished his 23 years of service in *Iudaea* with *legio X Fretensis*. At his death, aged 42, Claudia Ionice, his "freedwoman

281. *Tab. Vindol. II* 214 Pollard and Berry, *Complete Roman Legions*, 92.

282. *Tab. Vindol. II* 215.

283. *Tab. Vindol. II* 193.

284. Haynes, *Blood of the Provinces*, 184. Meyer suggests this was a *mutuum*, a "real contract" open to citizens and non-citizens: "the delivery of a thing obligated the recipient to return a thing of the same amount and quality as what had been received (*condimenta, halicae, ova*)" ("Law and Latinization," 193–94).

285. *Tab. Vindol. II* 313.

286. *Tab. Vindol. II* 343. Appendix Chapter 3.

287. *Tab. Vindol. II* 180, 181, 344. Johnston notes that "freedmen and freedwomen played a major role in the working of the Roman economy" and "are found . . . carrying out trading missions overseas" (*Roman Law*, 125).

288. *Tab. Vindol. II* 343; Appendix Chapter 3. A. R. Birley, "Vindolanda: Notes," 90–93; A. R. Birley, *Garrison Life*, 114–17; Bowman and Thomas, *Tab. Vindol. II*.

289. *Tab. Vindol. II* 343, Bowman and Thomas, *Tab. Vindol. II*. Appendix Chapter 3.

290. Cf. above, Chapter 2, nn., 160-167.

and heiress" (*lib(erta) et heres*) erected a tomb "on account of his merits" (*ob me|rita eius*) in Jerusalem.[291] Candidus, Spectatus and Firmus, centurions or *optiones*, were trading in large amounts with Octavius: 5,000 modii of cereal and hundreds of hides linked to Cataractonium (Catterick). The letter opens with an urgent plea from Octavius to Candidus: unless 500 denarii in cash is delivered promptly, he will lose his deposit (*arre*)[292] of 300 denarii and will "be embarrassed" or "blush with shame" (*erubescam*). His plea is heartfelt, "so, I ask you, send me some cash as soon as possible." Transactions referred to in this letter depend on the honor of all involved. According to du Plessis, this is "the only example where the Roman legal principle of *bona fides* is explained in concrete terms." Here we see the fundamental principle on which trade and so much of life depended throughout the empire: "much of Roman commerce was based on connections or 'networks' in which the parties trusted each other to behave in a trustworthy manner."[293] For Greg Woolf, it was by binding people into "networks of obligation and compliance" that Roman power was established.[294] The use of *erubesco*[295] is indicative of what du Plessis describes as "loss of face." The seriousness of what has happened financially means that the deposit (*arra*) that has been paid will be lost and Octavian will be shamed; the very use of *arra* depends upon the honor of all involved.[296] This is a good example of the Old Roman Cursive script used in the Vindolanda tablets:[297]

291. A. R. Birley, "Vindolanda: Notes," 93; Tiberius Claudius Fatalis: Zeichmann, "Database of Military Inscriptions," sec. 53.

292. A shortened form of *arrabo*, a transliteration of the Greek which also appears in Hebrew: *OLD*, 173. Entering Greek from Phoenician, its variant here is an example of a word that is spelled as it sounds. It occurs in a letter to do with another large deposit of 200 denarii in *Tab. Lond. Bloomberg* 35, in the Greek of 2 Cor 1:22; 5:5; Eph 1:14; and in the Hebrew and Greek of Gen 38:17, 18, 20. Cf. R. Cleaves, "Reading the New Testament in Roman Britain," 340–41. Appendix Chapter 2.

293. Du Plessis, "Provincial Law in Britannia," 16. Cf. Meyer, "Law and Latinization," 193; Johnston, *Roman Law*, 96. Cf. the appeal of the innocent man from overseas who had been beaten: *Tab. Vindol. II* 344. Appendix Chapter 3.

294. Woolf, "Rulers Ruled," sec. 30. Cf. Woolf, *Ancient Cities*, 358–62.

295. Literally, "go red in the face." Cf. *OLD*, 619: blush for shame, feel ashamed; in general, to become red.

296. Du Plessis, "Provincial Law in Britannia," 17; cf. R. Cleaves, "Reading the New Testament in Roman Britain," 340–41.

297. For an introduction to cursive scripts and how to read them, see Mullen and Bowman, *Scripts and Texts*, 1:41–83. Old Roman Cursive is also used in the Bloomberg tablets and in the Uley tablets.

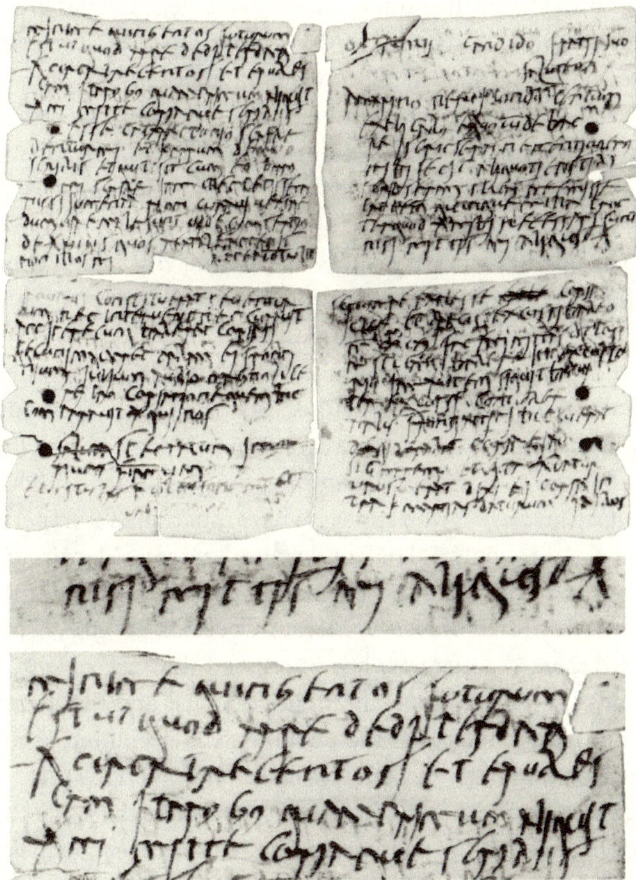

Figure 14. *Tab. Vindol. II* 343. Octavius writes a letter to Candidus regarding military supplies. a) W 182 × H 79; (b) W 179 × H 79. Appendix Chapter 3. © The Trustees of the British Museum. Lines 10–15, enlarged, illustrate Old Roman Cursive writing (line 10 is the bottom line of the top right leaf; line 11 is the first line of the top left leaf).

nisi mittis mi aliquit X
minime quingentos futurum
est ut quod arre dedi perdam
X circa trecentos et erubes
cam ita rogo quam primum aliquit
X mi mitte . . .

Unless you send me some cash, at least five hundred *denarii*, the result will be that I shall lose what I have laid out as a deposit, about three hundred *denarii*, and I shall be embarrassed. So, I ask you, send me some cash as soon as possible.
Note *X* is the symbol for *denarii*.

Later in the letter the honor code is in danger of being broken as Octavius expresses his frustration at the "messmate (*contubernalis*) of their friend Frontius" who had failed to keep an appointment and conclude a cash transaction for a significant number of hides. He has also heard that another acquaintance, Frontinius Iulius had been selling leather ware (?) at what, by implication, Octavius considers an excessive price.[298] The failure of their "messmate" to keep to the honor code means he will no longer be able to do business. To make matters worse, Octavius had to cope with the bad weather of northern Britannia and was unwilling to risk the well-being of his pack animals in adverse conditions.

There is evidence that imperial officials were involved with the grain supply. Trading in grain with his father, Maior writes to Cocceiius Maritimus seeking clarification about the arrangements for a transaction Maritimus has undertaken with the *Caesariani* (*cum Caesaria|n is*),[299] "members of the *familia Caesaris*"[300] who appear to have functioned as imperial officials linked to the grain supply.[301] His *gentilicium*[302] suggests Maritimus may have been "a freedman of Nerva, perhaps an imperial administrator,"[303] linked with another freedman of Nerva, Marcus Cocceius Vegetus,[304] perhaps the manumitted slave Vegetus who had purchased the enslaved girl Fortunata in Londinium.[305] The relationship hinges on trust and the honor of those involved but is in jeopardy: more documents are required as any further delay in completing the transaction will result in sanctions that will involve removing grain from the store. In a postscript written between the two columns at right angles to the main text, Maior adds a caveat, requesting that if Maritimus replies sending a slave (*puer*), he should bring with him a *chir(o)*

298. Abdy suggests there is possible evidence of deliberate cheating of local suppliers of grain in the discovery of a *modius*, a grain measure, from the reign of Domitian (81–95 CE) purporting to contain "exactly" 17½ *sextarii* (about 10 litres) of grain when it actually contained 20½ *sextarii* (about 11 ½litres) of grain (*Legion*, 247–48).

299. *Tab. Vindol. III* 645.

300. R. Birley and A. R. Birley, "Four New Tablets," 443.

301. Whittaker, "Supplying the Army," 93.

302. Bowman, *Life and Letters*, 50.

303. *Tab. Vindol. III* 645, Bowman and Thomas, *Tab. Vindol. III*.

304. *Tab. Vindol. II* 352.

305. Tomlin, "Girl in Question"; *Tab. Vindol. II* 352, cf. III Appendix: Bowman and Thomas, *Tab. Vindol. II*.

grafum, a note of hand. This may refer to a stylus tablet, a more appropriate form for legal documents.[306]

The local population are almost invisible in the tablets, and yet they are always there in the background. Probus acknowledges receipt of a large quantity of grain, 381 modii, from carts belonging to local Britons each of which carries fifty-three modii.[307] It seems that "the addressee was being promised a fee (or even payment in kind . . .) for his services in paying part of the carriage expenses":[308] "Furthermore(?), they have half(?) the payments for carriage (*dimi]dias uecturas*), that is one *denarius* each, and the full load for transportation as contracted (*et omnem uelaturam*); and the (part of the) payment for carriage which you will pay them, I(?) shall duly measure out to you as your fee(?)." That payment of the local population for transport was regulated is suggested in a bi-lingual Pisidian inscription from the time of Tiberius cited by Bowman and Thomas, stating that "no one should make use of carts without payment" (*ne quis gratuitis vehiculis utatur*).[309] In publishing the Pisidian inscription, Mitchell compares it with twenty-one papyri documenting similar regulations concerning the requisition of transport and suggests that many of them imply significant abuses of the system.[310] It is not clear from this Vindolanda tablet whether or not the payments were paid to local people; while there is no means of knowing how such a system was received by them, it is not unreasonable to suppose there were tensions with its imposition. It would seem some supplies were handled by the army and others contracted out to civilians. They were sourced locally and from further afield to the south and abroad for more exotic commodities.[311] In addition to an account mentioning "Brittanic civilian shoes and a Brittanic tunic" (*gallic [|].os ► Britt [anic]- |].. gallicula[| 5]cam Brit [tanic]-*),[312] a military memorandum describes the way the local Britons (*Brittones*) fight with cavalry before going on to speak of the

306. A. R. Birley, *Garrison Life*, 118–20; Meyer, "Writing in Legal Contexts," 86. Vindolanda's stylus tablets, far fewer than the ink tablets, have not yet been published.

307. *Tab. Vindol. III* 649.

308. J. N. Adams, "New Vindolanda Tablets," 561. The following reading is suggested by Bowman and Thomas, *Tab. Vindol. III* 649, n. line ii.11–12.

309. Bowman and Thomas, *Tab. Vindol. III* 649, n. i.2: S. Mitchell, "Requisitioned Transport," 107–9; Pritchard, *Atlas of Bible*, 172–73. In Acts Paul frequently traveled through Pisidia: Acts 13:13–52; 14:24; 16:4; 18:23.

310. S. Mitchell, "Requisitioned Transport," 111–12.

311. Whittaker, "Supplying the Army," 101.

312. *Tab. Vindol. III* 602.

way the "wretched Britons (*Brittunculi)* do not "mount in order to throw javelins."[313] It may have been an intelligence report regarding recruitment of locals to the army or (Bowman and Thomas's preference) an informative memo from a departing commander officer to his successor on the prowess of the Britons on horseback. In that case it may have been a note to Flavius Genialis from Haterius Nepos, a prefect who went on to be census officer for the Britons of the Anaviones (*censito[ri] | Brittonum Anavion[ens]*) and prefect of Egypt.[314]

Mention of a census[315] supports Tacitus in saying that Britons were conscripted as auxiliaries, involved at Mons Graupius (*expedito exercitu, cui ex Britannis fortissimos et longa pace exploratos addidderat, ad montem Graupium pervenit*: "with his army marching light, having reinforced it with the bravest of the Britanni whose loyalty had been proved during a long peace, he reached Mons Graupius.")[316] and later levied into units that served in Germania.[317] The imposition of regulations for transport, the use of the pejorative *Brittunculi* and reference to the census, remind us of the uneasy relationship with the local peoples. Tacitus had shortly before expressed a cynical view of that "long peace" the Britons experienced as they came to like fine buildings, education and Latin: "In their innocence they called this 'civilization', when in fact it was a part of their enslavement: *Idque apud imperitos humanitas vocabatur, cum pars servitutis esset*."[318] The words Tacitus puts into the mouth of Calgacus at Mons Graupius are a reminder that there was a brutality to the *imperium Romanum* they imposed and the *pax Romana* they celebrated: "Robbery, butchery, rapine, these the liars call 'empire' [*imperium*]: they create desolation and call it peace [*pax*]: *auferre trucidare rapere falsis nominibus imperium atque ubi solitudinem faciunt pacem appellant*."[319] The tensions that were to erupt into an uprising

313. *Tab. Vindol. II* 164.

314. Bowman and Thomas, *Tab. Vindol. III* 611, Introduction. Cf. Desau ILS, 1338: https://archive.org/details/inscriptioneslat01dessuoft/page/296/mode/2up.

315. *Tab. Vindol. II* 304.

316. Tacitus, *Agricola* 29.2, 110–11; *Agricola and Germania*, 19. See Map (Figure 1) note.

317. Southern, "Numeri of the Roman Army," 94–98.

318. Tacitus, *Agricola* 21.2, 107; *Agricola and Germania*, 15.

319. Tacitus, *Agricola* 30.5, 112, 257–58; *Agricola and Germania*, 20.

in the north of Britannia as Hadrian became emperor were never far from the surface.[320]

One informal account indicates that civilian traders worked with local producers of grain and other foodstuff and with *cohors I Tungrorum* after their return to Vindolanda between 105 and 120 CE. Working in close partnership with his brother and his father, the trader details loans and cash payments and refers to trade in wheat, oxen and pigs, naming centurions, a *beneficarius*, legionary soldiers and others. Wheat is supplied to oxherds in a nearby wood and to Amabilis at a shrine (*fanum*).[321]

On the reverse of two of the three sections of this account is the draft of another document written by the same person.[322] It suggests something had gone seriously wrong and that, although innocent, the trader had suffered a beating after claiming certain goods were worthless and after pouring others down the drain. He had the confidence to appeal to the military authorities. He sought redress from the prefect only to find him indisposed due to ill health; he turned to the *beneficarius*[323] and to other centurions but to no avail. He therefore appeals to "your majesty" (*tuam maies| [t] atem*). The form of address suggests an appeal at least to the provincial governor, possibly Flavius Proculus,[324] or even to the emperor Hadrian in anticipation of his visit.[325] Protesting his honesty and innocence he maintains that he should not have been beaten and he seeks redress. He repeats his claim to innocence and, addressing himself to "your mercifulness" (*tu] am misericord[ia]m*) he maintains that his good faith is open to full inquiry (*de cuius f[ide] |inquiras uirgis cruenṭ[at]u[m] |esse*).[326] Describing himself

320. A. R. Birley, *Garrison Life*, 95–97; D. J. Mattingly, *An Imperial Possession*, 119–21; S. R. Jackson, *Roman Occupation of Britain*, 143–55; Salway, *Roman Britain*, 173–84; Bruhn and Hodgson, "Impact of Hadrian's Wall," 133, 152–64.

321. Bowman and Thomas, *Tab. Vindol. II* 180, n. 10.

322. *Tab. Vindol. II* 344. Appendix Chapter 3.

323. Goldsworthy describes a *beneficarius* as an "experienced soldier attached to the staff of a provincial governor, often performing "policing functions" (*Complete Roman Army*, 215). Cf. Salway, *History of Roman Britain*, 372–73.

324. Bowman and Thomas, *Tab. Vindol. II* 344, Introduction, cf. III Appendix. Appendix Chapter 3.

325. A. R. Birley, *Garrison Life*, 75–76. *Tab. Vindol. II* 344 calls in question the statement made by Lentz that "Luke's description of Paul's calling on Caesar is the only example from the first century of the Common Era of such an appeal on a capital charge from the provinces" (*Luke's Portrait of Paul*, 108). Appendix Chapter 3.

326. Meyer comments that "'good-faith' contracts . . . could be undertaken by men who were not Roman citizens or by mixed citizen/non-citizen groups" ("Law and

as "a man from overseas and an innocent one" at that (*hominem trasmarinum |et innocentem*) he is certain he should not have been "bloodied by rods" as if he had "committed some crime" (*uirgis cruent[at]u[m] |esse ac si aliquid sceler[i]s |commisissem*).

Figure 15. *Tab. Vindol.* II 344. A trader from overseas protests his innocence and appeals to higher authority after being beaten by rods. W 171 mm × H 77 mm. Appendix Chapter 3. © The Trustees of the British Museum.

Centurions themselves could get into trouble. The prefect of a neighboring fort, Caecilius Secundus, wrote to Iulius Verecundus suggesting that some of his officers had taken affront at "little outbursts of anger" (*iracundiolae*) from one of Verecundus's centurions, Decuminus. Secundus was trying to put things right or perhaps to get Decuminus in trouble with his commanding officer.[327] Vocontius had been slow in organizing wagons and a delivery of stone and one letter-writer is sure he won't sort it out unless he is asked to.[328]

Legionary centurions could rise to positions of significant responsibility: "some were appointed to administer regions of a province where they were the most senior representative of Roman rule."[329] Valerius Maximus

Latinization," 193). Johnston states that "it was open to a judge to find that the failure of a party to act in accordance with ordinary commercial standards was not consonant with good faith" (*Roman Law*, 96). See above, Chapter 2, n. 60.

327. *Tab. Vindol. IV* 893 n. 5. Appendix Chapter 3.

328. *Tab. Vindol. II* 316. Two other centurions are mentioned by name: from 97–105 CE, Maximus (*Tab. Vindol. III* 680) and from 104–120 CE, Fortunatus (*Tab. Vindol. II* 351).

329. Goldsworthy, *Complete Roman Army*, 72; Salway, *A History of Roman Britain*, 384.

was such a regional centurion who corresponded with Flavius Cerialis, though only fragments of one letter remain (*ab Valerio Maxim [- |(centurione) reg(ionario))*.[330] Another was Annius Questor, the centurion who is "in charge of the region" at Luguvalium (Carlisle); his letters of recommendation supported Brigonius as he sought preferment and the support of his fellow prefect, Cerialis.[331]

Imagining Luke–Acts Through the Eyes of Centurions and Officers Associated with Vindolanda

Roman Law and Relationships Between the Military and Civilians

In Philippi, the magistrates ordered Paul and his companions to "be beaten with rods" (ῥαβδίζειν: *virgis caedi* Acts 16:22).[332] When the trader from overseas who protests his innocence describes the way he was "beaten with rods" (*uirgis cas[t]igatum |esse*), he might have been referring to a beating by a centurion using his cane.[333] Marcus Favonius Facilis was a legionary centurion who died in Camulodunum sometime in the 50s CE: his funerary monument, now in the Colchester museum, shows him holding in his right hand a *vitis*, the cane used by centurions for inflicting punishment.[334]

Commentators draw on the Valerian and Porcian Laws prohibiting the beating of citizens for the legal context of Acts 16:22.[335] Although in a far-flung empire law could not be centrally enforced,[336] *Tab. Vindol.* II 344 is part of a growing body of evidence of the way Roman law worked out in

330. *Tab. Vindol. III* 653.

331. *Tab. Vindol. II* 250, cf. III Appendix. Luguvalium, Appendix Chapter 3. Map (Figure 1) 37.

332. Keener suggests this may be a reference to the six lictors who walked in front of *duoviri* with bundles of six rods, *fasces* (*Acts*, 406).

333. Bowman and Thomas, *Tab. Vindol. II* 344, Introduction; Appendix Chapter 3. D. J. Mattingly, *An Imperial Possession*, 173.

334. Funerary inscription for the centurion Marcus Favonius Facilis, "*RIB*," 200. The original and a reconstruction are in Colchester Castle Museum: "Facilis Tombstone"; Abdy, *Legion*, 92–95; Tomlin, *Britannia Romana*, 19–20.

335. Sherwin-White, *Roman Society*, 144–56; Rapske, *Paul in Roman Custody*, 3:123–34; 139–47; Bruce, *Acts*, 366–67; 460–61; Lentz, *Luke's Portrait of Paul*, 120–23; Witherington, *Acts*, 407–502; 675–84; Pervo, *Acts*, 413–14; Keener, *Acts*, 402–8; 413–18; 540–43; Omerzu, "Roman Trial Against Paul."

336. Garnsey, "Lex Iulia," 189.

practice within the military community and in its relationship with local traders.[337] The picture that emerges would be recognized throughout the empire, not least in the eastern Mediterranean, as would the way in which Roman law adapted to local circumstances.[338] Richard Alston's study of 51 petitions presented by villagers in Egypt to centurions, decurions and *beneficarii*, between 20 BCE and 255 CE demonstrates that civilians like this Vindolanda trader, who was the link between local producers and the military community, expected to receive help from such officers[339] as they were "people of power who could get things done."[340]

In their relationships with civilians the centurions and other officers of Vindolanda have the capacity to help or to harm. However, this civilian trader is confident of their help, suggesting, as Richard Alston argues on the basis of papyrus evidence of the Roman army in Egypt, that the traditional image of the centurion as bully is mistaken.[341] Even though the pleas of the civilian trader of Vindolanda are not heeded he can still appeal to the governor or maybe the emperor himself.[342] Either way, this tablet bears out the view argued by Esler in the context of the Babatha documents that there are many instances of good relations between centurions and the local population.[343] There must be one caveat, however. Peachin points out that the discovery of the trader's appeal in the administrative quarters of a centurion gives rise to the possibility that a centurion intercepted the appeal and failed to pass it on. That would be another story![344]

A centurion following the Way of Jesus would be aware that people could be beaten, that centurions could be turned to for help, and that they

337. Peachin, "Vindolanda Tablets and Law"; Korporowicz, "Roman Law in Britain"; du Plessis, "Provincial Law in Britannia." Cf. Lentz, *Luke's Portrait of Paul*, 130–38.

338. Peachin, "Vindolanda Tablets and Law"; 231–33. Schellenberg suggests that Paul's imprisonments "are best explained by positing repeated coercive or judicial action by local magistrates" as "Paul was imprisoned not for being a Christian, nor as a threat to the Roman order, but rather for being a civic nuisance" ("Rest of Paul's Imprisonments").

339. Alston observes that more than half had to do with assault (*Soldier and Society*, 87–91). In P.Amh. II 77, 139 CE an Arab archer appealed to the *Beneficiarius* or *Epistrategus* when he stumbled across a fraud at a customs post and was beaten: https://papyri.info/ddbdp/p.amh; 2;77.

340. Alston, *Soldier and Society*, 95.

341. Alston, *Soldier and Society*, 53, 67–68.

342. *Tab. Vindol. II* 344. Appendix Chapter 3.

343. Esler, "Reading Matthew by the Dead Sea," 3–8.

344. Peachin, "Vindolanda Tablets and Law"; 227–31; Bowman and Thomas, *Tab. Vindol. II* 344, Introduction. Appendix Chapter 3.

could deny help to those who proclaimed their innocence. Reading about Paul in Philippi, they would note the way the authorities stepped back from their punishment of Paul when hearing his plea that he and Silas were "uncondemned, men who are Roman citizens" (ἀκατακρίτους, ἀνθρώπους Ῥωμαίους: *indemnatos homines romanos* Acts 16:37). Further they would notice in Jerusalem it is the Roman authorities who stop Paul being beaten by the crowds (Acts 21:32) and a centurion who prevents a scourging by the Roman authorities after hearing Paul's very similar plea that he is "a Roman citizen who is uncondemned" (ἄνθρωπον Ῥωμαῖον καὶ ἀκατάκριτον: *hominem romanum et indemnatum* Acts 22:25). The phrasing on both occasions is very similar to that of the writer of *Tab. Vindol.* II 344 who describes himself as "a man from overseas and an innocent one" (*hominem trasmarinum |et innocentem*).[345] Luke–Acts is written with the likes of our imagined readers in mind.[346] A centurion drawn to follow the Way of Jesus

345. Paul describes himself twice as a Roman man (ἀνθρώπος Ῥωμαίος: *hominis romanus*; Acts 16:37; 22:25); a centurion describes him likewise but the Vulgate translates ἀνθρώπος Ῥωμαίος as *civis romanus* (Acts 22:26). Paul is described by Luke as "a Roman" (Ῥωμαίος: *romanus* Acts 16:38), on the second occasion, however, the Vulgate translates the single word Ῥωμαίος as *civis romanus* (Acts 22:29). A tribune, and Claudius Lysias describe Paul as Ῥωμαίος: *romanus* (Acts 22:27; 23:27). Maloney and Reimer criticize the NRSV for translating each of these occurrences as "Roman citizen" and commend the Authorized Version for translating simply as "Roman." They call in question whether Paul is ever described as a "citizen" (*Acts*, 236–37). Interestingly, the NRSVue reverts to the Authorized Version usage and abandons the use of "citizen." Cf. Maloney and Reimer, *Acts*, 303–5. Keener, argues, to the contrary, that Paul is described as a Roman citizen, and was a Roman citizen (*Acts*, 415–17). Pervo maintains that Paul is described as a Roman citizen, but concludes that "on the whole, it does not seem probable that Paul was a Roman citizen, certainly not a citizen of the quality depicted in Acts" (*Acts*, 554–56). If someone acquainted with the phrase *hominis trasmarinus* were to encounter the phrase *hominis romanus*, or indeed the single word *romanus* it is reasonable to suppose they would conclude the person so described was a Roman citizen. That conclusion is perhaps reinforced by the occurrence of the *cognomen Paullus* in *Tab. Lond. Bloomberg* 65, (Tomlin, *Roman London's First Voices*, 206–7; Appendix Chapter 2) and in one other inscription on a piece of Samian ware from Londinium, *RIB* 2601.426. In the Bloomberg tablets and the Vindolanda tablets *romanus* occurs only once in the genitive plural, *Romanorum* (*Tab. Lond. Bloomberg* 75) and according to Tomlin might be translated "of the Romans" or "of Roman somethings" (*Roman London's First Voices*, 230). That confirms the argument put forward by Lentz: while it is inherently improbable that Paul was a citizen of Tarsus, a Roman citizen and a Pharisee, Luke's intention was to present Paul as "a man of high social standing" for the benefit of an audience who would take at face value that he was "an individual of the highest social and religious credentials" (*Luke's Portrait of Paul*, 60; cf. 23–61).

346. Schellenberg argues that in Acts "prison has been emptied of its essential social meaning—namely, the loss of dignity and self-determination" and has lost its horror; in

would not feel obliged to cease being a centurion. Aware of the kind of circumstances that led to the beating of the trader from overseas and to his appeal, he would be challenged to act fairly with those he met, to enquire about their good faith (*de cuius f[ide] |inquiras)*[347] and to avoid "threats and false accusation" (*concutiatis neque calumniam faciatis* Luke 3:14).

Inclusive Communities of Followers of the Way of Jesus in Luke–Acts

On the day the strength report was taken, of *cohors I Tungrorum* forty-six were absent serving as "guards of the governor," the emperor's representative in Britannia. In place of taxes, the Batavians supplied fighting men often under the command of Batavian nobles in different parts of the empire, contributing to "a new elite unit which served the Julio-Claudian emperors from Augustus to Nero as mounted bodyguards, stationed in Rome."[348] Whatever the historical justification for Cornelius's Italian cohort[349] and Julius's Augustan Cohort,[350] those designations would suggest to the likes of the Vindolanda centurions a close relationship to Rome and the emperor. The significance of the inclusion of someone of such high status as Cornelius among the followers of the Way would not be lost on our imagined readers.[351] It would demonstrate to them the inclusiveness of the Way and justify to them their decision to become followers. The repetition of the narrative underlines its significance (Acts 10; 11:1–18). Not only is Cornelius the first centurion in Luke–Acts to be named, suggesting he may himself have been the eye-witness source of this narrative,[352] but he is also the first non-Judean follower of the Way to be named in Acts. Clearly, for Luke his story is of great significance.

Paul's letters, on the other hand, the social meaning and horror are evident (*Abject Joy*, 9).

347. *Tab. Vindol. II* 344. Appendix Chapter 3.

348. A. R. Birley, *Garrison Life*, 43.

349. Keener is positive (*Acts*, 295); Zeichmann is doubtful. He maintains the only suggestion to receive substantial support is cohors *II Italica civium Romanorum* (*Roman Army and the New Testament*, chap. 3). Cf. Bruce, *Acts*, 252.

350. Zeichmann offers epigraphic support for an Augustan cohort under Agrippa II at around this time ("Military Forces in Judaea," 109–12); and in three inscriptions locating an auxiliary cohort of this name in the locality at this time ("Database of Military Inscriptions"). Speidel is positive about both cohorts ("Roman Army in Judaea").

351. Witherington, *Acts*, 340; cf. Pervo, *Acts*, 267–68.

352. Cf. on naming in the gospels Bauckham, *Jesus and the Eyewitnesses*, 39.

The centurions of Vindolanda were not just cogs in some military machine but part of a community with their own identities and varied responsibilities.[353] They would recognize the craftworkers of Acts: Simon the tanner (Acts 10:6); Aquila and Priscilla who, with Paul, were tentmakers or leatherworkers (Acts 18:1–4);[354] Demetrius and the silversmiths (Acts 19:23–25). Recognizing the skill of the leatherworker in creating leather tents, with which they would have been very familiar on campaigns, would give them respect for Aquila, Priscilla and Paul.[355] Knowing the importance of a good pair of shoes, John's reference to untying the thong of Jesus' sandals (Luke 3:16) would be readily understood by the centurions as an indication of the status accorded by John to Jesus.[356]

Literacy and the Way of Jesus

The centurions, their *principales*[357] and their administrative staff were literate. Regular reports ensured the whereabouts and activity of each member of the cohort were known; correspondence enabled officers and their superiors to keep in touch within the cohort and with other cohorts. Trade depended on keeping written accounts; loan notes ensured that debt was traceable. Literacy underpinned not only the work of those who themselves

353. James, "Community of Soldiers," 14.

354. Pervo reviews the alternative interpretations of "tentmaker" and one who "worked with leather," concluding "a general understanding of the term is preferable" (*Acts*, 452). Keener prefers the patristic "leatherworker" to the medieval "tentmaker" (*Acts*, 456). The discovery of a leather tent at Vindolanda makes this distinction redundant: van Driel-Murray, "Complete Roman Tent"; Abdy, *Legion*, 182–83. Reimer takes the view, espoused by Erasmus, that they made tents from pieces of leather: *erat autem illorum ars, e'pellibus confuere tabernacula*: Erasmus, *Paraphrasis In Acta XVIII*. Reimer also argues that "they belong to that very populous lower order of minor craftspeople in Corinth who earned their living with their own hands and thus were probably able to extend help to other people who were less well off than they (Acts 20:35)." (*Women in Acts*, 199–205). Witherington suggests they might have had a shop in front of their house (*Acts*). An example of such a shop can be seen in Caerwent: Brewer, *Caerwent*, 46–50; Map (Figure 1) 29.

355. Abdy, *Legion*, 183.

356. Cf. Wolter, *Luke I*, 169.

357. *Principales* served between the centurions and the soldiers, including the *optio*, *signifer* and *tessarrius*: Goldsworthy, *Complete Roman Army*, 68; Pollard and Berry, *Complete Roman Legions*, 228; Abdy, *Legion*, 95–98. On literacy of centurions and officers: Goldsworthy, *Complete Roman Army*, 72; Bowman, *Life and Letters*, 79–94; Speidel, "Learning Latin in Roman Army," 142.

were literate but the work of all those *milites* whose day-to-day work was described and accounted for in written records. The world of the centurions of Vindolanda was "essentially defined by writing."[358] Our imagined readers of Luke–Acts would assume literacy on the part of the centurions and others of higher status. They would notice the use by Zechariah of a small writing tablet that could be held in the hand (πινακίδιον: *pugillaris* Luke 1:63), an inscription (ἐπιγραφὴ: *superscriptio inscripta* Luke 23:38), a written loan note (τὰ γράμματα: *cautio*, Luke 16:6), ancient texts of the *Iudaei* (Luke 4:16–21; Acts 8:28–35; 13:14–15; 15:21), a letter of similar length to the ones they were used to (Acts 15:23–29)[359] and a legal document (Acts 23:25–30).[360] A distinctive characteristic of the followers of the Way of Jesus was their dependence on the "reading, writing and dissemination of texts."[361] Centurions such as we encounter in Vindolanda would recognize not only the importance of written texts to the followers of the Way but also the manner in which they shaped the lives of everyone whether or not they were literate: as long as one in a group of followers of the Way could read, all would be touched by the written word.[362] Just as their world of writing contributed to their sense of Roman identity,[363] the identity of those who followed the Way of Jesus was similarly shaped by the written words they shared.[364]

Travel and Identity Among Followers of the Way

The centurions of Vindolanda were not confined to that one location: their duties sometimes took them far from their base. They seem to have made use of itineraries as they traveled the network of roads connecting the newly

358. Haynes, *Blood of the Provinces*, 318. Cf. Bowman, *Life and Letters*, 79–80; Woolf, "Ancient Illiteracy?," 36–41.

359. Keener, *Acts*, 372: "only slightly longer than the average papyrus letter" which "ranged from 16 to 209 words."

360. Keener, *Acts*, 553. Pervo considers the wording of this letter to be Luke's but acknowledges that "a letter may have been written to accompany the transfer" (*Acts*, 583).

361. Luke 1:1–4; Acts 15:22–30; the letters of Paul et al. especially 1 Thess 5:27; Col 4:16, 1 Tim 4:13: Hurtado, "A Bookish Religion," 105. Cf. Haines-Eitzen, *Guardians of Letters*, 20.

362. Hurtado, "A Bookish Religion," 108.

363. D. J. Mattingly, *An Imperial Possession*, 199–204; Salway 2001, 360–63; Tomlin, "Literacy in Roman Britain"; Ingemark, "Literacy in Roman Britain," 26–27.

364. Kloppenborg, *Christ's Associations*, 335–39.

established towns and forts that had sprung up since the Claudian invasion of 43 CE.[365] The inter-connectedness of those forts and newly established towns secured the Roman presence in Britannia as it did throughout the empire.[366] It was not only their occupation of a fort, but also their traveling that gave Vindolanda's centurions a sense of their Roman identity. They knew the roads they used connected them with the whole empire. The very same network of roads gave the followers of Jesus an identity beyond the communities they belonged to. There is, especially in Acts, a correlation between the journeys recorded and ancient itineraries, mapping the network of roads connecting the cities of the empire.[367] The very act of traveling characterizes the Way of Jesus, and links the autonomous local churches.[368] The use of itineraries contributes to the overall impression in Luke–Acts "of the Jesus movement as an interconnected and harmonious whole."[369] Whether Luke is drawing on his own experience as a traveling companion of Paul,[370] on information contained in a travel source,[371] on his own reading of Paul's letters,[372] or indeed composing a fiction in order to

365. *Tab. Vindol. II* 185; Abdy, *Legion*, 37–43. See above, Chapter 3, nn. 244-50.

366. B. Jones and Mattingly, *Atlas of Roman Britain*, 23. Guest describes over 1,000 km of roads in Wales, connecting a web of 40 and more forts to the two legionary fortresses of Isca (Caerleon) and Deva (Chester), Map (Figure 1) 28, 47 (*Roman Frontiers in Wales*, 72); cf. Woolf, *Ancient Cities*, 25–30; Marquis argues it was not so much "ease" of travel as the Roman *regulation*, *administration*, or *control* of travel which could be enabling, restricting, or everything in between" ("Travel and Homelessness," 90).

367. Kloppenborg, "Luke's Geography"; Alexander, "Mapping Early Christianity"; Woolf, "Curse Tablets," 361–62. Contrast Maloney and Reimer, *Acts*, 180. Schellenberg reviews recent scholarship on Paul's travels, suggesting that it focuses either on the ease of travel due to Roman roads and the pax Romana or on the hardships involved in ancient travel ("Danger, Paul and Travel,"145). He suggests in Acts "travel is a narrative trope that allows Luke to emphasize the superior character of his hero," Paul, whereas Paul's "autobiographical comments [in the letters] suggest that his journeys were fraught with peril and that he did not always emerge unscathed" and that his travel plans were "characterized . . . by uncertainty and contingency" ("Danger, Paul and Travel," 141–42).

368. Alexander, "Mapping Early Christianity"; Alexander, "Pauline Itinerary."

369. Kloppenborg, "Luke's Geography"; 140. Cf. Leyerle, "Communication and Travel," 446. Contrast Schellenberg, "The travel narrative in Luke's gospel notoriously features Jesus always on the road but never getting anywhere; in Acts, Paul travels mile after mile but is never actually on the road." ("Danger, Paul and Travel," 142).

370. Keener, *Acts*, 383–85.

371. Barrett, *Acts*, vol. 2, xxv–xxx.

372. Schellenberg, "First Pauline Chronologist," 200, 202; Schellenberg, "Beatings and Imprisonments."

authenticate Paulinism,[373] is immaterial for our imagined reading. Were a centurion such as those we encounter in Vindolanda drawn to the Way of Jesus and to an encounter with Luke–Acts, he would notice that it is in the travels of Jesus, the twelve and the seventy-two that his teaching spreads (Luke 9:1–10; 10:1–20; 9:51—19:44); and in the travels of Philip, Peter, Paul and others (Acts 8:4–40; 10:1—11:18; 13–28) that the Way of Jesus is established.[374] With those journeys leading to Rome (Acts 28:30–31), and to the furthest frontiers of the empire, he would realize the followers of the Way had indeed been "witnesses in Jerusalem, in all Judea and Samaria, and to the ends of the earth" (Acts 1:8).[375] He would sense he was part of a movement that spanned the empire, linked together such groups of followers, and drew strength from its inter-connectedness.

Accountability

Accountability within the cohort was important. Daily postings and the completion of set tasks were reported by means of a brief *renuntium*[376] or a fuller account of work accomplished.[377] There is a similar accountability expected of those Jesus commissions: both the twelve and the seventy-two report back on all they have accomplished (Luke 9:10, 10:17). The process of sending out and reporting back was key to the consolidation and growth of the Way.[378]

Our imagined readers might recognize moments when Jesus speaks of his mission, and the mission he asks others to undertake, in military terms (Luke 14:31–33). The demands Jesus places upon those who would "follow" him "on the way" to Jerusalem (ἐν τῇ ὁδῷ: *in via*, Luke 9:57–62), are the demands the military community would be familiar with.[379] Involved as they

373. Pervo, *Acts*, 392–96.

374. Spencer, *Journeying through Acts*, 25–26; Barreto, "Gospel on the Move," Aymer suggests that in such travels "Luke replicates imperialism in the narrative of church growth, a narrative that would one day be accompanied by military might." ("Acts Women's Bible Commentary," 540).

375. Pervo, *Acts*, 44; cf. Keener refers to Thule beyond Britannia in the context of "the ends of the earth" (*Acts*, 108); Maloney and Reimer, *Acts*, 11.

376. E.g. *Tab. Vindol. II* 127–153; *Tab. Vindol. III* 574–579, 816, 849. See above, Chapter 3, nn. 256-59, Figure 13. Appendix Chapter 3.

377. E.g. *Tab. Vindol. II* 155–157. See above, Chapter 3, nn. 259-61.

378. Green, *Gospel of Luke*, 356, 362.

379. Wolter, *Luke II*, 49. Cf. the three comments made by John in Luke 3:10–14

were in construction, they would recognize the value of good foundations (Luke 6:46–49) and the need to cost a building project (Luke 14:28–30). Dependent on the local community for the supply of grain to provide for a great number of soldiers, they would appreciate the cost of purchasing food for 5,000 men (Luke 9:10–17), sitting in dining groups (κλισίας: *convivia*) of 50 and perhaps picture the scene as a fighting force[380] the approximate size of a legion.[381] Jesus arrives in Jerusalem to great acclamation in the manner of one leading a triumph which heralds the arrival of peace.[382] And yet he enters the city on a colt and proceeds to weep over its failure to "recognize the things that make for peace" (τὰ πρὸς εἰρήνην: *quae ad pacem,* Luke 19:28–44). In Jerusalem Jesus speaks of the destruction in store for the city, which was to take place in 70 CE and of which the Tungrian and Batavian cohorts would have been aware (Luke 13:31–35; 19:41–44; 21:5–36; 23:27–31).

Honor and Shame in Association

The writer who passes on his greetings to Felicio the centurion has a strong sense of collegiality and an equally strong sense of honor among the colleagues he is in correspondence with.[383] As he sets about righting a wrong by wrapping denarii in packages, he fears for his reputation which may lead to his resignation from the *schola*, the military association he belongs to. It is that connectedness that finds expression in the way he addresses his peers and appeals to his "lord." We can imagine readers such as these recognizing the connectedness of those who follow the Way of Jesus. Like

---

including the command to soldiers.

380. The suggestion that the 5,000 were a fighting force becomes more evident when comparing the accounts in Matthew, Mark and John. Matthew 14:21 tells us they were 5,000 men "besides women and children." Mark 6:39–40 describes the groups of 50 and 100 as *contubernia* (cf. *Tab. Vindol. III* 656, 657, 708; *contubernalis* [*contib*–] *Tab. Vindol. II* 181, 310, 311, 343, 346, 349, III 641, 658, 698). Andrew Lincoln comments that John 6:15 tells us "they were about to come and take him by force to make him king" (*John*, 214).

381. Pollard and Berry, *Complete Roman Legions*, 36–41; J. K. Knight, *Caerleon.*

382. Wolter, *Luke II*, 363–64. According to Beard coinage featuring many images of the triumph suggests this was "the age of the triumph" (*Roman Triumph*, 295–96). "*OCRE*": RIC I (2nd ed.) Claudius 34; South Warwickshire Hoard 1115, 1116: Ireland, *South-Warwickshire Hoard*, 32. Cf. Heilig, *Apostle and the Empire*.

383. *Tab. Vindol. III* 655, 656, 657. Appendix Chapter 3.

those who follow John (Luke 3:10–14), they are bound together by rules of conduct (Luke 6:20–49). Failure to follow that Way and, worse, causing others to stumble on the Way will lead to the shame of censure and possible exclusion (Luke 17:1–4). The betrayal of Jesus by Judas called Iscariot leads to his downfall and necessitates his replacement (Luke 22:1–6, 47–48; Acts 1:15–26). The small communities that are then set up among those who follow the Way are characterized by a commitment to each other that involves sharing and meeting the needs of one another (Acts 2:44–47, 4:32–37). Failure to abide by the ethos of that shared Way results in worse than expulsion, as Ananias and Sapphira find to their cost (Acts 5:1–11). John Kloppenborg argues that the sense of connectedness and belonging characteristic of associations in the cities of the Mediterranean is analogous to "the complexion and organization of various Christ groups,"[384] not least the community meeting in the house of Lydia the dealer in purple at Philippi (Acts 16:11–40; cf. Philippians), the group that included Aquila and Priscilla in Corinth (Acts 18:1–17; cf. 1 and 2 Corinthians) and the assembly in Thessalonica that included the leading women of the city (Acts 17:1–9; cf. 1 and 2 Thessalonians).[385] The auxiliary soldier was "essentially an urban creature"[386] and so we can imagine such passages through the eyes of Felicio's colleague and see how the connectedness and the sense of belonging they shared in their *schola* and *contubernium* had echoes in the communities of those following the Way of Jesus. Theirs too was a world where people came together in associations as did the silversmiths of Ephesus under the leadership of Demetrius (Acts 19:21–41).[387]

Honor and Shame in Relationships with Local People

The centurions of Vindolanda were often engaged away from the fort in work that involved the local peoples. The "clear and unequivocal reference to the organization of a census" in the frontier region,[388] suggests that our

384. Kloppenborg, *Christ's Associations*, 55.

385. Cf. Aymer, "Acts Women's Bible Commentary," 543.

386. Haynes, *Blood of the Provinces*, 145. Cf. chapter 6, "Military Service and the Urban Experience."

387. Kloppenborg, *Christ's Associations*, 55–96; Pervo, *Acts*, 491. Cf. *Tab. Vindol. III* 656; see above, Chapter 3, n. 271.

388. Bowman and Thomas, *Tab. Vindol. II* 304, Introduction. Cf. an earlier list of provincial censuses in Brunt, "Revenues of Rome," 171–72.

imagined reader would have an understanding of the implications of a census such as the one they would encounter in Luke 2:1–7 and the pressures it put on local people.[389] They would notice the way in which the centurion working in Capernaum (Luke 7:1–10) had earned the respect of the community as he built a synagogue for them (ἄξιός ἐστιν:. . . ἀγαπᾷ γὰρ τὸ ἔθνος ἡμῶν: *dignus est . . . diligit enim gentem nostram*).[390] He counts the local people as friends and is very conscious that he is a man with authority over others who is himself under authority. At the heart of the narrative is concern for a much valued slave (δοῦλος . . . ἔντιμος: *servus . . . pretiosus*) who is not well.[391] So too, Cornelius, a centurion of the Italian Cohort, has a close relationship with the local people and is described as "a devout man who feared God, with all his household" (εὐσεβὴς καὶ φοβούμενος τὸν θεὸν σὺν παντὶ τῷ οἴκῳ αὐτοῦ: *religiosus et timens Deum cum omni domo sua*) who "gave alms to the people and prayed constantly to God" (ποιῶν ἐλεημοσύνας πολλὰς τῷ λαῷ καὶ δεόμενος τοῦ θεοῦ διὰ παντός: *faciens elemosynas multas plebi et deprecans Deum semper*, Acts 10:2). Centurions such as those at Vindolanda, lived in a context that involved them with the local peoples; they were under the authority of the prefect and over their *principales* and *milites*;[392] they lived with sickness in a context where slaves also served among their administrative staff.[393] The presence of dedications to Celtic mother goddesses in Vindolanda as in many other locations in Britannia, suggests a willingness to adopt local practices as the centurion of Capernaum and Cornelius had done. They knew the need to give charitable donations perhaps in the context of religious ritual.[394] Just as the centurion of Capernaum was commended for his faith (Luke 7:9),

389. Wolter, *Luke I*, 116–17; Matthews and Reid suggest that "taking a census was not a benign act" (*Luke 1–9*, 64). On Roman Imperial censuses see Brunt, "Revenues of Rome."

390. Walter maintains that the centurion of Capernaum and Cornelius (Acts 10:1–2) "give financial expression to their connection to the Jewish communities" (*Luke I*, 295).

391. Wolter, *Luke I*, 293. Matthews and Reid describe this as a construct of Luke: "This portrayal of the centurion as friendly to the Jews and deferential to Jesus fits with Luke's aim to show that the values of the Jesus movement align with those of the empire" (*Luke 1–9*, 222).

392. Goldsworthy describes the *Principales* (principal officers below a centurion): *optio* (second in command), *signifer* (standard bearer) and *tessarius* (junior officer) whose title derives from the *tessara* tablet bearing the watchword for the day (*Complete Roman Army*, 68, 73, 215, 216); Abdy, *Legion*, 95–98.

393. *Tab. Vindol. II* 255.

394. Bowman and Thomas, *Tab. Vindol. II* 190, Introduction and note to lines 38–39.

so too Cornelius, together with his household, is drawn to follow the Way of Jesus (Acts 10:44–48).[395] Both are shaped not only by the web of Roman power of which they are a part, but also by the relationships they have with local people.[396]

Fresh from the campaigns under Agricola and his successors, the centurions of Vindolanda, would be only too conscious of a hostility among the vanquished Britons that would manifest itself in the rebellion that precipitated the building of the frontier wall around the time of Hadrian's visit (122 CE). At times, disparaging of the local peoples, the *Brittunculi*,[397] they would understand the role played by the centurion in the execution of Jesus.[398] The "sour wine" (ὄξος: *acetum*) the soldiers at the foot of the cross offered Jesus (Luke 23:36) was not the fine wine associated with the banquets of Vindolanda but the ordinary every day wine used by the *milites*.[399] The way they mocked this would-be *rex Iudaeorum* as they offered their own *acetum* makes all the more stark the response of the centurion as he declares the innocence of Jesus (ὁ ἄνθρωπος οὗτος δίκαιος ἦν: *vere hic homo iustus erat*, Luke 23:47).[400] They would recognize in Jesus that kind of justice, *iustitia*, for which Verecundus was, according to Andangius, very well known.[401]

395. Green suggests he is "in the good company of those who had responded positively to the good news (Luke 3:10–14)" (*Gospel of Luke*, 285). Witherington comments, "Even Roman soldiers found this new movement appealing and worth joining" (*Acts*, 347). Contrast Matthews and Reid who maintain that "the centurion's faith would seem to refer only to his belief that Jesus can heal." (*Luke 1–9*, 227).

396. Cf. Woolf, *The Rulers Ruled*, sec. 26. Keener maintains that Luke "would have known the stories of local believers" in Caesarea (*Acts*, 295); Maloney and Reimer argue that "Acts 10:1—11:18 is a Lukan composition structured for a particular purpose and without incidentals of 'local color.'" (*Acts*, 152).

397. *Tab. Vindol. II* 164.

398. The discovery of a British crucifixion in Fenstanton, Cambridgeshire, a roadside settlement dating to late first and early second century in 2018 illustrates the use of that form of execution in Britannia: Ingham and Duhig, *Crucifixion in the Fens*; Lewsey, "*Cambridgeshire Crucifixion*"; Abdy, *Legion*, 274. It is only the second crucifixion to be discovered, and the most complete. Note the body was laid in the grave carefully and respectfully. Map (Figure 1) 14.

399. *Tab. Vindol. II* 190, 202; III 589, 673.

400. Walter suggests that "it is the social connotation of this drink that lets it become an instrument of the mocking of Jesus." (*Luke II*, 527).

401. *Tab. Vindol. IV* 891, *rogamus te domin[e] | Verecunde per notis|simam iustitiam tuaṃ*: (we) ask you, lord Verecundus, by your very well known justice. Appendix Chapter 3.

Good standing and the respect of the local community was not something to be taken for granted; it was something to be worked at. When it was achieved it was something to be commended. The lengthy letter of Octavius to his brother Candidus, involving trade among civilians and centurions responsible for food supplies, enables us to see exactly how important honor was in securing good relations with the wider community.[402] Should Candidus fail again to come up with at least some of the payment he has promised, Octavius will lose face and will blush with shame (*erubescam*). In the same letter, the failure of Frontinius Iulius to attend a pre-arranged meeting and to conclude a cash transaction amounts to a break in that honor code and the destruction of the very trust on which relations with "messmates" and with the local community depend. In the same way in another context, Vocontius the centurion has clearly got a reputation for letting people down.[403]

Centurions play a part in the treatment of Paul following his arrest in Jerusalem. The centurions of Vindolanda would understand the reluctance of the centurion in Jerusalem to beat Paul, a Roman citizen, and the wisdom of his turning to the tribune of the cohort for advice (Acts 22:25–26). They would appreciate the instructions Felix gave to one of his centurions to keep Paul in custody "but to let him have some liberty and not to prevent any of his friends from taking care of his needs." (Acts 24:23).

The only other centurion in Luke–Acts to be named is Julius who, with the soldiers under his command, was to escort Paul and other prisoners on their journey to Rome. That kind of duty would have been familiar to the centurions of Vindolanda who occasionally had to make long journeys.[404] Sometimes, someone making a journey from Vindolanda would be asked to take letters.[405] Might it be that Julius was going to Rome anyway and his escorting duties were given to him in addition? The centurions of Vindolanda would recognize the way he negotiated passage in different ships dealing with ship owners and pilots (Acts 27:2, 6, 11; 28:11). They would have noticed once again how Julius "treated Paul kindly and" when in port "allowed him to go to his friends to be cared for" (Acts 27:3). Indeed, in the context of the storm at sea they would understand his initial response

402. *Tab. Vindol. II* 343. Appendix Chapter 3.

403. *Tab. Vindol. II* 316.

404. Cf. *Tab. Vindol. II* 154, 310; Appendix Chapter 3. Abdy, *Legion*, 37–43.

405. Cf. *Tab. Vindol. II* 263 (Appendix Chapter 3), *III* 670. Cf. A. R. Birley, *Garrison Life*, 36.

to the owner and captain of the ship but would have noticed the way Julius deferred to Paul's later advice (Acts 27:9–12, 31–38, 42–44). Our imagined readers would see in this named centurion of an auxiliary cohort an exemplar of virtue.[406] Having delivered Paul to Rome, Julius disappears to be replaced by an anonymous soldier who guards Paul in a house in Rome where followers of the Way are free to come and go (Acts 28:16, 30). Just as the seas had not stopped the advance of the Vindolanda cohorts through Britannia, so too the seas could not stop the advance of the Way of Jesus.[407]

Centurions such as those we encounter here and elsewhere in Vindolanda would be aware of the full import of the character assessments given in honor of the centurion of Capernaum (Luke 7:4,5),[408] Cornelius (Acts 10:2)[409] and Julius (Acts 27:3).[410] They would also be aware of the kind of shame the dishonest manager felt (Luke 16:3).[411] Luke makes it clear to our imagined readers not only that military personnel are "among those who hear the good news,"[412] but also that they are among those who follow the Way.[413]

Imagining Cerialis, Brocchus and Other Prefects

The correspondence of Flavius Cerialis, Lepidina's husband, prefect of *cohors VIIII Batauorum* (c. 95–105 CE) constitutes the largest collection of Vindolanda Tablets. Set alongside the letters of Iulius Verecundus, prefect of *cohors I Tungrorum* (c. 85–95 CE) and other prefects it helps us understand the kindliness of the tribune, Claudius Lysias, and his relationship with the tribunes of the other cohorts based in Caesarea, the provincial

406. Pervo, *Acts*, 645, 655, 657, 662–663, 666; For Schellenberg, "this story of [Paul's] remarkable courage provides for [Luke's] readers a lasting image of a man noble and virtuous when tested by the perils of travel" ("Danger, Paul and Travel," 143). According to Lentz, "in this telling of the shipwreck the readers/hearers are given an example of how Paul, the man of virtue, responds to adversity." (*Luke's Portrait of Paul*, 94).

407. Witherington, *Acts*, 757. Cf. Praeder, "Sea Voyages in Luke–Acts," 704–706.

408. As an honored benefactor: Green, *Gospel of Luke*, 285–87.

409. Witherington describes him as "a person of some status and rank," a man of piety and devout (*Acts*, 347).

410. Keener describes him as "positive" and respectful (*Acts*, 594).

411. For Green he was one who "would have enjoyed enviable status" for whom "loss of position as manager entails a forfeiture of social status" (*Gospel of Luke*, 590).

412. Green, *Gospel of Luke*, 566.

413. Witherington, *Acts*, 347.

governors, Felix and Festus, and King Agrippa and his sister, Bernice (Acts 21:27—26:32). Unlike Paul, Claudius Lysias had purchased his citizenship, taking the *gentilicum* Claudius after Claudius had encouraged the sale of citizenship (Acts 22:27–28).[414] Claudius had formalized the military service of those of equestrian rank enabling them to advance from the command of an auxiliary cohort to a cavalry *ala* and on to a legion (*Equestris militias ita ordinavit, ut post cohortem alam, post alam tribunatum legionis daret*: He arranged the military service of Roman knights in such a way that they first had charge of a cohort, then of a division of cavalry, and then served as tribune of a legion).[415] The tribunes who accompanied Agrippa II were, in all likelihood, drawn from the equestrian order, as were the prefects of the cohorts we meet in Vindolanda.[416] With a *gentilicum* going back to Augustus or even Julius Caesar, Iulius Verecundus was prefect of *cohors I Tungrorum* (circa early 90s CE); Flavius Genialis, possibly prefect of *cohors VIIII Batauorum* soon after their arrival in Vindolanda (c. early 90s CE), has a more recent *gentilicum* indicating "swifter success and mobility" during the Flavian dynasty.[417] He was succeeded by Flavius Cerialis (c. 97–104), perhaps a Batavian noble with a *cognomen* linking him to Petillius Cerialis who put down the first Batavian revolt (69–70 CE).[418] Emanating from a *praetorium* modelled on elite Mediterranean households the correspondence of Cerialis and other prefects enables us to glimpse high-status people such as Sergius Paulus, the proconsul of Cyprus (Acts

414. Keener, *Acts*, 542 citing Cassius Dio 60.17.5–6. Cf. Pervo, *Acts*, 569. Sherwin-White argues that the charge levelled by Cassius Dio that "Claudius allowed the citizenship to be bought and sold indiscriminately" has to be qualified. "The gift of honorary citizenship to individuals in return for services rendered" was already a long-established practice. Only a few examples of the purchase of citizenship, such as this in Acts 22:27–28, have emerged. Claudius did not enfranchise whole groups of people in the Eastern Provinces. But in the context of the Britannic campaign, he seems to have regularized and systematized "the practice of presenting auxiliary veterans with the citizenship upon discharge." In so doing Claudius "was following a definite plan . . . to establish little groups of Roman citizens up and down the provinces, which one day would form the basis for a large-scale extension of the citizenship" (*Roman Citizenship*, 245–50). According to Speidel, the numbers involved suggest this did not materialize ("Learning Latin in Roman Army," 135–38).

415. Suetonius, *Claudius* 25: *Vol. II*, 48–49; Suetonius, *Lives of the Caesars*, 183; Abdy, *Legion*, 129–31.

416. Keener, *Acts*, 580, citing Josephus, *Ant.* 19.364; Haynes, *Blood of the Provinces*, 52; A. R. Birley, *Garrison Life*, 46. Cf. Woolf, *Rome*, 195.

417. Bowman, *Life and Letters*, 50.

418. J. N. Adams, "Language of Vindolanda Tablets," 129.

13:7–12) and Dionysius the Areopagite (Acts 17:34), as followers of the Way.[419] Whether or not this is historically accurate (with Bruce, Barrett, and Keener)[420] or questionable (with Pervo, Kloppenborg, Matthews and Maloney, and Reimer),[421] Luke conveys to his readers that people of such standing were followers of the Way.[422]

Letters play a key part at two moments in Acts (15:23–29 and 23:26–30): the first is 112 words and the second seventy-four words in the Vulgate, "only slightly longer than the average papyrus letter" which ranged from sixteen to 209 words.[423] Many of the Vindolanda letters are a similar length or shorter; the length of one of the fullest letters from Vindolanda is 216 words.[424] Claudius Lysias writes a letter to the governor, Felix, explaining why he was handing Paul over to his charge (Acts 23:23–35). The prefect at Vindolanda was likewise part of a military network that extended to the governor of the province: letter writing enabled that network to be maintained and developed as much in Vindolanda as in Caesarea.

In their correspondence, honor and deference are shown to superiors and an intimacy maintained with peers. Using the formulaic greeting *salue, salute*,[425] Flavius Cerialis is addressed as *Ceriali suo* (his Cerialis),[426] and frequently as *domine me* (my lord);[427] on one occasion he is addressed by Valatta, a woman, as "her Cerialis" and "my lord."[428] The prefect of a neighboring cohort, Brocchus, addressed Cerialis as *frater* (brother);[429] *frater*

419. According to Keener, "Dionysius 'the Areopagite" was "a member of the town's highest aristocratic court" and as such "a municipal decurion." (*Acts*, 449).

420. Bruce, *Acts*, 296–99; C. K. Barrett, *Acts Volume 1*, 608–19; Keener, *Acts*, 334–35, 448–49.

421. Pervo, *Acts*, 323–27; Kloppenborg, *Christ's Associations*, 186–89; Maloney and Reimer maintain that "this journey is a construct throughout" (*Acts*, 180); Matthews suggests that "the claim that a Roman bearing the office of proconsul—one who had served as a consul and then, on senatorial appointment, received the governorship of a province—is a remarkably audacious assertion by Luke of the influence of Paul in the highest circles of Roman society." (*Acts*, 32).

422. Cf. Talbert, *Reading Acts*, 128.

423. Keener, *Acts*, 372.

424. *Tab. Vindol. II* 343. Appendix Chapter 3.

425. *Tab. Vindol. II* 248, 249, 261, 270, 287, *Tab. Vindol. III* 622. 623, 625, 631.

426. *Tab. Vindol. II* 250, 256, 259, 262, 263, 265, 270, 278, *Tab. Vindol. III* 625, 629, 631.

427. *Tab. Vindol. II* 247, 252, 255, 256, 260, 264, 289, 306, *Tab. Vindol. III* 628, 631.

428. *Tab. Vindol. II* 257. Appendix Chapter 3.

429. *Tab. Vindol. II* 252, 255, 259, 260, 165, 189.

carissime (dearest brother);[430] *mi frater k[ari]ssime* (my dearest brother);[431] and *domine] karissime* (dearest lord).[432] Iustinus and Brocchus write to Cerialis as to a "colleague" (*collega*).[433] Chrauttius expresses concern for his fellow prefect in a "prayer" for Cerialis that he should have "the best of fortune of which you are most worthy" (*opto domine sis |felicissimus quo |es dignissimus*).[434]

T. Haperius Nepos seems to have taken the pen into his own hand to conclude a letter to Genialis, regarding financial problems in a neat, left-justified greeting: *m2 uale [...] | 5 domine [...] |frater |karissime*: *m2* Farewell, my dearest lord and brother (*Tab. Vindol.* III 611). Evidence suggesting Nepos commanded the *ala Petriana*, a cavalry cohort, in Coria (Corbridge) in the mid-nineties and that he went on to become prefect of Egypt in the twenties of the second century means that this document is one of the very few to contain the handwriting of a prefect of such standing.[435]

In one letter Masclus, a decurion, writes to Cerialis and addresses him as "his king" (*regi suo*).[436] Citing the occurrence of this form of address in an early second century Egyptian papyrus, a letter from Claudius Tiberianus to Longinus Priscus, Bowman and Thomas suggest it simply means "his patron."[437] Anthony Birley, on the other hand, raises the possibility it implies Flavius Cerialis is "of royal stock."[438] David Cuff suggests the use of this form of address indicates a strong sense of Batavian identity with echoes of the time they were ruled by client kings.[439]

Observing that the most common forms of address in the Vindolanda tablets, *domine / domina, frater / soror and carissime/a*, are also the three most common forms of address in the Greek papyri of this period: κύριε/κύρια, ἀδελφέ/ἀδελφή, φίλτατε/φίλτατη, Eleanor Dickey maintains that

430. *Tab. Vindol. II* 306.

431. *Tab. Vindol. III* 622, and also *III* 632.

432. *Tab. Vindol. II* 285; *Tab. Vindol. III* 623.

433. *Tab. Vindol. II* 260; *Tab. Vindol. III* 623.

434. *Tab. Vindol. II* 264. Cf. 248, 260.

435. Bowman and Thomas, *Tab. Vindol. III* 611, note c–d.ii.4–7; A. R. Birley, *Garrison Life*, 95; Bowman, *Life and Letters*, 49. Map (Figure 1) 41.

436. *Tab. Vindol. III* 628.

437. "Letter from Claudius Tiberianus." See *Tab. Vindol. III* 628.

438. A. R. Birley, *Garrison Life*, 80.

439. Cuff, "King of the Batavians," 154–55; Roymans, *Ethnic Identity the Batavians*, 251.

"similarities like this can hardly be coincidental: . . . the two address systems are related."[440] Dickey goes on to argue for the influence of Latin on Greek in the period of imperial Rome, not least on the *koine* Greek of the New Testament where the forms of address in the parables and the letters are indebted to the Greek of the papyri and so have much in common with the Latin of the Vindolanda tablets.[441]

In all these forms of address we encounter the world of honor. Another who signed in his own hand was Brocchus as he joined Valerius Niger writing to Cerialis of an anticipated visit of the then governor.[442] Addressing Cerialis as "brother," they pray for success in a venture he is about to undertake (*óptamus frater it quot |acturus es felicis*), sure their prayers will bear fruit given that Cerialis is "most worthy" (*dignissimus*). Taking pen in hand Brocchus prays Cerialis would enjoy good health (*m2 op<t>amus frater |bene ualere te |domine*). Brocchus and Niger affirm the good standing and honor of their fellow-prefect Cerialis in anticipation of a visit from the governor.

According to the rough notebook listing significant events in the *praetorium* of Cerialis between 2 April 102 and 103 CE, preparations were being made on 1 May 103 CE for a lunch to greet the arrival of the governor (*K(alendis) Maiarum si n[gularibus.[|aduentu consu[laris] |in prandio),* perhaps Lucius Neratius Marcellus, and his bodyguards (*singulares*).[443] Within twelve years Hadrian was to become emperor and commemorate his extensive visitations around the empire in coins using the term *adventus*.[444] At around this time Cerialis draws on his formal training in "upper-class literary culture"[445] and drafts a letter to "his Crispinus" with great care, requesting his support as he approaches Marcellus seeking advancement, perhaps

440. Dickey, "Greek Address System," 502.

441. Dickey, "Greek Address System," 524.

442. Bowman and Thomas, *Tab. Vindol. II* 248, note lines 9–11; A. R. Birley, *Vindolanda:Notes*, 89.

443. Bowman and Thomas, *Tab. Vindol. III* 581, Introduction and note lines 95, 96. *Adventus* is used in the Vulgate New Testament to translate παρουσία on each occasion it refers to Jesus: Matt 24:3, 27, 37, 39; 1 Cor 15:23; 1 Thess 2:19; 3:13; 4:15; 5:23; 2 Thess 2:1; Jas 5:7, 8; 2 Pet 1:16: 3:4; 1 John 2:28. In the Vulgate New Testament it is used in Acts 7:52 of the coming Righteous One for ἐλεύσις and in Acts 13:24 of Jesus for the phrase πρὸ προσώπου τῆς εἰσόδου αὐτοῦ.

444. Kreitzer, *Striking New Images*, Appendix. Cf. "Llanvaches Hoard," 2008.19H/514. "*OCRE*," Hadrian Denarius, 133–135 CE.

445. J. N. Adams, "Language of Vindolanda Tablets," 129.

a transfer or a promotion.[446] It may be that he is trying his hand at his own patronage, seeking support as he anticipated recommending friends to higher posts.[447] It may be an instance of someone of equestrian rank at the center of a web of power, exercising influence through his own network.[448] Conscious of status and honor, he speaks of "his Crispinus" (*Crispino suo*) and addresses him in a fulsome way as "my lord" (*[d]ominum meum,*) "the man whom it is my very special wish to be in good health and master of all your hopes." (*quem saluom |[[habere]] esse et omnis spei |[[suae]] compotem*). He speaks of Marcellus as "the most distinguished of men" (*clarissi[mum ui]|[rum]*) and refers to him as "my governor" (*consularem meum*). Cerialis appeals to Crispinus, whom he holds in high esteem, to advance himself by building on the contacts he has with the circle of friends around the governor.

Prefects draw on one another seeking advancement. The prefect of one fort, (. . .) Brigonius, has approached the prefect of another, Claudius Karus wanting letters of recommendation as he seeks advancement from Annius Questor, the centurion who is "in charge of the region" at Luguvalium. He writes to Cerialis addressing his fellow prefect as "my lord" and praying that he is enjoying "the best of fortune" and that he is in "good health". Karus recognizes that this will place an obligation on him and says to Cerialis, by doing this "you will place me in debt to you both in his name (?) and my own (?)" (*digneris .[...] |[...].que nom[ine] |debetorem m[e tibi] |obligaturus*).[449] Here we glimpse a balanced reciprocity expecting a like return for a favor granted.[450]

When Clodius Super addresses Cerialis in familiar terms as "my dearest lord and brother" and says, "you know that I am smart in getting hold of this since I am the commissariat officer and am now on the point of acquiring transport" (*scis certe hoc me uor-/sute impetrare cum sim an-/ nonarius et iam adepturus / translationem*), that suggests to Bowman and

446. *Tab. Vindol. II* 225.

447. A. R. Birley, *Garrison Life*, 128.

448. Woolf, *The Rulers Ruled*, sec. 17.

449. Bowman and Thomas, *Tab. Vindol. II* 250, Introduction; Appendix Chapter 3. Goldsworthy, *Complete Roman Army*, 72. Alston points out that the Greek equivalent of *centurio regionarius*, ἐπι τῶν τόπων, occurs in five Egyptian petitions to centurions and *Beneficiarii* (*Soldier and Society*, 88, 89, 93).

450. Crook, *Reconceptualizing Conversion*, 54–58; Stegemann and Stegemann, *Jesus Movement*, 34–36; cf. Neyrey, "Ceremonies in Luke–Acts," 371–73; Paulraj, *Food Justice*, 100.

Thomas that he is of similar social standing, perhaps a legionary centurion *ex equite Romano.*[451]

As *cohors I Tungrorum* returned to Vindolanda, one letter of commendation lauds the virtues of the person commended in fine language, speaking of "a good man" (*uiri boni*) who has made "moral progress through love of liberal pursuits" (*accedit etiam libera|lium studiorum amore |profectus morum*) and is commended for his "moderation" (*denique | te[m] peramentum*).[452] A request for lodging adjacent to the fort appeals to "the goodness" of the recipient of the letter" (*peto domine de bon[itate |tuá ut mihi con[|hospitium*).[453] Andangius appeals to Verecundus, prefect of *I Cohors Tungrorum* on the grounds that he was very well known for his justice (*Andangius et Vel[|rogamus te domin[e] |Verecunde per notis|simam iustitiam tuam*).[454]

With honor goes the potential for shame. Wrongdoing is a serious matter: Flavius Genialis writes to Cerialis, "indicting . . . seven men"[455] and a colleague, Successor, writes to Cerialis concerning fighting.[456] That those who deserted brought shame upon themselves is suggested by the letter Celonius Iustus sends to his colleague, another prefect, requesting they be "immediately struck off the list" (*te ▸ rogo ▸ fra|ter ▸ continuo ▸ illos ▸ expun|gas*).[457]

As honor is accorded to others, so shame can be willed on others too. Following a formulaic greeting to "his Fadus" the unnamed writer of *Tab. Vindol.* II 321 goes on to wish ill on the one to whom he is writing: *opto male tibi.*

451. Bowman and Thomas, *Tab. Vindol.*II 255, note line 20. The text and translation follow the Appendix to *Tab. Vindol.* III. Cf. Pollard and Berry, *Complete Roman Legions*, 39–40: many legionary centurions "were recruited directly from the municipal landowning class and a few from the equestrian order in Rome."

452. *Tab. Vindol. III* 660, A. R. Birley, *Garrison Life*, 156.

453. *Tab. Vindol. IV* 880.

454. *Tab. Vindol. IV* 891. Appendix Chapter 3.

455. *Tab. Vindol. II* 256, cf. *III* Appendix.

456. *Tab. Vindol. II* 306, cf. *III* Appendix.

457. *Tab. Vindol.* 345. Cf. *Tab Vindol. II* 226, 320 for other possible references to deserters.

While courteousness (*civilitas*),[458] goodness (*bonitas*),[459] and justice (*iustitia*)[460] are celebrated, drunkenness (*ebriacum*) brings shame (*rumpantur inuidi[a]*).[461] When wages are paid it was important that a "suitable" (*idoneus*) person should bring the money.[462] There is an expectation that letters will be answered and a sense of frustration when they are not:[463] Sollemnis chastises his brother Paris as "a neglectful man" who has sent him "not even one letter" (*homo inpientissi|me qui mihi ne unam e|pistulam misisti*), while commending his own "more considerate behavior" in writing to his brother, his messmate (*putó me humanius |facere qui tibi scribó*).[464]

Arraigned by Ingenuus (*conuenit me Ingenus*), Suolcenus writes to Flavius Gentilis, maintaining he has not been neglectful (*non desum*); at issue is a problem concerning transport which he hopes Ingenuus will "quickly sort out" (*uidit Ingenus me non dese |de rotulis quas spero cito ex|[pl]icabit*), together with an outstanding debt he hopes Flavius Gentilis will collect.[465] That the prefect could be called upon to settle disputes arising from breaches of the honor code is evident in another fragmentary letter (*Tab. Vindol. II* 297). Writing to "his Priscinus," prefect after 105 CE, Firminius defends himself against accusations of malpractice and is adamant that he has done nothing with evil intent (*nihil ▸ malo ▸ animo ▸ feci*): indeed, all he has done has been with the "decency [of an honest man]" (*pudo[r hominis modesti]*).[466]

Words we encounter in these tablets go to the heart of the honor code: *sordide*, in a niggardly fashion; *opto male tibi eueniat uale*, it is my wish that it might turn out badly for you; *civilitas* and *bonitas*, politeness and goodness, are contrasted with one who was *ebriacum*, drunk; *homo inpientissime*, a neglectful man, in contrast to *putó me humanius | facere qui tibi scribó*, I think that I am behaving in a more considerate fashion in writing to you; *desum*, neglectful; *nihil malo animo feci*, I have done nothing with

458. *Tab. Vindol. II* 323.

459. *Tab. Vindol. IV* 880.

460. *Tab. Vindol. IV* 891. Appendix Chapter 3.

461. *Tab. Vindol. III* 662.

462. *Tab. Vindol. IV* 876.

463. *Tab. Vindol. II* 310. Appendix Chapter 3.

464. *Tab. Vindol. II* 311.

465. *Tab. Vindol. III* 648.

466. Bowman and Thomas, *Tab. Vindol. II* 297, note, a.9.

evil intent, contrasted with doing everything with *pudor [hominis modesti]*, with the decency [of an honest man].

In Vindolanda we glimpse people appealing to someone of higher authority when an injustice has been done or when they have been mistreated. When *cohors I Tungrorum* were first in Vindolanda a formal complaint (*accusatio*) was lodged although the details have been lost.[467] Following the theft from the baths of a military belt (*balteus*) and its subsequent discovery the person concerned sought justice from Cerialis in the hope of settling the matter.[468] Another writer, possibly Cerialis, informs "a higher official that he has sent a miscreant to be dealt with."[469] Ill health prevented the prefect from responding himself when the civilian trader sought help from him.[470]

Imagining Luke–Acts Through the Eyes of the Prefects Associated with Vindolanda

To the Most Excellent Theophilus

Whether or not Luke's opening dedication is characteristic of literary works appealing to those who were well read or technical works appealing to the kind of craftworkers who made up a significant number of those who followed the Way of Jesus, cannot be conclusively decided.[471] Whether the addressee, Theophilus was a specific individual, Luke's patron perhaps, or symbolic of every "friend of God," is again not possible to determine. At its simplest the dedication can be described as "a label with an address."[472] Wolter points out that Roman procurators are addressed as "most excellent" (κρατίστε, *optime*) in Acts 23:26; 24:3 and 26:25 and allows "the speculation that Theophilus was not without means and that he enjoyed a

467. *Tab. Vindol. II* 307.

468. Bowman and Thomas, *Tab. Vindol. II* 322; Peachin, "Vindolanda Tablets and Law"; 227.

469. Bowman and Thomas, *Tab. Vindol. II* 317, Introduction.

470. *Tab. Vindol. II* 344. Appendix Chapter 3.

471. Alexander, *Luke's Preface*; Green, *Gospel of Luke*, 34; Fitzmyer, *Luke I–IX*, 288; Tannehill, *Luke*, 1996, 33; Bonz, *Past as Legacy*, 129–32; Wolter, *Luke I*, 43. See above, Chapter 1, *The Genre of Luke–Acts; The First Readership or Audience of Luke–Acts.*

472. Alexander, *Luke's Preface*, 54.

certain social prestige."[473] Were a prefect from Vindolanda or someone of such standing to be a follower of the Way of Jesus and read Luke–Acts, they would, perhaps, sense that it was addressed to someone of their standing. Were they to discover the background to Luke 4:27, they would realize it was a commander of the Syrian army who is singled out by Jesus in his programmatic address in Nazareth.[474] Indeed, it is one of their peers, Claudius Lysias, who addresses the governor, Felix, in a letter structured in a way they would recognize (Acts 23:26).[475] The other letter in Acts is structured in a similar way with greetings familiar to the Vindolanda correspondents (Acts 15:23–29).[476]

Honor and Shame

They would recognize in the frequent use of κύριε[477] (*domine*) in addressing Jesus and ἀδελφός[478] (*frater*) in addressing fellow followers of the Way, the formality of addressing one's superiors as "lord" and one's equals as "brother." Would there also be a challenge here? Were the friends of the centurion right to honor Jesus with the designation κύριε (*domine*)? Implicit in its use is the notion of obedience, prompting Jesus to ask the question, "Why do you call me "Lord, Lord," and do not do what I tell you?" (Luke 6:46). For people of the status of the prefects of Vindolanda use of this form of address accords to Jesus the honor they owe to their superiors and with its use goes a willingness to obey and a mark of belonging.[479]

473. Wolter, *Luke I*, 52. Cf. Green, *Gospel of Luke*, 44; Fitzmyer, *Luke I–IX*, 299–300.

474. Cf. 2 Kgs 5:1–19, where Naaman acknowledges Yahweh but remains uncircumcised. Esler, *Community and Gospel in Luke–Acts*, 35.

475. Cf. Pervo, *Acts*, 584.

476. Alexander, "Acts Oxford Commentary," 1056; Keener, *Acts*, 553.

477. In addressing Jesus: Luke 5:8, 12; 6:46; 7:6; 9:54, 59, 61; 10:17, 40; 11:1; 12:41; 13:23; 17:37; 18:41; 19:8; 22:33, 38, 49; Acts 1:6, 24; 7:59, 60; 9:5, 10, 13; 22:8, 10, 19; 26:15.

478. Other than in a familial context: Luke 6:41, 42; 8:21; 17:3; 22:32; of fellow followers of the Way: Acts 1:15, 16; 6:3; 9:17, 30; 10:23; 11:1, 12, 29; 12:17; 14:2; 15:1, 3, 7, 13, 22, 23, 32, 33, 36, 40; 16:2, 40; 17:6, 10, 14; 18:18, 27; 21:7, 17, 20; 22:5, 13; 28:14, 15, 17, 21; of fellow *Iudaei*: Acts 2:29; 2:37; 3:17; 3:22; 7;2, 37; 13:15, 26, 38; 22:1; 23:1, 5, 6.

479. Brawley suggests this "is clearly an appeal to ingroup norms as an external pole of identity for those who have Jesus as their lord, and having Jesus as their lord is tantamount to a name for the ingroup" (*Luke*, 87–88).

The obverse of honor is shame. The prefects of Vindolanda were aware of shameful behavior and of occasions when things were done "with evil intent."[480] They would recognize the teaching of Jesus countering such shameful behavior, in the hypocrisy of those who judge others and in lives that bear bad fruit (Luke 6:37, 43–45). They would also recognize the way in which opponents of Jesus sought ill of him (Luke 4:28–29). They too would associate drunkenness with shame (Acts 2:15). They would have understood the shame brought on Ananias and Sapphira (Acts 5:1–11) and the sense of disappointment attached to Mark's desertion (Acts 15:36–41).

In the teaching of Jesus, lives touched by shame are blessed: the destitute, the hungry, those who weep, those who are hated. Lives honored in the world of the prefects are shamed by Jesus: the rich, the full, those who laugh, those who are spoken well of (Luke 6:20–26). The term "legion," honored in the world of Vindolanda is used as a term of shame (Luke 8:30). Indeed, Jesus changed the lives of those who had been shamed through circumstances beyond their control: the leprosy sufferer (Luke 5:12–16), the paralyzed man (Luke 5:17–26), the sinful woman (Luke 7:36–50), Legion himself (Luke 8:26–39).

Patron and Client

When Masclus, the decurion, addresses Cerialis as *rex* it may simply be a term of respect. If in some way, however, it comes from deep within the Batavian cultural identity and a time when they were a client kingdom of Rome, it may be that Cerialis would have some understanding of the rivalry between Herod and Pilate and the accord they eventually reached (Luke 23:12).[481]

In the hierarchical world of the military community of Vindolanda, Cerialis and his fellow prefects were fully aware of the deference due to them and the deference they owed to their superiors. Addressed once as *rex*, frequently as *domine*, Cerialis has authority over those beneath him, is at ease with his peers, and seeks advancement through a patronage that "ran through the Roman system from top to bottom."[482] The relationship of patron and client they were accustomed to, is explored and challenged in the teaching and storytelling of Jesus. One can imagine those responsible

480. *Tab. Vindol. II* 297, 321; *III* 648.

481. Wolter sees this as "an integral part of [Luke's] story of Jesus" (*Luke II*, 509).

482. Salway, *History of Roman Britain*, 371. Cf. *Tab. Vindol. II* 225.

for the provision of grain to a military community being drawn to the rich man whose land "produced abundantly"; the story is told, however, to challenge people to be on their guard "against all kinds of greed" (Luke 12:13–21). Our imagined readers are presented with a choice between "self-interest devoted to possessions" and "commitment to God."[483] The kind of household the prefects of Vindolanda would be familiar with is redefined by Jesus (Luke 12:32–40) as he urges those who belong to the household of faith to identify themselves with the slaves at the wedding banquet. In place of their possessions, they are to give alms. What Jesus advocates, however, is not a reversal of the hierarchies of the household but instead, a relationship of mutuality.[484] In the dealings of the "faithful and prudent manager" who is put in charge of his master's slaves pending his return (Luke 12:41–48), the status and privilege they were accustomed to is challenged by Jesus who uses apocalyptic language "to exhort disciples to live appropriately in the present."[485] One can imagine the parable of "the rich man who was dressed in purple" and Lazarus (Luke 16:19–31) and the encounter with the rich young ruler (Luke 18:18–30) resonating with our imagined readers accustomed to the luxuries of the *praetorium*. Theirs was, however, not a life of idleness: they presided over a military community whose structures were designed to ensure that every individual belonged to a supportive group right down to the eight-man *contubernium*, the smallest unit within the century. The Vindolanda tablets reflect the busy life of such a community not only within their fort but in the wider locality. Matthews and Reid observe that the "open-ended" nature of these stories would confront our imagined readers "with a difficult choice . . . . There is not a uniform way for disciples to deal with possessions, but Luke is relentless in his warnings about the dangers that wealth poses."[486]

On the eve of his execution, Jesus meets with his disciples to observe "the festival of Unleavened bread, which is called the Passover." It is at this meal that he instructs those who would follow his Way to stand apart from "the kings of the Gentiles" who "lord it over them" and from "those in authority over them" who "are called benefactors" (Luke 22:25). What marks out those who follow the Way of Jesus is that "the greatest" among them "must become like the youngest, and the leader like one who serves" (Luke

483. Brawley, *Luke*, 131; cf. Matthews and Reid, *Luke 10–24*, 397–98.

484. Green, *Gospel of Luke*, 498–502; Brawley, *Luke*, 133.

485. Brawley, *Luke*, 134.

486. Matthews and Reid, *Luke 10–24*, 500.

22:26). A highlight of the calendar at Vindolanda was the festival of *Saturnalia*.[487] The role reversal of slave and master it entailed lasted only for the duration of the feast and served to reinforce the status quo, leaving them in no doubt "who is greater, the one who is at table or the one who serves." It was most certainly "the one at the table." But for Jesus the role reversal is fundamental not only to his own self-awareness but to every community of those who follow his way. "I am among you," he says, "as one who serves," not for a season, but the year round. It is through such service that the greatest honor comes at his table in his kingdom (Luke 22:24–30).[488] Not only is this a reference to some future kingdom but in Acts it is made visible in the community life of those who follow the Way of Jesus. The movement that is to develop in Acts "will have its own institutions for a new identity that goes beyond established systems."[489] In similar vein Green argues this teaching is not concerned with removing abuses from the system but "with the nature of the system itself."[490] The whole system of private benefaction on which so much depended in the world to which the equestrian prefects of Vindolanda belonged is called in question. On the surface of it, that would make it impossible for people of the standing of Cerialis to become followers of the Way. Herein lies the paradox of Luke–Acts for it is evident in Acts that people of such standing were among those followers. Perhaps the challenge for our imagined reader would entail modifying his behavior.[491]

Roman Law

Were someone of the standing of a prefect to encounter Luke–Acts as a follower of the Way, they would recognize the respect shown by Luke to legal processes with which they were familiar. When he and his companions were given a severe flogging in Philippi and later when Claudius Lysias,

487. *Tab. Vindol. II* 301, *III* 622.

488. Green suggests that "Jesus uses normal social protocols from the Greco-Roman world [evident here in Vindolanda] in order to insist that standard categories will not do" (*Gospel of Luke*, 767); cf. Matthews and Reid, *Luke 10–24*, 401–2, 574–75.

489. Brawley, *Luke*, 189.

490. Green, *Gospel of Luke*, 768.

491. Green, *Gospel of Luke*, 767–69. Matthews and Reid suggest that Luke deliberately "casts the power of the rulers of the nations more positively by marking them as "benefactors" (εὐεργέται: *benefici*)"; the term is then used "in cognate form in Acts to speak of the good deeds of Peter and John (εὐεργεσίᾳ: *benefactum* Acts 4:9) and of Jesus himself (εὐεργετεω: *benefacio* Acts 10:38)" (*Luke 10–24*, 574).

the tribune of an auxiliary cohort in Jerusalem ordered his flogging, Paul sought redress as the proper judicial process had not been followed (Acts 16:22–24, 35–39; 22:22–29). Frustrated by the lack of progress of his case, his subsequent appeal to the emperor's tribunal (Acts 25:10) is reminiscent of the appeal the trader from overseas made to the emperor's representative, to the "majesty" of the governor in Vindolanda.[492]

It can be argued that the trials of Jesus (Luke 22:63—23:25) and of Paul (Acts 21:37—26:32) followed processes familiar to people of the standing of prefects.[493] There is a tension between the Roman authorities and the local peoples. Even though in the course of proceedings, the erstwhile enemies, Pilate (governor of *Iudaea*) and Herod (ruler of Galilee, a fourth part of the kingdom of Herod the Great) "became friends with each other" (Luke 23:12), a very real tension remains between Pilate and the representatives of the *Iudaei* (Luke 23:13–25). While Pilate is depicted negatively as one who "mingled" the blood of Galileans "with their sacrifices" (Luke 13:1–5), he is also presented as one who, when Jesus is on trial, declares his innocence three times: he found "no basis for an accusation against this

492. *Tab. Vindol. II* 344. Appendix Chapter 3. This tablet suggests the views expressed in some commentaries may be challenged: Lentz, suggests Luke's description of Paul's appeal is the only instance of such an appeal from the first century (*Luke's Portrait of Paul*, 108); Maloney and Reimer maintain, referring to an appeal to the emperor, "there is no basis in the historical record for this procedure" (*Acts*, 319); Pervo states that "the appeal presents legal difficulties that cannot be surmounted," observing that the appeal is not associated with Paul's citizenship (*Acts*, 611–613).

493. Sherwin-White views Luke's account as "technically correct" (*Roman Society*, 32, 68). Fitzmyer regards the hearing before Pilate as "of real political character" (*Luke X-XXIV*, 1474). For Green "the picture Luke paints is ... historically believable" (*Gospel of Luke*, 798). Wolter states that Luke's account is "common in judicial proceedings" (*Luke II*, 503, 511, 514). Bruce takes a similar position (*Acts*, 473–507). Witherington speaks of the "general plausibility of this account" (*Acts*, 679–84). Keener describes elements of Paul's trials as "customary" and "standard" and speaks of what "normally," "commonly" happened (*Acts*, 556–59). Maloney and Reimer say that "the shape of his trial scenes is standard fare from the historical and novelistic literature of the period" (*Acts*, 298). Lentz observes that "while these scenes in Acts demonstrate a knowledge of Roman law and the privileges . . . accorded to Roman citizens. . . this does not necessarily prove that the scenes in Acts are accurate historical reports of Paul's encounters with the Roman authorities" (*Luke's Portrait of Paul*, 105–70). Omerzu argues that processes implied in Acts 16 and 21–26 reflect the situation prevailing in the transition from Republican to Imperial law ("Roman Trial Against Paul"). Contrast Matthews and Reid who argue that "the Lukan trial scene contains details that are historically implausible" (*Luke 10–24*, 598). Schellenberg maintains that "The depiction of Paul is more propagandistic than it is historical. . . . Thus Luke does not report Paul's career; he commemorates it" (*Abject Joy*, 7).

man"; declared to the *Iudaei* and their leaders that he had "not found this man guilty of any of your charges against him"; and subsequently "found no ground for the sentence of death" (Luke 23:4,14,22). They would perhaps notice that it was not the empire itself but the weakness of its representative at fault when Pilate "gave his verdict that their demand should be granted" (Luke 23:24), though later he granted permission for the body's burial (Luke 23:52). A similar tension simmers beneath the surface as Paul is arrested and brought before the authorities of the *Iudaei* and of Rome (Acts 21:27—26:32). It nears resolution as Felix hands over to Festus who works more closely as governor of *Iudaea* with King Agrippa and his sister, Bernice (Acts 25:23—26:32). The prefects at Vindolanda were used to occasional visits from different governors: one can imagine them being unsurprised at the different approach of the governors of *Iudaea* to Paul. They would notice the way Felix was "rather well informed of the Way" (Acts 24:22) and be concerned at his seeking a bribe (Acts 24:26). As had been the case with Jesus, the governor, Festus, declares Paul's innocence three times (Acts 25:18, 25; 26:31), agreeing with Agrippa that Paul had done "nothing to deserve death or imprisonment" and that he could have been freed had he not appealed to Rome (Acts 26:30–32).

People of Standing Among the Followers of the Way

While the good news of Jesus is presented by Paul in Acts as an alternative to the practices of the empire in places such as Lystra (Acts 14:8–18), Athens (Acts 17:22–31) and Ephesus (Acts 19:21–40), readers such as those of standing in Vindolanda would notice among followers of the Way the court official in charge of the entire treasury of Candace, queen of the Ethiopians (Acts 8:26–40), Sergius Paulus, proconsul of Cyprus (Acts 13:4–12), Lydia, the "dealer in purple cloth" in Philippi (Acts 16:11–15, 40), not a few of the leading women in Thessalonica (Acts 17:4), Aquila and Priscilla "by trade . . . tentmakers" in Corinth (18:1–3), and Publius, the leading man of the island of Malta (Acts 28:7–10). They would recognize in Luke's account of Paul, the Roman citizen, "an individual of the highest social . . . credentials," capable of presenting himself before the governors Felix and Festus and king Agrippa (Acts 24–26) as "a man who possessed both social status and moral virtue."[494] He embodied before Felix and Drusilla "justice and self-

494. Lentz, *Luke's Portrait of Paul*, 60, 63. Lentz argues that Paul's use of a proverb with classical allusions in his account of his conversion (Acts 26:14), his claim to be

control" (Acts 24:25), before the "most excellent" Festus he was not out of his mind but spoke "the sober truth" (Acts 26:25).[495] Luke's narrative of Paul in custody makes it clear that arrest gives him the opportunity to witness to the elite who wield power (Acts 21–28).[496] As Acts comes to its climax with the arrival of Paul in Rome, it is as if Luke–Acts is written in such a way as to enable people of the standing of the prefects of Vindolanda to count themselves among the followers of the Way of Jesus.[497]

Negotiating the Way Through the World of a Military Community

A World Turned Upside Down

When we imagine one or more from the military community in Vindolanda becoming followers of the Way of Jesus and encountering Luke–Acts, there is much in the early chapters of Luke that they would find challenging. Mary speaks of "the Mighty One" who "has brought down the powerful from their thrones and lifted up the lowly," who "has filled the hungry with good things, and sent the rich away empty" (Luke 1:52–53). John explicitly exhorts soldiers not "to extort money from anyone by threats or false accusation" and to "be satisfied" with their wages (Luke 3:14). Jesus at the very outset speaks of himself as bringing "good news to the destitute, . . . release to the captives and recovery of sight to the blind"; he has come "to let the oppressed go free," and yet he commends Naaman, the Syrian army commander (Luke 4:18–19, 27).

An authoritative teacher, Jesus quickly draws many followers who are keen to be regarded as his disciples; by the time he chooses twelve from among them to be apostles, his travels have enabled him to attract people

---

speaking "the sober truth" (Acts 26:26) and his general demeanor would communicate to people of standing that Paul is their social equal; cf. Schellenberg, *Abject Joy*, 8.

495. Lentz, *Luke's Portrait of Paul*, 62–104. See above, Chapter 3, *Imagining Cerialis, Brocchus and Other Prefects*: Cerialis is "most worthy" (*Tab. Vindol. II* 248); Marcellus is "the most distinguished of men, *clarissi[mum ui]| [rum]* (*Tab. Vindol. II* 225); another is lauded as "a good man," *uiri boni* who has made "moral progress through love of liberal pursuits," *accedit etiam libera|lium studiorum amore |profectus morum* and is commended for his "moderation," *te[m]peramentum* (*Tab. Vindol. III* 660); Verecundus is "very well known for his justice," *per notis|simam iustitiam* (*Tab. Vindol. IV* 891); Appendix Chapter 3. Firminus defends himself to Priscinus "with the decency [of an honest man], *pudor [hominis modesti]* (*Tab. Vindol. II* 297).

496. Skinner 2003, 186.

497. See above, Chapter 2, *Conclusion: Negotiating the Way with a Radical Generosity.*

from all *Iudaea*, Jerusalem and the coast of Tyre and Sidon. It is as he addresses his disciples in Luke 6:17–49 that we read a résumé of the teaching that had made such an impact.

At the very outset there are things that would unsettle and disturb any readers in Vindolanda, the more so the higher up the hierarchy they are. Blessings for the destitute, the hungry, those who weep now and those who are hated and excluded because of their support for Jesus are matched by a declaration of woe on the rich, those who are full now, those who laugh and those who are highly regarded (Luke 6:20–26). This was teaching that reversed the things they held dear. And it went further. Fresh from a long period of campaigning, presiding over a peace that had been bitterly fought over and precariously held, the words of Jesus would come as a deeply unsettling challenge:

> But I say to you that listen, love your enemies, do good to those who hate you, bless those who curse you, pray for those who abuse you. If anyone strikes you on the cheek, offer the other also; and from anyone who takes away your coat do not withhold even your shirt. Give to everyone who begs from you; and if anyone takes away your goods, do not ask for them again. Do to others as you would have them do to you. (Luke 6:27–31)

It was not just their campaigning and the relationship they had with the local people that was called in question, but the very fabric of their social world built as it was on the cultivation of friendship among peers.

> If you love those who love you, what credit is that to you? For even sinners love those who love them. If you do good to those who do good to you, what credit is that to you? For even sinners do the same. If you lend to those from whom you hope to receive, what credit is that to you? Even sinners lend to sinners, to receive as much again. But love your enemies, do good, and lend, expecting nothing in return. Your reward will be great, and you will be children of the Most High; for he is kind to the ungrateful and the wicked. Be merciful, just as your Father is merciful. (Luke 6:32–36)

What remains of Jesus' teaching has a wisdom they might recognize about not judging, about forgiving and the need for a genuineness that springs from the heart. There could be no doubt that Jesus expected these words to be acted on (Luke 6:37–49). Jesus expected the obedience they were accustomed to.

> Why do you call me "Lord, Lord," and do not do what I tell you? I will show you what someone is like who comes to me, hears my words, and acts on them. (Luke 6:46)

Surely it would be impossible for them to remain as followers of the Way. How could they follow the teaching of Jesus that so reversed the values they held dear?

A Way That's Open to Those From a Military Community

It is precisely at this moment that they would be taken aback. Of all the people they should encounter "after Jesus had finished all his sayings in the hearing of the people" our imagined readers would have least expected to see one of their own. And yet it is at this moment that a centurion is introduced (Luke 7:1–10). It is telling that the centurion does not meet Jesus himself but instead sends friends: is that because he is unsure how he could be accepted by Jesus? He is presented as a model to be looked up to, as one who is concerned for the health of his slave, as one who is honored by the local population for the practical help he has given them and ultimately by Jesus himself for the faith he has shown.

At the very point at which readers such as we find in Vindolanda might have called in question their decision to follow Jesus, they find reassurance in the person of a centurion whose faith is commended so highly by Jesus. It is not long before they encounter women of high standing who provided for Jesus as they traveled with him (Luke 8:1–3); "not a few of the leading women" of Thessalonica "were persuaded" and became followers of the Way (Acts 17:4), as did people of the standing of Sergius Paulus, proconsul of Cyprus and Publius, the leading man of Malta (Acts 13:12, 28:7–10). Of the eight centurions who play a significant part in the narrative of Jesus in Luke and of the followers of the Way in Acts one is commended by Jesus for his faith (Luke 7:9); another, as Jesus is crucified, recognized that he was "innocent" (δίκαιος: *iustus*, Luke 23:47); and another, Cornelius of the Italian cohort, is baptized, becomes a follower of the Way and instrumental in initiating mixed table-fellowship (Acts 10:1—11:18). Two more centurions act properly in a way that is helpful to Paul (Acts 22:25–26; 23:16–22), two guard him effectively (Acts 23:23–35), and Julius of the Augustan cohort, with whom Paul travels under arrest to Rome, treats Paul "kindly" (φιλανθρώπως: *humane*, Acts 27:3). Whatever the historical background, Luke draws attention to Cornelius by repeating his story, by making him the first non-Judean convert to be named and by implication suggesting that he belongs to an elite Italian cohort.[498] He is emphatic that among the followers of the Way are people of such standing. However great the challenge of Jesus' words to his disciples (Luke 6:20–49), there is no expectation that they will overthrow the institutions of Rome to which such people belong.

Conclusion: Negotiating the Way with a Radical Inclusivity

Among the Vindolanda tablets we have focused on three archives, relating to the women, the centurions and the prefects of Vindolanda. Drawing on the multi-faceted imagination we explored in Chapter 1, and the process described in our adaptation of archival ethnography enables us to draw conclusions that are justifiable in the context of Vindolanda and the discovery there of so many ink writing tablets, informed by a careful study of the tablets themselves, and warranted by close attention to the text of Luke–Acts. As it is written, Luke–Acts demonstrates that people in the military community, women as well as men, can become followers of the Way of Jesus. They will find their peers among the followers of the Way whose story is told in Luke–Acts. Women such as Lepidina and Severa would find in Luke–Acts a familiar world where women of high-standing had a place and where women of agency traveled to accomplish their aims, took part in festivals and feasting, valued kinship in turbulent times, and had a part to play in responding to sickness and death. Centurions such as Felicio and Saecularis would find a world they knew well in Luke–Acts, where the practice of Roman law impacted on their relationships with civilians, where literacy was all-important, where a sense of identity came through travel, and where issues of honor and shame were all important within the collegiality of associations such as the *contubernium* and *schola*, and in their relationships with local people. The world of honor and shame, patrons and clients, literacy and law, evident in Luke–Acts would also be familiar to prefects such as Verecundus and Cerialis.

There would at the same time be no escaping the challenge brought by Luke–Acts. Luke addresses "the most excellent Theophilus" directly at the outset to explain why he has written his "orderly account": it is "so that you may know the truth (τὴν ἀσφάλειαν: *veritatem*) concerning the things

498. See above, Chapter 3, nn. 349-52.

about which you have been instructed" (Luke 1:4).[499] Towards the end Luke describes Paul seeking to persuade the "most excellent" Festus that he is speaking words of "sober truth" (ἀληθείας καὶ σωφροσύνης ῥήματα: *veritatis et sobrietatis verba*, Acts 26:25).[500] That "truth" carries with it at one and the same time the assurance that people from a military community can become followers of the Way, and the challenge that following the Way will impact on their conduct, their relationships with each other and the relationships they share with local people. That challenge, however, does not amount to an invitation from Jesus and his followers to contravene Roman law: to follow the Way is not a threat to the empire itself.

For such as Lepidina and Severa, Felicio and Saecularis, Cerialis and Brocchus the upside-down world of the *Saturnalia* and *Matronalia* which secured the place of master, mistress and slave for the remainder of the year, would be encountered in the table-fellowship of followers of the Way. Here the balanced reciprocity they were accustomed to gives way to a familial reciprocity that extends hospitality without expecting anything in return. They would be challenged to engage with the destitute beyond the fort differently. The collegiality enjoyed by centurion and prefect alike in the context of the *contubernium* and *schola* within the military community would extend to the followers of the Way as they met in association with each other. They would now be part of a different web of power, whose relationships could transform their lives. They would be challenged to build bridges not only with civilians engaged with the military community, but also with local peoples. For people from a military community, belonging to the Way of Jesus would involve a radical inclusivity that at times turns their world upside down.

499. The Greek supports Wolter's view that Luke's intention is "to give certainty to that which is generally accepted and recognized" (*Luke I*, 53). Cf. Esler, *Community and Gospel in Luke–Acts*, 67. The Latin suggests the appropriateness of the NRSV translation "truth," followed by Green, *Gospel of Luke*, 33,45. See above, Chapter 2, n. 214.

500. Keener, *Acts*, 591; Witherington, *Acts*, 749,751.

Figure 16. Uley. The temple of Mercury on the Hill of *Aruerius* with ancillary buildings.[1] A view from the north with a steep drop to the left, the Cotswold escarpment to the right, and the River Severn in the distance. In the foreground is a Neolithic burial chamber reused in Roman times, Hetty Pegler's Tump, and a possible Bronze Age round barrow. In the distance is Uley Bury Hill fort, possibly occupied into Roman times. The road is approximately followed by the modern road. Steve Smith. © and used with kind permission of Museum in the Park, Stroud.

1. Image of original painting by Steve Smith © and used with kind permission of Museum in the Park, Stroud.

CHAPTER 4

Imagining Luke–Acts in a Rural Community

Through the Eyes of the People of the Uley Tablets

"In attempting to contextualize 'indigenous' curse-texts in Latin it is important not merely to provide the best text one can manage and take material aspects and provenience into account, as is nowadays standard procedure, but also, in an act of historical imagination, to take seriously the situation of the writers as they represented it to themselves."

—Richard Gordon, "Imaginative Force and Verbal Energy in Latin Curse-Tablets"

Introducing the People of the Uley Tablets

HONORATUS HAD BEEN THE victim of a significant theft, losing two wheels, four cows and many small belongings from his house. He sought help at the nearby temple by presenting the god Mercury with a carefully worded message seeking the return of his property and reconciliation with the thief or, failing that, the physical punishment of whoever was responsible. The message was written in a practiced Old Roman Cursive hand with a sharp stylus on a lead sheet either by Honoratus himself or someone who helped him.[2]

2. *Tab. Uley* 72; Tomlin, *The Uley Tablets*, 286–90; Tomlin, "Roman Britain in 1991," 310–11; Sánchez Natalías, *Sylloge Defixiones*, 354–55 (*SD* 365). Figure 19 and Appendix to Chapter 4.

In a memorandum (*commonitorium*) to the god Mercury, Saturnina, a woman, asks that whoever has stolen a piece of linen should not rest unless they return it to the temple, at which point she will give a third part of its value to "the aforesaid god."[3] Someone else from that farming community demanded that whoever had stolen gold from his strong box should return it to "the temple of Mercury on the Hill of *Aruerius*" on pain of untold suffering.[4]

Unlike the Bloomberg tablets and the Vindolanda tablets, some of which are dated, all of which come from a dateable archaeological context, the Uley tablets span a period of about two hundred years. Originally deposited in the temple of Mercury on the hill of *Aruerius* near the modern village of Uley, they were scattered around the site during demolition and re-building.[5] In one sense they are even less like an archive, and yet they are a distinct corpus of texts, produced by individuals living in a rural community within reach of the temple of Mercury.[6] As we follow the process set out in Chapter 1, we shall discover they too enable us to re-enact a moment in history as we get to know individual people facing a time of crisis in their lives. In introducing the Uley tablets we will first look at Uley and its shrines, comparing other locations in Britain where curse tablets have been found. We will then go on to consider what curse tablets are and what is going on in writing such messages, asking whether they are curses or prayers for justice. It will then be possible to draw on our adaptation of archival ethnography and imagine the circumstances of the named people we encounter in the Uley tablets. While drawing on the various types of imagination explored in Chapter 1, we will find that Tilley's geographical imagination will help us to immerse ourselves at a particular moment in their lives, seeing with our inner eye something of their world. This is similar to the approach taken by Eleri Cousins in her study of *The Sanctuary at Bath* as she describes experiencing Aquae Sulis in a way that is "deliberately impressionistic, qualitative, and relatively brief" but at the same time

3. *Tab. Uley* 2; Tomlin, *The Uley Tablets*, 88–91; Tomlin, "Uley Inscribed Lead Tablets," 120–22; Sánchez Natalías, *Sylloge Defixiones*, 346–47 (SD 356). Figure 20 and Appendix to Chapter 4.

4. *Tab. Uley* 75; Tomlin, *The Uley Tablets*, 294–98. Appendix Chapter 4. Uley, temple of Mercury on the Hill of *Aruerius*, Map (Figure 1) 3.

5. Woodward and Leach, *Uley Shrines Excavation*, 113. .

6. Tomlin describes the Uley tablets and the Bath tablets as archives (*Britannia Romana*, 335).

"supported throughout by concrete archaeological evidence."[7] We will then be in a position to imagine what people such as these would have made of texts in Luke–Acts that have to do with temples, cursing, and praying.

Introducing the Uley Tablets

Introducing Uley and Its Shrines, Bath, and Other Curse Tablet Locations

The Uley tablets were found in a Romano-Celtic temple discovered in 1976 when a water pipe was being laid near the Gloucestershire village of Uley.[8] A sacred place long before the arrival of the Romans (43 CE), it remained so after their departure (410 CE).[9] Its lasting significance is glimpsed in the name of the nearby village of Nympsfield which means "the tract of open country belonging to a place called *Nymed* . . . the Celtic word for a shrine or holy place."[10] Neolithic standing stones or wooden posts in an oval enclosure were replaced in the late Iron Age with a wooden shrine encircled by ditches and banks and later rebuilt. Early in the second century CE a stone Romano-Celtic temple was built on the same spot and with the same alignment.[11] It was extended in the early fourth century within a complex of other buildings providing accommodation for those serving, visiting and trading in the temple.[12]

7. Cousins, *Sanctuary at Bath*, 50.

8. The site was excavated using modern scientific techniques in 1977, 1978 and 1979. Ann Woodward and Peter Leach published a full excavation report with illustrations of the temple site and many of the artefacts (*Uley Shrines Excavation*, https://doi.org/10.5284/1028203. In the excavation report Ann Woodward introduced the tablets and Roger Tomlin provided the detailed report, publishing five of the tablets and descripta of the remainder (*Uley Inscribed Lead Tablets*). Subsequently, he published more in *Britannia*; these were then brought together by Sánchez Natalías in *Sylloge Defixiones*. Tomlin published the full edition of the tablets in 2024 (*The Uley Tablets*). In due course they will be published in RIB. My account of the temple and its tablets is drawn primarily from *Uley Shrines Excavation* and from *The Uley Tablets*. Map (Figure 1) 3.

9. Woodward and Leach, *Uley Shrines Excavation*, xiii, 303–35.

10. Woodward and Leach, *Uley Shrines Excavation*, 303 citing Smith, *Place Names of Gloucestershire*, 244.

11. Woodward and Leach, *Uley Shrines Excavation*, 13–32.

12. Woodward and Leach, *Uley Shrines Excavation*, 33–62.

Figure 17. The temple of Mercury on the Hill of *Aruerius*, together with ancillary buildings. Artist's impression by Steve Smith. © and used with kind permission of Museum in the Park, Stroud.

An inner sanctuary (*cella*), surrounded by an ambulatory, contained a slightly more than life-size statue of Mercury sculpted with great skill in local oolitic limestone.[13] Three figurines of Mercury,[14] two altars with carvings showing Mercury flanked by a ram and cockerel,[15] six miniature *caducei* and a sketch of Mercury's characteristic *caduceus* (wand) on *Tab. Uley* 21[16] enable the sculpture to be visualized.[17] A rectangular pit from the pre-Roman shrine seems to have been retained in the temple; positioned in front of the statue, it may have contained water.[18]

13. Henig, et al., "Uley Votive Objects," 88–94.

14. Henig, et al., "Uley Votive Objects," 98–101.

15. Henig, et al., "Uley Votive Objects," 94–98.

16. *Tab. Uley* 21; Tomlin, *The Uley Tablets*, 144–49; cf. Henig, et al., "Uley Votive Objects," 102–3.

17. Henig, et al., "Uley Votive Objects," 92–93.

18. Tomlin, *The Uley Tablets*, 2; see a reconstruction of the cult statue and of the temple interior by Joanna Richards, Woodward and Leach, *Uley Shrines Excavation*, 93, 313.

Figure 18. The head of the high-quality oolitic limestone cult statue of Mercury, sculpted by a skilled craftsman from local stone in the late second century. and carefully buried after the temple fell out of use. Two stubs near the front of the head may be the remains of wings. Approximately 2m tall, the statue stood on a base with two of the god's animal companions, a ram and a cockerel, fragments of which were also discovered. © The Trustees of the British Museum.[19]

A quarter of a million animal bones, mainly sheep, goats and domestic fowl provide evidence of extensive ritual sacrifice, accompanied by feasting.[20] Towards the end of the fourth century CE the stone temple was demolished to be replaced by a smaller shrine in use for a short time. Early in the fifth century all signs of such a temple disappeared to be replaced first by a timber and then by a stone hall or basilican church on the same

19. British Museum number 1978, 0102.1. Woodward and Leach, *Uley Shrines Excavation*, 88–94.

20. Levitan, "Uley Vertebrate Remains"; Woodward and Leach, *Uley Shrines Excavation*, 300; Cousins, *Sanctuary at Bath*, 65; Tomlin cites Levitan's "estimate that 150 [sheep and goats] were sacrificed every autumn for fifty years, a reflection of 'the wealth of the region'" (*The Uley Tablets*, 330).

alignment.[21] It was during the late fourth or early fifth century demolition that the head of Mercury was carefully buried.[22] Artefacts from that last period, including a lead tablet with biblical scenes[23] and red-streaked window glass,[24] suggest it was Christian. That building was finally demolished in the seventh or eighth century CE and nothing of later date was discovered.[25]

One hundred and forty lead tablets were discovered, for the most part a little less than A6 in size, 105 x 148 mm. None was found at the point at which it had been deposited. All had probably been scattered during the demolition process at the end of the 4th century CE. 109 (76 percent) were rolled and flattened, five (3.6 percent) rolled but not flattened, nine (6.4 percent) not rolled at all, seventeen (14 percent) were indeterminate.[26] Eighty-six were found to have been inscribed using a pointed stylus in a hand familiar from the Latin papyri of the eastern Mediterranean, each in distinctive handwriting:[27] of the twenty-four using capitals one substantial text, short lists of names and a handful of fragments are written in "irregular capitals" reflecting a lower level of literacy; the other substantial texts are written in more formal "rustic capitals";[28] thirty-six tablets are written in Old Roman Cursive, of which one is written half in capitals and

21. Woodward and Leach, *Uley Shrines Excavation*, 63–79.

22. Woodward and Leach, *Uley Shrines Excavation*, xiii, 71–75.

23. Part of the sheeting from a casket on which four figured scenes remain: top left, Christ and the centurion (Matt 8:5–13; cf. Luke 7:1–10); top right Christ healing a blind man (Mark 8:22–26, cf. Luke 18:35–43; John 9); bottom left, Jonah under the bush (Jonah 4:6–8); bottom right, sacrifice of Isaac (Gen 22:1–14): Henig, et al., "Uley Votive Objects," 107–10; Bebbington, *History of Uley*, 24–25. For an image see British Museum online collection, museum number 1978,0102.70.

24. Price, "Uley Window Glass."

25. Woodward and Leach conclude their report with an overview of the sequence of pre-Roman, Roman and post-Roman shrines on the site of the temple at Uley. It is accompanied by sketches of the site at each stage of its development (*Uley Shrines Excavation*, 303–27).

26. Woodward and Leach, *Uley Shrines Excavation*, 113.

27. Tomlin, *The Uley Tablets*, 50–60. Tomlin tabulates Capital, ORC and NRC letter-forms by tablet in Figures 7.7, 7.8 and 7.9 (58–60) and in figure 7.10 (60) he illustrates ORC letter-forms in formulaic words to demonstrate the distinctive handwriting of each tablet. For illustrations of the unfolded tablets and of styluses used in Uley see Woodward and Leach, *Uley Shrines Excavation*, 113, 191; cf. Willi, *Writing Equipment*, 33–38, 62–64.

28. Tomlin, *The Uley Tablets*, 54–55, 58: Capitals: *Tab. Uley* 2, 3, 4, 7, 19, 24, 26, 30, 33, 43, 44, 49, 50, 56, 59, 60, 61, 66, 70, 75, 83, 84, 85, 86. Irregular capitals: a single substantial text, *Tab. Uley* 83; together with names, 33, 49, 61, 85, 86; and fragments, 56, 60, 66.

half in ORC, and a small number include one or two capitals;[29] one tablet is written in New Roman Cursive, five combine ORC and NRC and five fragments use NRC.[30] Until recently it was thought possible to date the tablets palaeographically, ORC second to third century, NRC third to fourth century, with a period of transition 275–325 CE; the discovery in 2016 of a mid-fourth century papyrus will in ORC, however, has called in question such dating.[31] One tablet contains a Latin text written in Greek letters;[32] seven of the tablets have writing which cannot be deciphered and may be described as "pseudo-inscriptions";[33] seventy-nine "once carried a literate text," of which twenty-seven can only be described. Of the remaining fifty-two, at least thirty-six are full enough to study in depth, two are possibly Celtic and the remainder fragmentary.[34] That the fifty-four blank tablets had been rolled or folded suggests they were deposited in the same way as the written tablets.[35] The fact that the remainder were practically all folded or rolled up after being inscribed indicates they were not intended for human eyes.[36]

The Uley tablets "preserve at least forty personal names representing thirty-four persons or more, at least six names being those of the person's

29. Tomlin, *The Uley Tablets*, 50–54, 59: ORC *Tab. Uley* 1, 5, 6, 8, 9, 17, 20, 21, 22, 23, 24, 28, 34, 35, 39, 40, 41, 47, 48, 54, 55, 57, 58, 62, 63, 71, 72, 73, 74, 76, 78, 79, 80, 81, 82, 84. The first ten lines of 84 are inscribed in capitals, the remaining twelve in ORC. A handful of ORC texts include capitals: *Tab. Uley* 24, 26, 41, 49.

30. Tomlin, *The Uley Tablets*, 50–51, 60: *Tab. Uley* 68 (Appendix Chapter 4) is in NRC; occasional NRC letters are included in ORC texts, *Tab. Uley* 8, 21, 34, 39, 77; and NRC letters occur on fragments, *Tab. Uley* 37, 51, 53, 65, 80.

31. In *The Uley Tablets*, Tomlin does not include any dating: Tomlin, *The Uley Tablets*, 51. Sánchez Natalías 2022, on the other hand, includes suggested dates based on handwriting.

32. *Tab. Uley* 52; Tomlin, *The Uley Tablets*, 230–34.

33. Tomlin, *The Uley Tablets*, 7: *Tab. Uley* 10, 26, 31, 39, 59, 66, 67.

34. Tomlin, *The Uley Tablets*, 7, 37. I have chosen to focus this study on *Tab. Uley* 1, 2, 3, 4, 5, 6, 8, 9, 17, 20, 21, 22, 24, 34, 40, 41, 43, 47, 50, 52, 55, 57, 58, 62, 68, 70, 71, 72, 75, 76, 78, 80, 81, 82, 83, 84. The Appendix to Chapter 4 includes the translation and transcript of thirteen of the tablets; Roger Tomlin emphasizes, however, that they are intended to be read alongside the commentary in *The Uley Tablets* and in due course in RIB. The two "un-Latin," possibly Celtic texts are *Tab. Uley* 7, 35; Tomlin, *The Uley Tablets*, 108–11, 182–83. See The Texts, xxiii-xxv, for an explanation of the conventions used in transcripts of the texts.

35. Tomlin, *The Uley Tablets*, 7, 37. See below, Appendix to Chapter 4.

36. Tomlin, "Fourth-Century Uley 'Curse Tablet,'" 73.

mother or father added for further identification."[37] The handwriting in each tablet is different suggesting that each individual wrote on the tablet themselves.[38] They are the work of "amateurs" not of "professional scribes." The use of formulaic language in many of the tablets implies that they each had some form of guidance; variations in the spelling and wording of those formulas, however, shows that they were not copying from a handbook, but seeking guidance in all likelihood from a priest at the temple: "petitioners made enquiry and were *told* what to say."[39] Behind that guidance was a tradition passed on by word of mouth that may at times have had access to handbooks.[40] The authors identify themselves by name on twenty-five tablets, although on nine of those their name has been lost; sixteen of the tablets have been written by people who wished to remain anonymous.[41] On five tablets eight intended victims are identified by name; eight tablets list by name nineteen people who in all likelihood were enemies of the writer or intended as victims, eight of those names are incomplete.[42] Approximately eleven women are named: five as mother for identification purposes; three appear to be wives, one of whom joins their husband in writing a tablet, one is named with their husband and son as an intended victim, and one is named with her husband in a list; only one woman names herself as the author of a tablet "in her own right," Saturnina.[43]

37. Tomlin, *The Uley Tablets*, 42.

38. For an analysis of the handwriting and tables tabulating each letter form on every tablet see Tomlin, *The Uley Tablets*, 47–60.

39. Tomlin, *The Uley Tablets*, 78. The formulas are listed 22–36.

40. Tomlin, *The Uley Tablets*, 22, 77–79. Cf. Tomlin, *Tabellae Sulis*, https://romaninscriptionsofbritain.org/tabsulis/formulas; https://romaninscriptionsofbritain.org/tabsulis/authorship; Tomlin, "Uley Inscribed Lead Tablets," 114, 117; Tomlin, "Writing to the Gods," 170; Tomlin, "Literacy in Roman Britain," 216.

41. Tomlin, *The Uley Tablets*, 42–43. Tablets preserving the name of the author: *Tab. Uley* 1, 2, 4, 8, 20, 34, 41, 43, 55, 62, 68, 70, 72, 74, 79, 83; tablets on which the name is lost: 3, 21, 22, 24, 40 (authors identified as *silvestres*), 47, 50, ?58, 71; anonymous tablets: 5, 9, 17, ?22, 30, ?47, ?50, 52, 58, 63, 75, 76, 78, 80, 81, 84.

42. Tomlin, *The Uley Tablets*, 43. Eight intended victims named: *Tab. Uley* 1, 20, 43, 68, 78; twelve complete names listed: 33, 39, 45, 49, 61, 86; eight incomplete names listed: 14, 20, 45, 85.

43. Tomlin, *The Uley Tablets*, 43. Four are mothers of suspected thieves or enemies listed: *Tab. Uley* 33, 49; another is probably the mother of a suspected thief or enemy whose name is lost: 61. One wife joins her husband as a petitioner: 20. One wife is named with her husband and son as an intended victim: 43. Saturnina identifies herself as a woman in writing her own tablet: 2.

While acknowledging that it is difficult to be precise, Tomlin lists twenty-eight "Roman" names, most of which are common cognomina and twenty-three "Celtic" names, a mix that can be seen in Bath and elsewhere by the end of the second century.[44] He goes on to say that "it is not worth speculating whether their bearers felt themselves to be 'Roman' or 'non-Roman.'" He does make the observation, however, "that 'Celtic' parents gave 'Celtic' names to their children, and 'Roman' parents 'Roman' names." While one writer uses a patronymic and may thereby identify himself as a *peregrinus*,[45] a provincial subject of the empire, none identifies themselves as a Roman citizen. Nonetheless, Tomlin suggests that the "educated command of Latin rhetoric and vocabulary" by the author of *Tab. Uley* 78 and the ability of the author of *Tab. Uley* 52 "to transliterate almost faultless Latin formulas into Greek letters" may indicate citizenship and possibly a connection with one of the fine villas in the vicinity of Uley, or with a nearby Roman city.[46] In the Uley tablets we encounter people from a farming community who keep beasts of burden, sheep, cows and other farm animals; they plough the land, deal in grain, keep bees, and weave pieces of cloth. We glimpse the household goods and clothing that are valuable to them, and the wealth some have accrued.[47]

In 1978, as Uley was being excavated, tragedy struck in Bath when a young girl died after bathing in the hot spring waters. When the sacred spring was subsequently drained 130 curse tablets were discovered alongside an enormous number of low-value coins and other deposits.[48] The language, handwriting and content of the tablets were similar to the Uley tablets.[49] 111 were literate texts, five were pseudo-inscriptions, six

44. Tomlin, *The Uley Tablets*, 44–45, 367: Roman names: Aeternus, [..]bicianus, Carin[ianus], ?Ociliaris, Docilinus, Honoratus, ?Lucilia, ?Manneius, Natalinus, Peregrina, Petronius, Primanus, Primulacus, Rufus, Sabinianus, Saturnina, ?Secura, Serenus, Seuerinus, ?Spectatus, Varianus, ?[Ve]nator, Vicariana, Virilis, Vitalinus, ?[. . .]aticus, ?[. . .]enta, ?[. . .]lanus. Celtic names: Aunillus, Bellenianus, Biccus, Cenacus, Corosulis, Couitius, Cunitus, Cunouinna, ?Lucila, ?Lucotius, ?Manneius, Maus[a]eus, Mellosus, Minidona, Minuassus, Minura, Pectillus, Satauacus, Senebellena, Senouarus, Varicillus, ?[. . .]benus, ?[. . .]bena. "A question mark precedes those which are of uncertain form, or where it is not clear from the context that they are personal names."

45. *Tab. Uley* 62; Tomlin, *The Uley Tablets*, 259–60.

46. Tomlin, *The Uley Tablets*, 44, 232, 308.

47. See below, *Imagining Honoratus, Saturnina and Many More.*

48. Cunliffe, *Roman Bath*, 36–38, 51–69; Cousins, *Sanctuary at Bath*, 110–49; Davenport, *Roman Bath*, 69–81, 157–62.

49. Tomlin, *Tabellae Sulis* (https://romaninscriptionsofbritain.org/tabsulis/language;

uninscribed, and eight still folded or otherwise illegible.[50] The temple to Sulis Minerva in Aquae Sulis was set in a very different location.[51] Classical in design, possibly built by Togidubnus, a friendly king of Rome, the temple may well have included imperial iconography.[52] It was dedicated to the Roman goddess Minerva and the Celtic goddess Sulis who had already gained a reputation for healing powers from the adjacent hot springs. Cousins differs from the view attributed to Henig, Cunliffe and Davenport that the erection of the temple and its dedication to Sulis and Minerva was, post Boudica, "an attempt to portray the incorporation of Britain into the empire in a positive light," and suggests "it seems more likely that we have here an imperial power placing beyond question or challenge its appropriation of an indigenous sacred spot."[53] Aquae Sulis itself was a cosmopolitan center that drew tourists as well as local people of every level in society.[54] Not only were there *sacerdotes* (priests) in attendance, but a *haruspex* (soothsayer)[55] as well; inscriptions on tombstones and altars indicate the presence in Aquae Sulis of the military, officers of state and the elite of the local society.[56] Initially the spring was open but as the temple developed it was enclosed in its own shrine.[57] With two exceptions, a ploughshare stolen

Tomlin, "Uley Inscribed Lead Tablets."

50. Tomlin, *Tabellae Sulis* (https://romaninscriptionsofbritain.org/tabsulis/texts).

51. Aldhouse-Green, *Sacred Britannia*, 111–15; Cunliffe, *Roman Bath*; Cousins, *Sanctuary at Bath*, 50–69; Allen and Bryan, *Roman Britain*, 74–76; Davenport, *Roman Bath*; Wilson, *A Guide to Roman Britain*, 158–70.

52. Henig suggests the link with Togidubnus ("New Star"); Cousins follows Cunliffe and Davenport in rejecting the link with Togidubnus (*Sanctuary at Bath*, 71–75).

53. Cousins, *Sanctuary at Bath*, 74.

54. Cunliffe, *Roman Bath*, 128–42; Davenport, *Roman Bath*, 148–65.

55. *Lucius Marcius Memor*: Cunliffe, *Roman Bath*, 128, 176–78; Davenport, *Roman Bath*, 155. Cousins suggests this is exceptional in Britannia: "This inscription [*RIB* 3049] has often been cited casually as evidence that Roman officiants such as haruspices existed in Britain, and thus that ritual in the province was 'Romanized'. In fact it would appear to support precisely the opposite conclusion" (*Sanctuary at Bath*, 176–78).

56. Cousins, *Sanctuary at Bath*, 92–109.

57. Cunliffe, *Roman Bath*, 51–66; Cousins, *Sanctuary at Bath*, 110–16; Davenport, *Roman Bath*, 56–69.

from Civilis[58] and items stolen from Deomiorix's house,[59] the tablets report the theft of items stolen in the baths.

Forty-six other tablets have been discovered east of Caerleon and the Severn and south of Ratcliffe on Soar.[60] They are from a mix of town and rural locations and, with only four exceptions, are not associated with military communities. Twelve tablets have been found in seven temples, five of which were near rivers,[61] and one in a shrine associated with the gods of the days of the week, a *septisonium*;[62] four have been found in or near rivers;[63] two were associated with burial sites;[64] two with amphitheaters near forts;[65] two with forts;[66] two were found in a house[67] or villa[68]; fourteen were found in unspecific locations in various Roman settlements.[69]

58. *Tab. Sulis* 31; Tomlin, *Tabellae Sulis*; Sánchez Natalías, *Sylloge Defixiones*, 285 (*SD* 236).

59. *Tab. Sulis* 99; Tomlin, *Tabellae Sulis*; Sánchez Natalías, *Sylloge Defixiones*, 321 (*SD* 304).

60. McKie, *Living and Cursing*, 14–15; Sánchez Natalías, *Sylloge Defixiones*, 77; D. J. Mattingly, *An Imperial Possession*, 310–15; Tomlin, *The Uley Tablets*, 3–5, 363–65. See Map (Figure 1) to the south and east of the broken line.

61. Brean Down, Weston-super-Mare (*SD* 447; Map (Figure 1) 57) now said by Tomlin to have been found at Uley (*The Uley Tablets*, 365); Lydney (*SD* 205; Map 56); Pagans Hill, Chew Stoke, Somerset (*SD* 443, 444, 445; Map 58); Ratcliffe-on-Soar (*SD* 349, 350, 351; Map 62); East Farleigh, Kent (*SD* 458; Map 59); Farley Heath, Surrey (*SD* 455; Map 60); Hockwold-cum-Wilton/Weeting-with-Broomhill, Norfolk (*SD* 450; Map 61).

62. Ratae Corieltavorum/Leicester (*SD* 457; Map (Figure 1) 63).

63. Little Ouse at Brandon (*SD* 449); River Tas at Venta Icenorum/Caistor St Edmund (*SD* 441; Map (Figure 1) 33); Hamble Estuary (*SD* 451); Thames at London Bridge (*SD* 340).

64. Clothall east of Baldock (*SD* 345); Towcester (*Britannia* (2007), 361.

65. Isca Silurum/Caerleon (*SD* 337); Londinium/London (*SD* 343; Map (Figure 1) 28 and 1).

66. Bravonium/Leintwardine (*SD* 347, 348).

67. Ratae Corieltavorum/Leicester (*SD* 456; Map (Figure 1) 63).

68. Eccles, Kent, Lidgate (*SD* 446).

69. Puckeridge Braughing (*SD* 448); Dodford (*SD* 453); Old Harlow (*SD* 353); Canonium/Kelvedon (*SD* 346); Londinium/London (*SD* 338, 339, 341, 342); Marlborough Downs (*SD* 452); Rothwell (Willis, *Roman Roadside Settlement*, 284–88); Calleva Atrebatum/Silchester (*SD* 454, Map (Figure 1) 20); Thetford (*SD* 442); Wanborough (*SD* 352); Weeting with Broomhill (*SD* 450). For many of these, the find-spots were not precisely identified.

The language of the curse tablets is one of the richest known sources of spoken or vulgar Latin and offers in microcosm an insight into the speech habits of Roman Britain.[70] However, such language is not indicative of low social status; phonetic misspellings and simple errors are evident across the empire and across all levels of society: writers who use "a vulgar spelling need not" themselves "be vulgar."[71] That suggests that literacy goes further and deeper than had hitherto been supposed,[72] and is not confined to the military,[73] to the urban or rural elite[74] but "extends to a moderately prosperous peasant community."[75] East meets west in one Uley tablet written in Latin but in Greek lettering, prompting Tomlin to observe, "to find such sophisticated literacy in the Romano-British countryside, even if only to maintain security of communication with the divine, is startling."[76] Another anonymous tablet he describes as "a literary tour de force" and "a surprisingly sophisticated text to come from a rural shrine," albeit one close to "the palatial villa at Woodchester" and the cities of Glevum (Gloucester) and Corinium (Cirencester).[77] There is evidence too of the continued use of a Celtic language. As at Bath, so in Uley, two tablets appear to be in a script that may well be Celtic.[78] There is also evidence of the influence of the Celtic language on the Latin used in Bath[79] and later in Uley.[80]

Mercury is addressed in at least twenty-six tablets, mentioned in five others and probably figures in many of those tablets that are too

70. Tomlin, *Tabellae Sulis*, 79, https://romaninscriptionsofbritain.org/tabsulis/language; Tomlin, *The Uley Tablets*, 65–73.

71. J. N. Adams, "British Latin," 24.

72. Mullen, "Linguistic Evidence for 'Romanization,'" 31.

73. Tomlin, "Cursing a Thief," 269.

74. Tomlin, "Uley Inscribed Lead Tablets," 116; Mullen "New Thoughts on British Latin," 271; J. Stevenson, "Beginnings of Literacy," 136.

75. Tomlin, "Uley Inscribed Lead Tablets," 116; Davenport, *Roman Bath*, 161–62; Wolff, "Education in Latinization," 178–79; Tomlin, *The Uley Tablets*, 74.

76. *Tab. Uley* 52; Tomlin, *The Uley Tablets*, 230–34.

77. *Tab. Uley* 78; Tomlin, *The Uley Tablets*, 306–12. Appendix Chapter 4.

78. Tomlin, *The Uley Tablets*, 44–46. Celtic tablets: *Tab. Uley* 7, 35; *Tab. Sulis* 14, 18; Mullen, "Evidence for Written Celtic"; cf. Mullen "New Thoughts on British Latin"; cf. *Tab. Uley* 39, 192.

79. J. N. Adams, "British Latin."

80. Tomlin, "Uley Inscribed Lead Tablets," 115; *Tab. Uley* 84; Tomlin, *The Uley Tablets*, 334.

fragmentary to interpret.[81] Very few refrain from using a name for the god.[82] There is some evidence that some of those responsible for the tablets were uncertain of the name of the god: four explicitly, and one implicitly, link Mars with Mercury;[83] and in one Saturnina "begins by referring to 'the god Mars Silvanus' (*deo Marti Siluano*), but then writes 'Mercury' (*Mercurio*) over 'Mars Silvanus,' only to refer once more to 'the god Silvanus' (*deo Siluano*) overleaf, without correcting it."[84] On one tablet, those who come to the temple describe themselves as *s[il]|uestres* (woodlanders), suggesting an on-going connection with the ancient sacred wood, *nymed* (Celtic) or *nemeton* (Latin).[85] In *The Uley Tablets* Roger Tomlin announced the name not only of the Celtic god associated with Mercury in the Uley shrines, but also the name of the location itself. In nine tablets a title immediately follows the name Mercury: *Aruerius* on six occasions and *Arueriacus* on three others.[86] In three other tablets the name *Aruerius* stands alone as if it is the equivalent of Mercury.[87] In two tablets *Aruerius* is used as a title of Mars.[88] In one tablet the petitioner asks a suspected thief to return stolen property "to the temple of Mercury on the Hill of *Aruerius*" (*ad tem[p]lum |Mer(curii) mont<e> Arueri*). As at Bath where the pre-Roman Celtic god, Sulis, is identified with the Roman god Minerva and often addressed as Sulis Minerva, so here in Uley "there was evidently a pre-Roman Celtic god [*Aruerius*] who became 'identified' with a Roman god [Mercury]."[89] That *Aruerius* was a name of some local significance is suggested by the appearance of *Arueri*, together with two spade-like symbols, on thirty-five

81. Tomlin, *The Uley Tablets*, 61, 368: Mercury is addressed in *Tab. Uley* 1, 2, 4, 9, 17, 21, 24, 28, 30, 34, 40, 43, 52, 55, 58, 62, 68, 70, 71, 72, 74, 76, 78, 79, 80, 81; the name of Mercury is restored in 50, 60 and named in the body of the text in 17, 39, 75.

82. Tomlin, *The Uley Tablets*, 61: *Tab. Uley* 5, 41, 83.

83. Tomlin, *The Uley Tablets*, 61: *Tab. Uley* 3, 8 19 are addressed to Mars Mercury; 24 equates Mars with Mercury; 84 addresses Mars alone, but gives him a title shared with Mercury, *Aruerius*.

84. Tomlin, *The Uley Tablets*, 61–62.

85. *Tab. Uley* 40; Tomlin, *The Uley Tablets*, 194–96.

86. Tomlin, *The Uley Tablets*, 62: Mercury *Aruerius* in 21, 28, 30, 75, 78, 81; Mercury *Arueriacus* in 40, 52, 78.

87. Tomlin, *The Uley Tablets*, 62: *Tab. Uley* 20, 47, 75.

88. Tomlin, *The Uley Tablets*, 62: *Tab. Uley* 63, 84.

89. Tomlin, The Uley Tablets, 63; Tomlin, *Britannia Romana*, 335–43; Tab. Uley 75, lines 7–8; Tomlin, *The Uley Tablets*, 294–98. Image at

https://www.britishmuseum.org/collection/object/H_1978-0102-151 Appendix Chapter 4.

stamped tiles discovered in and around nearby Cirencester (*Corinium*):[90] it may be linked to the proto-Celtic words *arwar* (grain) and *arweros* (host, army) and so have to do with a Celtic god linked to bountiful provision in an agricultural community, or linked to Mars the god of war. The discovery of miniature spears and iron projectile heads among deposits in the temple lend credence to the latter.[91] Mercury is connected with Mars and Silvanus elsewhere in Britannia suggesting to Tomlin that *Aruerius* may have had attributes linked with Mercury, Mars and Silvanus.[92] The Celtic interest in Mercury had been observed by Julius Caesar. Following the account of his two incursions into Britain and the quelling of revolts in Gaul, Caesar links the religious practices of the Britons with those of the Gauls and speaks of their high regard for Mercury.

> *Deum maxime Mercurium colunt. Huius sunt plurima simulacra: hunc omnium inventorem artium ferunt, hunc viarum atque itinerum ducem, hunc ad quaestus pecuniae mercaturasque habere vim maximam arbitrantur.*
>
> They especially honor the god Mercury. There are very many images of him: they describe him as the source of all knowledge, the guide on all roads and journeys; they consider he has the greatest power when it comes to the acquisition of wealth and the pursuit of commerce.[93]

There is nothing to see, yet everything to experience at "the temple of Mercury on the Hill of *Aruerius*." Approaching on foot one cannot help but feel the significance of its location.[94] Walk the kilometer from Nympsfield long barrow[95] along the edge of the Cotswold escarpment to Hetty Pegler's Tump, another Neolithic long barrow,[96] and within another hundred meters or so is the location of that Celtic sacred place that became home to the

90. "*RIB*," 2489.4A.i–xxxv; 4B.i; Darvill, "ARVERI."

91. Tomlin, *The Uley Tablets*, 63–64; cf. Woodward and Leach, *Uley Shrines Excavation*, 131–35.

92. Tomlin, "Uley Inscribed Lead Tablets," 115. Cf. Woolf, *Becoming Roman*, 212, 226.

93. Caesar, *Bellum Gallicum* VI.17: H. J. Edwards, ed. and trans., 340. Perring cites the prevalence of altars and statues to Mercury at the entrances to London as evidence for the association of Mercury with trade and travel in Britannia (*London in Roman World*, 174).

94. Tilley, *Phenomenology of Landscape*, 78ff.

95. "Nympsfield Long Barrow." Map (Figure 1) 53.

96. "Uley Long Barrow." Map (Figure 1) 52 and inset; Figure 16.

temple of Mercury *Aruerius*. To the west is a breath-taking view across the River Severn, with its tidal bore, to the Welsh mountains.[97] On the far side of the Severn and in a location that is just about visible is the Romano-Celtic temple at Lydney Park dedicated to the healing god Nodens.[98] Walking from a kilometer in the other direction, one skirts round Uley Bury, a large, multi-vallate Iron Age hill fort occupied from approximately 300 BCE to 100 CE and beyond[99] before arriving at the temple site. Walk from the rich agricultural land at the foot of the escarpment, past the spring line and the temple site comes into view as one reaches the top of the escarpment. There is evidence of a metaled Roman road at the foot of the escarpment that goes to the *colonia*, Glevum (Gloucester) 23 kilometers to the north.[100] East and then north on the Fosse Way is the major town of Corinium (Cirencester) in 26 kilometers; south, Aquae Sulis (Bath) with its sacred spring and temple dedicated to Sulis Minerva in 42 kilometers. Within 6 kilometers is the palatial villa of Woodchester with its enormous Orpheus mosaic.[101] One can sense why contemporaries of Honoratus and Saturnina valued this location as "the Hill of *Aruerius*," thinking of themselves as *siluestres*, woodlanders coming to what had from time immemorial been a sacred grove, overlooking *Sabrina*, the River Severn.[102] In their day this was an area of considerable agricultural activity where fertile land was being reclaimed from the tidal River Severn. It would appear that people lived not so much in villages as in substantial farmsteads:[103] in the vicinity there were many villas and

97. According to Tomlin it is remotely possible that *Tab. Uley* 59, an undeciphered spiral text, includes the word SABRINA, the Roman name for the River Severn (*The Uley Tablets*, 253).

98. Copeland, *Roman Gloucestershire*, 150–52; Lydney Park Estate, *Lydney Park*, 14–19; Wilson, *A Guide to Roman Britain*, 202–6; Allen and Bryan, *Roman Britain*, 87–89. Map (Figure 1) 56.

99. Lock and Ralson, "Atlas of Hillforts": EN0752 Uley Bury Camp, Gloucestershire; "Uley Bury Camp." Evans adduces evidence to suggest "the hillfort's use in the Roman period" and into the third century CE (*Uley Bury Gloucestershire*, Archaeological Background, 9–10). Map (Figure 1) 51.

100. Copeland, *Roman Gloucestershire*, 48. Glevum, Corinium, Aquae Sulis, Map (Figure 1) 26, 25, 55; Woodchester villa, Map (Figure 1) 54; Fosse Way, from Isca Dumnomniorum, through Corinium, and Ratae Corieltavorum to Lindum (Map (Figure 1) 24, 25, 63, 46.

101. Copeland, *Roman Gloucestershire*, 128–29.

102. Tomlin, *The Uley Tablets*, 63, 195; *Tab. Uley* 40, 59, 75.

103. Copeland, *Roman Gloucestershire*, 100–103.

other settlements.[104] From the grazing uplands of the escarpment to the lush pastures and arable lands below the spring-line, this was a rural community where Celtic and Roman worlds met and shaped the ritual practice of the local people.[105]

What Are Curse Tablets?

The people of Bath, Uley, and so many other sites in Britain east of the Severn and south of the Soar were not alone in what they were doing and yet what each did was an individualized response to a personal crisis.[106] Curse tablets first appeared in the Greek world in the fifth century BCE and in the Latin world in the second century BCE; they continue to appear until the fifth century CE. By 2019 over 1600 Greek and Latin curse tablets had been published, two-thirds in Greek and one third in Latin;[107] of the 520 Latin *defixiones* included in Celia Sánchez Natalías's *Sylloge of* defixiones *from the Latin West*, 256 are from Britannia.[108] They have a shared language that spans a thousand years and the entire Roman Empire,[109] draw on ideas current for "hundreds of miles and hundreds of years,"[110] are "a universal feature of Mediterranean culture in antiquity"[111] and "a part of everyday life even in the western provinces."[112] While the Latin tablets are widely distributed across the west in single finds or small groups, larger collections are limited to a few locations: Bath and Uley in Britannia, Mainz in Germania, Trier in Gallia, Rome in Italia, and Carthage in North Africa.[113] It is

104. Cleary, *Map of Roman Britain*.

105. Drinkwater, "Uley Geology and Geography," 3.

106. McKie, *Living and Cursing*, 3.

107. Franek and Urbanová, "Sympathetic Magic Part 1," 29; Eidinow, "Binding Spells," 353–55.

108. Sánchez Natalías, *Sylloge Defixiones* 265–383.

109. Faraone, "Agonistic Context," 3; Faraone, "Aeschylus," 151; Revell, "Religion and Ritual," 222; Scholz, "Round Curse Tablets," 39.

110. Tomlin, *Tabellae Sulis*, 62ff: "https://romaninscriptionsofbritain.org/tabsulis/formulas."

111. Gager, "Curse Tablets in Greco-Roman World," 72. Cf. Woolf, "Curse Tablets," 123.

112. Scholz, "Round Curse Tablets," 39.

113. McKie includes a distribution map of the 126 locations where curse tablets have been discovered in the western provinces (*Living and Cursing*, 12–18). Sánchez Natalías includes maps identifying the location of *defixiones* in the Republican period, the High

important, argues Celia Sánchez Natalías, to be wary of sweeping generalizations as if they represented a common phenomenon that spread through the Greek and then the Roman world: "these texts need to be seen in a more organic light and analyzed within particular social, historical, and cultural contexts."[114] They were, observes Woolf, "used in a matrix formed by personal relationships between humans" and "operated within a human social network."[115]

What's Going On in Writing Such Messages? Are They Curses or Prayers for Justice?

A definition proposed by D. R. Jordan has been widely accepted:[116] "*defixiones*, more commonly known as curse tablets, are inscribed pieces of lead, usually in the form of small, thin sheets, intended to influence, by supernatural means, the actions or welfare of persons or animals against their will."[117] That is further refined by Sánchez Natalías who stresses that "the true essence of a *defixio* is found neither in the material used nor in the inscribed message, but rather in its harmful nature and desire to manipulate."[118] Woolf argues that it is "the simple utility and versatility of the curse tablet form" that is important for any study of the curse tablets.[119] Originating with the binding spells of ancient Greece, there were three different styles according to C. A. Faraone: a direct binding formula in the first person singular amounting to a performative utterance accompanied by a significant ritual act; a prayer formula addressed to the chthonic underworld deities using the second person imperative, and a *similia similibus* formula often expressed as a wish that the victim should, for example,

Empire and Late Antiquity (*Sylloge Defixiones*, 69–79).

114. Sánchez Natalías, "Curse Tablets against Thieves," 103. Cf. Woolf, "Curse Tablets."

115. Woolf, "Curse Tablets," 133; cf. Cousins, *Sanctuary at Bath*, 176–86.

116. Tomlin, *Tabellae Sulis*, 59; Tomlin, "Writing to the Gods"; Urbanová, *Latin Curse Tablets*, 17; Franek and Urbanová, "Sympathetic Magic Part 1," 29, 28; Franek and Urbanová, "Sympathetic Magic Part 2," 205; Eidinow, "Binding Spells," 351; McKie, *Living and Cursing*, 12; Sánchez Natalías, *Sylloge Defixiones*, 5.

117. Jordan, "Survey of Greek Defixiones," 151.

118. Sánchez Natalías, *Sylloge Defixiones*, 5.

119. Woolf, "Curse Tablets," 133–34.

become as cold as this lead.[120] In this way *defixiones* were a means of binding or restraining enemies without killing them and were used in the context of "agonistic relationships between rival tradesmen, lovers, litigants or athletes concerned with the outcome of some future event."[121] Gager modified this classification suggesting three types: a direct binding formula, a prayer formula for supernatural assistance, and persuasive analogies.[122]

Faraone suggests that the use of *defixiones* can be traced "from the Levant to the Greek world and on to the Roman west."[123] He suggests Micah's mother's curse in Judg 17:1–4 is an ancient example of such a practice. One of thirteen Greek curse tablets from third or fourth century CE Antioch invokes Ιαω[124] to fill Babylas the greengrocer with evil fortune;[125] one of two from the fourth century CE found in the theater at Caesarea Maritima calls on the Egyptian Thoth and Isis to hinder the dance of Manna, a rival dancer; more than 60 were found in a well at Herod's palace in Caesarea Maritima;[126] in another fourth century CE example from a bath house in Jerusalem an unnamed person invokes Ιαω to [bind] the mind and otherwise harm five men with names that suggest a Christian milieu: Petros, Ioannes, ?Theodora, ?Anastasios.[127]

A handful of such agonistic curses against rivals, using the word, *defigo*, have been found in Britain. Tacita was accursed (*deficta*) and labelled old like putrid gore;[128] two Roman citizens, T(itus) Egnatius Tyran(n)nus and P(ublius) Cicereius Felix were accursed (*defictus*);[129] and someone wrote with feeling, "I curse (*defico*) Tretia Maria and her life and mind and memory and liver and lungs mixed up together, and her words, thoughts,

120. Faraone, "Agonistic Context," 9–10.

121. Faraone, "Agonistic Context," 11.

122. Gager, *Curse Tablets From Ancient World*, 13–14.

123. Faraone, "Curses," 31.

124. Hollman, "Curse Tablet from Antioch"; Skehan references a Qumran text of Lev 1–4 using *Iao* to translate the tetragrammaton ("Divine Name at Qumran," 28); Tov, "Texts from Judean Desert" with a discussion of the Qumran text, 4QpapLXXLev[b].

125. According to Hollman, the reference to the destruction of Pharaoh's chariots during the Israelites' crossing of the Red Sea, and to the cutting down of the first born of Egypt suggests acquaintance with the Judean YHWH and possible origin in a Judean community in Antioch ("Curse Tablet from Antioch").

126. Burrell, "Curse Tablets Caesarea."

127. Daniel and Sulimani, "New Curse Tablet from Jerusalem."

128. *SD* 345 (*RIB* 221), Sánchez Natalías, *Sylloge Defixiones*, 336–37.

129. *SD* 338 (*RIB* 6), Sánchez Natalías, *Sylloge Defixiones*, 331.

and memory; thus may she be unable to speak what things are concealed, nor be able . . . nor . . ."[130] In each of these instances, *defigo* has been used and the lead tablets have been pierced with five, one and seven nails respectively, as if they had been nailed figuratively and literally.[131]

Up until the late 1970s three of the ten curse tablets found in Britain were explicit curses, another four had to do with theft. With the discoveries at Uley and Bath that changed significantly. In publishing the Bath tablets Tomlin noticed that something subtly different was going on: in their concern for justice, the punishment of thieves, and the return of stolen property, almost all the tablets were in part prayers and in part legal documents.[132] Tomlin emphasizes the juridical nature of some of the language of the British tablets, with parallels to the *Digest* of Justinian,[133] a point taken up by Adams who draws parallels with German and Frankish law-codes.[134] Concerned with correcting the status quo rather than confronting an opponent,[135] prayers for justice gave people who did not have access to the legal system the opportunity to set matters right:[136] that may well be the reason why, in Britain, they are associated with neither the military nor the elite.[137] As a strategy for obtaining individual justice curse tablets enabled those who used them to seek redress for a wrong which could not be achieved in any other way "due to lack of knowledge, power or economic/legal resources."[138]

At the same time Henk Versnel suggested that some Greek and Latin curse tablets to do with the theft of items were not so much *defixiones* as judicial prayers.[139] The anonymity of a *defixio* which often seeks harm for

130. *SD* 339, (*RIB* 7), Sánchez Natalías, *Sylloge Defixiones*, 332.

131. Cf. Tomlin, *The Uley Tablets*, 13.

132. Tomlin, *Tabellae Sulis*, 60ff: https://romaninscriptionsofbritain.org/tabsulis/prayer-to-the-goddess.

133. Tomlin lists 17 legal formulae ("Uley Inscribed Lead Tablets," 116). *Justinian Digest* XLVII.2.19, Ulpian, *On Sabinus* XL, relating to the way property is described in an action for theft, "*Justinian Digest*." Tomlin describes the legal formulae used in the Bath tablets (*Tabellae Sulis*, 63–68: https://romaninscriptionsofbritain.org/tabsulis/formulas).

134. J. N. Adams, "British Latin," 2ff.

135. G. W. Adams, "Social and Cultural Implications of Curse Tablets," 13.

136. Versnel, "Beyond Cursing," 68; Veale, "*Defixiones* and Temple," 299–300; Meyer, "Law and Latinization," 199–205.

137. D. J. Mattingly, *An Imperial Possession*, 315.

138. Sánchez Natalías, *Sylloge Defixiones*, 5.

139. Versnel, "Beyond Cursing."

no specific reason by manipulating the chthonic gods of the underworld is contrasted with judicial prayers in which the petitioner often identifies themselves by name and addresses the god or goddess respectfully. Such judicial prayers use formulaic language like that used in courts of law, are directed to the recognized gods or goddesses of Rome and identified with local deities, Mercury, (identified with the Celtic god *Aruerius* and occasionally linked with Mars and Silvanus) in Uley and Sulis Minerva in Bath. They were folded and so unreadable by anyone else and deposited in a sacred place, such as a temple or a watery location. It is possible that the injured person mentioned the name of the suspect to make them aware of their indictment.[140] Versnel emphasized that he was using the minimal criteria of a prayer and that the distinction between a *defixio* and a judicial prayer is not always clear-cut. He spoke of a border area between the two and stressed that any such categorization is modern.[141] In 2005 Versnel reviewed the curse tablets discovered since 1991: modifying his terminology he spoke of eight of the fourteen as prayers for justice and suggested the other six fell into the border area, containing features characteristic both of prayers for justice and straight *defixiones*.[142] He defined prayers for justice as markedly emotional "pleas addressed to a god or gods to punish a (mostly unknown) person who has wronged the author (by theft, slander, false accusations or magical action), often with the additional request to redress the harm suffered by the author (e.g. by forcing a thief to return a stolen object, or to publicly confess guilt)."[143]

Martin Dreher rejected Versnel's categorization, suggesting such tablets should be thought of as "criminal curses"; that prompted a detailed rebuttal by Versnel who re-emphasized a border area between at one extreme binding spells and at the other prayers for justice.[144] In her study of *Latin Curse Tablets of the Roman Empire*, Daniela Urbanová reaffirms Versnel's approach and offers a detailed analysis that differentiates curses and prayers for justice.[145] According to Urbanová "prayers for justice were

140. Versnel, "Beyond Cursing," 90, cf. 68.

141. Versnel, "Beyond Cursing," 63.

142. Versnel, "Prayers for Justice," 322.

143. Versnel, "Prayers for Justice," 278; cf. 279–81.

144. Versnel, "Response to a Critique," 28.

145. Urbanová, *Latin Curse Tablets*: curses (102–179); prayers for justice (180–205). She categorizes curses and prayers for justice region by region (206–397) with a summary and distribution maps (398–425). While the prayers for justice coming from Italia (242–244), Hispania (258–262) and Gallia (274–278) "have several features in common,

made in the context of theft, fraud, injustice or other harm suffered by their authors":[146] 4 percent seek the return of the goods stolen without mentioning a punishment, 28 percent seek the return of the goods and the punishment of the culprit, and 55 percent seek only to punish or to take vengeance.[147] While Eleri Cousins maintains that "almost all British tablets meet Versnel's requirements for 'judicial prayers,'" she suggests they have to do not simply with the return of stolen property or the punishment of a thief, but also with the writer's desire "to reclaim their ability to control their lost property and its deposition."[148] In a sense the writing of a tablet is a reassertion by the victim of their own agency: "through the use of ritual, the petitioner goes from powerless victim to having agency over the fate of his or her possessions again."[149]

The publication of curse tablets from Rome,[150] Mainz,[151] Bolonia and Kempraten,[152] has confirmed the value of speaking of prayers for justice, although in her study of the Mainz tablets Sarah Veale emphasizes that it is not possible to draw neat boundaries between religious-oriented prayers for justice and *defixiones*.[153] That is also stressed by Eidinow, who speaks of prayers for justice as "personal expressions in the context of temple-religion."[154] Cousins stresses that "we should not think that all tablets in all places obeyed the same rules."[155] In her comprehensive *Sylloge Defixiones*,

and are more closely linked to curses," those found in Britannia (374–394) indicate "an autonomous and innovative development of this genre in this region" (203). She treats the prayers for justice in Germania, Raetia, Noricum, Pannonia (309–320) separately and notices there are no prayers for justice from the African provinces. Appendix I contains the corpus of Latin curses (426–504) and Appendix II the corpus of Latin prayers for justice (505–32), with texts and detailed classification.

146. Urbanová, *Latin Curse Tablets*, 180.

147. Urbanová, *Latin Curse Tablets*, 203.

148. Cousins, *Sanctuary at Bath*, 183–84.

149. Cousins, *Sanctuary at Bath*, 138.

150. Blansdorf, "Texts from Fons Annae Perennae."

151. Blansdorf, "*Defixiones* from Mainz."

152. Kellová, "Oriental Cults and Curse Tablets."

153. Veale, "*Defixiones* and Temple," 49.

154. Eidinow, "Binding Spells," 352.

155. Cousins, *Sanctuary at Bath*, 185. In seeking to explain the contrast between the few judicial prayers in curse tablets from the east and their "almost universal" presence in Britannia, Cousins observes that judicial prayers are "quite common" among Gallic or German tablets: it is as if they "represent a midway point between the extremes of British and Eastern practices, rendering the still undeniable uniqueness of the British texts a

Sánchez Natalías is critical of "the scholarly desire to classify and organize" as "most of the texts do not follow a general model."[156] Instead of using the phrase "prayers for justice," she uses what she considers a neutral phrase, *defixiones in fures*, to designate those that have to do with theft; her aim is to allow the texts to speak for themselves. Amina Kropp prefers to speak of requests rather than prayers as the latter implies "spoken not written language-use" and also a hierarchical relationship between "the orant and the addressee."[157]

With the publication of *The Uley Tablets*, Roger Tomlin, on the other hand, develops the thinking he first shared in 1988 in the publication of the tablets from Bath and entitles one introductory chapter "A Prayer to the God."[158] He calls in question the recent preference for the term *defixiones*, a word which occurs only once in Roman literature, and notes that the word *defigo* is not used in Bath or Uley in addressing the god.[159] Honoratus speaks of his "petition" (*petitio*) "with repeated prayers" (*pr{a}ecibus*), as he complains (*conqueror*) and "asks" deferentially (*rogauerim*) and simply (*rogo*), addressing Mercury as "the holy god" (*deo sanc\to/*) "your divinity" (*numen*) twice, "the *genius* of your divinity" (*genium numinis \tu{u}i/*), and "your Majesty" (*maiestate tua*).[160] One writer uses the word *peto*, I seek, and another possibly misspells the same word; another uses the word *oro*, I pray, though the context is entirely missing. Carinus (or Carinianus) uses a synonym, *obsecro*, I implore.[161] The god is "asked" for something in a number of tablets, and on occasion such requests are linked with complaints.[162] The use of such verbs to address the god leads Tomlin to the conclusion that "the Uley tablets are mostly 'prayers for justice,' not . . . 'pure' curses." He

---

little less jarring and exceptional" (*Sanctuary at Bath*, 182–83). It must always be remembered, however, that observed discrepancies may be due to the paucity of archaeological evidence.

156. Sánchez Natalías, *Sylloge Defixiones*, 30.

157. Kropp, "Magical Language," 365.

158. Tomlin, *The Uley Tablets*, 13–21; cf. https://romaninscriptionsofbritain.org/tabsulis/prayer-to-the-goddess.

159. Tomlin, *The Uley Tablets*, 13–14.

160. *Tab. Uley* 72; Tomlin, *The Uley Tablets*, 286–90; 15–16. Appendix Chapter 4.

161. Tomlin, *The Uley Tablets*, 15: *Tab. Uley* 75, 24, 6, 68.

162. Tomlin, *The Uley Tablets*, 15–16: *rogo*, *Tab. Uley* 43, 63, 72, possibly 34; *rogamus*, *Tab. Uley* 80; *queror* (I complain) is followed by *rogo* (I ask): *Tab. Uley* 1, 43, and implies *rogo*: *Tab. Uley* 76, 84.

acknowledges, however, that "the distinction is not absolute,"[163] and notes occasional tablets that are more akin to curses.[164]

The temptation to link curses with "magic" and prayers for justice with "religion" calls in question what is understood by "religion" in the Roman world, a subject too vast to cover here but one that must be touched on. At one time there was a willingness to systematize "Roman Religion" and differentiate religion and magic. In *Religion in Roman Britain* (1984), Mark Henig speaks of "the native religion of Britain," of Celtic and Roman religion as "separate though related systems" and of "compromise and fusion between the two systems."[165] Such an approach invites us to fit the practices we encounter into the systems of Roman religion that are primarily civic based and cult based. As the Uley and Bath tablets began to be published, Henig explored them in the context of "vows, requests and prayers." He regarded them as two considerable archives of "messages to the gods" that can be understood on analogy with the *nuncupatio* of a dedication in which the god addressed is named and a request is made. They have to do with redress for theft, with a stress on punishment, with gods enforcing moral behavior, and with piety. That distinguishes them significantly from "magic" which he suggests is "not religion but rather a debased offshoot from it which assumes that the gods can be controlled by man."[166] Whereas "religion was linked to morality, magic could be used to disturb society."[167] That means for Henig "the tablets help us to unify our view of religion in Britain."[168]

That approach has been called in question on two counts. First, instead of focusing on civic-centered state religion, Sarah Veale advocates a more "open-system" model: there is a constant process of negotiation going on, she suggests, as people draw on different traditions to engage in religious practices.[169] With its roots in a Celtic shrine, Uley enables us to glimpse the encounter between Roman practices and "the religious dimensions of iron age culture." What was important, suggests Woolf, was not so much "the propagation of a particular cosmology or theology, but rather of a

163. Tomlin, *The Uley Tablets*, 17.

164. Tomlin, *The Uley Tablets*, 14: *Tab. Uley* 43, 68, 76, 78.

165. Henig, *Religion in Roman Britain*, 24, 36.

166. Henig, *Religion in Roman Britain*, 32.

167. Henig, *Religion in Roman Britain*, 165.

168. Henig, *Religion in Roman Britain*, 145.

169. Veale, "*Defixiones* and Temple," 294. Cf. Rives, "Greco-Roman Religion," 284.

particular ritual tradition and its associated sensibilities."[170] As more becomes known of the name of the Uley shrine and its roots in a Celtic sacred place, Miranda Aldhouse-Green draws on that observation and maintains in the context of Britannia that "religion was not simply a matter of belief in and honor of the gods but was a highly complex affair involving negotiative power-relationships between groups and individuals and between Britain and Rome."[171] Second, it applies to the ancient world an anachronistic understanding of magic and religion formed in the modern world.

In 1998 Mary Beard, John North and Simon Price shifted the focus on to "the complex pattern of Rome's religious influence on its empire"[172] in a book with a tellingly different title, *Religions of Rome*.[173] In that volume and its companion source book,[174] they explore the changing perspectives on religious matters of different people in different places at different times. They consider the curse tablets to be on the boundaries of Roman religion. It is not true to say that in Roman religion there were no boundaries, and anything was permissible. There were boundaries but with regard to the construction and transgression of religious boundaries things are very much more complex than at first appears.[175] The boundary between religion and superstition was not so much about "truth" and "falsehood": rather, it had to do with the relationship between people and the gods. *Religio*, they suggest, was "an aspect of a Roman's *self*-description"; *superstitio*, on the other hand, "was always a slur against others." But, and this is the crucial thing as far as they are concerned, "they do not denote simple or easily definable opposites."[176] These terms must be understood in the context of contemporary Roman writers not of modern thinkers and Christian writers.[177] The same applies to the boundary between religion and magic. While there is an antipathy towards magic from writers such as Pliny the elder and Lucian, in official pronouncements and in early Christian writers, the reality of magical practice is more complex.[178] "so, for example, the

170. Woolf, *Becoming Roman*, 208, 215.

171. Aldhouse-Green, *Gallo-British Deities*, 194; Woolf, *Becoming Roman*.

172. Beard et al., *Religions of Rome Volume 1*, 314.

173. Beard et al., *Religions of Rome Volume 1*.

174. Beard et al., *Religions of Rome Volume 2*.

175. Beard et al., *Religions of Rome Volume 1*, 211–44.

176. Beard et al., *Religions of Rome Volume 1*, 215.

177. Beard et al., *Religions of Rome Volume 1*, 219.

178. Beard et al., *Religions of Rome Volume 1*, 218–21. Cf. Pervo, *Acts*, 207–9.

surviving Latin curses (often scratched on lead tablets, and so preserved) increase greatly in number under the empire, and the Greek magical papyri from Egypt are most common in the third and fourth centuries" CE.[179]

It may not be helpful to think in such cut and dried categories when considering the curse tablets. In his introduction to the Greek magical papyri in translation Hans Dieter Betz suggests they are of particular value in helping us to understand "what people are really thinking and doing in a particular time, geographical area, or cultural context."[180] The magical practices reflected in those papyri were so much a part of people's everyday lives that it is not possible to differentiate magical and religious practices: "the neat distinctions we make today between approved and disapproved forms of religion—calling the former "religion" and "church" and the latter "magic" and "cult"—did not exist in antiquity except among a few intellectuals."[181] In the context of *defixiones*, Faraone[182] and Gager[183] suggest that it is not correct to think in terms of a specific category of magic or of a clear-cut distinction between magic and religion.[184]

Richard Gordon in the last ten years has been part of a movement that rejects the approach of Henig and wants to go further than Beard, North and Price to focus on what has been called "Lived Ancient Religion," "a new approach to the religious practices, ideas and institutions of the distant past" that "emphasizes the social context of religious action."[185] Reflecting on the curse tablets he advocates abandoning "the abstract categories 'religion' and 'magic,' with their inescapable moral packaging": instead he suggests we should think "in terms of optional, semi-institutionalized strategies open to individuals in predicaments that for them were crisis-situations that threatened their social, economic, moral or emotional existence."[186] In so doing we must not overlook the efficacy of the supernatural power appealed to in the ritual of depositing a curse tablet. It was not only the personal

179. Beard et al., *Religions of Rome Volume 1*, 220.

180. Betz, *Greek Magical Papyri*, xli.

181. Betz, *Greek Magical Papyri*, xli; Jeffers, *Magic and Divination*; Mason, "Jews, Judaeans," 480–89; Mason comments that "it is only Western modernity that knows this category of religion" ("Jews, Judaeans," 488).

182. Faraone, "Agonistic Context," 20.

183. Gager, *Curse Tablets From Ancient World*, 25.

184. Woolf, "Curse Tablets," 127.

185. Gasparini et al., *Lived Religion*, 1, 3.

186. Gordon, "Gods, Guilt and Suffering," 255.

circumstances of those who had cause to use curse tablets that prompted their use: it was also the fact that that was what was done in that particular locality that prompted them to do so. Jörg Rüpke sees "Roman religion not as a set of cults, one of many localized 'religions,' but as a regional and temporal segment of lived religion in antiquity, serving individuals who employed religion as a resource for many a purpose."[187]

Stuart McKie has pursued this approach in his comprehensive study of 607 curse tablets, *Living and Cursing in the Roman West.*[188] Thinking in terms of Lived Ancient Religion, he advocates a shift from attention to the wording on the tablets to what was going on. Questioning the value of generalizations about the use of curse tablets throughout the Roman Empire, he focuses on the individual whose action is shaped by their own community, by friends and family, and by what they know is done locally. While it is helpful to glean from the text of the tablets itself the motives of the one using a curse tablet,[189] there is "more to be gained from a fine-grained approach that sees cursing within the contexts of the lives of the individuals who made" the curse tablets.[190] McKie suggests there are six steps in creating a curse tablet.[191]

1. An initial trigger prompts the decision to compose a curse tablet.
2. Acquisition of the physical materials needed (sheet of lead, stylus, in some cases one or more nails for piercing) and of advice regarding how to set about the process (circulating in the community, passed on by family and friends or from specialists based in a temple).
3. The act of writing transforms the tablet into an object with power.
4. That power is enhanced by folding, rolling, or nailing the tablet.
5. A prayer is spoken.
6. The tablet is deposited in a significant place, and in Britannia that is often a temple or a place near water.

187. Rüpke, *On Roman Religion*, 7.

188. McKie includes a select catalogue of curses (*Living and Cursing*, 133–244).

189. McKie observes that of the 607 curse tablets from the Roman west, 161 are not sufficiently legible to indicate a motive; 141 do not specify a motive; 145 are prayers for justice (of which 101 are from Britannia); 84 involve competition, e.g. in the amphitheater or on the chariot racing track; 43 are juridical to do with law cases; 30 are to do with love; and there are three others (*Living and Cursing*, 61).

190. McKie, *Living and Cursing*, 18. Cf. Cousins, *Sanctuary at Bath*, 134–40.

191. McKie, *Living and Cursing*, 29–58; cf. Cousins, *Sanctuary at Bath*, 134–38.

People engaging in that process wanted something to happen and their world to be changed. There was power in the ritual itself: for themselves something cathartic in all that needed to be done; for the culprit the potential of a psychosomatic effect related to the community's awareness of what was being done. There was power in gaining the knowledge to undertake the ritual. There was the supernatural power of the god appealed to in the temple context. In a situation of conflict or crisis the ritual restored their sense of agency; it enabled them to redefine their relationships with others and to regain control following the crisis they had experienced. It enabled them to preserve their own reputation and damage that of those they perceived as responsible.[192] In this ritual, for the most part, single names were used without identifying social status: there was "a subversion of normal power structures here, as curses worked to flatten the hierarchies of Roman society, bringing everyone down to the same level."[193]

It is noticeable that McKie tends to put to one side the terminology of "prayer" and instead speaks of "curses" and the act of depositing a curse tablet as a "cursing ritual." While acknowledging that the validity of categorizing some as "prayers for justice" remains an open question, Sánchez Natalías prefers the Latin phrase coined by Audollent, *defixiones in fures*, or *defixiones* against thieves.[194] The exclusive use of "curse" and the insistence on retaining the Latin *defixiones* obscures the association of many of the tablets, especially those at Uley and in Britannia, with the notion of prayer as a means of addressing a deity. As we have seen, Tomlin continues to speak of them as "prayers for justice."[195] In imagining Luke–Acts we will explore what happens when we think of them first as "curses" and then as "prayers for justice."

In the light of this discussion, we should avoid being too quick to categorize curse tablets, far less to fit them into some pre-conceived notion of Roman religion or a specific Roman "cult." Instead we should draw on a historical and archaeological imagination and allow the tablets to speak for themselves, giving voice to the people who wrote them. In so doing we will be drawing on the insights of Nancy Ammerman who speaks of "everyday

192. McKie, *Living and Cursing*, 83–103, 111–20.

193. McKie, *Living and Cursing*, 128.

194. Sánchez Natalías, *Sylloge Defixiones*, 60–61.

195. Tomlin, *The Uley Tablets*, 13–21.

religion"[196] and of Jeff Astley who speaks of "ordinary theology."[197] Roger Tomlin speaks of the Uley tablets as "petitions from the victims of theft and anti-social behavior in an under-policed world addressed to a superhuman patron"[198] and of the British tablets in general as "petitions to the gods inscribed on sheets of lead deposited in temples or running water."[199] Adopting "the Lived Ancient Religion approach," they offer "a privileged insight into individual appropriations of religious resources and lived religion in antiquity."[200] Fundamentally, suggests Sánchez Natalías, they are "a private and direct means of communicating with the divine."[201]

Imagining Honoratus, Saturnina and Many More

Whereas, in the limestone Cotswolds, the later "Saxons preferred to site their settlements on dry land above the springs, . . . the Romans constructed their villas below so that the water would run through their baths and wash-houses."[202] We can, therefore, imagine Honoratus farming the rich arable land watered by the springs that emerge from the slopes of the escarpment near Uley.[203] The theft of two wheels, four cows and belongings from his house or stable[204] has been a significant loss. He depended on the use of the two wheeled cart or more likely the two wheeled plough and the team of four that hauled them. He had no idea who had stolen them. Family, friends and neighbors in the local community were fully aware of what had happened and knew exactly what course of action Honoratus should take. He made his way up the steep slope to the temple overlooking the River

196. Ammerman, "Observing Religious Modern Lives"; Ammerman, "Finding Religion," 189.

197. Astley, *Ordinary Theology*.

198. Tomlin, "Fourth-Century Uley 'Curse Tablet,'" 73.

199. Tomlin, "Literacy in Roman Britain," 214.

200. Albrecht et al., "Religion in the Making," 576.

201. Sánchez Natalías, *Sylloge Defixiones*, 60.

202. Dreghorn, *Geology Explained*, 123. Map (Figure 1) 3 and Inset. Chedworth Roman Villa is a good example of this feature with a spring still flowing into a pool in the shrine and then into the bath house, the kitchen and finally the latrines (Map (Figure 1), 5).

203. *Tab. Uley* 72; Tomlin, *The Uley Tablets*, 286–90; Sánchez Natalías, *Sylloge Defixiones*, 354–55 (*SD* 365). Appendix Chapter 4. Cf. with reference to Aquae Sulis: Cousins, *Sanctuary at Bath*, 50–59 (Map (Figure 1) 55).

204. Cf. *Tab. Vindol. III* 362: J. N. Adams, *Anthology of Informal Latin*, chap. 37.

Severn. It had been a sacred place from time immemorial and was now known as "the temple of Mercury on the Hill of *Aruerius*."[205] The ramparts of the old settlement were visible to the south and an age–old burial mound had been re-used a little to the north.[206] The temple complex included living accommodation, guest accommodation and shops selling miniature copies of the statue of Mercury and other votive objects; it was a place where sheep, goats and fowl were sacrificed.[207] Perhaps he had purchased something before, made an offering, provided animals for a sacrifice, or shared in an ensuing meal. On this occasion he had a fixed purpose in mind. He knew it was a place to come to when something had gone wrong, and help was needed; it was a place to resolve conflicts and punish transgressions which would be hard to bring to court.[208] Knowing what it was that people did in similar circumstances he approached one of the stalls and purchased a blank sheet of lead. One side was patterned, the other ready to be inscribed with the stylus he chose to use. He needed help to get the wording right and perhaps with the writing itself.

205. *Tab. Uley* 75; Tomlin, *The Uley Tablets*, 294–98; Sánchez Natalías, *Sylloge Defixiones*, 363 (*SD* 386); Tomlin, "Uley Inscribed Lead Tablets," 130. Appendix Chapter 4.

206. Figure 16. Cf. Cousins, *Sanctuary at Bath*, chap. 3.

207. Cousins, *Sanctuary at Bath*, 122.

208. Gager, *Curse Tablets From Ancient World*, 102, citing Henig, *Religion in Roman Britain*, 38.

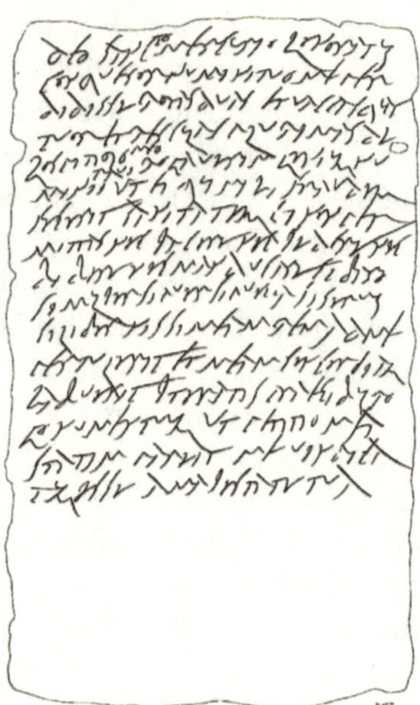

Figure 19. *Tab. Uley* 72. Honoratus complains of the theft of two wheels, four cows and other property. 76 by 131 mm; folded six times. Appendix Chapter 4. Photograph: © The Trustees of the British Museum. Drawing: R. S. O. Tomlin, "Roman Britain in 1991," 310–11, © Cambridge University Press.[209]

The choice of lead was deliberate. It was what was used for the purposes Honoratus had in mind and was readily available not too far away.[210] It was heavy and cold, soft and malleable, easy to write on and it produced a silvery text that was easy to read. "The stylus point cut through the grey surface patina of lead oxide and left a bright trace of pure metal; it would have been like writing on a waxed tablet, using a stylus to scratch through the black wax to the pale wood underneath."[211]

209. *Tab. Uley* 72; Tomlin, *The Uley Tablets*, 287; cf. Sánchez Natalías, *Sylloge Defixiones*, 354–55 (*SD* 365); Tomlin, "Roman Britain in 1991," 310–11; J. N. Adams, *Anthology of Informal Latin*, 314–15. Appendix Chapter 4.

210. According to B. Jones and Mattingly, Charterhouse-on-Mendip and Draethen (Lower Machen, Gwent), lead mines were nearby (*Atlas of Roman Britain*, 179–81, 184–90). Cf. Allen and Bryan, *Roman Britain*, 49–50; Wilson, *A Guide to Roman Britain*, 154–58.

211. Tomlin, "Voices from Sacred Spring," 13. Hunt demonstrated in a workshop the ease with which the tablet could be written and read: ("*Defixiones* Workshop"). McKie

Once he had completed writing the tablet, he was ready to enter the *cella* of the temple itself. Inside it was dark, lit by a few windows high up and perhaps candles near the life-size statue of Mercury, the focal point of the sanctuary.[212] Looking towards Mercury he spoke the words he had so carefully written before entering the shrine.

Honoratus addresses "the holy god Mercury" *deo sanc\to/ Mercurio* and "complains" to his "Divinity" (*conqueror numini tuo*) about the loss of "two wheels and four cows," perhaps a two-wheeled plough and "plough-team,"[213] and many small belongings" (*me per|didisse rotas duas et uaccas quat|tuor et resculas plurimas*) from his "little house" or "stable"[214] (*de |hospitiolo meo*). He has something to "ask" of "the *genius*" of his "Divinity" and makes his request with an air of politeness, "I would ask" (*rogaverim genium nu|minis \tu{u}i/*). It is, however, retribution that he seeks, that the *genius* of the Divinity of Mercury would not "permit health to the person" who has wronged him or permit "him to lie or sit or drink or eat," (*ut ei qui mihi fraudem |fecerit sanitatem ei non per|mittas nec iacere nec sedere nec |bibere nec manducare*); not knowing the identity of the culprit or suspecting anyone in particular he uses a series of catch-all phrases, "whether (he is) man or woman, whether boy or girl, whether slave or free" (*si baro*[215] *|si mulier*[216] *si puer si puella si seruus |si liber*). Such punishment will only be avoided if the property is returned and he gains his "concord," a reconciliation between Honoratus and the culprit, (*nis{s}i meam rem ad me*

experimented by writing on lead and then folding and manipulating the tablets to gain insights into "the experience of conducting a cursing ritual in the Roman world" (*Living and Cursing*, 30). On styluses and lead tablets: Willi, *Writing Equipment*, 33–38, 62–64.

212. For reconstructions of the interior of the temple and of the cult statue by Joanna Richards, see Woodward and Leach, *Uley Shrines Excavation*, 313 and 93.

213. Tomlin, *The Uley Tablets*, 288.

214. Tomlin, *The Uley Tablets*, 288; cf. *Tab. Vindol. III* 362: J. N. Adams, *Anthology of Informal Latin*, chap. 37.

215. Tomlin, *The Uley Tablets*, 34, 288; cf. *Tab. Sulis* 44, Sánchez Natalías, *Sylloge Defixiones*, 294 (*SD* 249). J. N. Adams differentiates between the Germanic term *baro* used positively of a man, and the classical term of abuse, *baro* = fool. He argues that *baro* "presumably meant 'warrior, fighting man,' and then in weakened senses, either 'valorous man' or 'man' (in general) . . . *Baro* (opposed to *mulier*) will have been brought to Britain either by soldiers or by other travelers." It develops into the old French word *baron* ("British Latin," 15–17).

216. Tomlin, *The Uley Tablets*, 34, 288; *mulier* is used opposite *baro* in *Tab. Sulis* 44 (*SD* 250); *Tab. Sulis* 57 (*SD* 262); *Tab. Sulis* 65 (*SD* 270); *Tab. Uley* 5 (*SD* 359), *Tab. Uley* 41; *Tab. Uley* 52; *Tab. Uley* 72 (*SD* 365); *Tab. Uley* 75 (*SD* 386) (Uley 75): J. N. Adams, "British Latin," 15.

|*pertulerit et meam concordiam* |*habuerit*). He spoke of his requests as "renewed prayers" (*iteratis pr{a)ecibus*) and as a "petition" (*petitio*). One senses the significance of the loss in the urgency of his final appeal to "your Divinity" (*numen tuum*) as he seeks an immediate response (*ut petitio mea* |*statim pareat*). He hopes it will be obvious to all that he has been vindicated or avenged "by your majesty" (*me vindica|tum esse a maiestate tua*).[217]

He rolled the tablet, leaving six folds, stepped forward and deposited it in the pool in front of the statue.[218] He left feeling he had accomplished something in the face of his loss and regained the initiative. No longer was he simply the victim. He had high hopes that something would happen soon. It was as if, once again he was in control of his possessions.

Such an imagined reconstruction poses many questions to which there are ultimately no answers. Did others know of the content of the tablet, reading it or hearing it being read out? What happened next? Was it simply that Honoratus went away feeling that he had at least done something about the damaging theft that had left him a victim, feeling a cathartic release of intolerable tension?[219] Did he indeed rediscover a sense of agency and feel he was no longer the "powerless victim"?[220] Did he expect his prayers to be heard?[221] Had he been trying to find out the identity of the thief? Was it public knowledge that he was going to the temple and would be making his request for restitution and failing that for retribution? Might that prompt such fear in the culprit as to take action to restore the stolen goods?[222] In the event of their falling ill might they associate it with the visit Honoratus made to the temple and the prayer he made to Mercury and so be shamed into taking action?[223] Did the power lie in the words[224] or in

217. *Tab. Uley* 72; Tomlin, *The Uley Tablets*, 286–90; Sánchez Natalías, *Sylloge Defixiones*, 354–55 (*SD* 365); Tomlin, "Roman Britain in 1991," 310–11; J. N. Adams, *Anthology of Informal Latin*, chap. 37; Cooley, *Manual of Latin Epigraphy*, 179–81. Appendix Chapter 4.

218. Woodward and Leach, *Uley Shrines Excavation*, 311–12; Tomlin, *The Uley Tablets*, 2.

219. Gager, *Curse Tablets From Ancient World*, 101; Gordon, "Gods, Guilt and Suffering," 269–72.

220. Cousins, *Sanctuary at Bath*, 138.

221. Veale, "*Defixiones* and Temple," 309.

222. Gordon, "Gods, Guilt and Suffering," 269–72.

223. Kiernan, "Did Curse Tablets Work?," 132f; Tomlin, *Tabellae Sulis*, 93f; 101f; Tomlin, "Voices from Sacred Spring," 22; Cunliffe, *Roman Bath*, 65.

224. Versnel, "Poetics of Magical Charm," 147.

the ritual itself?[225] Were those words performative, bringing about change themselves, or transformative, precipitating the desired change?[226] Are we under-estimating the belief that prompted Honoratus to go to the temple of Mercury and deposit his petition?[227]

In many ways we know next to nothing about Honoratus. There can be no answers to those questions. In other ways, however, we know an immense amount. We can in our imagining stand with him as he speaks of what has happened to him and seeks guidance in formulating this message to Mercury; we know enough from the wording of his plea to be sure that he was engaged in some way in a farming community not far from the temple itself; we sense his desire for the return of his property and the restitution of *concordia* with the one who has taken it; that the *concordia* that usually characterizes his community has been broken by the actions of a person or persons unknown; we sense his thirst for retribution should there be no restitution, no restored *concordia.* We can share in our imagination with Honoratus in that moment.

Women can also bring such complaints to the god: we can imagine Saturnina doing much the same thing. She too has been the victim of theft, losing a linen cloth. In choosing to come to the temple herself she takes back the initiative and asserts herself explicitly as "a woman," (*mulier*).[228] Acquiring a sheet of lead and a stylus she possibly sought help in getting the wording right. To describe what she is handing over in the temple she uses a technical, quasi-legal term, used of petitions to one's superior, to administrative officials or army officers.[229] She writes a "memorandum to the god," (*commonitorium deo*) as she names herself Saturnina and identifies herself as a woman, (*a Satur|nina muliere*). Initially she addresses the god as Mars Silvanus, ([[*Marti Siluano*]]) before correcting herself and addressing Mercury, (*Mercurio*), asking that the person responsible should themselves "not have rest before/unless/until" returning the linen cloth to the temple.

225. McKie, *Living and Cursing*, 111–12.

226. Kropp, "Magical Language," 357; Eidinow, "Binding Spells," 369.

227. Tomlin, "Cursing a Thief," 252–53.

228. *Tab. Uley* 2; Tomlin, *The Uley Tablets*, 88–91; Sánchez Natalías, *Sylloge Defixiones*, 346–47 (*SD* 356). Appendix Chapter 4.

229. Tomlin, "Uley Inscribed Lead Tablets," 121.

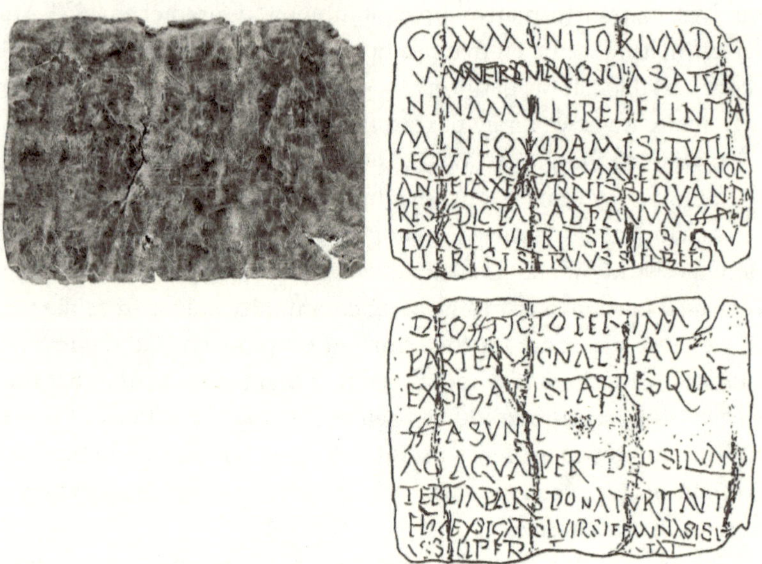

Figure 20. *Tab. Uley* 2. Memorandum from Saturnina. 85 x 62. Appendix Chapter 4. Photograph © The Trustees of the British Museum. Drawing: M. W. C. Hassall, *Britannia* 1979, 344 © Cambridge University Press.[230]

Saturnina uses legal language as she asks that whoever it was who has stolen the linen cloth, be they man or woman, slave or free (*si uir si mu|lier si seruus si liber*) should bring "the aforesaid property to the aforesaid temple" (*non |ante laxetur nis{s}i quando |res s(upra)s(criptas)dictas ad fanum s(upra)s(criptum)d[i]c|tum attul[e]rit*). Writing on the other side of the tablet she anticipates its return and "gives" (*donat*) a third part of its value to "the aforesaid god" (*deo s(upra)s(cripto)dicto*), as if she were wanting the god's success.[231] She repeats that statement addressing the god as *deo Siluano*. Her apparent confusion over names may have to do with the way in which the cult statue of Mercury is not only addressed as Mercury, but also as Mars Mercury, Mars, and, as both Mars and Mercury, linked with the local Celtic god *Aruerius* or *Arueriacus*. Another Celtic god, *Cocidius*, is "identified" sometimes with Mars and on one occasion with *Silvanus* in altars in the vicinity of Hadrian's Wall. From time immemorial this location

230. *Tab. Uley* 2; Tomlin, *The Uley Tablets*, 88–91; Sánchez Natalías, "Curse Tablets against Thieves," (*SD* 356). Appendix Chapter 4.

231. Sánchez Natalías, "Curse Tablets against Thieves," 102.

had been associated with a *nymed* (Celtic) or *nemeton* (Latin) or sacred wood; other petitioners described themselves as *siluestres*. Perhaps the location and its ancient associations meant something to Saturnina.[232] She then enters the shrine, approaches the pit in front of the statue, rolls the tablet leaving two folds and with a spoken prayer deposits her memorandum. No longer simply the victim she can leave the temple feeling she has done something about the loss she has suffered.

Saturnina was not alone in sensing how special the location of the temple was and its connection with age-old Celtic traditions. At an elevation of 250 meters the Temple of Mercury stands on what is now known as West Hill, Uley. It is a feature of the Cotswold escarpment which appears as a line of prominent hills when viewed from the west and the rich arable farmland that drops down to sea level at the River Severn. To the east the hill drops down to a steeply sided valley floor at 130 meters. The hilltop itself is stony ground and suitable mainly for grazing. It is a reasonable supposition, therefore, that the person who had lost "gold money" (*aurea{ca} pecunia*)" "and the ?interest from his crop" (*us(?uararia)* |*frumenta*) from his strongbox (*d(e) arca*) was living and farming below the escarpment (*Tab. Uley* 75; Appendix to Chapter 4). Commenting on the mistakes in his writing and his "uncertain" command of Latin, Tomlin supposes that he was engaged in trading with neighboring farmers: "perhaps he had lent, or was going to lend, money to a farmer who would then buy seed corn and sow it, this money to be repaid with interest when the corn was harvested." Faced with this significant loss of income, measured in gold coins, we can imagine him looking up towards the temple on the escarpment and deciding to make the walk up the side of the steep hill. Reaching the top of the climb, looking back, he would look down towards his rich farmland, and beyond to the Severn and the distant mountains of what is now Wales; in Roman times it was the land of the Silures. He knew the associations with this place went back a long way: it was so special that it had a name. Like so many others before him, he turned and approached the temple, purchasing

232. Tomlin, *The Uley Tablets*, 61–64, 89; Tomlin, "Uley Inscribed Lead Tablets," 121. Cocidius is associated with Mars: *RIB* 602, 993, 2015, 2024; and with Silvanus: *RIB* 1578. *Tab. Uley* 3, 8 19 are addressed to Mars Mercury; *Tab. Uley* 24 equates Mars with Mercury; Appendix Chapter 4. *Tab. Uley* 84 addresses Mars alone, but gives him a title shared with Mercury, *Aruerius*; Mercury is given the title *Arueriacus* in *Tab. Uley* 40, 52, 78 and *Aruerius* in *Tab. Uley* 21, 28, 30, 75, 78, 81; Mars is given the title *Aruerius* in *Tab. Uley* 84 and probably 63. In *Tab. Uley* 40 petitioners to Mercury *Arueriacus* describe themselves as *siluestres*, which Tomlin translates as "woodlanders" (*The Uley Tablets*, 195).

a small piece of lead and seeking the guidance of one of the priests. With the thieves in mind, he wrote with what Tomlin describes as an "uncertain" command of Latin, "I seek that, whether man or woman, whether boy or girl, they be not allowed to sleep or be wakeful, to sit or to lie, until he bring all those things to the temple of Mercury on the Hill of *Aruerius*" (*ad tem[p]lum |Mer(curii) mont<e> Arueri*). It seems as if he finished by "offering a reward to anyone who named the thieves." Rolling it up, leaving four folds, he deposited it in the pool in front of the statue and made his way out of the temple, past the stalls, the guest house and the other buildings. Perhaps the sun was setting now as he made his way back home down the hill which had age-old associations with the Celtic god *Aruerius*.[233] It is only now with the discovery of *Tab. Uley* 75 in excavations from 1976–1979 and its publication by Roger Tomlin in 2024 that West Hill can once again be known by its ancient name.

Saturnina is not the only woman to reclaim a sense of agency: another woman with a Celtic name, Cunouinna accompanies her husband Corosulis to the temple on the Hill of *Aruerius* and together they "give" the god "the property which they have lost, that is" various items of clothing including her underwear and cloak (*laena*), his cloak (*palleum*), sewing-thread, another garment, laces, leather and a pair of leg-bands "worn for protection in agricultural work." Speaking of the god as *Aruerius* they give (*don|[an] t*) "the property which they have lost" in the hope presumably that it will be returned to the temple and the thief or thieves will be appropriately punished; of those they suspect only the name of Bellenianus survives.[234] The "gift" of the property stolen or of the thief, in return for some form of "redemption," is characteristic of a number of the tablets and is unique to Britannia. On occasion the petitioner "gives" the god the responsibility to do something about the theft they have suffered.[235] On another occasion, a woman, Peregrina, with her husband and son, Varianus and Sabinianus,

233. *Tab. Uley* 75; Tomlin, *The Uley Tablets*, 294–98; see the image "The British Museum," 1978,0102.151 https://www.britishmuseum.org/collection/object/H_1978-0102-151. Zooming in, the phrase is clear: AD TEM[.]LVM are the last two words of line 7; MER MONT ΛRVERI are the first three words of line 8. Appendix Chapter 4.

234. *Tab. Uley* 20; Tomlin, *The Uley Tablets*, 138–42.

235. Tomlin, *The Uley Tablets*, 17–21. "Giving" to the god stolen property: *Tab. Uley* 4, 75, 78; giving a proportion of the property: 84 (one half), 2, 5 (one third). "Giving" the thief: 5, 9, 49 (probably), 52, 55, 78; "giving" the god the responsibility to intervene: 52, 78, 80.

is accused of malicious behavior,[236] while another woman and possibly her husband were suspected as enemies or thieves: Lucilla (daughter) of Mellossus and Minuassus (son) of Senebellena.[237]

We could in our "inner eye" stand with other people from that rural, agricultural community as they approach the god to complain about some theft or other harm and to ask for his help. Cenacus complains (*queritur*) about Vitalinus and his son, Natalinus, concerning "the beast of burden" (*iumento*) which has been stolen from him; he asks for himself the immediate return of the animal or its value and for Mercury the devotion he has demanded for himself (*deo |deuotionem qua[m] |ipse ab his ex|postulauerit*): it is not only theft they are guilty of but sacrilege as well.[238] Failing the return of the beast, he asks that they should be deprived of their health.[239]

In the first recorded instance of bee-keeping in Britain, the name of the bee-keeper whose hive had been stolen by someone, whether slave or free, is lost; as he approaches the temple, he prepares to deposit his tablet in much the same way as everyone else.[240] This is, after all, what you do here. Addressing first Mars and then Mercury, he seems to be confused about the identity of the god, suggesting it is the act of what he is doing that is all important, not the identity of the one he is addressing. He addresses his message formally in capitals on one side of the tablet "to the god Mars the Propitious," using *devo* which "could be borrowed from Celtic *deivos* meaning god"[241] (*DEVO MAR|TI .S PROPITIO*). On the other side

236. *Tab. Uley* 43; Tomlin, *The Uley Tablets*, 204–7; Appendix Chapter 4. A similar penalty is demanded of those who have thought evil towards the petitioner in *Tab. Uley* 76; Tomlin, *The Uley Tablets*, 300–303. Appendix Chapter 4.

237. *Tab. Uley* 33; Tomlin, *The Uley Tablets*, 174–75; Tomlin notes that "there is some evidence for the use of female lineage in British tablets, phylacteries, or curse tablets, notably the inscribed Bath plate (*Tab. Sulis* 30)." (*The Uley Tablets*, 175). According to Tomlin, at Uley the mothers of four sons are mentioned, and a fifth whose son's name is lost; three wives are named and the incomplete names of two other women are recorded. while at Uley, Saturnina is the only woman to be a petitioner, at Bath there are five or six women petitioners. (*The Uley Tablets*, 43).

238. Sánchez Natalías, "Curse Tablets against Thieves," 97.

239. *Tab. Uley* 1; Tomlin, *The Uley Tablets*, 84–87; Tomlin, "Uley Inscribed Lead Tablets," 118–20; Sánchez Natalías, *Sylloge Defixiones*, 344–46 (*SD* 355). Appendix Chapter 4. Versnel makes a link here with the Cnidian tablets in the use of the legal term "*queri*" — "to make a complaint before a court" ("Beyond Cursing," 88).

240. *Tab. Uley* 24; Tomlin, *The Uley Tablets*, 154–59; Tomlin, "Roman Britain in 2016," 462–64; Sánchez Natalías, *Sylloge Defixiones*, 361–62 (*SD* 373). Appendix Chapter 4.

241. Tomlin, *The Uley Tablets*,156; Sánchez Natalías, *Sylloge Defixiones*, 361; Tomlin,

he "complains" (*qu{a}erituR*) to the god Mars about whoever it was, slave or free, who has stolen his beehive (*uas apium*), in the hope that they will not be permitted to drink or eat, nor to have sleep or health unless "the said hive be returned to its proper place" (*nesi(!) ipsum |uas ad locum suum reuersetur*). There is an expectation that the thief will make some gift that will "gain the concord of Mercury" and repay the owner of the hive in some way.

One petitioner uses Greek letters to write his message in Latin.[242] Another opens his request, speaking of "the page" which is given to Mercury (*carta quae Mercurio dona|tur*).[243] Divisions extend beyond the individual to the family as Carinianus (*or* Carinus) names Primanus as thief and seeks vengeance with his blood (*san<g>uine suo conpliat |uendica[tionem]*) not only on him but on his ?wife and children too (*nec coniu. nec infantis*).[244] Redress is sought for the theft of a gold ring and an iron fetter.[245] In addressing Mercury, the Celtic-named Biccus thinks of himself as "giving" whatever he has lost to the god in the hope that it will be returned to the temple or Mercury; failing that he looks to the thief (whether man or male (*sic*)) not being able to "urinate, defecate, speak, sleep, stay awake, or (have) well-being or health."[246] Fraught with signs of a spoken Latin that departs from conventional grammar and orthography he does not want the thief to receive a pardon unless he himself intercedes or intervenes on his behalf (*ne co<n>|scientiam de |perferat ness[i] |me interceden|te*).[247] Someone else

"Roman Britain in 2016," 462. Cf. *SD* 205 (Lydney); *Tab. Uley* 9; Tomlin, *The Uley Tablets*, 119; Tomlin, "Roman Britain in 2019," 481–83. Appendix Chapter 4.

242. *Tab. Uley* 52; Tomlin, *The Uley Tablets*, 230–34; Sánchez Natalías, *Sylloge Defixiones*, 365 (*SD* 436).

243. *Tab. Uley* 80; Tomlin, *The Uley Tablets*, 316–20; Tomlin, *Roman Britain in 1995*, 439–41; Sánchez Natalías, *Sylloge Defixiones*, 356–57 (*SD* 367).

244. *Tab. Uley* 68; Tomlin, *The Uley Tablets*, 272–75; Tomlin, ""Tomlin, "Vindolanda's Other Inscriptions," 398–99; Sánchez Natalías, *Sylloge Defixiones*, 358–59 (*SD* 371). Appendix Chapter 4.

245. *Tab. Uley* 3; Tomlin, *The Uley Tablets*, 92–94; Tomlin, "Uley Inscribed Lead Tablets," 122–23; Sánchez Natalías, *Sylloge Defixiones*, 347 (*SD* 357).

246. *Tab. Uley* 4; Tomlin, *The Uley Tablets*, 96–100; Tomlin, "Uley Inscribed Lead Tablets," 124–26; Sánchez Natalías, *Sylloge Defixiones* (*SD* 358). Appendix Chapter 4.

247. Tomlin reflects on the difficulty of translating *intercedente*: "The verb *intercedo* has the Classical sense of "intervene," and is used in particular of a tribune of the plebs "interposing" his veto against the action of a magistrate. But the modern sense of "intercession" (with a god, to plead for clemency) is difficult to find outside Christian writers. This would suggest the usage is "late"; certainly it is the verb's first occurrence in a curse

makes the journey to the temple to seek redress for "one plaque and four rings."[248] An unnamed petitioner addresses the god as Mars *Aruerius* and registers a "complaint" at the theft of "two pewter plates." The one who is privy (to the theft) is to be permitted "neither sleep nor health, neither hope nor breath,[249] neither to stand nor sit, neither to drink nor to eat." Half their property is to be given to "you, Lord," that the property "should be paid in full through the blood of these (my) enemies."[250] On another occasion it is the name of the thief who has stolen the petitioner's bridle (whether slave or free, man or woman) that is "given" to the god; once again a proportion, one third, of the value of the items stolen is to be handed to the god, although as it stands the tablet makes little sense, the writer having conflated standard formulae.[251] Mention of his wife suggests the wider impact of this kind of theft on the families of those concerned.[252] Someone else has suffered the loss of his sheep and so has given (*donaui*) "the god Mercury" (*diu[o] Mercurio*) (the man) who of evil intent (*ma[li] consil{l}i*) has ?robbed him.[253] Virilis has also had trouble with stolen sheep: perhaps some had been intended for sacrifice in the temple. As he approached the *cella* and acquired his tablet ready to write, his concern was the return of the animals and failing that vengeance in the hope that whoever it was, slave [or free], man or woman, would not be permitted to eat or drink; indeed, he sought their blood.[254] Another person approached Mercury (Mercurio) suspicious that a weaver (*gerdi[um]*) had stolen wool and a jug (*res id est lanam et lagon[am]*)

tablet" (*The Uley Tablets*, 100); cf. Tomlin, "Uley Inscribed Lead Tablets," 126.

248. *Tab. Uley* 50; Tomlin, *The Uley Tablets*, 224–26; Tomlin, "Roman Britain in 1997," 433–34; Sánchez Natalías, *Sylloge Defixiones*, 352–53 (*SD* 363).

249. Tomlin notes that "while Christian writers link *spes* and *spiritus*, a Classical instance is still be to be found" (*The Uley Tablets*, 335).

250. *Tab. Uley* 84; Tomlin, *The Uley Tablets*, 332–36; Sánchez Natalías, *Sylloge Defixiones*, 365 (*SD* 431).

251. *Tab. Uley* 5; Tomlin, *The Uley Tablets*, 102–4; Tomlin, "Uley Inscribed Lead Tablets," 122–23; Sánchez Natalías, *Sylloge Defixiones*, 349 (*SD* 359).

252. Tomlin suggests *a FIMA* may be a transcription error perhaps for *a femina sua* (from his wife), "but if the thief is unknown so is his married status" (*The Uley Tablets*, 104); cf. Tomlin, "Writing to the Gods," 127.

253. *Tab. Uley* 9; Tomlin, *The Uley Tablets*, 118–21; Tomlin, "Roman Britain in 2019," 480–82; Sánchez Natalías, *Sylloge Defixiones*, 363 (*SD* 390). Appendix Chapter 4.

254. *Tab. Uley* 41; Tomlin, *The Uley Tablets*, 198–201; Tomlin, "Roman Britain in 2019," 481–83; Sánchez Natalías, *Sylloge Defixiones*, 364 (*SD* 411).

and pleads for vengeance in the hope that "the god is to recover the price of the stolen property."[255]

Recourse is made to Mercury not only when belongings are stolen or damaged but also when division and enmity find expression in less tangible, but no less hurtful ways. On two occasions, Tomlin suggests that petitioners attribute their personal misfortune "to someone else's witchcraft." Having experienced malicious behavior they seek to return like for like.[256] When Varianus, his wife Peregrina and their son Sabinianus engaged in malicious behavior, Docilinus complained to the god Mercury, accusing them of bringing "evil harm" on his "farm animal" (*peco|ri meo dolum malum in|tulerunt*) and of "pronouncing it in earth" (*et in t[e]rr[a] pro|locuntur*), thus causing its death and burial by means of incantation. Docilinus is forthright: "I ask that you drive them to the greatest death (*max[i]mo [le] to*), and do not permit them health or sleep unless they redeem from you what they have administered to me." That is to say, the whole family, Varianus, Perigrina and Sabinianus, are to suffer exactly what they have inflicted on Docilinus, a brutal death.[257]

On another occasion someone who is "the victim of malice by unknown persons" seeks retribution in like manner. He complains "to the holy god Mercury" because people have thought ill of him and have behaved badly towards him (*[deo] sancto Mercuri[o qu]er[or] |tibi de illis qui mihi male |cog[i]tant et male faciunt*): whoever they are, slave or free, male or female, they are not to be allowed to stand or sit, drink or eat or pay off these (causes of) anger" or "feelings of mutual displeasure, bad blood" unless they do so with their own blood (*n[e]c h[as] |iras redemere possit |nessi sanguine suo*).[258]

255. *Tab. Uley* 58; Tomlin, *The Uley Tablets*, 248–51; Sánchez Natalías, *Sylloge Defixiones*, 357–58 (*SD* 369). Appendix Chapter 4. According to Tomlin "the unusual script would suggest that 58 is the earliest tablet to survive from Uley, and it may have been inscribed quite soon after the temple was rebuilt in stone in the early second century" (*The Uley Tablets*, 248). He notes that *gerdius* (weaver) is a Greek loan-word, quite rare in Latin" (*The Uley Tablets*, 250).

256. According to Tomlin, *Tab. Uley* 43 and 76 "illustrate the classic anthropological thesis that personal misfortune is attributed to someone else's witchcraft" (*The Uley Tablets*, 301).

257. *Tab. Uley* 43; Tomlin, *The Uley Tablets*, 204–7. Appendix Chapter 4. While Docilianus in Bath and Docilinus in Uley use similar wording to seek "the greatest death," and there are other similarities of wording, Tomlin now rejects the earlier view that *Tab. Sulis* 10 and *Tab. Uley* 43 were written by the same individual (*The Uley Tablets*, 55–57).

258. *Tab. Uley* 76; Tomlin, *The Uley Tablets*, 300–303; Tomlin, "Roman Britain in 1994,"

In a "surprisingly sophisticated text to come from a rural shrine," another has been cheated of denarii he is owed by the "execrable Manneius": using six synonyms for "give" (*commendo, dono, obdo, of<f>ero, destino, deputo*) he offers the presumably exaggerated sum of 100,000 denarii to the god Mercury *Aruerius/Arueriacus*, in the hope that the thief would bring the stolen denarii "to the temple and treasury of the most mighty god." Vengeance reaches to the victim's family who are to "languish in sleeplessness with unknown ailments, adverse indispositions" (*uigiliam morbis |incognitis [u]a[l]itu|dinibus aduersis lege |[c]ontraria lan[gue]ant*). They are to "repel everybody, half-naked, toothless, trembling, gouty, without the pity of anyone" (*omnes auertant |seminudi edentuli tre|muli podagrici sine |cuiusque hominis mis|{s}erico<r>dia*). They are to "be finished out of the most disgusting state, and not find you merciful, Lord" (*ex situ turpissi|mo finiantur nec te |[d]omine prius propi|[ti]um habeant quam |[...].ium ha[be]|[ant]*).[259]

In the temple of Mercury on the Hill of *Aruerius* we encounter people from a rural community who in a time of personal crisis go to the temple, seeking restoration of their property, redress for the ills they have suffered, vengeance on those responsible. Whether what they write is described as a prayer for justice or part of a cursing ritual, the vindictive language they use serves as a reminder that it is impossible to draw hard and fast distinctions.[260]

Imagining Luke–Acts Through the Eyes of the People of the Uley Tablets

Imagining Luke–Acts through the eyes of a group of followers of the Way of Jesus from that rural community around the temple dedicated to Mercury at Uley, three important themes come to the fore. The first has to do with temples, what you do in them and what their significance is; the second with cursing and with what some would describe as magical practices; the third with praying and prayer.

373–76; Sánchez Natalías, *Sylloge Defixiones*, 355–56 (*SD* 366). Appendix Chapter 4.

259. *Tab. Uley* 78; Tomlin, *The Uley Tablets*, 306–12; Tomlin, "Writing to the Gods," 169; Sánchez Natalías, *Sylloge Defixiones*, 358 (*SD* 370). Appendix Chapter 4. Cf. Tab. Lond. Bloomberg 30 where Titus is accused of shameful behavior, *turpis*. See above, Chapter 2, n. 166. Appendix Chapter 2.

260. Sánchez Natalías, "Curse Tablets against Thieves," 92.

In the Temple

However different the temple in Jerusalem from the temple of Mercury on the Hill of *Aruerius*, there were some practices that would have resonated with the likes of Honoratus, Saturnina and our imagined readers. Prior to entering the *cella* they sought help in formulating the messages they had for the god Mercury; once inside they may have had help from a priest in depositing the tablet. The scent of incense mingled with the smell of sacrifices. They would have been familiar with the practice of sacrifice so prevalent there, and may have been called on to provide animals for sacrifice.[261] Some were concerned at the theft of sheep.[262] Zechariah brings to the Lord God of the Jerusalem temple the longing he and his wife Elizabeth have for a child (Luke 1:8–23); subsequently sacrifices are offered as the infant Jesus is brought to the temple (Luke 2:22–24) and on the day of Unleavened Bread (Luke 22:7). Concerns around pregnancy and childbirth were brought to the temple of Nodens the other side of the river where a small bone plaque representing a woman with her hands on her waist would have been purchased and pinned within the shrine as an offering to the god before or after childbirth.[263] Not far to the east a small gold tablet with wording in Greek familiar from the Greek magical papyri, expressing the hope and prayer that "Fabia whom Terentia her mother bore, being in full fitness and health, shall master the unborn child and bring it to birth; the name of the Lord and Great God being everlasting."[264] That the Jerusalem temple was a place of healing (Acts 3:1–10) would be familiar to people from this community who sought healing at the temple to Nodens at Lydney[265] and in the curative waters of Aquae Sulis, adjacent to the temple to Sulis Minerva.[266]

On entering the temple Jesus "drives out those who were selling things there" (Luke 19:45); later he sits opposite the treasury and contrasts the rich people who make their gifts and the poor, needy widow (χήραν πενιχρὰν : *viduam pauperculam*) who puts in "two small copper coins" that amounted to "all she had to live on" and so becomes poverty-stricken, destitute and

261. Woodward and Leach, *Uley Shrines Excavation*, 257, 258, 266.

262. *Tab. Uley* 9, 41, 83.

263. Lydney Park Estate, *Lydney Park*, 19. Map (Figure 1) 56.

264. Gold charm: Tomlin, "Graeco-Roman Gold Amulet," 222, 219–24.

265. Aldhouse-Green, *Sacred Britannia*, 94–96; Lydney Park Estate, *Lydney Park*. Map (Figure 1) 56.

266. Cunliffe, *Roman Bath*, 103. Map (Figure 1) 55.

a beggar (πτωχὴ: *pauper* Luke 21:1–4).[267] That a temple should have a treasury and expect payment is implicit in so many of the messages to Mercury as people dedicate to Mercury all or part of what has been stolen. In a tablet that refers to the theft of money by "the execrable Manneius," there is explicit reference to "the treasury" (*th<e>n|saurum*) of the Uley temple as 100,000 denarii are pledged to the god Mercury *Arueriacus* by a petitioner who does not give his name but writes in "a surprisingly sophisticated" way. Tomlin notes that the enormous amount involved is "unlikely to be a "real" sum" even when taking into account the loss of value of the denarius in the third century CE.[268]

Just as Peter healed the lame man at the Jerusalem temple (Acts 3:1–10), so Paul healed the lame man at Lystra (Acts 14:8–10). The reaction of the crowds was to shout with cries of adulation, hailing Paul and his companion Barnabas as "gods come down to us in human form": "Barnabas they called Δία: *Iovis* and Paul, Ἑρμῆν: *Mercurius*" (Acts 14:12),[269] bringing to our imagined readers' "inner eye" the sculpture of Mercury in the temple sanctuary. Julius Caesar's observations about the predilection of Celtic peoples in Gaul to "worship Mercury," together with the identification of the Roman god Mercury and the Celtic god *Aruerius*/*Arueriacus* in so many tablets, suggests that there was some association in the minds of the people of Uley between Mercury and a local Celtic divinity. They might well have understood the response of the people of Lystra and seen Paul as "the guide for every road and journey" as Julius Caesar suggests, and the discovery of altars and statues to Mercury at the entrances to London implies.[270] They

267. Paulraj describes the way "she moves from being πενιχρά [meaning very poor] to πτωχή [meaning utterly destitute with nothing] by giving away all that she has" (*Food Justice*, 92 see 89–92). He argues that the Πτωχοί are the expendables, those who live in abject poverty and are forced to beg (*Food Justice*, 94–104). Cf. Wolter, *Luke I*, 269; Matthews and Reid, *Luke 10–24*, 543–48; Schaberg and Ringe ask, "is she a model to be emulated or a cause for lament?" ("Luke," 494).

268. *Tab. Uley* 78; Tomlin, *The Uley Tablets*, 306–12; Tomlin, "Writing to the Gods," 169; Sánchez Natalías, *Sylloge Defixiones*, 358 (*SD* 370). Appendix Chapter 4.

269. Keener describes the way Zeus and Hermes were key and often paired deities in the region. Hermes is the messenger of the gods (Homer) and god of orators (Lucian) (*Acts*, 352). Pervo suggests "the story is inspired by a Greek myth known through Ovid's . . . tale of Baucis and Philemon (*Metamorphoses* 8.611–724)," citing many other commentators (*Acts*, 353–54).

270. Caesar *Bellum. Gallicum.* vi.17 H. J. Edwards, ed. and trans., 314–15, *hunc viarum atque itinerum ducem*. Perring cites the prevalence of altars and statues to Mercury at the entrances to London as evidence for the association of Mercury with trade and travel in Britannia (*London in Roman World*, 174). See above, Chapter 4, n. 93.

could perhaps imagine the priests coming from the temple to Zeus outside the gate with garlands and oxen to sacrifice. They would know only too well the importance of such sacrifice, using beasts from their nearby farms.

The temple of Mercury played its part in the local economy, not least in the provision of animals and other offerings from the rural neighborhood. There was also considerable trade in the complex of buildings surrounding the shrine of the temple itself. The discovery of fifty blank tablets suggests that they were on sale at the temple location itself; miniature statuettes of the god Mercury and other votive objects were also on sale. Miniatures of the god Nodens and of a fine, bronze, young wolfhound were on sale in the Lydney temple on the far side of the River Severn.[271] In Uley, as in Lydney, Honoratus and others would understand why Demetrius and the silversmiths of Ephesus objected to anything that threatened their livelihoods and may have appreciated the power of organized chants and the efficacy of acclamations in the context of ritual (Acts 19:21–41).[272]

The lived religious experience of the people of Uley is in some ways a world apart from the people whose stories are told in Luke–Acts and yet elements of that experience are shared. Both in Luke–Acts and in Uley, people have a connection with the temple in their locality that contributes to their sense of identity and provides them with a place to which they can turn in time of need.

At the very beginning of Luke, Zechariah is introduced as a priest who thereby can enter "the sanctuary of the Lord" (Luke 1:5–10) in the temple which we later learn is in Jerusalem (Luke 2:22–38, 41–51); he lives in the days of King Herod of *Iudaea* (Luke 1:5), whose jurisdiction is under the authority of the emperor Augustus and the governorship of Syria (Luke 2:1–2); his home, however, is in a town in the Judean hill country (Luke 1:23, 39–40). He shares a house with Elizabeth, his wife, in a tight-knit, supportive community, made up of neighbors and family (Luke 1:40, 58, 65). As a result of his prayers at the time of the incense offering (Luke 1:10) his wife, Elizabeth, gives birth to a son, John (Luke 1:57), who in adulthood heralds the coming of his relative Jesus in the fifteenth year of the emperor Tiberius when *Iudaea* is governed by Pontius Pilate and Galilee and neighboring regions by the brothers Herod and Philip, together with

271. Lydney Park Estate, *Lydney Park*, 19; Copeland, *Roman Gloucestershire*, 150–52; Wilson, *A Guide to Roman Britain*, 202–6. Map (Figure 1) 56.

272. Cf. Pervo, *Acts*, 494.

Lysanias while the Jerusalem temple is in the control of high priests, Annas and Caiaphas (Luke 3:1–2).

What is immediately apparent is that Zechariah's identity is found within a web of inter-connected relationships. Brawley draws on the insights of Harvey[273] and suggests that people have constantly to "negotiate where they belong" within the "nested hierarchy of spatial scales" and that for Zechariah those places include "at least the empire, nation, temple, local community and household, each of which puts constraints on him."[274]

A similar mapping exercise could be carried out with regard to each of the people we encounter in Luke–Acts who has to do with the Jerusalem temple. From Simeon and Anna to the Pharisee and tax collector of Jesus' parable; to its hierarchy of priests, police, moneychangers, benefactors, and authorities who sustain its system of sacrifices and ritual; to the rich and the poor who are expected to finance it; to the sick who seek help there; to Peter and John and Paul and his companions; each has to "negotiate where they belong." The same can be said of those we encounter in the temple of Zeus-outside-the-gate in Lystra, the many temples of Athens and the temple to Diana in Ephesus.

Honoratus's identity is found within a similar web of inter-connected relationships.[275] A householder, he lives in the rural community near the temple dedicated to the holy god Mercury from the *genius* of whose divinity he asks for help. He farms the land and is in possession of a number of cows, farming equipment and personal belongings. He lives in a locality where there are large villas, not far from the network of roads leading to Glevum (Gloucester), Aquae Sulis (Bath), Corinium (Cirencester) and beyond. Across the river the network of roads connects him with the temple to Nodens at Lydney, Venta Silurum (Caerwent), and the legionary fortress of Isca (Caerleon).[276] An unknown thief has stolen two wheels and four cows, perhaps a wheeled plough and its team, together with some of his personal belongings. He could have turned for help to one of those nearby towns. Second in size only to Londinium, Corinium was a *civitas* center where the complex web of Roman power interconnected with the local Dobunni

273. Harvey, Hart, *Spaces of Hope*, 75.

274. Brawley, *Luke*, 41.

275. McKie, *Living and Cursing*, 59–60; Woolf, *The Rulers Ruled*, secs. 25–30; Cousins, *Sanctuary at Bath*, 176–86.

276. Glevum, Aquae Sulis, Corinium, Lydney, Venta Silurum, Isca, Map (Figure 1) 26, 55, 25, 56, 29, 28.

peoples and their elite to such an extent that by the fourth century CE it probably became the capital of *Britannia prima*.[277] The *colonia*, Glevum, was by the third and fourth centuries CE declining and as far away, and the more remote Venta Silurum was the *civitas* capital of the Siluri, over the river and possibly unattractive to Honoratus. Some have supposed that recourse to the Roman legal system was not available to those who sought help using lead tablets;[278] it may have been simply a choice they made, their way of negotiating the complex web of power they were caught up in.[279] We may see here an example of the web of Roman power thinning towards the provinces and their hinterland.

For whatever reason, Honoratus turns instead to the nearby temple, connecting with traders, priests and others from his community. Restitution of his stolen property will lead to a reconciliation in relationships that have been fractured by the theft; failing that, he seeks retribution. The temple with its sacrifices and its associated buildings is closely connected to the agricultural community of which he is a part. Mercury links it to the Roman Empire as does the Latin language in everyday use there: Mercury has an association with Mars, Silvanus and *Aruerius/Arueriacus*, connecting with the Celtic peoples who for many generations had revered that sacred site.[280] His "Roman" name connects Honoratus with the empire, but, Tomlin suggests, by the end of the second Century the mixture of "Celtic" names and "Roman" names found in Bath and Uley "would have been general across south-eastern Britain."[281] Whether or not divisions were evident before the theft, Honoratus now lives in a fractured world in need of reconciliation (*concordia*). He hopes the awareness of family and friends and even those responsible for the theft will lead to a speedy resolution of his problem as things come into the open and people can see that he has been vindicated. Honoratus seeks to "negotiate" where he belongs within the "nested hierarchy of spatial scales": for him those places also include

277. Salway, *History of Roman Britain*, 419–21; D. J. Mattingly, *An Imperial Possession*, 262–63.

278. D. J. Mattingly, *An Imperial Possession*, 315.

279. McKie, *Living and Cursing*, 60; Woolf, *The Rulers Ruled*, 25–30; Cousins, *Sanctuary at Bath*, 176–86.

280. Tomlin, "Uley Inscribed Lead Tablets," 130; Tomlin, *The Uley Tablets*, 61–64.

281. Tomlin, *The Uley Tablets*, 45–46. D. J. Mattingly's view that Celtic names are narrowly in the majority in Bath and Uley (*An Imperial Possession*, 463) needs to be revised in the light of the full publication of the Uley Tablets. Tomlin lists twenty-three 'Celtic' names and twenty-eight 'Roman' names (*The Uley Tablets*, 44).

"the empire, [province], temple, local community and household, each of which puts constraints on him."[282]

We meet Honoratus and others seeking help from the "holy god Mercury" when the temple takes center stage because of some undesired action that has upset the equilibrium of their lives. It is one place that has the potential to restore the broken web of their relationships at best, and at worst to bring some kind of justice in the form of retribution. What they present in the temple gives them "the ability to define and alter their place in the world";[283] it restores that agency that had been taken away by the theft.[284] The temple is that kind of cultural center that can provide the focal point for the creation, preservation and restoration of social order. It can be said to perform for the likes of Honoratus a world-ordering function.

This is the role, Joel Green argues, that the Jerusalem temple is perceived to perform for the *Iudaei* in Luke–Acts. It is "the divinely legitimated hub that mirrors as well as communicates and sustains the boundaries of social relations": as a cultural center it has a "world-ordering" function.[285] Likewise, for the priest of Zeus-outside-the-gate in Lystra, for Demetrius in Ephesus and for so many in Athens, the temples they knew well carried out for each of them a similar function as a "world-ordering," "cultural center." In each context Luke–Acts offers a critique of the place of the temple, so much so that it is possible to maintain with John Elliott that "in the Lukan narrative the temple gradually emerges as an institution whose managers, interests, and ideology stand diametrically opposed to the ministry and mission of Jesus and his community."[286] That becomes evident in our imagined reading of Luke–Acts.

Not only does Luke itself begin and end in the Jerusalem temple, the last part of the opening section and the first part of the closing section of Luke also focuses on the identity of Jesus in relation to the temple. As a twelve-year-old he speaks of the temple as his "Father's house" (Luke 2:49), suggesting his identity relates not only to the temple as a cultural center but to the god of the temple. As he reaches his long-awaited destination in Jerusalem he makes for the temple, expecting to enter "his Father's house"

282. Brawley, *Luke*, 41.

283. McKie, *Living and Cursing*, 104–5.

284. Cousins, *Sanctuary at Bath*, 138.

285. Green, *Gospel of Luke*, 509–10, referencing Geertz, *Local Knowledge*, 122–23.

286. Elliott, "Temple versus Household," 223; but contrast Matthews and Reid, *Luke 10–24*, 522.

as a house of prayer only to find it desecrated as a "den of robbers" by "those who were selling things there" (Luke 19:46). It then becomes a place of controversy and tension (Luke 19:47—20:44), where Jesus witnesses the financial ruin of a poverty-stricken widow who becomes destitute at the hands of the temple authorities (Luke 20:45–21:4). He tells of its forthcoming destruction (Luke 21:5–38, especially 5–6, 20–24), presaged at his death when "the sun's light failed, and the curtain of the temple was torn in two" (Luke 23:45).

As Luke concludes and Acts opens the Jerusalem temple is seen to be a place of praise, prayer and healing (Luke 24:53; Acts 3:1–26; 5:12–16), but also of tension and conflict (Acts 4:1–22; 5:17–42; 6:8–15). That conflict comes to a head as Stephen is dragged out of the city and stoned to death after addressing the council (Acts 7:54—8:1). *Iudaei* reading Luke–Acts as followers of the Way of Jesus would recognize numerous allusions to the Hebrew Scriptures and writing in the style of those scriptures in translation.[287] It may be that Honoratus, Saturnina and their contemporaries had some scant knowledge of the *Iudaei*: Aquae Sulis (Bath) drew travelers from far across the empire;[288] *Iudaea Capta* coins minted by Vespasian were in circulation in the vicinity of the River Severn into the later second century CE and beyond;[289] Aaron, a Judean name, and Iulius, two of the three Christian martyrs from second century CE Britannia are associated with Venta Silurum (Caerwent) and Isca (Caerleon), on the other side of the River Severn;[290] a gold amulet in Greek lettering, using the divine name associated with the *Iudaei* was found in Segontium (Caernarfon)[291] suggesting the possible presence or influence of diaspora *Iudaei*.[292]

It is equally possible that they had no awareness of the *Iudaei*, in which case background information within the text itself enables such readers to appreciate the significance of what is going on. In Stephen's speech (Acts 7:2–53) they would find an account of the origins of the *Iudaei* with Abraham, Isaac, Jacob, Joseph and his brothers, how they came to be in Egypt

287. Pervo, *Acts*, 180.

288. Cunliffe, *Roman Bath*, 128–42; Cousins, *Sanctuary at Bath*, 64–69; Davenport, *Roman Bath*, 148–65. Map (Figure 1) 55.

289. "Llanvaches Hoard," 2008.19H/19; 2008.19H/20. Five reported to PAS.

290. Seaman, "Martyrs of Caerleon"; J. R. Davies, "OT Personal Names." Venta Silurum, Isca, Map (Figure 1) 29, 28.

291. *RIB* 436. Cf. Tomlin, "Graeco-Roman Gold Amulet," 219; Tomlin, "Bilingual Roman Charm." Segontium, Map (Figure 1) 49.

292. J. N. Adams, "British Latin," 12 n. 41.

and were led by Moses and Joshua into the land of *Iudaea*, where David's idea of building a temple, a house for the God of Jacob, was realized by Solomon. We can imagine the people of the rural community around Uley for whom the temple was their "cultural center" reading this speech as an account of the origin of the Jerusalem temple. At its climax, however, the speech is critical of the temple:

> Yet the Most High does not dwell in houses made by human hands; as the prophet says, "Heaven is my throne, and the earth is my footstool. What kind of house will you build for me, says the Lord, or what is the place of my rest? Did not my hand make all these things?"
>
> ἀλλ' οὐχ ὁ ὕψιστος ἐν χειροποιήτοις κατοικεῖ, καθὼς ὁ προφήτης λέγει· ὁ οὐρανός μοι θρόνος, ἡ δὲ γῆ ὑποπόδιον τῶν ποδῶν μου· ποῖον οἶκον οἰκοδομήσετέ μοι, λέγει κύριος, ἢ τίς τόπος τῆς καταπαύσεώς μου; οὐχὶ ἡ χείρ μου ἐποίησεν ταῦτα πάντα;
>
> *sed non Excelsus in manufactis habitat sicut propheta dicit caelum mihi sedis est terra autem scabillum pedum meorum quam domum aedificabitis mihi dicit Dominus aut quis locus requietionis meae est nonne manus mea fecit haec omnia* (Acts 7:48–50)

Stephen then turns to address the Council in particular. The ensuing death of Stephen results in "a severe persecution . . . against the church in Jerusalem" as a result of which "all except the apostles were scattered throughout the countryside of *Iudaea* and Samaria" (Acts 8:1).

From this point on the Jerusalem temple ceases to play a significant role in the narrative in Acts. There is no mention of the temple: when Saul visits Jerusalem following his conversion (Acts 9:26–29); when Peter reports to the church in Jerusalem following the conversion of Cornelius (Acts 11:1–18); when James is executed and Peter imprisoned at the time of the Passover (Acts 12:1–19); when the apostles and elders meet together in Jerusalem to consider the question of the circumcision of Gentile followers of the Way (Acts 15:1–29); or when Paul visits fleetingly, returning from Athens and Corinth (Acts 18:22–23). It is on his last visit to Jerusalem that Paul is seen visiting the temple on seven consecutive days, sharing in its sacrifices and other rituals. It becomes for him a scene of tension and conflict as "*Iudaei* from Asia, who had seen him in the temple stirred up the whole crowd" who "seized Paul and dragged him out of the temple" where the Tribune and soldiers and centurions intervene (Acts 21:17–36).

Recalling his own experience of conversion Paul mentions returning from Damascus to Jerusalem where he "was praying in the temple" (Acts 22:17).

It is telling that the very last glimpse we have of the Jerusalem temple in Luke–Acts is as Paul is seized and dragged out of the temple: "and immediately the doors were shut" (Acts 21:30).[293] We can imagine the people of Uley registering that for all its positive value to the followers of the Way of Jesus who continued to pray and sacrifice in the temple, ultimately its doors were shut to them. Whether or not they knew of the destruction of the temple, they could be in no doubt of the likelihood of it happening. More than that, they were confronted with the stark message that the God at the heart of the narrative of Luke–Acts was the God of heaven and earth who could not be contained in a house made with human hands.

That is precisely the critique made of the three other settings in which reference is made to a temple. When in Lystra Paul healed the man who could not use his feet and had never walked, the crowds shouted in the Lycaonian language, "The gods have come down to us in human form" identifying Barnabas as *Iovis* and Paul as *Mercurius*. The priest of the temple dedicated to *Iovis* outside the city wall "brought oxen and garlands to the gates and . . . wanted to offer sacrifice." Paul would have none of it:

> Friends, why are you doing this? We are mortals just like you, and we bring you good news, that you should turn from these worthless things to the living God, who made the heaven and the earth and the sea and all that is in them.
>
> Καὶ λέγοντες· ἄνδρες, τί ταῦτα ποιεῖτε; καὶ ἡμεῖς ὁμοιοπαθεῖς ἐσμεν ὑμῖν ἄνθρωποι εὐαγγελιζόμενοι ὑμᾶς ἀπὸ τούτων τῶν ματαίων ἐπιστρέφειν ἐπὶ θεὸν ζῶντα, ὃς ἐποίησεν τὸν οὐρανὸν καὶ τὴν γῆν καὶ τὴν θάλασσαν καὶ πάντα τὰ ἐν αὐτοῖς.
>
> *et dicentes viri quid haec facitis et nos mortales sumus similes vobis homines adnuntiantes vobis ab his vanis converti ad Deum vivum qui fecit caelum et terram et mare et omnia quae in eis sunt.* (Acts 14:15)

As Paul arrives in Athens with its many temples he was "deeply distressed to see that the city was full of idols," finding "an altar with the inscription to an unknown god" (Acts 17:16, 22–23). He then makes a comment very similar to the comments made by Stephen of the Jerusalem temple and by Paul of the temple in Lystra:

293. Bruce, *Acts*, 450; Witherington, *Acts*, 655; Pervo, *Acts*, 551.

> The God who made the world and everything in it, he who is Lord of heaven and earth, does not live in shrines made by human hands, nor is he served by human hands, as though he needed anything, since he himself gives to all mortals life and breath and all things.
>
> ὁ θεὸς ὁ ποιήσας τὸν κόσμον καὶ πάντα τὰ ἐν αὐτῷ, οὗτος οὐρανοῦ καὶ γῆς ὑπάρχων κύριος οὐκ ἐν χειροποιήτοις ναοῖς κατοικεῖ 25οὐδὲ ὑπὸ χειρῶν ἀνθρωπίνων θεραπεύεται προσδεόμενός τινος, αὐτὸς διδοὺς πᾶσιν ζωὴν καὶ πνοὴν καὶ τὰ πάντα·
>
> *Deus qui fecit mundum et omnia quae in eo sunt hic caeli et terrae cum sit Dominus non in manufactis templis inhabitat nec manibus humanis colitur indigens aliquo cum ipse det omnibus vitam et inspirationem et omnia.* (Acts 17:24–25)

This is the very accusation levelled at Paul by Demetrius on behalf of the silversmiths of the temple to Diana in Ephesus:

> You also see and hear that not only in Ephesus but in almost the whole of Asia this Paul has persuaded and drawn away a considerable number of people by saying that gods made with hands are not gods.
>
> καὶ θεωρεῖτε καὶ ἀκούετε ὅτι οὐ μόνον Ἐφέσου ἀλλὰ σχεδὸν πάσης τῆς Ἀσίας ὁ Παῦλος οὗτος πείσας μετέστησεν ἱκανὸν ὄχλον λέγων ὅτι οὐκ εἰσὶν θεοὶ οἱ διὰ χειρῶν γινόμενοι.
>
> *et videtis et auditis quia non solum Ephesi sed paene totius Asiae Paulus hic suadens avertit multam turbam dicens quoniam non sunt dii qui manibus fiunt.* (Acts 19:26)

As we imagine reading Luke–Acts through the eyes of those who went up to the imposing temple of Mercury on the Hill of *Aruerius* looking west over the River Severn towards the Welsh mountains, the point made in Luke–Acts with reference to each location associated with temples becomes even more powerful. In "identifying" Mercury with the Celtic god associated with the "*nemeton* or Celtic place of extreme importance," the significance of place is very much to the fore.[294] It is in a temple's location that one can appreciate so much more of the religious experience of those who frequented it.[295]

294. Tomlin, *The Uley Tablets*, 63.

295. Aldhouse-Green, *Gallo-British Deities*, 208–10; Aldhouse-Green, *Sacred Britannia*, 95; Tilley, *Phenomenology of Landscape*, 74.

Luke–Acts challenges people from a community such as this, drawn to follow the Way of Jesus, to call in question the temple they are so much a part of and to think further about the God of heaven and earth at the heart of the Luke–Acts narrative.[296] But that gives rise to the question, is there an alternative? Whether in the parables and Jesus' teaching or on his journey to Jerusalem, the household is an alternative focus for the ministry of Jesus in Luke and comes to the fore among the first followers of the Way of Jesus in Acts. Indeed, Acts opens in the upper room of a house in Jerusalem, takes the reader to the homes where the first followers of Jesus met in Jerusalem and in so many other places, and ends in the house Paul occupies in Rome. On four occasions Luke reports a household conversion (the households of Cornelius, Acts 10:44–48, 11:14–15; Lydia, Acts 16:11–15; the Philippian jailer, Acts 16:25–34; Crispus, Acts 18:1–11) signifying "the shift from temple to home as the focus of Christian life and worship."[297] As Elliott argues, "temple and household represent distinctly different and contrasted types of social institutions with conflicting sets of structures, interests, values, beliefs and behaviors."[298] This, suggests Pervo, is "a basic inversion of apocalyptic proportions": he suggests that for Luke "the locus of God's saving message and actions" is the house(hold), "while the temple constitutes the center of resistance to grace."[299] Honoratus, Saturnina and others would be presented with an alternative focal point for their religious experience, not in the temple but in the home. Their source of strength would be in their meeting together in one another's homes or other locations which facilitated such gatherings.[300] The God of heaven and earth who could not be contained in buildings or worshipped with things made with the hand was with them in a shared household setting as they looked to him as "Father."[301] More significantly, he was able to offer the help they sought, though in quite a different way: in prayers addressed to the

296. Pervo argues that "for Luke, all shrines and sacrifices are marks of bad theology" (*Acts*, 191, 434).

297. Pervo, *Acts*, 283.

298. Elliott, "Temple versus Household," 230.

299. Pervo, *Acts*, 94.

300. E. Adams, *Earliest Christian Meeting Places.*

301. Elliott, "Temple versus Household," 229; cf. Matthews and Reid, *Luke 10–24*, 366–69.

Father (Luke 11:1–12); and in prayers shared as they met together (Acts 4:23–31).[302]

Cursing?

When people of the rural community around Uley approached the temple, they knew they had been wronged and needed help; knowing what needed to be done, they were confident help would be forthcoming from the temple and the god Mercury *Aruerius*. If, with McKie, we think of their actions as a "cursing ritual,"[303] involving "theft curses,"[304] and with Sánchez Natalías categorize them as *Defixiones in fures* (*defixiones* against thieves) that reveal with all *defixiones* or curse tablets emotions such as "anger, wrath and desperation,"[305] then it is clear we can reflect on texts in Luke–Acts that have to do with cursing. That remains the case even when, with Tomlin, we differentiate "prayers for justice" from "pure curses": the fierceness of the punishment envisaged in so many of the tablets comes very close to cursing.[306]

While at Uley there is nothing of the simplicity of the curse or *defixio* proper found in Londinium against Titus Egnatius Tyranus and Publius Cicereius Felix,[307] there are echoes of the directness of another London curse: "I curse (*defico*) Tretia Martia and her life and mind and memory and liver and lungs mixed up together, and her words, thoughts, and memory; so may she be unable to speak."[308] The victim of a theft, as so many of the community around Uley are, Biccus asks that the one responsible "may not urinate nor defecate nor speak nor sleep nor stay awake nor [have] well-being or health,"[309] while Honoratus addresses the holy god Mercury and

302. See section below, *Praying?*

303. McKie, *Living and Cursing*, 26.

304. McKie, *Living and Cursing*, 67.

305. Sánchez Natalías, *Sylloge Defixiones*, 61.

306. Tomlin observes that "often the thief is to be forced by ill health" to surrender the stolen property; but for curses the ill health is an end in itself" (*The Uley Tablets*, 17). He notes that eight tablets have to do with vengeance: *Tab. Uley* 17, 41, 58, 62, 68, 72, 80, 83.

307. *SD* 338 (*RIB* 6), Sánchez Natalías, *Sylloge Defixiones*, 331.

308. *SD* 339 (*RIB* 7), Sánchez Natalías, *Sylloge Defixiones*, 332.

309. *Tab. Uley* 4; Tomlin, *The Uley Tablets*, 96–100; Tomlin, "Uley Inscribed Lead Tablets," 124–26; Sánchez Natalías, *Sylloge Defixiones*, 348–49 (*SD* 358). Appendix Chapter 4.

asks "the genius of your divinity that you do not allow health to the person who has done me wrong, nor allow him to lie or sit or drink or eat."[310] Another unnamed person, whose sheep have been stolen by someone "of evil intent" asks that "the god himself kill (him) with his vile blood."[311] Docilinus attributes the evil harm suffered by his farm animal to the malice of Varianus, Peregrina and Sabinianus and their imprecations and seeks like for like retribution in return as they are to be driven "to the greatest death" and not permitted "health or sleep."[312] In the world of the people of Uley there was an expectation that failure to comply with the god of the temple to whom they appealed for help would result in personal distress and extreme suffering. This is close to the language of cursing.

As we imagine the likes of Honoratus and Saturnina becoming followers of the Way of Jesus and encountering Luke–Acts they would feel very much at home with some of the language used by Jesus in Luke and by his followers in Acts. Their ritual vests them with a power and an agency they had been denied because of what had happened to them; they expect their words to make a difference and result in something happening. When Jesus utters the word "woe" (οὐαὶ: nae) to those who are rich, full, laughing and honored (Luke 6:24–26), to those who do not welcome him (Luke 10:13–16), to those who neglect justice and the love of God, seek honor, load people with burdens too hard to bear, and have denied others knowledge (Luke 11:37–52), to those who cause people to stumble (Luke 17:1), and to the one who was to betray him (Luke 22:22), our imagined readers would expect such declarations to make a difference and to effect change. The hunger, mourning, weeping (Luke 6:25), the destruction (Luke 10:13–15), the death (Luke 11:44,47), the drowning (Luke 17:2), the distress and destruction (Luke 21:23–24), are not simply far off in the future but have to do with what will happen in the world as it is. Followers of the Way are not simply to rejoice at the welcome they receive but when they are rejected, they are to "shake the dust from their feet" (Luke 9:5 and 10:11). For our imagined readers the utterance of a woe is not about matters eschatological as some suggest,[313] neither does it amount to "ethical exhortation": instead,

310. *Tab. Uley* 72; Tomlin, *The Uley Tablets*, 286–90; Tomlin, "Roman Britain in 1991," 310–11; Sánchez Natalías, *Sylloge Defixiones*, 354–55 (*SD* 365). Appendix Chapter 4.

311. *Tab. Uley* 9; Tomlin, *The Uley Tablets*, 118–21; Tomlin, "Roman Britain in 2019," 480–82; Sánchez Natalías, *Sylloge Defixiones*, 363 (*SD* 390). Appendix Chapter 4.

312. *Tab. Uley* 43; Tomlin, *The Uley Tablets*, 204–7. Appendix Chapter 4.

313. Fitzmyer, *Luke I–IX*, 637.

it is performative and effects change.[314] These are the things our imagined readers would expect to happen.

Honoratus, Saturnina and the others who sought help from Mercury and engaged in what has been described as "a cursing ritual" were not only aware of the harm they had experienced individually, but they were also all too conscious of the divisions those actions had caused within their community. Concord was broken and needed to be restored.[315] Where suspects are named, we glimpse real and identifiable divisions that are all too evident in this fractured community.[316] The use of catch-all formulae when the names of the perpetrators are not known indicates divisions that are no less real and as disturbing despite their anonymity.[317] The vehemence of the language reflects the depth of those divisions. While these texts from Luke–Acts do not have to do with theft or damage to property, there is a similar vehemence which reflects divisions between those who follow the Way and those who do not. Divisions, however, would also have been evident to such imagined readers within the community of those who followed the Way.

Followers of the Way of Jesus in Uley would see early in Acts how that community was built on principles of sharing that involved mutual commitment to one another:

> All who believed were together and had all things in common; they would sell their possessions and goods and distribute the proceeds to all, as any had need.
>
> πάντες δὲ οἱ πιστεύοντες ἦσαν ἐπὶ τὸ αὐτὸ καὶ εἶχον ἅπαντα κοινὰ καὶ τὰ κτήματα καὶ τὰς ὑπάρξεις ἐπίπρασκον καὶ διεμέριζον αὐτὰ πᾶσιν καθότι ἄν τις χρείαν εἶχεν·
>
> *omnes etiam qui credebant erant pariter et habebant omnia communia possessiones et substantias vendebant et dividebant illa omnibus prout cuique opus erat* (Acts 2:44–45)

314. Brawley, *Luke*, 82.

315. *Tab. Uley* 8, 24, 57, 72.

316. *Tab. Uley* 1, 20, 43, 68, 78; cf. Tablets that simply list names: Tab. Uley 33, 39, 45, 49, 61, 86.

317. *Tab. Uley* 2, 4, 5, 8, 12, 21, 24, 34, 41, 52, 53, 55, 62, 72, 75, 76: *si seruus/ancella si liber/libertus/liberta* (whether slave or free) *Tab. Uley* 5, 8, 21, 24, 34, 52, 53, 62; *si paganus si miles* (whether soldier or civilian) *Tab. Uley* 52; *si uir/baro/mascel si femina/mulier* (whether man or woman) *Tab. Uley* 2, 4, 8, 21, 41, 53, 55, 62, 75, 76; *si puer si puella* (whether boy or girl) *Tab. Uley* 12, 52, 72, 75.

That was given concrete expression in the example of Joseph of Cyprus, named Barnabas by the Apostles (Acts 4:32–37). It is when Ananias and Sapphira fail to share the proceeds of the sale of a piece of property that dire consequences follow for Ananias and subsequently Sapphira (Acts 5:1–11). In a sequence of four rhetorical questions Peter confronts Ananias with what he has done, and "when Ananias heard these words, he fell down and died." Three hours later, Peter asks Sapphira to confirm the payment; when she repeats Ananias's lie Peter declares,

> Look, the feet of those who have buried your husband are at the door, and they will carry you out.
>
> *ἰδοὺ οἱ πόδες τῶν θαψάντων τὸν ἄνδρα σου ἐπὶ τῇ θύρᾳ καὶ ἐξοίσουσίν σε.*
>
> *ecce pedes eorum qui sepelierunt virum tuum ad ostium et efferent te.* (Acts 5:9)

Keener cites anthropological literature that "documents suffering and death caused by curses" but goes on to suggest that Peter's words are "more like a prophecy or pronouncement of a divine verdict."[318] Likewise Witherington maintains that Peter's words are "not a curse formula, but rather a prophetic word."[319] Reimer maintains that Peter speaks more in sorrow than in anger, outlining the consequences of their joint decision to break the agreement on which the community is based: "his function is not that of a judge, but rather that of a legal representative of the community of saints."[320] That Peter predicts Sapphira's death is evident, "whether he causes it is not expressly stated" according to Barrett.[321] Benedict Kent has argued that it is helpful to read Peter's words to Sapphira, together with his words to Simon Magus (Acts 8:4–25), and to Bar-Jesus (Acts 13:4–12) from the perspective of "a selection of Greek and Coptic 'magical' texts."[322] In a careful analysis of the wording of Peter's questions to Ananias and his confrontation with Sapphira, Kent argues that there is the suggestion within the text that the words Peter uses effect the outcome that results. There is, he suggests, a "relation between the [apostle's] pronouncements

318. Keener, *Acts*, 206.

319. Witherington, *Acts*, 218.

320. Reimer, *Women in Acts*, 16–23.

321. C. K. Barrett, *Acts Volume 1*, 270 cf. 262–64.

322. Kent, "Curses in Acts," 413.

and the subsequent afflictions" suffered first by Ananias and then by Sapphira.[323] Were people from the Uley community to encounter this text they would bring to it the assumption that words uttered could result in adverse effects in the people concerned. What is at stake here, however, is not a theft from Peter, to which he responds with words of power, but an action that has broken the spirit of community that binds together those who follow the Way of Jesus.[324] That too connects with the fractured community life that has prompted the likes of Honoratus to engage in their cursing ritual.

One of those drawn to the Way of Jesus as Philip "went down to the city of Samaria, proclaiming the Messiah to them" was Simon who "had previously practiced magic in the city: προϋπῆρχεν ἐν τῇ πόλει μαγεύων: *qui ante fuerat in civitate magus*" (Acts 8:9). However, when he offered Peter and John money after seeing "that the Spirit was given through the laying of the apostles' hands" Peter responded with words which according to Kent, following Barrett,[325] are akin to the language of cursing in that they start and finish with a ferocity that penetrates to Simon's heart,

> May your silver perish with you . . . your heart is not right before God . . . For I see that you are in the gall of bitterness and the chains of wickedness.
>
> *ὁ ἀργύριόν σου σὺν σοὶ εἴη εἰς ἀπώλειαν . . . ἡ γὰρ καρδία σου οὐκ ἔστιν εὐθεῖα ἔναντι τοῦ θεοῦ . . . εἰς γὰρ χολὴν πικρίας καὶ σύνδεσμον ἀδικίας ὁρῶ σε ὄντα.*
>
> *pecunia tua tecum sit in perditionem . . . cor enim tuum non est rectum coram Deo . . . in felle enim amaritudinis et obligatione iniquitatis video te esse.* (Acts 8:20–23)

The opportunity Peter gives to Simon to repent and make confession (Acts 8:22) is, Kent argues, most characteristic of that category of cursing that is associated with prayers for justice.[326] Peter's words here are not in response to anything that has been done against him: he seeks rather to demonstrate that God's Spirit cannot be "bought" but is a gift of God. These

323. Kent, "Curses in Acts," 434; cf. Tomlin who compares *Tab. Sulis* 94 with its condemnation of perjury: *Tab.Sulis*, https://romaninscriptionsofbritain.org/tabsulis/power-of-the-goddess.

324. Witherington is clear that "it is not said that Peter . . . uttered a curse that killed him" (*Acts*, 215–16).

325. C. K. Barrett, *Acts Volume 1*, 617; cf. Pervo, *Acts*, 214; Talbert, *Reading Acts*, 87.

326. Kent, "Curses in Acts," 427.

words suggest "a marked dislike for those who make money out of their dealings with the supernatural."[327]

In this instance there is no indication of the effect Peter's words had on Simon either for good[328] or ill.[329] The fate of Herod, on the other hand, is reminiscent of the fate sought for the perpetrators of ill by the people of Uley and would suggest to them that he had been subject to a curse and the consequent retribution:

> an angel of the Lord struck him down, and he was eaten by worms and died.
>
> πάταξεν αὐτὸν ἄγγελος κυρίου . . . καὶ γενόμενος σκωληκόβρωτος ἐξέψυξεν.
>
> *percussit eum angelus Domini . . . et consumptus a vermibus exspiravit*) (Acts 12:23)

Accustomed to the kind of petition contained in the curse tablets they might sense that he had done something to deserve such divine retribution.[330]

In seeking to "place the curses of Acts in the context of cursing traditions in the wider ancient Mediterranean world," Kent gives priority to the narrative of the encounter Saul and Barnabas had with "a Judean false prophet, named Bar-Jesus," "the magician Elymas" (Acts 13:4–12). Drawing especially on the work of Faraone, Gager and Versnel, he suggests that for all the differences between the words attributed here to Saul and the variety of binding spells, *defixiones* proper and so-called prayers for justice they are nonetheless useful for comparison.[331] Laura Nasrallah argues they are "an underutilized source for investigation of philosophical, theological ideas about the agency, the will, and the efficacy of human and nonhuman actors, whether gods or the materiality of the lead on which a *defixio* is incised."[332] She has developed Kent's work further and drawn on curse tablets classified by Versnel as prayers for justice from the Sanctuary of Demeter and Kore

327. C. K. Barrett, *Acts Volume 1*, 413.

328. Bruce, *Acts*, 219.

329. Witherington, *Acts*, 287.

330. Bruce, *Acts*, 289; Pervo, *Acts*, 314.

331. Kent, "Curses in Acts," 419.

332. Nasrallah, "*Defixiones* and 1 Corinthians," 355.

to throw light on the world of the first Christ-followers in Corinth and on Paul's use of curse language in 1 Cor 5:1–5.[333]

Saul has a sense of being wronged by Elymas (Acts 13:8) which prompts him to respond in the way he does. He addresses his words directly to Elymas and then declares,

> And now listen—the hand of the Lord is against you, and you will be blind for a while, unable to see the sun.
>
> καὶ νῦν ἰδοὺ χεὶρ κυρίου ἐπὶ σὲ καὶ ἔσῃ τυφλὸς μὴ βλέπων τὸν ἥλιον ἄχρι καιροῦ.
>
> *et nunc ecce manus Domini super te et eris caecus non videns solem usque ad tempus* (Acts13:11a)

According to Barrett "the magus is roundly cursed."[334] This declaration is very similar to the ill health sought from those who had wronged the petitioners at the temple of Mercury, indeed "blindness" is wished on one perpetrator at the nearby temple to Sulis Minerva in Bath.[335] What would be striking for readers from the Uley community would be the immediate consequence:

> Immediately mist and darkness came over him, and he went about groping for someone to lead him by the hand.
>
> παραχρῆμά τε ἔπεσεν ἐπ' αὐτὸν ἀχλὺς καὶ σκότος καὶ περιάγων ἐζήτει χειραγωγούς.
>
> *et confestim cecidit in eum caligo et tenebrae et circumiens quaerebat qui ei manum daret* (Acts 13:11b)

The wrong that has been perpetrated, unlike the wrongs experienced by the people of Uley, was not personal to Saul, but to the message he was sharing with the proconsul, Sergius Paulus, who "when he saw what had happened, . . . believed, for he was astonished at the teaching about the Lord" (Acts 13:12). What matters here is that, as in each of the other narratives that would resonate with the people of Uley, the purpose of the curse for the apostles is not so much to punish as to "demonstrate God's power

333. Nasrallah, "*Defixiones* and 1 Corinthians," 350–62. Cf. 1 Cor. 16:22 and possibly 12:3.

334. C. K. Barrett, *Acts Volume 1*, 617; cf. Pervo, *Acts*, 326–27.

335. *Tab. Sulis* 45; Tomlin, *Tabellae Sulis*, https://romaninscriptionsofbritain.org/inscriptions/TabSulis45; Sánchez Natalías, *Sylloge Defixiones*, 294–95 (*SD* 250).

and the authority of their message."[336] For those living in the vicinity of the temple of Mercury on the Hill of *Aruerius*, one can imagine this narrative confirming the decision they had taken to become followers of the Way of Jesus.

Defixiones proper were often found in an agonistic context where adversaries were pitched against each other.[337] There is a strong sense here of a perceived opposition between Saul and the other apostles and those who practice "magic." This comes to a head in Ephesus when Paul's encounter with "some itinerant Jewish exorcists" prompts "a number of those who practiced magic" (*κανοὶ δὲ τῶν τὰ περίεργα πραξάντων*: *multi autem ex his qui fuerant curiosa*) to collect their books and burn them publicly (Acts 19:19).[338] That the texts of the curse tablets of Uley and indeed of Bath and elsewhere are formulaic and resemble the text of curse tablets across the empire suggests an oral transmission shaped by a tradition that itself was influenced by the use of handbooks.[339] At this point might our imagined readers of Luke–Acts have been challenged to call in question the language of cursing they were accustomed to?

As our imagined readers from the community around Uley encounter Luke–Acts it is not long before they arrive at words of Jesus that go to the heart of what it takes to be a follower of the Way, words that speak into the world they know so well. Hearing Jesus pronounce a blessing on those who are poor, those who are hungry now, those who laugh and declaring a woe on those who are rich, those who are full now and those who are laughing now, they would be immediately aware of a "way" that challenged the world they knew (Luke 6:20–26). With a couple of possible exceptions, they were neither among the elite nor among the poor: they farmed and had possessions.[340] When we encounter them, they had become the vic-

336. Kent, "Curses in Acts," 423.

337. Faraone, "Agonistic Context"; Kent, "Curses in Acts," 423.

338. Keener suggests that "Magical papyri contain many of the same curse formulae found in *defixiones*, lead tablets inscribed with curses intended to harm others" (*Acts*, 476–78). Pervo speaks of the way "Luke strongly deprecated any utilization of magical and other syncretistic practices" and of the way the "*agora*/forum was the place of choice for" book-burning, an action which "for Luke was a trope for the apocalyptic destruction of the demonic powers" (*Acts*, 480).

339. Tomlin, *The Uley Tablets*, 77–78; cf. Tomlin, *Tabellae Sulis*, 62ff, https://romaninscriptionsofbritain.org/tabsulis/authorship; Meyer, "Law and Latinization," 201.

340. The sophistication of *Tab. Uley* 52 and 78 suggests to Tomlin that the petitioners may have been people of some standing from nearby Woodchester villa, Glevum or Corinium (Map (Figure 1) 54, 26, 25) (*The Uley Tablets*, 230–34, 306–12).

tim of wrongs that had the potential to threaten their livelihood as beasts, farm implements, beehives and clothing were stolen. They had come to the temple dedicated to Mercury to redress the injustice they had experienced. They sought punishment on those who had wronged them in the hope that Mercury would be able to redeem their losses for them. They know full well that they have been wronged; in some instances they know the names of those they suspect of having wronged them and they know exactly what should befall them. It is the next words of Jesus that challenge the very basis on which they have written their "curses."

> But I say to you that listen, love your enemies, do good to those who hate you, bless those who curse you, pray for those who abuse you.
>
> Ἀλλ' ὑμῖν λέγω τοῖς ἀκούουσιν· ἀγαπᾶτε τοὺς ἐχθροὺς ὑμῶν, καλῶς ποιεῖτε τοῖς μισοῦσιν ὑμᾶς, εὐλογεῖτε τοὺς καταρωμένους ὑμᾶς, προσεύχεσθε περὶ τῶν ἐπηρεαζόντων ὑμᾶς.
>
> *sed vobis dico qui auditis diligite inimicos vestros benefacite his qui vos oderunt benedicite maledicentibus vobis orate pro calumniantibus vos.* (Luke 6:27–28)

The very reaction they have in seeking redress is what is called in question by Jesus here. It is even more explicit in the words that follow:

> If anyone strikes you on the cheek, offer the other also; and from anyone who takes away your coat do not withhold even your shirt. Give to everyone who begs from you; and if anyone takes away your goods, do not ask for them again.
>
> τῷ τύπτοντί σε ἐπὶ τὴν σιαγόνα πάρεχε καὶ τὴν ἄλλην, καὶ ἀπὸ τοῦ αἴροντός σου τὸ ἱμάτιον καὶ τὸν χιτῶνα μὴ κωλύσῃς. Παντὶ αἰτοῦντί σε δίδου, καὶ ἀπὸ τοῦ αἴροντος τὰ σὰ μὴ ἀπαίτει.
>
> *ei qui te percutit in maxillam praebe et alteram et ab eo qui aufert tibi vestimentum etiam tunicam noli prohibere omni autem petenti te tribue et qui aufert quae tua sunt ne repetas* (Luke 6:29–30)

This very different approach that no longer seeks retribution and vengeance is then encapsulated in the words of Jesus:

> Do to others as you would have them do to you.
>
> Καὶ καθὼς θέλετε ἵνα ποιῶσιν ὑμῖν οἱ ἄνθρωποι ποιεῖτε αὐτοῖς ὁμοίως.
>
> *et prout vultis ut faciant vobis homines et vos facite illis similiter* (Luke 6:31)

This is a major departure from what they are accustomed to. Here below the Hill of *Aruerius* as much as anywhere in the world of the Roman Empire something different is happening for those who seek to follow the Way of Jesus. Wolter's comment on this verse is as applicable in Uley as anywhere. To follow the Way of Jesus and belong to those some call "Christians" involves a fundamental reorientation of their values: "Christians receive their ethically unique position through the fact that in their interpersonal actions they do not orient themselves towards the principle of reciprocity, but one-sidedly do what all humans wish from one another."[341] It involves belonging to a community whose norms are different, giving to others without expecting anything in return, what could be described as a "familial reciprocity."[342] What this does, suggests Robert Brawley, in the Eastern Mediterranean context can also be imagined in the Uley community: there is "an inversion of the hidden hierarchies of dominance formed by enmity, hate and conflict" that applies even to violence and force. It is not, he suggests, a submissive acceptance of wrongdoing, but an alternative way of responding to it that has the potential to take the initiative from the offender and shape an alternative kind of community.[343]

Praying?

If we think of our imagined readers as approaching Mercury with a prayer, then we can imagine another set of passages catching their eye. Characteristic of Luke's account of Jesus and of the first followers of the Way of Jesus is a focus on prayer.[344] For the priest, Zechariah (Luke 1:10), for the

341. Wolter, *Luke I*, 282.

342. Green, *Gospel of Luke*, 271; cf. Crook, *Reconceptualizing Conversion*, 56–59; 34–36.

343. Brawley, *Luke*, 84; Wink, *Engaging the Powers*, 127, 185–93; Matthews and Reid, *Luke 1–9*, 206–13.

344. Wolter, *Luke I*, 176. Cf. Wolter, *Luke II*, 86–101; Matthews and Reid, *Luke 10–24*, 366. Works on prayer in Luke-Acts: Crump, "Jesus the Intercessor"; Kloppenborg, "Lord's Prayer"; O'Brien, "Prayer in Luke-Acts"; Trites, "Prayer Motif in Luke-Acts"; Walton, "A Spirituality of Acts?," 197. Luke commentaries on prayer: Brawley, *Luke*, 81, 120–23; Fitzmyer, *Luke I–IX*, 244–47; Fitzmyer, *Luke X–XXIV*, 896–916; Green, *Gospel of Luke*, 439–50; Kuecker, "*Luke*," 139; Matthews and Reid, *Luke 10–24*, 363–74, 487–96. Acts commentaries on prayer: Alexander, *Acts People's Commentary*, 17, 44–45; Alexander, "Acts Oxford Commentary," 1031, 1033, 1034; C. K. Barrett, *Acts Volume 1*, 88–89, 166, 245–50; C. K. Barrett, *Acts Volume 2*, 781; Bruce, *Acts*, 106; Talbert, *Reading Acts*, 42, 107, 119; Fitzmyer, *Acts*, 215; Keener, *Acts*, 114–15; Kuecker, "*Acts*," 218.

righteous and devout Simeon (Luke 2:25–35), for the prophet Anna (Luke 2:36–38), for the Pharisee and the tax collector of the parable (Luke 18:10), for the first followers of the Way of Jesus, Peter, John (Acts 2:46; 3:1) and Paul (Acts 21:26; 22:17), the Jerusalem temple was a place of prayer; for Jesus it was his father's house (Luke 2:49), a house of prayer (Luke 19:46). The temple, however, was not the only location for prayer: Jesus prays on the mountain (Luke 6:12; 9:28; 22:39–46) and in deserted places (Luke 5:16); his followers pray in their houses (Acts 1:13–14; 2:42, 46; 4:23–21; 9:11, 36–43; 10:1–3, 9; 12:5, 12). Jesus prays at significant moments in his life: at his baptism (Luke 3:21); prior to his first clash with the scribes and Pharisees (Luke 5:16); prior to his choice of the twelve apostles (Luke 6:12–16); prior to Peter's confession of faith (Luke 9:18); at the transfiguration (Luke 9:28); in anticipation of Peter's denial (Luke 22:31–34); on the Mount of Olives (Luke 22:39–46); on the cross (Luke 23:34, 46); and at the resurrection (Luke 24:30). It is in the context of prayer that the Spirit is given (Luke 3:21–22; 11:2, 13). Such is the impression made on the disciples by Jesus' practice of prayer that they ask him to teach them how to pray just as John had taught his disciples: Jesus offers them a pattern prayer and draws on two analogies from the home, (Luke 11:1–13), later followed by one from the judicial process and one from the temple (Luke 18:1–14). Prayer became a "characteristic element" of the first followers of the Way of Jesus as they followed his example and "engaged in this same petitionary activity."[345] They receive the Spirit in the context of prayer (Acts 1:14; 2:1–4; 8:15–17); it is with prayer that Matthias is appointed an apostle (Acts 1:24); Stephen's prayers at the point of death echo the prayers of Jesus (Acts 7:59, 60); prayer accompanies the appointment of the seven (Acts 6:1–6), the commissioning of Barnabas and Saul (Acts 13:1–3), and their appointment of elders in the churches (Acts 14:23). The followers of the Way are constantly at prayer (Acts 1:14; 2:41–42, 47; 6:4); the hours of prayer at the temple are observed (Acts 3:1; cf. 10:3, 30), while Peter prays at noon (Acts 10:9), the Jerusalem church at night (Acts 12:5,6) and Paul and Silas at midnight (Acts 16:25). Cornelius and Lydia are drawn to prayer before becoming followers of the Way (Acts 10:1–4; 16:13, 16).

In his survey of prayer in Luke–Acts, O'Brien suggests that it is not simply that Jesus is repeatedly seen at prayer but that this becomes an example for those who follow his Way: as they too are continuously at prayer

345. O'Brien, "Prayer in Luke–Acts," 122–23.

it becomes clear that prayer is the means by which God guides his people.[346] That, Trites argues, is Luke's primary concern: not simply to cultivate prayer on the part of his readers but "to show that prayer is the instrument by which God has directed the course of holy history."[347] It is Jesus' habit of withdrawing for prayer that empowers all he does[348] and becomes the model for the life of discipleship in the church.[349] It is such prayer that galvanizes the church together into a new community of disciples looking to God as Father.[350] Just as they share things in common, so they pray with one mind (Acts 1:14; 4:24). While there is an inference that prayer is answered,[351] not least in Jesus' prayer of thanksgiving (Luke 10:21–22) prompted by his perception that "his earlier prayers have been answered by his Father,"[352] the text of Luke–Acts is more nuanced. Crump[353] differentiates between the many occasions when there is no reference to the content of the prayer,[354] and the far fewer occasions when the wording of a prayer is recorded.[355] In Luke it is not that prayers receive answers, it is rather that praying binds the pray-er and God together.[356] It also binds the pray-er and God's people together in community. As people pray there is a closer alignment with the will of God. Crump concludes that it is "better to speak of prayer as an activity in and of itself,"[357] quoting G. W. H. Lampe: "prayer is . . . the point at which the communication of divine influence becomes effective for its

346. O'Brien, "Prayer in Luke–Acts," 120–21, 126–27.

347. Trites, "Prayer Motif in Luke–Acts," 169.

348. Green, *Gospel of Luke*, 238.

349. Green, *Gospel of Luke*, 439.

350. Green, *Gospel of Luke*, 440.

351. Trites, "Prayer Motif in Luke–Acts"; O'Brien, "Prayer in Luke–Acts."

352. Crump, "Jesus the Intercessor," 132.

353. Crump, "Jesus the Intercessor," 223–29.

354. Luke. 1:10–13; 2:37; 3:21–22; 5:16; 6:12; 9:18, 28–29; 11:1; Acts 1:14; 2:42; 6:4, 6; 9:11, 40; 10:2, 9, 30–31; 11:5; 12:5, 12; 14:23; 16:25; 20:36; 21:5; 22:17; 28:8, although it may be possible to infer the content in some of these examples: Luke 1:10–13; 9:18, 28–29; Acts 9:40; 12:5, 12; 14:23; 20:36.

355. Verbatim: Luke 2:28–32; 10:21–22; 11:2–4; 22:42; 23:34, 46; Acts 1:24–25; 4:24–30; 7:59,60; implicitly: Luke 22:40; Acts 8:15; 26:29; 27:29; 28:15.

356. Cf. R. W. Cleaves: "the nature of prayer is not the pragmatics of production, not a matter of putting a coin in the slot and pulling out the drawer, it is not a computer card or a silicon chip. It is the practice of the communion of the soul with the soul of God" (*Love of the Lover of Souls*, 12).

357. Crump, "Jesus the Intercessor," 227.

recipients."[358] There is no correlation between specific prayers and specific answers to prayer: instead, as Fitzmyer argues, prayer is the setting in which things happen.[359] As Wolter observes, "time and again important events take place while Jesus prays or after he has just stopped praying."[360] For Luke, according to Crump, "prayer is not a guaranteed means of acquiring whatever one asks for, it is the means by which God gives what he determines to be good."[361] There is no hint in Luke–Acts of the pray-er seeking "to control or compel divine forces to operate in a desired fashion through the careful use of specific techniques."[362] Rather, prayer is "for Luke one of the most important marks of an existence oriented toward God."[363]

What would our imagined readers make of the prayers and the praying of Luke–Acts? They had the confidence to approach the god in the temple of Mercury on the Hill of *Aruerius* and seek help. In the opening chapters of Luke, they would not only recognize the temple in Jerusalem as a place of prayer but also sense the sacredness of the mountain top as a location for prayer. By the time they arrived at the words of Jesus' prayer in Luke 10:21–22, they could not but notice the place of answered prayer in the story of Jesus. They knew the importance of seeking guidance as they arrived at the temple: they needed to follow the correct process, acquiring a tablet to write on, a stylus to write with, and the correct wording for their prayer. They were willing to learn of those more experienced than themselves. It is telling that in the narrative of Luke–Acts it is only once prayer has been established as a central part of the life of Jesus that one of the disciples asks him to teach them to pray. As part of a community of those following the Way of Jesus, our imagined readers would be open to being taught. There is something familiar and at the same time radically different in the pattern prayer Jesus offers his disciples and Luke passes on to his readers (Luke 11:2–4).

The prayer opens by directly addressing God as "father" (Πάτερ: *Pater*), goes on to hallow his name (hallowed be your name: ἁγιασθήτω τὸ ὄνομά σου: *sanctificetur nomen tuum*) and speak of his coming kingdom

358. Lampe, "Holy Spirit," 169.

359. Fitzmyer, *Luke I–IX*, 244–47.

360. Wolter, *Luke I*, 176.

361. Crump, "Jesus the Intercessor," 264.

362. Crump, "Jesus the Intercessor," 268.

363. Wolter, *Luke I*, 176: Luke 1:10; 2:37; 5:16; 6:12; 9:18; 9:28–29; 11:1; 18:1; 22:41, 44, 46.

(your kingdom come: ἐλθέτω ἡ βασιλεία σου: *adveniat regnum tuum*). This would be familiar to Honoratus who addresses Mercury as "holy god" (*deo sanc\to/ Mercurio*), "your Divinity" (*numini tuo*), the "*genius* of your Divinity" (*genium nu|minis \tu{u}i/*), "your Divinity" (*numen tuum*) and "your Majesty" (*maiestate tua*).[364] This use of *maiestas* bears close comparison with the use of kingdom language in this prayer and elsewhere in the teaching of Jesus.

The prayer of Jesus then includes three petitions: "give us" (δίδου ἡμῖν: *da nobis*), "forgive us" (ἄφες ἡμῖν: *dimitte nobis*), "do not bring us" (μὴ εἰσενέγκῃς ἡμᾶς: *ne nos inducas*). Honoratus petitions the holy Mercury, using the language of complaint, request, prayer, and petition: "I complain" (*conqueror*), "I would ask" (*rogauerim*), "with renewed prayers I ask" *(iteratis pr{a}ecibus ro|go)*; finally speaking of "my petition" (*petitio mea*). Whereas the petition Honoratus makes is specifically related to the loss of "two wheels and four cows and many small belongings from my house" (*rotas duas et uaccas quat|tuor et resculas plurimas de |hospitiolo meo*), and asks for their return (*meam rem ad me |pertulerit*), the petition in the prayer of Jesus relates to the provision of daily needs (give us each day our daily bread: τὸν ἄρτον ἡμῶν τὸν ἐπιούσιον δίδου ἡμῖν τὸ καθ' ἡμέραν: *panem nostrum cotidianum da nobis cotidie*). Honoratus is aware of the divisions that have occurred in his community because of the actions of the thief and so he also asks that there be "concord," reconciliation with the thief (*et meam concordiam |habuerit*). In the same way, the second petition of the prayer of Jesus seeking the forgiveness of sins reflects the need to restore a community divided not by theft but by debt: (and forgive us our sins, for we ourselves forgive everyone indebted to us: καὶ ἄφες ἡμῖν τὰς ἁμαρτίας ἡμῶν, καὶ γὰρ αὐτοὶ ἀφίομεν παντὶ ὀφείλοντι ἡμῖν: *et dimitte nobis peccata nostra siquidem et ipsi dimittimus omni debenti nobis*). The sense of urgency in the petition of Honoratus, asking that it "immediately ?be evident" (*ut petitio mea |statim pareat*)[365] is in accord with the final petition of the prayer of Jesus that seeks to avoid temptation, the time of testing or trial (and do not bring us to the time of trial: καὶ μὴ εἰσενέγκῃς ἡμᾶς εἰς πειρασμόν: *et ne nos inducas in temptationem*).

364. *Tab. Uley* 72; Tomlin, *The Uley Tablets*, 286–90; Sánchez Natalías, *Sylloge Defixiones*, 354–55 (*SD* 365). Appendix Chapter 4.

365. For a discussion of the meaning of *pareat* see Tomlin, *The Uley Tablets*, 290. Tomlin now translates "may immediately ?be evident."

Honoratus expects an answer to his prayer: either the return of the goods and a reconciliation with the one responsible for the theft, or the severe sickness of the thief. Drawing on two analogies that would be familiar to Honoratus, the householder and the father, the teaching of Jesus goes on to speak of needs that are met because of persistence in prayer (Luke 11:5–8). While "everyone who asks receives, and everyone who searches finds, and for everyone who knocks, the door will be opened" there is not a direct, quantifiable answer to each petition. Instead, the Spirit is given as people engage in prayer (Luke 11:11–13).

At the heart of the prayer of Jesus, however, is something radically different from the main thrust of the prayer of Honoratus. Failing the granting of his requests, Honoratus spells out what he wants to happen to the one who has wronged him, whether they be "man or woman, boy or girl, slave or free" (*si baro |si mulier si puer si puella |si seruus si liber*): "I would ask the *genius* of your divinity that you do not allow health to the person who has done me wrong, nor (permit) him to lie or sit or drink or eat" (*rogaverim genium nu|minis \tu{u}i/ ut ei qui mihi fraudem |fecerit sanitatem ei non per|mittas nec iacere nec sedere nec |bibere nec manducare*). In seeking the forgiveness of sins in the context of the forgiveness of "those indebted to us," the prayer of Jesus turns on its head the vindictiveness or negative reciprocity that becomes even more explicit as Honoratus prays that his "petition may immediately ?be evident," making it obvious that he has been avenged or vindicated "by your Majesty (*ut petitio mea |statim pareat me uindica|tum esse a maiestate tua*). Here we have an example of that kind of negative reciprocity we encountered in the context of the Bloomberg tablets.[366] In place of the retribution sought by the people of the rural community around Uley who had been wronged, there is to be a spirit of forgiveness that breaks the cycle of indebtedness implicit in the retribution sought in their petitions.[367] "The experience of forgiveness by God is inseparably bound up with the granting of forgiveness in relation to other human beings."[368]

The vindictiveness or negative reciprocity characteristic of the prayers for justice is absent from the prayers and the praying of Luke–Acts. Docilinus holds Varianus, Peregrina and Sabinianus responsible for bringing "evil harm" on his beast and asks that the god Mercury "drive them to the

366. See above, Chapter 2, n. 189.

367. Brawley, *Luke*, 120f; Green, *Gospel of Luke*, 439–44.

368. Wolter, *Luke II*, 94.

greatest death and do not allow them health or sleep."[369] Likewise, in her "memorandum" to the god Mercury, otherwise known as Silvanus or Mars Silvanus, Saturnina asks that whoever has stolen her linen cloth "should not have rest."[370] Tomlin observes that "the 'justice' for which they ask merges easily into 'vengeance'" which "is explicit in nine of the Uley tablets."[371] Behind the prayers of Docilinus and Saturnina there is a strong element that seeks some kind of restoration of the relationships that have been broken by the wrong that has been done. In his prayer Docilinus allows for the possibility that the perpetrator acknowledges their offence and at Uley reimburses the value of the damage done in the blood of a wounded animal as "they redeem from you what they have administered to me" (*a te quod mi[hi] ad[mi]|ni[strau]erint |redem[e]rint*).[372]

One can see in these prayers the kind of bargaining that is absent from the prayers of Luke–Acts, but a central tenet of Roman prayer: *do ut des* (I give so that you might give).[373] Saturnina makes an offering to Mercury of one third of the value of the linen cloth that has been stolen to prompt the god to help recover the stolen property: "she gives a third part to the aforesaid god on condition that he exact the property above-written. And the property which has been lost ... a third part is given to the god Silvanus on condition that he exact it, whether man or woman, whether slave or free..." (*deo s(upra)s(cripto)dicto tertiam |partem donat ita ut |ex{s}igat istas res quae |s(upra)s(crip)ta sunt* uacat *|ac [e]a quae peri<i>t deo Siluano |tertia*

369. *Tab. Uley* 43; Tomlin, *The Uley Tablets*, 204–7; Sánchez Natalías, *Sylloge Defixiones*, 350–51 (*SD* 361). Appendix Chapter 4. In Bath a person with a similar sounding name, Docilianus, asks "the most holy goddess Sulis" to inflict whoever it is who has stolen his hooded cloak "with the greatest death and not allow him sleep or children now nor in the future" (*Tab. Sulis* 10; Tomlin, *Tabellae Sulis*,

https://romaninscriptionsofbritain.org/inscriptions/TabSulis10. See above, Chapter 4, n. 257; Tomlin, *The Uley Tablets*, 55–57. Sánchez Natalías, *Sylloge Defixiones*, 274–75 (*SD* 215).

370. Tab. Uley 2; Tomlin, *The Uley Tablets*, 88–91; Sánchez Natalías, *Sylloge Defixiones*, 346–47, SD 356. Appendix Chapter 4.

371. Tomlin, *The Uley Tablets*, 17: Tab. Uley 17, 41, 58, 62, 68, 72, 80, 82, 83.

372. *Tab. Uley* 43; Tomlin, *The Uley Tablets*, 204–7. Appendix Chapter 4.

373. Esler, pers. comm. Cf. Davenport, *Roman Bath*,73. Beard et al., *Religions of Rome Volume 1*, 32. Beard et al. *Religions of Rome Volume 2*: 5.5a, Pliny, *Natural History* XXVIII.10–11 (129); 5.7b, stone inscription regarding The Saecular Games, ILS 5050, CIL VI.32323 lines 90–168 (139–40); 6.3a, Cato, *On Agriculture* 141 (152–53); but contrast 13.5e, Marcus Aurelius, *Communings with Himself* IX.40 (358–59).

pars donatur ita ut |hoc ex{s}igat si uir si femina si seru|us si liber).[374] She is not alone in proposing such an arrangement. Biccus "gives" (*dat*) Mercury "whatever he has lost," seeking all manner of ill health unless the thief "has brought (it) in the temple of Mercury."[375] All that is lost is given (*data*) by an anonymous petitioner who seeks similar suffering "until he bring all those things to the temple of Mercury on the Hill of *Aruerius*."[376] A very literate petitioner commits (*commendo*) the execrable Manneius who has done wrong by failing to repay a debt and goes on to "give, offer, destine, assign (*obd[o] of<f>ero destino deputo*) to the god Mercury *Arueriacus*" 100,000 denarrii which he describes as a proportion of the debt so that the thief should "bring this to the temple and the treasury of the most powerful god." Should he fail to do that not only the thief but their family as well is to be cut short and "languish in sleeplessness with unknown ailments, adverse indispositions" repelling everybody, "half naked, toothless, trembling, gouty, without the pity of anyone." In that event they are not to find the Lord "merciful."[377] Another complains "to the god Mars *Aruerius*, most holy Divinity," concerning those who have stolen their property, that is two pewter plates; the arrangement is that the petitioner gives half their property (*dimidiam [re]rum |mearum tibi dono*) and in return a full payment is made "through the blood of these (my) enemies" (*per sangu<in>em |eorum hos[tium]*]).[378] On occasions the thieves themselves are "given" to the god and punishment is sought in return.[379]

Prayers that are transactional,[380] seek the harsh punishment of the perpetrator,[381] the restoration of the loss[382] and entail some element of persuasion[383] are characteristic of the prayers to the god Mercury at Uley. Our imagined readers would be challenged by the very different response advocated by Jesus to the kind of crisis they experienced. He had challenged his followers to love those considered enemies by doing good to those who

374. *Tab. Uley* 2; Tomlin, *The Uley Tablets*, 88–91. Appendix Chapter 4.

375. *Tab. Uley* 4; Tomlin, *The Uley Tablets*, 96–100. Appendix Chapter 4.

376. *Tab. Uley* 75; Tomlin, *The Uley Tablets*, 294–98. Appendix Chapter 4.

377. *Tab. Uley* 78; Tomlin, *The Uley Tablets*, 306–12. Appendix Chapter 4.

378. *Tab. Uley* 84; Tomlin, *The Uley Tablets*, 332–36.

379. Tomlin, *The Uley Tablets*, 19: *Tab. Uley* 5, 9, 49, 52, 55, 58, 78.

380. Cf. *Tab. Uley* 2, 4, 5, 9, 49, 52, 55, 58, 78, 79, 84.

381. Cf. *Tab. Uley* 1, 2, 4, 5, 24, 34, 41, 43, 52, 68, 72, 76, 80, 84.

382. Cf. *Tab. Uley* 1, 2, 4, 24, 34, 52, 72, 78, 83, 84.

383. Cf. *Tab. Uley* 1, 2, 4, 5, 52, 55, 76, 78, 80, 83, 84.

hate you, blessing those who curse you and praying for those who abuse you (Luke 6:27–28). One specific instance he gives speaks directly to those accustomed to addressing their god with prayers for justice:

> from anyone who takes away your coat do not withhold even your shirt . . . if anyone takes away your goods, do not ask for them again.
>
> ἀπὸ τοῦ αἴροντός σου τὸ ἱμάτιον καὶ τὸν χιτῶνα μὴ κωλύσῃς . . . καὶ ἀπὸ τοῦ αἴροντος τὰ σὰ μὴ ἀπαίτει.
>
> *ab eo qui aufert tibi vestimentum etiam tunicam noli prohibere . . . et qui aufert quae tua sunt ne repetas* (Luke 6:29–30)

Instead of seeking retribution against those perpetrating wrong against them, followers of Jesus are to follow a very different path which shapes their identity as followers of the Way. This spirit of forgiveness in the face of adversity expressed in this prayer is actualized in two further passages one can imagine catching the attention of people from the rural community around Uley drawn to follow the Way of Jesus: Jesus' prayer on the cross echoed in the words of Stephen as he is stoned to death:

> Father, forgive them; for they do not know what they are doing.
>
> πάτερ, ἄφες αὐτοῖς, οὐ γὰρ οἴδασιν τί ποιοῦσιν
>
> *Pater dimitte illis non enim sciunt quid faciunt* (Luke 23:34)

> Lord, do not hold this sin against them.
>
> κύριε, μὴ στήσῃς αὐτοῖς ταύτην τὴν ἁμαρτίαν.
>
> *Domine ne statuas illis hoc peccatum* (Acts 7:60)

For our imagined readers the spirit of the prayer Jesus taught, with its focus on forgiveness, went to the heart of the Way they sought to follow. In the context of their rural community, it would become a type of boundary marker and "engrave itself into the life of the community" in a way that differentiated them as followers of the Way of Jesus.[384]

Negotiating the Way Through the World of a Rural Community

In the written petitions in the temple of Mercury on the Hill of *Aruerius* we glimpse the circumstances of named people from a rural community,

384. Green, *Gospel of Luke*, 440.

their response to adversity and their relationship to the temple shrine in the vicinity of their homes. Whether we regard those petitions as curses, prayers for justice or somewhere in the grey area between, we witness people engaged in a practice that spanned the empire in space and time. Should people such as these have been drawn to follow the Way of Jesus, we can imagine how they might have responded to passages in Luke–Acts that touch on what you do when you go to a temple, on cursing, and on the practice of prayer. While some aspects of Luke–Acts would resonate with them, others would significantly challenge them.

We can test that conclusion in two ways. First, we can bring together the Lived Ancient Religion approach to such a practice with the discipline of Ordinary Theology. Second, we can draw on archaeological evidence that shows Christians engaging in this practice.

Ordinary Theology and an Analytic Framework

In his study of the Bath tablets, Tomlin makes a connection between those petitions to Sulis Minerva and "the naively written and touching requests for prayer that can sometimes be seen in an English parish church";[385] Versnel makes a similar link to what he describes as "letters to heaven" encountered in churches today,[386] as does Guy de la Bédoyère.[387] Taking seriously the contemporary Christian practice of leaving written prayer requests in a church context offers us a point of comparison with the practice found at Uley, Bath, and elsewhere. The study of those prayer requests gives us a direct insight into the thinking of ordinary people as they engage in an ordinary, everyday religious practice.

In his seminal work *Ordinary Theology: Looking, Listening and Learning in Theology*, Jeff Astley defines Ordinary Theology as "the theological beliefs and processes of believing that find expression in the God-talk of those believers who have received no scholarly theological education."[388]

385. Tomlin, *Tabellae Sulis*, 100: https://romaninscriptionsofbritain.org/tabsulis/authorship.

386. Versnel, "Beyond Cursing," 81.

387. Accompanying a photograph of prayer requests on a noticeboard in Exeter Cathedral in 2002, de la Bédoyère writes, "At this stand, visitors to the church can write and post prayers, messages and requests to the Christian God recalling how, in similar ways, the men and women of Roman Britain sought pagan divine intervention in their lives" (*Gods with Thunderbolts*, 239).

388. Astley, *Ordinary Theology*, 1.

Ordinary Theology takes seriously the thinking and reflection that "ordinary people" undertake with reference to what they believe: it is a term that can be used of the study of that thinking.[389]

Adapting the methodology of Ordinary Theology, several studies have been made of prayer requests left in local churches today.[390] Alec Brown and Lewis Burton examined 58 prayer requests on the prayer board, and 419 entries in the visitors' book, in a large medieval church popular with visitors in a small village in the north of England. They drew three conclusions. First, the location, the setting and the ambience of the church itself is important: 72 percent of the recorded entries in the visitors' book referred to the beauty, peace and tranquility of the church.[391] There is a pronounced connection here with the location of temples where curse tablets have been found: the breath-taking experience of seeing the sun setting over the Welsh mountains from the site of the Uley temple on the Cotswold escarpment has not changed since Honoratus deposited his prayer text long ago.[392] Second, it is important to respect the semi-articulate and semi-formed God-talk of those whose perception of the divine has not been informed by the formal theological training of the academy or seminary. It is important not to be disparaging of those around Uley, Bath, and elsewhere who petitioned the gods, but to take seriously their writings as a glimpse of their ordinary practice. This accords with the Lived Ancient Religion approach. Third, the God profiled by the ordinary theology of the prayers pinned to the prayer board is a personal God who cares about the vicissitudes of life experienced by the individual; shows love towards the sick, the disturbed, the dying and the bereaved; listens to human requests; and may influence significant events, even by intervening on the stage of human history.[393] Those who petitioned the gods using curse tablets sought their intervention when they had been wronged in their everyday lives.

389. Astley, *Ordinary Theology*, 97.

390. A. Brown and Burton, "Learning from Prayer Requests"; Burton, "Prayers on a Prayer Tree"; ap Siôn, "Ordinary Prayer."

391. A. Brown and Burton, "Learning from Prayer Requests," 50; cf. ap Siôn, 2020.

392. Tilley, *Phenomenology of Landscape*, 74; Aldhouse-Green notes that other temples where curse tablets have been found are also in breathtaking locations, especially those in the vicinity of the River Severn: Uley, Lydney and Brean Down: Map (Figure 1) 3, 56, 57 (*Gallo-British Deities*, 208–10). Note that Tomlin reports that "the Brean Down tablet, according to a local informant, was actually found at Uley, but given a false provenance" (*The Uley Tablets*, 365).

393. A. Brown and Burton, "Learning from Prayer Requests," 51.

Tania ap Siôn has come to similar conclusions in a variety of different settings, rural and urban, using an analytic framework she has devised for intercessory prayer. First, "the prayer intention" identifies what the prayer request is about; second, "the prayer reference" identifies who the prayer is focused on; third, "the prayer objective" differentiates prayer requests that are explicit about the desired outcome from those that are unspecific.[394] In an initial study of a rural church the prayer intention of 29 percent of 917 prayer cards studied were non-specific, 21 percent had to do with illness and 16 percent with death. The prayer reference of 90 percent of the prayer requests was for people known personally to the prayer author or for global issues and only 4 percent were for the authors themselves. The prayer objective of 57 percent of the prayer authors placed the outcome in the hands of another and 43 percent indicated their desired outcome.[395] Studies in other rural settings[396] and in three urban settings[397] produced interestingly nuanced variations, but much the same kind of result.

While it is not possible to make a direct comparison between these studies of intercessory prayers and the prayer requests of the Uley community that arise from a crisis in the life of each prayer author, the application of ap Siôn's framework to the Uley tablets highlights the transactional, manipulative and vindictive nature of these prayers:

Tablet	Prayer Intention	Prayer Reference	Prayer Objective
Tab. Uley 1	Theft of beast of burden.	Petitioner, Cenacus, complains to, and asks, the god Mercury.	Return of beast of burden; failing that deprivation of health of thieves, full payment of devotion demanded by god.

394. Ap Siôn, "Ordinary Prayer," 21.

395. Ap Siôn, "Ordinary Prayer," 20.

396. Ap Siôn, "Ordinary Prayer," 22–29; ap Siôn, "Power of Place."

397. Ap Siôn, "Prayers from the Inner City."

Tablet	Prayer Intention	Prayer Reference	Prayer Objective
Tab. Uley 2	Theft of linen cloth.	Petitioner, "Saturnina, a woman" writes a memorandum to the god Mercury (*written over* "Mars Silvanus"), the god Silvanus.	Return of linen cloth to the temple by thief, "whether man or woman, whether slave or free"; failing that deprivation of rest of thief. Gift to the god of a third part of the value on condition he (having "been made part-creditor") "exact the debt" and give it to "the god Silvanus."
Tab. Uley 3	Theft of gold ring from [my] house and an iron fetter.	Petitioner "to the god Mars Mercury."	"If anyone has done the wrong," god to discover the property.
Tab. Uley 4	Theft of property.	Petitioner, Biccus, gives to Mercury whatever he has lost.	Return of property to the temple of Mercury and gift to Mercury of property; failing that the thief, "whether man or male" should not urinate, defecate, speak, sleep, stay awake, have well-being or health, gain consciousness . . . unless the petitioner intercedes.

Tablet	Prayer Intention	Prayer Reference	Prayer Objective
Tab. Uley 5	Theft of a bridle.	Petitioner speaks of unnamed god.	Name of thief given to the god. Abbreviated formulae suggest return of two thirds of property and gift of one third to the god. Failing that possibly ill health to the thief.
Tab. Uley 6		Petitioner to the god, I pray.	
Tab. Uley 8	Wrong done to petitioner and theft.	Petitioner, Primulacus, to the god Mars Mercury, describing himself as "author."	Return of property to the temple of Mercury; failing that wrong-doer, whether man or woman, slave [or free], freedman or freedwoman, to be unable to eat or drink. Concord with the god through the author; failing that Mercury to deny them health.
Tab. Uley 9	Theft of a sheep, with evil intent.	Petitioner to the god Mercury.	Gives the thief of evil intent to the god Mercury. Possibly seeks the return of stolen property; failing that, let the god kill the thief with his vile blood, whether slave or free, boy or girl.

Tablet	Prayer Intention	Prayer Reference	Prayer Objective
Tab. Uley 17	[Theft]	Petitioner [asks] Mercury, the god, Divinity.	Gift to Mercury. seeks vengeance on the thief, unless with his own blood . . .
Tab Uley 20 Only Uley tablet to mention two petitioners	Theft of stolen property including clothes: women's underwear, a cloak (*pallium*), a cloak (*laena*), sewing thread, a . . . garment, laces, leather, two leg-bands.	Petitioners, Cunouinna and Corosulis, presumably husband and wife mention *Aruerius*.	Conouinna and Corosulis give the property lost perhaps to *Aruerius*, naming suspects.
Tab. Uley 21	Theft of 35,000 denarii.	Petitioner to the god Mercury *Aruerius* (or *Arueriacus*), [I ask [your] majesty] – with line drawing of *caduceus*.	Possible return of stolen money; failing that asks for vengeance, and that the thief, whether free or slave, woman [or man] be permitted neither to drink nor to eat, nor to defecate, neither sleep nor health, unless (restitution is made).
Tab. Uley 22	Theft.	Petitioner possibly a woman, presumably addressed to the god.	Vengeance, thief or stolen property given to god.

Tablet	Prayer Intention	Prayer Reference	Prayer Objective
Tab. Uley 24	Theft of a beehive.	Petitioner (whose name is now lost) to the god Mars. Complains, asks, ?petitions. Second side, to the god Mars the Propitious.	Complains (of the man) whether slave or free who has stolen (his) beehive. Asks for the return of hive to its proper place, and (the thief) gain the concord of Mercury. Failing that for the thief not to be permitted to drink or eat, nor sleep or have health. ?Petitions that something (perhaps vengeance?) be made evident to the thief.
Tab. Uley 34	Has done me wrong; theft of a ring.	Petitioner, Cunitus to the *genius* Mercury . . . (I ask your) holy *genius*.	Payment at "your temple"; failing that the thief, "whether [man slave] or slave-girl, whether free man or [free woman] . . . of a woman . . . whether boy or girl]" be ? shamed and not permitted to sit, to eat, to urinate.
Tab. Uley 40		Petitioner(s) to the god Mercury *Arueriacus* describing themselves as *s[il] uestres ei[us]*, his woodlanders. Possibly a description of votaries of Silvanus, with whom Mercury is identified in *Tab. Uley* 2.	Possible return of the stolen property; failing that the loss of health to the thief; the "discovering" of the thief or a reference to "vengeance."

Tablet	Prayer Intention	Prayer Reference	Prayer Objective
Tab. Uley 41	Theft of a sheep from private property of Virilis.	Petitioner, Virilis, to [god].	The thief to make restitution and return the stolen property; failing that the thief "whether slave [or free], whether man or woman, whether slave [or free]," be not permitted to drink or eat, and to be bloodless within nine days; seeks vengeance.
Tab. Uley 43	Evil harm done to farm animal (*pecus*: sheep, goat, pig or bovine). "The act of causing death and burial ("in earth") by means of incantation."	Petitioner, Docilinus, complains to and asks the god Mercury.	Restitution involving "redeeming" what has been done. Failing that the death and burial as they are driven "to the greatest death" and not permitted health. Close to a curse.
Tab. Uley 47	Theft of the greatest . . ., and of silver coins, possibly fourteen in number.	Petitioner complains to [Mercury] *Aruerius*.	Restitution suggested; failing that, the thief, "[whether slave] or free have "execrable" health and forfeit his blood.
Tab. Uley 50	Theft of one plaque (perhaps a gold amulet) and four rings. "No doubt they were silver or gold bullion in a convenient form."	Petitioner [to the god Mercury . . .].	[No indication – but probably return; failing that retribution.] the god is to find the guilty person and the stolen property.

Tablet	Prayer Intention	Prayer Reference	Prayer Objective
Tab. Uley 52 Note: use of Greek letters to write Latin text may have demonstrated scribe's bilingualism: "startling" to find "such sophisticated literacy in the Romano-British countryside." Tomlin.	Theft of linen cloth, cloak and two silver coins.	Petitioner to the holy god Mercury *Arueriacus*.	The thief, whether boy or girl, whether male or female slave, whether man or woman, whether soldier or civilian, given to god. The stolen property to be returned to the god's temple; failing that, "the marrow, blood, life" to be taken from the thief by the god.
Tab. Uley 55	Theft of the material of a cloak, presumably the woollen cloth from which it was made.	Petitioner, *mintla* Rufus, to the god Mercury.	"gift" to the god of the stolen property and the thief whether woman or [man].
Tab. Uley 57	Theft implied.	Petitioner unnamed, to the god implied.	The thief is to be denied [sleep/well-being] or health, unless he make good with his own blood this gift so as to gain the concord of the petitioner. Note: This amounts to "a bogus concession" as the thief is to lose his life whatever he does.

Tablet	Prayer Intention	Prayer Reference	Prayer Objective
Tab. Uley 58 Note: possibly earliest tablet, early second century. Tomlin.	Theft of wool and a jug.	Petitioner to [the god] Mercury.	Commits the weaver and the stolen property to Mercury and asks Mercury to give the weaver no rest; seeks vengeance; the god is to recover "the price of the (stolen) property."
Tab. Uley 62	Theft of a cloak of *sagum* type, and a band (or scarf) [and ?thread] and a cap that was "sudden, unexpected and (perhaps) violent"; a description that "might well refer to a "break-in" . . . in a place in which the petitioner was staying, perhaps "an isolated hut, or shepherd's shelter."	Petitioner, Senouarus the son of Senouarus to the god Mercury, to *Aruerius*, a tablet.	"Mercury is not to "permit" health and well-being to the thief, either to see with his eyes nor to have children, whether man or woman, whether free or slave, until he returns the stolen goods to the temple. Mercury is to punish, avenge, anyone who tries to stop the tablet (*pittacium*) from working.
Tab. Uley 68	Unspecified theft.	Petitioner, Carin[ianus] (or Carinus), to the holy god Mercury, I implore you.	Carinus implores Mercury to permit Primanus the thief neither sun, nor moon, neither ?wife nor children; and that he fulfil (my) vengeance with his blood. Close to a curse.

Tablet	Prayer Intention	Prayer Reference	Prayer Objective
Tab. Uley 70 Tablet re-used	Implied theft.	Petitioner, Severinus, to the god Mercury.	May he (Mercury) find the thief *or* the stolen property. The gifts of Severinus.
Tab. Uley 71	Theft.	Petitioner to the god Mercury.	Mercury not to permit thief "to drink nor to eat, [and not to have] sleep or [health] (until he makes restitution).
Tab. Uley 72	Theft of two wheels, four cows and many small belongings from my house.	Petitioner, Honoratus, to the holy god Mercury, I complain to your Divinity; I would ask the *genius* of your Divinity; with renewed prayers I ask your Divinity; my petition; your Majesty.	Return of property to Honoratus and concord regained with him; failing that, that the person who has "done me wrong," whether (he is) man or woman, boy or girl, whether slave or free, be not permitted health, nor to lie or sit or drink or eat. Asks "your Divinity" "that my petition may immediately ?be evident that I have been vindicated by your Majesty.

Tablet	Prayer Intention	Prayer Reference	Prayer Objective
Tab. Uley 75	Property stolen from strongbox, that is gold money and my ?interest on the crop. (Possibly, the petitioner "had lent, or was going to lend, money to a farmer who would then buy seed corn and sow it, this money to be repaid with interest when the corn was harvested.")	Petitioner to Mercury (implied), I seek. The temple of Mercury on the Hill of *Aruerius*.	That the thief, whether man or woman, whether boy or girl, be not permitted to sleep or be wakeful, to sit or to lie, until everything stolen is returned to "the temple of Mercury on the Hill of *Aruerius*." Property ? given to god. Possibly, appeal for information leading to the discovery of the thief, perhaps a reward for anyone who named the thief.
Tab. Uley 76	Those who are thinking evil towards me and doing evil to . . . beasts of burden.	Petitioner to the holy god Mercury, I complain.	May those responsible, whether slave or free, male or female, not be permitted to stand or sit, to drink or eat, or to redeem these (causes of) anger unless with their own blood, a "bogus concession." Close to a curse.

Tablet	Prayer Intention	Prayer Reference	Prayer Objective
Tab. Uley 78 Note: "eschews formulae," is "a literary tour de force," and "is a surprisingly sophisticated text to come from a rural shrine." Tomlin.	Wrongdoing involving unpaid debt, or a deposit denied, of more than 100,000 denarii.	Petitioner to "the holy god Mercury *Aruerius*"; to the god Mercury *Arueriacus*; you, Mercury *Arueriacus;* Lord.	The execrable Manneius is committed to the holy god Mercury *Aruerius*. He is to bring the stolen denarii "to the temple and the treasury of the most powerful god"; and present it "to the god Mercury *Arueriacus*." Failing that Mercury Arueriacus to cut short his life. And impose untold sufferings on his family who will not find him merciful. A bogus concession if they make concord with the god or the author, and give their blood. Close to a curse.
Tab. Uley 80	Theft of gloves.	Petitioner, the page given to Mercury; we are asking the god Mercury.	That Mercury exact vengeance for the theft of gloves; take blood and health from thief; that this be evident to the thief "as quickly as possible."

Tablet	Prayer Intention	Prayer Reference	Prayer Objective
Tab. Uley 81	Theft.	Petitioner to the holy god [Mercury] *Aruerius* [I complain . . .].	Complaint addressed to the holy god [Mercury] *Aruerius*, possibly that they do not have ?health unless they restore the stolen goods; failing which they will pay with their blood. Has given whoever has stolen from him, whether slave or free. . . .
Tab. Uley 82	[Theft]	Petitioner to the god.	Gives to the god, a plea for vengeance.
Tab. Uley 83	Theft of wethers ("castrated male sheep eaten as mutton").	Petitioner, Pectillus, to the god.	That thief return them unharmed without bloodshed. Gives perhaps "the god's duty of intervening."

Tablet	Prayer Intention	Prayer Reference	Prayer Objective
Tab. Uley 84	Theft of two pewter plates.	Petitioner, complaint to the god Mars *Aruerius*, most holy Divinity; Lord.	Complains concerning those who have stolen the two pewter plates. May the one privy (to the theft) be permitted neither sleep nor health, neither hope nor breath, neither to stand nor sit, neither to drink nor to eat. Half the property given to the Lord; property should be paid in full through the blood of these enemies.

Table 7. Tania ap Siôn's analytic framework for intercessory prayer adapted for the Uley tablets[398]

First, of thirty-six prayer requests detailed enough to study, all have a clear prayer intention: one has to do with thinking evil against the petitioner and doing evil to beasts of burden; one has to do with evil harm done to a farm animal (sheep, goat, pig or bovine); one has to do with unpaid debt or a deposit denied. Thirty-three have to do with theft, in five of which the theft is implied, and in two of which the theft is accompanied by wrong

398. Of the eighty-six inscribed Uley tablets, at least seventy-nine once carried a literate text. The other seven or so are "pseudo-inscriptions" or lettering which apparently did not form a real text (10, 26, 31, 39, 59, 66, 67). Twenty-seven tablets remain *descripta*, although inscribed they can only be described (11, 13, 14, 16, 18, 19, 23, 25, 27, 28, 29, 32, 36, 37, 38, 42, 44, 46, 51, 54, 56, 65, 69, 73, 77, 85, 87); fourteen have very few decipherable words (12, 15, 30, 33, 45, 48, 49, 53, 60, 61, 63, 74, 79, 86); two are described as having an un-Latin text, probably Celtic (7, 35). The remaining thirty-six with a substantial text have been included in Table 7 and have been chosen as the basis of this study. This, however, serves only as a summary. It is essential to refer to the full published drawing, transcript, translation and commentary. See Tomlin, *The Uley Tablets*, 7–12. N.B. there is no *Tab. Uley* 64 as the same tablet was recorded twice as 64 and 67 in the excavation report (Tomlin, *The Uley Tablets*, 266; cf. Woodward and Leach, *Uley Shrines Excavation*, 129.

done: five of animals (one of a beast of burden, one of four cows, three of sheep or wethers); three of farm implements (two wheels or a plough, one an iron fetter, one a bridle); one of a beehive; one of wool and a jug; six of cloth, woolen material and clothing; three of rings; one of a plaque, possibly a gold amulet; two of pewter plates; four of money (one of 35,000 denarii, one of fourteen silver coins, one of two silver coins, one of gold money from a strongbox); seven of unspecified property.

Second, the prayer reference is in each case to the prayer author themselves as they address the god of the temple: thirteen name themselves (including one woman two co-petitioners, and a husband and wife); seventeen address Mercury explicitly (of which one is written over Mars Silvanus and also addressed to Silvanus); one speaks of "the temple of Mercury on the Hill of *Aruerius*," one mentions the votaries as *siluestres*; seven address Mercury *Aruerius/Arueriacus*, one with a line drawing of a *caduceus*; one mentions *Aruerius*; two address Mars Mercury; one addresses Mars *Aruerius*; one addresses Mars as Mars the Propitious; five address the god; one addresses the god as Lord, *genius*, Divinity and Majesty; one as Lord and Divinity; one as *genius*; one as Majesty; six address the god as holy and one as most holy; one speaks of a petition and renewed prayers; in one the petitioner implores, in another prays, in six asks, in four complains.

Third, the prayer objective is explicit in all prayers: five name the perpetrators; seventeen use catch-all phrases of the suspects; twenty-five seek return of the item stolen or payment to the temple; ten give the property stolen to the god (of which four also give the thief, two give one third and one a half of the property); two give the thief or the property; four seek concord with the perpetrator or the god; twenty-six seek physical suffering or death of the perpetrator in the event of the stolen property not being returned (of which three seek what Tomlin describes as a "bogus concession," demanding the blood of the perpetrator); nine (and possibly two others) seek vengeance; four are close to curses.

That analytic framework brings into stark relief the observations we have made. Our imagined readers would be challenged to respond to theft in a different way and to have different concerns in prayer. They would find themselves questioning their emphasis on retribution and would be turned away from manipulating the god they address in their praying.

Archaeological Evidence of the First Followers of the Way in Britannia

Secondly, we can turn to archaeological evidence. The petitions to Mercury were deposited at the temple in Uley over a long period of time. The nature of their deposition makes it impossible to date them precisely.[399] The use of capitals, Old Roman Cursive script and New Roman Cursive suggests a range of dates from second to fourth centuries CE. By the end of this period there is evidence of the formation of groups of followers of the Way of Jesus in the vicinity of the River Severn. The *ROTAS SATOR* word square etched into the plaster of a house in Corinium, Cirencester, could possibly indicate the presence of followers of the Way of Jesus who valued the words of the prayer Jesus taught: the palindromic word square can be rearranged to spell out *PATER NOSTER* with Latin transliterations of the alpha and omega associated with Christ.[400] The *Chi Rho* symbol has been found etched on paving slabs around the sacred spring at the Chedworth Roman villa suggesting the presence of followers of the Way of Jesus.[401] A pewter bowl with a rough *Chi Rho* monogram on the base was discovered in a house within the walled town of Venta Silurium (Caerwent); a nearby house may have been re-fashioned as a church.[402] Tradition going back to Gildas (c. sixth century) *martyrium* has it that nearby Isca (Caerleon) had witnessed the execution of Julius and Aaron, followers of the Way of Jesus, in the third century CE.[403] In the fifth century CE the temple of Mercury was demolished and replaced with first a wooden, and later a stone basilica,

399. See above, Chapter 4, n. 5.

400. *RIB* 2247.20; Atkinson, "'SATOR' Word-Square"; Atkinson, "Cirencester Word-Square"; "Acrostic"; Kidd and Stevenson, *A New Eusebius*, 7–8; Map (Figure 1) 25. Cf. the same inscription on the shoulder of a late second century CE amphora found in Manchester (Mamucium, Map (Figure 1) 6): *RIB* 2494.98; B. Jones and Mattingly, *Atlas of Roman Britain*, 295, 297. Commenting on *Tab. Uley* 72, Tomlin says that "it is striking that "wheels" (*rotas*) should be associated with "the sower" (*sator*) in the famous word-square . . . but this more likely reflects the exigencies of palindrome than Cotswolds agriculture" (*The Uley Tablets*, 288). Appendix Chapter 4.

401. Cleary, *Chedworth Roman Villa*, 97.

402. Brewer, *Caerwent*, 23; Manning, *Roman Wales*, 94. Map (Figure 1) 29.

403. Seaman, "Martyrs of Caerleon" referencing Gildas, *De Excidio Britanniae*, circa 535 CE (Map (Figure 1) 28); A. Breeze, suggests a stronger case can be made for York and stronger still for Leicester (Map (Figure 1) 45, 63) "British Martyrs Aaron and Julius." The only other Christian martyr tradition from Roman Britain is Alban of Verulamium, St Albans (Map (Figure 1) 17).

possibly a Christian church. During that demolition and re-building, fragments of the statue to Mercury were used in the stone walls and its head carefully buried in a pit outside the south-eastern corner.[404] Perhaps that community of followers of the Way of Jesus were asserting their identity and at the same time honoring what had gone before.

It may well be that followers of Jesus at nearby Aquae Sulis (Bath) continued to present petitions to Sulis Minerva. Dated c. 275–400 CE, *Tab. Sulis* 98 (*SD* 303) contains the first extant use of the word *Christianus* (albeit misspelled) in Roman Britain. It appears as the first of a sequence of catch-all phrases, *seu gen(tili)s seu C|h(r)istianus.*

> *seu gen(tili)s seu C|h(r)istianus quaecumque utrum vir |[u]trum mulier utrum puer utrum puella |utrum s[er]vus utrum liber mihi Annia[n]|5 o Ma{n}tutene de bursa mea s(e)x argente[o]s |furaverit tu d[o]mina dea ab ipso perexi[g]|e. [eo]s si mihi per [f]raudem aliquam in DEP|REG [.]STVM dederit nec sic ipsi dona sed ut sangu|inem suum (r)eputes qui mihi hoc inrogaverit*
>
> Whether pagan or Christian, whether man or woman, whether boy or girl, whether slave or free, whoever has stolen from me, Annianus (son of) Matutina (?), six silver coins from my purse, you, lady Goddess, are to exact (them) from him. If through some deceit he has given me . . . and do not give thus to him but reckon as (?) the blood of him who has invoked this upon me.[405]

Tomlin suggests this text is important for "its casual reference to Christianity." Henig presumes the tablet was written by a pagan and suggests the use of this word implies an ordinary person as opposed to the specially designated *Christianus.*[406] However, the use of the word *gentilis* by Christians to designate pagans, makes it far more likely that Annianus, the author of this text, belonged to a group of Christians and was still prepared to use a prayer for justice so like the many other prayers from Britannia.[407]

404. Woodward and Leach, *Uley Shrines Excavation*, 71, 73, 75; Aldhouse-Green, *Sacred Britannia*, 192–93.

405. *Tab. Sulis* 98; Tomlin, *Tabellae Sulis*, https://romaninscriptionsofbritain.org/inscriptions/TabSulis98; Sánchez Natalías, *Sylloge Defixiones*, 319–21 (*SD* 303); Tomlin, *Tabellae Sulis*: this is the only tablet to be reversed, "with the sequence of letters reversed from beginning to end"; it contains misspellings.

406. Henig, *Religion in Roman Britain*, 71.

407. *Tab. Sulis* 98: Tomlin, *Tabellae Sulis*,

https://romaninscriptionsofbritain.org/inscriptions/TabSulis98; Sánchez Natalías, *Sylloge Defixiones*, 320 (*SD* 303). Tomlin observes that "Christian writers link *spes* and

He was not alone, the use of the repeated phrase "in the house of god" (*in do|[mo dei (?)]* suggests the prayer for justice discovered in the Eccles Roman villa was also written by a Christian.[408]

J. N. Adams calls in question Tomlin's reconstruction *gen[tili]s* and suggests *gens* is more probable, though unusual as a generic term. Drawing on evidence on its use by Pelagius and Theodore of Mopsuestia (who in a comment on Col 3:11 uses it to differentiate "gentile" from *Iudaeus*) and on its use in an old Latin manuscript of Matthew 18:17, he explores the possibility there may be a usage represented in this tablet that can be traced back to the Greek Bible and the Hebrew Scriptures. In making this argument he refers to a gold phylactery discovered in Caernarfon from the Roman period with Hebrew written in Greek characters.[409]

It can be argued that such a practice made more urgent the need for the kind of imagined reading of Luke–Acts we have been envisaging. In the second and third centuries CE followers of the Way had been developing the use of the codex to facilitate the reading of books such as Luke–Acts.[410] With the circulation of codices including Matthew, Mark, Luke, John and Acts in the third century CE[411] the followers of the Way of Jesus were becoming a "bookish" people.[412] On the one hand followers of the Way of Jesus who described themselves as *christiani* would notice the first use of the word to identify the disciples of Jesus in Antioch-on-the Orontes (Acts 11:26).[413] It was perhaps because they continued to use prayers for justice that they needed to heed the challenge of Luke–Acts. We can imagine Luke–Acts serving as a corrective for communities such as the one Annianus belonged to: it was written

> so that you may know the truth concerning the things about which you have been instructed

---

spiritus" (hope and spirit), words which are linked in *Tab. Uley* 84; he also notes "a Classical instance is still to be found" (*The Uley Tablets*, 335). Might the petitioner have heard those words linked by Christians?

408. *SD* 446 (Eccles), Sánchez Natalías, *Sylloge Defixiones*, 370–71; Tomlin, "Roman Britain in 1985," 428–31.

409. J. N. Adams, "British Latin," 11 and n. 41. See *RIB* 436.

410. Hurtado, *Earliest Christian Artifacts*, 88.

411. Chester Beatty Papyrus 45: Hurtado, *Earliest Christian Artifacts*, 218. See above Chapter 1, nn. 191–99.

412. Hurtado, "A Bookish Religion."

413. Pervo suggests its use "encapsulates the cosmopolitan background of emergent Christianity" (*Acts*, 294–95).

ἵνα ἐπιγνῷς περὶ ὧν κατηχήθης λόγων τὴν ἀσφάλειαν.

ut cognoscas eorum verborum de quibus eruditus es veritatem (Luke 1:4)

Their community was to be shaped by the spirit of prayer seen in the life of Jesus and among the first followers of the Way and narrated in Luke–Acts: it was to be characterized by a rejection of retribution, vindictiveness and manipulation. Theirs was to be a community in which the kind of fracturing experienced under the escarpment at Uley was replaced with a sharing (Acts 2:44; 4:32–37) in which God shows no partiality (Acts 10:34–35; 15:7–8).

It is just possible they might have encountered a codex containing letters of Paul addressed to churches whose roots were described in Acts[414] that spoke of being baptized into one body and drinking of one Spirit whether Jews or Greeks, slaves or free (εἴτε Ἰουδαῖοι εἴτε Ἕλληνες εἴτε δοῦλοι εἴτε ἐλεύθεροι: *sive Iudaei sive gentiles sive servi sive liberi* 1 Cor 12:13) where all are one in Christ Jesus since

> there is no longer Jew or Greek, there is no longer slave or free, there is no longer male and female.
>
> οὐκ ἔνι Ἰουδαῖος οὐδὲ Ἕλλην, οὐκ ἔνι δοῦλος οὐδὲ ἐλεύθερος, οὐκ ἔνι ἄρσεν καὶ θῆλυ·
>
> *non est Iudaeus neque Graecus non est servus neque liber non est masculus neque femina* (Gal 3:28)

> Where there is no longer Greek and Jew, circumcised and uncircumcised, barbarian, Scythian, slave and free; but Christ is all and in all!
>
> ὅπου οὐκ ἔνι Ἕλλην καὶ Ἰουδαῖος, περιτομὴ καὶ ἀκροβυστία, βάρβαρος, Σκύθης, δοῦλος, ἐλεύθερος, ἀλλὰ [τὰ] πάντα καὶ ἐν πᾶσιν Χριστός.
>
> *ubi non est gentilis et Iudaeus circumcisio et praeputium barbarus et Scytha servus et liber sed omnia et in omnibus Christus.* (Col 3:11)

Drawing on insights from "Ordinary Theology" and from archaeological discoveries in the vicinity, there is evidence to suggest that followers of the Way of Jesus in and around the River Severn had an identity

414. E.g. Chester Beatty Papyrus 45: Hurtado, *Earliest Christian Artifacts*, 221; *Tab. Sulis* 98 (*SD* 303), Tomlin suggests "it is tempting to think that a novel *gentilis/Christianus* pair was added as a tribute to the universal power of Sulis by someone who knew both the traditional formulae and the words of St Paul" (*Tabellae Sulis*, https://romaninscriptionsofbritain.org/inscriptions/TabSulis98.

that differentiated them from others.[415] We can imagine such followers encountering Luke–Acts and being challenged to strengthen that sense of identity as they are confronted with "the truth concerning the things about which" they "had been instructed" (Luke 1:4). Where once they had turned to the temple for help in time of need, now they turned to a house which, like Lydia's house in Philippi, "became a center of Christian life," a house church where "people lived according to the baptismal confession of Gal. 3:28" and modelled "a "contrast society," on a small scale in which "all can be equal sisters and brothers."[416] It would be a community where enslaved women and men would have a part to play.[417]

Conclusion: Negotiating the Way with a Radical Spirituality

Though smaller in number and from a much longer period of time, the curse tablets of the temple of Mercury on the Hill of *Aruerius* can, in the looser sense, be described as an archive. Drawing on each aspect of the imagination we explored in Chapter 1 and the process we outlined there, our adaptation of archival ethnography has helped us to imagine not simply the individuals we encounter in the curse tablets, but also the network of relationships of which they were part. What we have seen with our inner eye has been informed by attention to the location of the temple shrine and the nature of the tablets themselves. Our imagined reading of passages from Luke–Acts to do with temples, cursing and prayer has been warranted by close attention to the biblical text. We have been able to test those conclusions with reference to the discipline of Ordinary Theology and to the archaeological evidence of early followers of the Way who were

415. Matthews advocates reading Acts "against the grain," suggesting that in Acts Luke was deliberately suppressing "strands of the early Christian movement that . . . struggled for inclusiveness, justice and equality" (*Acts*, 82–88). She argues that Gal. 3:28 reflects that tendency among some early followers of Jesus to strive after "a democratic utopian society" that "gestures toward equality" even though it cannot attain it (*Acts*, 89–91).

416. Reimer, *Women in Acts*, 126. Cf. Schaberg and Ringe, "Luke," 498.

417. Reimer suggests that the possibility that in Philippi the enslaved woman (παιδίσκη: *puella* Acts 16:16) "was accepted into the community at that time and was able to participate in its life" (*Women in Acts*, 151–94). In a Leicester curse tablet, listing the names of twenty slaves in a courtyard house, the Greek παιδίον/παιδίσκη comes into Latin in the word *paedogogium* referring to the slave quarters. Among the twenty named are three women, Vorvena, Vendicina and Nigella: Tomlin, "Paedagogium and Septizonium"; Savani et al., *Roman Leicester*, 49 (Map (Figure 1) 63).

contemporary with some of those responsible for the curse tablets. That there is evidence of the use of curse tablets by some Christians reinforces our imagined reading of Luke–Acts and takes us back to Luke 1:1–4. Luke–Acts is written so that such as these "may know the truth concerning the things about which" they "have been instructed."

In moments of crisis Honoratus, Saturnina and others from that rural community around the temple of Mercury on the Cotswold escarpment turned not to the law for redress, but to the local temple. Were such as these to become followers of the Way and encounter Luke–Acts they would recognize the significance of the temple to the *Iudaei* and of other temples in the context of Paul's travels. However, on the Hill of *Aruerius*, experiencing a sunset over the Severn and the Welsh mountains, we can imagine the words of Acts 7:48–50; 14:15; and 17:24–25 having the power to challenge them profoundly. A new and radically different source of help was to be found in the God of creation and in a new network of relationships centered not on the local temple, but on a house meeting of followers of the Way and reaching far beyond.

They would expect the words of Jesus in declaring woe upon certain people to effect change and to make a difference. The wrong they experienced had caused divisions in their community for which they sought redress: they would recognize the reaction of Peter to the divisions caused by the actions of Ananias and Sapphira. They would particularly have been struck by the effect the words of the first followers of the Way of Jesus had. However, they would be challenged by the words of Jesus teaching his followers to bless those who curse them: heeding such words had the potential to shape an alternative kind of community. While at home with the emphasis in Luke–Acts on prayer they would be challenged to turn away from the transactional nature of the prayers for justice they brought to Mercury *Aruerius*. Prayer for those following the Way of Jesus was very different. It had at its heart not the longing for retribution, but the challenge of forgiveness. This is nothing less than a radical spirituality, rooted in the teaching and practice of Jesus in Luke's Gospel and of the first followers of the Way in Acts.

CHAPTER 5

Conclusion

Imagining Luke–Acts in Roman Britain

"to live and act and serve the future hour."

—Wordsworth, *Poems of the Imagination*

Imagining Luke–Acts in Roman Britain has demonstrated in general that the archaeology and history of Roman Britain opens windows on to the world of the New Testament, and specifically, that the Bloomberg tablets, the Vindolanda tablets, and the Uley tablets from an urban, a military, and a rural context function as "gateways into a lost world," giving us that sense of "overwhelming closeness,"[1] that enables us to engage with real people from the past and give an account of their everyday lives.[2] Though not archives in the strict sense, they lend themselves to the disciplines of archival ethnography and enable us to construct a new interpretation of the meanings Luke–Acts conveyed to its first audiences.

Key to our adaptation of archival ethnography has been the use of a multi-faceted imagination that in Wordsworth's words, sees "into the life of things," is "formed by patient observation," hears with "the inward ear," and sees with "that inward" and "inner eye."[3] Understanding imagination as "that which creates images"[4] and "the faculty which makes sense of

1. Lennartsson, "Notes on Not Being There," 109.

2. Esler, *Babatha's Orchard*, 4.

3. Poems of the Imagination XXVI, Preface to the edition of 1815, *Poems of the Imagination* XXIX, XII, XIX, Wordsworth, *Poetical Works*, 164, 753, 166, 149, 157.

4. Warnock, *Imagination*, 10.

things,"[5] we have guarded against flights of fancy by careful study of each corpus of texts, cultivating "a fact-based imaginative empathy."[6] We have glimpsed the story of their discovery, outlined their historical context, and studied the words written in each tablet. Such an archival ethnography is "the eye of the needle through which the threads of the imagination must pass."[7] With imagination's "inward ear" we have heard Roman London's first voices in the Bloomberg tablets; with its "inward eye" we have seen the people of a military community engaging with each other and with local people, happily and under duress, in the Vindolanda tablets; with its "inner eye" we have seen the anguish of people from a rural community seeking help in time of crisis from the temple of Mercury on the Hill of *Aruerius* in the Uley tablets.

Among the first followers of the Way of Jesus we meet within Luke–Acts itself, we encounter people from the world of commerce and trade we glimpse in the Bloomberg tablets, from the military world we see in the Vindolanda tablets and from the kind of rural community we meet in the Uley tablets. We have argued, therefore, that it is appropriate to imagine how people from these communities, were they to become followers of the Way of Jesus, would have responded to a reading of Luke–Acts. Our imagined readings are justifiable in the locations and with the writings chosen, informed by careful study of the data available, and warranted by close attention to the biblical text.

We can imagine a trader or merchant from first century Londinium, drawn to follow the Way of Jesus, recognizing in Luke–Acts a familiar world of commerce and trade, of wealth and poverty, of honor and shame. In the teachings of Jesus and in the community life shared by his first followers they would be challenged to a radical generosity that reaches out to the poor, addresses the issue of debt and builds community in a spirit of familial reciprocity.

A centurion, a woman of standing, or a prefect from the military community of Vindolanda drawn to follow the Way would also discover a familiar world in Luke–Acts, where centurions engaged with the local community far from their base, where women of agency had something to contribute, where identity was found, and power asserted through a network of relationships that bound communities together and extended

5. Warnock, *Imagination*, 10.

6. Maloney and Reimer, *Acts*, lxi.

7. Willis, *Ethnographic Imagination*, viii.

to Rome and the emperor. Encountering Luke–Acts they would be challenged to a radical inclusivity within a community of followers of the Way that would involve a year-round reversal of roles that includes others at the table, reaches out to the destitute, builds bridges with local peoples, and seeks justice for all.

Were someone from the rural community in the vicinity of the temple of Mercury at Uley to become a follower of the Way of Jesus and encounter Luke–Acts we can imagine them also finding a new identity in a different network of relationships. The breath-taking views from the Hill of *Aruerius* over the Severn as the sun sets over the Welsh mountains may still be experienced. In that location the challenge of Luke–Acts to a Way rooted in the practice and teaching of Jesus and in the community spirit of the first followers of the Way would entail a radical spirituality: communicating with God in the community of the Way; blessing those who curse; and replacing the spirit of vindictive retribution that sought to manipulate the god of the local temple, with a spirit of forgiveness that was neither vindictive nor manipulative.

The challenge we imagine in all three contexts would be radical in the sense that it takes seriously the introductory words of Luke–Acts and looks to Jesus and the first followers of the Way. Our imagined reading makes clear that Luke's Gospel, together with the Acts of the Apostles, functions as a book that is intended to be read or heard in its entirety. Whether or not it was intended for an individual of standing who is addressed as the "most excellent Theophilus," a generic "friend of God," or a specific community of followers of the Way, our imagined reading makes it clear that it is entirely plausible to maintain that Luke–Acts was written for communities of the Way anywhere in the Roman Empire, and to see it functioning as a corrective to guide people in the Way. As such, Luke–Acts is written so that those who already follow the Way "may know the truth about which" they had been instructed (Luke 1:4).

People such as we encounter in mid-first century Londinium, in late first and early second century Vindolanda, and in the later temple of Mercury on the Hill of *Aruerius*, would, on becoming followers of the Way, find their world turned upside down with a radical generosity, a radical inclusivity and a radical spirituality. They would not, however, be prompted to engage in revolution against Rome. It is as one imagines them reading or hearing the narrative of Luke–Acts unfold that this paradox becomes apparent. It is precisely at the point at which he has encountered Mary's song

(Luke 1:46–55), Jesus' programmatic sermon in Nazareth (Luke 4:16–30), and his teaching to his disciples (Luke 6:20–49), that our imagined centurion of Vindolanda would encounter the centurion of Capernaum (Luke 7:1–10). Our imagined traders of Londinium would have encountered the bleak parable of the rich fool (Luke 12:13–21) and the narrative of the ruler challenged to sell all that he has (Luke 18:18–30) only to find that the wealthy Zacchaeus is able to retain half his possessions (Luke 19:1–10). They would go on to read of a community where all is shared (Acts 2:44–45; 4:32—5:11), only to find that there was room for Lydia, Aquilla, Priscilla, and Paul himself, all of whom continue to be involved in the world of trade (Acts 16:11–40; 18:1–4).

Within the community of followers of the Way they would find an upside down world, where it was the norm for the exalted to be humbled, the destitute welcomed to the table (Luke 14:7–24) and everything shared (Acts 2:44–45); where a spirit of forgiveness replaced the longing for retribution (Luke 11:1–13).

I finish as I started, by extending to the reader the invitation Graham Ward shared as he came to the end of his celebration of imagination: "the exercise of my imagination as a writer is an invitation to exercise your mind as a reader."[8] It must, however, be an informed imagination. That invites further research. I have offered a broad-brush approach that has taken in three disparate archives and a range of passages from Luke–Acts. The same approach could be used of other gospels, letters and the book of Revelation. With the Bloomberg tablets only published in 2016 and the full corpus of Uley tablets in 2024, a full ethnographic study of the people responsible for those tablets has yet to be undertaken; there is always more to be done as more Vindolanda tablets are discovered and published. The inter-connectedness apparent among many of the people responsible for the Vindolanda tablets and implied among the people responsible for the Bloomberg tablets, and in a different way in the rural community around Uley, suggests that the kind of Social Network Analysis of archival material developed by Lena Tambs and others for studying socio-economic realities could contribute much.[9] More detailed study of one or all of these archives, would lend itself to a thematic approach to the New Testament. Using the insights of Jeannine Brown's narrative method, it would be possible to produce an imagined reading of Luke–Acts or any other New Testament book

8. Ward, *Unimaginable*, 237.

9. Tambs, "Social Network Analysis"; Tambs, "Social and Symbolic Boundaries."

from beginning to end, from the perspective of those who produced these texts.[10]

I have imagined reading Luke–Acts through the eyes of those responsible for the Bloomberg tablets, the Vindolanda tablets and the Uley tablets. The implied presence of non-elite women as well as men, slaves as well as free, in each of the communities represented in these three archives invites an imagined reading through their eyes that goes "against the grain," building on the approach taken by Matthews and Reid.[11] Recent research suggests it most unlikely that Claudius marched with elephants into Camulodunum in 43 CE as Cassius Dio seems to imply.[12] There has, however, been an elephant in the room throughout our imagined reading. There is scarcely any mention of local peoples in any of the three archives. It would be useful to draw on research that seeks to give them a voice in developing our imagined reading further.[13]

For those who have an eye to see, the accessibility online of all manner of Roman inscriptions from Britain,[14] and coins discovered in Britain,[15] together with accompanying publications[16] and continuing archaeological research,[17] can open up many windows on to the world of the New Testament in Roman Britain. That means there is ample scope for popularizing

10. J. K. Brown, *Narrative Method*; J. K. Brown, *Gospels as Stories*.

11. Matthews and Reid, *Luke 1–9*, xli–xlvii; Matthews and Reid, *Luke 10–24*, 403; Matthews, *Acts*, 82–91; Reid, *Do You See This Woman?*, 117–20. Cf. Allason-Jones, *Women in Roman Britain*.

12. Charles and Singleton, "Claudius, Elephants and Britain"; Cassius Dio LX.21.2, Cary and Foster 1914ff., Vol. VIII, 420–21. Map (Figure 1) 16.

13. Figure 1, Map of Britannia, is based in part on the *Ordnance Survey Map of Roman Britain* which is criticized by David Mattingly for being a map of Roman Britain and not a map of Britain in the Roman Empire as it limits itself primarily "to the features of government and domination, and of elite society" (*An Imperial Possession*, 356–69).

14. "Roman Inscriptions of Britain"; Roger Tomlin, *Britannia Romana* is an excellent place to start.

15. "Portable Antiquities Scheme"; "Llanvaches Roman Coin Hoard"; Ireland, *South-Warwickshire Hoard*.

16. Roger Tomlin has brought together transcripts, translations and commentary on the whole range of inscriptions available in Roman Britain, reflecting on what they reveal of Britannia in *Britannia Romana*. Sam Moorhead has opened a window on to the world of Roman coins illustrated by finds recorded with the Portable Antiquities Scheme, *Roman Coinage in Britain*.

17. The Roman Society's journal, *Britannia* gives an insight into current research in Roman Britain.

the contextual study of the New Testament among adults and children in church and school settings.

Re-enacting in our minds' eye the world of the Bloomberg tablets, the Vindolanda tablets and the Uley tablets has enabled us to connect with people from an urban, a military, and a rural community in Roman Britain. Little did they imagine that something they had hand-written would, nearly two thousand years later, still have the power "to live and act and serve the future hour."[18] It is that service that has enabled us to imagine Luke–Acts through the eyes of those who were contemporaries of its first readers and see afresh its challenge to a radical generosity, a radical inclusivity and a radical spirituality.

18. *The River Duddon* XXXIV "After-thought": Wordsworth, *Poetical Works*, 303.

APPENDIXES

A Select Catalogue of the Tablets

> "It is crucial not to mislead the reader into thinking that letters in a text are more legible than they really are."
>
> —Alison Cooley, *The Cambridge Manual of Latin Epigraphy.*

The key texts referred to in Chapters 2, 3, and 4 are reproduced here for ease of reference. However, they tell only part of the story. The transcripts and translations were published alongside photographs, drawings, introductions, notes and commentary for each tablet. When studying any tablet it is essential to refer to the full publication. The Bloomberg tablets and the Vindolanda tablets (together with the Bath curse tablets) are available online at *Roman Inscriptions of Britain* (*RIB*): https://romaninscriptionsofbritain.org/. The Uley tablets have been published in Roger S. O. Tomlin, *The Uley Tablets* and in due course will appear, together with all other curse tablets from Britain, in *RIB*. Images of the Bloomberg tablets and the Uley tablets are available at British Museum Online Collections (https://www.britishmuseum.org/collection/).

Appendix to Chapter 2: A Selection of the Bloomberg Tablets

The site period date range represents the context in which the tablet was found (see Table 4). Explicit dates and other internal evidence sometimes indicate that tablets are older. The find spot is indicated by OA: Open Area; B: Building; S: Structure.[1]

No.	Tab. Lond. Bloomberg
27	Correspondence: Letter-text with first line. Period 3 phase 1 (late), 80–90/5 CE. OA22: found in waste dumped from vicinity, forming new building platforms (Fig. 30). W 142.9 × H (35.7) × Th R: 5.0 × Th F: 4.9 mm. 1 Secundionis liberto Vialico | *vacat* sal(utem) |accipias c<h>irographum seru[i] |M(arci?) S[a]luii M[... ...]tandi | 5 *traces* |. . . To Vialicus, the freedman of Secundio, greetings. Would you receive the note of hand of the slave of ?Marcus Salvius M[. . .] . . .
29	Letter-text with first line. Period 3 phase 1 (late), 80–90/95 CE. OA22: found in waste dumped from vicinity, forming new building platforms (Fig. 30). W 139.4 mm x H 113.7 mm x Th R: 5.9 mm x Th F: 4.5 mm. Reconstruction: Figure 4 1 Taurus ⟦Taurinus⟧ Macrino domino | *vacat* [ca]riss[imo] salute<m> | *traces* recte esse | *traces* | 5 cum uenerat Catarrius et |⟦ni [o]ccas{s}ionem non adii[s]ses⟧ |iumenta a<b>duxerat, conpe<n>dia |quae messibus tribus reficere |non possum [?adf]ueram [?he]re | 10 a[d D]iadumenum set ille |superuenit unum diem Taurus (*written over* Taurinus) to Macrinus his dearest lord, greetings. . . . in good health . . . when Catarrius had come and had taken the beasts of burden away, investments which I cannot replace in three months. ?Yesterday I was at (the house of) Diadumenus, but he (Catarrius) arrived unexpectedly for a single day ...

1. See Table 4. The information about find spots is taken from Bryan et al., "The Archaeological Context," 34–53; see site diagrams, Figures 22–36.

No.	Tab. Lond. Bloomberg
30	Correspondence: letter-text, first line lost. Period 2 phase 1, 43–53 CE. OA2: found in discarded waste on natural gravels close to Walbrook (Fig. 24). W 127.4 × H (58.7) × Th R: 7.4 × Th F: 6.0 mm. *outer* 1 dabis Tito auia|rius *inner* . . . 1 quia per forum totum |gloriantur se te faene|ras<s>e itaque te rogo tua |causa ne tu turpis appar<e>|5 as in ...cus non sic |res tuas ?ama[bis] |et. put[a]s *traces* *outer* You will give (this) to Titus ... *inner* . . . because they are boasting through the whole market that you have lent them money. Therefore I ask you in your own interest not to appear shabby . . . you will not thus favour your own affairs . . .
31	Correspondence: letter-text, first line lost. Period 2 phase 3 (late), 62–65/70 CE. OA12 phase 1: found in landfill that created the platform for buildings (Fig. 27). W 127.0 × H (44.0) × Th R: 7.1 × Th F: 6.1 mm. *outer* . . . | 1 At<t>icus *vacat* *inner* . . . | 1 *traces* |rogo [te] per panem et sal|em ut quam primum mit|tas (denarios) uiginti sex in uictoriat(is) | 5 et (denarios) decem Paterionis |. . . *outer* . . . (from) Atticus. *inner* . . . I ask you by bread and salt that you send as soon as possible the twenty-six denarii in victoriati and the ten denarii of Paterio . . .

<table>
<tr><th>No.</th><th>Tab. Lond. Bloomberg</th></tr>
<tr><td>35</td><td>Correspondence: letter-text, first line lost.
Period 3 phase 1 (early), 65/70–80 CE. OA15: found in levelling dumps for buildings (Fig. 29).
W 140.7 × H (90.3) × Th R: 9.3 × Th F: 5.2 × W seal-groove: 25.0 mm.

. . . | 1 [...] traces |[...] soluere | traces [e]st non ?m<i>ratus tueri |in eam (denarios) CC quos dedi arram | 5 traces mittas mihi quod |debes [...]eris ...tere | traces

. . . to pay . . . ?he was not surprised to watch over . . . for it 200 denarii which I have given (as) deposit . . . would you send me what you owe . . . you will . . .</td></tr>
<tr><td>38</td><td>Correspondence: letter-text, first line lost.
Period 3 phase 1 (late), 80–90/5 CE. OA22: found in waste dumped from vicinity, forming new building platforms (Fig. 30).
W 147.0 × H (46.0) mm.

. . . | 1 mal[..]m res id est ads[..]cer[.]i succurri | traces |fussum emerent ues traces [do]|mine f(rater), cum vacat | 5 quibus quam primum uenient | vacat a Tincori[.]

. . . property, that is . . . to be helped . . . that they buy the fussum . . . lord brother, with which [or whom, plural] they will come as soon as possible from Tincori[. . .]. [Note: fussum: spindle, grain, barley poured out.]</td></tr>
<tr><td>39</td><td>Correspondence: letter-text, first line lost.
Period 3 phase 1 (late), 80–90/5 CE. OA22: found in waste dumped from vicinity, forming new building platforms (Fig. 30).
W 136.7 × H (58.0) × Th R: 11.5 × Th F: 7.9 mm.

1 traces |erat in Icenis castello |?Epocuria eamque traces |in se recepit Iulius Suavis | 5 ... neque se ... |. . .

. . . was in (the canton of) the Iceni at the fort of ?Epocuria, and Julius Suavis has accepted it for himself ... nor he ...</td></tr>
</table>

No.	Tab. Lond. Bloomberg
44	Financial or legal document, dated 8 January 57 CE. Period 2 phase 2, 53–60/1 CE. S5: found in rectilinear earthen banks on cleared site forming an enclosure (Fig. 25). W 137.3 × H (56.2) × Th R: 7.6 × Th F: 4.6 mm. Photograph and drawing: Figure 6. Nerone Claudio Caesare Augusto |Germanico ii L(ucio) Calpurnio Pisone | *vacat* co(n)s(ulibus) ui Idus Ianuarias *vacat* |Tibullus Venusti l(ibertus) scripsi et dico me | debere Grato <S>puri l(iberto) (denarios) CV ex{s} pretio |mercis quae uendita et tradita <est> |quam pecuniam ei reddere debeo |eiue ad quem ea res pertinebit | . . . In the consulship of Nero Claudius Caesar Augustus Germanicus for the second time and of Lucius Calpurnius Piso, on the 6th day before the Ides of January (8 January 57 CE). I, Tibullus the freedman of Venustus, have written and say that I owe Gratus the freedman of Spurius 105 denarii from the price of the merchandise which has been sold and delivered. This money I am due to repay him or the person whom the matter will concern . . .
45	Financial or legal document, dated 21 October 62 CE. Period 2 phase 3 (early), 60/1–62 CE. S36: found wedged in wattle lining of a drain (Fig. 26). W 142.0 × H (81.0) × Th R: 7.4 × Th F: 4.2 mm. P(ublio) Mario Celso L(ucio) Afinio Gallo co(n)s(ulibus) XII Kal(endas) Nouembr(es) |M(arcus) Renn[iu]s Venustus me condux{s}isse |a C(aio) Valerio Proculo ut intra |Idus Nouembres perferret a ⟦Londi⟧ | Verulamio penoris onera uiginti |in singula (denarii) quadrans uecturae |ea condicione ut per me mora |(asses) i Londinium quod si ulnam |om[n]e[m] *traces* |. . . In the consulship of Publius Marius Celsus and Lucius Afinius Gallus, on the 12th day before the Kalends of November (21 October 62 CE). I, Marcus Rennius Venustus, (have written and say that) I have contracted with Gaius Valerius Proculus that he bring from Verulamium by the Ides of November (13 November) twenty loads of provisions at a transport-charge of one-quarter denarius for each, on condition that . . . one *as* . . . to London; but if . . . the whole . . .

No.	Tab. Lond. Bloomberg
50	Financial or legal document, dated 64 CE. Period 3 phase 1 (late), 80–90/5 CE. OA22: found in waste dumped from vicinity, forming new building platforms (Fig. 30). W 147.0 × H (61.0) × Th R: 7.1 × Th F: 6.9 mm. 1 M(arco) Licinio Crasso [F]r[u]gi et C(aio) Lae|[cani]o Basso co(n) s(ulibus) [...]embr[e]s. |Florentinus Sex(ti) Cassi [...]ti |seru[u]s scrips[i] iussu domini | 5 mei eum accepisse pension|es duas ex fundo uodatio | *traces* In the consulship of Marcus Licinius Crassus Frugi and Gaius Laecanius Bassus (64 CE), on the [... day before the ...] of [...]ember. I, Florentinus, the slave of Sextus Cassius [...]tus, have written by order of my master that he has received the two payments from the ... farm ...
51	Financial or legal document, dated 22 October 76 CE. Period 3 phase 1 (late), 80–90/5 CE. OA23: found in a yard, containing two hearths, separating Buildings 10 and 11 (Fig. 31). W 133.7 × H (77.7) × Th R: 8.3 × Th F: 5.4 mm. 1 imper(atore) Ca[e]sare Vespasiano VII |Tit[o] V c[o](n)s(ulibus) XI K(alendas) Nou(embres) |opera in u Id(us) Nouembres |inter Litugenum et | 5 Magunum data ab |Ca[e]sare praeiudico |. . . In the consulship of the Emperor Caesar Vespasian for the seventh time (and) of Titus for the fifth time, on the 11th day before the Kalends of November (22 October 76 CE). Responsibility (for the case) between Litugenus and Magunus on the fifth day before the Ides of November (9 November) having been given by the emperor, my preliminary judgement is [...]

No.	Tab. Lond. Bloomberg
55	Financial or legal document, date lost. Period 3 phase 1 (early), 65/70–80 CE. OA14: found in initial dumps, followed by the construction of cribwork, timber boxes retaining further, similar dumps (Fig. 28). W 146.0 × H (77.8) × Th R: 8.2 × Th F: 5.8 mm. Photograph and drawing: Figure 7. [et] sor[tem et eorum u]s{s}uras |qua[s] debuerit probos recte |curari qua(n) documque peti[eri]t | *traces* [...]runt | Nar[cisso] Rogati Lingonis |[rec]te [p]robe dari fide promis{s}it |Atticus *traces* ?[I]ng[e]nuo ...illis |eiue ad quem ea res pertinebit |eosque [m]anu q(ui) s(upra) s(cripti) s(unt) coram dix{s}it se | debere et <h>abere et accepisse |ante hanc diem Atticus | *traces* |. . . . . . and the principal and the interest on them which he shall have owed . . . to be properly managed in good (coin) whenever he shall have requested . . . To Narcissus (the slave) of Rogatus the Lingonian, Atticus . . . has properly, truly, faithfully promised (it is) to be given, to Ingenuus . . . or to him to whom the matter will pertain. And in the presence of those who have been written in (their own) hand above, Atticus has said that he owes and holds and has received before this day . . .
57	Financial or legal document, date lost. Period 3 phase 1 (late), 80–90/5 CE. B9: found in situ on the trampled earth floors of a building including industrial premises, adjoining Buildings 10 and 11 (Fig. 31). W 142.3 × H 112.0 × Th R: 7.0 × Th F: 6.3 mm. *traces* | *traces* |de... [r]erum suar[u]|m agendarum persequen|darumque omnium sponsion|em facere iudicio certare |permis(i)sti *vacat* |item autem praesens ille |rem procurationem r... | [i]ngenuos d... ius ... you have permitted [*name*] to enter into an undertaking of doing and pursuing all his business (and) to contend in judgement. But likewise, he (being) present ... the matter, the management . . . free-born (persons) . . .

No.	Tab. Lond. Bloomberg
65	Financial or legal document, list of witnesses Period 3 phase 1 (late), 80–90/5 CE. OA22: found in waste dumped from vicinity, forming new building platforms (Fig. 30). W 137.5 × H 114.6 × Th R: 9.0 × Th F: 5.7 × W seal-groove: 22.2 mm. Photograph and drawing: Figure 8.

(i)	(ii)
Mari	*traces*
Paulli	*traces*
Sacc[i]	*traces*
traces	*traces*
Verecu[n]	d[i...]
vacat	*vacat*

(Seal) of Marius (*perhaps* Marus) . . . (seal) of Paullus . . . (seal) of Saccus . . . (seal) of . . . (seal) of Verecundus.

Appendix to Chapter 3: A Selection of the Vindolanda Tablets

The site period date range represents the context in which the tablet was found (see Table 6). The site context identifies the specific location in which the tablet was discovered: period 1 outside west wall of earliest wooden fort; periods 2 and 3 in the *praetorium* of the enlarged fort; period 4: barracks; period 5: workshop.[2] The find date relates to specific periods of excavation (see Table 5). Numbering of the Vindolanda tablets begins with Tab. Vindol. II 118 because the 117 tablets published in *Tab. Vindol. I* were revised and republished in *Tab. Vindol. II*, starting with number 118. The transcripts were heavily dependent on Alison Rutherford's photography. Between the publication of *Tab. Vindol. II* and *Tab. Vindol. III* the digital revolution in photography occurred. All the tablets published in *Tab. Vindol. II* were revised in the light of that new technology and amendments listed in the Appendix to *Tab. Vindol. III*. Transcripts published in that Appendix are not alternative interpretations, but definitive revisions made as a result of vastly improved photographic techniques. The texts reproduced here take into account those revisions.

No.	Tab. Vindol.
II 118	Literary and sub-literary text; writing practice, verse. W 100 × H 15. Find date: 1985. Site period 3 (97–105 CE). Site context: WVIA (southern part of the *via principalis*, west of the yard in the *praetorium*, VIA). . . . |interea pavidam volitans pinna|ta .ubem *m2* seg. *vacat* |. . . Meanwhile winged Rumour flew in haste through the settlement (in a different hand) ? slack

2. The descriptions of the site context are based on R. Birley, *Vindolanda: Roman Frontier Fort*, 52, 64, 93; Anthony Birley, *Garison Life*, 60, 63, 70; and for the 2017 excavations from Bowman et al., "Vindolanda Tablets IV," tablets-context.

No.	Tab. Vindol.
II 154	Military document; strength report of *I cohors Tungrorum.* W 86 × H 394. Find date: 1988. Site period: 1 (92–97 CE). Site context: Ditch (near southern end of western wall of earliest wooden fort).[3] XV K(alendas) Iunias n(umerus) p(urus) [co]h(ortis) i Tungro– rum cui prae<e>st Iulius Vere– cundus praef(ectus) DCCLII in is (centuriones) VI ex eis absentes singulares leg(ati) XLVI officio Ferocis Coris CCCXXXVII in is (centuriones) II Londinio *vacat* (centurio) [I] uas ... in scir..[... e]xtra prouinciam. VI in is (centurio) I [prof]ecti in Gallia[m] VIIII in is (centurio) I . [Ebura]co stipendiatum XI in.a I XXXXV summa absentes CCCCLVI in is (centuriones) V reliqui praesentes CCLXXXXVI in is (centurio) I ex eis aegri XV uolnerati VI lippientes [X] summa eor[um] XXXI reliqui ualent[es CC]LXV in [is (centurio) I] 18 May, net number of the First Cohort of Tungrians, of which the commander is Iulius Verecundus the prefect 752, including 6 centurions of whom there are absent: 46 guards of the governor at the office of Ferox 337 at Coria, including 2 (?) centurions at London, 1 (?) centurion 6 [. . . outside the province], including 1 centurion 9 [going ahead into Gaul], including 1 centurion

3. Difficulties in the interpretation of this tablet underline the importance of consulting the full publication, especially Appendix III. Note: some figures are difficult to read.

No.	Tab. Vindol.
	11 [in York to collect pay] 1 (?) at (?) 45 total 456 absentees, including 5 centurions remainder, 296 present, including 1 centurion from these: 15 sick 6 wounded 10 suffering from inflammation of the eyes total of these 31 remainder, 265 fit for active service, including 1 centurion
II 250	Correspondence of Flavius Cerialis; private document: letter of recommendation from Karus, amended in III Appendix. Dimensions unrecorded. Find date: 1973–1975. Site period 3 (97–105 CE). Site context VIA (large open yard in *praetorium*). *i* [*c*.4]ius Karus C[e]r[iali] | *vacat* s[alutem] |[*c*.4]brigionus petit a me |[domi]ne ut eum tibi com| mendarem rogo ergo do|mine si quod a te petierit |[u]elis ei subscribere |Annio Questori (centurioni) regi|onario Luguualio ro| go ut eum commen| *ii* [*c.* 4] digneris .[...] |[...].que nom[ine] |debetorem m[e tibi] |obligaturus op[to] | te felicissimum |bene ⟦f⟧ ualere | *vacat* | *m2* uale frater *Back* *m1* [C]eriali |praef(ecto) |*traces*

The references to locations outside the province, in Gaul and in York are particularly difficult to interpret. This summary also takes into account revised readings in the Appendix to Tab. Vindol. III as a result of the advent of digital scanning.

No.	Tab. Vindol.
	Front ...ius Karus to his Cerialis, greetings. . . . Brigionus (?) has requested me, my lord, to recommend him to you. I therefore ask, my lord, if you would be willing to support him in what he has requested of you. I ask that you think fit to commend him to Annius Questor, centurion in charge of the region, at Luguvalium, [by doing which] you will place me in debt to you both in his name (?) and my own (?). I pray that you are enjoying the best of fortune and are in good health. *m2* Farewell, brother. *Back* *m1* To Cerialis, prefect. *traces* of name of sender.
II 257	Correspondence of Flavius Cerialis; private document: letter from Valatta, probably a woman, amended in III Appendix. W 96 × H 52. Find date: 1985. Site period 3 (97–105 CE). Site context: WVIA (southern part of the *via principalis*, west of the yard in the *praetorium*, VIA). Valatta [Ceriali suo] |s[alutem] |rogo domin[e per pos|teritat[e]m tuam. [| 5 et per Lepidinam quod [|mihi concedas *vacat* |].[|. . . Valatta to her Cerialis, greetings. I ask you, my lord, by your posterity and by your (wife) Lepidina that you grant me what I ask (?) ...

No.	Tab. Vindol.
II 263	Correspondence of Flavius Cerialis; Private document: letter from Vitalis, a decurion, in the auxiliary cavalry of Augustus, amended in III Appendix. Dimensions unrecorded. Find date: 1973–1975. Site period: 3 (97–105 CE). Site context II (one of the prefect's public rooms in the *praetorium*). *i* [Ceriali su]o | *3? lines lost* |]. |[...]si |]m |. . . *ii* [Perp]etuó com|m[iliton]e et epistu|las .[..].s ► quas acceperas |ab Equestre centurione | coh(ortis) ► III ► Batauorum [re]mi|si |ad te pr(idie) K(alendas) Ma.... .nos |..e.[.] benefi[carius]amus | *m2*? dominam tuam a me salu|ta uitali[..]opto te bene ualere *Back* *m1* Flauio Ceriali |praef(ecto) coh(ortis) VIIII Bat(auorum) a Vitale dec(urione) alae |Aug(ustae). *Front* ... to his Cerialis ... ... and those letters which you (?) had received from fellow-soldier Perpetuus and from Equester, centurion of the 3rd Cohort of Batavians, I sent back (?) to you on 30 April (?) ... (2nd hand?) greetings from me to your) mistress (?) I wish you good health *Back* *m1* To Flavius Cerialis, prefect of the 9th Cohort of Batavians, from Vitalis, decurion of the Augustan cavalry.

No.	Tab. Vindol.
II 291	Birthday invitation of Sulpicia Lepidina; private document: letter, amended in III Appendix. W 223 x H 96. Find date 1985. Site period 3 (97–105 CE). Site context VIA (large open yard in *praetorium*). Photograph: Figure 12. i Cl(audia) ► Seuerá Lepidinae [suae] |[sa]l[u]tem |iii Idus Septembr[e]s soror ad diem ′ |sollemnem natalem meum rogó | libenter faciás ut uenias |ad nos iucundiorem mihi ii [diem] interuentú tuo facturá si |[.].[c.3]s *vacat* |Cerial[em t]uum salutá Aelius meus [te] | et filiolus salutant *vacat* | *m2 vacat* sperabo te soror |uale soror anima |mea ita ualeam |karissima et haue Back *m1* Sulpiciae Lepidinae |Cerialis |a Cl(audia) ► Seuerá. *Front* Claudia Severa to her Lepidina greetings. On 11 September, sister, for the day of the celebration of my birthday, I give you a warm invitation to make sure that you come to us, to make the day more enjoyable for me by your arrival, if you are present (?). Give my greetings to your Cerialis. My Aelius and my little son send *you* (?) their greetings. *m2* I shall expect you, sister. Farewell, sister, my dearest soul, as I hope to prosper, and hail. *Back* *m1* To Sulpicia Lepidina, wife of Cerialis, from Claudia Severa.

No.	Tab. Vindol.
II 292	Correspondence of Sulpicia Lepidina; private document: letter from Severa to Lepidina, amended III Appendix. a) W 190 × H 31; (b) W 193 × H 36; (c) W 96 × H 32. Find date: 1985. Site period 3 (97–105 CE). Site context: IV (well-furnished room with access to state room II, perhaps quarters of prefect's scribes and his archive). *a* *col. i* |. . . |salutem |ego soror sicut tecum locuta fueram et promiseram |ut peterem a Brocchó et uenirem at te peti |et res[po]ndit mihi <i>ta corie semp[er li]citum uná *b* *col. ii* |. . . | *traces* |quomodocumque possim |at te peruenire sunt enim |necessariá quaedam qua[e] *col. iii* |. . . | *traces*? |rem meum epistulas meas |accipies quibus scies quid |sim actura haec tibi *c* *col. v* |. . . | *traces* |ra eram et Brigae mansura |Cerialem tuum a me saluta | *vacat* *b.Back* *m2* ual]e mi soror |karissima et anima |ma desideratissima | *vacat traces* *c.Back* *m1* Sulpiciae Lepidi|nae Ceria[li]s *traces*? |a Seuera B[rocchi] *Front* ... greetings. Just as I had spoken with you, sister, and promised that I would ask Brocchus and would come to you, I asked him and he gave me the following reply, that it was always permitted to me to meet at Coria, together with .... to come to you in whatever way I can. For there are certain essential things which . . . you will receive my letters by which you will know what I am going to do . . . I was . . . and will remain at Briga. Greet your Cerialis from me. *Back* *m2* Farewell my sister, my dearest and most longed-for soul. *m1* To Sulpicia Lepidina, wife of Cerialis, from Severa, wife of Brocchus (?).

<table>
<tr><th>No.</th><th>Tab. Vindol.</th></tr>
<tr><td>II 294</td><td>Correspondence of Sulpicia Lepidina; Private documents: letter from a woman to Lepidina.
W 65 × H 65. Find date: 1985. Site period 3 (97–105CE). Site context: VIA (large open yard in praetorium).

].a...na(?) Lepidin[ae suae] |s[alutem... |ita sim salua domi[na... |ut ego duas an.[...] | feram tibi alter[am |alteram febric.[...] |et ideo me tibi e[...] |sed quatenus m.[|. . .

. . . Paterna (?) to her Lepidina, greetings. So help me God, my lady [and sister?], I shall bring (?) you two remedies (?), the one for ..., the other for fever (?) and therefore ... myself to you ... but insofar as ...</td></tr>
<tr><td>II 310</td><td>Private document: miscellaneous, letter from Chrauttius to Veldedeius, amended III Appendix.
W 189 × H 70. Find date: 1986. Site period 3 (97–105 CE). Site context: VIA (large open yard in praetorium).

i
Chrauttius Veldeio suó fratri |contubernali antiquo pluri|mam salutem |et rogo te Veldei frater miror | quod mihi tot tempus nihil |rescripsti a parentibus nos|tris si quid audieris aut |Quot.m in quo numero |sit et illum a me salutabis | ⟦s⟧ uerbis meis et Virilem |ueterinarium rogabis |illum ut forficem
ii
quam mihi promissit pretio |mittas per aliquem de nostris | et rogo te frater Virilis |salutes a me Thuttenam |sororem Velbutenam |rescribas nobis cum... |se habeat vacat | m2? opt<o> sis felicissimus |uale
Back
m1 Londini |Veldedeio |equisioni co(n)s(ularis) | a Chrauttio |fratre

Chrauttius to Veldeius his brother and old messmate, very many greetings. And I ask you, brother Veldeius—I am surprised that you have written nothing back to me for such a long time—whether you have heard anything from our elders, or about ... in which unit he is; and greet him from me in my words and Virilis the veterinary doctor. Ask him (sc. Virilis) whether you may send through one of our friends the pair of shears which he promised me in exchange for money. And I ask you, brother Virilis, to greet from me our sister Thuttena. Write back to us how Velbutena is (?). m2? It is my wish that you enjoy the best of fortune. Farewell.
Back
m1 (Deliver) at London. To Veldedeius, groom of the governor, from his brother Chrauttius.</td></tr>
</table>

No.	Tab. Vindol.
II 343	Private document: miscellaneous, letter from Octavius to Candidus, amended III Appendix. a) W 182 × H 79; (b) W 179 × H 79. Find date: 1988. Site period: 4 (104–120 CE). Site context: XIV (barracks, centurion's quarters). Photograph: Figure 14. *i* Octauius Candido fratri suo |salutem |a Marino nerui pondo centum |explicabo e quo tu de hac | re scripseras ne mentionem |mihi fecit aliquotiens tibi |scripseram spicas me emisse |prope m(odios) quinque milia prop|ter quod (denarii) mihi necessari sunt | nisi mittis mi aliquit (denariorum) *ii* minime quingentos futurum |est ut quod arre dedi perdam |(denarios) circa trecentos et erubes|cam ita rogo quam primum aliquit | (denariorum) mi mitte coria que scribis |esse Cataractonio scribe |dentur mi et karrum de quo |scribis et quit sit cum eo karro |mi scribe iam illec petissem | nissi iumenta non curaui uexsare |dum uiae male sunt uide cum Tertio |de (denariis) VIII s(emisse) quos a Fatale accepit |non illos mi *vacat* accepto tulit *iii* scito mae explesse ⟦exple⟧ coria | CLXX et bracis excussi habeo |m(odios) CXIX fac (denarios) mi mittas ut possi|m spicam habere in excusso|rio iam autem si quit habui |perexcussi contuber|nalis Fronti amici hic fuerat |desiderabat coria ei ad|signarem et ita (denarios) datur|{ur}us erat dixi ei coria in|tra K(alendas) Martias daturum Idibus *iv* Ianuariis constituerat se uentur|um nec interuenit nec curauit |accipere cum haberet coria si |pecuniam daret dabam ei Fronti|nium Iulium audio magno lice|re pro coriatione que[m] hic |comparauit (denarios) quinos |saluta Spectatum I...|rium Firmum |epistulas a Gleucone accepi | ual (e) *Back* Vindol(anda) *Front* Octavius to his brother Candidus, greetings. The hundred pounds of sinew from Marinus – I will settle up. From the time when you wrote about this matter, he has not even mentioned it to me. I have several times written to you that I have bought about five thousand *modii* of ears of grain, on account of which I need cash. Unless you send me some cash, at least five hundred *denarii*, the result will be that I shall lose what I have laid out as a deposit, about three hundred *denarii*, and I shall be embarrassed. So, I ask you, send me some cash as soon as possible. The hides which you write are at Cataractonium – write that they be given to me and the wagon about which you write. And write to me what is

No.	Tab. Vindol.
	with that wagon. I would have already been to collect them except that I did not care to injure the animals while the roads are bad. See with Tertius about the 8½ *denarii* which he received from Fatalis. He has not credited them to my account. Know that I have completed the 170 hides and I have 119 *modii* of threshed *bracis*. Make sure that you send me cash so that I may have ears of grain on the threshing-floor. Moreover, I have already finished threshing all that I had. A messmate of our friend Frontius has been here. He was wanting me to allocate (?) him hides and that being so, was ready to give cash. I told him I would give him the hides by 1 March. He decided that he would come on 13 January. He did not turn up nor did he take any trouble to obtain them since he had hides. If he had given the cash, I would have given him them. I hear that Frontinius Iulius has for sale at a high price for leather-making (the things) which he bought here for five denarii apiece. Greet Spectatus and ... and Firmus. I have received letters from Gleuco. Farewell. *Back* (Deliver) at Vindolanda.
II 344	Private document, miscellaneous. Appeal of the man from overseas after being beaten with rods. Amended in III Appendix. W 171 mm × H 77 mm. Find date: 1988. Site Period: 4 (104–120 CE). Site Context: XIV (barracks: centurion's quarters). Photograph: Figure 15. i eo magis me ca[c.12] |d...[.]em mercem [c.8] |r[.] uel effunder [c.3] r[...]|[..]mine probo tuam maies| [t]atem imploro ne patiaris me |[i]nnocentem uirgis cas[t]igatum |esse et domine Procle prae|[fe] cto non potui queri quia ua|[let]udini detinebatur | ques[tu]s sum beneficiario ii [c.8 cen]turionibu[s] |[c.7] numeri eius [...] |[c.3 tu]am misericord[ia]m |imploro ne patiaris me | hominem trasmarinum |et innocentem de cuius f[ide] |inquiras uirgis cruent[at]u[m] |esse ac si aliquid sceler[i]s |commisissem *vacat*

No.	Tab. Vindol.
	. . . he beat (?) me all the more . . . goods . . . or pour them down the drain (?). As befits an honest man (?) I implore your majesty not to allow me, an innocent man, to have been beaten with rods and, my lord, Proculus, I was unable to complain to the prefect because he was detained by ill-health I have complained in vain (?) to the *beneficiarius* and the rest (?) of the centurions of his (?) unit. Accordingly (?) I implore your mercifulness not to allow me, a man from overseas and an innocent one, about whose good faith you may inquire, to have been bloodied by rods as if I had committed some crime.
II 452	Private document. First line of Virgil's *Aeneid* twice, a writing exercise. Dimensions: unrecorded. Find date: 1986. Site period: 4 (105–120 CE). Site context XI (barracks). *A* [arma] uirum que [c]anó Tro|[iae qu]i primus ab oris *B* arma [ui]r[um que cano] |Troiae qui primu[s ab oris] Arms and the man I sing, who first from the coasts of Troy
III 574	Military document. *Renuntium* of Cohors viiii Batavorum. W 83mm x H 82 mm. Find date: 1993. Site period: 3 (100–105CE). Site context: SG, South Gate of enlarged wooden fort (bonfire site). Photograph: Figure 13. XVII K(alendas) Maias | renuntium *vacat* | coh(ortis) VIIII Batauo|rum omnes ad loca qui | 5 debunt et inpedimenta | renuntiarunt optiones |et curatores |detulit Arcuittius optio |(centuriae) Crescentis. [Note: there is an overbar above the number VIIII]. 15 April. Report of the Ninth Cohort of Batavians. All who should be are at duty stations, as is the baggage. The *optiones* and *curatores* made the report. Arcuittius, *optio* of the century of Crescens, delivered it.

No.	Tab. Vindol.
III 629	Correspondence of Flavius Cerialis; private document: letter from Super to Cerialis. W 204 × H 50. Find date: 1993. Site period: 3 (97–105 CE). Site context: SG, South Gate of enlarged wooden fort (bonfire site). *i* [Cl]odius Super Ceriali suo |salutem |libentissime frater sicut uoluer[as] |Lepidinae tuae [....]a.. interf[u]| issem utique te ⟦*traces*⟧ *m2* ..le.te. *m1* .. [...]|. . . *ii* reddere. utique enim scis |iucundissime mihi esse quo|[ti]ens pariter sumus simi- |[...]..iam non putaui mit| [......]m ne antequam u[...]|. . . *Back* *m3*? Flauio Ceria[li] |. . . *Front* Clodius Super to his Cerialis greetings. Most willingly, brother, just as you had wanted, I would have been present for your Lepidina's birthday(?). At any rate ... For you surely know that it pleases me most whenever we are together. If(?)... I did not think ... lest before ... *Back* *m3*? To Flavius Cerialis ...

No.	Tab. Vindol.
III 655	Private document: letter in the same hand as *Tab. Vindol. II* 346, *III* 656, 657. W 99 × H 45. Find date: 1993. Site period: 3 (97–105 CE). Site context SG/NE, to north east of South Gate of enlarged wooden fort (*intervallum* road). *A* apsistas misi tibi seiun[-... ...]]|liorum(?) denariorum du[-...] |quae sigulas in cartas inse[-...] |ges det[.]r[.]....s mihi s.[...] |tanquam utique mihi [...]|non sit gratum .[.].[...] |. . . *B* t.m mea erratio quem |.]. optestor inutiliter |ita rogo credas mihi |m..... eme sic re|cedere ut integer |sim quod est primu(m) |. . . *A* ... you may stop(?) I have sent you separately(?)... additional(?) *denarii*, which ... into individual wrappings ... as if at any rate ... were not pleasing to me ... B ... my mistake(?) ... , whose help I am also(?) asking for(?) to no purpose. So please believe me ... that I retire thus so that my reputation is intact, which is the chief point ...
III 656	Private document: letter in the same hand as *Tab. Vindol. II* 346, *III* 655, 657. W 184 mm × H 33 mm. Find date: 1993. Site period: 3 (97–105 CE). Site context: SG, South Gate of enlarged wooden fort (bonfire site). *i* . . . ..[.].[|ac tamen uolo liqueat |tibi me nec a contiber|nio recedere nec a sco|la nisi c..ius rationem |. . . *ii* . . . illud in..c.... domi|no uidit autem me |potest fieri apud auri|fices aut apud argen|tarios et haec est pr. |. . . *Back* ka]r[is]|sime. *vaca*t And yet I want it to be clear to you that I am withdrawing neither from the mess nor from the club unless ... that ... to the chief. But he saw me, perhaps(?), at the goldsmiths' or the silversmiths' and this is ...

No.	Tab. Vindol.
III 663	Private document: letter to the wife of Priscinus. W 180 mm × H 50 mm. Find date: 1993. Site period: 3 (97–105 CE). Site context: SG, South Gate of enlarged wooden fort (bonfire site). *i* . . . |].[...] |[.]e.ina fecit qua ► me |[.].cunde ► consolaris |sicut mater faceret | hunc enim ► adfec|tum ► animus meus |. . . *ii* . . . |diebus ► am.[*c.*5] |ram et comm[ode] |conualescebam ► tu[...]|quid agas cum Pris|cinó tuo quam |. . . ... has made(?), with which you agreeably(?) comfort me just as a mother would do. For my mind ... this sympathy(?)... within [a few(?)] days I had ... and I was beginning to recover nicely. As to you(?), ... what you are doing with your Priscinus ...
IV 891	Letter of Andangius and Vel[...] to Verecundus; Private document: letter. W 185 × H 56. Find date: 2017. Site period 1 (85–92 CE). Site context V17–52B, from the residence of the first known commanding officer at Vindolanda, Iulius Verecundus. Find context: above Period 1 extramural road. *i* Andangius et Vel[|rogamus te domin[e] |Verecunde per notis|simam iustitiam tuam | dignos nos habe[a]s [et] |praestes ut ci[uem et] *ii* [amicum] nostrum nomi|[ne] Crispum mensorem |facias ut possit bene|ficio tuo leuius militare |e[t] genio tuo gratias age|[re d]ebemus *vacat* Andangius and Vel[...] (we) ask you, lord Verecundus, by your very well known justice, to consider us worthy and to undertake that you make it that our [fellow-countryman and friend], by name Crispus the *mensor*, may be able by your kindness to have a lighter military service; and we (will) owe thanks to your *gen*ius.

No.	Tab. Vindol.
IV 893	Letter of Caecilius Secundus to Iulius Verecundus; private document: letter. W 192 × H 32. Site period: 1 (c. 85–92 CE). Find date: 2017. Site context: V17–52B, from the residence of the first known commanding officer at Vindolanda, Iulius Verecundus. Find context: above period 1 extramural road. *Front.i* Caecilius Secundus ► Verecundó |suó ► salutem |Decuminó ► (centurioni) ► ti[li]as ► quas ► mihi ► scri|pseras ► oste[ndi ut] sciret se id |. . . *Front.ii* corporis ► sed ► iracundiolae ► quae ► cas|tigationem ► a senioribus ► merentur |de qua re commod[i]us ► est ► ut tecum |praesens ► a[ga]m ► in ► praesentia ► | scito ► omn[es] decuriones ► huius ► numeri | *traces* [|. . . *Back* Iulió Verecundó |. . . *Back* Caecilius Secundus to his Verecundus, greetings. The tablets which you had written to me I have shown to the centurion Decuminus, that he might know that he ... it [...] || [... ?not] of body [...] but little outbursts of anger which merit castigation by one's seniors. Concerning which matter, it is more convenient that I discuss it with you in person. For the moment know that all the decurions of this unit ... *Back* To Iulius Verecundus [...]

Appendix to Chapter 4: A Selection of the Uley Tablets

When they were discovered all the Uley tablets had been dispersed across the site; there is, therefore, no useful information about site finds and context.

No.	Tab. Uley
1	Theft of a beast of burden. Petitioner: Cenacus. Stylish Old Roman Cursive, seventeen lines, two-sided, folded three times. 85 by 135 mm. *(a)* deo Mercurio |Cenacus queritur |de Vitalino et Nata|lino filio ipsius de |iumento |quod ei rap|tum est et rogat |deum Mercurium |ut nec ante sa|nitatem *(b)* habeant nis{s}i |[[nissi]] repraesen|tauerint mihi iu|mentum quod ra|puerunt et deo |deuotionem qua[m] |ipse ab his ex|postulauerit To the god Mercury Cenacus complains of Vitalinus and Natalinus his son concerning the beast of burden which has been snatched from him, and asks the god Mercury that they do not have health before/unless they pay in full to me the beast of burden which they have snatched and (pay in full) to the god the devotion which he has demanded from them.

No.	Tab. Uley
2	Memorandum from Saturnina. Petitioner: Saturnina. 'rustic capitals', seventeen lines, two sided, folded three times. 85 by 62 mm. *a)* commonitorium deo |[[Marti Siluano]] Mercurio a Satur|nina muliere de lintia|mine quod amisit ut il|le qui hoc circumuenit non |ante laxetur nis{s}i quando |res s(upra)s(criptas)dictas ad fanum s(upra) s(criptum)d[i]c|tum attul[e]rit si uir si mu|lier si seruus si liber. *(b)* deo s(upra)s(cripto)dicto tertiam |partem donat ita ut |ex{s}igat istas res quae |s(upra)s(crip)ta sunt *uacat* |ac [e]a quae peri<i>t deo Siluano |tertia pars donatur ita ut |hoc ex{s}igat si uir si femina si seru|us si liber [.]te[...].at. A memorandum to the god Mercury (*written o*ver 'Mars Silvanus') from Saturnina, a woman, concerning the linen cloth which she has lost. May he who has acquired it wrongly not have rest before/unless/until he has brought the aforesaid property to the aforesaid temple, whether man or woman, whether slave or free. She gives a third part to the aforesaid god on condition that he exact the property abovewritten. And the property which has been lost ... a third part is given to the god Silvanus on condition that he exact it, whether man or woman, whether slave or free...
4	Biccus curses a thief. Petitioner: Biccus. 'rustic capitals', sixteen lines, folded several times. 66 by 124 mm. Biccus dat M|ercurio quidquid |pe<r>d<id>it si uir si m|ascel ne maiet(!) |ne cacet ne loqua|tur ne dormiat |n[e] uig<i>let nec sa|[l]utem nec s[a]|nitatem ne|ssa(!) in templo |Mercurii per|tulerit ne co<n>|scientiam de |perferat ness[i] |me interceden|te Biccus gives to Mercury whatever he has lost, (that the thief), whether man or male (*sic*), may not urinate nor defecate nor speak nor sleep nor stay awake nor (have) well-being or health, unless he has brought (it) in the temple of Mercury; (and) may not gain consciousness (*sic*) concerning ... unless with me interceding.

No.	Tab. Uley
9	Theft of a sheep. Petitioner: anonymous. Old Roman Cursive, twelve lines inscribed on hammered lead sheet, two-sided, folded twice. 92 by 79 mm. *(a)* diu[o] Mercurio donaui |qui me ma[li] consil{l}i |desputauerit ouem |inuolauerit ipse |deus interscia<t> sangu<i>n[e] |uili si ser<u>us si liber si |puer si puel<l>a *(b)* licet qu[o]d [n]escio |aput .e[...].muican |diui ipseu[s...] me |inp[.] ope[...] nessi |ips.[.]seu[.]s[...] To the god Mercury I have given (the man) who of evil intent has ?robbed me (and) has stolen (my) sheep. Let the god himself ?kill (him) with his vile blood, whether (he is) slave or free, whether boy or girl, even if, which I do not know, at the ... of the god himself ... me ... unless ...
24	Theft of a beehive. Petitioner: name lost. inner face one line of capitals followed by ten of Old Roman Cursive (a), outer face two lines of capitals, two-sided, folded four times. 125 by 92 mm. *(a)* DEVO MARTI .[ ]. RVS[|qu{a}erituR, si ser<u>us si liber [|qui uas apium inualauit(!) ?[u]ere |si comodia(!) erat ne illi permittatur |nec bib[er]e nec mandu<ca>re nec |{nec} somnum nec sanitate<m> nesi(!) ipsum |uas ad locum suum reuersetur |et congortiam(!) Mercur<i>i agat |*SEPET* deum u[t] illi qui [fraudem] |fecit ut illi si .. pariat [|qui *traces* *(b)* DEVO MAR|TI .S PROPITIO (a) To the god Mars [*name lost*] complains (of the man) whether slave or free, who has stolen (his) beehive. Truly, if it was ?convenient, may he not be permitted to drink or eat, nor sleep or health, unless the said hive be returned to its proper place and (the thief) gain the concord of Mercury. He ?petitions the god that to this (man) who has done [the wrong], that to this man ?it be evident ... who ... (b) To the god Mars the Propitious...

No.	Tab. Uley
34	Theft of a ring. Petitioner: Cunitus. Old Roman Cursive; eighteen lines, folded four times. 53 by 88 mm. Cunitus |Mercurio |[g]enio qui mihi |[...]dum fecerit an|ulum inuolaverit |sa..t genium si [seruus si] a[n]]cilla si liber si [libera] |[mu]lieris si puer si [pue]lla |[non] permitt<as> eum |[...]..ernat pudorem |[...]iat pede [...] |[...]mbllat [...] |nec manducat nec |sedit(!) nec magiat(!) n[i]|si ad templum |tuum repraese|ntauerit OP |TI.EI.. Cunitus to the *genius* Mercury. (He) who has done me ?wrong, has stolen (my) ?ring ... (I ask your) ?holy *genius* that whether [man slave] or slave-girl, whether free man or [free woman] ... of a woman ... whether boy or girl ... you do [not] permit him ... shame ... with his foot ... nor to eat nor to sit (?at stool) nor to ?urinate, unless he pays in full ... at your temple.
43	Docilinus curses Varianus, Peregrina and Sabinianus for doing harm to his farm animal. Petitioner: Docilinus. Well-formed 'rustic capitals', thirteen lines, hammered flat before being inscribed, folded once. 84 by 98 mm. deo Mercurio |Docilinus qu{a}eri[t]ur |Varianus et Peregrina |et Sabinianus qu[i] peco|ri meo dolum malum in|tulerunt et in t[e]rr[a] pro|locuntur rogo te ut eos |max[i]mo [le]to adigas nec |eis sanit[atem nec] som|num perm[itt]as nisi |a te quod mi[hi] ad[mi]|ni[strau]erint |redem[e]rint Docilinus complains to the god Mercury. Varianus and Peregrina and Sabinianus who have brought evil harm on my farm animal and are pronouncing it in earth. I ask you that you drive them to the greatest death, and do not permit them health or sleep unless they redeem from you what they have administered to me.

<table>
<tr><th>No.</th><th>Tab. Uley</th></tr>
<tr><td>58</td><td>Theft of wool and a jug. Petitioner: ?name lost or anonymous.
Old Roman Cursive in unusual script typical of stylus-tablet texts (c. 75–150 CE), eight lines and trace of a ninth, not folded, possibly “the earliest tablet to survive from Uley, ... it may have been inscribed quite soon after the temple was rebuilt in stone in the early second century.”
120 by 71 mm

[deo] Mercurio [ ].[ ] |datur(!) est M[ercur]io .[...] |illum gerdi[um] s(upra)s(criptum) [co]m[m]endo m[eas] |res id est lanam et lagon[am] |rogatum te habeo ut gerdium [ ]. |[...]reos huius acti quas id es[t] |me uindicas .. traces |traces pretium rerum qu[|[...]ls[...]

To [the god] Mercury ... is given to Mercury ... I commit the above-written weaver (and) my property, that is wool and a jug ... I have asked you that the weaver ... those guilty of this act ... that is ... you avenge me ... the price of the property which ...</td></tr>
<tr><td>68</td><td>Primanus is cursed for theft. Petitioner: Carin[ianus] (or Carinus).
fluent New Roman Cursive with a broad nib-like point, fourteen lines, two-sided, folded twice.
47 by 38 mm.

(a)
deo sancto Mercurio |Carin[... ?obs]ec|ro de furdo(!) {uo} quod |mihi factum est Pri|manus nec [e]i per|mitt[a]t [deu]s Mercuriu|s nec ...

(b)
nec ... |... |nec solem nec lun[am] |nec coniu. nec infantis |... ..neum |san<g>uine suo conpliat |uendica[tionem]

To the holy god Mercury. I, Carinianus (or Carinus), implore you concerning the theft which has been done to me (by) Primanus. And [the god] Mercury is to permit him neither ... nor ... nor ... neither sun nor moon, neither ?wife nor children ... that he fulfil (my) vengenace with his blood.</td></tr>
</table>

No.	Tab. Uley
72	Theft of two wheels and four cows (etc.). Petitioner: Honoratus. Old Roman Cursive by a practised hand, seventeen lines, folded six times. 76 by 131 mm. Deo sanc\to/ Mercurio Honoratus |conqueror numini tuo me per|didisse rotas duas et uaccas quat|tuor et resculas plurimas de |hospitiolo meo |rogauerim genium nu|minis \tu{u}i/ ut ei qui mihi fraudem |fecerit sanitatem ei non per|mittas nec iacere nec sedere nec |bibere nec manducare si baro |si mulier si puer si puella si seruus |si liber nis{s}i meam rem ad me |pertulerit et meam concordiam |habuerit iteratis pr{a}ecibus ro|go numen tuum ut petitio mea |statim pareat me uindica|tum esse a maiestate tua. Honoratus to the holy god Mercury. I complain to your Divinity that I have lost two wheels and four cows and many small belongings from my house. I would ask the *genius* of your Divinity that you do not permit health to the person who has done me wrong, nor (permit) him to lie or sit or drink or eat, whether (he is) man or woman, whether boy or girl, whether slave or free, unless he brings my property to me and gains my concord. With renewed prayers I ask your Divinity that my petition may immediately ?be evident that I have been vindicated by your Majesty.
75	On the Hill of Aruerius. Petitioner: anonymous. Capitals, competetent and fairly regular, 10 lines, folded four times. c.110 (max. 120) by 59 mm. data VAECOGNATO |res d(e) arca perd<i>d<i> id est |aurea{ca} pecunia et mea us(?uraria) |frumenta peto s(i) b(aro) s(i) m(ulier) s(i) p(uer) s(i) p(uella) |ut his non [li]ceat nec dorm[i]re |nec uig(ilare) nec [s]ed(ere) nec iacer[e] |donec ista omnia ad tem[p]lum |Mer(curii) mont<e> Arueri perferat |?[f]ec[i] indiciuas quod |[s]ortis i<n>dicauerint. Given ?to ... the property (which) I have lost from (my) strongbox, that is gold money and my ?interest on the crop. I seek that, whether man or woman, whether boy or girl, they be not allowed to sleep or be wakeful, to sit or to lie, until he bring all those things to the temple of Mercury on the Hill of Aruerius .... rewards for information ...?they shall have informed.

No.	Tab. Uley
76	Malice towards beasts of burden. Petitioner: anonymous. fluent Old Roman Cursive, eight lines on the inner face (a), four lines on the outer face (b), folded twice. 79 by 75 mm. *(a)* [deo] sancto Mercuri[o qu]er[or] |tibi de illis qui mihi male |cog[i]tant et male faciunt |supra ed[iti]s iumen[tis] |si servus si liber si m[ascel] |si [fem]ina ut [n]on illis per|mittas nec stare nec |sedere nec bibere *(b)* nec manducar[e] n[e]c h[as] |iras redemere possit |nessi sanguine suo *AENE* |*traces* |*uacat* To the holy god Mercury. I complain to you about those who are thinking evil towards me and doing evil to the above-mentioned beasts of burden, whether slave or free, whether male or female. May you not permit them to stand or sit, to drink or eat, or be able to redeem these (causes of) anger unless with their own blood ...

No.	Tab. Uley
78	Reclaiming 100,000 denarii. Petitioner: anonymous. Old Roman Cursive by a practised hand, seventeen lines on the inner face (a); fourteen lines on the outer face (b), rolled up. 63 by 144 mm. *(a)* deo sa<n>cto Mercurio Arue|rio t[ib]i commendo Mannei|um <exec>rabile<m> qui mihi frau|dem fecit de denar<i>is illis |quos [mih]i debebat dono |et t[ib]i de pecunia huius |temporis denarium |centum milia quae obd[o] |of<f>ero destino deputo |deo Mercurio Arueriaco |ut hoc in fanum et th<e>n|saurum potent{en}issi[mi] |dei perferat quod [si] |hoc facere contem[pse]|rit tunc tu Mercuri[e] |Arueriace u[t int]|ercepera[s...] *(b)* uigiliam morbis |incognitis [u]a[l]itu|dinibus aduersis lege |[c]ontraria lan[gue]ant |su{u}i omnes auertant |seminudi edentuli tre|muli podagrici sine |cuiusque hominis mis|{s}erico<r>dia ex situ turpissi|mo finiantur nec te |[d]omine prius propi|[ti]um habeant quam |[...].ium ha[be]|[ant] (a) To the holy god Mercury Aruerius. I commit to you the execrable Manneius who has done me wrong concerning those *denarii* which he owed me. And from the money of this time I give you one hundred thousand *denarii,* which I give, offer, destine, assign to the god Mercury Arueriacus, that he bring this to the temple and the treasury of the most powerful god. But [if] he shall scorn to do this, then you, Mercury Arueriacus, ... had cut short ... (b) May his (family) languish in sleeplessness with unknown ailments, adverse indispositions, the law against them. May they repel everybody, half-naked, toothless, trembling, gouty, without the pity of anyone. May they be finished out of the most disgusting state, and not find you merciful, Lord, before they have ...

Bibliography

Primary Sources

Bloomberg Tablets

Tomlin, Roger S. O. *Roman London's First Voices: Writing Tablets from the Bloomberg Excavations, 2010–14*. London: Museum of London Archaeology, 2016. https://romaninscriptionsofbritain.org/tablondbloomberg.

Vindolanda Tablets

Bowman, Alan K., and J. David Thomas. "Tabulae Vindolandenses – Vol. I (1983) | Roman Inscriptions of Britain." 2019. https://romaninscriptionsofbritain.org/tabvindol/vol-I.

———. "Tabulae Vindolandenses – Vol. II (1994) | Roman Inscriptions of Britain." 2019. https://romaninscriptionsofbritain.org/tabvindol/vol-II.

———. "Tabulae Vindolandenses – Vol. III (2003) | Roman Inscriptions of Britain." 2019. https://romaninscriptionsofbritain.org/tabvindol/vol-III.

Bowman, Alan K., J. David Thomas, and Roger S. O. Tomlin. "Tabulae Vindolandenses – Vol. IV, Parts 1 (2010), 2 (2011), and 3 (2019) | Roman Inscriptions of Britain." 2019. https://romaninscriptionsofbritain.org/tabvindol/vol-IV. All at https://romaninscriptionsofbritain.org/tabvindol.

Uley Tablets

Tomlin, Roger S. O. *The Uley Tablets: Roman Curse Tablets from the Temple of Mercury at Uley (Gloucestershire)*. Oxford Studies in Ancient Documents. Oxford: Oxford University Press, 2024.

———. "The Inscribed Lead Tablets: An Interim Report." In *The Uley Shrines: Excavation of a Ritual Complex on West Hill, Uley*, edited by Ann Woodward and Peter E. Leach,

17:113–30. Archaeological Report (English Heritage). London: English Heritage in association with British Museum, 1993.

———. *Britannia*, 1989, 1992, 1993, 1995, 1996, 1998, 2015, 2016, 2017, 2020, 2021.

———. "Writing to the Gods in Roman Britain." In *Becoming Roman, Writing Latin? Literacy and Epigraphy in the Roman West*, edited by A. E. Cooley, 48:165–79. Journal of Roman Archaeology Supplementary Series. Portsmouth, Rhode Island: Journal of Roman Archaeology, 2002.

Sánchez Natalías, Celia. *Sylloge of Defixiones from the Roman West. Volumes I and II: A Comprehensive Collection of Curse Tablets from the Fourth Century BCE to the Fifth Century CE.* Oxford: British Archaeological Reports, 2022.

Urbanová, Daniela. *Latin Curse Tablets of the Roman Empire.* Translated by Natalia Gachallova. Innsbruck: Innsbrucker Beiträge zur Kulturwissenschaft, 2018.

History of Rome and Britannia

Augustus, *Res Gestae divi Augusti: πράξεις τε καὶ δωρεαὶ Σεβαστοῦ θεοῦ*. Cooley, Alison E. *Res Gestae Divi Augusti: Text, Translation and Commentary*. Cambridge: Cambridge University Press, 2009.

Caesar. *Bellum Gallicum. The Gallic War.* Edited and translated by H. J. Edwards. Loeb Classical Library 72. Cambridge: Harvard University Press, 1917.

———. *War Commentaries of Caesar.* Translated by Rex Warner. New York: Mentor Books, 1960.

Cassius Dio. *Roman History, Books: 39, 40, 49, 53, 59, 60, 62, 66; Volumes III, V, VI, VII, VIII.* Translated by Earnest Cary and Herbert B. Foster. Loeb Classical Library 53, 82, 83, 175, 176. Cambridge: Harvard University Press, 1914, 1917, 1917, 1924, 1925.

Josephus. *The Jewish War, Volume I: Books 1–2; Volume II: Books 3–4; Volume III: Books 5–7.* Translated by H. St J. Thackeray. Loeb Classical Library 203, 487, 210. Cambridge: Harvard University Press, 1927.

———. *The Jewish War.* Revised. Translated by G. Williamson and E. Mary Smallwood. London: Penguin, 1981.

Justinian. "Institutiones." https://www.thelatinlibrary.com/gaius.html.

———. "Digest." https://www.thelatinlibrary.com/justinian.html.

———. *Digest Volume 1.* Translated by Alan Watson. Philadelphia: University of Pennsylvania Press, 1998.

Pliny the Elder. *Natural Histories*, Volume IV, Books XII–XVI. Translated by H. Rackham. Loeb Classical Library 370. Cambridge: Harvard University Press, 1945.

Strabo. *Strabo: Geography, Vols. I, II.* Translated by Horace Leonard Jones. Loeb Classical Library 49–50. Cambridge: Harvard University Press, 1917, 1923.

Suetonius, *Lives of the Caesars, Volume I: Julius, Augustus, Tiberius, Gaius, Caligula; Volume II: Claudius, Nero, Galba, Otho, Vitellius, Vespasian, Titus, Domitian.* Translated by J. .C. Rolfe. Loeb Classical Library 31 and 38. Cambridge: Harvard University Press, 1914.

———. *Lives of the Caesars.* Translated by Catharine Edwards. Oxford: Oxford University Press, 2008.

Tacitus. "Agricola". In *Agricola, Germania, Dialogue on Oratory*, translated by M. Hutton and W. Peterson, 3–115. Loeb Classical Library 35. Cambridge: Harvard University Press, 1914.

———. *Agricola. Text, Introduction and Commentary*. Edited by R. M. Ogilvie and I. A. Richmond. Oxford: Oxford University Press, 1967.

———. *Agricola and Germania*. Revised. Translated by Harold Mattingley and J. B. Rives. London: Penguin Classics, 2009.

———. *Annals: Books 1–3; Books 4–6, 11–12; Books 13–16*. Translated by Clifford H. Moore and John Jackson. Loeb Classical Library 249, 312, 322. Cambridge: Harvard University Press, 1931, 1937, 1937.

———. *The Annals of Imperial Rome*. Revised. Translated by Michael Grant. London: Penguin, 1996.

———. *Histories, Books 1–3; Books 4–5*. Translated by Clifford H. Moore. Loeb Classical Library 111, 249. Cambridge: Harvard University Press, 1925, 1931.

———. *The Histories*. Revised. Translated by W. H. Fyfe and D. S. Levene. Oxford: Oxford University Press, 1999.

Virgil. *Aeneid: Books 1–6* and 7–12. Revised by G. P. Goold. Translated by H. Rushton Fairclough. Loeb Classical Library 63 and 64. Cambridge: Harvard University Press, 1916 and 1918.

———. *The Aeneid*. Revised. Translated by W. F. Jackson Knight. Penguin Classics. London: Penguin, 1958.

Ireland, Stanley. *Roman Britain: A Sourcebook*. 3rd edn. Routledge Sourcebooks for the Ancient World. London: Routledge, 2008. A collection of all the main literary sources in translation for the Romans in Britain.

The Bible

Aland, B. and K. et al. *Nestle-Aland, Novum Testamentum Graece*, 28th Revised Edition. Stuttgart. Stuttgart: Deutsche Bibelgesellschaft. 2012.

Weber, Robert, *Biblia Sacra Iuxta Vulgatam Versionem*. 3rd rev. ed. Stuttgart: Deutsche Bibelgesellschaft. 1983.

New Revised Standard Version Bible (NRSV). 1989. Division of Christian Education of the National Council of the Churches of Christ in the United States of America.

Earliest Papyrus Codex containing Luke and Acts

Chester Beatty Papyrus Codex of the Gospels, Acts and the Catholic Epistles (Apostolos), P.45, 3rd Century: Centre for the Study of New Testament Manuscripts. "Manuscript P45 Centre for the Study of New Testament Manuscripts." https://manuscripts.csntm.org/manuscript/View/GA_P45.

The Alexandrian text, Greek manuscript of Luke and Acts

Codex Sinaiticus (London, British Library, Add MS 43725).
Luke: https://codexsinaiticus.org/en/manuscript.aspx?book=35,
Acts: https://codexsinaiticus.org/en/manuscript.aspx?book=51.

The Western text, bi-lingual Old Latin and Greek manuscripts of Luke and Acts

Codex Bezae (Cambridge, University Library, MS Nn.2.41).
Luke: https://cudl.lib.cam.ac.uk/view/MS-NN-00002-00041/345.
Acts: https://cudl.lib.cam.ac.uk/view/MS-NN-00002-00041/679.
The Laudian Acts (Bodleian Library MS. Laud Gr. 35).
https://digital.bodleian.ox.ac.uk/objects/55b2e494-4845-403e-9ba6-d812bda79329/

General Bibliography

Abdy, Richard Anthony. *Legion: Life in the Roman Army*. London: The British Museum, 2024.

———. *Romano-British Coin Hoards*. Shire Archaeology 82. Princes Risborough: Shire, 2002.

Adams, Edward. *The Earliest Christian Meeting Places: Almost Exclusively Houses?* London: T&T Clark, 2013.

Adams, Geoff W. "The Social and Cultural Implications of Curse Tablets [Defixiones] in Britain and on the Continent." *Studia Humaniora Tartuensia* 7 (2006) 1–15.

Adams, J. N. *An Anthology of Informal Latin, 200 BC–AD 900: Fifty Texts with Translations and Linguistic Commentary*. Cambridge: Cambridge University Press, 2016.

———. "British Latin: The Text, Interpretation and Language of the Bath Curse Tablets." *Britannia* 23 (1992) 1–26.

———. "Latin and Punic in Contact? The Case of the Bu Njem Ostraca." *Journal of Roman Studies* 84 (1994) 87–112.

———. "The Language of the Vindolanda Writing Tablets: An Interim Report." *Journal of Roman Studies* 85 (1995) 86–134.

———. "The New Vindolanda Writing-Tablets." *Classical Quarterly* 53.2 (2003) 530–75.

Albrecht, Janico, et al. "Religion in the Making: The Lived Ancient Religion Approach." *Religion* 48.4 (2018) 568–93.

Aldhouse-Green, Miranda. "Gallo-British Deities and Their Shrines." In *A Companion to Roman Britain*, edited by Malcolm Todd, 193–219. Blackwell Companions to British History. Oxford: Blackwell, 2004.

———. *Sacred Britannia: The Gods and Rituals of Roman Britain*. London: Thames & Hudson, 2018.

Alexander, Loveday. "Acts." In *The Oxford Bible Commentary*, edited by John Barton and John Muddiman, 1028–61. Oxford: Oxford University Press, 2001.

———. *Acts*. The People's Bible Commentary. Oxford: The Bible Reading Fellowship, 2006.

———. "Luke's Political Vision." *Interpretation* 66.3 (2012) 283–93.

———. "Luke's Preface in the Context of Greek Preface-Writing." *Novum Testamentum* 28.1 (1986) 48–74.

———. "Mapping Early Christianity: Acts and the Shape of Early Church History." *Interpretation* 57.2 (2003) 163–73.

———. "The Pauline Itinerary and the Archive of Theophanes." In *The New Testament and Early Christian Literature in Greco-Roman Context*, edited by John Fotopoulos, 148–62. Supplements to Novum Testamentum 122. Leiden: Brill, 2010.

Allason-Jones, Lindsay. "Health Care in the Roman North." *Britannia* 30 (1999) 133–46.

———. *Women in Roman Britain*. 2nd ed. York: Council for British Archaeology, 2005.

Allen, Denise, and Mike Bryan. *Roman Britain and Where to Find It*. Stroud, UK: Amberley, 2020.

Alston, Richard. *Soldier and Society in Roman Egypt: A Social History*. London: Routledge, 1995.

Ammerman, Nancy T. "Finding Religion in Everyday Life." *Sociology of Religion* 75 (2014) 189–207.

———. "Introduction: Observing Religious Modern Lives." In *Every Day Religion: Observing Modern Religious Lives*, edited by Nancy Ammerman, 3–18. Oxford: Oxford University Press, 2007.

Ammirati, Serena. "The Use of Wooden Tablets in the Ancient Graeco-Roman World and the Birth of the Book in Codex Form: Some Remarks." *Scripta* 6 (2013) 9–15.

Andreau, Jean. *Banking and Business in the Roman World*. Key Themes in Ancient History. Cambridge: Cambridge University Press, 1999.

ap Siôn, Tania. "Ordinary Prayer and the Rural Church: An Empirical Study of Prayer Cards." *Rural Theology* 7.1 (2009) 17–31.

———. "Prayers from the Inner City: Listening to the Prayer Board in Southwark Cathedral." *Research in the Social Scientific Study of Religion* 26 (2015) 99–119.

———. "The Power of Place: Listening to Visitors' Prayers Left in a Shrine in Rural Wales." *Rural Theology* 18.2 (2020) 87–100.

Arzt-Grabner, Peter, et al. *More Light from the Ancient East: Understanding the New Testament Through Papyri*. Papyri and the New Testament 1. Paderborn: Brill Schöningh, 2023.

Ascough, R. S. *Lydia: Paul's Cosmopolitan Hostess*. Paul's Social Network: Brothers and Sisters in Faith. Collegeville, MN: Liturgical, 2009.

"Ashmolean Museum, Heberden Coin Room." 2023. https://www.ashmolean.org/heberden-coin-room.

Astley, Jeff. *Ordinary Theology: Looking, Listening and Learning in Theology*. Explorations in Practical, Pastoral, and Empirical Theology. Farnham, VT: Ashgate, 2002.

Atkinson, Donald. "The Cirencester Word-Square." *Transactions of the Bristol and Gloucestershire Archaeological Society* 76 (1957) 21–34.

———. "The Origin and Date of the 'SATOR' Word-Square." *Journal of Ecclesiastical History* 2.1 (1951) 1–18.

Aymer, Margaret. "Acts of the Apostles." In *Women's Bible Commentary*, 3rd ed., edited by Carol A. Newsome et al., 536–45. Louisville: Westminster John Knox, 2012.

Bailey, Kenneth E. *Paul through Mediterranean Eyes: Cultural Studies in 1 Corinthians*. London: SPCK, 2011.

Baker, Patricia. "Medicine." In *The Oxford Handbook of Roman Britain*, edited by Martin Millett, Louise Revell, and Alison Moore, 555–72. Oxford Handbooks. Oxford: Oxford University Press, 2016.

Barclay, John M. G. *Jews in the Mediterranean Diaspora: From Alexander to Trajan (323 BCE–117 CE)*. Berkeley: University of California Press, 1996.

———. "Why the Roman Empire Was Insignificant to Paul." In *Pauline Churches and Diaspora Jews*, edited by John M. G. Barclay. Wissenschaftliche Untersuchungen zum Neuen Testament 275. Tübingen: Mohr Siebeck, 2011.

Barreto, Eric D. "A Gospel on the Move: Practice, Proclamation, and Place in Luke–Acts." *Interpretation* 72.2 (2018) 175–87.

Barrett, A. A. "Claudius' British Victory Arch in Rome." *Britannia* 22 (1991) 1–19.

Barrett, C. K. *Acts*. Vol. 1. International Critical Commentary. London: Bloomsbury, 1994.

———. *Acts*. Vol. 2. International Critical Commentary. London: Bloomsbury, 1998.

Batten, Alicia. "God in the Letter of James: Patron or Benefactor?" In *The Social World of the New Testament*, edited by Jerome H. Neyrey, 40–61. Peabody, MA: Hendrickson, 2008.

Bauckham, Richard. *The Gospels for All Christians: Rethinking the Gospel Audiences*. Grand Rapids: Eerdmans, 1998.

———. "For Whom Were Gospels Written?" In *The Gospel for All Christians: Rethinking the Gospel Audiences*, edited by Richard Bauckham, 9–48. Grand Rapids: Eerdmans, 1998.

———. *Jesus and the Eyewitnesses: The Gospels as Eyewitness Testimony*. Grand Rapids: Eerdmans, 2006.

Beard, Mary. *SPQR—A History of Ancient Rome*. London: Profile, 2017.

———. *The Roman Triumph*. Cambridge: Harvard University Press, 2009.

Beard, Mary, et al. *Religions of Rome*. Vol. 1, *A History*. Cambridge: Cambridge University Press, 1998.

———. *Religions of Rome*. Vol. 2, *A Sourcebook*. Cambridge: Cambridge University Press, 1998.

Bebbington, Alan. *A History of Uley Gloucestershire*. Uley, UK: The Uley Society, 2003.

Betz, Hans Dieter. *The Greek Magical Papyri in Translation*. Chicago: University of Chicago Press, 1986.

Billings, Drew W. *Acts of the Apostles and the Rhetoric of Roman Imperialism*. Cambridge: Cambridge University Press, 2017.

Binford, Lewis R. "Archaeology as Anthropology." *American Antiquity* 28.2 (1962) 217–25.

Binford, Lewis R., and Sally R. Binford. "Archaeological Perspectives." In *New Perspectives in Archaeology*, edited by Lewis R. Binford and Sally R. Binford, 5–32. Chicago: Aldine, 1968.

Birley, Andrew, and Justin Blake. *Vindolanda Research Report: The Excavations of 2005–2006*. Hexham, UK: Vindolanda Trust, 2007.

Birley, Anthony R. "A Case of Eye Disease (Lippitudo) on the Roman Frontier in Britain." *Documenta Ophthalmologica* 81 (1992) 111–19.

———. *Garrison Life at Vindolanda: A Band of Brothers*. Stroud, UK: Tempus, 2002.

———. "Officers of the Second Augustan Legion in Britain." In *Birthday of the Eagle: The Second Augustan Legion and the Roman Military Machine*, edited by Richard J. Brewer, 103–7. Cardiff, UK: Amgueddfeydd ac Orielau Cenedlaethol Cymru: National Museums and Galleries of Wales, 2002.

———. "A Review of the Tablets by Periods." In *The Early Wooden Forts. Reports on the Auxiliaries, the Writing Tablets, Inscriptions, Brands and Graffiti*, edited by Eric Birley, Robin Birley, and Anthony R. Birley, 26–88. Carvoran, UK: Roman Army Museum, 1993.

———. "Vindolanda: Notes on Some New Writing Tablets." *Zeitschrift für Papyrologie und Epigraphik* 88 (1991) 87–102.

Birley, Barbara. "The Curator's Favourite Shoes." *The Collection*, https://www.vindolanda.com/blog/the-curators-favourite-shoes.

Birley, Robin. *Vindolanda: Extraordinary Records of Daily Life on the Northern Frontier.* Greenhead, UK: Roman Army Museum Publications for the Vindolanda Trust, 2015.

———. *Vindolanda: A Roman Frontier Fort on Hadrian's Wall.* Stroud, UK: Amberley, 2009.

———. *Writing Materials.* IV. Vindolanda Research Reports New Series. Carvoran, UK: Roman Army Museum Publications for the Vindolanda Trust, 1999.

Birley, Robin, and Anthony R. Birley. "Four New Writing Tablets from Vindolanda." *Zeitschrift für Papyrologie und Epigraphik* 100 (1994) 431–46.

Blair, Ian, et al. "Wells and Bucket-Chains: Unforeseen Elements of Water Supply in Early Roman London." *Britannia* 37 (2006) 1–52.

Bland, Roger. "Coin Hoards and Hoarding (4): The Denarius Period, AD 69–238." *British Numismatic Journal* 86 (2016) 68–95.

Blansdorf, Jurgen. "The Defixiones from the Sanctuary of Isis and Mater Magna in Mainz." In *Magical Practice in the Latin West*, edited by Richard Lindsay Gordon and Marco Simón Francisco, 141–90. Religions in the Graeco-Roman World 168. Leiden: Brill, 2010.

———. "The Texts from the Fons Annae Perennae." In *Magical Practice in the Latin West*, edited by Richard Lindsay Gordon and Marco Simón Francisco, 215–44. Religions in the Graeco-Roman World 168. Leiden: Brill, 2010.

Bonz, Marianne Palmer. *The Past as Legacy: Luke–Acts and Ancient Epic.* Minneapolis: Fortress, 2000.

Bowman, Alan K. *Life and Letters on the Roman Frontier: Vindolanda and Its People.* Rev., exp. and upd. Ed. London: British Museum, 2003.

Bowman, Alan K., and J. David Thomas. "New Writing Tablets from Vindolanda." *Britannia* 27 (1997) 299–328.

———. "The Format of the Vindolanda Tablets | Roman Inscriptions of Britain." 1983. https://romaninscriptionsofbritain.org/tabvindol/vol-I/introduction/ch2-c.

———. "Tabulae Vindolandenses – Vol. I (1983) | Roman Inscriptions of Britain." 2019. https://romaninscriptionsofbritain.org/tabvindol/vol-I.

———. "Tabulae Vindolandenses – Vol. II (1994) | Roman Inscriptions of Britain." 2019. https://romaninscriptionsofbritain.org/tabvindol/vol-II.

———. "Tabulae Vindolandenses – Vol. III (2003) | Roman Inscriptions of Britain." 2019. https://romaninscriptionsofbritain.org/tabvindol/vol-III.

———. *Vindolanda: The Latin Writing-Tablets.* Britannia Monograph Series 4. London: Society for the Promotion of Roman Studies, 1983.

Bowman, Alan K., et al. *Vindolanda Writing-Tablets: (Tabulae Vindolandenses II).* London: British Museum, 1994.

Bowman, Alan K., et al. *The Vindolanda Writing-Tablets (Tabulae Vindolandenses III).* London: British Museum, 2003.

Bowman, Alan K., et al. "Roman Inscriptions of Britain / Vindolanda Tablets / Vol. IV." 2019. https://romaninscriptionsofbritain.org/tabvindol/vol-IV/texts.

———. "Tabulae Vindolandenses – Vol. IV, Parts 1 (2010), 2 (2011), and 3 (2019) | Roman Inscriptions of Britain." 2019. https://romaninscriptionsofbritain.org/tabvindol/vol-IV.

———. "The Vindolanda Writing-Tablets (Tabulae Vindolandenses IV, Part 1)." *Britannia* 41 (2010) 187–224.

———. "The Vindolanda Writing-Tablets (Tabulae Vindolandenses IV, Part 2)." *Britannia* 42 (2011) 113–44.

———. "The Vindolanda Writing-Tablets (Tabulae Vindolandenses IV, Part 3): New Letters of Iulius Verecundus." *Britannia* 50 (2019) 225–51.

Box, Roger. "Plated Roman Denarii and Unofficial Coin Production in Claudian Britain." BA thesis, University of Birmingham, 1999.

Bradley, Keith. *Slavery and Society at Rome*. Key Themes in Ancient History. Cambridge: Cambridge University Press, 1994.

Brawley, Robert L. *Luke: A Social Identity Commentary*. T&T Clark Social Identity Commentaries on the New Testament. London: T&T Clark, 2020.

Breeze, Andrew. "Legionum Urbs and the British Martyrs Aaron and Julius." *Voprosy Onomastiki* 13 (2016) 30–42.

Breeze, David J., ed. "Collection: Frontiers of the Roman Empire." 2025. https://www.archaeopress.com/Archaeopress/Collection/Frontiers-of-the-Roman-Empire.

———. *The Frontiers of Imperial Rome*. Barnsley, UK: Pen & Sword Military, 2011.

———. *Frontiers of the Roman Empire: Hadrian's Wall*. Oxford: Archaeopress Archaeology, 2023.

———. *Frontiers of the Roman Empire: The Hinterland of Hadrian's Wall*. Oxford: Archaeopress Archaeology, 2023.

———. "Hadrian's Wall Today and in the Future." In *Hadrian's Wall: A Study in Archaeological Exploration and Interpretation. The Rhind Lectures 2019*, 151–73. Oxford: Archaeopress, 2019.

———. "The Impact of Rome: Life on and around the Frontier." In *Hadrian's Wall: A Study in Archaeological Exploration and Interpretation. The Rhind Lectures 2019*, 122–50. Oxford: Archaeopress, 2019.

———. "Life in the Fort." In *Bearsden: The Story of a Roman Fort*, 42–58. Oxford: Archaeopress, 2016.

———. "The Purpose and Operation of Hadrian's Wall under Hadrian." In *Hadrian's Wall: A Study in Archaeological Exploration and Interpretation. The Rhind Lectures 2019*, 61–92. Oxford: Archaeopress, 2019.

———. "The Value of Studying Roman Frontiers." *Theoretical Roman Archaeology Journal* 1.1 (2018) 1–17.

Breeze, David J., et al. *Frontiers of the Roman Empire: The Eastern Frontiers*. Oxford: Archaeopress, 2022.

Breeze, David J., and Peter Guest. *Frontiers of the Roman Empire, Ffiniau'r Ymerodraeth Rufeinig: The Roman Frontiers in Wales, Ffiniau Rhufeinig Cymru*. Oxford: Archaeopress, 2022.

Breeze, David J., et al. *A History of the Congress of Roman Frontier Studies 1949–2022*. Oxford: Archaeopress, 2022.

Breeze, David J., et al. *Frontiers of the Roman Empire: The African Frontiers*. Edinburgh: Society for Libyan Studies, 2013.

Brewer, Richard J. *Caerwent Roman Town*. Cardiff: Cadw, Welsh Assembly Government, 2006.

"British Museum, Department of Coins and Medals." London: The British Museum, 2023. https://www.britishmuseum.org/our-work/departments/coins-and-medals.

"The British Museum." 2025. https://www.britishmuseum.org.

Brown, Alec, and Lewis Burton. "Learning from Prayer Requests in a Rural Church: An Exercise in Ordinary Theology." *Rural Theology* 5.1 (2007) 45–52.

Brown, Jeannine K. *The Gospels as Stories.* Grand Rapids: Baker Academic, 2020.

Bruce, F. F. *The Acts of the Apostles.* 3rd revised and enlarged. Leicester: Apollos, 1990.

Bruhn, James, and Nick Hodgson. "The Social and Economic Impact of Hadrian's Wall on the Frontier Zone in Britain." *Britannia* 53 (2022) 125–57.

Brunt, P. A. "The Revenues of Rome." *Journal of Roman Studies* 71 (1981) 161–72.

Bryan, Jessica, et al. "The Archaeological Context." In *Roman London's First Voices: Writing Tablets from the Bloomberg Excavations 2010–2014*, 31–51. London: Museum of London Archaeology, 2016.

Burrell, Barbara. "'Curse Tablets' from Caesarea." *Near Eastern Archaeology* 61.2 (1998) 128.

———. "Herod's Caesarea On Sebastos: Urban Structures and Influences." In *Herod and Augustus: Papers Presented at the IJS Conference, 21st–23rd June 2005*, edited by David Jacobson and Nikos Kokkinos, 215–34. IJS Studies in Judaica. Leiden: Brill, 2009.

Burridge, Richard A. "The Genre of Acts – Revisited." In *Reading Acts Today: Essays in Honour of Loveday C. A. Alexander*, edited by Steve Walton, Thomas E. Phillips, Lloyd K. Pietersen, and F. Scott Spencer, 3–28. The Library of New Testament Studies. London: T&T Clark, 2011.

———. *What Are the Gospels? A Comparison with Graeco-Roman Biography.* 25th anniversary edition. Waco, Texas: Baylor University Press, 2018.

Burton, Lewis. "Prayers on a Prayer Tree: Ordinary Theology from a Tourist Village." *Rural Theology* 8.1 (2010) 62–77.

Cadbury, Henry Joel. *The Making of Luke–Acts.* 2nd ed. London: S.P.C.K., 1968.

Caird, G. B. *The Language and Imagery of the Bible.* Philadelphia: Westminster, 1980.

———. *Saint Luke.* Pelican Gospel Commentaries. London: Penguin, 1963.

Calpino, Teresa J. "Crafting Gender in Acts: Tabitha and Lydia." In *Acts of the Apostles*, edited by Linda M. Maloney and Ivoni Richter Reimer, 45:222–26. Wisdom Commentary. Collegeville, MN: Liturgical, 2022.

Campbell, Douglas A. "Chronology." In *T&T Clark Handbook to the Historical Paul*, edited by Ryan S. Schellenberg and Heidi Wendt, 265–86. London: T&T Clark, 2022.

Carter, Warren. "Aquatic Display: Navigating the Roman Imperial World in Acts 27." *New Testament Studies* 62 (2016) 79–96.

———. *Jesus and the Empire of God: Reading the Gospels in the Roman Empire.* Cascade Companions. Eugene, OR: Cascade Books, 2021.

———. *The Roman Empire and the New Testament: An Essential Guide.* Nashville: Abingdon, 2006.

Cassidy, Richard J. *Christians and Roman Rule in the New Testament: New Perspectives.* New York: Crossroad, 2001.

———. *Jesus, Politics, and Society: A Study of Luke's Gospel.* 1978. Reprint, Eugene, Oregon: Wipf & Stock, 2015.

———. *Society and Politics in the Acts of the Apostles.* 1987. Reprint, Eugene, OR: Wipf & Stock, 2015.

"Celtic Coin Index." 2022. https://cci.arch.ox.ac.uk/.

"Centre for the Study of Ancient Documents." 2015. http://www.csad.ox.ac.uk/.

Charles, Michael B., and Michael Singleton. "Claudius, Elephants and Britain: Making Sense of Cassius Dio 60.21.2." *Britannia* 53 (2022) 173–84.

"Chi Rho Dish from Caerwent: BBC – A History of the World." A History of the World, 2022. https://www.bbc.co.uk/ahistoryoftheworld/objects/EU7DWYC6R4uI4_Su_nB2aw.

Clark, John, and Harvey Sheldon. *Londinium and Beyond: Essays on Roman London and Its Hinterland for Harvey Sheldon*. CBA Research Report 156. York: Council for British Archaeology, 2008.

Cleary, S. E. *Chedworth: Life in a Roman Villa*. Stroud, UK: History, 2013.

———. *Map of Roman Britain*. 6th ed. Southampton, UK: Ordnance Survey, 2011.

Cleaves, R. W. *The Love of the Lover of Souls: Last Sermons*. Leicester: Clarendon Park Congregational Church, 1980.

Cleaves, Richard. "Reading the New Testament in Roman Britain." In *The Early Christian World*, 2nd ed., edited by Philip F. Esler, 329–54. Abingdon: Routledge, 2017.

"*Colchester Castle*." Colchester Museums, 2023. https://colchester.cimuseums.org.uk/visit/colchester-castle/.

Collingwood, R. G. *The Idea of History*. Oxford: Oxford University Press, 1946.

Collingwood, R. G., and John Nowell Linton Myres. *Roman Britain and English Settlements*. Oxford: Oxford University Press, 1936.

Conzelmann, Hans. *Acts of the Apostles: A Commentary on the Acts of the Apostles*. Hermeneia. Philadelphia: Fortress, 1987.

Cooley, Alison E. *The Cambridge Manual of Latin Epigraphy*. Cambridge: Cambridge University Press, 2012.

———. *Res Gestae Divi Augusti: Text, Translation and Commentary*. Cambridge: Cambridge University Press, 2009.

———. "The Role of the Non-Elite in Spreading Latin in Roman Britain." In *Social Factors in the Latinization of the Roman West*, edited by Alex Mullen, 99–116. Oxford: Oxford University Press, 2023.

Cooley, Alison E., and M. G. L. Cooley. *Pompeii and Herculaneum: A Sourcebook*. 2nd edn. Routledge Sourcebooks for the Ancient World. London: Routledge, 2014.

Copeland, T. *Roman Gloucestershire*. Stroud, UK: History, 2011.

"Corinium Museum Acrostic." Corinium Museum, Cirencester, 2021. https://coriniummuseum.org/object/b950-2/.

"Corinium Museum." Corinium Museum, Cirencester, 2022. https://coriniummuseum.org/.

Cotton, Hannah. "A Cancelled Marriage Contract from the Judaean Desert." *Journal of Roman Studies* 84 (1994) 64–86.

———. "The Guardianship of Jesus Son of Babatha: Roman and Local Law in the Province of Arabia." *Journal of Roman Studies* 83 (1993) 94–108.

Cousins, Eleri H. *The Sanctuary at Bath in the Roman Empire*. Cambridge Classical Studies. Cambridge: Cambridge University Press, 2020.

Creighton, John. *Coins and Power in Late Iron Age Britain*. New Studies in Archaeology. Cambridge: Cambridge University Press, 2000.

Crook, Zeba A. *Reconceptualising Conversion: Patronage, Loyalty, and Conversion in the Religions of the Ancient Mediterranean*. Berlin, Boston: De Gruyter, 2004.

Crossan, John Dominic. *God and Empire: Jesus Against Rome, Then and Now*. New York: Harper Collins, 2007.

Crossan, John Dominic, and Jonathan L. Reed. *Excavating Jesus: Beneath the Stones, Behind the Texts*. Revised and Updated. San Francisco: HarperOne, 2001.

———. *In Search of Paul*. London: SPCK, 2005.

Crummy, Philip. *City of Victory: The Story of Colchester – Britain's First Roman Town*. Colchester: Colchester Archaeological Trust, 1997.

Crummy, Philip, and H. R. Hurst. *The Coloniae of Roman Britain: New Studies and a Review, Papers of the Conference Held at Gloucester on 5–6 July 1997*. Journal of Roman Archaeology Supplementary Series 36. Portsmouth, Rhode Island: Journal of Roman Archaeology, 1999.

Crump, David Michael. "Jesus the Intercessor: Prayer and Christology in Luke–Acts." PhD diss., University of Aberdeen, 1988.

Cruse, A. *Roman Medicine*. Stroud, UK: Tempus, 2004.

———. Review of *Roman Medicine*, by Rebecca Flemming. Britannia 37 (2006) 502–3.

Cuff, David B. "The King of the Batavians: Remarks on Tab. Vindol. III, 628." *Britannia* 42 (2011) 145–56.

Cunliffe, Barry W. *Britain Begins*. Oxford: Oxford University Press, 2012.

———. *Fishbourne Roman Palace*. Rev. and upd. ed. Stroud, UK: Tempus, 1998.

———. *Roman Bath Discovered*. New. Stroud, UK: Tempus, 2000.

D'Angelo, Mary Rose. "The ANHP Question in Luke–Acts." In *A Feminist Companion to Luke*, edited by Amy-Jill Levine and Marianne Blickenstaff, 44–69. Feminist Companion to the New Testament and Early Christian Writings 3. London: Sheffield Academic, 2002.

———. "Women in Luke–Acts: A Redactional View." *Journal of Biblical Literature* 109.3 (1990) 441–61.

Daniel, Robert W., and Gideon Sulimani. "A New Curse Tablet from Jerusalem." *Zeitschrift für Papyrologie und Epigraphik* 171 (2009) 123–28.

Dannell, Geoffrey B., and John Peter Wild. *Longthorpe II: The Military Works-Depot: An Episode in Landscape History*. Vol. 8. Britannia Monograph Series. London: Society for the Promotion of Roman Studies, 1987.

Darvill, Timothy. "The ARVERI and TPLF Stamped Roman Ceramic Tiles in the Cotswolds and Severn Valley." *The Transactions of the Bristol and Gloucestershire Archaeological Society* 100 (1982) 47–63.

Davenport, Peter. *Roman Bath: A New History and Archaeology of Aquae Sulis*. Stroud, UK: History, 2021.

Davies, John Reuben. "Old Testament Personal Names among the Britons: Their Occurrence and Significance before the Twelfth Century." *Viator* 43.1 (2012) 175–92.

Davies, R. W. "The Medici of the Roman Armed Forces." *Epigraphische Studien* 8 (1969) 83–99.

———. "Some More Military Medici." *Epigraphische Studien* 9 (1972) 1–11.

———. "The Roman Military Diet." *Britannia* 2 (1971) 122–42.

de Boer, Esther A. "The Lukan Mary Magdalene and the Other Women Following Jesus." In *A Feminist Companion to Luke*, edited by Amy-Jill Levine and Marianne Blickenstaff, 140–60. Feminist Companion to the New Testament and Early Christian Writings 3. London: Sheffield Academic, 2002.

de la Bédoyère, Guy. *Gladius: Living, Fighting and Dying in the Roman Army*. London: Abacus, 2021.

———. *Gods with Thunderbolts: Religion in Roman Britain*. Tempus Series. Stroud, UK: History, 2007.

———. *The Real Lives of Roman Britain*. New Haven: Yale University Press, 2016.

———. *Roman Britain: A New History*. Revised. London: Thames & Hudson, 2013.

Dickey, Eleanor. "The Greek Address System of the Roman Period and Its Relationship to Latin." *Classical Quarterly* 54.2 (2004) 494–527.

Dingle, Charlie. "Market Hall Museum." Warwickshire Heritage and Culture, 2023. https://heritage.warwickshire.gov.uk/markethallmuseum.

Dolansky, Fanny. "Celebrating the Saturnalia: Religious Ritual and Roman Domestic Life." In *A Companion to Families in the Greek and Roman Worlds*, edited by Beryl Rawson, 488–503. Blackwell Companions to the Ancient World. Chichester: Wiley-Blackwell, 2011.

———. "Reconsidering the Matronalia and Women's Rites." *Classical World* 104.2 (2011) 191–209.

Dreghorn, William. *Geology Explained in the Severn Vale and Cotswolds*. Newton Abbott: David and Charles, 1967.

Drinkwater, John. "Geology and Geography." In *The Uley Shrines: Excavation of a Ritual Complex on West Hill, Uley, Gloucestershire 1977–9*, edited by Ann Woodward and Peter E. Leach, 3–5. London: English Heritage in association with British Museum, 1993.

du Plessis, Paul J. "The Bloomberg Tablets and Roman Law." The Edinburgh Legal History Blog, 2016.

———. *Letting and Hiring in Roman Legal Thought: 27 BCE–284 CE*. Leiden: Brill, 2012.

———. "'Provincial Law' in Britannia." In *Law in the Roman Provinces*, edited by Kimberley Czajkowski, Benedikt Eckhardt, and Meret Strothmann, 436–61. Oxford: Oxford University Press, 2020.

———. "The Roman Concept of Lex Contractus." *Roman Legal Tradition, a Journal of Ancient Medieval and Modern Civil Law* 3 (2006) 79–94.

Dupertuis, Ruben R., and Todd Penner. *Engaging Early Christian History: Reading Acts in the Second Century*. Bible World. London: Routledge, 2013.

Edwards, Brian, and Clive Anderson. *Through the British Museum: With the Bible*. 6th edn. Leominster: Day One, 2019.

Edwards, Douglas R. "Surviving the Web of Roman Power: Religion and Politics in the Acts of the Apostles, Josephus, and Chariton's Chaereas and Callirhoe." In *Images of Empire*, edited by Loveday Alexander, 179–201. Journal for the Study of the Old Testament Supplement Series 122. Sheffield: Sheffield Academic, 1991.

Eidinow, Esther. "Binding Spells on Tablets and Papyri." In *Guide to the Study of Ancient Magic*, edited by David Frankfurter, 351–87. Leiden: Brill, 2019.

Elliott, John H. *Social Scientific Criticism of the New Testament*. London: SPCK, 1995.

———. "Temple versus Household in Luke–Acts: A Contrast in Social Institutions." In *The Social World of Luke–Acts: Models for Interpretation*, edited by Jerome H. Neyrey, 211–40. Peabody, MA: Hendrickson, 1993.

Erasmus, Desiderius. *Paraphrasis D. Erasmi Roterodami In Acta Apostolorum*. Antwerp: Apud Ioannem Steelsium sub scuto Burgundiae, 1541.

Esler, Philip F. *Babatha's Orchard: The Yadin Papyri and an Ancient Jewish Family Tale Retold*. New York, NY: OUP Oxford, 2017.

———. *Community and Gospel in Luke–Acts: The Social and Political Motivations of Lucan Theology*. Cambridge: Cambridge University Press, 1987.

———. "The Dead Sea Legal Papyri, Babatha and the Gospel of Matthew." University of Gloucestershire, 2024.

———. *The Early Christian World*. 2nd ed. London: Routledge, 2017.

———. *The First Christians in Their Social Worlds: Social-Scientific Approaches to New Testament Interpretation*. London: Routledge, 1994.

———. *Modelling Early Christianity: Social-Scientific Studies of the New Testament in Its Context*. London: Routledge, 1995.

———. "Reading Matthew by the Dead Sea: Matthew 8:5–13 in Light of P. Yadin 11." *HTS Teologiese Studies / Theological Studies*, 2014. http://www.hts.org.za/index.php/HTS/article/view/2773.

———. "The Righteousness of Joseph: Interpreting Matthew 1:18–25 in Light of Judean Legal Papyri." University of Gloucestershire Eprints, 2022. https://eprints.glos.ac.uk/id/eprint/10090

Evans, Derek. *Uley Bury Gloucestershire: Programme of Archaeological Recording*. Kemble, Cirencester: Cotswold Archaeology, 2005.

"Facilis Tombstone," Colchester Castle Museum, COLEM:PC.129: https://cim-web.adlibhosting.com/ais6/Details/collect/169897.

Faraone, Christopher A. "Aeschylus' Ὕμνος Δέσμιος (Eum. 306) and Attic Judicial Curse Tablets." *Journal of Hellenic Studies* 105 (1985) 150–54.

———. "The Agonistic Context of Early Greek Binding Spells." In *Magika Hiera: Ancient Greek Magic and Religion*, edited by Christopher A. Faraone and Dirk Obbink, 3–32. Oxford: Oxford University Press, 1991.

———. "Curses, Crime Detection and Conflict Resolution at the Festival of Demeter Thesmophoros." *Journal of Hellenic Studies* 131 (2011) 25–44.

Ferrándiz, Emilia Mataix. "What Is Law? In the Context of Roman Trading Ports." Presented at the Institute of Classical Studies, Classical Archaeology Seminar Series, University of London School of Advanced Studies, 2021.

Fitzmyer, Joseph A. *The Acts of the Apostles*. The Anchor Bible. New York: Doubleday, 1998.

———. *The Gospel According to Luke I–IX*. The Anchor Bible. New York: Doubleday, 1970.

———. *The Gospel According to Luke X–XXIV*. The Anchor Bible. New York: Doubleday, 1985.

Franek, Juraj, and Daniela Urbanová. "'As Isis Loved Osiris, So Let Matrona Love Theodoros. . .': Sympathetic Magic and Similia Similibus Formulae in Greek and Latin Curse Tablets (Part 2)." *Philologia Classica* 14.2 (2019) 177–207.

———. "'May Their Limbs Melt, Just as This Lead Shall Melt . . .': Sympathetic Magic and Similia Similibus Formulae in Greek and Latin Curse Tablets (Part 1)." *Philologia Classica* 14.1 (2019) 27–55.

Frere, Sheppard. *Britannia: A History of Roman Britain*. 3rd ed. London: Pimlico, 1987.

Frere, Sheppard et al. *Inscriptions of Roman Britain*. 3rd ed. London Association of Classical Teachers Original Records 4. London: London Association of Classical Teachers, 1995.

Frere, Shepard, and Roger S. O. Tomlin, eds. *The Roman Inscriptions of Britain, Volume II Instrumentum Domesticum, Fascicule 4*. Gloucester: Alan Sutton, 1992.

Frier, Bruce W. *A Casebook on the Roman Law of Contracts*. New York: Oxford University Press, 2021.

Gager, John G. *Curse Tablets and Binding Spells from the Ancient World*. Oxford: Oxford University Press, 1992.

———. "Curse Tablets and Binding Spells in the Greco-Roman World." In *The Meanings of Magic from the Bible to Buffalo Bill*, edited by Amy Wygant, 69–87. Oxford: Berghahn, 2006.

Gamble, Clive. *Archaeology: The Basics*. London: Routledge, 2001.

Gardner, Carlotta. "Metalworking Crucibles in Roman Britain." PhD diss., University College London, 2018.

Garnsey, Peter. "The Lex Iulia and Appeal under the Empire." *Journal of Roman Studies* 56 (1966) 167–89.

Gasparini, Valentino, et al., eds. *Lived Religion in the Ancient Mediterranean World: Approaching Religious Transformations from Archaeology, History and Classics*. Berlin; Boston: De Gruyter, 2020.

"Gateway to Britannia: Richborough's Monumental Arch." *English Heritage*. https://www.english-heritage.org.uk/visit/places/richborough-roman-fort-and-amphitheatre/history-and-stories/gateway-britannia/.

Gaventa, Beverly Roberts. *The Acts of the Apostles*. Abingdon New Testament Commentaries. Nashville, Tennessee: Abingdon, 2003.

Geertz, Clifford. *Local Knowledge: Further Essays in Interpretive Anthropology*. New York: Basic Books, 1983.

Gilbert, Gary. "Roman Propaganda and Christian Identity in the Worldview of Luke–Acts." In *Contextualizing Acts: Lukan Narrative and Greco-Roman Discourse*, edited by Todd Penner and Caroline Vander Stichele, 233–56. SBL Symposium Series 20. Atlanta: Society of Biblical Literature, 2003.

Goldsworthy, Adrian. *The Complete Roman Army*. London: Thames & Hudson, 2015.

Goldsworthy, Adrian, et al., eds. *The Roman Army as a Community*. Journal of Roman Archaeology Supplementary Series 34. Portsmouth, RI: Journal of Roman Archaeology, 1999.

Goodburn, Damian, and Owen Humphreys. "The Manufacture of Waxed Stylus Writing Tablets in Roman London." In *Roman London's First Voices*, edited by Roger S. O. Tomlin, 8–15. MOLA Monograph 72. London: Museum of London Archaeology, 2016.

Goodburn, Roger. *The Roman Villa, Chedworth*. London: The National Trust, 1979.

Gordon, Richard. "Gods, Guilt and Suffering: Psychological Aspects of Cursing in the North-West Provinces of the Roman Empire." *Acta Classica Universitatis Scientiarum Debreceniensis* 49 (2013) 255–81.

———. "Imaginative Force and Verbal Energy in Latin Curse-Tablets." In *Litterae Magicae: Studies for R. S. O. Tomlin*, edited by Celia Sánchez Natalías, 111–30. Supplementa MHNH. Zaragosa: Libros Portico, 2019.

Grabbe, Lester L. *Judaism from Cyrus to Hadrian*. London: SCM, 1994.

Green, Joel B. "Luke–Acts, or Luke and Acts? A Reaffirmation of Narrative Unity." In *Reading Acts Today: Essays in Honour of Loveday C. A. Alexander*, edited by Steve Walton et al. 101–19. The Library of New Testament Studies. London: T&T Clark, 2011.

———. *The Gospel of Luke*. New International Commentary on the New Testament. Grand Rapids: Eerdmans, 1997.

Greene, Elizabeth M. "Female Networks in Military Communities in the Roman West: A View from the Vindolanda Tablets." In *Women and the Roman City in the Latin West*, edited by Emily Hemelrijk and Greg Woolf, 369–90. Leiden; Boston: Brill, 2013.

———. "Sulpicia Lepidina and Elizabeth Custer: A Cross-Cultural Analogy for the Social Roles of Women on a Military Frontier." In *Theoretical Roman Archaeology Conference 2011*, edited by Mary Duggan et al., 105–14. Oxford: Oxbow, 2012.

———. "Women and Families in the Auxiliary Military Communities of the Roman West in the First and Second Centuries AD." PhD diss., University of North Carolina at Chapel Hill, 2011.

Gregson, Fiona J. R. *Everything in Common? The Theology and Practice of the Sharing of Possessions in Community in the New Testament*. Eugene, OR: Pickwick Publications, 2017.

Guéraud, Octave. "Ostraca Grecs et Latins de l'Wâdi Fawâkhir." *Bulletin de l'Institut Français d'Archéologie Orientale* 41 (1941) 141–96.

Guest, Peter. "The Forum-Basilica at Caerwent (Venta Silurum): A History of the Roman Silures." *Britannia* 53 (2022) 227–67.

———. *The Roman Frontiers in Wales: Ffiniau Rhufeinig Cymru*. Oxford: Archaeopress, 2022.

Haines-Eitzen, Kim. *Guardians of Letters: Literacy, Power, and the Transmitters of Early Christian Literature*. Oxford: Oxford University Press, 2000.

"Hallaton Treasure." *Harborough Museum*. https://www.harboroughmuseum.org.uk/the-museum/collections/the-hallaton-treasure/.

Hanson, K. C., and Douglas E. Oakman. *Palestine in the Time of Jesus: Social Structures and Social Conflicts*. 2nd ed. Minneapolis: Fortress, 2008.

Haran, Menahem. "Codex, Pinax and Writing Slat." *Scripta Classica Israelica* 15 (1996) 212–22.

Harlizius-Kluck, Ellen. "Textile Technology." In *A Companion to Science, Technology, and Medicine in Ancient Greece and Rome*, edited by Georgia L. Irby, 747–67. Blackwell Companions to the Ancient World: Ancient History. Oxford: Wiley Blackwell, 2016.

Harrill, J. Albert. "Paul and Slavery." In *Paul in the Greco-Roman World: A Handbook Volume II*, edited by Paul Sampley, 301–45. 2 vols. 2nd ed. London: T&T Clark, 2016.

———. *Slaves in the New Testament: Literary, Social, and Moral Dimensions*. Minneapolis: Fortress, 2006.

Harrington, Joy. *Paul of Tarsus*. Leicester, UK: Brockhampton, 1961.

Hart, Trevor. *Between the Image and the Word: Theological Engagements with Imagination, Language and Literature*. Ashgate Studies in Theology, Imagination and the Arts. London: Ashgate, 2013.

———. "Imagination and Responsible Reading." In *Renewing Biblical Interpretation*, edited by Craig Bartholomew et al., 307–34. Scripture and Hermeneutics Series. Carlisle, UK: Paternoster, 2000.

Harvey, David. *Spaces of Hope*. Edinburgh: Edinburgh University Press, 2000.

Hassall, Mark. "London: Britain's First 'University'? Education in Roman Britain." In *Londinium and Beyond: Essays on Roman London and Its Hinterland for Harvey Sheldon*, edited by John Clark, 117–20. CBA Research Report 156. London: Council for British Archaeology, 2008.

Haverfield, F. *The Romanization of Roman Britain*. 3rd ed. Oxford: Clarendon Press, 1915.

Hawkes, Jacquetta. "The Proper Study of Mankind." *Antiquity* 42.168 (1968) 255–62.

Haynes, Ian. *Blood of the Provinces: The Roman Auxilia and the Making of Provincial Society from Augustus to the Severans*. Illus. ed. Oxford: Oxford University Press, 2013.

———. "The Roman Army as a Community." In *The Roman Army as a Community*, edited by Adrian Goldsworthy, Ian Haynes, and Colin E. P. Adams. Journal of Roman Archaeology Supplementary Series 34. Portsmouth, RI: Journal of Roman Archaeology, 1999.

Heilig, Christoph. *The Apostle and the Empire*. Grand Rapids: Eerdmans, 2022.

Hemelrijk, Emily A. "City Patronesses in the Roman Empire." *Historia: Zeitschrift für Alte Geschichte* 53.2 (2004) 209–45.

Hendin, David. *Guide to Biblical Coins*. 6th ed. New York: American Numismatic Society, 2021.

Henig, Martin. "A New Star Shining over Bath." *Oxford Journal of Archaeology* 18.4 (1999) 419–25.

———. *Religion in Roman Britain*. London: Batsford, 1984.

Henig, Martin, et al., "Votive Objects: Images and Inscriptions." In *The Uley Shrines: Excavation of a Ritual Complex on West Hill, Uley, Gloucestershire 1977–9*, edited by Ann Woodward and Peter E. Leach, 89–112. London: English Heritage in association with British Museum, 1993.

Higgins, Charlotte. *Under Another Sky: Journeys in Roman Britain*. London: Random House, 2014.

Hill, Julian, and Peter Rowsome. *Roman London and the Walbrook Stream Crossing: Excavations at 1 Poultry and Vicinity, City of London*. MOLA Monograph 37. London: Museum of London Archaeology, 2011.

Hill, Stephen, and Stanley Ireland. *Roman Britain*. London: Bristol Classical, 1996.

Hillam, Jennifer. "Tree-Ring Analysis of Roman Timbers from Vindolanda, Northumberland." In *Vindolanda: The Early Wooden Forts*, edited by Carol van Driel-Murray, 3:124–36. Vindolanda Research Reports, New Series. Carvoran, Northumberland: Roman Army Museum, 2003.

Hingley, Richard. *Conquering the Ocean: The Roman Invasion of Britain*. Ancient Warfare and Civilization. Oxford: Oxford University Press, 2022.

———. "Early Studies in Roman Britain 1610–1906." In *The Oxford Handbook of Roman Britain*, edited by Martin Millett, Louise Revell, and Alison Moore, 3–21. Oxford Handbooks. Oxford: Oxford University Press, 2016.

———. *Londinium: A Biography: Roman London from Its Origin to the Fifth Century*. London: Bloomsbury Academic, 2018.

Hobbs, Richard, and Ralph Jackson. *Roman Britain: Life at the Edge of Empire*. London: British Museum, 2010.

Holford, Matthew. "The Travels of the Laudian Acts." Manuscripts from German-Speaking Lands—A Polonsky Foundation Digitization Project, 2020. https://hab.bodleian.ox.ac.uk/en/blog/blog-post-28/.

Hollman, Alexander. "A Curse Tablet from Antioch against Babylas the Greengrocer." *Zeitschrift für Papyrologie und Epigraphik* 177 (2011) 157–65.

Hopewell, David. *Roman Roads in North West Wales*. Bangor: Gwynedd Archaeological Trust, 2013.

Horsley, Richard A., ed. *Paul and Empire: Religion and Power in Roman Imperial Society*. London: Bloomsbury Academic, 1997.

Hoskins, W. G. *The Making of the English Landscape*. Pelican Books. Harmondsworth, UK: Penguin, 1970.

Houghton, H. A. G. *The Latin New Testament: A Guide to Its Early History, Texts and Manuscripts*. Oxford: Oxford University Press, 2016.

———. *A Textual Commentary on the Greek New Testament (UBS6): A Companion to the 6th Edition of the United Bible Societies' Greek New Testament*. Stuttgart: German Bible Society, 2025.

Howell, Ray. *Silures: Resistance, Resilience, Revival*. Cheltenham, UK: History, 2022.

Huebner, Sabine R. *Papyri and the Social World of the New Testament*. Cambridge: Cambridge University Press, 2019.

Hunt, Yvette. "Defixiones Workshop: Making Ancient Curse Tablets." The University of Queensland, 2014.

Hurtado, Larry W. "A 'Bookish Religion.'" In *Destroyer of the Gods: Early Christian Distinctiveness in the Roman World*, 105–41. Waco: Baylor University Press, 2016.

———. *The Earliest Christian Artifacts: Manuscripts and Christian Origins*. Illus. ed. Grand Rapids: Eerdmans, 2006.

Hylen, Susan E. *Women in the New Testament World*. Essentials of Biblical Studies. Oxford: Oxford University Press, 2019.

"I Went to Rome and All I Got You Was This Stylus!" Museum of London Archaeology, 2019. https://www.mola.org.uk/discoveries/news/i-went-rome-and-all-i-got-you-was-stylus-rare-inscribed-roman-writing-implement.

Ingemark, Dominic. "Literacy in Roman Britain: The Epigraphical Evidence." *Opuscula Romana* 25–26 (2000) 19–30.

Ingham, David, and Corinne Duhig. "Crucifixion in the Fens: Life and Death in Roman Fenstanton." *British Archaeology* (Jan–Feb, 2022) 18–29.

Ireland, Stanley. *Roman Britain: A Sourcebook*. 3rd ed. London: Routledge, 2008.

———. *The South-Warwickshire Hoard of Roman Denarii: A Catalogue*. British Archaeological Reports Series 585. Oxford: Archaeopress, 2013.

"Iron Age Coins in Britain." 2022. https://iacb.arch.ox.ac.uk/results.

"IVDAEA CAPTA Coins Reported to the Portable Antiquities Scheme." Portable Antiquities Scheme, 2022. https://finds.org.uk/database/search/results/q/ivdaea/broadperiod/ROMAN.

Jackson, Sir Rupert. *The Roman Occupation of Britain and Its Legacy*. London: Bloomsbury Academic, 2020.

Jagersma, H. *A History of Israel from Alexander the Great to Bar Kochba*. London: SCM, 1985.

James, Simon. "The Community of Soldiers: A Major Identity and Centre of Power in the Roman Empire." *Theoretical Roman Archaeology Journal* (1999) 14–25.

———. *Exploring the World of the Celts*. London: Thames & Hudson, 2005.

———. "Soldiers and Civilians: Identity and Interaction in Roman Britain." In *Britons and Romans: Advancing an Archaeological Agenda*, edited by Simon James and Martin Millett, 77–89. CBA Research Report 125. York: Council for British Archaeology, 2001.

Jarmy, Clare. "'Neath the Moth-Eaten Rag': Do Artefacts Play a Special Role for Historical Knowledge?" *Journal of Philosophy of Education* 53.2 (2019) 425–39.

Jeffers, Ann. *Magic and Divination in Ancient Palestine and Syria*. Studies in the History and Culture of the Ancient Near East 8. Leiden: Brill, 1996.

Jervell, Jacob. *The Theology of the Acts of the Apostles*. New Tesament Theoogy. Cambridge: Cambridge University Press, 1996.

"Jewry Wall—A Real Roman Experience." 2025. https://www.jewrywall.com.

Johnson, Tom. "The Use of Celtic Coinage in Early Roman London: A Re-Interpretation of Bloomberg Wax Tablet 31." *Britannia* 54 (2023) 3–22.

Johnston, David. *Roman Law in Context*. 2nd ed. Key Themes in Ancient History. Cambridge: Cambridge University Press, 2022.

Jones, Barri, and David Mattingly. *An Atlas of Roman Britain*. Oxford: Blackwell, 1990.

Jones, David. *The Bankers of Puteoli: Financing Trade & Industry in the Roman World*. Stroud, UK: Tempus, 2006.

Jordan, D. R. "A Survey of Greek Defixiones not Included in the Special Corpora." *Greek, Roman, and Byzantine Studies* 26.2 (1985) 151–97.

Kahl, Brigitte. "Acts of the Apostles: Pro(to)-Imperial Script and Hidden Transcript." In *In the Shadow of Empire: Reclaiming the Bible as a History of Faithful Resistance*, edited by Richard A. Horsley, 137–56. Louisville: Westminster John Knox, 2008.

———. "Reading Luke Against Luke: Non-Uniformity of Text, Hermeneutics of Conspiracy and the 'Scriptural Principle' in Luke 1." In *A Feminist Companion to Luke*, edited by Amy-Jill Levine, 70–88. Feminist Companion to the New Testament and Early Christian Writings 3. London: Sheffield Academic, 2002.

Karris, Robert J. "Women and Discipleship in Luke." In *A Feminist Companion to Luke*, edited by Amy-Jill Levine and Marianne Blickenstaff. Feminist Companion to the New Testament and Early Christian Writings 3. London: Sheffield Academic, 2002.

Keener, Craig S. *Acts*. New Cambridge Bible Commentary. Cambridge: Cambridge University Press, 2020.

Keith, Chris. *Jesus' Literacy: Scribal Culture and the Teacher from Galilee*. Library of New Testament Studies. London: T&T Clark, 2011.

———. *The Pericope Adulterae, the Gospel of John, and the Literacy of Jesus*. New Testament Tools, Studies and Documents 38. Leiden: Brill, 2009.

Keller, Otto, ed. *Pseudacronis Scholia in Horatium Vetustiora*. Bibliotheca scriptorum Graecorum et Romanorum Teubneriana. Leipzig: Teubner, 1902.

Kellová, Michaela. "Oriental Cults and Curse Tablets in Europe." *Graeco-Latina Brunensia* 24.2 (2019) 97–111.

Kent, Benedict H. M. "Curses in Acts: Hearing the Apostles' Words of Judgment Alongside 'Magical' Spell Texts." *Journal for the Study of the New Testament* 39.4 (2017) 412–40.

Kidd, B. J., and James Stevenson. *A New Eusebius: Documents Illustrative of the History of the Church to AD 337*. London: SPCK, 1965.

Kiernan, P. "Did Curse Tablets Work?" In *TRAC 2003 Proceedings of the Thirteenth Annual Theoretical Archaeology Conference (Leicester 2003)*, edited by Ben Croxford, 123–34. Oxford: Oxbow, 2003.

Klinghardt, Matthias. "Meals in the Gospel of Luke." In *T&T Clark Handbook to Early Christian Meals in the Greco-Roman World*, edited by Soham Al-Suadi and Peter-Ben Smit, 108–20. T&T Clark Handbooks. London: T&T Clark, 2019.

Kloppenborg, John S. *Christ's Associations: Connecting and Belonging in the Ancient City*. New Haven: Yale University Press, 2019.

———. "The Dishonoured Master (Luke 16:1–8a)." *Biblica* 70.4 (1989) 474–95.

———. "The Lord's Prayer and Debt Recovery: Insights from Graeco-Egyptian Papyri." In *Prayer in the Sayings Gospel Q*, edited by Daniel A. Smith and Christoph Heil, 201–18. Wissenschaftliche Untersuchungen zum Neuen Testament 425. Tübingen: Mohr Siebeck, 2019.

———. "Luke's Geography: Knowledge, Ignorance, Sources, and Spatial Conception." In *Luke on Jesus, Paul, and Christianity: What Did He Really Know?*, edited by Joseph Verheyden and John S. Kloppenborg, 101–43. Biblical Tools and Studies 29. Leuven: Peeters, 2017.

Knight, J. K. *Caerleon Roman Fortress*. 3rd ed. Cardiff: Cadw: Welsh Historic Monuments, 2003.

Knox, John. *Marcion and the New Testament*. Chicago: University of Chicago Press, 1942.

Kochenash, Michael. "Taking the Bad with the Good: Reconciling Images of Rome in Luke–Acts." *Religious Studies Review* 41 (2015) 43–51.

Kolb, Anne. "Mobility, Roads, and Milestones: Aspects of the Use of Latin in the Roman Empire." In *Social Factors in the Latinization of the Roman West*, edited by Alex Mullen, 117–32. Oxford Studies in Ancient Documents. Oxford: Oxford University Press, 2023.

Korporowicz, Łukasz Jan. "Roman Law in Roman Britain: An Introductory Survey." *Journal of Legal History* 33.2 (2012) 133–50.

Kreitzer, L. Joseph. *Striking New Images: Roman Imperial Coinage and the New Testament World*. Journal for the Study of the New Testament Supplement Series 134. Sheffield: Sheffield Academic, 1996.

Kropp, Amina. "How Does Magical Language Work? The Spells and Formulae of the Latin Defixionum Tabellae." In *Magical Practice in the Latin West*, edited by Richard Gordon and Francisco Marco Simón, 357–80. Religions in the Graeco-Roman World 168. Leiden: Brill, 2010.

Kuecker, Aaron. "Acts." In *T&T Clark Social Identity Commentary on the New Testament*, edited by J. Brian Tucker and Aaron Kuecker, 211–56. London: T&T Clark, 2020.

———. "Luke." In *T&T Clark Social Identity Commentary on the New Testament*, edited by J. Brian Tucker and Aaron Kuecker, 103–68. London: T&T Clark, 2020.

LaFosse, Mona Tokarek. "Women, Children and House Churches." In *The Early Christian World*, edited by Philip F. Esler, 385–405. 2nd ed. Abingdon: Routledge, 2017.

Lampe, G. W. H. "The Holy Spirit in the Writings of St. Luke." In *Studies in the Gospels*, edited by Dennis E. Nineham. Oxford: Blackwell, 1955.

"LatinNow." 5 December 2023. https://latinnow.eu/.

Lawrence, Louise J. "Appearance and Health." In *T&T Clark Handbook to the Historical Paul*, edited by Ryan S. Schellenberg and Heidi Wendt, 141–54. T&T Clark Handbooks. London: T&T Clark, 2022.

Leins, Ian, and Julia Farley. "A Changing World, c. 150 BC – AD 50." In *Celts: Art and Identity*, edited by Julia Harvey and Fraser Hunter, 109–27. London: British Museum, 2015.

Lennartsson, Rebecka. "Archival Ethnography: Reflections on a Lost Note." *Historische Anthropologie. Historisches Forum* (Berlin) 14 (2012) 77–92.

———. "Notes on Not Being There." *Ethnologia Europaea* 41.1 (2011) 105–14.

Lents, Hannah. "Third Space in Paul's Areopagus Speech." In *Acts of the Apostles*, edited by Linda M. Maloney and Ivoni Richter Reimer, 45:247–53. Wisdom Commentary. Collegeville, MN: Liturgical, 2022.

Lentz, John Clayton. *Luke's Portrait of Paul*. Society for New Testament Studies Monograph Series 77. Cambridge: Cambridge University Press, 1993.

"Letter from Claudius Tiberianus to Longinus Priscus. P.Mich.Inv. 5392." 2020. http://quod.lib.umich.edu/a/apis/x-2446/1.

Levitan, Bruce. "Vertebrate Remains." In *The Uley Shrines: Excavation of a Ritual Complex on West Hill, Uley, Gloucestershire 1977–9*, edited by Ann Woodward and Peter E. Leach, 257–63. London: English Heritage in association with British Museum, 1993.

Lewis, Naphtali, ed. *The Documents of the Bar Kokhba Period in the Cave of Letters – Greek Papyri*. Jerusalem: Israel Exploration Society, 1989.

Lewsey, Fred. "Evidence of a Roman Crucifixion Found in Cambridgeshire." University of Cambridge, 2021. https://www.cam.ac.uk/stories/romancrucifixion.

Leyerle, Blake. "Communication and Travel." In *The Early Christian World*, 2nd ed., 442–64. London: Routledge, 2017.

Lincoln, Andrew T. *The Gospel According to Saint John*. London: Continuum, 2005.

"Llanvaches Hoard: Collections Online." National Museum Wales, 2019. https://museum.wales/collections/online/.

"Llanvaches Roman Coin Hoard | Museum Wales | Amgueddfa Cymru." 2023. https://museum.wales/articles/1171/The-Llanvaches-Roman-coin-hoard/.

Lock, G., and I. Ralson. "Atlas of Hillforts of Britain and Ireland." https://hillforts.arch.ox.ac.uk.

"London Mithraeum." 2023. https://www.londonmithraeum.com/.

"London Museum." 2026. https://www.londonmuseum.org.uk.

Longenecker, Bruce W. *In Stone and Story: Early Christianity in the Roman World*. Grand Rapids: Baker Academic, 2020.

Lydney Park Estate. *Lydney Park Spring Gardens and Roman Remains*. Lydney: Lydney Park Estate, 2000.

MacMullen, Ramsay. *Roman Social Relations 50 BC to AD 284*. New Haven: Yale University Press, 1974.

"Magna Roman Fort." The Vindolanda Trust, 2022. https://www.vindolanda.com/blog/magna-roman-fort.

Malina, Bruce J. *The New Testament World: Insights from Cultural Anthropology*. 3rd ed. Louisville: Westminster John Knox, 2001.

———. *Windows on the World of Jesus: Time Travel to Ancient Judea*. Louisville: Westminster John Knox, 1993.

Malina, Bruce J., and Jerome H. Neyrey. "Honor and Shame in Luke–Acts: Pivotal Values of the Mediterranean World." In *The Social World of Luke–Acts*, edited by Jerome H. Neyrey, 25–65. Peabody, MA: Hendrickson, 1991.

Maloney, Linda M., and Ivoni Richter Reimer. *Acts of the Apostles*. Wisdom Commentary 45. Collegeville, MN: Liturgical, 2022.

Manning, William. *Roman Wales: A Pocket Guide*. Cardiff: University of Wales Press, 2001.

Marquis, Timothy Luckritz. "Travel and Homelessness." In *T&T Clark Handbook to the Historical Paul*, edited by Ryan S. Schellenberg and Heidi Wendt, 87–102. London: T&T Clark, 2022.

Marshman, Ian J. "Making Your Mark in Britannia: An Investigation into the Use of Signet Rings and Intaglios in Roman Britain." PhD thesis, Leicester University, 2016.

Mason, Steve. "Jews, Judaeans, Judaizing, Judaism: Problems of Categorization in Ancient History." *Journal for the Study of Judaism in the Persian, Hellenistic and Roman Period* 38 (2007) 457–512.

Mastrocinque, Attilio. "A Defixio from Caesarea Maritima Against a Dancer." In *Litterae Magicae. Studies in Honour of Roger S. O. Tomlin*, edited by Celia Sánchez Natalías, 59–75. Supplementa MHNH 2. Zaragosa: Libros Portico, 2019.

Matthews, Shelly. *The Acts of the Apostles: Taming the Tongues of Fire*. T&T Clark Study Guide to the New Testament. London: T&T Clark, 2017.

Matthews, Shelly, and Barbara E. Reid. *Luke 1–9*. Vol. 43a. Wisdom Commentary. Collegeville, MN: Liturgical, 2021.

———. *Luke 10–24*. Vol. 43b. Wisdom Commentary. Collegeville, MN: Liturgical, 2021.

Mattingly, D. J. *An Imperial Possession: Britain in the Roman Empire, 54 BC-AD 409*. London: Penguin, 2007.

———. *Imperialism, Power, and Identity: Experiencing the Roman Empire*. New ed. Princeton: Princeton University Press, 2014.

Mattingly, Harold. *Roman Coins: From the Earliest Times to the Fall of the Western Empire*. 2nd ed. London: Methuen, 1960.

McDonnell, Myles. "Writing, Copying, and Autograph Manuscripts in Ancient Rome." *Classical Quarterly* 46.2 (1996) 469–91.

McKie, Stuart. *Living and Cursing in the Roman West: Curse Tablets and Society*. London: Bloomsbury Academic, 2022.

Metzger, Bruce. *A Textual Commentary on the Greek New Testament*. 2nd ed. Stuttgart: United Bible Societies, 1994.

Meyer, Elizabeth A. "Law and Latinization in Rome's Western Provinces." In *Social Factors in the Latinization of the Roman West*, edited by Alex Mullen, 182–205. Oxford Studies in Ancient Documents. Oxford: Oxford University Press, 2023.

———. *Legitimacy and Law in the Roman World: Tabulae in Roman Belief and Practice*. Cambridge: Cambridge University Press, 2004.

———. "Writing in Roman Legal Contexts." In *The Cambridge Companion to Roman Law*, edited by David Johnston, 85–96. Cambridge Companions to the Ancient World. Cambridge: Cambridge University Press, 2015.

Millett, Martin. "Roman Britain since Haverfield." In *The Oxford Handbook of Roman Britain*, edited by Martin Millett et al., 22–42. Oxford: Oxford University Press, 2016.

Millett, Martin, et al., eds. *The Oxford Handbook of Roman Britain*. Oxford: Oxford University Press, 2016.

Mills, C. Wright. *The Sociological Imagination*. Oxford: Oxford University Press, 1959.

Mitchell, Stephen. "Requisitioned Transport in the Roman Empire: A New Inscription from Pisidia." *Journal of Roman Studies* 66 (1976) 106–31.

Mitchell, T. C. *The Bible in the British Museum: Interpreting the Evidence*. 2nd ed. London: British Museum, 2004.

Moorhead, Sam. *A History of Roman Coinage in Britain*. Witham, Essex: Greenlight, 2013.

Mount, Christopher. "Acts." In *T&T Clark Handbook to the Historical Paul*, edited by Ryan S. Schellenberg and Heidi Wendt, 23–38. London: T&T Clark, 2022.

Mullen, Alex. "Evidence for Written Celtic from Roman Britain: A Linguistic Analysis of Tabellae Sulis 14 and 18." *Studia Celtica* 41 (2007) 31–45.

———. "Linguistic Evidence for 'Romanization': Continuity and Change in Romano-British Onomastics: A Study of the Epigraphic Record with Particular Reference to Bath." *Britannia* 38 (2007) 35–61.

———. "New Thoughts on British Latin: A Curse Tablet from Red Hill, Ratcliffe-on-Soar (Nottinghamshire)." *Zeitschrift für Papyrologie und Epigraphik* 187 (2013) 266–72.

———, ed. *Social Factors in the Latinization of the Roman West*. Oxford Studies in Ancient Documents. Oxford: Oxford University Press, 2023.

Mullen, Alex, and Alan Bowman. *Scripts and Texts*. Vol. 1. Manual of Roman Everyday Writing. Nottingham: LatinNow ePubs, 2021. https://library.oapen.org/handle/20.500.12657/56666.

"Museum of Gloucester." 2023. https://www.museumofgloucester.co.uk.

Nasrallah, Laura Salah. "Judgment, Justice, and Destruction: Defixiones and 1 Corinthians." *Journal of Biblical Literature* 140.2 (2021) 347–67.

Neusner, Jacob, and Bruce Chilton. *Judaism in the New Testament: Practices and Beliefs*. New York: Routledge, 1995.

Neusner, Jacob, et al., eds. *Judaisms and Their Messiahs at the Turn of the Christian Era*. Cambridge: Cambridge University Press, 1988.

"Newport Museum and Art Gallery: Archaeology." (2022). https://www.newport.gov.uk/heritage/en/Museum-Art-Gallery/Collections/Archaeology.aspx.

Neyrey, Jerome H. "Ceremonies in Luke–Acts: The Case of Meals and Table Fellowship." In *The Social World of Luke–Acts: Models for Interpretation*, edited by Jerome H. Neyrey, 361–87. Peabody, MA: Hendrickson, 1991.

———. *Imagining Jesus in His Own Culture: Creating Scenarios of the Gospel for Contemplative Prayer.* Eugene, OR: Cascade Books, 2018.

———. *The Social World of Luke–Acts: Models for Interpretation*. Peabody, MA: Hendrickson, 1991.

Neyrey, Jerome H., and Eric C. Stewart, eds. *The Social World of the New Testament, Insights and Models*. Peabody, MA: Hendrickson, 2008.

Niblett, Rosalind. *Verulamium: The Roman City of St Albans*. Stroud, UK: History Press, 2001.

Novenson, Matthew V. "Ioudaios, Pharisee, Zealot." In *T&T Clark Handbook to the Historical Paul*, edited by Ryan S. Schellenberg and Heidi Wendt, 167–82. London: T&T Clark, 2022.

Nutton, Vivian. "Medicine and the Roman Army: A Further Reconsideration." *Medical History* 13.3 (1969) 260–70.

"Nympsfield Long Barrow." (2021). https://www.english-heritage.org.uk/visit/places/nympsfield-long-barrow/.

Oakes, Peter. *Empire, Economics, and the New Testament*. Grand Rapids: Eerdmans, 2020.

———. *Reading Romans in Pompeii, Paul's Letter at Ground Level*. London: SPCK, 2009.

———. *Rome in the Bible and the Early Church*. Carlisle, UK: Paternoster, 2002.

Oakes, Peter, and Benedict Kent. "Entering Early Christianity via Pompei: A Virtual Guide to the World of the New Testament." (2019). https://www.alc.manchester.ac.uk/religions-and-theology/research/centres/centre-for-biblical-studies/virtual-guide/.

Oakman, Douglas E. "Jesus and Agrarian Palestine: The Factor of Debt." In *The Social World of the New Testament*, edited by Jerome H. Neyrey, 65–82. Peabody, MA: Hendrickson, 2008.

O'Brien, P. T. "Prayer in Luke–Acts." *Tyndale Bulletin* 24.1 (1973) 111–27.

Oliver, Andrew, and John Shelton. "Silver on Papyrus: A Translation of a Roman Silver Tableware Inventory." *Archaeology* 32.1 (1979) 21–28.

Omerzu, Heike. "The Roman Trial Against Paul According to Acts 21–28." In *The Last Years of Paul: Essays from the Tarragona Conference, June 2013*, edited by A. Puig i Tàrrech et al., 187–200. Wissenschaftliche Untersuchungen Zum Neuen Testament. Tübingen: Mohr Siebeck, 2015.

"Online Coins of the Roman Empire." 2018. https://numismatics.org/ocre/.

Osiek, Carolyn, et al., eds. *A Woman's Place: House Churches in Earliest Christianity*. Minneapolis: Fortress, 2006.

Parsons, Mikeal C. *Acts*. Paideia. Grand Rapids: Baker Academic, 2008.

———. "Empowering, Empire-Ing or Engaging? Acts in the Discourse of Politics: A Response." In *Reading Acts in the Discourses of Masculinity and Politics*, edited by Eric D. Barreto et al., 141–47. The Library of New Testament Studies. London: T&T Clark, 2017.

Paulraj, Gideon S. S. *Food Justice and Hospitality in Luke–Acts: A Historical and Contemporary Interpretation*. Eugene, OR: Pickwick Publications, 2023.

Peachin, Michael. "View of Five Vindolanda Tablets, Soldiers, and the Law." *Tyche: Beiträge zur Alten Geschichte Papyrologie und Epigraphik* 14 (1999) 223–36.

Pearce, John. "Archaeology, Writing Tablets and Literacy in Roman Britain." *Gallia* 61 (2004) 43–51.

———. "Food as Substance and Symbol in the Roman Army: A Case Study from Vindolanda." In *Limes XVIII - Proceedings of the XVIIIth International Congress of Roman Frontier Studies Held in Amman, Jordan (September 2000)*, edited by Philip Freeman et al., 931–44. Oxford: Archaeopress, 2002.

———. "Imagining Roman London: A Global Neighbourhood by the Walbrook." 15th Congress of the Féderation Internationale des Associations d'Études Classiques and the Classical Association Conference, 2019.

Penner, Todd C., and Caroline Vander Stichele, eds. *Contextualizing Acts: Lukan Narrative and Greco-Roman Discourse*. SBL Symposium Series 20. Atlanta: Society of Biblical Literature, 2003.

Perring, Dominic. *London in the Roman World*. Oxford: Oxford University Press, 2022.

———. "Recent Advances in the Understanding of Roman London." In *The Towns of Roman Britain: The Contribution of Commercial Archaeology since 1990*, edited by Michael Fulford and Neil Holbrook. London: Society for the Promotion of Roman Studies, 2015.

———. *Roman London*. The Archaeology of London. London: Seaby, 1991.

Perring, Dominic, and Trevor Brigham. "Londinium and Its Hinterland: The Roman Period." In *The Archaeology of Greater London*, edited by Trevor Brigham, 119–70. London: Museum of London Archaeology Service, 2000.

Perring, Dominic, S. P. Roskams, and Patrick Allen. *The Archaeology of Roman London. Vol. 2, Early Development of Roman London West of the Walbrook*. CBA Research Report 70. London: Museum of London and the Council for British Archaeology, 1991.

Pervo, Richard I. *Acts: A Commentary*. Hermeneia – a Critical and Historical Commentary on the Bible. Minneapolis: Fortress, 2009.

———. *Dating Acts: Between the Evangelists and the Apologists*. Santa Rosa, California: Polebridge, 2006.

———. *The Gospel of Luke*. Salem, OR: Polebridge, 2014.

———. *The Mystery of Acts*. Santa Rosa, CA: Polebridge, 2008.

———. *Profit with Delight: The Literary Genre of the Acts of the Apostles*. Philadelphia: Fortress, 1987.

Following Schellenberg and Wendt, I do not wish to cite Pervo's work "without acknowledging his 2001 conviction for the possession and distribution of child pornography and the violence entailed in these actions" (*Handbook to Historical Paul*, 3).

Pollard, Nigel, and Joanne Berry. *The Complete Roman Legions*. London: Thames & Hudson, 2012.

"Portable Antiquities Scheme Website." http://finds.org.uk/.

Powery, Emerson B. "Roman Slavery and the New Testament: Engaging the Work of Keith Bradley." *Biblical Interpretation* 21.4/5 (2013) 495–96.

Praeder, Susan Marie. "Acts 27:1—28:16: Sea Voyages in Ancient Literature and the Theology of Luke–Acts." *Catholic Biblical Quarterly* 46.4 (1984) 683–706.

Price, Jennifer. "Window Glass." In *The Uley Shrines: Excavation of a Ritual Complex on West Hill, Uley, Gloucestershire 1977–9*, edited by Ann Woodward and Peter E. Leach, 188–92. Archaeological Report (English Heritage) 17. London: English Heritage in association with British Museum, 1993.

Pritchard, James B. *The Times Atlas of the Bible*. London: Times, 1987.

Rapske, Brian. *Paul in Roman Custody*. The Book of Acts in Its First Century Setting 3. Carlisle, UK: Paternoster, 1994.

"Record ID: BH-1DD9E4 - Victoriatus." *The Portable Antiquities Scheme / British Museum, 2022*. http://finds.org.uk/database/artefacts/record/id/508805.

Reece, Richard. *The Coinage of Roman Britain*. Stroud, UK: Tempus, 2002.

Reed, Jonathan L. *The HarperCollins Visual Guide to the New Testament: What Archaeology Reveals about the First Christians*. New York: HarperOne, 2007.

Reid, Barbara E. "'Do You See This Woman?' A Liberative Look at Luke 7:36–50 and Strategies for Reading Other Lukan Stories against the Grain." In *A Feminist Companion to Luke*, edited by Amy-Jill Levine and Marianne Blickenstaff, 106–20. Feminist Companion to the New Testament and Early Christian Writings 3. London: Sheffield Academic, 2002.

Reimer, Ivoni Richter. *Women in the Acts of the Apostles*. Minneapolis: Fortress, 1995.

Revell, Louise. "Religion and Ritual in the Western Provinces." *Greece & Rome*, second series, 54.2 (2007) 210–28.

Richmond, I. A. "Roman Legionaries at Corbridge, Their Supply-Base, Temples and Religious Cults." *Archaeologia Aeliana*, 4, 21 (1943) 127–224.

Rives, James B. "Graeco-Roman Religion in the Roman Empire: Old Assumptions and New Approaches." *Currents in Biblical Research* 8.2 (2010) 240–99.

Robbins, Vernon K. "Luke–Acts: A Mixed Population Seeks a Home in the Roman Empire." In *Images of Empire*, edited by Loveday Alexander, 202–21. Journal for the Study of the Old Testament Supplement Series 122. Sheffield: Sheffield Academic, 1991.

———. "The Social Location of the Implied Author of Luke–Acts." In *The Social World of Luke–Acts: Models for Interpretation*, edited by Jerome H. Neyrey, 305–32. Peabody, MA: Hendrickson, 1991.

Robinson, John A. T. *Redating the New Testament*. London: SCM, 1976.

"Roman Britain." https://www.roman-britain.co.uk/.

"Roman Baths of Bath." https://www.romanbaths.co.uk/.

"Roman Inscriptions of Britain." 2019. https://romaninscriptionsofbritain.org/.

"Roman London Gallery in the Museum of London." Museum of London, 2022. https://www.museumoflondon.org.uk/museum-london/permanent-galleries/roman-london.

"Roman Vindolanda Fort and Museum." https://www.vindolanda.com/roman-vindolanda-fort-museum

Rowe, C. Kavin. *World Upside Down: Reading Acts in the Graeco-Roman Age*. Oxford: Oxford University Press, 2009.

Rowe, Rosemary. *The Ghosts of Glevum*. London: Headline, 2004.

Rowsome, Peter. *Heart of the City: Roman, Medieval and Modern London Revealed by Archaeology at 1 Poultry*. London: Museum of London Archaeology, 2000.

———. "Londinium—A New Map and Guide to Roman London." London: Museum of London Archaeology, 2011.

———. "Mapping Roman London: Identifying Its Urban Patterns and Interpreting Their Meaning." In *Londinium and Beyond: Essays on Roman London and Its Hinterland for Harvey Sheldon*, edited by John Clark, 25–32. CBA Research Report 156. York: Council for British Archaeology, 2008.

Roymans, Nico. *Ethnic Identity and Imperial Power: The Batavians in the Early Roman Empire*. Amsterdam Archaeological Studies. Amsterdam: Amsterdam University Press, 2004.

Rüpke, Jörg. *On Roman Religion: Lived Religion and the Individual in Ancient Rome*. Ithaca: Cornell University Press, 2016.

Sahlins, Marshall. *Stone Age Economics*. New York: Aldine, 1972.

Salway, Peter. *A History of Roman Britain*. Oxford: Oxford University Press, 2001.

———. *The Oxford Illustrated History of Roman Britain*. Oxford: Oxford University Press, 1993.

———. *Roman Britain*. Oxford: Clarendon, 1981.

———. *Roman Britain: A Very Short Introduction*. Oxford: Oxford University Press, 2015.

Sánchez Natalías, Celia. "Curse Tablets against Thieves in Roman Britain: The Social and Legal Influences on a Magical-Religious Technology." *Greece & Rome* 69.1 (2022) 88–103.

Savani, Giacomo et al. *Life in the Roman World: Roman Leicester*. Leicester: School of Archaeology and Ancient History, University of Leicester, 2018.

Schaberg, Jane D., and Sharon H. Ringe. "Gospel of Luke." In *Women's Bible Commentary*, edited by Carol A. Newsom et al., 493–511. 3rd ed. Louisville: Westminster John Knox, 2012.

Scheidel, Walter. "Marriage, Families, and Survival: Demographic Aspects." In *A Companion to the Roman Army*, edited by Paul Erdkamp, 417–34. Blackwell Companions to the Ancient World: Ancient History. Oxford: Blackwell, 2007.

Schellenberg, Ryan S. *Abject Joy: Paul, Prison, and the Art of Making Do*. New York: Oxford University Press, USA, 2021.

———. "Beatings and Imprisonments." In *T&T Clark Handbook to the Historical Paul*, edited by Ryan S. Schellenberg and Heidi Wendt, 123–39. T&T Clark Handbooks. London: T&T Clark, 2022.

———. "Danger in the Wilderness, Danger at Sea: Paul and the Perils of Travel." In *Travel and Religion in Antiquity*, edited by P. Harland, 141–61. Waterloo, ON: Wilfrid Laurier University Press, 2011.

———. "The First Pauline Chronologist? Paul's Itinerary in the Letters and in Acts." *Journal of Biblical Literature* 134.1 (2015) 193–213.

———. "The Rest of Paul's Imprisonments." *Journal of Theological Studies* 69.2 (2018) 533–72.

Schellenberg, Ryan S., and Heidi Wendt, eds. *T&T Clark Handbook to the Historical Paul*. T&T Clark Handbooks. London: T&T Clark, 2022.

Scholz, Markus. "Round Curse Tablets: Correlation of Form and Content." In *Litterae Magicae: Studies in Honour of R. S. O. Tomlin*, edited by Celia Sánchez Natalías, 39–50. Zaragoza: Libros Pórtico, 2019.

Schwartz, Saundra. "The Trial Scene in the Greek Novels and in Acts." In *Contextualizing Acts: Lukan Narrative and Greco-Roman Discourse*, edited by Todd C. Penner and Caroline Vander Stichele, 103–35. SBL Symposium Series 20. Atlanta: Society of Biblical Literature, 2003.

Score, Vicki. *Hoards, Hounds and Helmets: A Conquest-Period Ritual Site at Hallaton, Leicestershire*. Leicester Archaeology Monographs 21. Leicester: University of Leicester Archaeological Services, 2011.

———. *Hoards, Hounds and Helmets: The Story of the Hallaton Treasure*. Leicester: University of Leicester, 2013.

Seaman, Andy. "Julius and Aaron 'Martyrs of Caerleon': In Search of Wales' First Christians." *Archaeologia Cambrensis* 164 (2015) 201–19.

Seccombe, David. "Dating Luke–Acts: Further Arguments for an Early Date." *Tyndale Bulletin* 71.2 (2020) 207–27.

Seim, Turid Karlsen. "The Virgin Mother: Mary and Ascetic Discipleship in Luke." In *A Feminist Companion to Luke*, edited by Amy-Jill Levine and Marianne Blickenstaff, 89–105. Feminist Companion to the New Testament and Early Christian Writings 3. London: Sheffield Academic, 2002.

Shanks, Michael. *The Archaeological Imagination*. Walnut Creek, CA: Left Coast, 2012.

Shanks, Michael, and Christopher Tilley. *Reconstructing Archaeology: Theory and Practice*. 2nd ed. London: Routledge, 1992.

Sherwin-White, A. N. *The Roman Citizenship*. 2nd ed. Oxford: Oxford University Press, 1973.

———. *Roman Society and Roman Law in the New Testament*. The Sarum Lectures 1960–1961. Oxford: Oxford University Press, 1963.

Sherwood, Harriet. "Roman Gateway Rebuilt in 'Exact Spot' at Site of Invasion of Britain." *The Guardian, 18 April 2023*. https://www.theguardian.com/uk-news/2023/apr/18/roman-gateway-rebuilt-exact-spot-invasion-britain.

Silva, Moisés. *New International Dictionary of New Testament Theology and Exegesis*. Michigan: Zondervan, 2014.

Skehan, Patrick W. "The Divine Name at Qumran, in the Masada Scroll, and in the Septuagint." *Bulletin of the International Organization for Septuagint and Cognate Studies (BIOSCS)* 13 (1980) 14–44.

Skinner, Matthew L. "Who Speaks For (Or Against) Rome? Acts In Relation To Empire." In *Reading Acts in the Discourses of Masculinity and Politics*, edited by Eric D. Barreto et al., 107–25. The Library of New Testament Studies. London: T&T Clark, 2017.

Smith, A. H. *The Place Names of Gloucestershire, Part 2*. Vol. 39. English Place-Name Society. Cambridge: Cambridge University Press, 1965.

Smith, R. E. "The Army Reforms of Septimius Severus." *Historia: Zeitschrift für Alte Geschichte* 21.3 (1972) 481–500.

Souter, A. et al., eds. *Oxford Latin Dictionary*. Oxford: Oxford University Press, 1968.

Southern, P. "The Numeri of the Roman Imperial Army." *Britannia* 20 (1989) 81–140.

Speidel, M. A. "Learning Latin in the Roman Army." In *Social Factors in the Latinization of the Roman West*, edited by Alex Mullen, 133–58. Oxford Studies in Ancient Documents. Oxford: Oxford University Press, 2023.

———. *Die Römischen Schreibtafeln von Vindonissa*. Veröffentlichungen Der Gesellschaft Pro Vindonissa. 1996.

Speidel, Michael P. "The Roman Army in Judaea under the Procurators: The Italian and the Augustan Cohort in the Acts of the Apostles". In *Essential Essays for the Study of the Military in First-Century Palestine*, edited by Christopher B. Zeichmann. Eugene, OR: Pickwick Publications, 2019.

Spencer, F. Scott. *Journeying through Acts: A Literary and Cultural Reading*. Peabody, MA: Hendrickson, 2004.

Standing, Giles. "The Claudian Invasion of Britain and the Cult of Victoria Britannica." *Britannia* 34 (2003) 281–88.

Stegemann, E. W., and W. Stegemann. *The Jesus Movement: A Social History of Its First Century*. Translated by O. C. Dean. Minneapolis: Fortress, 1999.

Stevenson, Angus, and Maurice Waite, eds. *Concise Oxford English Dictionary*. 12th ed. Oxford: Oxford University Press, 2011.

Stevenson, Jane. "The Beginnings of Literacy in Ireland." *Proceedings of the Royal Irish Academy. Section C: Archaeology, Celtic Studies, History, Linguistics, Literature* 89C (1989) 127–65.

Stevenson, Leslie. "Twelve Conceptions of Imagination." *British Journal of Aesthetics* 43.3 (2003) 238–59.

Talbert, Charles H. *Reading Acts: A Literary and Theological Commentary on the Acts of the Apostles*. New York: Crossroad, 1997.

Tambs, Lena. "Social Network Analysis as Tools for Studying Socio-Economic Realities in the Upper Egyptian Town of Pathyris (186–88 BCE)." International Centre for Biblical Interpretation, 2021.

———. "Social and Symbolic Boundaries in the Upper Egyptian Town of Pathyris (2nd to Early 1st Century BCE)." *Fronteiras - Revista Catarinense de História* 40 (2022) 164–205.

Tannehill, Robert C. *Luke*. Abingdon New Testament Commentaries. Nashville: Abingdon, 1996.

Thompson, Michael B. "The Holy Internet: Communication Between Churches in the First Christian Generation." In *The Gospels for All Christians*, edited by Richard Bauckham, 49–70. Grand Rapids: Eerdmans, 1998.

Tilley, Christopher. *A Phenomenology of Landscape*. Oxford: Berg, 1994.

———. Review of *A Phenomenology of Landscape*, by Timothy Darvill. Times Higher Education Supplement 1893 (2009) 34–35.

Todd, Malcolm. *A Companion to Roman Britain*. Blackwell Companions to British History. Oxford: Blackwell, 2007.

———. *Roman Britain*. 3rd ed. Blackwell Classic Histories of England. Oxford: Blackwell, 1999.

Tomlin, Roger S. O. "A Bilingual Roman Charm for Health and Victory." *Zeitschrift für Papyrologie und Epigraphik* 149 (2004) 259–66.

———. *Britannia Romana: Roman Inscriptions and Roman Britain*. Oxford: Oxbow Books, 2018.

———. "Cursing a Thief in Iberia and Britain." In *Magical Practice in the Latin West*, edited by R. L. Gordon and F. M. Simón, 245–74. Religions in the Graeco-Roman World 168. Leiden: Brill, 2010.

———. "A Five Acre Wood in Roman Kent." In *Interpreting Roman London: Papers in Memory of Hugh Chapman*, edited by Joanna Bird, Mark Hassall, and Harvey Sheldon, 209–15. Oxford: Oxford University Press, 1996.

———. "A Fourth-Century 'Curse Tablet' from Uley." In *Celtic Religions in the Roman Period*, edited by Ralph Haeussler and Anthony King, 71–78. Aberystwyth: Celtic Studies, 2017.

———. "'The Girl in Question': A New Text from Roman London." *Britannia* 34 (2003) 41–51.

———. "The Inscribed Lead Tablets: An Interim Report." In *The Uley Shrines: Excavation of a Ritual Complex on West Hill, Uley*, edited by Ann Woodward and Peter E. Leach,

17:113–30. Archaeological Report (English Heritage). London: English Heritage in association with British Museum, 1993.

———. "Literacy in Roman Britain." In *Literacy in Ancient Everyday Life*, edited by Anne Kolb, 201–20. Berlin: De Gruyter, 2018.

———. "Not to Mention the Tablets: Vindolanda's Other Inscriptions." *Archaeologia Aeliana* 41 (2012) 207–15.

———. "'Paedagogium and Septizonium': Two Roman Lead Tablets from Leicester." *Zeitschrift für Papyrologie und Epigraphik* 167 (2008) 207–18.

———. "Roman Britain in 1985 II Inscriptions." *Britannia* 17 (1986) 428–54.

———. "Roman Britain in 1988 II Inscriptions." *Britannia* 20 (1989) 327–45.

———. "Roman Britain in 1990 II Inscriptions." *Britannia* 22 (1991) 293–311.

———. "Roman Britain in 1991 II Inscriptions." *Britannia* 23 (1992) 309–23.

———. "Roman Britain in 1994 II Inscriptions." *Britannia* 26 (1995) 371–90.

———. "Roman Britain in 1995 II Inscriptions." *Britannia* 27 (1996) 439–57.

———. "Roman Britain in 1997 II Inscriptions." *Britannia* 29 (1998) 433–45.

———. "Roman Britain in 2014 III Inscriptions." *Britannia* 46 (2015) 383–420.

———. "Roman Britain in 2016 III Inscriptions." *Britannia* 48 (2017) 457–90.

———. "Roman Britain in 2018 III Inscriptions." *Britannia* 50 (2019) 495–524.

———. "Roman Britain in 2019 III Inscriptions." *Britannia* 51 (2020) 471–525.

———. "Roman Britain in 2020 III Inscriptions." *Britannia* 52 (2021) 471–72.

———. *Roman London's First Voices: Writing Tablets from the Bloomberg Excavations, 2010–14*. London: Museum of London Archaeology, 2016. www.romaninscriptionsofbritain.org/tablondbloomberg.

———. 'A Roman Will from Wales'. *Archaeologia Cambrensis* (Cymru) 150 (2004) 143–56.

———. "Special Delivery: A Graeco-Roman Gold Amulet for Healthy Childbirth." *Zeitschrift für Papyrologie und Epigraphik* 167 (2008) 219–24.

———. "Stylus Writing Tablets." In *Roman London and the Walbrook Stream Crossing: Excavations at 1 Poultry and Vicinity, City of London*, edited by Julian Hill and Peter Rowsome, 37:514–17. MOLA Monograph. London: Museum of London Archaeology, 2011.

———. *Tabellae Sulis: Roman Inscribed Tablets of Tin and Lead from the Sacred Spring at Bath*. Vol. 16 fasc. 1. Monograph (University of Oxford Committee for Archaeology). Oxford: Oxford University Committee for Archaeology, 1988. https://romaninscriptionsofbritain.org/tabsulis.

———. *The Uley Tablets: Roman Curse Tablets from the Temple of Mercury at Uley (Gloucestershire)*. Oxford Studies in Ancient Documents. Oxford: Oxford University Press, 2024.

———. "The Vindolanda Tablets." *Britannia* 27 (1996) 459–63.

———. "Voices from the Sacred Spring." In *Bath History, Volume IV*, 7–24. Bath: Millstream, 1992.

———. "Writing to the Gods in Roman Britain." In *Becoming Roman, Writing Latin? Literacy and Epigraphy in the Roman West*, edited by A. E. Cooley, 48:165–79. Journal of Roman Archaeology Supplementary Series. Portsmouth, Rhode Island: Journal of Roman Archaeology, 2002.

Tov, Emanuel. "The Greek Biblical Texts from the Judean Desert." In *Hebrew Bible, Greek Bible, and Qumran*, 339–64. Tübingen: Mohr Siebeck, 2008.

Trites, Allison A. "The Prayer Motif in Luke–Acts." In *Perspectives on Luke–Acts*, edited by Charles H. Talbert, 5:168–86. Perspectives in Religious Studies: Special Studies Series. Danville, VA: Association of Baptist Professors of Religion, 1978.

Turner, C. H. "A Laon Ms. in 1906 and 1920. Sermo De Flvxv Sangvinis (Cod. 113, Fol. 36 b)." *Journal of Theological Studies* 22.85 (1920) 1–5.

Tyers, Ian. "A Gazeteer of Tree-Ring Dates from Roman London." In *Londinium and Beyond: Essays on Roman London and Its Hinterland for Harvey Sheldon*, edited by John Clark, 156:69–74. CBA Research Report. London: Council for British Archaeology, 2008.

Tyson, Joseph B. *Marcion and Luke–Acts: A Defining Struggle*. Columbia: University of South Carolina Press, 2006.

"Uley Bury Camp, Uley – 1004866 | Historic England." Historic England, 2015. https://historicengland.org.uk/listing/the-list/list-entry/1004866.

"Uley Long Barrow, Also Known as Hetty Pegler's Tump." Historic England, 2016. https://historicengland.org.uk/listing/the-list/list-entry/1008195.

van Arsdell, R. D. "*Celtic Coinage of Britain*, 3rd Edition." 2017. https://www.vanarsdellcelticcoinageofbritain.com/index.html.

van Driel-Murray, Carol. "The Leatherwork." In *Vindolanda: The Early Wooden Forts: Preliminary Reports on the Leather, Textiles, Environmental Evidence and Dendrochronology*, edited by Carol van Driel-Murray, 15–81. Vindolanda Research Reports, New Series. Carvoran, UK: Roman Army Museum, 2003.

———. "Warm and Dry: A Complete Roman Tent from Vindolanda." In *Roman Frontier Studies 1989: Proceedings of the XVth International Congress of Roman Frontier Studies (at Canterbury)*, edited by Valerie A. Maxfield and Michael J. Dobson, 367–72. Exeter: University of Exeter Press, 1991.

Veale, Sarah. "*Defixiones* and the Temple Locus: The Power of Place in the Curse Tablets at Mainz." *Magic, Ritual, and Witchcraft* 12.3 (2017) 279–313.

Vermes, Geza. *Jesus in the Jewish World*. London: SCM, 2010.

Versnel, H. S. "Beyond Cursing: The Appeal to Justice in Judicial Prayers." In *Magika Hiera: Ancient Greek Magic and Religion*, edited by Christopher Faraone and Dirk Obbink, 60–106. Oxford: Oxford University Press, 1991.

———. "Prayers for Justice in East and West: Recent Finds and Publications." In *Magical Practice in the Latin West*, edited by Richard L. Gordon and Francisco Marco Simón, 275–356. Religions in the Graeco-Roman World 168. Leiden: Brill, 2010.

———. "Response to a Critique." In *Contesti Magici / Contextos Mágicos*, edited by Marina Piranomonte and Francisco Marco Simón, 33–45. Rome: De Luca, 2012.

———. "The Poetics of the Magical Charm: An Essay in the Power of Words." In *Magic and Ritual in the Ancient World*, edited by Paul Mirecki and Marvin Meyer, 105–58. Leiden: Brill, 2002.

———. *Inconsistencies in Greek and Roman Religion*. Vol. 2: *Transition and Reversal in Myth and Ritual*. Studies in Greek and Roman Religion 6/2. Leiden: Brill, 1993.

"Verulamium Museum: The Museum of Everyday Life in Roman Britain, St Albans." St Albans Museums, 2022. https://www.stalbansmuseums.org.uk/visit/verulamium-museum.

"Vindolanda Fact-File: Roman Forts." 2022. https://www.vindolanda.com/blog/fact-file-roman-fort.

"Vindolanda Tablets – Home | Roman Inscriptions of Britain." 2020. https://romaninscriptionsofbritain.org/tabvindol.

"The [Vindolanda] Tablets and Their Context (2010–11) | Roman Inscriptions of Britain." 2021. https://romaninscriptionsofbritain.org/tabvindol/vol-IV/tablets-context.

"Vindolanda Trust." 2023. https://romanarmymuseum.com/about-vindolanda/.

"Vindolanda & the Roman Army Museum." The Vindolanda Trust, 2020. https://www.vindolanda.com/.

Waal, Willemijn. "They Wrote on Wood. The Case for a Hieroglyphic Scribal Tradition on Wooden Writing Boards in Hittite Anatolia." *Anatolian Studies* 61 (2011) 21–34.

Walaskay, Paul W. *And So We Came to Rome: The Political Perspective of St Luke*. Society for New Testament Studies Monograph Series 49. Cambridge: Cambridge University Press, 2010.

Walker, Peter. *In the Steps of Jesus: An Illustrated Guide to the Places of the Holy Land*. Oxford: Lion Hudson, 2007.

———. *In the Steps of Saint Paul: An Illustrated Guide to Paul's Journeys*. Oxford: Lion Hudson, 2008.

Walton, Steve. "A Spirituality of Acts?" In *Reading Acts Today: Essays in Honour of Loveday C. A. Alexander*, edited by Steve Walton et al., 186–201. Library of New Testament Studies 427. London: T&T Clark, 2011.

———. "The State They Were In: Luke's View of the Roman Empire." In *Reading Acts in the Discourses of Masculinity and Politics*, edited by Eric D. Barreto, Matthew L. Skinner, and Steve Walton, 75–106. Library of New Testament Studies 559. London: T&T Clark, 2017.

Walton, Steve, and David Wenham. *Exploring the New Testament: The Gospels and Acts: Volume 1*. 2nd rev. ed. Barnsley: SPCK, 2011.

Ward, Graham. *Unimaginable: What We Imagine and What We Can't*. London: Tauris, 2018.

Warnock, Mary. *Imagination*. London: Faber & Faber, 1976.

Watson, Sadie. "Roman Britain in 2020: Southern Counties (East)." *Britannia* 52 (2021) 431–34.

Webley, Robert. "Styli, Pencils and Parchment-Prickers." Portable Antiquities Scheme Finds Recording Guides, 2019. https://finds.org.uk/counties/findsrecordingguides/styli-pencils-and-parchment-prickers/.

Whiteley, D. E. H. *The Theology of St. Paul*. Oxford: Blackwell, 1964.

Whittaker, C. R. "Supplying the Army: The Evidence from the Frontier Fort of Vindolanda." In *Rome and Its Frontiers: The Dynamics of Empire*, 88–114. London: Routledge, 2004.

Wild, John-Peter. "Vindolanda and Its Textiles: Gavvo and His Tosseae." In *III Symposium Internacional Sobre Textiles y Tintes Del Mediterráneo En El Mundo Antiguo*, edited by C. Alfaro, 69–93. Valencia: University of Valencia, 2011.

Wilkes, Isobel. "The SATOR Square." Corinium Museum, 2021. https://coriniummuseum.org/2021/07/the-sator-square-by-isobel-wilkes/.

Willi, Anna. *Writing Equipment*. Vol. 2. Manual of Roman Everyday Writing. Nottingham: LatinNow ePubs, 2021. https://library.oapen.org/handle/20.500.12657/56668.

Willis, Paul. *The Ethnographic Imagination*. Cambridge: Polity, 2000.

Willis, Steven. *The Roman Roadside Settlement and Multi-Period Ritual Complex at Nettleton and Rothwell, Lincolnshire*. London: Pre-Construct Archaeology, 2014.

Wilmott, Tony, and Philip Smither. "The Plan of the Saxon Shore Fort at Richborough." *Britannia* 51 (2020) 147–74.

Wilson, Andrew. "Latin, Literacy, and the Roman Economy." In *Social Factors in the Latinization of the Roman West*, edited by Alex Mullen, 78–98. Oxford Studies in Ancient Documents. Oxford: Oxford University Press, 2023.

Wilson, Brittany. *Unmanly Men: Refigurations of Masculinity in Luke–Acts*. Oxford: Oxford University Press, 2015.

Wilson, Roger J. A. *A Guide to the Roman Remains in Britain*. Rev. ed. London: Constable, 2002.

Wink, Walter. *Engaging the Powers: Discernment and Resistance in a World of Domination*. Minneapolis: Fortress, 1992.

Witherington, Ben III. *The Acts of the Apostles: A Socio-Rhetorical Commentary*. Grand Rapids: Eerdmans, 1998.

———. "On the Road with Mary Magdalene, Joanna, Susanna, and Other Disciples—Luke 8:1–3." In *A Feminist Companion to Luke*, edited by Amy-Jill Levine and Marianne Blickenstaff, 133–39. Feminist Companion to the New Testament and Early Christian Writings 3. London: Sheffield Academic, 2002.

Wolff, Catherine. "The Role of Education in the Latinization of the Roman West." In *Social Factors in the Latinization of the Roman West*, edited by Alex Mullen, 158–81. Oxford Studies in Ancient Documents. Oxford: Oxford University Press, 2023.

Wolter, Michael. *The Gospel According to Luke*. Vol. I: *Luke 1—9:50*. Translated by Wayne Coppins and Christoph Heilig. Baylor–Mohr Siebeck Studies in Early Christianity. Tübingen: Mohr Siebeck, 2016.

———. *The Gospel According to Luke* Volume II: *Luke 9:51—24*. Translated by Wayne Coppins, Simon Gathercole, and Christoph Heilig. Baylor–Mohr Siebeck Studies in Early Christianity. Tübingen: Mohr Siebeck, 2017.

Woodward, Ann, and Peter E. Leach. *The Uley Shrines: Excavation of a Ritual Complex on West Hill, Uley, Gloucestershire 1977–9*. Archaeological Report (English Heritage) 17. London: English Heritage in association with British Museum, 1993.

Woolf, Greg. "Ancient Illiteracy?" *Bulletin of the Institute of Classical Studies* 58.2 (2015) 31–42.

———. *Becoming Roman: The Origins of Provincial Civilization in Gaul*. Cambridge: Cambridge University Press, 1998.

———. "Curse Tablets: The History of a Technology." *Greece and Rome* 69.1 (2022) 120–34.

———. "Female Mobility in the Latin West." In *Women and the Roman City in the Latin West*, edited by Emily A. Hemelrijk and Greg Woolf, 351–68. Mnemosyne Supplements: History and Archaeology of Classical Antiquity 360. Leiden: Brill, 2013.

———. *The Life and Death of Ancient Cities*. Oxford: Oxford University Press, 2020.

———. *Rome: An Empire's Story*. 2nd ed. Oxford: Oxford University Press, 2022.

———. "The Rulers Ruled." In *Reconsidering Roman Power: Roman, Greek, Jewish and Christian Perceptions and Reactions*, edited by Katell Berthelot. Rome: Publications de l'École française de Rome, 2020. https://books.openedition.org/efr/4773.

Wordsworth, William. *Wordsworth Poetical Works*. Edited by Thomas Hutchinson and Ernest de Selincourt. Oxford Standard Authors. London: Oxford University Press, 1934.

Wright, N. T. "Paul's Gospel and Caesar's Empire." 2001. https://ntwrightpage.com/1998/01/01/pauls-gospel-and-caesars-empire/.

Wright, Susan M., ed. *Archaeology at Bloomberg*. London: Museum of London Archaeology, 2017.

Yadin, Y. *Bar-Kokhba: The Rediscovery of the Legendary Hero of the Last Jewish Revolt against Imperial Rome*. London: Weidenfeld & Nicholson, 1971.

———. *The Documents from the Bar Kokhba Period in the Cave of Letters: Hebrew, Aramaic and Nabatean-Aramaic Papyri*. Judean Desert Studies. Jerusalem: Israel Exploration Society, Institute of Archaeology, Hebrew University and the Shrine of the Book, Israel Museum, 2002.

———. "The Expedition to the Judean Desert, 1960 (1961): Expedition D." *Israel Exploration Journal* 11.1/2 (1961) 36–52.

Yamazaki-Ransom, Kazuhiko. *The Roman Empire in Luke's Narrative*. Library of New Testament Studies 404. London: T&T Clark, 2010.

Zeichmann, Christopher B. "Database of Military Inscriptions and Papyri of Early Roman Palestine." 2018. https://armyofromanpalestine.com/.

———, ed. *Essential Essays for the Study of the Military in First-Century Palestine: Soldiers and the New Testament Context*. Eugene, OR: Pickwick Publications, 2019. [AQ: OK to add?]

———. "Military Forces in Judaea 6–130 CE: The Status Quaestionis and Relevance for New Testament Studies." *Currents in Biblical Research* 17.1 (2018) 86–120.

———. *The Roman Army and the New Testament*. Lanham, MD: Fortress Academic, 2018.

Ancient Document Index

Luke (*continued*)

Acts (*continued*)

Romans

1 Corinthians

2 Corinthians

Galatians

Ephesians

Other Ink on Wood Writing Tablets

Lead Tablets

Tab. Uley

Other Curse Tablets

Gold Amulet

Subject Index

www.ingramcontent.com/pod-product-compliance
Lightning Source LLC
La Vergne TN
LVHW100502110826
845146LV00002B/490

* 9 7 9 8 3 8 5 2 6 2 8 8 5 *